For
Pat, Tricia, and Julie

RN

"A fascinating portrait . . .
the voice of the prose reflects its author more distinctly than does that of any other American political memoir I can think of . . . that voice continues to hypnotize throughout."

— Christopher Lehmann-Haupt,
New York Times

"Deeply impressive . . . splendidly readable . . . remarkably persuasive. There is a disarming frankness about this book that is very rare in the memoirs of a public man . . . there is a dimension of true drama and real tragedy which raises it to the realm of literature . . . My guess is that posterity will come to acclaim this work as a political classic."

—Peregrine Worsthorne, Associate Editor of
The London Sunday Telegraph, in a special book
review essay for *The American Spectator*

Also by Richard Nixon

Memoirs Volume II
Six Crises

Published By
WARNER BOOKS

THE MEMOIRS OF RICHARD NIXON

VOLUME 1

WARNER BOOKS

A Warner Communications Company

WARNER BOOKS EDITION

Copyright © 1978 by Richard Nixon
All rights reserved.

Some of the factual events in this book were treated
in greater detail in *Six Crises* (Doubleday & Company, Inc.
copyright © 1962 by Richard M. Nixon).

Book design: H. Roberts

Warner Books, Inc., 75 Rockefeller Plaza,
New York, N.Y. 10019

 A Warner Communications Company

Printed in the United States of America

First Printing: October, 1979

10 9 8 7 6 5 4 3 2 1

Library of Congress Cataloging in Publication Data

Nixon, Richard Milhous, 1913–
  RN, the Memoirs of Richard Nixon.

  Reprint of the ed. published by Grosset & Dunlap,
New York.
  Includes index.
  1. Nixon, Richard Milhous, 1913–   2. United
States—Politics and government—1945–   3. Presi-
dents—United States—Biography.   I. Title.
[E856.A35 1979]   973.924'092'4 [B]   79-9271
ISBN 0-446-93259-0 (v. 1)

CONTENTS

Early Years 1913-1946   1

Congressman and Senator 1947-1952   37

Vice President 1953-1960   141

Private Citizen 1961-1967   283

1968 Campaign and Election   365

The Presidency 1969-1971   451

Index   671

SOURCES AND ACKNOWLEDGMENTS

This is a memoir—a book of memories. Since memory is fallible and inevitably selective, I have tried whenever possible to check my recollections against the available records and to supplement them with contemporary sources. Some of these sources—memos, correspondence, public papers—are self-evident. A few of them need further elaboration.

Throughout my public career I have had the habit of making extensive handwritten notes about my ideas, conversations, activities, and speeches. These notes, most of them made on yellow legal pads, total more than 20,000 pages extending from my outlines for the debates in the 1946 campaign to the outlines of my resignation speech in 1974. They range from offhand observations to extremely detailed passages of dialogue.

Between 1954 and 1957, while I was Vice President, I made diary-type dictations covering 112 different meetings, conversations, or events. I cannot remember why I started or why I stopped making them, and they cover such a wide variety of subjects and personalities that there does not seem to have been any single purpose behind them. These diaries, which were dictated on Edison Voicewriter platters, were transcribed in 1961 when I wrote *Six Crises*, but I did not use them directly in that book and they are quoted here for the first time.

By historical necessity some of the events in the pre-presidential years that were treated in *Six Crises* are also dealt with in this book. The reader will find, however, that while the facts concerning the events have not changed, the passage of time has enabled me to analyze them with greater perspective, and the new context has made it necessary for me to treat them in a substantially different and more condensed manner than they were treated in that earlier account.

During the presidency, from November 1971 until April 1973 and again in June and July 1974, I kept an almost daily dictated diary. In this book these passages are introduced by the heading *Diary*. With the exception of a few that were subpoenaed by the Watergate Special Prosecutor, none of these diary cassettes was transcribed until the summer of 1976 in San Clemente. While I have excerpted the passages from them that appear in this book, no word has been changed without adding brackets to indicate the change. These dictated diaries do not have the orderliness of a written diary—often I would dictate on a subject one day and then expand on the same subject a day or two later. Because of this, in some cases, I have combined entries that deal with the same subjects but were dictated on different days. Diary entries dealing with Watergate, however, are always from the same dictating session on the same day.

For the Watergate period I have used some of the tape transcripts that are already public or that were used by the Special Prosecutor in different investigations and trials. In an effort to reconstruct as completely as possible what I knew and what I did in the crucial period immediately following the Watergate break-in, I asked Mrs. Marjorie Acker, a member of my staff since the Senate years, to type transcripts as well of the tapes of every conversation I had with H. R. Halderman, John Ehrlichman, and Charles Colson for the month after my return to Washington following the break-in, June 20-July 20, 1972. I asked her to do the same for my conversations with Haldeman in May 1973, when we were discussing what we remembered of the events of June 23, 1979, when I authorized the meeting in which the CIA was asked to limit the FBI's investigation of Watergate.

There were many unintelligible passages on these new tapes. Even so, I believe that they have enabled me to give the most complete account of those days that has ever been given.

In this book I recount many conversations, some of them as direct quotes. Those dealing with Watergate are largely based on the language recorded on the White House tapes. Others are based on my handwritten notes or my dictated diaries. There are also extensive memoranda of conversations—"memcons"—covering most talks with foreign leaders, and I have been able to use these to confirm and supplement my notes and recollections. Conversations in which I did not take part are obviously dependent upon reports from the participants or on secondary sources. In a few cases, I have had to depend solely upon my memory of a conversation in re-creating it, but I have tried to limit this to exchanges in which the vividness of the words lodged them unforgettably in my mind.

This book could not have been written or published without the help of dozens of people, and I am deeply grateful to all of them.

The wonderful volunteer women who work every day taking care of the mail that comes into La Casa Pacifica spent many hours on the laborious but important proofreading of three drafts of the manuscript.

Cathy Price, Marnie Pavlick, Nora Kelly, Cindy Serrano-Mesa, and Meredith Johnson worked late hours and many weekends in order to type the manuscript and then proof galleys against original documents. Judy Johnson helped with a variety of typing and research tasks; Meredith Khachigian helped to proof the manuscript against the originals of my diary. When all the papers of my administration were impounded, Howard W. Smith, a private citizen, kindly sent us his complete set of the daily press office news releases and special briefing transcripts.

Robert Huberty and Mark Jacobsen, of the University of California, Irvine, did much of the detailed library research and newspaper checking.

In a work of this size the copy editors perform an enormous and vital task. I want to thank David C. Frost and Nancy Brooks of Grosset & Dunlap for their patience, diligence, and professional expertise. Others who assisted in various tasks were Jack Brennan, Carl Howell, Bernard Shir-Cliff, Larry Gadd, Diana Price, and Robert and Cara Ackerman. The index was compiled by Robert Daugherty, and the photographs were assembled with the help of Ann Grier. I also appreciate the interest and encouragement I have received from my publishers: Harold Roth and Bob Markel of Grosset & Dunlap and Bill Sarnoff and Howard Kaminsky of Warner Books.

I am grateful to the dozens of former staff members and friends who took part in the events chronicled in this book and who gave hours of time to me and my staff as we worked to reconstruct those events fairly and accurately. I am also grateful to those who read different parts of the manuscript and gave valuable advice and assistance: General Brent Scowcroft, who concentrated on the sections dealing with international affairs and foreign policy; Ray Price, who gave editorial assistance and advice, particularly on the domestic policy sections of the presidency; and Herb Stein, who provided editorial assistance on the section dealing with the economy.

Rose Mary Woods was able to spend several months in San Clemente sharing her memories of the twenty-three years during which she served as my personal secretary and applying painstaking attention to detail in reading and checking the manuscript. Marje Acker also came out to help with these tasks. Loie Gaunt, who first joined my staff when I was in the Senate, has served tirelessly as a limitless source of information and help throughout the past three years.

Finally, there are the three people who have worked with me on this project from the beginning. My deep gratitude goes to Ken Khachigian and Diane Sawyer for their research and for pulling together much of the source material. And to Frank Gannon, my chief editorial assistant who organized the research and directed the project, my special appreciation.

RN

La Casa Pacifica
March 1978

Early Years
1913-1946

I was born in a house my father built. My birth on the night of January 9, 1913, coincided with a record-breaking cold snap in our town of Yorba Linda, California. Yorba Linda was a farming community of 200 people about thirty miles from Los Angeles, surrounded by avocado and citrus groves and barley, alfalfa, and bean fields.

For a child the setting was idyllic. In the spring the air was heavy with the rich scent of orange blossoms. And there was much to excite a child's imagination: glimpses of the Pacific Ocean to the west, the San Bernardino Mountains to the north, a "haunted house" in the nearby foothills to be viewed with awe and approached with caution—and a railroad line that ran about a mile from our house.

In the daytime I could see the smoke from the steam engines. Sometimes at night I was awakened by the whistle of a train, and then I dreamed of the far-off places I wanted to visit someday. My brothers and I played railroad games, taking the parts of engineers and conductors. I remember the thrill of talking to Everett Barnum, the Santa Fe Railroad engineer who lived in our town. All through grade school my ambition was to become a railroad engineer.

My first conscious memory is of running. I was three years old, and my mother was driving us in a horse-drawn buggy, holding my baby brother Don on her lap while a neighbor girl held me. The horse turned the corner leading to our house at high speed, and I tumbled onto the ground. I must have been in shock, but I managed to get up and run after the buggy while my mother tried to make the horse stop. The only aftereffect of this accident was that years later, when the vogue of parting hair on the left side came along, I still had to comb mine straight back to hide a scar caused by the fall.

Our life in Yorba Linda was hard but happy. My father worked at whatever jobs he could find. Thanks to a vegetable garden and some of our own fruit trees, we had plenty to eat despite our low income. We also had a cow that provided milk from which my mother made our butter and cheese.

I started first grade in Yorba Linda's schoolhouse when I was six. My mother had already taught me to read at home, and this head start enabled me to skip the second grade.

After homework and chores, I often sat by the fireplace or at the kitchen table immersed in a book or magazine. We took the Los Angeles *Times,* the *Saturday Evening Post,* and the *Ladies' Home Journal.* Aunt Olive, my mother's youngest sister, and her husband, Oscar Marshburn, lived in nearby Whittier and subscribed to the *National Geographic.* Nearly every time I visited them I borrowed a copy. It was my favorite magazine.

In 1922 my father sold our house and lemon grove in Yorba Linda, and we moved to Whittier. He did roustabout work in the oil fields, but although it paid well, this physical labor offered no challenge to a man of his ambition, intelligence, and lively imagination. Early on, my father could see that even though there were still very few automobiles and only one paved road in the area, the horseless carriage was an idea whose time was about to come. He borrowed $5,000 to buy some land on the main road connecting the growing towns of Whittier and La Habra. He cleared the lot, put in a tank and a pump, and opened the first service station in the eight-mile stretch between the two towns.

The enterprise was an almost instant success, and he soon opened a general store and market. He added a small counter for my mother's home-baked pies and cakes. One of her specialties was angel food cake. She insisted that it was at its best only when she beat fresh outdoor air into the batter before putting it into the oven. I remember her standing outside the kitchen door in the chilly predawn air, beating the batter with a big wooden spoon.

The grocery business expanded rapidly, and had it not been for the illnesses that struck our family, we would have been modestly well off by the standards of those times.

The Nixon Market was a "mom and pop" operation; the whole family worked in the store. In addition to waiting on the customers and keeping the accounts, inventory had to be taken, orders placed, and the shelves kept stocked. The store had to be cleaned and swept each night and sprayed for flies each day.

When I was older, I took over the fresh fruit and vegetable buying. Each morning I got up at four in order to be at the Seventh Street market in Los Angeles by five o'clock. I chose the best fruits and vegetables, bargained with the farmers and wholesalers for a good price, and then drove back to East Whittier to wash, sort, and arrange the produce in the store and be off to school by eight. It was not an easy life, but it was a good one, centered around a loving family and a small, tight-knit, Quaker community. For those who were willing to work hard, California in the 1920s seemed a place and time of almost unlimited opportunity.

The principle that opposites attract aptly describes my father and my mother. In the most important ways they were very much alike. Both were deeply religious. They were completely devoted to one another, and no sacrifice was too great for them to make for their children. But two more temperamentally different people could hardly be imagined.

My father, Francis Anthony Nixon, was known

throughout his life as Frank. He was born on a farm in Ohio on December 3, 1878. His mother died of tuberculosis when he was eight, and her long illness left the family almost penniless. After her death the family moved to a small barren plot of land in eastern Ohio, where my father had to walk several miles each day to the nearest school. A newcomer, small in stature and dressed in ragged clothes, he was taunted by his schoolmates. He responded with a quick tongue and a ready pair of fists, and he soon became known as a natural fighter.

The family fortunes did not improve, and after he had finished the sixth grade he quit school and went to work. It was a necessary decision, but one he regretted all his life. Over the next few years he held many jobs, acquiring new skills with each. He drove an ox team hauling logs to a sawmill, worked as a carpenter, managed a potato farm, sheared sheep in Colorado, and installed early hand-crank telephones.

Throughout his life my father tried to better himself through work. He moved to Columbus, Ohio, and became a streetcar motorman. The insides of those early trolleys were heated by pot-bellied stoves, but the vestibules where the motormen stood were open. During the winter of 1906 his feet became frostbitten. Complaints to the company went unheeded, so he organized a protest by the motormen and conductors. They managed to get a bill passed in the state legislature requiring that the vestibules be enclosed and heated.

Nonetheless, the battle had left him frustrated and discouraged, and he decided to move to Southern California, where at least frostbite would not be a problem. In 1907 he got a job as a motorman on the Pacific Electric streetcar line that ran between Los Angeles and Whittier. In 1908 he met Hannah Milhous at a Valentine's Day party, and despite the reservations of her family because she had not finished college and because her suitor was not a Quaker, they were married four months later.

My father had an Irish quickness both to anger and to mirth. It was his temper that impressed me most as a small child. He had tempestuous arguments with my brothers Harold and Don, and their shouting could be heard all through the neighborhood. He was a strict and stern disciplinarian, and I tried to follow my mother's example of not crossing him when he was in a bad mood. Perhaps my own aversion to personal confrontations dates back to these early recollections.

He often argued vehemently on almost any subject with the customers he waited on in the store. His outbursts were not personal; they were just his way of putting life into a discussion. Unfortunately some of our customers did not appreciate this, and it was a standing family joke that my mother or one of us boys would rush to wait on some of our more sensitive customers before he could get to them.

Whatever talent I have as a debater must have been acquired from my father, from his love of argument and disputation. When I was on the debating team in college, he would often drive me to the debates and sit in the back of the room listening intently. On the way home he would dissect and analyze each of the arguments.

My father had a deep belief in the "little man" in America. He opposed the vested interests and the political machines that exercised so much control over American life at the beginning of the century. Because he thought that the Standard Oil trust was a blight on the American landscape, he chose to be supplied by the less well known Richfield Oil Company when he opened his service station in Whittier. As the Nixon Market grew, he became a vociferous opponent of chain stores. He feared that through their volume buying they would crush the independent operator and the family grocery store.

In those days before television and when radio was still in its infancy, conversation within the family and among friends was a major source of recreation. Lively discussions of political issues were always a feature of our family gatherings. My father started out as a hard-line Ohio Republican. In 1924, however, he became disenchanted with the stand-pat Republicanism of Harding and Coolidge. A populist strain entered his thinking, and that year he deserted his party to vote for the great Wisconsin Progressive Senator Robert "Fighting Bob" La Follette. He even became an ardent supporter of the Townsend Plan, which proposed paying $200 a month to everyone over sixty who would spend the money and agree to retire, a program which was too liberal even for the New Deal. He supported Hoover in 1932 because Hoover was a "dry" and FDR a "wet" on prohibition. He never told me how he voted in 1936, but I always suspected that in the midst of the Depression he voted for Franklin D. Roosevelt rather than Alf Landon, whom he once described as a "stand-patter."

The dignity of labor was the keystone of my father's philosophy of life. He said that taking too seriously the biblical invitation to lean on the Lord encouraged laziness, and his favorite biblical passage was, "in the sweat of thy face shalt thou eat bread." During the long period when my brother Harold had tuberculosis—the years of the Great Depression—my father refused to let him go to the county tuberculosis hospital, one of the best in the country, on the ground that going there would be taking charity.

My father's temper may have been exacerbated by a partial deafness that became almost total as he grew older. There were times I suspected him of provoking a commotion just so he could turn off his hearing aid and watch the drama unfold before him like a silent movie. But it is the love beneath his brusque and bristling exterior that I remember best. When he and my mother came to New York to see me off on the Herter Committee trip to Europe in 1947, Pat and I arranged a special treat for them. He particularly loved musical comedy, and I was able to get the best seats for the Broadway hit *Oklahoma!* We had to rush from the hotel to the theatre, and on the way he discovered that he had left his hearing aid in his room. He was determined that he would not spoil our evening, and I remember how intently he followed the play and how he laughed and applauded with the rest of the audience so that we would think he was having a good time, even though he could not hear a single word or a single note.

My father's interest in politics made him the most enthusiastic follower of my career from its beginnings. My success meant to him that everything he had worked for and believed in was true: that in America, with hard work and determination a man can achieve anything. During the years I was in Congress, I sent home copies of the daily *Congressional Record*. He read them cover to cover—something that

8

no congressman or senator I knew ever took the time to do. When I was running for Vice President, he wrote a typically straightforward letter to one of the newspapers he had read years before, suggesting that it support me: "This boy is one of five that I raised and they are the finest, I think, in the United States. If you care to give him a lift I would say the *Ohio State Journal* is still doing some good."

Everyone who ever knew my mother was impressed with what a remarkable woman she was. She was born March 7, 1885, in southern Indiana into an Irish Quaker family of nine children. When she was twelve, her father decided to move to a new Quaker settlement in California. They loaded a railroad boxcar with many of their possessions, including horses and saddles, doors, and window frames, and arrived at Whittier in 1897, where my grandfather opened a tree nursery and planted an orange grove. After graduating from Whittier Academy, my mother went on to Whittier College. She loved history and literature, and she majored in languages, concentrating in Latin, Greek, and German. When she met and married my father, she had completed her second year of college. They had five sons and, with the exception of one named for my father, she named us after the early kings of England: Harold, born in 1909; Richard, born in 1913; Francis Donald, born in 1914; Arthur, born in 1918; and Edward, born in 1930.

My mother was always concerned and active in community affairs, but her most striking quality was a deep sense of privacy. Although she radiated warmth and love for her family, indeed, for all people, she was intensely private in her feelings and emotions. We never had a meal without saying grace, but except for special occasions when each of us boys would be called on to recite a verse from the Bible, these prayers were always silent. She even took literally the injunction from St. Matthew that praying should be done behind closed doors and went into a closet to say her prayers before going to bed at night.

Often when I had a difficult decision to make or a speech to prepare, or when I was under attack in the press, my mother would say, "I will be thinking of you." This was her quiet Quaker way of saying, "I will be praying for you"—and it meant infinitely more to me because of its understatement.

Many people who knew my mother in Whittier referred to her, even during her lifetime, as a Quaker saint. My cousin Jessamyn West recently wrote to me about my mother. She said, "I don't think of Hannah as a 'saint.' Saints, I feel, have a special pipeline to God which provides them a fortitude not given ordinary mortals. Hannah was not ordinary; but she did what she did and was what she was through a strength and lovingness which welled up out of her own good heart and because of her own indomitable character." The quality that made my mother so special, and that made people want to be close to her, was that although the inner serenity religion gave her shone through, she never wore her religion on her sleeve.

As a child I spent hours sitting at the piano in our living room picking out tunes. Shortly after I began school, I started taking piano lessons from my Uncle Griffith Milhous. He also taught me the fundamentals of the violin.

Probably because of Uncle Griffith's urgings, my parents decided to give my musical abilities a real test. My mother's sister Jane had studied piano at the Metropolitan School of Music in Indianapolis and was an accomplished performer and teacher. She lived with her own family in Lindsay, another Quaker enclave, in central California. It was decided that I should live with them for half a year and take lessons from her. Right after a family reunion at my grandmother's house in December 1924, I went home with Aunt Jane and Uncle Harold Beeson and my cousins Alden and Sheldon.

For six months I took daily piano lessons from Aunt Jane and violin lessons from a teacher in nearby Exeter, and walked a mile and a half each way to school with Alden and Sheldon. I enjoyed studying music, and I was able to memorize quite easily. Even today, more than fifty years later, I still remember some of the music I learned back in Lindsay.

Playing the piano is a way of expressing oneself that is perhaps even more fulfilling than writing or speaking. In fact, I have always had two great—and still unfulfilled—ambitions: to direct a symphony orchestra and to play an organ in a cathedral. I think that to create great music is one of the highest aspirations man can set for himself.

My parents came to bring me home in June 1925. Like any twelve-year-old I was happy to see them after what seemed like a very long time. As soon as he saw me alone, my youngest brother, Arthur, greeted me with a solemn kiss on the cheek. I later learned that he had asked my mother if it would be proper for him to kiss me since I had been away. Even at that early age he had acquired our family's reticence about open displays of affection.

A short time after we returned to Whittier, Arthur complained of a headache. The family doctor thought it was flu and ordered him to bed. Arthur's condition deteriorated quickly, and the doctor was unable to find the cause. He prescribed a series of tests, including a spinal tap. After that most painful of tests had been taken, I remember my father coming downstairs. It was the first time I had ever seen him cry. He said, "The doctors are afraid that the little darling is going to die."

Because Arthur required constant care and attention, Don and I were sent to stay with my Aunt Carrie Wildermuth in Fullerton. Just before we left, we went upstairs to see our brother. He had asked for one of his favorite dishes, tomato gravy on toast; we brought some up with us, and I remember how much he enjoyed it. Two days later he died.

The doctor said that it was tubercular encephalitis, but those words were too big, too cold, and too impersonal for us to grasp or understand. My father, who had been keeping the service station open on Sundays to accommodate the increasing weekend traffic on Whittier Boulevard, half believed that Arthur's death represented some kind of divine displeasure, and he never again opened the station or the market on a Sunday.

For weeks after Arthur's funeral there was not a day that I did not think about him and cry. For the first time I had learned what death was like and what it meant.

As a freshman in college I wrote a short essay about Arthur for an English composition course. I described the photograph of Arthur that my mother always kept in our living room, and I wrote, "Let me tell you, in a few words, something of my brother as I remember him."

The first two or three years of my baby brother's life are rather indistinct in my memory for I was engrossed in the first years of my grammar school education. However, there were certain things concerned with my little brother's early development which did impress me. For example, I remember how his eyes changed from their original baby-blue to an almost black shade; how his hair, blond at first, became dark brown; how his mouth, toothless for five months, was filled with tiny, white teeth which, by the way, were exceedingly sharp when applied on soft fingers or toes which happened to get within their reach; how those little incoherent sounds of his finally developed into words and then into sentences; and how he learned to roll over, then to crawl, and finally to walk.

Although I do not remember many incidents connected with my brother's early childhood, there were some which made a clear imprint on my mind. There was one time when he was asked to be a ring bearer at a wedding. I remember how my mother had to work with him for hours to get him to do it, because he disliked walking with the little flower girl. Another time, when he was about five years old, he showed the world that he was a man by getting some cigarettes out of our store and secretly smoking them back of the house. Unfortunately for him, one of our gossipy neighbors happened to see him, and she promptly informed my mother. I have disliked that neighbor from that time. . . .

Again, I shall never forget how he disliked wearing "sticky" wool suits. As soon as he was able to read, he used to search the mail order catalogues for suits which weren't "sticky." . . .

There is a growing tendency among college students to let their childhood beliefs be forgotten. Especially we find this true when we speak of the Divine Creator and his plans for us. I thought that I would also become that way, but I find that it is almost impossible for me to do so. Two days before my brother's death, he called my mother into the room. He put his arms around her and said that he wanted to pray before he went to sleep. Then, with closed eyes, he repeated that age-old child's prayer which ends with those simple yet beautiful words:

"If I should die before I awake, I pray Thee, Lord, my soul to take."

There is a grave out now in the hills, but, like the picture, it contains only the bodily image of my brother.

And so when I am tired and worried, and am almost ready to quit trying to live as I should, I look up and see the picture of a little boy with sparkling eyes, and curly hair; I remember the childlike prayer; I pray that it may prove true for me as it did for my brother Arthur.

My oldest brother Harold's long bout with tuberculosis began several years before Arthur died, but it continued for more than ten years. It was especially hard for us to accept because he had always had such a robust enjoyment of life. He was tall and handsome with blue eyes and blond hair. At one point he grew a moustache that made him look quite rakish. In high school he had a stripped-down Model T Ford that he raced with his friends.

It was during Harold's long illness that my mother showed the depth of her character and faith. In those days, TB was almost always incurable, and the long, losing fight left its tragic mark on our whole family. First, Harold went to an expensive private sanatorium, and then he spent a few months in a cottage in the Antelope Valley in California, which is considerably drier than the Whittier area.

Finally, my mother decided to take him to live in Prescott, Arizona, which was supposed to be excellent for tubercular cures because of its dry climate and high elevation. She stayed with Harold in Prescott for almost three years. To make ends meet, she took care of three other bedridden patients. She cooked and cleaned, gave them bed baths and alcohol rubs, and did everything that a nurse does for a patient. Later, as she heard that one by one each had died, I could tell that she felt their deaths as deeply as if they had been her own sons'.

In addition to the wrenching physical and emotional strain of nursing, the very fact of separation from the rest of us was very hard on my mother. My father regularly made the fourteen-hour drive to Prescott with Don and me during Christmas and spring vacations, and we spent part of our summers there. During those two summers in Prescott, I worked at any odd job I could find. I was a janitor at a

13

swimming pool, and once I helped pluck and dress frying chickens for a butcher shop. I also worked as a carnival barker at the Frontier Days festival that is still celebrated in Prescott every July.

Harold's illness continued to drag on. He became so thin it was almost painful to look at him. He was terribly unhappy and homesick in Prescott, so it was finally decided to let him come home, hoping that the familiar surroundings would compensate for the damper climate. He had a desperate will to live and refused to comply with the doctor's orders that he stay in bed. It was especially painful for us all because Harold was still so full of hope and had so much life in him. We kept hoping against hope that some mental lift might start him on the way back to physical recovery. When he said that he would like to go through the San Bernardino Mountains to see the desert, my father dropped everything to make plans for the trip. He rented one of the first house trailers on the market—a wooden structure built on a Reo truck chassis—and spent hours with Harold planning their route and their itinerary.

We saw them off one morning, expecting them to be gone for almost a month. They were back three days later. Harold had had another hemorrhage, and despite his insistence that they go on, my father knew that Harold would not be able to stand the rigors of living in the trailer. Harold told me that he was nevertheless glad they had taken even this short trip. I can still remember his voice when he described the beauty of the wild flowers in the foothills and the striking sight of snow in the mountains. I sensed that he knew this was the last time he would ever see them.

On March 6, 1933, Harold asked me to drive him downtown. He had seen an ad for a new kind of electric cake mixer he wanted to give our mother for her birthday the next day. He barely had the strength to walk with me into the hardware store. We had them wrap the mixer as a birthday present, and we hid it at home at the top of a closet.

The next morning he said that we should postpone giving our presents to mother until that night because he did not feel well and wanted to rest. About three hours later I was studying in the college library when I received a message to come home. When I got there, I saw a hearse parked in front of the house. My parents were crying uncontrollably as the undertaker carried out Harold's body. My mother said that right after I left for school Harold asked her to put her arms around him and hold him very close. He had never been particularly religious, but he looked at her and said, "This is the last time I will see you, until we meet in heaven." He died an hour later. That night I got the cake mixer out and gave it to my mother and told her that it was Harold's gift to her.

I loved my parents equally but in very different ways, just as they were very different people. My father was a scrappy, belligerent fighter with a quick, wide-ranging raw intellect. He left me a respect for learning and hard work, and the will to keep fighting no matter what the odds. My mother loved me completely and selflessly, and her special legacy was a quiet, inner peace, and the determination never to despair.

Three words describe my life in Whittier: family, church, and school.

The Milhous family was one of the oldest in the town, and counting sisters and cousins and aunts, it included scores of people. It was a matriarchy headed, first, by my great-grandmother Elizabeth Price Milhous. This remarkable woman, along with a forebear of hers, was the model for Eliza Cope Birdwell in Jessamyn West's charming novel *The Friendly Persuasion*. She died in 1923 at the age of ninety-six, when I was only ten, but I can remember her well.

My grandmother, Almira Burdg Milhous, lived to be ninety-four. At our traditional Christmas family reunions at her house she sat regally in her best red velvet dress as all the grandchildren brought their very modest presents to her. She praised them all equally, remarking that each was something she had particularly wanted. She seemed to take a special interest in me, and she wrote me verses on my birthday and on other special occasions. On my thirteenth birthday, in 1926, she gave me a framed picture of Lincoln with the words from Longfellow's "Psalm of Life" in her own handwriting beneath it: "Lives of great men oft remind us/We can make our lives sublime,/And departing, leave

15

behind us/Footprints on the sands of time." I hung the picture above my bed at home, and to this day it is one of my fondest possessions. When I was in college my grandmother gave me a biography of Gandhi, which I read from cover to cover. Gandhi's concept of peaceful change and passive resistance appealed to her, and she had a deep Quaker opposition to any racial or religious prejudice.

Grandmother Milhous belonged to the generation of Quakers who used the plain speech. She would say, "Is thee going today?" or "Is this thine?" or "What are thy wishes?" I loved to listen when my mother and my aunts, none of whom used the plain speech in their own homes, would slip back into it while talking with her or with each other.

I grew up in a religious environment that was at once unusually strict and unusually tolerant. My mother and her family belonged to a branch of the Friends Church that had ministers, choirs, and virtually all the symbols of other Protestant denominations. The differences were the absence of water baptism and communion, and the heavy Quaker emphasis on silent prayer. My father had converted to Quakerism from his own rather robust Methodism at the time of his marriage, and he had the typical enthusiasm of a convert for his new religion. Our family went to church four times on Sunday—Sunday school, the regular morning service, Christian Endeavor in the late afternoon, and another service in the evening—and to Wednesday night services as well. During my high school and college years I also played the piano for various church services each week. My mother gave me a Bible when I graduated from eighth grade, and I never went to bed at night without reading a few verses.

Even the extensive religious activities of the Friends meetings in Yorba Linda and Whittier were not enough to satisfy my parents. They were both fascinated by the evangelists and revivalists of those times, and often we drove to Los Angeles to hear Aimee Semple McPherson at the Angelus Temple and Bob Shuler, her great competitor, at the Trinity Methodist Church.

While religion and prayer were very much a part of our family life, they were essentially personal and private. Perhaps because of this I never fell into the common practice of quoting the Bible in the speeches I made during my school years or later in my political life. When I was Vice President, President Eisenhower urged me to refer to God from time to time in my speeches, but I did not feel comfortable doing so.

I suffered my first political defeat in my junior year at Whittier High School, when I lost the election for president of the student body. I was appointed student body manager by the faculty, and it was my responsibility to handle the sale of tickets to football games and to persuade local businessmen to advertise in the school yearbook.

Our senior year, 1930, was the 2000th anniversary of the poet Vergil's birth, and the Latin teachers at school decided to put on a special dramatization of the *Aeneid* to commemorate the event. I was chosen to play Aeneas, and my girl friend, Ola Florence Welch, was his beloved Dido. It was my first experience in dramatics, and it is amazing that it was not my last.

The performance was sheer torture. First, the audience was bored stiff—Vergil obviously had not written the *Aeneid* for a high school assembly in Whittier, California. Second, the dramatically tender scene in which I embraced Dido evoked such catcalls, whistles, and uproarious laughter that we had to wait until they subsided before we could continue. Third, whoever rented the costumes had not taken into account the size of my feet—11D! I would guess that the silver boots I had to wear with my costume were no bigger than size 9. It took both Latin teachers and me several minutes to get them on and almost as long to get them off, and the hour on stage in them was agony beyond description and almost beyond endurance.

I had dreamed of going to college in the East. I finished third in my high school class, won the constitutional oratorical contests in my junior and senior years, and received the Harvard Club of California's award for outstanding all-around student. There was also a possibility of a tuition scholarship to Yale, but travel and living expenses would amount to even more than tuition, and by 1930 the Depression and the enormous expenses of Harold's illness had stripped our family finances to the bone. I had no choice but to live at home, and that meant that I would have to attend

Whittier College. I was not disappointed, because the idea of college was so exciting that nothing could have dimmed it for me.

In college, as in high school, I continued to plug away at my studies. For the first time I met students who were able to get good grades without working very hard for them, but I needed the steady discipline of nightly study to keep up with all the courses and reading.

Each of my teachers made a great impression on me, but a few in particular touched my mind and changed my life.

Dr. Paul Smith was probably the greatest intellectual inspiration of my early years. I took his courses in British and American civilization, the American Constitution, and international relations and law. He was a brilliant lecturer, who always spoke without notes. His doctorate was from the University of Wisconsin, where he had studied under the great Progressive historian Glenn Frank. Dr. Smith's approach to history and politics was strongly influenced by the Progressive outlook, and it came as a revelation to me that history could be more than a chronicle of past events—that it could be a tool of analysis and criticism.

Albert Upton, who taught English and was the director of the drama club, was an iconoclast. Nothing was sacred to him, and he stimulated us by his outspoken unorthodoxy.

At the end of my junior year he told me that my education would not be complete until I read Tolstoy and the other great Russian novelists. That summer I read little else. My favorite was *Resurrection,* Tolstoy's last major novel. I was even more deeply affected by the philosophical works of his later years. His program for a peaceful revolution for the downtrodden Russian masses, his passionate opposition to war, and his emphasis on the spiritual elements in all aspects of life left a more lasting impression on me than his novels. At that time in my life I became a Tolstoyan.

Dr. J. Herschel Coffin influenced me in a different way. He taught a course called "The Philosophy of Christian Reconstruction," which I took in my senior year. This course was better known by its subtitle, "What Can I Believe?" It involved a weekly written self-analysis based on questions raised in class. We studied the theory of evolution, the literal authenticity of the Bible, and the nature of democracy, and at the beginning, middle, and end of the course, we had to write an essay answering the question, "What Can I Believe?"

On October 9, 1933, I described some of my impressions and problems at the beginning of the course. This composition gives a clearer picture of my beliefs, questions, and uncertainties as a college student than anything I could reconstruct today.

> Years of training in the home and church have had their effect on my thinking. . . . My parents, "fundamental Quakers," had ground into me, with the aid of the church, all the fundamental ideas in their strictest interpretation. The infallibility and literal correctness of the Bible, the miracles, even the whale story, all these I accepted as facts when I entered college four years ago. Even then I could not forget the admonition to not be misled by college professors who might be a little too liberal in their views! Many of those childhood ideas have been destroyed but there are some which I cannot bring myself to drop. To me, the greatness of the universe is too much for man to explain. I still believe that God is the creator, the first cause of all that exists. I still believe that He lives today, in some form, directing the destinies of the cosmos. How can I reconcile this idea with my scientific method? It is of course an unanswerable question. However, for the time being I shall accept the solution offered by Kant: that man can go only so far in his research and explanations; from that point on we must accept God. What is unknown to man, God knows.

I thought that Jesus was the Son of God, but not necessarily in the physical sense of the term: "He reached the highest conception of God and of value that the world has ever seen. He lived a life which radiated those values. He taught a philosophy which revealed those values to men. I even go so far as to say Jesus and God are one, because Jesus set the great example which is forever pulling men upward to the ideal life. His life was so perfect that he 'mingled' his soul with God's."

I wrote that the literal accuracy of the story of the resurrection was not as important as its profound symbolism: "The important fact is that Jesus lived and taught a life so perfect that he continued to live and grow after his death—in the hearts of men. It may be true that the resurrection story is a myth, but symbolically it teaches the great lesson that men who achieve the highest values in their lives may gain immortality. ... Orthodox teachers have always insisted that the physical resurrection of Jesus is the most important cornerstone in the Christian religion. I believe that the modern world will find a real resurrection in the life and teachings of Jesus."

The populist elements of my father's politics, the Progressive influence of Paul Smith, the iconoclasm of Albert Upton, and the Christian humanism of Dr. Coffin gave my early thinking a very liberal, almost populist, tinge.

Thanks to my teachers I studied hard and received a first-rate education at Whittier. But academic pursuits were by no means the only—or the most important—part of my four years there. From the first week of school on, I was involved in extracurricular activities.

Whittier did not have any fraternities, but there was one social club, the Franklin Society, whose members had high social status on campus. One of the first students I met at college was Dean Triggs, who had just transferred to Whittier after two years at Colorado College, where he had belonged to a fraternity. He thought it undemocratic to have only one such club at Whittier, and he suggested that we start another. Albert Upton agreed to be our sponsor, and we decided to call ourselves the Orthogonian Society—the "Square Shooters."

While the Franklins were socially oriented, the Orthogonians recruited mostly athletes and men who were working their way through school. The Franklins posed for their yearbook pictures wearing tuxedos; we posed for our pictures wearing open-necked shirts. We were officially dedicated to what, with our collegiate exuberance, we called the Four B's: Beans, Brawn, Brain, and Bowels. Our motto was *Écrasons l'infâme*—"Stamp out evil"—and our symbol was a boar's head. Although only a freshman, I was elected the first president of the Orthogonians, and I wrote our constitution and our song.

College debating in those days was a serious pursuit and a highly developed art, and to me it provided not only experience with techniques of argument but also an intensive introduction to the substance of some issues I would deal with in later years.

Because of the way our college debates were organized, the team had to be prepared to argue either side of a question. This sort of exercise turned out to be a healthy antidote to certainty, and a good lesson in seeing the other person's point of view. Because of this debate training I became used to speaking without notes, a practice that was of great importance to me later in my political career. During my senior year I won the intercollegiate extemporaneous speaking contest of Southern California.

One of the topics we debated was free trade versus protectionism. Once I had thoroughly researched—and argued—both sides, I became a convinced free-trader and remain so to this day. Another topic was whether the Allied war debts should be canceled. Although once again I debated both sides, I became convinced that the economic recovery of Europe was more important than our insisting on payment of war debts. We also debated whether a free economy was more efficient than a managed economy. Though this was at the height of the early enthusiasm for the experiments of the New Deal, I surfaced from my immersion in both sides of that topic thoroughly persuaded of the superior merits of a free economy.

During the winter of my second year in college, the debate team made a 3,500-mile tour through the Pacific Northwest. My father let us take our family's eight-year-old, seven-passenger Packard for the trip. The leader of our debating team was Joe Sweeney, a red-headed Irishman with loads of self-assurance.

One of our stops was San Francisco. In those days shortly before the repeal of Prohibition, San Francisco was a wide-open town. We followed Sweeney down winding, colorful streets to a drugstore. He showed the man behind the counter a card one of the bellboys at the hotel had given him, and the man led us over to a wall covered with shelves of drugs. He pushed the wall and it opened like a door into a speakeasy. It was not a particularly boisterous place, although the smoky air and the casual attitude of the patrons made us feel that we had wandered into a veritable den of iniquity. I did not have the slightest idea what to drink, so Sweeney ordered a Tom Collins for me. Except for him, none of us had been in a speakeasy before, and I had never tasted alcohol, so it was a lark just to sit there watching the people, listening to their conversation, and admiring the barmaid who served our drinks.

I tried out for several plays in college, and I was usually given the character parts. I was the dithering Mr. Ingoldsby in Booth Tarkington's *The Trysting Place,* the Innkeeper in John Drinkwater's *Bird in Hand,* an old Scottish miner in a grim one-act play, *The Price of Coal,* and a rather flaky comic character in George M. Cohan's *The Tavern.* I also served as stage manager for the college productions of *The Mikado* and *The Pirates of Penzance.*

Student politics was necessarily low-keyed in a small school where everyone knew one another. My only major "campaign" was for president of the student body at the end of my third year. I was the candidate of the Orthogonian Society, and my opponent was Dick Thomson of the Franklin Society. We were good friends and did not feel much enthusiasm for running against each other.

I based my campaign on the controversial issue of allowing dancing on campus. I had no personal stake in it since I had not even known how to dance until Ola Florence forced me to learn a few steps at a party. My argument was strictly pragmatic: whether or not one approved of dancing—and most of the members of Whittier's board of trustees did not, as a matter of religious principle—most of the students were going to dance. Surely, I argued, it would be better to have dances on campus where they could be supervised, rather than off campus in some second-rate dance hall.

I won the election and then had to deliver on my promise. Herbert Harris, acting president of the college, helped me work out a compromise with the board of trustees whereby the board would rent the nearby Whittier Women's Club building, which had a fine ballroom. We held eight successful dances there during the year. The only problem now was that I had to attend. Ola Florence and several other coeds were very patient with me, but I fear that many new pairs of slippers were scuffed as a result of my attempts to lead my partners around the dance floor.

My happiest memories of those college days involve sports. In freshman year I played on the Poetlings basketball team, and we had a perfect record for the year: we lost every game. In fact, the only trophy I have to show for having played basketball is a porcelain dental bridge. In one game, jumping for a rebound, a forward from La Verne College hit me in the mouth with his elbow and broke my top front teeth in half.

Two factors have always motivated great interest in sports. First, sports have provided necessary relief from the heavy burdens of work and study that I have assumed at every stage of my life. Second, I have a highly competitive instinct, and I find it stimulating to follow the great sports events in which one team's or one man's skill and discipline and brains are pitted against another's in the most exciting kind of combat imaginable.

Ever since I first played in high school, football has been my favorite sport. As a 150-pound seventeen-year-old freshman I hardly cut a formidable figure on the field, but I loved the game—the spirit, the teamwork, the friendship. There were only eleven eligible men on the freshman team, so despite my size and weight I got to play in every game and to wear a team numeral on my sweater. But for the rest of my college years, the only times I got to play were in the last few minutes of a game that was already safely won or hopelessly lost.

College football at Whittier gave me a chance to get to know the coach, Wallace "Chief" Newman. I think that I admired him more and learned more from him than from any man I have ever known aside from my father.

Newman was an American Indian, and tremendously proud of his heritage. Tall and ramrod-straight, with sharp features and copper skin, from his youngest days he was nicknamed Chief. He inspired in us the idea that if we worked hard enough and played hard enough, we could beat anybody. He had no tolerance for the view that how you play the game counts more than whether you win or lose. He believed in always playing cleanly, but he also believed that there is a great difference between winning and losing. He used to say, "Show me a good loser, and I'll show you a loser." He also said, "When you lose, get mad—but get mad at yourself, not at your opponent."

There is no way I can adequately describe Chief Newman's influence on me. He drilled into me a competitive spirit and the determination to come back after you have been knocked down or after you lose. He also gave me an acute understanding that what really matters is not a man's background, his color, his race, or his religion, but only his character.

One day during my last year at Whittier I saw a notice on the bulletin board announcing twenty-five $250 tuition scholarships to the new Duke University Law School in Durham, North Carolina. I applied, and only after I had won and accepted one did I learn that the students called this offer the "meat grinder," because of the twenty-five scholarships available for the first year, only twelve were renewed for the second.

When I arrived in Durham in September 1934, the photographs I had seen had not prepared me for the size and beauty of the Duke campus. For someone accustomed to California architecture and a small college like Whittier, Duke was like a medieval cathedral town. There were spires and towers and stained glass everywhere. Dozens of buildings were set in clusters amid acres of woods and gardens.

From the first day I knew that I was on a fast competitive track. Over half the members of my class were Phi Beta Kappas. Duke had adopted the Harvard case method, which involved memorizing the facts and points of law in hundreds of different cases and being able to stand up in class, recite them, and respond to sharp questioning. My memory was a great asset here, but I had never been faced with such an overwhelming mass of material. I sometimes despaired of pulling the memorized facts together into any meaningful knowledge of the law.

One night when I was studying in the library I poured

out my fears and doubts to an upperclassman, Bill Adelson, who had noted the long hours I spent studying in the law library. He heard me out, sat back, looked me in the eye, and told me something I shall never forget: "You don't have to worry. You have what it takes to learn the law—an iron butt."

During my first two years at Duke I lived in a $5-a-month rented room; for my third year I joined three friends and moved into a small house in Duke Forest, about two miles from the campus. "Small house" is really an overstatement: it was a one-room clapboard shack without heat or inside plumbing, in which the four of us shared two large brass beds. As I look back, I am amazed that we lived so long and so contentedly in such primitive conditions, but at the time it seemed exciting and adventurous. We called the place Whippoorwill Manor, and we had a great time there.

There was a metal stove in the middle of the room, which we stuffed with paper at night; the first one up in the morning lighted it. While the paper burned, we pulled on our clothes by the fire's warmth. In order to save money, for breakfast I usually had a Milky Way candy bar. I left my razor behind some books in the law school library and shaved each morning in the men's room, enjoying the luxury of central heating and hot and cold running water. Each afternoon I played handball and then took a shower in the gym.

I was able to maintain the grades I needed to keep my scholarship, and I became a member of Duke's law review, a quarterly journal called *Law and Contemporary Problems.* My scholarship covered only tuition but I was able to supplement my income by working in the law library and doing research for Dean H. Claude Horack. I even found time for some political activity and was elected president of the Student Bar Association.

My three years at Duke provided an excellent legal background. Despite the fact that we had some intense discussions on the race issue, and while I could not agree with many of my Southern classmates on this subject, I learned in these years to understand and respect them for their patriotism, their pride, and their enormous interest in national issues. After my years at Duke I felt strongly that it was time to bring the South back into the Union.

As the last year at Duke Law School began, I had to think about what I would do after graduation. I expected to finish near the top of my class, but the job market was very bad. The recession of 1937 was about to wipe out what few gains had been made since the Depression began, and good jobs with good salaries were few. During the Christmas vacation of 1936 I decided to go to New York with my classmates Harlan Leathers and William Perdue and try my luck with some of the big law firms there. The only firm that showed any interest in me was Donovan, Leisure, Newton and Lombard. They wrote to me a month after the interview, but by that time I was no longer so keen on the idea of starting out in that cold and expensive city. At least we made use of our time in New York to see some plays—*Tobacco Road* was one—and to get the only seats we could afford in the upper reaches of the Metropolitan Opera House.

The Federal Bureau of Investigation recruited at Duke. I submitted an application and was called in for an interview. After that I never heard anything further from them. Many years later, when I was Vice President, I saw J. Edgar Hoover at a party at Alice Roosevelt Longworth's house and mentioned to him that I had once applied for a position as a special agent. He called me a few days later and said that he had looked up the file and found that my application had been approved. Just before the notification was to be mailed their appropriation request for the next year was cut; if it had come through, I might have had a career as a G-man for the FBI.

I decided to return home to Whittier and begin practicing law there. My family, including my eighty-eight-year-old grandmother, drove East for my graduation in June 1937. It was a proud day for them, made more so by the fact that on the day they arrived an announcement was made that I had finished third in my class and had been named a member of the prestigious national legal honor society, the Order of the Coif.

I arrived back in Whittier with good prospects but an uncertain future. First I had to pass the California bar. I would have just six weeks to study for the test for which most candidates allowed over two months; even worse, the three-day exam would include the extensive California code, which we had not studied at all at Duke.

Waiting for the results was an unnerving experience for me and my family. The scuttlebutt was that those who had passed received a simple notice in a regular envelope; those who failed received a large envelope containing all the papers necessary for applying to take the exam again. During the weeks of waiting for the results we eagerly checked the mailbox each day. Then one morning my mother returned from the mailbox in tears, holding the long-awaited envelope. It was a large one, obviously filled with papers. I did not want her to see my distress, so I went into the bathroom and shut the door before opening the envelope. Scuttlebutt notwithstanding, I had passed the exam: the letter was accompanied by voluminous instructions about making arrangements to be sworn in and other technical matters. I walked back to the kitchen and announced the good news.

I got a job in Whittier's oldest law firm, Wingert and Bewley. The first legal work I did involved the usual estate and divorce cases that fall to many young lawyers. I found the divorce cases unhappy and unsettling. At first I was surprised by some of the intimate matters people argued about, and equally surprised by the fact that they could calmly sit down and tell a stranger, even their lawyer, about them. I always tried to talk my clients into a reconciliation but seldom succeeded.

I enjoyed being a lawyer, and after a year the firm became Wingert, Bewley, and Nixon. Now for the first time I was no longer Frank and Hannah Nixon's son—I was Mr. Nixon, the new partner in Wingert and Bewley.

Young lawyers trying to get business for their firms are expected to join local clubs, so I began to participate extensively in community affairs. I joined the Kiwanis Club of La Habra and the 20-30 Club, a group for young business and professional men between those ages. By 1941 I had pretty well established myself in the community. I had been elected president of the 20-30 Club, and was president of the Whittier College Alumni Association, president of the Duke University Alumni of California, president of the Orange County Association of Cities, and the youngest member ever chosen for the Whittier College board of trustees. I was approached by several of the town's Republican leaders about running for the state assembly. I was flattered and interested by this suggestion, but the war intervened.

One day in 1938, Mrs. Lilly Baldwin, the director of the local amateur theatre group, telephoned me to ask if I would like to play the part of a prosecuting attorney in their upcoming production of Ayn Rand's courtroom drama, *The Night of January 16th.* I took the part and thoroughly enjoyed this experience in amateur dramatics.

Several months later I went to the casting tryouts for a production of George S. Kaufman and Alexander Woollcott's play, *The Dark Tower.* I thought I knew everyone in Whittier, but that night a beautiful and vivacious young woman with titian hair appeared whom I had never seen before. I found I could not take my eyes away from her. This new girl in town was Pat Ryan, and she had just begun teaching at Whittier High School. For me it was a case of love at first sight.

I got a friend to introduce us and then offered them both a ride home. On the way I asked Pat if she would like a date with me. She said, "I'm very busy." I said, "You shouldn't say that, because someday I am going to marry you!" We all laughed because it seemed so unlikely at that time. But I wonder whether it was a sixth sense that prompted me to make such an impetuous statement.

Pat's life deserves a volume of its own, and perhaps someday she will write that volume herself. It is an exceptional story, just as she is an exceptional woman with great independence, keen intelligence, and a warm sense of humor. She was born on March 16, 1912, in the little mining town of Ely, Nevada, and was christened Thelma Catherine Ryan. When she was a year old, her father decided to quit the mines and bring his family to a small ranch about twenty miles southwest of Los Angeles, near Artesia, California. There, the family of seven—her parents, a sister, and three brothers—lived in a house very much like the Nixons' in nearby Yorba Linda.

She decided to adopt the name her Irish father liked to call her, and became known to everyone as Pat. It is deeply irritating to be burdened with a name you dislike, and when our daughters were born Pat suggested that we give them only one name each, Patricia and Julie, so that they could change them or add to them when they were old enough to decide.

Her mother died of cancer when Pat was only thirteen, and Pat had to take her place, cooking and keeping house for her father and brothers. About the time she graduated from high school the long years in the mine took their toll and her father became ill with silicosis. Pat gave up her plans for college and nursed him until his death two years later. With her father gone and her brothers away at college, she was now completely on her own.

After her father died, Pat continued to live in the family house. She worked part-time as a teller in a bank and began attending classes at Fullerton Junior College. During the summer she heard that an elderly couple she knew was moving to New York and wanted someone to drive them across the country. Much to their surprise, this pretty, young girl asked for the job—and much to her surprise, she got it.

Pat was completely captivated by New York, and after only a few days she decided to stay there. She became a secretary and then took an X-ray technicians' course at Seton Hospital, which was run by the Sisters of Charity. She lived in the hospital annex and chauffeured the nuns around town when they went shopping.

Pat's goal had always been to continue her education, and after two years she returned to Los Angeles and registered at the University of Southern California. She supported herself by working forty hours a week as a research assistant to a professor. For a year she also worked as a salesperson in Bullock's Wilshire department store, and from time to time she was hired as an extra for crowd scenes in the movies. If you look closely, you can spot her in *Becky Sharp* and *Small Town Girl*. Offers of bigger parts and even a career in the movies could not distract her from her education, and she received a B.S. degree with honors from USC in 1937, the same year I graduated from Duke.

Pat's interest was marketing, and she expected to work for a department store. But jobs were hard to find, and when the opportunity arose to teach business courses at Whittier High School for $190 a month, she jumped at it. She was an immediate hit at the school, charming students and faculty alike. She was faculty adviser for the Student Pep Club and prepared programs for school assemblies and rallies. Because of her interest in dramatics, she decided to audition for the local theatre group. That was where she met the intense young man with the dark curly hair and the prominent nose who could not take his eyes away from her at the tryouts for *The Dark Tower*.

Pat and I began to see each other regularly. We went ice skating at the new indoor rink near Artesia, swimming at nearby beaches, and skiing in the mountains just outside Los Angeles. We were both movie fans and we often drove up to the large movie theatres in Hollywood. Fortunately Pat also liked football, so we went to as many Whittier and USC games as we could. She met my parents and they both liked her immediately. They were particularly impressed by her obvious strength of character and indomitable spirit.

In 1940 I sent Pat a May basket with an engagement ring set among the flowers. We were married on June 21, at a small family ceremony at the Mission Inn in Riverside, California. For our honeymoon we drove for two weeks through Mexico. We had very little money, so we had stocked up on canned foods in order to avoid the expense of restaurants. After we were on our way, we discovered that our friends had removed the labels from all the cans, and thus every meal became a game of chance. Several times we ended up having pork and beans for breakfast and grapefruit slices for dinner.

Back in Whittier I returned to my law office and Pat returned to teaching. Our life was happy and full of promise. As the 1940 elections approached, I strongly supported Wendell Willkie because, while I favored some of Roosevelt's domestic programs, particularly Social Security, I opposed his attempt to break the two-term tradition. I even made a couple of speeches for Willkie before small local groups in Whittier.

In 1941 Pat and I saved enough money to take a Caribbean cruise on the United Fruit Company's freight and passenger ship *Ulua*. Except for the fact that I was seasick for almost the entire trip, we enjoyed what turned out to be our last vacation for several years. My sharpest recollection of the trip is of the evening of June 22, 1941, when our elderly black steward told us that word had just come over the ship's radio that Hitler had invaded Russia. We both hoped this would lead to a Russian victory and Hitler's downfall. I despised Hitler, and despite my disenchantment with Stalin over the Hitler-Stalin pact, had no particular anti-Soviet or anticommunist feelings.

In December 1941, thanks to the recommendations of one of my professors from Duke, David Cavers, I was offered a job with the Office of Price Administration in Washington. The pay was only $3,200 a year, not nearly so much as Pat and I were making together with her teaching and my law practice. But it seemed a good opportunity to go to Washington and observe the working of the government firsthand. I also think that my mother was secretly relieved by this decision. Although it would take me far from Whittier again, she probably thought that if war came I would stay working in the government rather than compromise our Quaker principles by deciding to fight in the armed services.

One Sunday shortly before we were to leave for Washington, Pat and I decided to go to the movies in Hollywood. On the way we stopped for a visit at her sister Neva's house. When we arrived, Neva's husband, Marc, said that he had just heard on the radio an unconfirmed report that the Japanese had bombed Pearl Harbor. I said I was sure that it was just one more of the frequent scare stories we all had been hearing, and we went on to the matinee. Shortly before the film was finished, the theatre manager interrupted with an announcement that all servicemen had been called to their units immediately. When we left the theatre, I saw the headline: *Japs Bomb Pearl Harbor*. The newsboy held up the paper as I walked over. He said, "We're at war, mister."

Early in January 1942 Pat and I drove across the country to a Washington that was now the capital of a nation at war. We found a small apartment nearby in Virginia, and I reported to the OPA office in one of the "temporary" buildings on Independence Avenue a few blocks from the Capitol.

I cannot say that my eight months at OPA were particularly happy ones, but at least they were instructive. I was an assistant attorney for the rationing coordination section, which dealt primarily with rationing rubber and automobile tires. One of the first lessons I learned was how government bureaucrats work. I went to Washington as a P-3 at $3,200 a year. I found that others with lesser academic records and not as much legal experience had come in as P-4s, a step higher, and some even as P-5s, at $4,600 a year. I made no complaints, but I did talk it over with some of the people I knew in personnel. One of my superiors, David Lloyd, who later became one of President Truman's top advisers, said, "Build a little staff. Request two or three people to assist you, and then we can raise you to a P-5." I said, "But I don't need a staff." "Then you won't get a promotion," he replied.

As a junior lawyer in the tire rationing division, I cannot say that I had much effect on OPA. But the experience had an enormous effect on the policies I later developed during my political career.

One impression that stayed with me was that while some career government workers were sincere, dedicated, and able people, others became obsessed with their own power and seemed to delight in kicking people around, particularly those in the private sector. It was hard enough to make rationing work even when we had the incentive of the war and the appeal to patriotism to back it up. I knew that once the war was over, rationing and price control would be almost impossible to enforce, and that the black marketeers, just like the bootleggers during the days of Prohibition, would be the only ones to profit from a continuation of the government-controlled system.

Many men in OPA were able to get draft deferments and spent the war in their offices. Despite my Quaker background and beliefs, I never considered doing this. When I heard that young lawyers were being recruited as officers for the Navy, I talked to Pat about it and applied for a commission. I was sent to the naval officer indoctrination school at Quonset Point, Rhode Island, in August 1942.

After two months at Quonset, where I learned to stand straight and keep my shoes shined, I listed "Ships and Stations" as my first choice for active duty. I expected to be assigned to a battle fleet in the South Pacific or the North Atlantic. I could hardly believe my eyes when I opened my orders and found that I was being sent to the Naval Air Station in Ottumwa, Iowa. When I reported for duty, I found that the station was still under construction. Its uncompleted runway stopped abruptly in the middle of a cornfield. My disappointment with this assignment was soon overcome by the warmth and friendliness of our new neighbors. Pat got a job in town as a bank teller and we settled in for an enjoyable taste of Midwest life.

Just when it began to seem that I might be landlocked in Iowa for the rest of the war, I saw a notice that applications for sea duty would be accepted from officers aged twenty-nine or younger. I was exactly twenty-nine, and I sent the application in immediately. Pat was worried about my safety, but she supported my decision to try to play a real part in the war effort.

I received orders to report to San Francisco for assignment overseas, and we went back to Whittier so that I could say goodbye to my family. It was a very painful visit. Although nothing was ever said, I knew that my mother and grandmother were deeply troubled by my decision. In World War I my Uncle Oscar had gone to France with the American Friends Service Committee and worked with the Red Cross as an orderly, tending wounded soldiers on both sides of the lines. I am sure that this was the kind of service they had hoped I would choose. It was a difficult decision for me to make, but I felt that I could not sit back while my country was being attacked. The problem with Quaker pacifism, it seemed to me, was that it could only work if one were fighting a civilized, compassionate enemy. In the face of Hitler and Tojo, pacifism not only failed to stop violence—it actually played into the hands of a barbarous foe and weakened home-front morale.

Family and friends came to see Pat and me off on the

train to San Francisco. The Bewleys were there, along with my former secretary, Evlyn Dorn, and her husband, and some friends of Pat's and mine. My mother and father were there, along with Don and his wife, Clara Jane, and my youngest brother, Eddie, who was now twelve and looked like a carbon copy of me at that age. We all had breakfast at the Harvey House in Union Station. It was a painful meal, full of sad silences beneath the superficially cheerful conversation, and I was relieved when the train was finally announced. As Pat and I stood on the wooden block getting ready to board the train, I turned to take one last look. I think we all realized that we might never see each other again. My mother held her sorrow in, but my father began to sob. Pat and I watched them waving to us while the train pulled slowly out of the station until they disappeared in the distance.

Almost as soon as I left San Francisco I realized that I did not have a recent photograph of Pat to carry with me. I wrote to her and she went to a portrait studio and had one taken. I was happy when it arrived, but it made the separation even more painful for me.

I was assigned to the South Pacific Combat Air Transport Command at Nouméa on the island of New Caledonia. We were officially known as SCAT from our initials. Our unit was responsible for preparing manifests and flight plans for C-47 cargo and transport planes as they flew from island to island. The planes brought supplies in and flew the wounded out. We would unload the boxes and crates of supplies and then carefully carry aboard the stretchers of the critically wounded.

Like many assigned "down the line," I wanted to get where the action was, and I spent a lot of my time trying to get a battle-station assignment. Finally, in January 1944, I was assigned to Bougainville, which was a target for occasional Japanese bomber attacks. Shortly after I arrived, the Japanese staged an assault. When it was over, we counted thirty-five shell holes within a hundred feet of the air raid bunker six of us shared. Our tent had been completely destroyed.

Many fighter and bomber pilots came through Bougainville on their way to battle missions, and I felt that they deserved the best we could possibly give them. I used my SCAT resources to get small supplies of chopped meat and beer. Everyone in the unit had a nickname, and I was known as Nick Nixon. Whenever I received a fresh shipment, I opened "Nick's Hamburger Stand" and served a free hamburger and a bottle of Australian beer to flight crews who probably had not tasted anything to remind them of home in many weeks.

After serving on Bougainville, I requested and received an assignment as officer in charge of the SCAT detachment that was to support the invasion of Green Island. We landed in the bay in a PBY seaplane. The Japanese had already retreated, however, and the only danger came from a few straggling snipers and the ever-present giant centipedes.

The Seabees immediately went to work constructing an airstrip. A few days before it was completed, an Army B-29 bomber that had been seriously damaged flying over Rabaul had to use it for a crash landing even though some of the Seabees' equipment was still standing on it. It was dusk, almost dark, and we all cheered as the plane came in on its belly. Then we watched in horror as it crashed head-on into a bulldozer and exploded. The carnage was terrible. I can still see the wedding ring on the charred hand of one of the crewmen when I carried his body from the twisted wreckage.

My poker playing during this time has been somewhat exaggerated in terms of both my skill and my winnings. In Whittier any kind of gambling had been anathema to me as a Quaker. But the pressures of wartime, and the even more oppressive monotony, made it an irresistible diversion. I found playing poker instructive as well as entertaining and profitable. I learned that the people who have the cards are usually the ones who talk the least and the softest; those who are bluffing tend to talk loudly and give themselves away. One night in a stud poker game, with an ace in the hole, I drew a royal flush in diamonds. The odds against this are about 650,000 to 1, and I was naturally excited. But I played it with a true poker face, and won a substantial pot.

It was a lonely war for most of the men in the South Pacific, filled with seemingly interminable periods of waiting while the action unfolded thousands of miles away. We devoured the copies of *Life* magazine that filtered through to us, and, as much out of boredom as out of piety, I read and reread the old illustrated Bible that I had brought with me. Letters from home were the only thing we really had to look forward to, and I wrote to Pat every day during the fourteen months I was away. She has kept all those letters to this day.

When I was on Green Island I met Charles Lindbergh, who was flying combat missions testing new planes for the Air Force. The CO invited me to a small dinner in Lindbergh's honor, but I had to decline because a month before I had agreed to host a poker game. Today it seems incredible to me that I passed up an opportunity to have dinner with Charles Lindbergh because of a card game. But in the intense loneliness and boredom of the South Pacific our poker games were more than idle pastimes, and the etiquette surrounding them was taken very seriously. A quarter of a century later I was able to rectify this error when Charles and Anne Morrow Lindbergh accepted our invitation to attend a state dinner at the White House.

In July 1944 my overseas tour of duty was completed and I was ordered back to the States. I caught a cargo plane from Guadalcanal to Hawaii, and when we made a fueling stop at Wake Island in the middle of the night I got out to stretch my legs. For the first time I saw one of our war cemeteries. I shall never forget those white crosses, row after row after row of them, beginning at the edge of the runway and stretching out into the darkness on that tiny island so far away from home. I thought of all the men who were still out there fighting for these little bits of unfriendly and often barren ground, and I wondered, as I often had before, why Americans or the Japanese thought they were worth fighting and dying for. Of course, I knew that they were the essential stepping-stones for bringing the war home to Japan, and that we had to capture them just as the enemy had to defend them. But standing on Wake, waiting for the plane to be refueled, I was overcome with the ultimate futility of war and the terrible reality of the loss that lies behind it.

Congressman and
Senator
1947-1952

As soon as I reached San Diego I phoned Pat, and she flew down from San Francisco, where, during my time overseas, she had been working as a price analyst for the OPA. I was at the airport gate waiting for her. She wore a bright red dress, and when she saw me standing there her eyes lighted up, and she ran to the barrier and threw her arms around me.

Although I was home now, I was still in the Navy. In January 1945 I received orders to go East to work on Navy contract terminations. During these last months of the war and the first months of peace we lived in Washington, Philadelphia, New York, and Baltimore.

Those were momentous times for Americans. In April Pat and I were in Bookbinders Restaurant in Philadelphia when our waiter came over and said he had just heard on the radio that FDR had died. Like everyone else, we were shocked and saddened by the news. A month later the war in Europe was over, and we saw the newsreels of Soviet and American troops shaking hands at the Elbe. In August Pat and I joined the throng in Times Square to celebrate V-J Day.

Pat was expecting our first child, and now that the war was over we began to think seriously about what I should do in civilian life. The answer came in September in the form of a letter I received in Baltimore from Herman Perry. Manager of the Bank of America's Whittier branch, Perry was one of the community's Republican leaders. He had been a classmate of my mother's at Whittier College and was an old family friend. His letter was to the point:

Dear Dick:

I am writing you this short note to ask if you would like to be a candidate for Congress on the Republican ticket in 1946.

Jerry Voorhis expects to run—registration is about 50-50. The Republicans are gaining.

Please airmail me your reply if you are interested.

Yours very truly,
H. L. Perry

P.S. Are you a registered voter in California?

Perry knew of my interest in politics from our discussions before the war about my running for the state assembly. But in 1941 I had been a newly married young lawyer just starting a career; in 1946 I would be a demobilized Navy lieutenant commander with a wife and child. It was clear that if I were to go after the congressional nomination seriously, it would require my full-time effort and attention. Pat and I would have to be able to support ourselves and finance the campaign at least until the primary in June. If I won the nomination, we could count on campaign funds from the party organization, although we would still have to pay all our personal expenses. With my pay, Pat's salary, and my poker winnings, we had managed to save $10,000 during the war. We had planned to use it to buy a house. Pat was dubious about spending our savings on what was at best a risky political campaign. But the more we thought about the possibility of returning to Washington as a congressional family, the more enthusiastic we became.

Two days later I called Perry and said that I was honored by his letter and excited by the prospect of running for Congress. When I told him that I could be in California to begin campaigning by the first of the year, he poured some cold water on my enthusiasm by saying that the nomination was not his to offer. He had written to me on behalf of a candidate search committee, known as the Committee of 100, established by the Twelfth District's Republican leaders to try to find someone who had a chance of beating Voorhis. He felt that if I were interested I would have a good chance, but the committee would probably interview several other candidates before deciding which one to endorse.

The next morning I wrote Perry a letter confirming my interest. I added: "I feel very strongly that Jerry Voorhis can be beaten, and I'd welcome the opportunity to take a crack at him. An aggressive, vigorous campaign on a platform of *practical* liberalism should be the antidote the people have been looking for to take the place of Voorhis's particular brand of New Deal idealism. My brief experience in Washington with the bureaucrats and my three and a half years in the Navy have given me a pretty good idea of what a mess things are in Washington."

I flew back to Whittier for the Committee of 100 dinner meeting at the William Penn Hotel on November 2, 1945. The group's search had produced six prospective candidates, and each of us was to make a speech describing the reasons for his candidacy. I wore my Navy uniform; I didn't own a civilian suit.

Since I drew the lot as last speaker on a long program, I decided that brevity would be as much appreciated as eloquence. In the first speech of my political career I described my view of the two conflicting opinions about the nature of the American system.

One advocated by the New Deal is government control in regulating our lives. The other calls for individual freedom and all that initiative can produce.

I hold with the latter viewpoint. I believe the returning veterans, and I have talked to many of them in the foxholes, will not be satisfied with a dole or a government handout.

41

They want a respectable job in private industry where they will be recognized for what they produce, or they want the opportunity to start their own business.

If the choice of this committee comes to me I will be prepared to put on an aggressive and vigorous campaign on a platform of practical liberalism and with your help I feel very strongly that the present incumbent can be defeated.

I returned to Baltimore to wait for the committee's decision. It was after two o'clock in the morning on November 29 when the phone rang in our apartment. Roy Day, a member of the committee, shouted into the phone, "Dick, the nomination's yours!" I had received sixty-three votes. My closest competitor, Sam Gist, a furniture store owner from Pomona, received twelve.

While I was waiting to be discharged from the Navy I began a crash course in politics and public affairs. Each night when I got home from work I pored over magazines, newspapers, and books about Congress and campaigns. I wrote to House Minority Leader Joe Martin, introducing myself as the prospective Republican nominee for the Twelfth District, and I visited him in his office in the Capitol. I talked with several Republican congressmen, seeking their evaluations of Voorhis. Through the Republican Campaign Committee I obtained his complete voting record, and I spent several days familiarizing myself with it. By the time of my discharge and return to California in January, I was confident that I knew Voorhis's record as well as he did himself. As it turned out, I knew it even better.

In the initial meetings with my campaign advisers, we agreed that the first thing I had to do was to become known throughout the district. While I was well known in the Whittier area, I was a stranger in all the other towns.

We began holding a series of "house meetings" in which Republican supporters would open up their houses to as many—or as few—of their friends and neighbors as were interested in coming to meet me. Over tea and coffee, I made brief remarks and then answered questions. These house meetings permitted me to meet hundreds of voters and helped me to enlist the women volunteers whose dedicated work is so important to any campaign. They also let me know what was really on the minds of the voters.

Pat was my best helper. Very soon after Tricia was born on February 21, she volunteered her time for typing press releases, mailing pamphlets, and keeping track of my schedule. She went to many of the house meetings with me and afterward gave thoughtful and sometimes quite persistent critiques of my performances.

Primary day was June 4. At that time California law permitted cross-filing, which meant that a candidate could enter the primaries of both parties. Thus the primary served as a trial heat for the later general election. Voorhis and I took advantage of this, and each of us was on the ballot as a candidate for both the Republican and Democratic nominations. When the votes were counted, each of us, as expected, had won the nomination of his own party. But in the combined vote totals, he had beaten me by about 7,500 votes. I knew I faced an uphill fight if I were to defeat him in November.

I was disappointed at not having done better, but I considered it significant and promising that this was Voorhis's weakest primary showing since 1936. The Twelfth District was basically conservative and Republican, and I was confident that we could recapture it if we could just maintain the intensity of the primary campaign right through the general election in November. "All we need," I wrote to Roy Day, now a key campaign adviser, "is a win complex and we'll take him in November."

The greatest advantage I had in 1946 was that the national trend that year was Republican. People were tired of the privations and shortages of four years of war, and in the burst of postwar prosperity they were beginning to bridle against the governmental regulations and interference that were written into so much of the New Deal legislation. In the Twelfth District, as in many others across the country, returning veterans could not find homes at prices or rents they could afford; many could not find housing at all. The shortage of consumer goods was exacerbated by the many long strikes in 1946, and prices skyrocketed as a result. Some butcher shops in the district put signs in the window: "No meat today? Ask your congressman." My ads asked: "Are you satisfied with present conditions? Can you buy meat, a new car, a refrigerator, clothes you need? A vote for Nixon is a vote for change. Where are all those new houses you were promised? A vote for Nixon is a vote for change." The nationwide Republican campaign slogan in 1946 was, "HAD ENOUGH?" And the answer from the voters was clearly going to be a resounding "Yes!"

In anticipation of a Republican landslide, many Democrats tried to dissociate themselves from their party, and some even campaigned as critics of Truman and his policies. But Jerry Voorhis was far enough to the left of Truman that this was one problem I did not have to worry about.

Shortly before the campaign officially began in September, I received a request from a group called the Independent Voters of South Pasadena to participate in a debate with Voorhis. Most of my advisers were dubious about the idea, especially after they discovered that the Independent Voters group consisted predominantly of New Deal liberals. I felt, however, that as a challenger I could hardly turn down an invitation to debate my opponent.

As it turned out, the debate was not really a debate at all. It was more a joint public meeting in which each of us made an opening statement and then responded to questions from the floor. Voorhis spoke first in a rambling, discursive way about the nature of the executive-legislative relationship and the need for progressive legislation. He defended the record of the Truman administration. In my opening statement I made a hard attack on the bureaucratic red tape and bungling involved in the meat and housing shortages, and I called for strong action to prevent more of the strikes and labor disputes that had been hurting the economy so badly.

In the question period we were allotted three minutes for each answer. I tried to give brisk, concise responses, but Voorhis had trouble keeping within the time limit. There was one question, however, to which he had no trouble giving a short answer. He was asked whether he had once been a registered Socialist. He answered that he had, but only in the 1920s and during the early years of the Depression, when he felt that the two major parties weren't doing the job.

Then one of my supporters asked Voorhis to explain his "peculiar ideas about money"—a reference to his pet ideas on monetary reform, which had been known as his "funny money" program ever since he presented it in his book *Out of Debt, Out of Danger.* His colleagues in Congress had not been able to understand his program, and neither could the voters in Pasadena that night.

When it was my turn, one of Voorhis's supporters accused me of making false charges against Voorhis by claiming that he had been endorsed by the Political Action Committee of the Congress of Industrial Organizations. This question opened what became—at least after the fact—the most famous and controversial issue of the 1946 campaign.

The PAC had been established as a political arm of organized labor to support Franklin Roosevelt in the 1944 election. A sister organization, the National Citizens Political Action Committee (NCPAC), was set up to permit non-union participation. Until his death, labor leader Sidney Hillman served as chairman of both groups, and many other leaders of CIO-PAC also served on NCPAC. Both groups interviewed candidates and then made funds and campaign workers available to those whom they endorsed. It was estimated that in 1944 the two PAC organizations contributed over $650,000 to political campaigns. Although the leadership of both groups was non-Communist, the organizations were known to be infiltrated with Communists and fellow travelers who, because of their discipline, wielded an influence disproportionate to their numbers. Such influence was viewed as a problem because there was an emerging concern about Soviet postwar intentions and a corresponding apprehension about the communist movement in America.

Voorhis had been endorsed by CIO-PAC in 1944. In 1946, however, CIO-PAC decided to withhold its endorsement—ostensibly because he had not supported some measures in Congress considered important by the union leadership. In the spring of 1946, the Los Angeles County chapter of the NCPAC circulated a bulletin indicating that it was going to endorse Voorhis regardless of what

CIO-PAC did. The May 31, 1946, issue of *Daily People's World,* the West Coast Communist newspaper, ran an article with the headline: *Candidates Endorsed by "Big Five."* The "Big Five" labor and progressive coalition was made up of CIO-PAC, NCPAC, the railroad brotherhoods, the Progressive AFL, and the Hollywood Independent Citizens Committee of the Arts, Sciences, and Professions. The *Daily People's World* article reported that the Big Five had interviewed the candidates and included the list of endorsements for the June 4 primary. The first name on the list was H. Jerry Voorhis. Following his name was this note: "No CIO endorsement." In answer, then, to my charge that he was endorsed by PAC, Voorhis had replied that he was not—that year—endorsed by *CIO*-PAC. To me that was an irrelevancy. The Los Angeles County chapter of NCPAC had a large number of Communists and fellow travelers, and, considering the close ties between the two PACs, I thought that the question of which PAC had endorsed him was a distinction without a difference.

When the question was raised in the South Pasadena debate, I pulled from my pocket a copy of the NCPAC bulletin announcing its endorsement recommendation and walked across the stage to show it to Voorhis. Reading aloud the names of the board members of each organization, many of which were the same, I demonstrated that there was little practical difference between a CIO-PAC endorsement and an NCPAC one.

Voorhis repeated his claim that CIO-PAC and NCPAC were separate organizations, but I could tell from the audience's reaction that I had made my point. A few days later Voorhis himself underscored it by sending a telegram to NCPAC headquarters in New York requesting that "whatever qualified endorsement the Citizens PAC may have given me be withdrawn." Had he repudiated the endorsement before he was backed onto the defensive and forced to act, the issue might never have developed. But since he had not, I thought then and still think that the endorsement was a legitimate issue to raise. Communist infiltration of labor and political organizations was a serious threat in those early postwar years, and a candidate's attitude toward endorsements by heavily infiltrated organizations was a barometer of his attitude toward that threat.

Repudiation was also an essential weapon against infiltration.

After this debate, the PAC became a peripheral but heated issue in the campaign. While Voorhis equivocated, my campaign director, Harrison McCall, came up with the idea of passing out plastic thimbles saying: "Nixon for Congress—Put the Needle in the PAC."

This first "debate" was so successful that many of my supporters urged me to challenge Voorhis to other joint appearances. I had some reservations, because each one would require two or three days of concentrated preparation, and I did not want to take off any more time from campaigning. Murray Chotiner, the brilliant and no-nonsense public relations man who was running Bill Knowland's senatorial campaign and advising me part-time on mine, went straight to the point. "Dick," he said, "you're running behind, and when you're behind, you don't play it safe. You must run a high-risk campaign." He paused for a moment until I nodded my agreement, and then he said, "Good. I've already arranged for an announcement challenging Voorhis to more debates."

Voorhis accepted my challenge, and during the course of the campaign there were four more debates held in various towns in the district. They became very popular and drew overflow crowds. When the last one was held in San Gabriel the week before the election, more than a thousand people were crammed into the hall and loudspeakers had to be set up for the several hundred standing outside.

My research into Voorhis's record showed that of the more than a hundred bills he had introduced in Congress during the previous four years, only one had actually been passed into law. The effect of this bill was to transfer jurisdiction over rabbit breeders from the Department of the Interior to the Department of Agriculture. I began running a newspaper advertisement pointing out this rather insignificant legislative achievement. Voorhis replied with an ad under the headline: *Deception of the Voter Has No Place in American Politics.* He listed several of his congressional accomplishments, but they were either resolutions or speeches, not bills enacted into law.

47

At our fourth debate, at the Monrovia high school, Voorhis raised this issue and charged that my statements about his record were lies. I pointed out that none of the examples he cited was an actual bill that had been passed into law. To the delight of my supporters in the overflow audience of 1,200, I suggested that one had to be a rabbit to get effective representation in this congressional district.

Voorhis kept the issue alive, continuing to charge that I had lied about his record. In my opening remarks at our final debate I turned to him and said: "Congressman, I flatly challenge you to name one public bill of your authorship which passed both houses of Congress during the last four years." In his reply, he referred to a measure he wrote establishing National Employ the Physically Handicapped Week. My research into his record paid off again. In my rebuttal I produced a copy of the measure, handed it to Voorhis, and pointed out that this too was a resolution, not a bill.

Since no polls had been taken, I had no idea on Election Day how close the race might be. There were no voting machines, and the counting of the paper ballots lasted long into the following morning. But before we went to bed at about 4 A.M., it was clear that I had won. By the next afternoon the totals were complete. I had received 65,586 votes, and Voorhis received 49,994.

I was thirty-three years old, and the Twelfth District's new congressman.

In 1950, 1952, 1956, 1968, and 1972 I was again to experience the satisfaction of winning, and most of those campaigns were tough ones. But nothing could equal the excitement and jubilation of winning the first campaign. Pat and I were happier on November 6, 1946, than we were ever to be again in my political career.

By defeating a well-known figure like Voorhis, I briefly became a minor national celebrity. *Time* reported that I "turned a California grass-roots campaign (dubbed 'hopeless' by wheelhorse Republicans) into a triumph over high-powered, high-minded Democratic incumbent Jerry Voorhis" and added that I had "politely avoided personal attacks" on my opponent. *Newsweek* said, "In five

Lincoln-Douglas debates, [Nixon] bested his opponent, New Dealer Jerry Voorhis, who admitted: 'This fellow has a silver tongue.' "

Despite later—and widespread—misconceptions, communism was not the central issue in the 1946 campaign. The PAC controversy provided emotional and rhetorical excitement, but it was not the issue that stirred or motivated most voters. The central issue in the 1946 campaign was the quality of life in postwar America. The loudest and longest applause given any line in any of the debates came when I said in the first one that "the time has come in this country when no labor leader or no management leader should have the power to deny the American people any of the necessities of life." Voorhis himself later wrote in his autobiography, *Confessions of a Congressman:* "The most important single factor in the campaign of 1946 was the difference in general attitude between the 'outs' and 'ins.' Anyone seeking to unseat an incumbent needed only to point out all the things that had gone wrong and all the troubles of the war period and its aftermath. Many of these things were intimate experiences in the everyday lives of the people." I took advantage of a nationwide phenomenon *Time* called "a cold but nonetheless angry voice raised against many things: price muddles, shortages, black markets, strikes, government bungling and confusion, too much government in too many things."

It was also true that although Voorhis was a hardworking and generally respected congressman, he was not really in tune with the voters of the district. I have no doubt that the Committee of 100 was right in its belief that any good Republican candidate would have had a chance of unseating Voorhis in 1946 despite his popularity and his incumbency.

Voorhis, the former Socialist, believed in large-scale government intervention, and I did not. He saw dark conspiracies among "reactionaries" and "monopolies," and I did not. He was generally an uncritical supporter of the labor unions, while I considered myself their critical friend. He advocated policies that I believed shackled and restricted

American industry. His political views were 180 degrees away from mine. Most important, his votes in Congress on a wide range of issues did not represent the wishes of the voters in his district.

Since Voorhis was the front-runner and I a newcomer, I ran an especially vigorous campaign. I challenged his judgment and his voting record, a record that I appeared to know better than he did himself. If some of my rhetoric seems overstated now, it was nonetheless in keeping with the approach that seasoned Republican politicians were using that year. For example, when Henry Wallace campaigned for Democrats in California, Governor Earl Warren called him a spearhead of an attack "by leftist organizations that are attuned to the communist movement." Earlier in the year, Ohio Senator Robert Taft charged that Democratic congressional proposals "bordered on communism," while Joe Martin called for Republican victories in order to oust the Communists and fellow travelers from the federal government.

One of the most distorted charges subsequently made about the 1946 campaign involved my supporters. As I moved up the political ladder, my adversaries tried to picture me as the hand-picked stooge of oil magnates, rich bankers, real estate tycoons, and conservative millionaires. But a look at the list of my early supporters shows that they were typical representatives of the Southern California middle class: an auto dealer, a bank manager, a printing salesman, an insurance salesman, and a furniture dealer. What united them was no special vested interest but the fierce desire of average people to regain control of their own lives. Along with a majority of the voters in the Twelfth District, they had "had enough," and they decided to do something about it.

My first choice for a committee assignment was the prestigious Judiciary Committee. I was not surprised when I did not receive it, and I was pleased to be assigned to my second choice, the Education and Labor Committee. By one of those curious coincidences of history, another freshman assigned to that committee was a good-looking, good-humored young Democrat from Massachusetts named John Fitzgerald Kennedy. The newly elected members on the committee drew straws to determine their positions in the all-important seniority ranking. Kennedy drew the shortest straw among the Democrats, and I drew the shortest straw among the Republicans. As a result, he and I shared the dubious distinction of sitting at the opposite ends of the committee table, like a pair of unmatched bookends.

The Education and Labor Committee's work took up most of my time during 1947, my first year in Congress. We held months of hearings on legislation, which I supported, that passed into law as the Taft-Hartley Act in June 1947.

A public affairs group in McKeesport, Pennsylvania, asked the district's Democratic congressman, Frank Buchanan, to select the freshman from each party who seemed to have the brightest political future, and to invite them to debate the Taft-Hartley bill at a public meeting. Buchanan chose Kennedy and me, and on April 21, 1947, we had the first Kennedy-Nixon debate. McKeesport is near Pittsburgh, and for this meeting the normally Republican and conservative audience was augmented by a substantial number of anti-Taft-Hartley union men who introduced some acrimonious moments into the question period.

We took the *Capital Limited* back to Washington after the debate. We drew straws for the lower berth, and—this time—I won. We sat up late, talking far more about foreign policy than domestic issues. Kennedy and I were too different in background, outlook, and temperament to become close friends, but we were thrown together throughout our early careers, and we never had less than an amicable relationship. We were of the same generation—he was only four years younger than I; we were both Navy veterans; we both came to the House the same year; and we were both committed to devoting enormous energy to our work. Our exchanges in committee meetings and our discussions in the cloakrooms were never tinged with the personal acerbity that can make political differences uncomfortable. In those early years we saw ourselves as political opponents but not political rivals. We shared one quality which distinguished us from most of our fellow congressmen: neither of us was a backslapper, and we were both uncomfortable with boisterous displays of superficial camaraderie. He was shy, and that sometimes made him appear aloof. But it was shyness born of an instinct that guarded privacy and concealed emotions. I understood these qualities because I shared them.

Pat and I saw the inside of the White House for the first time on February 18, 1947, when we attended a reception the Trumans gave for the new members of the Eightieth Congress. On July 2 I was included in a group of four freshmen Republican congressmen for whom Representative Charles Kersten of Wisconsin had arranged a private meeting with the President. In the notes I made later that day, I described the Oval Office as a "big pleasant room," with "no gadgets" except for a pony express confidential pouch that Truman pointed out to us. Pictures of his family were on the table behind his desk, and also a model airplane that I assumed to be the presidential aircraft—an Air Force Constellation that Truman had named the *Sacred Cow*.

Truman made us all feel welcome and relaxed as we shook hands with him. We sat around the desk, and he spoke very earnestly about the necessity of rehabilitating Europe and emphasized his concern that peaceful German production should be encouraged. He said he was glad to see us even though we were Republicans, because he always considered it necessary for the two parties to cooperate in foreign affairs. He said, "Some of my best friends never agree with me politically."

He led us over to a big globe where he pointed to Manchuria and remarked on how rich it was in oil and mineral deposits. He said that the Soviets had devastated the whole region but that Manchuria would recover and become the next great productive area for the world. Then he turned the globe with the palm of his hand and pointed to the great mass of the Soviet Union. He said, "The Russians are like us, they look and act like us. They are fine people. They got along with our soldiers in Berlin very well. As far as I am concerned, they can have whatever they want just so they don't try to impose their system on others." He mentioned the accounts of Mrs. Roosevelt attending an international conference where the Soviet delegate was always obstructing action by saying that he had to clear the issue with the Kremlin. "That's just the way it was at Potsdam where I went with charitable feelings in view of their contributions in the war," Truman remarked. He said he could not understand what the Russians wanted as far as their policy toward Germany and toward Europe was concerned.

He told us that dropping the atomic bomb was an awful decision for him to make. Speaking of his job, he said, "It's the greatest show on earth, and it doesn't cost anything to the weekly newsman who covers the White House." I observed in my notes that Truman's strength was "his hominess, his democratic attitude, and his sincerity."

Twenty-two years later, when I was President, Pat and I flew to Independence to present Truman the piano he had played in the White House, for his presidential library. He was fighting a rough bout with flu, but his flair for pithy plain speaking was undiminished. I knew that he had long since changed his opinion of the Soviets. In 1969 he told me, "The Russians are liars—you can't trust them. At Potsdam they agreed to everything and broke their word. It's too bad the second world power is like this, but that's the way it is, and we must keep our strength."

Most freshmen received only one committee assignment, but Joe Martin, the new Republican Speaker, asked if I would be also willing to sit on the House Committee on Un-American Activities. Now that the Republicans controlled Congress, we would be held accountable for the committee's frequently irresponsible conduct. "We need a young lawyer on that committee to smarten it up," he said, and he added that he would consider my acceptance a personal favor. Put in this way, it was an offer I could not very well refuse. I accepted with considerable reluctance, however, because of the dubious reputation the committee had acquired under its former chairman, Martin Dies, a flamboyant and at times demagogic Texas Democrat.

My own attitude toward communism had recently changed from one of general disinterest to one of extreme concern. I do not recall being particularly disturbed when Roosevelt recognized the Soviet Union in 1934. During the Spanish Civil War the concerted press campaign against

Franco—who was always described as a fascist rebel—led me to side with the Loyalists, whose communist orientation was seldom mentioned in the newspapers. At the time of the Hitler-Stalin pact I was strongly against Stalin, not because he was a Communist but because he was allied with Hitler, whom I despised; during the war I was pro-Russian, not because the Russians were Communists but because they were helping us fight Hitler. I was elated when both the United States and the Soviet Union supported the founding of the United Nations. As an admirer of Woodrow Wilson I felt that we had made a serious mistake in not joining the League of Nations, and I believed that the UN offered the world's best chance to build a lasting peace.

It was Churchill's Iron Curtain speech, delivered in Fulton, Missouri, in March 1946 that profoundly affected my attitude toward communism in general and the Soviet Union in particular. He said:

> From Stettin in the Baltic to Trieste in the Adriatic, an iron curtain has descended across the Continent. Behind that line lie all the capitals of the ancient states of Central and Eastern Europe. Warsaw, Berlin, Prague, Vienna, Budapest, Belgrade, Bucharest, and Sofia, all these famous cities and the populations around them lie in what I must call the Soviet sphere, and all are subject in one form or another, not only to Soviet influence, but to a very high, and, in many cases, increasing measure of control from Moscow.

I was jolted by these words, and at first I wondered if he had gone too far. But as the Communist subjugation of Eastern Europe became more and more apparent—with the takeover of Hungary in 1947 and Czechoslovakia in 1948—I realized that the defeat of Hitler and Japan had not produced a lasting peace, and freedom was now threatened by a new and even more dangerous enemy.

My maiden speech in the House on February 18, 1947, was the presentation of a contempt of Congress citation against Gerhart Eisler, who had been identified as the top Communist agent in America. When he refused to testify before the committee, he was held in contempt. I spoke for only ten minutes, describing the background of the case, and

I concluded: "It is essential as members of this House that we defend vigilantly the fundamental rights of freedom of speech and freedom of the press. But we must bear in mind that the rights of free speech and free press do not carry with them the right to advocate the destruction of the very government which protects the freedom of an individual to express his views."

The only member who voted against the contempt citation was Vito Marcantonio of New York.

Eisler was finally indicted for passport fraud. Before he could be tried, however, he jumped bail and fled to East Germany, where he eventually became director of propaganda for the Communist regime.

At the end of 1947 I was appointed to a special legislative subcommittee of the Committee on Un-American Activities. We held some wide-ranging hearings into the nature of communist philosophy and practice, and on the basis of these I prepared a report outlining a new approach to the complicated problem of internal communist subversion. Most of the dedicated anticommunists felt that the best way to stop internal subversion was to outlaw the Communist Party. I believed that this approach would be inefficient and counterproductive. The practical effect of outlawing the party would only be to drive the hard core of true believers underground. I thought it made more sense to drive the Communist Party into the open so that we could know who its members were.

Another problem in this area was finding an objective way to define and identify Communist front organizations. Too many conservatives and other anticommunists applied broad and imprecise criteria, with the result that many extremely liberal and left-wing organizations were unfairly tarred with the communist brush. I felt that no matter how abhorrent the beliefs of any individuals or groups might be, as long as they did not receive financial support or orders from foreign governments, or engage in illegal activities, their right to their beliefs must be protected.

Working closely together, Karl Mundt of South Dakota and I prepared a bill that was introduced in the spring of 1948 and became known as the Mundt-Nixon bill. It was the first piece of legislation to emerge in ten years from the

House Committee on Un-American Activities. It provided for the registration of all Communist Party members and required a statement of the source of all printed and broadcast material issued by organizations that were found to be Communist fronts. Under our bill, the identification of a group as a Communist front would be made by a Subversive Activities Control Board, which would investigate a group at the request of the Attorney General.

I was made floor manager for the debate on the bill; Vito Marcantonio was the floor leader for the Democrats. At the end of the first day's debate, I spoke briefly: "There is too much loose talk and confusion on the Communist issue. By passing this bill the Congress of the United States will go on record as to just what is subversive about communism in the United States. . . . It will once and for all spike many of the loose charges about organizations being Communist fronts because they happen to advocate some of the same policies which the Communists support."

The Mundt-Nixon bill passed the House on May 19, 1948, by a vote of 319 to 58. The Senate let it die in committee, and it was not until 1950 that some of its provisions were embodied in the McCarran Act. By then, of course, the nature of the question of internal communism had changed because of the Hiss case, and the harsher terms of the McCarran Act reflected that change.

It is important to remember that the perception of communism in American politics changed completely in the early postwar years. During the war, the Soviets were our allies against Hitler. The photographs of American and Russian soldiers shaking hands at the Elbe made a strong impression on many Americans, who looked forward to a new dawn of international peace and cooperation.

In the main, anticommunism in postwar America meant opposition to the kind of dictatorial state socialism that existed in Russia and that many Americans saw as a negation of everything America stood for. In the 1946 campaign, for example, when I talked about the "communist-dominated PAC," my remarks were generally understood in this context of dictatorial socialism versus free enterprise.

In the years 1946 to 1948 domestic communism was a

peripheral issue. Until the Hiss case, it was generally not seen as a clear and present danger to our way of life. A poll in January 1948, for example, found that 40 percent of those questioned felt the American Communist Party posed no threat, while 45 percent believed that it posed a potential threat.

As the presidential election of 1948 approached, however, Truman must have begun to worry about the issue of internal security. Now that the Committee on Un-American Activities was in Republican hands, he may have decided that the best way to handle the issue was to cover up the evidence. On March 15, 1948, he ordered all federal departments and agencies to refuse future congressional requests or subpoenas for information regarding loyalty or security matters. This decision backfired because instead of defusing the issue it made it appear that Truman was trying to cover something up. Instead of admitting an error of judgment, Truman decided to tough it through. His course led him into the shoals of red herring that caused him so many problems, not only in the Hiss case but also two years later when McCarthy began his anticommunist career with the ostensible purpose of getting Truman to rescind this executive order.

It was the Hiss case that completely changed the public's perception of domestic communism. People were now alerted to a serious threat to our liberties. At the same time this new awareness unfortunately led to emotional excesses and demagogic imprecisions that clouded the issue more than they illuminated it.

THE HERTER COMMITTEE

On Monday, July 30, 1947, I was probably the most surprised man in Washington when I opened the morning newspaper and read that I had been chosen by Speaker Joe Martin to be one of the nineteen members of a select committee headed by Congressman Christian Herter of Massachusetts to go to Europe and prepare a report in connection with the foreign aid plan that the Secretary of State, General George C. Marshall, had unveiled at a Harvard commencement speech in June. I had not even spoken to Martin or anyone else about the committee because I had not thought there was any chance of being appointed to it.

The appointment was an unexpected honor and opportunity for me. My determination to work hard had paid off unexpectedly soon. I was also modest enough to recognize that geography and age had played a part in my selection. Martin wanted the committee to represent a cross section of the House, and I was the only Westerner and the youngest member appointed to it. I would now have an opportunity to work with some of the most senior and influential men in the House and a chance to show what I could do in the field of foreign affairs.

Most of my advisers in California were pleased with my appointment, but they wanted the committee's report to disown the bipartisan Truman-Vandenberg foreign policy that was being promoted in Washington to support the Marshall Plan. Just before we sailed for Europe, I received a long letter signed by half a dozen of my strongest supporters. It began, "We feel it appropriate to state our views at this time inasmuch as you are embarking on a trip on which you will be subjected first, to a skillful orientation program by the State Department and later, to no less skillfully prepared European propaganda. It is our hope and belief that, even in the midst of these powerful influences, you will be able to maintain the level-headed course you have followed in Congress." The conclusion was a straightforward partisan reminder that a presidential election was little more than a year away: "We believe there is only one fundamental cure for this whole situation—that is to rid ourselves of all the hangover philosophies of the New Deal by making a clean sweep in Washington and electing a Republican administration in 1948. This can be done provided the Republican members of Congress are wise enough to refuse to be drawn into support of a dangerously unworkable and profoundly inflationary foreign policy and, provided further, that the Democrats do not succeed in so dividing our party by bipartisan internationalism that there no longer is any way to tell who is a Republican."

The committee sailed from New York on the *Queen Mary* at the end of August. Despite all our briefings and studying, I do not think that any of us was really prepared for what we found in Europe. From the minute we stepped off the luxurious ship in Southampton it was clear that we had come to a continent tottering on the brink of starvation and chaos. In every country we visited the situation was the same: without American aid, millions would starve or die of diseases caused by malnutrition before the winter was over. The political facts were equally evident: without our food and aid, Europe would be plunged into anarchy, revolution, and, ultimately, communism.

Britain's Prime Minister, Clement Attlee, invited us to tea at 10 Downing Street, and we spent an hour with the Falstaffian Foreign Secretary, Ernest Bevin, whose recent speech advocating that all the gold at Fort Knox be divided up among the nations of the world tended to get the discussion off on the wrong foot.

If London was depressing, Berlin seemed hopeless. What once had been a great city was now block after block, mile after mile of charred desolation. It hardly seemed possible that three million people were still living amidst the rubble. As we stood in the vast ruined hall of what had been Hitler's Chancellery, small thin-faced German boys tried to sell us their fathers' war medals as souvenirs.

Despite the cautious reluctance of some of our embassy people, I insisted that we meet with the Communist Party leaders in each country we visited. We found that these men were usually more vigorous and impressive than their democratic counterparts. I was curious to see how their minds worked, and I also wanted to assess their relationship to the Soviet Union. I particularly remember our meeting with Giuseppe Di Vittorio, the Communist Secretary General of the Italian Labor Confederation. His office was decorated with red curtains and red walls, and he wore a small red flag in his lapel. I had seen most of the American labor leaders in action before the House Labor Committee, and Di Vittorio could have held his own with the best of them.

I asked him what kind of government policy he favored for Italian unions, and he replied that he would like to see labor be free from government control and have the right to strike.

"From your answer," I said, "I assume that you favor the kind of government we have in the United States, where labor is striking at this very moment, rather than the kind of government they have in Russia, where labor is dominated by the state and they haven't had a strike in the last twenty years."

After the translation, Di Vittorio gave me an icy look and said, "The gentleman and I are not speaking the same language. In a country like the United States the workers must strike to obtain their rights from the capitalist reactionaries and employers. In Russia there are no capitalist reactionaries and employers and therefore the right to strike need not exist."

I asked him if he had any criticisms to offer regarding American foreign policy. In the notes I made of the conversation, I wrote that "he proceeded to give our foreign policy a going over which would make Henry Wallace look like a piker." When he finished, I said, "We always welcome criticism of our policy, but may I ask whether you have ever criticized Russian policy so closely and in such detail?"

Di Vittorio gave me the same look as before and said, "Again the gentleman and I are not speaking the same language. The reason the foreign policy of the United States is necessarily imperialistic is that it is dominated by capitalists, reactionaries, and employers. In Russia there are no capitalists, reactionaries, and employers, and therefore it is impossible for the foreign policy of Russia to be imperialistic. Therefore it is not subject to criticism."

He was right: we were not speaking the same language. It struck me that Di Vittorio's expression of the party line was almost identical—right down to the phraseology—to that of the Communist leaders we had met in England and France. In my notes I concluded that "this indicates definitely then that the Communists throughout the world owe their loyalty not to the countries in which they live but to Russia."

If we saw the false face of an ostensibly patriotic communism in Britain, France, and Italy, we saw its true and brutal face in Greece and Trieste. In Greece we used an old cargo plane to fly up to the northern mountains to assess the military situation and the morale of the loyalist soldiers fighting against the Communist rebels. When we walked down the main street of a mountain town, the mayor introduced us to a girl whose left breast had been cut off by the

Communists because she had refused to betray her brother, one of the loyalist leaders.

In Trieste, the large port on the Italian-Yugoslav border that was about to become a UN-mandated free city, I witnessed firsthand the violence that sometimes accompanied the communist threat.

We arrived the day before the UN mandate was to become effective. I was at the hotel, just beginning to unpack, when I heard loud singing. I looked out the window and saw a parade of about five hundred men and women. They were young, vigorous, and full of fight. Many were carrying red flags, and they were singing the stirring "Internationale" at the top of their lungs. The Communist Party headquarters was opposite the hotel, and as the parade passed by, each marcher raised his arm in a clenched-fist salute. I went down to see what was going on. Suddenly there was an explosion at the end of the block. The crowd cleared and I saw the body of a young man whose head had been blown off by a grenade thrown from a second-story window. For a frozen moment everyone stood looking at the blood gushing from his neck, but then rocks and bottles started flying. The police arrived and began chasing the Communist leaders.

A fleeing Communist, barreling through the crowd like a college fullback, hit an old woman and knocked her halfway across the street against the curb, where she lay motionless. This sort of thing continued all afternoon and evening. That day five people were killed and seventy-five were wounded by bombs and gunfire. I was sure that what was happening in Trieste would soon be re-enacted throughout Western Europe unless America helped to restore stability and prosperity.

A few weeks after we returned to Washington, the Herter Committee issued a number of reports based on the truckload of notes and papers we brought back with us. The common denominator of each report was a strong recommendation for economic aid for Europe. In the meantime I had taken a poll and found that 75 percent of my constituents in the Twelfth District were resolutely opposed to any foreign aid. This was the first time I had personally experienced the classic dilemma, so eloquently described by Edmund Burke, that is faced at one time or another by almost any elected official in a democracy: how much should his votes register his constituents' opinions, and how much should they represent his own views and convictions? After what I had seen and learned in Europe, I believed so strongly in the necessity of extending economic aid that I felt I had no choice but to vote my conscience and then try my hardest to convince my constituents.

I immediately prepared a series of columns for the local newspapers, and as soon as I could I went home and began an active round of speeches throughout the district describing what I had seen on the trip and why I felt that economic assistance was necessary if we were to save Europe from the twin specters of starvation and communism.

Fortunately, my appearances in the district were successful, and the whole experience ended up enhancing my popularity. On December 15, 1947, the House voted 313 to 82 in favor of the Marshall Plan. As everyone now knows, it was successful in every way: it saved Europe from starvation, it ensured Europe's economic recovery, and it preserved Europe from communism.

I learned a great deal from the Herter Committee trip. Above all, I now understood the reasons for the success of communism in Europe.

First, the Communist leaders were strong and vigorous: they knew what they wanted and were willing to work hard to get it. After this visit, I would never make the mistake of thinking, either because of the doubletalk party line jargon or because their manners are often crude, that Communist leaders are not very intelligent and very tough men.

Second, I saw how the leaders of postwar European communism understood the power of nationalism and were appropriating that power. While we were in Rome, for example, Communist posters for the upcoming municipal elections were plastered all over the city. These posters did not feature the hammer and sickle, or any other Communist symbol, nor did they depict the joys of some future workers' state. Instead, they were huge heroic pictures of the nineteenth-century patriot Garibaldi—who would have turned over in his grave had he known that his life's devotion to Italy and freedom was being manipulated by an international statist ideology ruled from Moscow.

Third, I saw how European communism was rolling in Soviet money. Unlike most of their democratic counterparts, the European Communist parties were well financed from Moscow.

Fourth, I saw that most of democratic Europe was either leaderless or, worse still, that many in the leadership classes had simply capitulated to communism. For the first time, I understood the vital importance of strong leadership to a people and a nation, and I saw the sad consequences when such leadership is lacking or when it fails. From just this brief exposure, I could see that the only thing the Communists would respect—and deal with seriously—was power at least equal to theirs and backed up by willingness to use it. I made a penciled note in Trieste that is as true today as it was thirty years ago: "One basic rule with Russians—never bluff unless you are prepared to carry through, because they will test you every time."

THE HISS CASE

Just before the House's summer recess in 1948, the Committee on Un-American Activities, chaired by J. Parnell Thomas of New Jersey, had heard testimony from Elizabeth Bentley, a courier for a Communist spy ring in Washington during the war. Looking for witnesses to corroborate her testimony, Robert Stripling, the committee's highly intelligent and dynamic young chief investigator, suggested that we subpoena a man who had been identified as a Communist functionary in the 1930s but who had left the party and was now a professionally well-respected and well-paid senior editor of *Time* magazine. That man was Whittaker Chambers.

When I first saw Chambers on the morning of August 3, just before he testified in public session, I could hardly believe this man was our witness. Whittaker Chambers was one of the most disheveled-looking persons I had ever seen. Everything about him seemed wrinkled and unpressed.

He began his testimony with the story of how, as a disaffected intellectual, he became a Communist in 1924. He told of his growing disillusion with Stalinism, and of his

63

eventual break with the party in the late 1930s. Like many former Communists, Chambers had undergone a religious conversion. Now he feared and hated Communism with an almost mystical fervor. He said that he had been part of a Communist group whose primary aim was to infiltrate the government. Among the members of this group, he said, was Alger Hiss. He described their last meeting, in 1938, when Hiss had tearfully refused to join Chambers in leaving the Communist Party.

A ripple of surprise went through the room, because Hiss, who had not been mentioned in Miss Bentley's testimony, was a well-known and highly respected figure in New York and Washington. He had made a brilliant record at Harvard Law School and then served as a secretary to Supreme Court Justice Oliver Wendell Holmes. After a few years with private law firms in Boston and New York, Hiss had returned to Washington in 1933; like so many others he was drawn by the excitement and opportunities of the New Deal. He occupied a number of important government posts, ultimately becoming assistant to the Assistant Secretary of State and serving as one of President Roosevelt's advisers at the Yalta Conference with Stalin and Churchill. Hiss was acknowledged as one of the primary architects of the United Nations; he served as Secretary-General of the San Francisco Conference, at which the UN charter was drafted, and was then an adviser to the American delegation at the first General Assembly meeting in London. In 1947 he left the State Department to become president of the prestigious Carnegie Endowment for International Peace. John Foster Dulles, chairman of the Endowment's board of directors, was among those who had recommended and endorsed his selection.

Now here was Whittaker Chambers testifying that he had known Alger Hiss as a member of the Communist Party underground.

It may seem surprising in light of later events that Chambers's testimony that morning did not cause more of a stir. This was partly because his story was totally unexpected. Also, Chambers was such an unprepossessing figure that his story was not taken as seriously as it would have been had he been more forceful and impressive.

The next morning we received a telegram from Hiss

asking to appear before us in order to deny Chambers's charge. We invited him to appear the next day.

As Alger Hiss stood to be sworn in on the morning of August 5, the difference between him and Chambers could not have been more striking. Hiss was tall, elegant, handsome, and perfectly poised as he categorically denied Chambers's charge. In a firm voice he said, "I am here at my own request to deny unqualifiedly various statements about me which were made before this committee by one Whittaker Chambers the day before yesterday." He lowered his voice for dramatic emphasis when he stated: "I am not and never have been a member of the Communist Party. I do not and never have adhered to the tenets of the Communist Party. I am not and never have been a member of any Communist front organization. I have never followed the Communist Party line, directly or indirectly."

He denied everything Chambers had said and added that he did not even know anyone named Chambers and, as far as he could remember, never had. When Mundt, as acting chairman, pointed out that Chambers had testified under oath when he said that he knew him, Hiss boldly rejoined, "I do know that he said that. I also know that I am testifying under those same laws to the contrary."

When Hiss finished his testimony people surged around him, to shake his hand and congratulate him on his performance, and to commiserate with him on the damage the committee had done him.

That same morning, President Truman held an informal press conference in the Oval Office. One of the reporters asked about our hearings. "Mr. President," he said, "do you think that the Capitol Hill spy scare is a 'red herring' to divert public attention from inflation?" After agreeing with the reporter's "red herring" characterization, Truman read a prepared statement that the hearings were doing "irreparable harm to certain people, seriously impairing the morale of federal employees, and undermining public confidence in the government."

While Truman's contemptuous dismissal of our hearings as a "red herring" had the effect of throwing his political weight against the investigation, he wielded still more effective powers. In his statement he reaffirmed his earlier order that all administrative agencies of the government refuse to turn over to a congressional committee information relating to the loyalty of any government employee.

Truman had honed his political skills in the rough and scandal-tainted Kansas City Democratic machine, and he never shied away from using any weapon available. Without question his goal throughout the Hiss case was to obstruct our efforts to uncover the facts.

The attack by the President, the impact of his executive directive, and Hiss's highly effective testimony combined to throw the committee into a panic by the time we met again in executive session that afternoon. The audience in the hearing room and the press seemed to have been completely convinced by Hiss, and we knew that we were in for a rough time for allowing Chambers to testify without having first verified his story. No one on the committee wanted to undergo such an assault from the President and the press right before the election. One of the members summed up the general opinion when he said, "We're ruined." I was the only member of the committee who argued in favor of holding our ground and pursuing the case further. Stripling, whose judgment was highly respected by all the members, strongly supported my position.

My reasoning was pragmatic. I felt that as far as the reputation of the committee was concerned, Chambers's testimony had already done its damage. Our critics would not be silenced just because we decided to drop the case, and I argued that we had more to gain than we had left to lose by seeing it through. I pointed out that the formulation of Chambers's charges and Hiss's response provided us with a unique angle to pursue. In most cases we were in the almost impossible position of having to prove whether or not an individual had actually been a Communist. This time, however, because of Hiss's categorical denials, we did not have to establish anything more complicated than whether the two men had known each other. I suggested that we examine Chambers again to see if he could substantiate his story. If he could, the committee would be vindicated; if he could not, we might then find out what bizarre or sinister motives had led him to lie about Hiss and thus at least be able to make a better defense for our mistake.

I already had some doubts about Hiss because for all the vehemence of his denials, he never actually said unequivocally that he did not know Chambers. There was always some qualifier. When Mundt described Chambers as a man "whom you say you have never seen," Hiss had interrupted and said, "As far as I know, I have never seen him."

The British sometimes say that someone is "too clever by half." That was my impression of Hiss: he was too suave, too smooth, and too self-confident to be an entirely trustworthy witness.

Stripling and I were finally able to convince the committee of the uncomfortable truth that we had indeed little left to lose, and it was decided that John McDowell, a thoughtful Republican from Pennsylvania, Eddie Hébert, a Louisiana Democrat who had been a newspaper reporter before entering politics, and I would take a crack at testing Chambers's story. We questioned him on August 7, a quiet Saturday morning, in a room in the deserted Federal Court House on Foley Square in lower Manhattan. I had made a long list of the kinds of things that a man would be likely to know and remember about a friend.

I began by giving him a chance to pull back, gently asking if we had correctly understood him to say that Hiss was a Communist.

"Could this have possibly been an intellectual study group?" I asked.

"It was in no wise an intellectual study group," Chambers firmly replied. "Its primary function was to infiltrate the government in the interest of the Communist Party."

Chambers had a wealth of detailed and intimate information about Hiss; virtually all of it turned out to be correct. He told us that in private Hiss called his wife Dilly or Pross and she called him Hilly; he told us about the cocker spaniel they had boarded in a kennel on Wisconsin Avenue in Washington when they took their summer holidays on the Eastern Shore in Maryland; he mentioned Hiss's simple tastes in food. He described Mrs. Hiss as a short, highly nervous woman who had a habit of blushing a fiery red when she became excited. He told us about the location and layout of the three houses and apartments Hiss had lived in during the years that he had known him, and described the several occasions on which he had stayed overnight in them.

Chambers told us that one of Hiss's hobbies was ornithology, and that he could still remember Hiss's excitement when he came home one morning after having seen a prothonotary warbler, a rare species.

After over two hours of exhaustive examination, I asked Chambers if he would be willing to take a lie detector test. Without hesitation, he said that he would. "You have that much confidence?" I asked. "I am telling the truth," he calmly replied.

If there turned out to be substance to Chambers's charges, Truman would be terribly embarrassed, and ordinarily this possibility alone might have spurred the Republicans on in an election year. But special factors in the Hiss case favored a cautious approach. Governor Thomas Dewey of New York was the Republican nominee for President. John Foster Dulles, one of those who had recommended Hiss for his job as president of the Carnegie Endowment, was Dewey's chief foreign policy adviser and was expected to be Secretary of State in a Dewey administration. The Hiss case, with its disturbing questions about "softness on communism," might become a two-edged sword that could hurt Dewey as much as Truman. I was aware that the Dewey campaign organization would undoubtedly be grateful if I decided to go along with the rest of the committee and let the case pass into a pre-election limbo.

On the basis of the testimony, I felt strongly that Hiss was lying. But before the case went any further, I wanted to follow up on a number of points that I did not think had been fully covered even in our marathon session. So I decided to visit Chambers at his farm in Westminster, Maryland, where I met Esther Chambers for the first time. She was a strikingly dark woman, who said very little but looked deeply sad and worried.

Once again, the richness and fullness of the detail of Chambers's memory were overwhelming. I told him point-blank that many people were charging that he had some hidden grudge or motive for what he was doing to Hiss. He was silent for a long time and then said: "Certainly

I wouldn't have a motive which would involve destroying my own career." He said that privacy was almost an obsession with him and that appearing in public was one of the most painful things he had ever done in his life.

I happened to mention that I was a Quaker, and he said that Mrs. Hiss had been a Quaker when he knew her and that since then he had become a Quaker himself. He snapped his fingers and said, "That reminds me of something. Priscilla often used the plain speech in talking to Alger at home." From my own family, I knew how unlikely it would be for anyone but a close friend to know such an intimate detail. Of course, it was still possible that he could have learned it from someone, but the way he blurted it out convinced me that he was telling the truth.

Charles Kersten, an expert on Communist activities, urged that I discuss my findings with John Foster Dulles. On August 11, I called the Dewey campaign headquarters at the Roosevelt Hotel in New York and told Dulles that I thought he should look at Chambers's testimony before he made any kind of public statement on the case. That afternoon Kersten and I took the train up to New York to see him.

Kersten and I sat on a sofa in Dulles's suite while Foster and his brother, Allen, read through the transcripts of the three hearings. After they both had finished, Foster Dulles stood and paced back and forth across the room. "There's no question about it," he said. "It's almost impossible to believe, but Chambers knows Hiss." Allen Dulles agreed, and both felt that the case should be brought into the open by a public confrontation between the two men as soon as possible. Foster did not for a moment flinch from the potential embarrassment to himself as one of Hiss's sponsors for the presidency of the Carnegie Endowment. I told them I would keep them informed of any new developments.

After visiting Chambers's farm, I had called Bert Andrews, the Pulitzer Prize-winning head of the New York *Herald Tribune*'s Washington bureau. I knew that Andrews was an outspoken critic of the committee; he had recently written a book, *Washington Witch Hunt,* which was highly critical of the administration's loyalty program. I told Andrews that I believed Chambers was telling the truth, but that I wanted to put his story to every possible test. He agreed to go up with me and question Chambers thoroughly.

Andrews asked Chambers tough questions and bore down hard about the rumors that had begun to sweep Washington that he was an alcoholic and that he had a history of mental illness and institutional confinement. Chambers was unfazed and pointed out that rumors of this sort were typical of Communist smear campaigns.

By the time we got back to Washington, Andrews was more excited than I. He was convinced that Chambers was telling the truth, and he was now worried that Hiss would get off because of the careless methods and inefficient staff work that he felt had characterized committee hearings in the past. So was I.

Because of Truman's executive order we were not able to get any direct help from J. Edgar Hoover or the FBI. However, we had some informal contacts with a lower-level agent that proved helpful in our investigations.

When we called Hiss back before an executive session on August 16 he was in a very different temper than during our first encounter.

I told him that there were substantial areas of difference between his testimony and Chambers's, and that we wanted to give him an opportunity to explain these in executive session before we arranged a public confrontation. Hiss straightened his back and said, "I have been angered and hurt by the attitude you have been taking today that you have a conflict of testimony between two witnesses—one of whom is a confessed former Communist and the other is me—and that you simply have two witnesses saying contradictory things as between whom you find it most difficult to decide on credibility. I do not wish to make it easier for anyone who, for whatever motive I cannot understand, is apparently endeavoring to destroy me. I should not be asked to give details which somehow he may hear and then may be able to use as if he knew them before."

Then he introduced what was to become the main theme of his subsequent testimony: the idea that the *details* of the case were not important. He said, "The issue is not whether this man knew me and I don't remember him. The issue is whether he had a particular conversation that he has said he had with me, and which I have denied, and whether I am a member of the Communist Party or ever was, which he has said and which I have denied."

This was a crucial point. I had persuaded the committee to continue the hearings on precisely the ground that the details of the case *were* important because only the details could prove whether Hiss had lied when he said he did not know Chambers. His denial of even knowing Chambers was the primary factor that had discredited Chambers and the committee as well. If Hiss could now shift the hearings to the question of whether or not we could prove he was a Communist, we were finished.

I said that Chambers had been told that every answer he gave would be subject to the laws of perjury. Details concerning his alleged relationship with Hiss could be confirmed by third parties. That, I said, was the purpose of these questions.

Hiss asked if he could say something for the record. "Certainly," I replied.

With elaborate deliberation, he wrote something on the pad of paper in front of him. He said that he had written the name of a man he had known in the mid-1930s and who, he now remembered, had in fact done some of the things that Chambers claimed to have done. This man had spent several days in Hiss's house, sublet his apartment, borrowed money from him, and taken his car. But, Hiss said, he was reluctant to reveal the name directly because it might be leaked back to Chambers, who could then incorporate it into his perjurious tale.

The questioning resumed and once again Hiss quibbled about answering the questions Stripling and I asked him about the places he had lived on the grounds that his answers might get back to Chambers and be used against him. This coy reticence proved too much for the crusty Hébert. He said bluntly to Hiss, "Either you or Mr. Chambers is lying." Hiss coolly replied, "That is certainly true." Hébert came back, "And whichever one of you is lying is the greatest actor that America has ever produced."

The committee took a five-minute recess, and when the session resumed Hiss said he would reveal the name that he had earlier written on the pad.

He said, "The name of the man I brought in—and he may have no relation to this whole nightmare—is a man named George Crosley."

Thus George Crosley, the man who never was, the real red herring of the Hiss case, made his first appearance.

Hiss spent the better part of an hour and a quarter answering questions about George Crosley. Crosley was, he said, a free-loading free-lance journalist who had approached Hiss when he was counsel for the Senate's Nye Committee on Munitions and Armaments and asked for information for magazine articles he purported to be writing on the committee's activities. Hiss added that he frequently dealt with such requests from writers.

They had lunch a couple of times, he said, and Crosley asked for his help in finding a place to live because he wanted to bring his wife and baby down from New York for the rest of the summer while he wrote his articles. It happened that Hiss was about to move into a new house in Georgetown, with three months remaining in the lease of his old apartment. So he sublet the apartment to Crosley. When the Crosleys' furniture was late arriving from New York, Hiss said, he even let them stay in his new house for a few days. He added that in the end Crosley had welshed on the rent, and they had parted on less than friendly terms. Since 1935, Hiss said, he had never seen or heard from Crosley.

It was hard to believe that Hiss could have forgotten and then suddenly remembered someone like "Crosley," but we took the story at face value and questioned him about this mysterious journalist.

I asked him what Mrs. Crosley looked like, and he replied that she was "strikingly dark." I was the only member of the Committee who had ever seen Mrs. Chambers, and I knew that this described her perfectly. Now I felt sure that Hiss had known Chambers. Whether or not he had known him as George Crosley was the only question that remained to be answered. Next, I took him through a catalogue of Crosley's physical appearance, beginning with his height and weight. Then I asked, "How about his teeth?"

"Very bad teeth. That is one of the things I particularly want to see Chambers about. This man had very bad teeth, did not take care of his teeth."

"Did he have most of his teeth or just weren't well cared for?" Stripling asked.

"I don't think he had gapped teeth, but they were badly taken care of. They were stained and I would say obviously not attended to," Hiss replied.

Then, using Chambers's testimony as a guide, we took Hiss back over the ground of his life in the 1930s. We asked him the same questions that we had asked Chambers, and in almost every instance we got the same answers.

For most members of the committee, the exchange that clinched the case arose late in the day over the least likely subject. I asked Hiss if he had any hobbies, and he replied that he was interested in tennis and amateur ornithology. "Did you ever see a prothonotary warbler?" McDowell asked casually.

Hiss virtually lit up with excitement. "I have, right here on the Potomac."

"I saw one in Arlington," McDowell said.

"They come back and nest in those swamps," Hiss continued. "Beautiful yellow head, a gorgeous bird . . ."

There was a moment of telling silence as the significance of this exchange hit the committee.

We had promised Hiss a public confrontation with Chambers for August 25, which was still a week away. Now, however, there might be a third man in the mix—George Crosley—and with him a strange new twist had been added to the possibilities of mistaken identity. I felt that we had to have the meeting between Hiss and Chambers right away. If the whole thing were a mistake, it should be put right before any more damage was done. On the other hand, if Hiss had manufactured Crosley out of whole cloth to explain Chambers's damning testimony, I thought that it was equally important to flush him out before he had time to fill in more details of his deception.

I stayed very late at the office trying to decide the best

thing to do. At 2 A.M. I phoned Stripling and said we could not wait a week and that I wanted a session arranged for that very afternoon. He said that he had reached the same conclusion and agreed to make the necessary arrangements.

The first Hiss-Chambers confrontation took place on August 17 at 5:35 P.M. in suite 1400 of the Commodore Hotel in New York.

The suite consisted of a living room and bedroom. The living room walls were decorated, ironically, with Audubon prints of birds. We put three chairs behind a table near the window for the committee members, and placed a single chair about eight feet away facing the table. There was a sofa against the wall, to the right of the chair.

When Hiss arrived, along with a friend from the Carnegie Endowment, he was pettish and irritable. When he was finally seated in the chair facing us, I told him that instead of waiting until August 25 we had decided that the cause of truth would be better served if he and Chambers could meet right away. We had therefore brought Chambers to this suite.

I asked that Chambers be brought in. The bedroom door behind Hiss opened, and Chambers walked through.

Hiss did not so much as look around while Chambers walked up behind him and then sat down on the sofa. He stared straight ahead at the window.

I began, "Mr. Chambers, will you please stand? And will you please stand, Mr. Hiss?"

The two men now stood and Hiss turned to face Chambers; they could not have been more than four or five feet apart.

"Mr. Hiss," I said, "the man standing here is Mr. Whittaker Chambers. I ask you now if you have ever known that man before?"

I do not think that I have ever seen one man look at another with more hatred in his eyes than did Alger Hiss when he looked at Whittaker Chambers. We opened the blinds so that there could later be no suggestion that bad light had hampered the identification.

Hiss now seemed genuinely uncertain and confused. He looked at me and said, "Will you ask him to say something?"

I asked Chambers to state his name and business. He

said, "My name is Whittaker Chambers."

With this, Hiss took a step toward him, saying, "Would you mind opening your mouth wider?"

Chambers repeated his name, and Hiss became very impatient. "I said, would you open your mouth"—and he made a gesture with his fingers to show what he wanted him to do. Looking over at me, he said, "You know what I am referring to, Mr. Nixon." What he meant was that he wanted to look at Chambers's teeth; Hiss's hand was not more than six inches from Chambers's mouth, and at that moment I wondered whether Chambers was tempted to bite his finger.

"May I ask whether his voice, when he testified before, was comparable to this?" Hiss asked. I looked around for something Chambers could read. The only reading matter in the room was a copy of *Newsweek*. As Chambers read from the magazine, Hiss studied his mouth intently, like a horse trader trying to guess the age of a potential purchase. Chambers paused, and Hiss said that the voice sounded a little different from the way he remembered Crosley's, and that the teeth were obviously much improved. Therefore, he said, without further checking he could not take an oath that Chambers was Crosley.

I asked Chambers whether he had had any major dental work done, and he mentioned some extractions and a plate made by his dentist, a Dr. Hitchcock. Hiss seemed satisfied with this information and said, "That testimony of Mr. Chambers, if it can be believed, would tend to substantiate my feeling that he represented himself to me in 1934 or 1935 or thereabouts as George Crosley, a free-lance writer of articles for magazines. I would like to find out from Dr. Hitchcock if what he has just said is true, because I am relying partly—one of my main recollections of Crosley was the poor condition of his teeth."

I said, "Mr. Hiss, do you feel that you would have to have the dentist tell you just what he did to the teeth before you could tell anything about this man?"

Hiss changed the subject and I began questioning Chambers.

"Mr. Chairman—" Hiss interrupted.

"Just a moment," I said, and returned to Chambers.

When Chambers said that he had stayed in Hiss's

apartment for approximately three weeks, Hiss interrupted again and said, "Mr. Chairman, I don't need to ask Mr. Whittaker Chambers any more questions. I am now perfectly prepared to identify this man as George Crosley."

I have studied the testimony very closely, but I have never been sure why Hiss suddenly decided at this point to give up the charade. Just a few minutes earlier his "visual memory" had been so bad that he insisted on consulting dental charts before he could be sure of Chambers's identity. Now, he was so emphatic about his identification that when he was asked if he were absolutely certain, he said, "If he had lost both eyes and taken his nose off, I would be sure." He still, however, claimed that he had not known that Chambers/Crosley was a Communist.

Chambers was asked whether he could make a positive identification of Hiss as the Communist he had known and in whose house he had stayed. He answered, "Positive identification." Hiss suddenly shot up out of his chair and moved toward him, shaking his fist. His voice quavered with anger as he said, "May I say for the record at this point that I would like to invite Mr. Whittaker Chambers to make those same statements out of the presence of this committee, without their being privileged for suit for libel. I challenge you to do it, and I hope you will do it damned quickly."

Chambers had shown no fear at all when Hiss came toward him, but Hiss now was completely unnerved. I regretted that we had agreed to let him go early so he could keep a dinner appointment. I believe that if we had continued to press him we might have gotten even more contradictions out of him, if not an actual break. But as it was, we had quite enough.

The public confrontation between the two men came the following week on August 25, in the Caucus Room of the Old House Office Building. The room overflowed with people crowded in to witness the scene, and the heavy air was superheated by television lights.

Hiss used three basic tactics. At first he tried to confuse and belabor the details of the evidence. He once again brought up the importance of the dental work to explain his initial reluctance to identify Chambers as Crosley.

I said, "You have made much of the point of the bad

76

teeth. You even asked the name of his dentist and wanted to consult with the dentist before you made the identification positive. My question may sound facetious, but I am just wondering: didn't you ever see Crosley with his mouth closed?"

He replied, "The striking thing in my recollection about Crosley was not when he had his mouth shut, but when he had his mouth open." With this answer the audience, which had started out on Hiss's side but had become restive because of his constant evasiveness, burst out laughing. Chairman Thomas called for order and said to Hiss, "If you've got any very humorous remarks in the way of answers, call me out later on and give them to me. I always like a good laugh, but let's not have any more laughing in here if we can possibly avoid it." Hiss was flailing about now, and he replied haughtily, "I understood the laughter to be at the question, not at the answer, Mr. Chairman. Maybe you or Mr. Nixon would like to withdraw to tell your jokes."

Equally ludicrous was Hiss's performance when he was shown a photostatic copy of a document bearing his signature and was asked to identify it. He hesitated and hedged, and said that he could not do so without seeing the original.

Mundt was completely exasperated by this reply and asked incredulously, "Could you be sure if you saw the original?"

"I could be surer," Hiss replied. Again there was laughter from the audience, and even his friends sitting in the front rows shook their heads uncomfortably.

His second tactic was to remind us of all the well-known and unquestionably patriotic people with whom he had worked and who thought highly of him. He named thirty-four, from John Foster Dulles and Harold Stassen to Cordell Hull and James Byrnes, and suggested that we consult them about his loyalty. This line of "innocence by association" did not get him anywhere with the committee, and did not seem to impress many people in the audience either.

His third tactic involved a renewed attempt to insist that the details of his and Chambers's conflicting stories made no difference because the only real issue was whether he had been a Communist. Once again I tried to expose the false logic behind this premise and to keep the hearings firmly on the ground of establishing whether he had committed perjury when he said he had not known Chambers.

"Mr. Hiss," I said, "you yourself have made an issue of the fact as to (1) whether you knew Chambers at all—that issue has now been resolved; and (2) how well you knew Chambers and whether you knew him as a Communist. That is the purpose of this questioning now."

The part of Hiss's testimony that seriously discredited him in the eyes of many was his story about his car. Chambers had testified that Hiss was such a dedicated Communist that when he bought a new Plymouth in 1936 he wanted to give his old car, a 1929 Ford roadster, to the Communist Party. It was strictly against party rules for a member of the underground to do anything that might publicly link him with the party, but Chambers said that Hiss had been so insistent that an exception was made, and an arrangement was worked out whereby the car was transferred through an intermediary.

Hiss's version was completely different. At one point in his testimony about George Crosley, he had said, "I sold him an automobile"; at another, "I gave him the use of the car"; at another, "I let him have it along with the rent." I pointed out these discrepancies to him, and said that it was hard to believe that he could not remember more precisely what he had done about the ownership of something as substantial as a car.

Thanks to some superb investigative work and a great stroke of luck, we accomplished the one thing Hiss had clearly never imagined possible: we found the papers he had signed transferring ownership of the car more than ten years before. The transaction turned out to have been highly unusual. Hiss had signed the car over to an automobile dealership for $25, and it had then immediately been signed over in the name of the dealership, for the same amount, to a man who turned out to have a record as a Communist organizer and who used a false address on the transfer papers. Nowhere did the name George Crosley appear; and we established that the transfer had not taken place in June 1935, when Hiss testified he had last seen Crosley, but almost a year later, in July 1936—exactly when Chambers had testified it happened.

The car transaction was incontrovertible evidence that Hiss had not been telling the truth and that he had known Chambers (or "Crosley") far better, far longer, and far later than he had testified. After his first appearance before the committee, Hiss had been besieged by well-wishers. At the end of this testimony, however, he and his attorney made their solitary way out of the hearing room. James Reston, who knew Hiss personally and was among those who had recommended him for his job at the Carnegie Endowment, reported in the New York *Times*, "Throughout these questions Mr. Hiss was calm, elaborately polite, but always he answered with a caution which angered members of the committee and, in the opinion even of his friends, hurt his case."

Chambers followed Hiss to the witness chair. When asked for his reaction to Hiss's testimony, he said simply, "Mr. Hiss is lying." His straightforward answers made Hiss's appear even more evasive and misleading.

I asked Chambers whether he might not have some kind of grudge against Hiss which would explain his apparent determination to tear him down and destroy him. To me, this exchange was the high point of the hearings, both as history and as drama.

I said, "Mr. Chambers, can you search your memory now to see what motive you can have for accusing Mr. Hiss of being a Communist at the present time?"

"What motive I can have?" he asked.

"Yes, do you, I mean, is there any grudge you have against Mr. Hiss over anything he has done to you?"

"The story has spread that in testifying against Mr. Hiss I am working out some old grudge, or motives of revenge or hatred," he said. "I do not hate Mr. Hiss. We were close friends, but we are caught in a tragedy of history. Mr. Hiss represents the concealed enemy against which we are all fighting, and I am fighting. I have testified against him with remorse and pity, but in a moment of history in which this nation now stands, so help me God, I could not do otherwise."

*   *   *

As soon as I had a chance to study all the testimony, I sent a four-page letter to John Foster Dulles summarizing my opinions and conclusions. I wrote: "Whether [Hiss] was guilty of technical perjury or whether it has been established definitely that he was a member of the Communist Party are issues which still may be open for debate, but there is no longer any doubt in my mind that for reasons only he can give, he was trying to keep the committee from learning the truth in regard to his relationship with Chambers."

This was the end of the committee's direct involvement in the Hiss case. The next step would depend on how Chambers reacted to Hiss's challenge to repeat his statements where they would not be protected by congressional immunity, so that Hiss could sue for libel. Two days after the public session on August 25, Chambers appeared on *Meet the Press*. The first question was about Hiss's challenge.

"Are you willing to repeat your charge that Alger Hiss was a Communist?" Chambers was asked.

"Alger Hiss was a Communist and may still be one," Chambers replied.

Hiss's friends assumed that he would sue Chambers immediately. Much to their consternation, he took no action for a month. Finally the Washington *Post*, one of his staunchest supporters, bluntly called his bluff in an impatient editorial declaring that Hiss himself had "created a situation in which he is obliged to put up or shut up."

Three weeks later, Hiss sued Chambers for libel. Legally Hiss's position seemed strong, because without corroborative evidence to back up his allegations Chambers could never prove them to any court's satisfaction. Hiss probably assumed that if Chambers had any such proof, it would have been produced during the committee hearings.

The case, which had already provided so many bizarre surprises, had not yet exhausted its supply.

Chambers was called by Hiss's lawyers for a pretrial deposition and in the course of routine questioning they asked him whether he had any documentary proof of his charges. He made no reply at the time, but he began agonizing over what he might have to do to defend his position.

Hiss's lawyers also questioned Mrs. Chambers. Chambers never told me specifically what had happened, but only that they had been very rough on her and had made her cry. He said that from that moment he realized that they were out to destroy him and that he must react accordingly. He told his lawyer that when the pretrial hearing resumed the next day, he had decided to introduce some documents he had recently retrieved from his wife's nephew in New York.

On November 17, Chambers turned over an envelope containing sixty-five pages of typewritten copies of State Department documents and four memos in Alger Hiss's handwriting. He explained to the stunned lawyers that when he decided to leave the party he had hidden these papers away as a sort of life insurance against any Communist attempts to blackmail or kill him.

The head of the Justice Department's Criminal Division was immediately summoned from Washington. He impounded the papers and obtained a court order enforcing secrecy on everyone concerned. Chambers returned to his farm assuming that it would only be a matter of a few days before the Justice Department brought the case to a grand jury and Hiss would be indicted. Two weeks passed, however, and nothing happened. On December 1, a small United Press story appeared in the Washington *Daily News* reporting that the Justice Department was considering dropping the case against Hiss. Another article stated that there were rumors that a perjury charge against Chambers was under consideration. It was hard to believe, but it appeared that the Justice Department was going to use the papers Chambers had produced not to prove that Hiss was a spy but as the basis for indicting Chambers for perjury because he had lied when he testified that he himself had never been involved in espionage.

These shattering new developments came at the worst possible time for me personally. Our second daughter, Julie, had been born on July 5, 1948. We had hoped to spend a few weeks with her and Tricia out of the sweltering heat of summertime Washington, but once again we were forced to cancel a planned vacation when the Hiss case had completely taken up the month of August. I promised Pat that we would take our first vacation in three years as soon as

Congress recessed. We made reservations for a two-week Caribbean cruise at the beginning of December, and both of us looked forward to the trip.

On the day before we were to leave, I saw the article in the *Daily News*, and I was shocked that the Justice Department would be party to such a cynical maneuver. That afternoon Stripling and I drove to Chambers's farm.

I showed Chambers the newspaper report. He said, "This is what I have been afraid of."

He explained that he had turned over a considerable amount of documentary evidence, which had then been impounded by the Justice Department, and a court order prohibited him from disclosing the contents. "I will only say that they were a real bombshell," he told us.

We tried unsuccessfully to get some idea of what the papers contained. Finally I asked whether we were facing a situation in which the Justice Department alone would decide if any further action were to be taken.

"No, I wouldn't be that foolish," Chambers replied. "My attorney has photostatic copies, and also, I didn't turn over everything I had. I have another bombshell in case they try to suppress this one."

"You keep that second bombshell," I told him. "Don't give it to anybody except the committee."

When Stripling and I got back to Washington I was uncertain about what to do. I spent much of that night trying to decide whether to issue a subpoena for the rest of Chambers's material. I could not understand why Chambers would have withheld any important information from the committee hearings, and I could not help thinking that there might be some good reason the Justice Department was acting in this way.

After weighing all the factors, however, I decided that the case was too important to risk losing it now, so I asked Stripling to have subpoenas served on Chambers immediately for everything he had. "I mean *everything*," I said.

Our ship sailed from New York that afternoon. Pat and I relaxed in the lazy shipboard routine and enjoyed the company of the other members of Congress and their wives who were on board. We felt a sense of relief from the tremendous tension that had surrounded us in Washington.

The next evening, however, I received a cable from Stripling:

SECOND BOMBSHELL OBTAINED BY SUB-POENA 1 A.M. FRIDAY. CASE CLINCHED. IN-FORMATION AMAZING. HEAT IS ON FROM PRESS AND OTHER PLACES. IMMEDIATE AC-TION APPEARS NECESSARY. CAN YOU POSSI-BLY GET BACK?

The next morning, I received a cable from Andrews:

DOCUMENTS INCREDIBLY HOT. LINK TO HISS SEEMS CERTAIN. LINK TO OTHERS IN-EVITABLE. RESULTS SHOULD RESTORE FAITH IN NEED FOR COMMITTEE IF NOT IN SOME MEMBERS. . . . NEW YORK JURY MEETS WEDNESDAY. . . . COULD YOU ARRIVE TUES-DAY AND GET DAY'S JUMP ON GRAND JURY. IF NOT, HOLDING HEARING EARLY WEDNESDAY. MY LIBERAL FRIENDS DON'T LOVE ME NO MORE. NOR YOU. BUT FACTS ARE FACTS AND THESE FACTS ARE DYNA-MITE. HISS'S WRITING IDENTIFIED ON THREE DOCUMENTS. NOT PROOF HE GAVE THEM TO CHAMBERS BUT HIGHLY SIGNIFI-CANT. STRIPLING SAYS CAN PROVE WHO GAVE THEM TO CHAMBERS. LOVE TO PAT. VACATION-WRECKER ANDREWS

I radioed Stripling to make arrangements for my return. The next morning I was picked up from the ship by a Coast Guard seaplane that took me to Miami, where I caught a flight to Washington. At the Miami airport reporters asked if I had any comment on the "pumpkin papers." I had no idea what they were talking about. When I reached Washington, Stripling filled me in on the latest turn of this extraordinary case.

I learned that Chambers had been in Washington on the day our subpoena was served on him, and he arranged to meet two of our investigators that night and drive back to his farm with them. They arrived very late. He led them into a frost-covered pumpkin patch. The flabbergasted investigators watched while he took the top off one of the pumpkins, reached inside, and pulled out three small metal microfilm cylinders. He explained that he had not wanted to leave anything in the house in case any other subpoenas or search warrants arrived in his absence. That morning, therefore, he had hollowed out a pumpkin and used it as a hiding place.

When the "pumpkin" microfilms were developed they yielded hundreds of pages of photostats. These represented a sampling of the classified documents Hiss gave to Chambers in the period just before Chambers left the party; they ran the gamut from inconsequential bureaucratic trivia to top-secret ambassadorial cables. Hiss's defense later claimed that the documents were unimportant and represented no threat to national security. That contention was shot down by expert testimony before the committee and at both trials. Some of the documents were relatively unimportant, but the State Department still felt in 1948, ten years after they had been taken from the government files, that publication of the complete "pumpkin papers" would be injurious to the national security. As important as the specific contents of the documents was the fact that many of even the substantively unimportant ones were coded, and anyone able to obtain copies of them could thus break our secret codes.

The "pumpkin papers" completely captured public attention. The uproar was tremendous, and even many of Hiss's erstwhile defenders had to admit that they had been wrong and the committee had been right.

Since the statute of limitations made prosecution for espionage impossible, the grand jury unanimously voted to indict Hiss on two counts of perjury. The first was for having lied when he testified that he had not unlawfully taken classified documents from the State Department and given them to Chambers; the second was for having lied when he testified that he had not seen Chambers after January 1, 1937.

There were two trials. The first ended with a hung jury divided 8 to 4 for conviction. At the second trial, the jury on January 21, 1950, unanimously found Hiss guilty. Shortly after the verdict had been announced, I received a telegram from Herbert Hoover. It read:

THE CONVICTION OF ALGER HISS WAS DUE TO YOUR PATIENCE AND PERSISTENCE ALONE. AT LAST THE STREAM OF TREASON THAT HAS EXISTED IN OUR GOVERNMENT HAS BEEN EXPOSED IN A FASHION ALL MAY BELIEVE.

Hiss was sentenced to five years in prison. After serving forty-four months he was released on parole and sank into obscurity, working as a stationery and printing supplies salesman in New York.

To this day, Alger Hiss has emphatically insisted on his innocence and makes periodic attempts to clear himself. This tenacity, together with the passage of time and the vagaries of memory, has now and then been rewarded with favorable publicity and increasing acceptance. In 1975, for example, he was readmitted to the Massachusetts bar. Whenever the Hiss case is considered on the facts and the testimony, however, the verdict is the same: the evidence against him is still overwhelming.

It was very difficult for me to understand President Truman's conduct during our investigation of the Hiss case. I knew that he had defied his liberal advisers and supporters by proposing aid to the anticommunist governments in Greece and Turkey, and I considered him to be someone who understood the threat of communism and recognized the need to oppose its subversive spread.

Yet in the face of overwhelming evidence that Hiss was at best a perjurer and at worst a spy, Truman persisted in condemning our investigation as a "red herring" and, through his public statements and executive orders, doing everything in his power to obstruct it. Before the 1948 presidential election I could understand that he would do everything possible to contain the investigation in order to avoid political embarrassment. But I was surprised when, even after he had won the election, he continued this same stubborn course.

Bert Andrews, who had excellent sources in the White House, told me that when a Justice Department official showed Truman the typewritten documents that clearly seemed to implicate Hiss in espionage, Truman had furiously paced the floor in the Oval Office, saying over and over, "The son of a bitch—he betrayed his country!" At a press conference after Hiss was indicted, reporters asked Truman whether he still believed our investigation was a "red herring." Truman cut off one reporter abruptly and snapped: "I have made my position perfectly clear on that subject, and I have nothing further to say on it. My position hasn't changed. Period." When one of his aides later asked him about this, he replied, "Of course Hiss is guilty. But that damn committee isn't interested in that. All it cares about is politics, and as long as they try to make politics out of this communist issue, I am going to label their activities for what they are—a 'red herring.'"

Truman honestly believed that the investigation was politically motivated, and in return his motives were political. He finally approved a full Justice Department and FBI investigation, but for months he used the power and prestige of his office to obstruct the committee's work. But I did not think then, and I do not think now, that his actions were motivated by anything other than the political instincts of an intensely political man.

The Hiss case proved beyond any reasonable doubt the existence of Soviet-directed Communist subversion at the highest levels of American government. But many who had defended Hiss simply refused to accept the overwhelming evidence of his guilt. Some turned their anger and frustration toward me, as if I were somehow responsible for the fact that Hiss had taken them in. While there is no doubt that my reputation from the Hiss case launched me on the road to the vice presidency, it also turned me from a relatively popular young congressman, enjoying a good but limited press, into one of the most controversial figures in Washington, bitterly opposed by the most respected and influential liberal journalists and opinion leaders of the time.

I think that Foster Dulles expressed the real lesson of the Hiss case when he said, "The conviction of Alger Hiss is human tragedy. It is tragic that so great promise should have come to so inglorious an end. But the greater tragedy is that seemingly our national ideals no longer inspire the loyal devotions needed for their defense."

This, to me, went to the heart of the problem we faced then and in the years ahead: how could we instill in brilliant young Americans the same dedication to the philosophy of freedom that the Communists seemed to be able to instill in people like Hiss.

RUNNING FOR SENATOR: 1950

I attended the 1948 Republican National Convention in Philadelphia as an observer. I had great respect for the front-runners, Senator Robert Taft of Ohio and Governor Thomas Dewey of New York, but I believed that the Republicans needed a fresh face and a change in 1948, and I supported Harold Stassen of Minnesota—the one-time "boy wonder" of the Republican Party—for the presidential nomination. Dewey won the nomination on the third ballot, and he chose Earl Warren as his running mate.

Since I had won both the Democratic and Republican nominations for re-election to the House, I did a great deal of speaking for the national ticket across the country in the fall campaign. Although there was nothing specific I could put my finger on, I was not as optimistic about our chances as most Republicans were. The crowds I spoke to were large and friendly, but they did not convey the electricity that so often means the difference between victory and defeat. I was also bothered by Dewey's gingerly approach to Truman and by his refusal to rebut Truman's attacks on what he labeled the "do-nothing Eightieth Congress." Because of his temperament, overconfidence, and misjudgment, Dewey ran a lofty and detached campaign, while Truman behaved as if he really wanted the job. Truman won an eleventh-hour victory that stunned the forecasters. While I was deeply disappointed by Dewey's loss, I thought that our complacency had caught up with us.

Dewey's defeat and our loss of both houses of Congress turned me overnight into a junior member of the minority party, a "comer" with no place to go. For the first time I began to consider the possibility of trying to move up on my own instead of patiently waiting for seniority or party preferment in the House of Representatives.

The term of Sheridan Downey, California's Democratic senator, was to expire in 1950, and not long after the 1948 election I began to consider challenging Downey for his seat. At first glance the prospects were not promising. Downey was a popular and uncontroversial incumbent, and it was by no means clear that anyone could beat him.

Virtually all my political friends and advisers told me that running for the Senate would be tantamount to political suicide. But I recognized the worth of the nationwide publicity that the Hiss case had given me— publicity on a scale that most congressmen only dream of achieving. Running for the Downey seat was the only possibility for me to move up the political ladder at a time when my political stock was high. On August 11, 1949, I wrote to my friend and political adviser, Frank Jorgensen, summing up the situation as I saw it:

> I have built up quite a file of people who have written me pro and con on the Senate matter. Most of those who are against it, incidentally, are afraid of the risk of my losing the House seat. As I wrote you before, however, I have virtually reached the conclusion that although it is admittedly a long shot, it presents such an unusual opportunity that the risk is worth taking, provided, of course, that we do not have too determined an opposition in the primary. As I have told several of my friends here, unless the Republicans do make substantial gains in both the House and Senate in 1950, which necessarily would mean a Republican trend, I seriously doubt if we can ever work our way back into power. Actually, in my mind, I do not see any great gain in remaining a member of the House, even from a relatively good district, if it means that we would be simply a vocal but ineffective minority.
>
> On the other hand, if the trend is on, the chances for winning the Senate seat in California will be good. If the trend is not on, rewinning the House seat might prove to be a rather empty victory.

At the beginning of October Representative Helen Gahagan Douglas announced that she was going to run against Downey in the Democratic primary. Her entry brightened my prospects considerably. If Downey won the primary, he would be weakened by her attacks; if Mrs. Douglas won, she would be easier to beat than Downey.

During the fall I learned from Kyle Palmer, the astute political editor of the Los Angeles *Times,* that if I became a candidate for the Senate I would be endorsed by the *Times*. I received similar assurances about the San Francisco *Chronicle* and the Oakland *Tribune*. These endorsements were vital not only for the boost they would give my candidacy but because they would virtually assure that I would not face any opposition in the Republican primary.

On November 3, 1949—exactly one year before the election—I announced my candidacy for the Senate before a crowd of more than five hundred supporters in Pomona. I made a hard-hitting speech that foreshadowed the kind of campaign I planned to run. I said that the central issue of the campaign would be "simply the choice between freedom and state socialism." I charged that "the Democratic Party today, nationally and in our own state of California, has been captured and is completely controlled by a group of ruthless, cynical seekers-after-power who have committed that party to policies and principles which are completely foreign to those of its founders." I ended my speech with some lines that would be quoted frequently in later years: "There is only one way we can win," I said. "We must put on a fighting, rocking, socking campaign and carry that campaign directly into every county, city, town, precinct, and home in the state of California."

Thus began one of the most hectic and heated campaigns of my career. It had been hard enough to convince the voters in one traditionally Republican congressional district to elect me; now I had to campaign all through the second most populous state in the nation, seeking the support of millions of voters—most of them registered Democrats.

I decided to campaign all over California, and to get around I used a second-hand wood-paneled station wagon with "Nixon for Senator" signs nailed on each side. It was fitted with portable sound equipment, and as we came into a town we played a phonograph record of a popular song over the loudspeaker. That usually attracted at least half a dozen people at a busy street corner. Once a small crowd had gathered, I would speak for a few minutes and then answer questions.

At the beginning I often spoke to no more than a handful of bemused passersby. When the campaign began to gather steam, however, the crowds began to grow, and before long the presence of hecklers assured a large and lively audience at every stop. These hecklers were tightly organized bands sent out from local left-wing labor and political organizations. They tried to disrupt my speeches by a continuous counterpoint of critical questions and derisive observations. On one occasion in San Francisco, they even brought their own sound truck, and we engaged in an amplified debate. When a small band of them arrived outside a rally at Long Beach Municipal Auditorium, my driver turned up the loudspeaker and played a recording of one of the popular songs of the day, "If I Knew You Were Coming I'd've Baked a Cake." My supporters roared their approval.

While I was beginning my campaign treks around the state, sparks were flying in the Democratic primary. Senator Downey had withdrawn from the race, citing health problems, and Mrs. Douglas was now opposed by Manchester Boddy, publisher of the Los Angeles *Daily News*. Boddy was well financed, and he campaigned with the genuine fervor of a lifelong Democrat who despised Mrs. Douglas's left-wing leanings. He referred to her and her followers as a "small subversive clique of red hots." His supporters attacked her voting record by comparing it with that of Vito Marcantonio, the only openly procommunist member of Congress.

Anyone could see that the Douglas and Marcantonio records were strikingly similar and the attacks coming from within her own party were as damaging as anything I could say. The subsequently controversial "pink sheet" that my campaign committee issued was, in fact, inspired by these earlier comparisons of the two voting records. Whatever interpretation was later placed on these facts, no one was ever able to challenge their accuracy. All we added was the mordant comment of the color of the paper.

The most serious damage to Mrs. Douglas was done by Senator Downey. On May 22, he publicly stated: "It is my opinion that Mrs. Douglas does not have the fundamental ability and qualifications for a United States Senator. . . . She has shown no inclination, in fact no ability, to dig in and do the hard and tedious work required to prepare legislation and push it through Congress." Referring to her voting record in the House, he said, "Mrs. Douglas gave comfort to the Soviet tyranny by voting against aid to both Greece and Turkey. She voted against the President in a crisis when he most needed her support and most fully deserved her confidence."

Mrs. Douglas ended up with less than 50 percent of the vote in the Democratic primary. Boddy got about 30 percent and, because crossover voting was still allowed, I received 20 percent. On the Republican side, I ran unopposed and received 740,000 votes—a record primary turnout. Thus the lines for the general election were clearly drawn. I had a completely unified Republican Party behind me, while the Democrats were divided and dispirited after a bitter primary.

Helen Gahagan had been a popular light opera and Broadway musical star during the 1920s. In 1931 she married Melvyn Douglas, one of Hollywood's most popular leading men. When the Democratic congressman from the Fourteenth District in Los Angeles retired in 1944, Helen Douglas ran for his seat and won. She entered the House of Representatives in January 1945.

Mrs. Douglas was a handsome woman with a dramatic presence. She had many fans among the public and many admirers in the press and in the entertainment industry, but she was not, to put it mildly, the most popular member of the House of Representatives. Generally when two members of the House run against each other for another office their fellow congressmen maintain a friendly attitude and wish both of them well. But in our case, even many of the House Democrats let me know that they hoped I could defeat Helen Douglas.

One afternoon in 1950, I was working in my office when Dorothy Cox, my personal secretary, came in and said, "Congressman Kennedy is here and would like to talk to you."

Jack Kennedy was ushered in and I motioned him into a chair. He took an envelope from his breast pocket and handed it to me. "Dick, I know you're in for a pretty rough campaign," he said, "and my father wanted to help out."

We talked for a while about the campaign. As he rose

to leave, he said, "I obviously can't endorse you, but it isn't going to break my heart if you can turn the Senate's loss into Hollywood's gain."

After he left. I opened the envelope and found it contained a $1,000 contribution. Three days after I won in November, Kennedy told an informal gathering of professors and students at Harvard that he was personally very happy that I had defeated Mrs. Douglas.

The Douglas victory in the primary called for some rethinking of my strategy. My original plans had been geared to running against Downey, a popular moderate as well as an entrenched incumbent.

Now I found myself running against one of the most left-wing members of Congress—and a woman. I knew that I must not appear ungallant in my criticism of Mrs. Douglas. Consequently, I felt that the best strategy was to let her record do my work for me. She was out of step with the voters of California, and if I could prevent her formidable dramatic skills from clouding the issues, I was almost certain to win.

Throughout the campaign I kept her pinned to her extremist record. I pointed out that she had voted against Truman on military aid to Greece and Turkey, the key plank of the Truman Doctrine, which I had supported. She had also voted against bills requiring loyalty checks for federal employees and was one of only fourteen members of Congress who had voted against the security bill that allowed the heads of key national defense agencies, such as the Atomic Energy Commission, to discharge government workers found to be poor security risks. In a speech before the Conference on American-Soviet Cultural Cooperation, she had claimed that the obstacles to unity between the two countries were "deliberately created by sinister and dangerous forces in this country who have never given up their allegiance to the ideas of Hitler."

Mrs. Douglas had often appeared at meetings and addressed organizations that had been cited by the Attorney General's office during Truman's administration as "Communist and subversive." The Communist *Daily Worker* had selected Mrs. Douglas as "one of the heroes of the Eightieth Congress." Although I constantly questioned her wisdom and judgment in light of such a record, I never questioned her patriotism.

One of the most peculiar ineptitudes of the Douglas campaign was the attempt to charge that my voting record was actually more procommunist than hers. In her speeches she began saying that she was more anticommunist than I, and that I was the one who had voted with Marcantonio against key anticommunist issues. The decision to pursue this particular attack was clearly rooted more in desperation than in logic, because the charge that I was a communist sympathizer had no public credibility whatever. She made the further mistake of careless research on my voting record when she accused me of having voted five times with Marcantonio on key matters. In two of the five votes in question, I had not done so—although she had. In the third there was no vote of record. In the other two cases, she had seized on procedural technicalities to distort the record. She accused me of opposing aid to Korea when I had actually supported it, and of voting to cut a Korean aid program in half when in fact I had voted for a one-year bill rather than a two-year bill.

I made a statewide radio speech accusing her of glaring misstatements in a flyer that her campaign was circulating. I refuted each charge and repeated my challenge that she cite one instance in which I had misrepresented her record. Her side replied with a newspaper ad headed, *Thou Shalt Not Bear False Witness!*

Prominently placed in the ad was a desperate, ludicrous attack:

NIXON-MARCANTONIO ISOLATIONISM
Nixon's record of blind stupidity on foreign policy gave aid and comfort to the Communists. On every key vote Nixon stood with party liner Marcantonio against America in its fight to defeat Communism.

On October 12, four weeks before the election, a California poll was released showing that I had a 12 percent lead over Mrs. Douglas, with 34 percent still undecided. Panic must have swept the Douglas camp when this poll came out, because as the campaign entered its last weeks her attacks became more viciously personal. One of her campaign flyers printed on yellow paper read: "THE BIG LIE! Hitler invented it. Stalin perfected it. Nixon uses it. . . . YOU pick the Congressman the Kremlin loves!" She told one audience, "The temporary success of the Republican Party in 1946, with its backwash of young men in dark shirts, was short lived." She told an interviewer that she hated "Communist totalitarianism and Nazi totalitarianism and Mundt-Nixon totalitarianism." She called me a "peewee who is trying to scare people into voting for him" and customarily referred to me as a "pipsqueak."

In a campaign dispatch, the San Francisco *Chronicle* reported that "Nixon was dubbed 'tricky Dick' by Mrs. Douglas. She warned her listeners that if they want a depression again, elect Nixon. . . . She charged that Nixon had voted along with Congressman Vito Marcantonio on foreign affairs issues and the New Yorker always followed the Communist Party line. She said Nixon was attempting to 'steal' Democratic votes by 'harping' on her record." On October 23, she said that I was smearing her and denounced what she termed my "reaction at home and retreat abroad." She charged that I was "throwing up a smokescreen of smears, innuendos, and half-truths to try to confuse and mislead the voters." I responded immediately: "If it is a smear, it is by the record, and Mrs. Douglas made that record."

The New York *Times* captured the flavor of the campaign in a report from California that "Mrs. Douglas has been depicting her opponent as a red-baiting, reactionary enemy of labor and the common man. . . . Mr. Nixon has been assailing Mrs. Douglas as a flighty left-winger and an exponent of a regime that failed."

In addition to issues of foreign policy and internal security, the 1950 campaign involved several important California-related issues: offshore oil rights, water rights, and federal farm controls. On each, Mrs. Douglas held highly unpopular views. For example, on the question of rights to oil and mineral deposits in the tidelands just off the California coast, she alone of the twenty-three-member California congressional delegation voted to oppose state ownership and favor federal control.

Near the end of the campaign we scheduled a massive old-fashioned torchlight parade and rally in Los Angeles. I was introduced by movie actor Dick Powell. His wife, June Allyson, then pregnant, made a short and moving speech about the future of her unborn child.

I won the election by a margin of 680,000 votes, the largest plurality of any Senate winner that year. It was a good night for Republicans throughout the country as we picked up 30 House seats and 5 Senate seats.

Mrs. Douglas sent no personal message or even the traditional congratulations to me, although she did issue a brief statement: "It now seems certain that Richard Nixon has been elected and that California has two Republican senators." I did, however, receive a telegram from Senator Downey:

PLEASE ACCEPT MY CONGRATULATIONS ON YOUR NOTABLE VICTORY AND MY BEST WISHES AND REGARDS.

The 1950 campaign became highly controversial because of the "rocking, socking" way in which I was said to have waged and won it. Mrs. Douglas and many of her friends and supporters claimed that I had impugned her loyalty and smeared her character, thus depriving the voters of the opportunity to make an honest choice.

Anyone who takes the trouble to go back through the newspapers and other sources of the period, however, will find that things happened as I have described them here.

Helen Gahagan Douglas waged a campaign that would not be equaled for stridency, ineptness, or self-righteousness until George McGovern's presidential campaign twenty-two years later. In the long run, however, even this probably made little difference. Helen Douglas lost the election because the voters of California in 1950 were not prepared to elect as their senator anyone with a left-wing voting record or anyone they perceived as being soft on or naive about communism. She may have been at some political disadvantage because she was a woman. But her fatal disadvantage lay in her record and in her views.

PRESIDENTIAL POLITICS: 1952

Although the 1952 presidential election was still two years away, Republicans in Congress and across the country were already beginning to gear up for it. We had come so close to winning with Dewey in 1948 that there was an almost desperate determination not to fail again. After twenty years out of power, Republicans could almost taste the victory we knew must be ours if only we could enter the election as a party united behind a strong candidate. As the new senator from the nation's second most populous state, I was caught up in this activity from my first days in the Senate.

Truman at this point was a tremendously unpopular President. After a humiliating defeat in the New Hampshire primary in March 1952, he decided not to run again. Even so, whoever the Democrats selected would still have to counter the weight of Truman's unpopularity and the public's disgust with the blatant corruption that even Adlai Stevenson, in reply to a question from the *Oregon Journal,* referred to as "the mess in Washington."

Truman stood in the eye of a hurricane of scandals that swirled around him while he did nothing. His military assistant presided over an influence-peddling scheme of such proportions that the free-lance agents trading in government contracts that grew up as a result came to be known, after their customary fee, as "5 percenters." Payoffs in the form of deep freezes went to Truman's Appointments Secretary, his naval aide, and his Treasury Secretary, among others.

A Senate investigation of the Reconstruction Finance Corporation revealed that its directors had been subject to manipulation for personal gain by top Democratic Party officials and by at least one member of the White House staff. But the tax scandals were the worst of all. A congressional inquiry produced a list of charges against officials in the then Bureau of Internal Revenue that included extortion, evading income tax, and preventing the audit of their own returns.

Of nine district tax collectors removed, one was a personal friend of Truman's, had figured in the RFC scandal, was sent to jail, and was later pardoned by President

Johnson. Truman's Appointments Secretary was convicted of conspiracy in a tax case, sent to prison, and later pardoned by President Kennedy. The head of the Justice Department's Tax Division was convicted in the same case and was also pardoned by President Johnson.

In 1951 alone, 166 Internal Revenue officials were fired or forced to resign. It was no overstatement, then, when I kicked off my Western campaign in Pomona, to charge Truman with heading a "scandal-a-day" administration.

The two major Republican candidates were General Dwight Eisenhower and Senator Robert Taft of Ohio. Taft, the son of a President, had been in the Senate since 1939. He was known as "Mr. Republican" and would clearly be the choice of the party organizers and workers. He was generally described as a conservative, but his beliefs were far too complex—and he was far too intelligent and complicated a man—for any simple label. He was, to be sure, a strong anticommunist with an isolationist streak. Domestically, however, he was constantly trying to find creative solutions to America's social problems without having to resort to big government spending programs. Taft was universally respected in Congress, and perhaps his most ardent supporter was Bill Knowland, my senior colleague from California.

Eisenhower had been the Supreme Allied Commander in Europe during World War II. Immediately after the war he served as Army Chief of Staff. He was named president of Columbia University in 1948, but in 1950 he returned to the military as Supreme Commander of the North Atlantic Treaty Organization forces.

Throughout his military career, Eisenhower had been determinedly non-political, but after the war his heroic image made him a prize sought after by both political parties. According to Eisenhower, Truman had offered to back him for the Democratic presidential nomination in 1948. Eisenhower never told me why he refused Truman's offer. I feel there may have been several reasons. He probably felt the time wasn't right for him; he was reluctant to run as Truman's protégé, and—to the limited extent that he thought in partisan terms—he considered himself a Republican rather than a Democrat. Unlike Taft, Eisenhower could claim no grass roots base among the party faithful.

But his engaging personality, his dazzling smile, and his great military successes had made "Ike" a genuine popular hero who could almost certainly win the election if he could first win the nomination.

By 1951 several small groups of influential Republicans were trying to persuade Eisenhower to run for the Republican nomination. Many of the more liberal elements of the party coalesced behind him. His leading supporter on Capitol Hill was Senator Henry Cabot Lodge of Massachusetts.

There were two other candidates, each of whom hoped that if the convention became deadlocked over Eisenhower and Taft it might turn to him: Harold Stassen and Earl Warren. Stassen's chances of nomination were remote at best. Warren, on the other hand, had been Dewey's running mate in 1948 and as a result of having won the California presidential primary as a favorite son, he would arrive at the convention in Chicago with a solid bloc of seventy delegates bound to stay with him until he decided to release them.

The first time I ever saw Dwight Eisenhower was on his triumphant return to the States after V-E Day in 1945. I was doing Navy contract termination work on Church Street in lower Manhattan, and the windows of my twentieth-floor office overlooked the route of his ticker-tape parade up Broadway. I could just make him out through the snowstorm of confetti, sitting in the back of his open car, waving and looking up at the cheering thousands like me who filled every window of the towering buildings. His arms were raised high over his head in the gesture that soon became his trademark.

I saw him closer up in 1948, when he briefed the members of the House of Representatives on the situation in Europe at a meeting held in the Library of Congress. In the summer of 1950, I saw him at even closer quarters at the Bohemian Grove, the site of the annual summer retreat of San Francisco's Bohemian Club, where each year members of this prestigious private men's club and their guests from all over the country gather amidst California's beautiful redwoods. Herbert Hoover used to invite some of the most distinguished of the 1,400 men at the Grove to join him at his "Cave Man Camp" for lunch each day. On this occasion Eisenhower, then president of Columbia University, was the honored guest. Hoover sat at the head of the table as usual, with Eisenhower at his right. As the Republican nominee in an uphill Senate battle, I was about two places from the bottom.

Eisenhower was deferential to Hoover but not obsequious. He responded to Hoover's toast with a very gracious one of his own. I am sure he was aware that he was in enemy territory among this generally conservative group. Hoover and most of his friends favored Taft and hoped that Eisenhower would not become a candidate.

Later that day, Eisenhower spoke at the beautiful lakeside amphitheatre. It was not a polished speech, but he delivered it without notes and he had the good sense not to speak too long. The only line that drew significant applause was his comment that he did not see why anyone who refused to sign a loyalty oath should have the right to teach in a state university.

After Eisenhower's speech we went back to Cave Man Camp and sat around the campfire appraising it. Everyone liked Eisenhower, but the feeling was that he had a long way to go before he would have the experience, the depth, and the understanding to be President. But it struck me forcibly that Eisenhower's personality and personal mystique had deeply impressed the skeptical and critical Cave Man audience.

In May 1951 I went as a Senate observer to the World Health Organization conference in Geneva. Senator Frank Carlson of Kansas, one of Eisenhower's early supporters, arranged for me to meet Eisenhower at NATO headquarters in Paris. An aide ushered me into Eisenhower's office, and he rose from his desk to greet me. He was erect and vital and impeccably tailored, wearing his famous waist-length uniform jacket, popularly known as the "Eisenhower jacket." He motioned me to a large sofa against the wall, and his informality put me so completely at ease that we were able to talk very freely.

He spoke optimistically about the prospects for European recovery and development. Warming to the topic, he said, "What we need over here and what we need in the States is more optimism in order to combat the defeatist attitude that too many people seem to have."

99

He carefully steered away from American politics, but it was clear he had done his homework. He said that he had read about the Hiss case in *Seeds of Treason* by Ralph de Toledano and Victor Lasky. "The thing that most impressed me was that you not only got Hiss, but you got him fairly," he said. He also liked the emphasis I placed in some of my speeches on the need to take into account economic and ideological as well as military factors in fashioning foreign policy. "Being strong militarily just isn't enough in the kind of battle we are fighting now," he said. This impressed me because, then as now, it was unusual to hear a military man emphasize the importance of non-military strength.

It was not the substance of Eisenhower's conversation so much as his manner that most impressed me that afternoon. It was easy to see how he had been able to bring the leaders of the great wartime alliance together despite their many differences. I felt that in terms of experience and ability in handling foreign policy, Eisenhower was by far the best qualified of the potential presidential candidates. I felt that I was in the presence of a genuine statesman, and I came away convinced that he should be the next President. I also decided that if he ran for the nomination I would do everything I could to help him get it.

I did not know Bob Taft well, although I had met him several times while I was in the House of Representatives, particularly during the debates on the Taft-Hartley bill. He was highly respected in Washington, but even his strongest supporters acknowledged that he lacked some of the personality traits needed by a presidential candidate. He was an intelligent, high-minded patriot, but he was also very proud and very shy. This combination unfortunately made many people feel that he was arrogant. Taft was visibly uncomfortable with the personal "small change" of presidential politics—the handshaking and backslapping and endless importuning of local party leaders, and he was honest in a way that could be painfully blunt. I shall never forget seeing him on television during the New Hampshire primary. As he emerged from a building he began shaking hands. A little girl held out a pen and a piece of paper and asked for his autograph. Right on camera, he explained to her with devastating reasonableness that handshaking took less time than signing autographs, and since he had a very busy schedule he could not interrupt it to sign anything for her.

I think that next to Pat, Martha Taft was the most exceptional political wife I have ever known. She was as gracious and vivacious as her husband was shy and stiff. She had suffered a crippling stroke in 1950 and was confined to a wheelchair; Taft, who was completely devoted to her, took her everywhere with him, and at a dinner party it was a touching sight to see him cut her food and help feed it to her. People in Washington who knew these things about Taft admired him and made allowances because of them. But when it came to choosing a nominee the fact had to be faced that his abrasive personality would be a serious disadvantage in a presidential campaign.

I believed that the President elected in 1952 had first and foremost to be an expert in dealing with the serious international challenges facing America, and I had some serious reservations about Taft in this regard.

Before the election in 1950 I had been invited to be the major speaker at the 36th Annual McKinley Day Dinner in Dayton, Ohio. My subject was the threat of communism at home and abroad. Taft had followed me with a short speech in which he said that, as he saw it, the greatest problem facing America at home or abroad was not communism but socialism. He urged therefore that we concentrate our efforts on fighting and defeating socialism. I did not like socialism any more than he did. What concerned me was his failure to recognize that many socialists were dedicated anticommunists. The major threat we faced was not socialism, but communist subversion supported by the international Communist movement, and Taft's failure to understand this distinction raised questions in my mind about his grasp of the whole international situation.

One day early in 1952, Taft came to see me. He was a man no more interested in small talk than I was, so he got right to the point. He said that we had many mutual friends in California and some of them had urged him to drop by and simply ask me for my support for his candidacy. "It wasn't something *I* felt I ought to do," he added with complete sincerity, "but I don't want to have any misunderstanding about my desire to have your support if you feel that my candidacy is consistent with your point of view."

I told him that I had enormous respect for his leadership in the Senate and had no doubt that in terms of domestic affairs he was the best qualified man to lead the country. It was with a great deal of sadness that I told him I personally felt that international affairs would be more important for the next President and that I had concluded Eisenhower was the best qualified in that area. Therefore I would be supporting his candidacy. I said I had already informed Knowland and Warren of my decision. I added that if Taft won the nomination he would have my wholehearted support and assured him that under no circumstances would I lend myself to a "stop Taft" movement at the convention.

He said that although he was naturally disappointed with my decision, he appreciated my frankness, and he was generous and respectful in his comments about Eisenhower. Bob Taft was a fine gentleman, and it was a great loss to the party, the Congress, and the nation when he died of cancer just a few months after Eisenhower was inaugurated.

On July 1, I flew to Chicago to take part in the platform hearings being held the week before the Republican National Convention.

I had first become aware that I might be considered as the nominee for Vice President a few months earlier when clues and signs began appearing in the press and the political rumor mills. However, I considered my chances almost impossibly remote. In retrospect, I see that the road to the ticket had begun on May 8, 1952, when, at Governor Dewey's invitation, I was the main speaker at the New York State Republican Party's annual fund-raising dinner at the Waldorf-Astoria. Because it was a presidential year, and because Dewey was both the former standard-bearer and one of the principal people behind Eisenhower, the dinner was a major occasion, and my speech would be broadcast on radio. I spent several hours making outlines, to be sure that I could say everything within the allotted half-hour radio time. I delivered it without notes in exactly twenty-nine minutes, and the audience gave me a standing ovation when it was over.

When I sat down next to Dewey after acknowledging the applause, he very deliberately snuffed out his cigarette, which he always held in a cigarette holder, grasped my hand, and earnestly said, "That was a terrific speech. Make me a promise: don't get fat, don't lose your zeal, and you can be President someday." I did not take him seriously, much less literally, because such compliments are commonplace in politics. But later that evening, during a small reception in his suite for some of his close friends, he asked me if I would object to his suggesting my name as a possible candidate for Vice President.

A few weeks later I was invited to meet with Eisenhower's inner circle of advisers in a suite at the Mayflower Hotel in Washington. The group included Herbert Brownell, the lawyer whom Eisenhower was later to name Attorney General, and General Lucius Clay, and Harold Talbott, Dewey's chief fund-raiser. We had a wide-ranging discussion of foreign and domestic policy that lasted most of the afternoon. Nothing was said about the vice presidency, but it was clear that they were trying to get to know me better and to size me up.

Word of this meeting quickly made its way through the Washington grapevine, and rumors that I might be Eisenhower's running mate began to appear in the papers. One evening a few weeks before the convention, Pat and I had dinner with Alice Longworth, the witty, acerbic daughter of Teddy Roosevelt. I asked her if she thought I should take the nomination if Eisenhower offered it to me. I knew that Mrs. Longworth was an all-out Taft supporter. She did not like Eisenhower, and as far as I could tell she never did develop any liking for him.

In her typically outspoken way, she said, "Father used to tell me that being Vice President was the most boring job in the world. However," she added, "if Eisenhower gets the nomination, someone will have to go on that ticket who can reassure the party regulars and particularly the conservatives that he won't take everyone to hell in a handcart, and you are the best man to do it."

As we were leaving, Mrs. Longworth brought up the subject again and asked me whether I was giving it serious thought. I said that the prospect was too unlikely for me to take it very seriously. "I thought as much," she said disapprovingly. "you should be giving it a lot of thought, and you should talk to Pat about it so that just in case it does happen you aren't caught with your drawers down! If you ask me, and since you did I'll tell you again, if you're thinking of your own good and your own career you are probably better off to stay in the Senate and not go down in history as another nonentity who served as Vice President. Of course, Father's experience was different, and by some act of God you might become President too, but you shouldn't plan on it. For the good of the party, however, I think that you should take it if you have the chance."

Until this conversation, I had never taken the possibility of nomination seriously enough to consider that I might not want the job. The vice presidency had traditionally been a political dead end, and most Vice Presidents were old party wheelhorses or regional politicians added to balance the ticket. Theodore Roosevelt referred to the vice presidency as "taking the veil," and Harry Truman described the office as being about as useful as a fifth teat on a cow. Until Eisenhower completely changed the concept of the office, the Vice President was almost exclusively a ceremonial figure who went to the receptions and dedicated the dams the President didn't have time for. His only important functions were to cast occasional tie-breaking votes in the Senate and to be constantly ready to take over if the President died or were incapacitated. Today we think of the vice presidency as a stepping-stone to the presidency, but before 1952 it was more often a stepping-stone to political oblivion.

I did not have to know Eisenhower well to know that he would expect his Vice President to subordinate any personal ambitions to the President's programs and policies. It was one thing for me to believe that Eisenhower was the best man for the job; it was quite another to renounce my own political career just as it reached a national stage in the Senate. If I had had presidential ambitions—which I did not at that point—I probably would not have considered becoming Vice President.

When the Republican National Convention opened in Chicago on July 7, Bill Knowland, Minnesota Congressman Walter Judd, Colorado Governor Dan Thornton, and I were being touted as the most likely running mates for Eisenhower. Two days before the nominating session, Jack Knight, publisher and editor of the Chicago *Daily News*, went out on a political limb and predicted that Eisenhower and I would be the Republican nominees. A headline across the top of page one proclaimed: *GOP Ticket: Ike and Nixon, Predicts Knight.* I still considered this so unlikely that I sent someone out to buy a half a dozen copies of the paper. I said, "That will probably be the last time we'll see that headline, and I want to be able to show it to my grandchildren."

When I got back to the hotel around midnight, Pat was waiting up for me. For her, the worst part of politics was campaigning, and through two strenuous California campaigns in 1946 and 1950 she had been at my side every step of the way and took it all with good grace. Although campaigning did not come easily to her because of her deep-rooted sense of privacy, she did it superbly. But now that we actually had to consider the possibility of a long and grueling nationwide campaign, she was having second thoughts about what accepting the nomination could mean to us and to our young daughters.

About 4 A.M., after we had talked for hours, I suggested that we talk to Murray Chotiner. As a political professional, he might have a different perspective about the whole question.

When he arrived at our room I filled him in on our discussion and asked for his opinion. He answered in his usual blunt way. "There comes a point," he said, "when you have to go up or go out." He pointed out that even if I ran for Vice President and lost, I would still have my Senate seat. Or, if I became Vice President and did not like it, I could step down after the first term. "Think of it, Dick," he said, "any man who quits political life as Vice President as young as you are certainly hasn't lost a thing."

After Murray left, Pat and I talked about what he had said and we agreed that he was right. "I guess I can make it through another campaign," she said.

Eisenhower was nominated on the first ballot. The Taft forces were unhappy not just because they had been defeated but because of the strong-arm tactics they felt had been used on many delegates by Eisenhower's supporters under the direction of his floor manager, Governor Sherman Adams of New Hampshire.

When the convention adjourned for lunch, I decided to go back to my room at the Stock Yard Inn and sleep until the evening session when Eisenhower and his running mate would make their acceptance speeches. I had been up nearly all night talking to Pat and Murray, and the morning had been tiring because of the final frantic shiftings and maneuverings before the balloting. The room was not air-conditioned, and the temperature must have been 100 degrees when I opened the door. I stripped down to my shorts and lay on top of the covers, trying to think cool thoughts. Chotiner arrived a few minutes later, and he could scarcely contain his excitement. He told me that Eisenhower had approved a final list of acceptable running mates and then turned the actual selection over to his inner circle of advisers. One of them, Herb Brownell, had told Chotiner that I was on the list and asked where I could be reached if the need arose.

"It's still wishful thinking, Murray," I said.

I had just started to drift to sleep when the bedside phone rang. I could recognize Brownell's voice coming over the line, but it sounded very distant. I pressed the receiver against my ear and realized that he was talking to someone else.

"Yes, General," he was saying, "we have agreed unanimously, and it's Dick Nixon."

Then Brownell came on the line with me. He said simply, "We picked you."

For one of the few times I can remember, I was speechless.

"The general asked if you could come see him right away in his suite at the Blackstone Hotel," Brownell continued. "That is, assuming you want it!"

I felt hot, sleepy, and grubby, but there wasn't even time to shower or shave. I pulled my clothes on again and started down to the lobby. The ever-resourceful Chotiner somehow produced a limousine and a police motorcycle escort which sped us across town to Eisenhower's headquarters at the Blackstone.

Eisenhower beamed as he shook my hand and led me

into the large sitting room of his suite. He introduced me to Mrs. Eisenhower, and the three of us chatted for a few minutes before she left us.

Almost immediately Eisenhower seemed to shift gears. He became very serious and formal. He said that he wanted his campaign to be a crusade for the things he believed in and the things he believed America stood for. "Will you join me in such a campaign?" he asked. I was a little taken aback by his formality, but I answered, "I would be proud and happy to."

"I'm glad you are going to be on the team, Dick," he said. "I think that we can win, and I know that we can do the right things for this country."

Suddenly he hit his forehead with the palm of his hand. "I just remembered," he said. "I haven't resigned from the Army yet!" He called in his secretary and dictated a letter to the Secretary of the Army. A few minutes later she brought the typed letter back to him.

While I watched as he read it over and signed it, I wondered what must be going through his mind. He had spent his entire adult life in the Army and had reached the pinnacle of fame and success. Now he was giving it up to plunge into politics. My guess is that if he could have known of the agonies he was to go through over the next eight years he would have had serious second thoughts.

As we talked, I was struck by Eisenhower's beguiling mixture of personal savvy and political naïveté. He began by telling me all the reasons he had not wanted to run for President, and how he had finally decided that it was his duty to run. Then, turning abruptly to his plans for his administration, he said, "Dick, I don't want a Vice President who will be a figurehead. I want a man who will be a member of the team. And I want him to be able to step into the presidency smoothly in case anything happens to me. Of course," he added with a grin, "we have to win the election first."

Eisenhower wanted his campaign to be waged as a crusade against the corruption of the Truman administration and against its foreign policy, which he felt had played into the Communists' hands in both Europe and Asia. It was clear that he envisaged taking an above-the-battle position, and that whatever hard partisan campaigning was required would be pretty much left to me. He said that as an upstanding young man and a good speaker I should be able not only to flail the Democrats on the corruption issue but also to personify the remedy for it. As for the communist threat, he said that the Hiss case was a text from which I could preach everywhere in the country.

Years later, in 1964, he told me my name had been first on the list he had submitted to his advisers for consideration. He added a bit sheepishly, "I must admit I thought at the time that you were two or three years older than you were."

I think there were several reasons that Eisenhower had put me on his list and that his advisers had chosen me. In 1952 Republican Party stalwarts viewed Eisenhower as the candidate of the Eastern liberal establishment. In order to hold the party together, he needed a moderate conservative from the Midwest or West who could serve as a bridge to the regular Republican Party organization, which had been sorely disappointed by Taft's defeat. Eisenhower also knew that to maintain his above-the-battle position he needed a running mate who was willing to engage in all-out combat, and who was good at it. In a sense, the hero needed a point-man.

There was undoubtedly a geographic element in his choice—the recognition of the postwar power and influence of the western United States and particularly of California. More than anyone else under serious consideration, I would also be able to appeal directly to the large number of younger voters and veterans.

I knew that some of Eisenhower's more liberal advisers had preferred Earl Warren to me, and that some of his more conservative advisers had preferred Bill Knowland, or even Bob Taft if he would accept. Perhaps my anticommunist credentials from the Hiss case were what most tilted the decision to me, because it was already clear that the communist challenge would be an important issue in the campaign.

Eisenhower finally looked at his watch. "We had both better begin getting ready for tonight," he said.

As we shook hands again at the door, two things were foremost in my mind. First, within a few hours I would be addressing the convention and millions of Americans on radio and television, and I had not yet prepared a single word or thought. Second, this possibility had seemed so remote that the only suit I had brought to Chicago was the wrinkled light gray one I was wearing. Pat too had been caught by surprise. She was lunching in a nearby restaurant when she heard a news bulletin that I was to be Eisenhower's running mate.

Chotiner and I went directly to the convention hall. We arrived shortly before the delegates were to begin the balloting for Vice President. I found Bill Knowland and asked him if he would do me the honor of placing my name in nomination. Knowland was not only a personal friend, but also the man whom Taft probably would have chosen as his running mate. Knowland said that he would be proud and happy to nominate me. I walked down the aisle to the Ohio delegation, and immediately spotted Senator John Bricker by his massive mane of white hair. When I asked if he would second my nomination, tears filled his eyes: "Dick," he said, "there isn't anybody in the world I would rather make a speech for, but after what they have said and done to Bob Taft over the last few months, I just cannot bring myself to do it. I would appreciate it if you would ask somebody else." I was taken aback by the depth of his feeling against the Eisenhower forces, and for the first time I realized how difficult and how important my role as a bridge between the party factions was going to be. I told Bricker that I appreciated his candor. I asked Governor Alfred Driscoll of New Jersey to deliver the main seconding speech in his place.

Since there was no opposition to my nomination, a motion was made that the rules be suspended and I be nominated by acclamation. At 6:33 P.M. I became the convention's nominee for Vice President. Joe Martin asked me to come up to the rostrum. Pat joined me on the convention floor and kissed me twice—the second time at the insistence of the photographers who had missed the first time.

It was to happen many times over the next two decades, but both Pat and I still remember that first time, and our surprise and elation at the thunderous sound of several thousand people shouting themselves hoarse and stamping their feet and clapping for us. I felt exhilarated—almost heady—as I looked out across the moving, shifting mass that filled the convention floor and galleries. Pat said later that for those few minutes it actually made her forget the long campaign that we would have to endure.

Joe Martin was beaming broadly. Pat kissed him, and his face flushed boyishly. I asked him whether he should not try to calm the people down, and he had to yell in my ear to make himself heard above the noise: "You know the old saying—gather in the hay while the sun is shining."

That night Eisenhower delivered his acceptance speech proclaiming his crusade. My acceptance speech followed his and closed both the evening and the convention. Standing before the delegates and the television cameras, still in my rumpled gray suit, I pledged myself to put on a "fighting campaign for the election of a fighting candidate," and also to work for a Republican-controlled House and Senate. In an attempt to begin healing wounds right away, I praised Joe Martin and Styles Bridges—both considered to be either pro-Taft or at best neutral toward Eisenhower—for their work at the convention and said how important it was that they be Speaker and Majority Leader in the next Congress.

The raucous audience suddenly grew still in anticipation of what it knew must be coming. "And then may I say this one word about a man that I consider to be a very great man. I am a relatively young man in politics. . . . But I do think I know something about the abilities of men in legislative life. And it seems to me that one of the greatest tragedies of the past two years, in the past four years, has been this: that one of the really great senators, one of the greatest legislative leaders in the history of America at the present time, instead of being chairman of the majority policy committee is chairman of the minority policy committee. And I say let's be sure that Senator Bob Taft is chairman of the majority policy committee after next January."

The frustration of the Taft supporters at having lost was added to the general sentiment for "Mr. Republican," and the convention went wild for him. In fact, it went too wild for the taste of some of Eisenhower's liberal advisers, who felt that Taft's ovation was more enthusiastic than Eisenhower's. Some of them even suggested that I had done this purposely in order to belittle Eisenhower and build myself up. This was my first, but by no means my last, run-in with this small but determined group.

The next evening I called on Taft at his hotel. He was

obviously a terribly disappointed man, but not a beaten man. He took his defeat with good grace, and reassured me that he would work for Eisenhower's election. He told me that he was genuinely pleased that I was on the ticket.

My major job in the campaign, as I saw it, was to help heal the breach which had developed during the pre-convention period between the Taft and Eisenhower supporters. The problem was not the men at the top: Taft was a team player and he went all out in his support of the ticket. But many of Taft's partisans were bitter over their defeat and seemed likely to sit out the campaign. Most of the resentment was not aimed at Eisenhower personally, but at the men around him, and particularly the Eastern liberal faction that had managed his nomination, symbolized by Cabot Lodge, Sherman Adams, and Tom Dewey.

While they all knew that I had been for Eisenhower, they appreciated the fact that I had not been involved in any of the pre-convention attacks on Taft. Also, the Taft people tended to be organization minded, and they considered me to be a good organization man because both as congressman and senator I had spoken for party fund-raising and other affairs all over the country and thus was known personally to many of them. They knew that I would hit hard against communism and corruption, and they believed that it was essential to develop those issues if we were to pull in the candidates for the House and Senate who would assure us majorities in Congress.

That was why I was asked to keynote the Ohio State Republican Convention held in Columbus three weeks after the national convention. Two weeks later I made a similar speech on Republican Day at the Illinois State Fair. Illinois was a Taft state, and it was felt that through my speech I could stimulate the interest of the organization people on behalf of the ticket.

Right after the convention, Eisenhower went to Denver for a vacation, and I returned to Washington in a kind of daze. One of the many thousands of letters that poured in to my office was a handwritten one from a 1947 House classmate.

111

Dear Dick:

I was tremendously pleased that the convention selected you for V.P. I was always convinced that you would move ahead to the top —but I never thought it would come this quickly. You were an ideal selection and will bring to the ticket a great deal of strength.

Please give my best to your wife and all kinds of good luck to you.

Cordially,
Jack Kennedy

Campaigns in those days still used whistle-stop trains, and that is how we began ours. Eisenhower's train, the *Look Ahead, Neighbor Special,* set out first for a tour of the Midwest. My own more prosaically named *Nixon Special* left on September 17 from Pomona, the town near Whittier where I had kicked off my campaigns for the House and Senate.

Nearly all the Nixons and Milhouses were on hand at the station that night. Even Earl Warren was carried away by the excitement. He introduced me graciously and concluded by saying, "I now present to you the next President of the United States." The laughter and applause which broke loose after his uncharacteristic slip of the tongue drowned out his embarrassed correction.

From the back platform of my train, I described the corruption in Truman's administration and lambasted "the mess in Washington." Eisenhower would change all that, I said, and I promised to bring the message of Eisenhower's crusade to every corner of the country during the next two months.

THE FUND CRISIS

A few days before the Pomona kickoff, I had appeared in Washington on *Meet the Press.* After the broadcast, one of the reporters on the panel, the syndicated columnist Peter Edson, took me aside and said, "Senator, what is this 'fund' we hear about? There is a rumor to the effect that you have a supplementary salary of $20,000 a year, contributed by a hundred California businessmen. What about it?"

I told Edson that immediately after my election to the Senate I had met with several of my California supporters to discuss the best ways of being an effective senator. The biggest problem was the great distance between Washington and California. Everyone agreed that to be effective I should spend as much time as possible traveling around the state, making speeches and keeping in touch with the people in person and through the mail. But the statutory allowance provided for only one round trip between California and Washington per session, and since personal or strictly political material could not be sent free under the Senate frank, I would also have to pay for printing and postage of political mailings from my own funds. This could be expensive; for example, it had cost me over $2,000 a year just to send a Christmas card to each of the 20,000 people who had done volunteer work or made a contribution to my Senate campaign.

Murray Chotiner suggested that we think in terms of running a "permanent campaign" all through my six-year term, and Dana Smith, an attorney from Pasadena who had been finance chairman of my Senate campaign, suggested that we do some public fund-raising for it. He said that if we limited contributions to a relatively small amount and then had everything handled through a trustee, there could be no question about people trying to buy influence or about my gaining any personal profit.

In late 1950 Smith sent a letter to a few hundred campaign contributors outlining the purposes of this new fund. Several weeks later Smith sent out a second and more widely distributed mailing—this time an open letter to several thousand people on our campaign mailing lists. In the end, seventy-six had contributed an average of $240 each. No single contribution was more than $500, the limit Smith had set. The total amount we received for my fund was $18,235. Throughout the two years of its existence, all transactions were handled by Smith and paid by check. All expenditures were for mailing, travel, and other political activities. Not a cent was used for solely personal purposes.

I told Edson to call Smith for any information he needed for his story and gave him Smith's phone number in Pasadena.

Edson called Smith, who was happy to explain the fund to him. The same day, three other reporters also asked Smith about it, and he explained it to them. One of the three was Leo Katcher, a Hollywood movie writer who also covered the Los Angeles area for the New York *Post*.

On September 18, the day after our Pomona kickoff, the fund story exploded across the front page of the late morning edition of the New York *Post*. *Secret Nixon Fund!* the banner screamed; inside, another headline said: *Secret Rich Men's Trust Fund Keeps Nixon in Style Far Beyond His Salary.*

The story, written by Katcher, did not support the sensationalism of these headlines. In fact, the *Post*'s play of the story was so excessive that many editors dismissed it as a partisan ploy or relegated accounts of it to an inside page. The *Post*'s extreme liberal-left politics and Katcher's Hollywood gossip background lent weight to this interpretation. The editors of *Newsweek* decided that the story was a political stunt and that it would either be ignored or would backfire. Peter Edson's long and objective story on the fund appeared in many papers on the same day as Katcher's "exclusive," but its sober recounting of the facts sounded pale alongside the *Post*'s bombastic fantasy.

The Democrats, whose presidential nominee was Governor Adlai Stevenson of Illinois, tried to keep the *Post*'s version of the fund story going. They succeeded in making it a national issue when the Democratic National Chairman, Stephen Mitchell, demanded that I be thrown off the ticket or that we at least keep quiet about public morals. Other Democrats quickly chimed in that the whole Eisenhower crusade had been exposed as a phony.

About the only silence concerning the fund came from the Eisenhower train, where his staff had kept the story from him until early Friday morning so that he could devote his full attention to a major speech outlining his farm policy at Omaha on Thursday night. When they told him, he was surprised and upset. Concerned because his next scheduled speeches were on corruption, he told his staff, "Let's find out the facts before I shoot my mouth off."

After meeting with his principal advisers, Eisenhower released a statement:

> I have long admired and applauded Senator Nixon's American faith and determination to drive communist sympathizers from offices of public trust.
>
> There has recently been leveled against him a charge of unethical practices. I believe Dick Nixon to be an honest man. I am confident that he will place all the facts before the American people fairly and squarely.
>
> I intend to talk with him at the earliest time we can reach each other by telephone.

Meanwhile, the *Nixon Special* moved up through the central California valley toward Oregon. Large crowds continued to turn out as hecklers transformed my speeches into sparring matches.

We delayed our departure from Chico, in northern California, to make telephone contact with the Eisenhower train in Nebraska. Senator Fred Seaton, who was acting as liaison between the Eisenhower and Nixon campaign trains, told me that he had a message that Eisenhower had penciled out that morning, recommending that I publish all documentary evidence I had to back up my position. He added that the general said he was ready to consult with me as soon as physically possible, explaining that our train schedules had apparently prevented a telephone conversation up to now. It was clear to me that Eisenhower was not committing himself.

By the beginning of the weekend, the whole nation was saturated with stories and rumors about the Nixon fund—and with speculation about Nixon's future. Late Friday night, after our train had pulled into a siding until morning, I ran into a reporter in the corridor, and he asked if I had any comment on the Washington *Post* and New York *Herald Tribune* editorials.

"What editorials?" I asked.

"Both the *Post* and *Herald Tribune* have editorials tomorrow morning saying that you ought to offer your resignation to General Eisenhower."

I felt as much of a jolt as if the train had suddenly started to move. I said I would not comment without having read the editorials and went back to my private car. I asked to see Murray Chotiner and Bill Rogers, who told me it was true. Since there was nothing that we could do about it, the staff had decided not to ruin my sleep by telling me. They showed me a copy of the *Herald Tribune* editorial. Although it avoided the question of whether I was actually guilty of anything, it concluded: "The proper course of Senator Nixon in the circumstances is to make a formal offer of withdrawal from the ticket. How this offer is acted on will be determined by an appraisal of all the facts in the light of General Eisenhower's unsurpassed fairness of mind."

For the first time I was struck by the enormity of the impending crisis. So far I had viewed it as a typical partisan attempt by the Democrats to derail my whistle-stopping attacks on the corruption issue. I had felt secure that I was on firm ground on the merits of the case and that I would therefore have nothing to worry about in the long run.

The demand for my resignation by the Washington *Post* was neither a surprise nor a particular concern. But the *Herald Tribune* was something altogether different. It was generally considered to be the most influential Republican paper in the East, if not in the country. Bert Andrews, who had worked so closely with me during the Hiss case, was traveling with Eisenhower as head of the *Trib*'s Washington bureau; I thought of the publishers and the editor as personal friends, and I knew that they were close to Eisenhower. If the *Herald Tribune* was calling for my resignation from the ticket, the fat was in the fire.

Chotiner was furious. "If those damned amateurs around Eisenhower just had the sense they were born with, they would recognize that this is a purely political attack and they wouldn't pop off like this," he said. He was assuming, as was I, that the *Herald Tribune* would not have published such an editorial unless people high in the councils of the Eisenhower campaign had indicated that it reflected their point of view.

It was essential that I get some firsthand information about where the people around Eisenhower—and, of course, Eisenhower himself—stood. We agreed that first thing in the morning, Rogers would call Dewey, and Chotiner would call Fred Seaton.

Perhaps the staff had been right in trying to protect my night's sleep, because by the time our discussion was over it was after 2 A.M. When I returned to our compartment, Pat woke up and I told her what had happened.

I was very tired and very discouraged by this time. "Maybe I am looking at this too much from my own standpoint," I said. "If the judgment of more objective people around Eisenhower is that my resignation would help him to win, maybe I ought to resign."

"You can't think of resigning," she said emphatically. With a typically incisive analysis she said flatly that if Eisenhower forced me off the ticket he would lose the election. She also argued strongly that unless I fought for my honor in the face of such an attack, I would mar not only my life but the lives of our family and particularly the girls.

The *Herald Tribune* editorial appeared on Saturday morning and had a predictable effect. Speculation began as to how much longer I could last on the ticket. One bright spot in a bleak day came when I learned that Bob Taft, when asked about the fund in an interview the day before, had replied bluntly: "I see no reason why a senator or representative should not accept gifts from members of his family or his friends or his constituents to help pay even personal expenses which are not paid by the government. The only possible criticism would arise if these donors asked for or received legislative or other favors. I know that no such motives inspired the expense payments in the case of Dick Nixon. Those who contributed to the fund probably agreed one hundred percent with his legislative position anyway." Karl Mundt had branded the *Post* story a "left-wing smear" and a "filthy" maneuver by a patently pro-Stevenson paper.

Before the day was over, Senator George Aiken of Vermont and former President Herbert Hoover had also come to my defense.

On Saturday afternoon the train arrived in Portland, Oregon. The crowd outside the hotel there was the ugliest we had met so far. They threw pennies into our car, and Pat was pushed and jostled as she walked alongside me. Our path was obstructed by people from the local Democratic organization with canes and dark glasses shaking tin cups labeled "Nickels for poor Nixon."

A message was waiting for me at the hotel switchboard: Sherman Adams, Eisenhower's campaign manager, had called me on an urgent matter. I told Chotiner to pass along the message that I would not talk with anyone except Eisenhower himself. Whatever happened, I was not going to be fobbed off on staff aides.

Jim Bassett, my press secretary, informed me that there had been an unofficial reaction from Eisenhower. During an off-the-record press conference on his train, the reporters traveling with Eisenhower had told him that the results of an informal poll taken among themselves had come out 40 to 2 in favor of dropping me from the ticket. Eisenhower told them, "I don't care if you fellows are 40 to 2. I am taking my time on this. Nothing's decided, contrary to your idea that this is a setup for a whitewash of Nixon." Then he added, "Of what avail is it for us to carry on this crusade against this business of what has been going on in Washington if we, ourselves, aren't clean as a hound's tooth?" Word of this inevitably leaked out, and the colorful phrase captured the public's imagination. Nixon would have to be clean as a hound's tooth.

Pat couldn't get over how unfair the whole thing was. "Not only isn't the fund illegal," she said, "but you know how you bent over backward to keep it public and to make sure that every cent was accounted for."

My mother was in Washington taking care of the girls when the crisis broke. On Saturday night, after reading the papers and listening to the radio news, she wrote out two telegrams. One I was not to hear about for several days. The other she sent to me:

GIRLS ARE OKAY. THIS IS TO TELL YOU WE ARE THINKING OF YOU AND KNOW EVERY-THING WILL BE FINE. LOVE ALWAYS, MOTHER.

In our family, as I have said, the phrase "we are thinking of you" meant "we are praying for you." I was deeply touched by this message, but it also reminded me of all the people who were watching me and depending on me.

By Sunday morning there was still no direct word from Eisenhower. The tension had become so great that I could almost feel it in the air. The night before, Chotiner had suggested that since the Republican National Committee had allotted television time to the vice presidential candidate, I should ask for part of it to deliver a defense of the fund.

I spent the afternoon talking with my staff about the different possibilities for a television program. We were deep in this discussion when Tom Dewey called from New York. Dewey was never one to mince words. He said that he had been in touch with the Eisenhower train and confirmed what I already suspected: with only one or two exceptions, the circle around Eisenhower was a hanging jury as far as I was concerned. They wanted me to offer Eisenhower my resignation. Dewey was still one of my supporters, however, and he said that Eisenhower himself had not yet made a decision. "I think you ought to go on television," he said. "I don't think Eisenhower *should* make this decision. Make the American people do it. At the conclusion of the program, ask people to wire their verdict in to you. You will probably get over a million replies, and that will give you three or four days to think it over. At the end of that time, if it is 60 percent for you and 40 percent against you, say you are getting out as that is not enough of a majority. If it is 90 to 10, stay on. If you stay on, it isn't blamed on Ike, and if you get off, it isn't blamed on Ike. All the fellows here in New York agree with me."

I told him that was exactly what we had been discussing when he called. He urged me to start making plans right away, since the situation was too tense to wait much longer for a favorable resolution.

Later that night, I finally heard from Eisenhower. I took his telephone call without asking the others in the room to leave. They were all so intimately involved that I felt they had a right to be present at what might be the end of my vice presidential candidacy.

I could tell from Eisenhower's voice that although he was trying to buck me up, he was deeply troubled.

"You've been taking a lot of heat the last couple of days," he said. "I imagine it has been pretty rough."

"It hasn't been easy," I replied.

He said that it was very difficult for him to decide what was the best thing to do. "I have come to the conclusion," he said, "that you are the one who has to decide what to do. After all, you've got a big following in this country, and if the impression got around that you got off the ticket because I forced you off, it is going to be very bad. On the other hand, if I issue a statement now backing you up, in effect people will accuse me of condoning wrongdoing."

He paused as if waiting for me to fill the gap, but I let the line hang silent. After a moment he said that he had just been out to dinner with some of his friends. None of them knew what to do, but all of them agreed that I should have an opportunity to tell my side of the story to the country. "I don't want to be in the position of condemning an innocent man," he said. "I think you ought to go on a nationwide television program and tell them everything there is to tell, everything you can remember since the day you entered public life. Tell them about any money you have ever received."

"General," I asked, "do you think after the television program that an announcement could then be made one way or the other?"

He hesitated. "I am hoping that no announcement would be necessary at all," he replied, "but maybe after the program we could tell what ought to be done."

"General," I told him, "I just want you to know that I don't want you to give any consideration to my personal feelings. I know how difficult this problem is for you." I told him that if he thought my staying on the ticket would be harmful, I would get off it and take the heat. But I also told him that there comes a time to stop dawdling, and that once I had done the television program he ought to decide. "There comes a time in matters like this when you've either got to shit or get off the pot," I blurted out. "The great trouble here is the indecision," I added.

The language I used startled the men in the room with me, and I can only assume it had a similar effect on Eisenhower, who was certainly not used to being talked to in that manner. But he obviously remained unconvinced. He said,

"We will have to wait three or four days after the television show to see what the effect of the program is."

There was nothing more to discuss. I would have to stake everything on a successful television speech. The conversation trailed off. His last words were, "Keep your chin up."

It seemed clear that Eisenhower would not have objected if I had told him that I was going to submit a resignation to him, which he could then choose to accept or not as the circumstances indicated. As I had told him, I was perfectly willing to do this, but the decision must be his. I felt that his indecision or his unwillingness to come out and ask for it relieved me of any obligation in that regard. It is one thing to offer to sign your own death warrant; it is another to be expected to draw it up yourself.

I told Pat about Eisenhower's call and asked her what she thought I should do. This whole episode had already scarred her deeply. The stress was so great that she had developed a painfully stiff neck and had to stay in bed. She was worried about how the girls would be affected by it, and she was constantly on the phone to my mother in Washington to make sure that things there were all right.

"We both know what you have to do, Dick," she said. "You have to fight it all the way to the end, no matter what happens."

That night I sat alone in my room and made my decision: I would stay and I would fight.

The Republican National Committee and the Senatorial and Congressional Campaign Committees agreed to put up $75,000 to buy a half hour of television time for me on Tuesday night, September 23. In those days, nationwide network broadcasts could originate only in New York, Chicago, and Los Angeles, so on Monday we flew from Portland back to Los Angeles. On the plane, I took some postcards from the pocket of the seat in front of me and began to put down some thoughts about what I might say.

I remembered the Truman scandal concerning a $9,000 mink coat given to a White House secretary, and I made a note that Pat had no mink—just a cloth coat. I thought of

DNC Chairman Mitchell's snide comment that people who cannot afford to hold an office should not run for it, and I made a note to check out a quotation from Lincoln to the effect that God must have loved the common people because he made so many of them. I also thought about the stunning success FDR had in his speech during the 1944 campaign, when he had ridiculed his critics by saying they were even attacking his little dog Fala, and I knew it would infuriate my critics if I could turn this particular table on them. I made a note: "They will be charging that I have taken gifts. I must report that I did receive one gift after the nomination—a cocker spaniel dog, Checkers, and whatever they say, we are going to keep her."

During the flight Chotiner stopped by my seat for a brief chat and repeated something he had first observed three days earlier. He had shrewdly noted that all the Democrats except Stevenson were attacking me. "I smell a rat. I bet he has something to hide," Chotiner had said.

That evening, news arrived that proved Chotiner to be a prophet. Kent Chandler, a Chicago manufacturing executive, had sent a telegram to Stevenson charging that as governor of Illinois, Stevenson had promoted a "cash fund contributed by private individuals, which was paid to various of your official appointees to state jobs in order to supplement the salaries paid them by the state."

Within hours, Stevenson had issued a statement acknowledging the existence of such a fund saying: "The funds used for this purpose were left over from the 1948 campaign for governor, together with subsequent general contributions." His spokesman declined to elaborate, and Stevenson himself refused to meet with reporters.

Stevenson's statement did not address the subject of yet another revelation that day. A former Illinois state purchasing agent, William J. McKinney, revealed that he had made up a monthly list of business corporations and state suppliers who were solicited for expenses Stevenson felt could not be charged to the taxpayers. The amounts contributed reportedly ranged from $100 to $5,000. "They figured it would help them get business," McKinney said. Two men who had engaged in this solicitation admitted their roles while denying any impropriety.

Stevenson refused any further comment. Frustrated

reporters signed a petition asking him for a news conference, but he said he doubted that it would be possible to hold one. At the end of the week, Stevenson finally released some information about his fund, showing that $18,744.96 had been turned over to him from his 1948 campaign. To this amount was added $2,900 in contributions from Chicago businessmen, for a total of $21,644.96. In fact, during the campaign the public never learned the real extent or disposition of these Stevenson funds; it was only revealed twenty-four years later, by Stevenson's official biographer, John Bartlow Martin, in *Adlai Stevenson of Illinois*, that Stevenson's disclosure had been less than candid. He had not stated that additional sums totaling almost $65,000 had been added to this fund in 1950, 1951, and 1952, bringing it to a total of $84,026.56. On September 26, 1952, long after the Stevenson-for-Governor Committee had been disbanded, and four days after the existence of the fund had been revealed, Stevenson wrote a personal check for more than $10,500 as reimbursement to the committee.

The final audit of this fund showed that $13,429.37 was expended for some rather broadly defined political purposes, including annual Christmas parties, gifts to newsmen, and an orchestra to play at a dance for Stevenson's sons. In one instance Stevenson used this political fund to make a small contribution to the Lake County Tuberculosis Association and then claimed the contribution as a personal deduction on his income tax returns.

The press treated Stevenson with kid gloves. His refusals to talk to reporters received only a mild reproach, and the obvious impropriety involved was all but ignored editorially. Johnson Kanady of the Chicago *Tribune* later wrote, "No newspaper was ever able to get details of the 1950 and 1951 Stevenson funds, and so far as I know no newspaperman with Stevenson, except me, tried very hard."

For me, one of the most depressing and infuriating aspects of the entire fund controversy was to see the blatant double standard that most of the press applied to reporting the Nixon fund and the Stevenson fund. But that would not become fully apparent until later, and in the meantime I had to concentrate all my efforts on trying to prepare my speech and master its delivery in the twenty-four hours before the broadcast.

The first part of the fund speech was the easiest to write. Paul Hoffman, chairman of Citizens for Eisenhower, had commissioned the firm of Price Waterhouse to make a complete audit of the fund and had retained the distinguished Los Angeles law firm of Gibson, Dunn, and Crutcher to prepare an opinion on its legality. I planned to present the summaries of these reports as part of my speech. Because the charges against me had become so bitter and so excessive, however, I knew that something more would be needed. I remembered Eisenhower's advice on the telephone: "Tell them everything you can remember," he had said. "Tell them about any money you have ever received."

I was proud of the way Pat and I had worked hard to earn what little we had. Knowing how closely the left and its sympathizers in the press would scrutinize everything about me after the Hiss case, I had been especially careful in my financial dealings. I knew that I could document and support everything I said. Up to that time, I doubt that any candidate had ever detailed his personal finances so thoroughly during an election campaign. Despite the repugnance I felt for such an invasion of our family's privacy, I could not help thinking about the dramatic impact such an unprecedented financial disclosure would have.

I told Pat what I was considering doing. It was too much for her. "Why do you have to tell people how little we have and how much we owe?" she asked.

"People in political life have to live in a fish bowl," I said, but I knew it was a weak explanation for the humiliation I was asking her to endure.

Now that I knew what I wanted to do with the speech, the writing became much easier. I worked all through the afternoon and evening in a suite in the Ambassador Hotel, scarcely bothering to touch the hamburgers that were ordered from room service.

By noon the next day the report from Gibson, Dunn, and Crutcher had arrived, confirming that there was nothing illegal about the fund. The accountants' report was taking longer than expected, however. Without it, the impact of whatever I said would be considerably lessened. It was essential that the crucial question of whether I had personally profited from the fund be independently and authoritatively answered.

Although I did not see any of the hundreds of telegrams that poured into the hotel on the afternoon before the speech, I was touched and heartened when I read many of them later that night.

Congressman Jerry Ford wired: "Over radio and newspapers I am in your corner 100 percent. Fight it to the finish just as you did the smears by the Communists when you were proving charges against Alger Hiss. All Michigan representatives feel as I do. I will personally welcome you in Grand Rapids or any other part of Michigan. Best personal regards."

The Minnesota lawyer and Republican Party leader, Warren Burger, and his wife, Vera, sent word that "your Minnesota friends have complete confidence in your personal and political integrity. We are looking forward to your speech tonight. Please call if there is anything we can do."

Whittaker Chambers sent an eloquent message: "Attack on you shows how deeply the enemy fears you as he always fears and seeks to destroy a combination of honesty and fighting courage. Be proud to be attacked for the attackers are the enemies of all of us. To few recent public figures does this nation owe so much as to you. God help us if we ever forget it."

An hour before we had to leave for the studio, a call came through from "Mr. Chapman" in New York. This was the codename that Tom Dewey had told us he would use for very sensitive calls. The long-distance line crackled as I heard Dewey's voice.

"Dick?"

"Yes."

"There has just been a meeting of all of Eisenhower's top advisers, and they have asked me to tell you that it is their opinion that at the conclusion of the broadcast tonight you should submit your resignation to Eisenhower. As you know, I have not shared this point of view, but it is my responsibility to pass this recommendation on to you."

I was stunned. "What does Eisenhower want me to do?" I asked in as even a voice as I could summon.

Dewey hedged, saying that he did not want to give the impression that he had spoken directly to Eisenhower or that the decision had been approved by Eisenhower himself. But in view of the close relationship between Eisenhower and those with whom Dewey had spoken, he felt that they would not have asked him to call me unless what he was suggesting represented Eisenhower's view as well.

"It's kind of late for them to pass on this kind of recommendation to me now," I said. "I've already prepared my remarks, and it would be very difficult for me to change them now."

Dewey said that he thought I should go ahead with my explanation of the fund as he had originally suggested. At the end, however, I should say that although I felt that I had done no wrong, I did not want my presence on the ticket to be in any way a liability to the Eisenhower crusade. Therefore, I should submit my resignation to Eisenhower and insist that he accept it.

"I've got another suggestion as to how you can follow this up and come out of all of it the hero rather than the goat," Dewey continued. "What you might do is announce not only that you are resigning from the ticket, but that you're resigning from the Senate as well. Then, in the special election which will have to be called for the Senate, you can run again and vindicate yourself by winning the biggest plurality in history."

The conversation was becoming unreal. Silence was the only possible response to this mind-boggling suggestion.

Dewey finally said, "Well, what shall I tell them you are going to do?"

I could barely control my temper. "Just tell them," I said, "that I haven't the slightest idea what I am going to do, and if they want to find out they'd better listen to the broadcast. And tell them I know something about politics too!" I slammed the receiver back into its cradle.

When I told Chotiner and Rogers about Dewey's suggestion, they were dumbfounded.

"You certainly aren't going to do it, are you?" Murray asked.

"I just don't know," I replied. "You two had better get out of here and give me a chance to think."

A few minutes later, it was time to go to the studio. As

126

Pat and I emerged from our room, all activity came to a halt. Everyone came out into the corridor in a show of support, but not a word was spoken.

On the way, I went over my notes one final time. The figures from Price Waterhouse had arrived at the last minute, but I was worried about being able to memorize them and get them straight. One slip, or one mistake, and the credibility of the whole speech would be undermined.

Ted Rogers led us onto the stage of the empty 750-seat El Capitan theatre, which had been converted into a television studio by NBC. I had ordered that no one was to be there during the speech except for the director and technical crew. We arranged for the reporters to watch on a monitor in a separate room.

Ted showed me the set. It was a flimsy-looking, nondescript room with only a desk, a chair, and a bookcase set into the wall. I asked him to remove a small vase of flowers because I thought it looked out of place.

After a brief lighting and sound check we were ushered into a small room at the far side of the stage. Soon Ted was back, saying that there were only three minutes before we went on the air. I was suddenly overwhelmed by despair. My voice almost broke as I said, "I just don't think I can go through with this one." "Of course you can," Pat said matter-of-factly. She took my hand and we walked back onto the stage together.

"My fellow Americans," I began, "I come before you tonight as a candidate for the vice presidency and as a man whose honesty and integrity have been questioned."

As I continued to talk I began to feel that surge of confidence that comes when a good speech has been well prepared. I began to feel instinctively the rhythm of its words and the logic of its organization. I hardly had to look down at my notes at all. I felt warmed by the bright lights, and I opened up and spoke freely and emotionally. I talked as if only Pat were in the room and no one else were listening.

The speech was divided into four parts. I began by giving the facts about the fund and describing my personal finances. Then I went on the counterattack against Stevenson. The third section praised Eisenhower, and the fourth requested that my audience send letters and wires to the Republican National Committee in Washington to indicate whether they thought I should remain on or step down from the ticket.

I saw Ted Rogers come out of the director's booth and crouch down beside the camera in front of me. He held up the fingers of both hands and I knew that this was the signal that I had ten minutes left. I saw him when he held up one hand for five minutes, and then three fingers. By that time I was so wrapped up in what I was saying that I didn't see his signal for "ten seconds," "five seconds," or "cut." I was still talking when time ran out, standing in front of the desk with my arms stretched out toward the camera.

Suddenly I saw Ted Rogers stand up, and I realized that I had gone overtime. I couldn't believe it. I hadn't even given people the address of the Republican National Committee so that they would know where to send their telegrams. I felt almost dazed. I took a few steps forward and my shoulder grazed the side of the camera. I could hear Ted Rogers saying that they had waited until what sounded like the end of a sentence and faded the picture although I was still talking. Then Pat, Murray Chotiner, Pat Hillings, and Bill Rogers were standing in front of me. Pat embraced me, and I could only say, "I'm sorry I had to rush at the last; I didn't give the National Committee address. I should have timed it better." Everyone insisted that it had been a tremendous success, and I tried to smile and thank them for their support; but I felt drained and depressed.

While I was shaking hands with the cameramen, Ted Rogers ran in and said, "The telephone switchboard is lit up like a Christmas tree."

By the time we got back to the hotel and began to read some of the messages that were pouring in, I realized that, despite the problem with the ending, the speech had in fact been a great success. Apparently my emotional nerve endings had been rubbed so raw by the events of the previous few days that I was able to convey the intensity of my feelings to the audience.

Eisenhower was speaking in Cleveland that night. Along with Mamie and about thirty friends and staff members, he watched my speech on a television set in the manager's office above the hall where he was to speak. He sat on a chair directly in front of the set, with Mamie nearby.

I was told there was a brief silence in the small room in Cleveland when the television program was over. Mamie was sobbing and several others were holding back tears. Suddenly, the audience in the auditorium below, which had been listening to the speech on a radio hookup, began to chant, "We want Nixon! We want Nixon!" With the voice of the people literally ringing in his ears, Eisenhower turned to RNC Chairman Arthur Summerfield and said, "Well, Arthur, you certainly got your $75,000 worth tonight!"

After taking a few minutes alone to collect his thoughts, Eisenhower went down to the auditorium and told the cheering crowd, "I happen to be one of those people who, when I get into a fight, would rather have a courageous and honest man by my side than a whole boxcar of pussyfooters. I have seen brave men in tough situations. I have never seen anyone come through in better fashion than Senator Nixon did tonight." The crowd roared its approval.

But instead of declaring the case closed and affirming my place on the ticket, Eisenhower said that one speech was not enough to settle all the important questions that had been raised and that he would meet with me before reaching his final decision. He told the crowd that he was sending me a telegram asking me to fly to see him the next day in Wheeling, West Virginia, where he would be campaigning.

It turned out that Eisenhower's telegram, which got lost among the thousands of others that arrived that night, read:

YOUR PRESENTATION WAS MAGNIFICENT. WHILE TECHNICALLY NO DECISION RESTS WITH ME, YOU AND I KNOW THE REALITIES OF THE SITUATION REQUIRE A PRONOUNCEMENT WHICH THE PUBLIC CONSIDERS DECISIVE. MY PERSONAL DECISION IS GOING TO BE BASED ON PERSONAL CONCLUSIONS. I WOULD MOST APPRECIATE IT IF YOU CAN FLY TO SEE ME AT ONCE. TOMORROW I WILL BE AT WHEELING, W. VA.

WHATEVER PERSONAL AFFECTION AND ADMIRATION I HAD FOR YOU—AND THEY ARE VERY GREAT—ARE UNDIMINISHED.

All I heard that night was a wire service bulletin quoting Eisenhower as saying that one speech wasn't enough. I despaired when I heard this. "What more can he possibly want from me?" I angrily asked Chotiner. I had done everything I could, and if that were not enough I would do the only thing left and resign from the ticket. I would not humiliate myself further by going to Wheeling. I said that we would fly to my next scheduled campaign stop in Missoula, Montana, and wait there for Eisenhower to accept and announce my resignation.

I called Rose Mary Woods into my room, dictated the resignation, and told her to send it immediately. She typed it up, but instead of sending it she took it to Murray Chotiner, who read it and ripped it up. He said to Rose, "I don't blame him for being mad, and it would serve them right if he resigned now and Ike lost the election. But I think we ought to let things settle a little bit longer before we do anything this final."

A little later a call came through from Bert Andrews in Cleveland. He was enthusiastic in his praise for my speech, but when I filled him in on everything that had happened, his voice darkened and he spoke in flat, measured words. He even changed his form of address.

"Richard," he said, "you don't have to be concerned about what will happen when you meet Eisenhower. The broadcast decided that, and Eisenhower knows it as well as anyone else. But you must remember who he is. He is the general who led the Allied armies to victory in Europe. He is the immensely popular candidate who is going to win this election. He is going to be President, and he is the boss of this outfit. He will make this decision, and he will make the right decision. But he has the right to make it in his own way, and you must come to Wheeling to meet him and give him the opportunity to do exactly that."

I was impressed by Andrews's reasoning and chastened by his tone. In the aftermath of a tremendously emotional event I had failed to consider Eisenhower's point of view. For one thing, he hardly knew me. I should also have realized that it was perfectly logical for Eisenhower as a newcomer to politics to stand back and see what happened before he committed himself. I changed my mind and asked the staff to make arrangements for us to fly directly from Missoula to Wheeling.

We had landed at Wheeling, and I was just helping Pat on with her coat, when Chotiner rushed up to us.

It was one of the few times I ever heard awe in Murray Chotiner's voice. "The general is coming up the steps!" he said. No sooner were the words out than Eisenhower strode down the aisle behind him, hand outstretched, flashing his famous smile.

"General, you didn't need to come out to the airport," I said.

"Why not?" he grinned, "You're my boy!"

It was a cold night, with a heavy, dank smog covering Wheeling as we drove to the stadium for a rally. During the entire ride, Eisenhower never made any reference to the harrowing crisis we both had just been through. As I got to know him better, I discovered that this was characteristic, but I still recall the surreal quality of that twenty-minute drive during which he blithely talked about the comparative merits of whistle-stopping and rallies, as if nothing unusual had happened.

When we got to the stadium the roof of our convertible was put down and we sat together in the back, waving to the cheering crowds as the car drove around the track.

Eisenhower spoke first. He described me as "a man of courage and honor" who had been "subjected to a very unfair and vicious attack," and said that before I came to the podium he wanted to read to the audience two telegrams he had received. I had no idea what they were, so I listened as intently as everyone else in the crowd while he read:

DEAR GENERAL: I AM TRUSTING THAT THE ABSOLUTE TRUTH MAY COME OUT CONCERNING THIS ATTACK ON RICHARD, AND WHEN IT DOES I AM SURE YOU WILL BE GUIDED RIGHT IN YOUR DECISION, TO

131

PLACE IMPLICIT FAITH IN HIS INTEGRITY AND HONESTY. BEST WISHES FROM ONE WHO HAS KNOWN RICHARD LONGER THAN ANYONE ELSE. HIS MOTHER.

He then read a telegram from Arthur Summerfield informing him that all 107 of the 138 members of the Republican National Committee they had been able to reach had supported my staying on the ticket:

THE COMMENT ACCOMPANYING THEIR UNANIMOUS RESPONSE WAS OVERWHELM-INGLY ENTHUSIASTIC. . . . AS A MEMBER OF THE REPUBLICAN NATIONAL COMMIT-TEE IT GAVE ME GREAT SATISFACTION TO JOIN WITH MY COLLEAGUES IN THIS STIR-RING TRIBUTE TO A TRULY GREAT AMERI-CAN WHO WALKED UNAFRAID THROUGH THE VALLEY OF DESPAIR AND EMERGED UNSCATHED AND UNBOWED. LET THERE BE NO DOUBT ABOUT IT—AMERICA HAS TAKEN DICK NIXON TO ITS HEART.

When I stood up to speak the ovation was overpower-ing. Everything I had to say was expressed in one sentence: "I want you to know that this is probably the greatest moment of my life."

After the speeches I saw Bill Knowland's familiar bulky form in the crowd of well-wishers, and when I reached him he grinned, grasped my hand, and said, "That was a great speech, Dick." All the pent-up emotion of the whole week burst out and tears filled my eyes. Knowland put his arm around me and I hid my face on his shoulder.

Afterward, Eisenhower invited Pat and me to see his private car on his campaign train. It turned out that he wanted a chance to talk to me alone because he had heard rumors of several other scandals involving my personal finances. In my response, I drew an analogy that would be familiar to him. "This is just like war, General," I said. "Our opponents are losing. They mounted a massive attack against me and have taken a bad beating. It will take them a little time to regroup, but when they start fighting back, they will be desperate, and they will throw everything at us, including the kitchen sink. There will be other charges, but none of them will stand up. What we must avoid at all costs is to allow any of their attacks to get off the ground. The minute they start one of these rumors, we have to knock it down just as quickly as we can." As a popular hero, Eisenhower had been treated extremely well by the press. I do not think he completely grasped what I was saying that night until he reached the White House and began to be treated as a politician.

In the car on the way to our hotel, Pat took my hand and held it without saying a word. I knew how fiercely proud she was that we had come through this painful crisis. But I also knew how much it had hurt her, how deeply it had wounded her sense of pride and privacy. I knew that from that time on, although she would do everything she could to help me and help my career, she would hate politics and dream of the day when I would leave it behind and we could have a happy and normal life for ourselves and our family.

I had begun the campaign feeling vigorous and enthusiastic. The fund crisis made me feel suddenly old and tired. It is said that you can live a year in a day. That is how I felt about this period: I lived several years during that single week.

I was deeply dispirited by much of the reaction to the fund. I was not surprised that the story was exploited by partisan Democrats. But I was disappointed and hurt that so many Republicans prejudged me without waiting for the facts, and I was bitterly disillusioned by the performance of the press. I regarded what had been done to me as character assassination, and the experience permanently and powerfully affected my attitude toward the press in particular and the news media in general.

While the fund was the most egregious press and partisan smear of the campaign, it was by no means the only one.

Less than a week before the election, the St. Louis *Post-Dispatch*, a staunchly pro-Stevenson newspaper, ran a front-page story charging that I had accompanied Dana Smith, the fund's trustee, to a Havana gambling club some six months earlier. The charge was a blatant lie. At the time the story put me in Havana, I was on a vacation thousands of miles away in Hawaii.

On October 28, just days before the election, the Democratic National Committee charged that my family and I owned real estate "conservatively valued at more than a quarter of a million dollars." In reaching this sum, they included the allegation that my brother Don owned a "swanky new drive-in restaurant" appraised at $175,000. In fact, Don was renting the property. What really infuriated me over this particular series of charges was the inclusion in the DNC calculations of a small farm in Pennsylvania and a modest house in Florida that my parents had bought for their retirement. These properties, which were not lavish by any standards, reflected the sum total of an entire life of hard work by my mother and father. I considered it despicable to attack my parents and suggest that they had unethically acquired expensive real estate.

Two days later, a Drew Pearson column appeared, characteristically teeming with innuendo and loose facts, which included information from my tax returns. Partisans in the Bureau of Internal Revenue had obviously leaked them to Pearson. Included in his laundry list of charges was one that Pat and I had falsely sworn to a joint property value of less than $10,000 in order to qualify for a $50 veterans' tax exemption on our California taxes. The charge was totally false. It turned out that a Mrs. Pat Nixon had filed for such an exemption on behalf of her husband, Richard—but they were a couple who coincidentally had the same names as ours. Pearson had not bothered to check with me before printing this lie five days *before* the election and he did not retract it until three weeks *after* it.

Also only after the election did information surface about a criminal scheme designed to malign my character and integrity. Someone forged a letter purporting to be from one oil company executive to another suggesting that I had been bought off for more than $52,000 a year to serve the oil industry in Washington. On the eve of the election, this patent forgery was delivered to the Democratic National Committee, which sent it to the New York *Post*. Even the *Post* decided not to risk printing such an obvious libel.

After the election, Drew Pearson continued trying to stir up interest in the story, so I called for a full investigation by the Senate Subcommittee on Privileges and Elections. The investigation proved conclusively that the letter was a forgery, and referred the matter to the Justice Department.

The fund smear had fallen short, and lies and forgery had also missed the target. But they all took their emotional toll on me and my family. It was not until long afterward that I found out that my proud and combative father had been reduced to bouts of weeping as each new smear surfaced.

The taste for politics soured, but my only recourse —and my instinct—was to fight back. I quickly came to feel a kinship with Teddy Roosevelt's description of the man in the arena "whose face is marred by dust and sweat and blood." Forgetful critics would later remember my counterattacks without recalling the lies and distortions that often bred them.

It would be many months before I could begin to put the agony of the fund crisis in perspective. I think that Eisenhower was impressed both by my toughness and by the political acumen I showed. He appreciated that from the start I had offered to resign if he wanted me to and that I had never consciously done anything to embarrass him.

I also learned some important lessons about politics and friendship. In politics, most people are your friends only as long as you can do something for them or something to them. In this respect I don't suppose that politics is much different from other walks of life—but the openly competitive nature of elections probably makes that fact stand out more starkly. Still, I shall never forget my surprise and disappointment about those who turned against me overnight when it looked as if I would have to leave the ticket.

THE 1952 ELECTION

After the fund crisis, the rest of the 1952 election campaign seemed tame. Voter studies and opinion polls showed that the demand for change and disgust with the corruption in the federal government were still among the most potent issues we had going for us. President Truman was extremely unpopular in 1952, as President Johnson was later in the dark days of Vietnam and as I was to become during Watergate. As with Johnson and me, some of Truman's unpopularity rubbed off on his party. Even Adlai Stevenson began putting distance between himself and the Truman administration.

By surviving the fund crisis, I forestalled the Democrats' attempt to short-circuit the corruption issue. In fact I emerged a far more effective and sought-after campaigner. My prominence after the fund speech revived public interest in the Hiss case and I reminded audiences across the country that Stevenson had given a deposition used in Hiss's first perjury trial that vouched for his reputation for veracity, integrity, and loyalty. This was *after* our committee hearings had proved that Hiss had lied about his relationship with Chambers.

I also criticized Secretary of State Dean Acheson, whose policies toward international Communism, I said, had lost us China, much of Eastern Europe, and had invited the Communists to begin the Korean war. I used a phrase that caught the public's attention—and the commentators' wrath—when I charged that Stevenson was a graduate of Acheson's "Cowardly College of Communist Containment."

Many years later, when I was President, Acheson and I became friends, and he was one of my most valued and trusted unofficial advisers. In this campaign, however, his clipped moustache, his British tweeds, and his haughty manner made him the perfect foil for my attacks on the snobbish kind of foreign service personality and mentality that had been taken in hook, line, and sinker by the Communists. Today I regret the intensity of those attacks. While I still believe that Acheson was wrong about Asia, he was right about Europe, where he helped make NATO a strong, durable bastion against Communist aggression.

In most elections, obviously, the opposing candidates are not overly fond of each other, but there is usually little or no personal antagonism. I felt instinctively negative toward Stevenson. I considered him to be far more veneer than substance, and I felt that beneath his glibness and mocking wit he was shallow, flippant, and indecisive. He reminded me of Oscar Wilde's definition of a cynic as a man who knows the price of everything and the value of nothing. Eisenhower shared my feelings. As late as 1957, when Dulles brought Stevenson into the State Department in an effort to assure the success of the NATO summit after the shock caused by *Sputnik*, Eisenhower was adamant against receiving him at the White House or having him attend the summit meetings in Paris. In fact, after Eisenhower's stroke the doctors ordered us to steer clear of discussion of Stevenson because it always caused the President's blood pressure to rise alarmingly.

Although he was not running himself, and although an embarrassed Stevenson tried to keep him in the background, President Truman was one of the main actors in the drama of the 1952 campaign. Harry Truman thrived on the cut and thrust of politics, and it was impossible for Stevenson to keep him out of the campaign. After Truman's unsuccessful attempt to interest Eisenhower in becoming his Democratic successor in the White House, the relations between the two men became strained and in the 1952 campaign, Truman attacked Eisenhower with a vengeance. Unlike most of the Democrats, who did not challenge Eisenhower's heroic status, Truman made typically dramatic—and typically irresponsible—charges about Eisenhower's expertise and even about his motives. Eisenhower was deeply offended by Truman's intimation that he had been politically involved in the Yalta and Potsdam agreements, which had effectively given Eastern Europe to the Communists. The charge was demonstrably untrue, but Eisenhower never got over his anger that Truman would even countenance, much less spread, such a deliberate slander.

As a result of this bitterness, Eisenhower would not have the traditional coffee at the White House with his predecessor before going to the Capitol for his inauguration. Instead, the two men met under the North Portico and, but for a bit of casual conversation, rode together in icy silence. Except for a chance meeting at the funeral of Chief Justice Fred Vinson in 1953, they did not meet again until 1961, after Eisenhower had left the White House.

Pat and I traveled 46,000 grueling miles during the 1952 campaign. I made 92 speeches, 143 whistle-stop appearances, visited 214 cities, and held several press conferences. Because of the fund episode, and because I took the partisan lead that Eisenhower had avoided, I received much more attention than the usual vice presidential candidate—certainly far more than Stevenson's running mate, Senator John Sparkman of Alabama. In some areas I even outdrew Stevenson.

Everywhere I went I blasted the Democrats, linking Stevenson with Truman and Acheson and asking how the same people who had created the mess in Washington could be expected to clean it up. I called Acheson the "architect of striped-pants confusion." I told a Boston audience that if Stevenson were elected, "We can expect four more years of this same policy, because Mr. Stevenson received his education from Dean Acheson's wishy-washy State Department." I told another cheering audience that I would rather have a "khaki-clad President than one clothed in State Department pinks."

A week before the election, in a speech on October 27 at Texarkana, Arkansas, I said that Truman, Stevenson, and Acheson were "traitors to the high principles in which many of the nation's Democrats believe." In 1954 and in subsequent campaigns Truman charged that I had called him a traitor in this speech. Even when a tape recording was found and an exact transcript of my words was shown him, he refused to accept that what I had said was not as he had apparently remembered it.

Some of the rhetoric I used during this campaign was very rough. Perhaps I was unconsciously overreacting to the attacks made against me during and after the fund crisis; perhaps I was simply carried away by the partisan role Eisenhower had assigned me and the knowledge that someone had to fire up the party faithful and let them know a presidential campaign was being fought.

By the time the last Gallup poll appeared, a few days before the election, the trend was fairly clear:

Eisenhower-Nixon	47%
Stevenson-Sparkman	40%
Undecided	13%

Both Eisenhower and I campaigned right down to the wire, however, ending with a televised election eve rally at the Boston Garden. Later that night Pat and I flew to California.

I knew from my experiences in 1946 and 1950 that the longest day of a politician's life is Election Day, when millions are deciding his fate and he can do nothing whatever about it. After Pat and I voted early in the morning in East Whittier, I asked Bill Rogers if he would like to take a ride. We drove down to Laguna Beach, where we parked the car and walked several miles along the shore.

Some Marines from Camp Pendleton were throwing a football around on the beach, and we joined them for an impromptu game of touch football. One of the Marines had been staring at me for several minutes before he walked over to Rogers and said, "Say, isn't he some kind of a celebrity or something?" Rogers responded, "No, he is just Senator Nixon, running for Vice President." When I dropped a pass later in the game, one of the Marines jokingly remarked, "You'll make a better Vice President than a football player." Suddenly he caught himself and sheepishly added, "Sir."

We got back to the Ambassador Hotel in Los Angeles around four o'clock and I went straight to my room, got into my pajamas, and tried to take a nap. I told the staff that I did not want to hear any results until at least six, because anything before then would be too fragmentary and would just make everyone nervous. At six o'clock sharp there was a knock on my door, and about a dozen people burst into the room all talking at once. The polls had been closed only for an hour in the East, but already it looked like a landslide.

In the end, we won by over 6½ million votes: 55.1 percent to 44.4 percent. We picked up 22 seats in the House; and the final tally was 221 to 213 and 1 independent. In the Senate we picked up 1 seat, which gave us a bare majority of 1.

Vice President
1953-1960

January 20, 1953, the day of my first inauguration as Vice President, was mild and sunny. For the swearing-in ceremony my mother brought two Bibles that had been in the Milhous family for several generations.

That night we had a small family dinner at home before the inaugural balls. While the others were all talking about the great events of the day, my mother quietly took me aside and gave me a small piece of paper on which she had written a message for me. No one else saw her give it to me, and I did not read it until I was alone later that night. I put it in my wallet, and I have carried it with me ever since:

To Richard

You have gone far and we are proud of you always— I know that you will keep your relationship with your maker as it should be for after all that, as you must know, is the most important thing in this life.

With love, mother

Eisenhower's election ended twenty years of Democratic control of the White House. Winning control of the House and Senate made the victory doubly satisfying. But the tasks we faced were monumental.

The most immediate problems lay in the area of foreign policy. We were fighting an unpopular war in Korea, and Eisenhower had pledged in the election campaign to bring it to an honorable conclusion.

Although the U.S.S.R. was still far behind the United States in nuclear arms, it was moving dramatically forward. In Eastern Europe, the Soviet satellite nations formed a monolithic power bloc controlled from Moscow. The rigorously ideological Communist Chinese, still friendly with the Soviets and dependent upon them for economic and technological aid, were in an expansionist phase of their foreign policy.

Following World War II, the great free world alliance had been formalized by the establishment of NATO, and Europe had been rebuilt with American aid. But it was now becoming clear that both Britain and France had been so weakened by the war that it would not be long before their ability to help maintain security beyond their borders would be limited. The war had marked the beginning of the end —if not the end—of European colonialism. Symptomatic of this phenomenon was the crisis that would plague not only the Eisenhower administration but its successors as well: the deterioration of French control in Indochina. The tide of anticolonialism had not yet swept over Africa when Eisenhower took office. But eight years later, by the time he left, there were more than twenty new independent countries on that continent.

Other problem areas soon became apparent. The creation of the state of Israel in 1948 had planted seeds of hatred that would eventually explode into three full-scale wars. Nearby Iran, with its enormous oil reserves, was under the control of a left-leaning government that most observers feared would inevitably fall under Soviet domination. Latin America appeared secure on the surface, yet long years of dictatorships had laid the foundation for a period of instability and revolution.

At home Eisenhower's first task was to fulfill his pledge to clean up the "mess in Washington" by restoring confidence in the honesty of those serving in government. No less important was the job of rooting out security risks in the government—those who by reasons of disloyalty or poor judgment might subvert the policies of the United States.

The new President was also confronted with a massive problem in trying to develop an economic policy that would bring prosperity without war. He had to mediate the classic debate between those who urged him to cut spending and taxes and those who demanded that more money be spent for housing, health, education, and welfare.

Eisenhower was to find all these foreign and domestic issues less perplexing than his new duties as head of a divided political party. The division had been stark at the Chicago convention: the Eisenhower wing versus the so-called Old Guard Republicans led by Bob Taft.

Eisenhower had no taste for many of the rituals of politics. He recognized that he had the almost superhuman job of getting Republicans to think positively after having been the opposition for twenty years. In addition, while he had Republican majorities in both houses of Congress, those majorities were very thin, and in large measure they were based on Eisenhower's personal popularity rather than his party's strength. He recognized that it was his responsibility to broaden the base of the party so that it would be as strong as its leader, but he never felt at ease with most of the things he had to do to achieve that end.

INTERNATIONAL DIPLOMACY: 1953

Late in the spring of 1953, Eisenhower asked me to undertake a major trip to Asia and the Far East. He suggested that Pat come with me, and he urged that we visit as many countries as we possibly could.

From his wartime experiences, Eisenhower knew Europe and its leaders better than almost any other non-European in the world. But he did not know Asia or the Middle East well, and he was never one to overestimate his experience or knowledge. He also felt that Truman had seriously neglected both these important areas, and he tried to remedy this neglect during his own administration.

In the early 1950s most of the nations on our trip still knew very little about America or Americans. None of these nations had ever received an official visit from a President or Vice President. Their impressions of us were largely formed through bits and pieces of rumors and news, by contacts with individual Americans, and from exported Hollywood films about Chicago gangsters and cowboys and Indians. In those days the good will trip had not yet become a diplomatic cliché.

There were four specific purposes that my trip was meant to serve. It was intended to honor and reassure our friends and allies. It would also provide an opportunity for me to explain American policies in countries that had adopted a policy of neutrality. It would give me a firsthand look at the rapidly developing situation in Indochina. And it would give me an opportunity to assess Asian attitudes toward the emerging colossus of Communist China.

On October 5 Pat and I said goodbye to Tricia and Julie and boarded an Air Force four-engine Constellation at National Airport. It was a painful farewell, especially for Pat, who had never been away from the girls for more than two weeks; now we would be away from them for more than two months.

Our official party consisted of a chief of staff, Phil Watts; my administrative assistant, Chris Herter, Jr.; my secretary, Rose Woods; a Navy doctor; and a military aide to handle protocol matters. Only two Secret Service agents accompanied us on the trip. In comparison with what is provided for official trips today, this would be considered a pitifully small staff, but they more than made up in dedication what they lacked in numbers. There was relatively little press interest in the trip, and only one reporter from each of the three wire services came with us.

We had sent wires ahead to all our embassies indicating that I wanted strictly social events to be kept to a minimum. I let it be known that I was bringing only one dinner jacket and would not be packing a white tie or striped pants. Since we would not have more than four formal dinners in any one country, Pat took four formal gowns so that she could wear a different one on each occasion.

I also asked the State Department to arrange my schedule so that I could meet as many different kinds of people as possible—students, laborers, businessmen, intellectuals, politicians in and out of office, military men, farmers. I was told that this would be very unusual, very unorthodox, and very undiplomatic. I replied that unless these meetings were arranged for me I would have to arrange them on my own. There was the same kind of resistance when Pat requested her own itinerary. Wives of visiting officials from Washington customarily spent most of their days shopping or socializing. But Pat wanted to play an active part in the trip, visiting schools, hospitals, orphanages, clinics, museums, and marketplaces to meet the people and to let the people meet her. We deliberately ruled out shopping parties except on the few occasions when our embassy officials told us that our hosts would be offended if she did not purchase the local handicrafts.

Pat also asked to meet with representatives of women's organizations, and her visits gave great impetus to the new respect for women that was slowly beginning to develop in many of the countries we were visiting.

Phil Watts worked out a procedure whereby we were met at each stop by a senior foreign service officer from the embassy in the next country on our itinerary. During the flight the officer would update the briefings I had received before we left. This enabled me to conduct my meetings without using notes, a practice I had begun on the Herter Committee trip, when I found that using or making notes seems to inhibit spontaneous conversation. Some of the most useful conversations I have had during my visits with foreign leaders have been during automobile rides to and from airports, when only they and I and an interpreter were present.

Our first stops were in New Zealand and Australia, where we were warmly received. Of the many political leaders I met on this trip, by far the most impressive was Australia's Prime Minister Sir Robert Menzies. His extraordinary intelligence and profound understanding of issues, not only in the Pacific but throughout the world, made an indelible impression on me. Had he been born in Britain rather than in Australia, I am convinced that he would have been a great British Prime Minister in the tradition of Winston Churchill.

We plunged into Asia when we landed at Djakarta,

Indonesia. We were greeted by President Sukarno, whose tastes were as rich as his people were poor. In no other country we visited was the conspicuous luxury of the ruler in such striking contrast to the poverty and misery of his people. Djakarta was a collection of sweltering huts and hovels. An open sewer ran through the heart of the city, but Sukarno's palace was painted a spotless white and set in the middle of hundreds of acres of exotic gardens. One night we ate off gold plate to the light of a thousand torches while musicians played on the shore of a lake covered with white lotus blossoms and candles floating on small rafts.

Sukarno was well educated and acutely aware that he exerted a magnetic hold over his people. He had led them to independence by ousting the hated Dutch rulers, and had given them a battle cry that stirred their pride and touched their hearts: *merdeka*—"freedom." But as a leader of almost unlimited power, Sukarno had become a mixture of political brilliance and corrosive vanity. He was very proud of his sexual prowess, which was the subject of countless rumors and stories—many of which he probably started himself. Be that as it may, his palaces were filled with some of the most exquisite women I have ever seen. My briefings had stressed this side of his character and his great susceptibility to flattery along these lines.

Sukarno was the main personification of a common problem in the newly created nation-states of Asia and Africa. He was a brilliant revolutionary leader but he was totally inept as a nation-builder once independence was achieved. Like Nasser in Egypt and Nkrumah in Ghana, he could be very successful in tearing down the old system, but he could not concentrate his attention on building a viable new one to replace it. These men could not lead their nations as effectively as they had led their revolutions, and their nations—and the world—are still paying the price for that failing.

Sukarno ruled with such an iron hand that the Communists had not been able to make much headway in Indonesia. But at our next stop, Malaya, we came face to face with the new kind of Communist warfare that was already threatening the stability of the entire region. Communist guerrilla forces were challenging the struggling Malayan government, which was just getting ready to make the break from British colonialism. The British were not making the mistake that the Americans made in the early days of the war in Korea and were to make later in Vietnam, of trying to fight a guerrilla war with conventional tactics and traditional strategy. Instead, the British trained the natives and enlisted their wholehearted support in the fight against the insurgents.

In Kuala Lumpur I met with the High Commissioner, Field Marshal Sir Gerald Templer, a wiry, tough, emotional leader who had served under Eisenhower in North Africa. He told me, "What I am trying to do is convince all the native leaders and the native troops that this is *their* war, that they are fighting for *their* independence, and that once the guerrillas are defeated it will be *their* country and *their* decision to make as to whether they desire to remain within the British Commonwealth."

Both Templer and his wife worked closely with the local leaders and treated them with respect and dignity—something that had never occurred to the Dutch in Indonesia, that the French never learned in Vietnam, and that the Americans there learned only too late. We talked about the situation in Indochina and Templer shook his head sadly. "I hate to admit this because he's a real SOB, but what they need there is a Rhee." Events proved Templer right. Until strong leaders capable of providing stability appeared in Vietnam—first Diem and later Thieu— there was no solid opposition to Communist infiltration.

We spent six fascinating and frustrating days visiting Cambodia, Laos, and Vietnam, the three countries of French Indochina. Vietnam at that time was a nominal monarchy ruled by the emperor Bao Dai, whom the French had restored as a figurehead in 1949. He refused to lend his presence or even his support to the French military effort against the Communist Vietminh guerrilla forces unless France would make a guarantee of independence for Vietnam. This the French refused to do, and the result was a demoralizing standoff that benefited only the Communists.

Bao Dai rarely saw foreigners, but while I was in Saigon he invited me to visit him at his luxurious mountain resort in Dalat. He received me in a long room whose windows looked out at the jungle hills. Barefoot servants padded in noiselessly carrying silver trays laden with fresh fruit and cups of tea.

Bao Dai was opposed to any negotiations with the Communists. He said, "There is no point in trying to negotiate with them. At the least we would end up with a conference which would divide my country between us and them. And if Vietnam is divided, we will eventually lose it all."

From Saigon we flew to Vientiane, the capital of Laos, where I had a long meeting with Prince Souvanna Phouma, a young, Paris-educated member of the Laotian ruling family, who was then Prime Minister. Sixteen years later, when I was President, Souvanna Phouma was again Prime Minister, and we worked closely together trying to prevent the Communists from taking over all of Indochina.

From Vientiane we flew to Hanoi. A brilliant sunset bathed the land below in gold as we flew above the muddy Red River snaking its way through the jungle toward the city. Driving to the residence of the French Commissioner General of Indochina, where we were to spend the night, I could see something of the city. Unlike Saigon, which was a sprawling cosmopolitan city teeming with the diversity of the many races that lived and traded there, Hanoi was like a prosperous provincial town in France. We drove down wide tree-shaded boulevards, and through ornate wrought-iron gates I caught glimpses of large villas set amidst lawns and gardens.

That night the Governor of North Vietnam, a French-educated Vietnamese, gave a dinner in our honor. In retrospect, my toast that night in Hanoi seems sad and ironic:

> The threat to this nation, although it has taken the form of a civil war, still derives its strength from an alien source. This source, to call it by its name, is totalitarian communism. . . .
>
> The struggle against the Vietminh in this country, therefore, is important far beyond the boundaries of Vietnam. On this battleground, stained with the blood of Vietnamese and Frenchmen and the peoples associated with France, are being defended the liberties and the continued national existence not

only of Vietnamese, but also of Cambodians, Laotians, and of their neighbors to the west, to the south, and to the east. . . .

We know that you are determined to resist aggression, even as we are determined to resist it. And we are resolved, as our past actions have proved, that you shall not fight unaided.

The next morning I boarded a French military transport plane. We were in the air before the sun was up, flying low over the dense jungle. We landed on a small airstrip, where several French commanding officers waited to greet us. As soon as the engines of our plane had stopped, I could hear what I had not heard for nine years: the thudding reverberation of artillery.

After I had met the French officers, one of them took me to the edge of the field and introduced me to their Vietnamese counterparts. I saw immediately a basic problem of the war. The French did nothing to hide the disdain they felt toward the Vietnamese. During the rest of my brief stay, without unnecessarily offending the French or embarrassing the Vietnamese, I made a point of trying to spend equal time with both groups.

I put on battle fatigues and a helmet and we drove to the front in a convoy of jeeps. There we watched an artillery barrage against a Vietminh division holding out in the jungle around Lai Cac, a hamlet about fifty miles from the Chinese border. I talked to both the French and the Vietnamese troops, and with the sound of the mortar fire raging around us, I told them that they were fighting on the very outpost of freedom and that the American people supported their cause and honored their heroism. I could see the inspiration this gave the Vietnamese soldiers, and I reflected that the French had forfeited their loyalty by not talking to them in this way.

When we returned to the airfield, I had lunch with the French officers in their mess. There, in the middle of the Vietnamese jungle, we had *boeuf bourguignon* washed down with an excellent Algerian red wine. When I thanked them for arranging such a fine meal in my honor, they replied that it was nothing special for them. I said that I would like to visit the Vietnamese soldiers' mess. This was an unpopular suggestion, but I persisted. Finally I was led to another

151

cluster of tents, where the Vietnamese lived and ate. As we approached the mess tent, a sharp, unpleasant odor struck our noses. "What is that they're cooking?" I asked. One of the French officers crinkled his nose haughtily and said, "It's probably monkey." The Vietnamese soldiers were clearly moved by the fact that I had come to see them, and I repeated the things I had said to the officers in the French mess.

We were back in Hanoi by one o'clock. That afternoon Pat and I made a journey about twenty-five miles northwest of Hanoi to a large refugee camp at the town of Sontay. In every village along the way the provincial officials had turned out schoolchildren and Boy Scouts to cheer us. Banners with greetings in English and Vietnamese were stretched across the road.

Sontay was both heartrending and hopeful. Thousands of refugees, driven from their homes by the Communist guerrillas, lived in the crowded tents. Even during our short visit a steady stream of people carrying all they owned on their shoulders kept coming through the gate. These people seemed so at home with their sorrow that they conveyed a sense of dignity and even optimism which made me feel that, if the Communists could be defeated, the people of Vietnam could build a strong and successful nation. I never imagined that seventeen years later this war would still be going on, but fought by American troops instead of French, and that this very town Pat and I were visiting would serve as a prison camp for American prisoners of war.

That night, our last in Hanoi, the Commissioner General, Maurice Dejean, gave a formal dinner for us at his official residence. Except for the sprinkling of Vietnamese faces and the lush palms and orchids in the garden outside, the occasion might have been a mayoral banquet in Dijon or Toulouse, with starched linen napkins, sparkling crystal goblets, and silver candelabra.

Dejean was a polished and able diplomat, but his attitude displayed the same condescension that kept the French from dealing with the Vietnamese in a way that would have allowed a working partnership. In his toast, he referred to the toast delivered the night before by the Governor at the dinner he had given for us, remarking, "I could not stop myself on hearing it from feeling great pride in listening to a

Vietnamese expressing himself with such clarity in a French so pure."

In my reply, I tried to stress the important part the Vietnamese would have to play if there were to be a victory against communism. Then I closed the toast on a personal note.

> Tomorrow morning we will leave this country. I do not know when we will return, but there is one final thought that I have, and I am sure Mrs. Nixon will have as we leave, and that is the thought of what a happy and great land this could be if only the aggressors in this land would stop their aggression. I realize that there has been talk of negotiation with the aggressors. We all want peace, but I think that we all realize too that the aggressors have not asked for peace, they have not asked to negotiate, and we all also realize that under no circumstances could negotiations take place which would in effect place people who want to be free and independent in perpetual bondage. Under the circumstances we leave with the confidence that this struggle which creates so much unhappiness and so much sorrow in this land will finally come to a victorious end.

In Cambodia we visited the haunting and majestic ruins at Angkor Wat, and I talked with King Sihanouk. I had met him earlier in the year when he was in Washington on an unofficial visit, and my first impressions were unfortunately confirmed. He was an intelligent man, but vain and flighty. He seemed prouder of his musical talents than of his political leadership, and he appeared to me totally unrealistic about the problems his country faced.

I left Vietnam, Laos, and Cambodia convinced that the French had failed primarily because they had not sufficiently trained, much less inspired, the Indochinese people to be able to defend themselves. They had failed to build a cause—or a cadre—that could resist the nationalist and anticolonialist appeals of the Communists.

The Vietnamese forces lived in deplorable conditions. They had no confidence in themselves, and they had no leader to inspire them. Most important, they did not have a battle cry, a *merdeka*, to make the difference between having to fight and wanting to fight.

But for this very reason, if the French were to pull out, Vietnam—and possibly Laos and Cambodia as well—would fall like husks before the fury of the communist hurricane. I decided, therefore, that the United States would have to do everything possible to find a way to keep the French in Vietnam until the Communists had been defeated.

The Chinese Communists were training and supplying the Vietminh forces in Vietnam, but nowhere was their presence more ominously felt than on Formosa, where Generalissimo and Madame Chiang Kai-shek nurtured dreams and prepared plans for ousting the Communists from the mainland. I met with Chiang in his magnificent residence in Taipei. We talked for seven hours, Madame Chiang serving as our interpreter. When he talked about "China," Chiang made a sweeping gesture that made it clear that he did not mean just this small island to which his rule had been reduced, but the whole country beyond the horizon. I could not tell Chiang outright that his chances of reuniting China under his rule were virtually nonexistent, but I made it clear that American military power would not be committed to support any invasion he might launch. Although I felt his plans to return to the mainland were totally unrealistic, I was impressed by his high intelligence and his total dedication to the goal of freeing the Chinese people from Communist domination.

I arrived in Korea bearing a letter from Eisenhower to President Syngman Rhee. Rhee was unhappy with the Korean armistice that had been concluded in July. He refused to accept the division of his country, and he still cherished hopes of ruling a united nation.

Our ambassador in Seoul, Ellis Briggs, suspected that unless Rhee were made to understand our position, he might provoke an incident or even launch an attack against North Korea because of a mistaken belief that America would not leave him to fight alone. At the embassy I talked with Arthur Dean, our special negotiator in Korea, who knew that I was bringing a message for Rhee. Dean described him with great admiration. "I hope you aren't here to completely pull Rhee's teeth and take the fire out of him," he said. "He's a great leader, and a great friend in a part of the world where most of our friends are of the fair-weather variety."

Everywhere in Seoul I could see the legacy of wartime pain and privation. Small children in thin cotton pajamas shivered outside tarpaper huts that offered no protection from the freezing wind. It was obvious that South Korea—always a bleak, poor land—had paid a high price for its survival.

I met President Rhee the next day. He was a thin, small man wearing a dark blue suit and a dark blue tie. His firm handshake and spry walk belied his seventy-eight years. After some general conversation I said that I had some matters I would like to discuss with him personally. He nodded, and everyone else left the room.

Rhee studied me with a penetrating gaze while I told him that I was not only a representative of Eisenhower but someone who had a long and consistent record as a friend of Korea. I took Eisenhower's letter from my jacket and handed it to him. He held it gingerly with his fingers, almost as if he were weighing it.

With slow and deliberate movements he opened the envelope and unfolded the letter. In an even voice he read it aloud. In dignified but unmistakable language, Eisenhower made it clear that the United States would not tolerate any actions that might lead to a reopening of war and asked for specific reassurances from Rhee.

When he reached the end Rhee put the letter in his lap and stared down at it without saying anything. When he looked up his eyes were glistening with tears. "That is a very fine letter," he said.

Then he began to talk as if the letter did not exist. He described his attitude toward Japan; he talked about the future of Asia and the Pacific basin; he criticized the way we had administered the economic aid program. I tried to avoid pressing him too hard, but I finally brought him back to a discussion of the letter and of the assurances Eisenhower wanted. I said that I was speaking frankly to him because I thought it was of the highest urgency that he understand Eisenhower's position and make the commitment the President had requested in his letter.

"I too want to speak frankly to you," Rhee replied. "I am deeply appreciative of the aid my country has received from the United States and of my personal relationship with President Eisenhower. Because of this friendship I would not want to do anything that would not be in accord with the policies of the United States. On the other hand, I must think of Korea and, particularly, of the three million enslaved Koreans in the North. My obligation as a leader of the Korean people is to achieve unification of our country by peaceful means if possible but by force if necessary."

He paused. Then, as he continued, he ran his finger along the creases of the letter in his lap.

"I understand why the United States is anxious to maintain peace, and I am in basic agreement with that objective," he said. "But on the other hand a peace which leaves Korea divided would inevitably lead to a war which would destroy both Korea and the United States and I cannot agree to such a peace."

Suddenly he leaned toward me. "I pledge to you that before I take any unilateral action at any time I shall inform President Eisenhower first."

This was hardly the assurance Eisenhower had asked for, and I said firmly that it was essential for him to understand that under no circumstances should he take any action except by mutual agreement with Eisenhower. The meeting ended on this inconclusive note.

When I returned to the embassy I made extensive notes of our conversation. I had felt uncomfortable going as far as I did, but I knew that my mission would be a failure if because of any reticence or ineptness on my part, Rhee did not understand that the United States would not support any unilateral military attempt he might undertake to reunite his country.

My uncertainty increased the next day when Rhee told an interviewer, "I hope I will be able to convince President Eisenhower, through Vice President Nixon, that it is the right policy to finish this thing in Korea."

On the last night of our visit, Pat and I were the guests of honor at a show of Korean dancing and music. Midway through the performance there was a sharp crack, and the wooden platform at the back of the stage, on which a children's choir was standing, began to collapse. The audience gasped. When the children realized what was happening, they began screaming and crying.

Within a minute it was clear that no one had been hurt, and the audience's concern for the children's safety gave way to embarrassment that such a thing should have happened at a performance honoring foreign visitors. I knew that throughout the Far East, to lose face is the worst humiliation. It seemed as if Korea had lost face in this incident. The conductor threw up his hands and walked off the stage in embarrassment.

I suddenly thought of a way to rescue the evening from disaster. I jumped up from my seat and began to applaud. Pat saw what I was doing and immediately followed my lead. One by one, and then in larger groups, the audience joined us, and the applause grew louder and louder. The children, who had been frightened and then embarrassed by the accident, responded to the applause and began to smile. Finally the conductor returned, and the show went on.

When I paid a farewell call on Rhee the next day, he was very warm and friendly; I have no doubt he had been told about the incident with the choir. When we settled down alone again to talk, he took two pages of thin paper from his jacket. As he unfolded them, he said that he had typed them himself to ensure complete security. "The moment the Communists are certain that the United States controls Rhee," he said, "you will have lost one of your most effective bargaining points, and we will have lost all our hope. The fear that I may start some action is a constant check on the Communists. We are being very frank now, you and I, so you should know that the Communists think that America wants peace so badly that you will do anything to get it. At times, I am afraid that they are right. But they do not think that this is true as far as I am concerned, and I believe that you would be wrong to dispel their doubts in that respect. I shall send my reply to President Eisenhower's letter when you are in Tokyo tomorrow. I would like it to be delivered to President Eisenhower personally and then destroyed once he has seen it."

He handed me the notes he had been reading from and

said, "You may want to use these in preparing your report of our meeting." At the end was an addition in his own handwriting: "Too much newspaper reports say Rhee has promised not to act independently. Such impression is not in line with our propaganda idea." As we shook hands at the door of his office, he said, "Any statements I have made about Korea acting independently were made to help America. In my heart I know that Korea cannot possibly act alone. We must act together with America. We realize that we will get everything as long as we travel together, and that we will lose everything if we do not."

I left Korea impressed by the courage and endurance of its people, and by the strength and intelligence of Syngman Rhee. I also gave much thought to Rhee's insight about the importance of being unpredictable in dealing with the Communists. The more I traveled and the more I learned in the years that followed, the more I appreciated how wise the old man had been.

Pat and I were Japan's first state guests since World War II. Everywhere we went in Japan we were cheered enthusiastically by hundreds of thousands who lined our motorcade routes. Those people were demonstrating a deep feeling I shared: that the war had been a tragedy and the time had come to re-establish the tradition of Japanese-American friendship that had previously existed for so many years.

In Tokyo I delivered a speech that made headlines around the world and stirred up a mild controversy at home. Before I left Washington, Foster Dulles and I had discussed what I should say about the touchy question of Japanese rearmament. Japanese disarmament had begun in 1946 and was formalized, at American insistence, by the Japanese Constitution in 1947. Privately we felt that some kind of Japanese armed defense force would soon be necessary to resist Communist domination of the Pacific. But in 1953 World War II was still a painfully recent memory, and we knew that the first mention of Japanese rearmament would raise storms of protest. Dulles thought that raising the subject first in Japan itself might help blunt the political impact in America, and I decided that an invitation to address a luncheon sponsored by the America-Japan Society and several other groups would provide the idea forum. I said:

> Now if disarmament was right in 1946, why is it wrong in 1953? And if it was right in 1946 and wrong in 1953, why doesn't the United States admit for once that it made a mistake? And I'm going to do something that I think perhaps ought to be done more by people in public life. I'm going to admit right here that the United States did make a mistake in 1946.
>
> We made a mistake because we misjudged the intentions of the Soviet leaders. . . . We recognize that disarmament under present world conditions by the free nations would inevitably lead to war and, therefore, it is because we want peace and we believe in peace that we ourselves have rearmed since 1946, and that we believe that Japan and other free nations must assume their share of the responsibility of rearming.

The reaction in America to the speech was exactly what we had wanted: there was some speculation that I was launching a trial balloon, but many commentators simply assumed that I had gone too far on my own. Also as we had hoped, the speech had an enormously positive effect on the anticommunist leaders of Japan. What impressed all the Japanese, including the opposition parties, was that the United States admitted having made a mistake by imposing too harsh restrictions on their right to develop their ability to defend their country.

The highlight of my visit to the Philippines was my meeting with the President-elect, Ramon Magsaysay. We hit it off extremely well, and Pat remarked afterward that she had never seen two men of different cultural backgrounds who seemed to have so much in common. Magsaysay was dedicated to giving the Filipino people the kind of honest and efficient government very few of their postwar leaders had provided. He had the enthusiastic support of the young people, and he was a magnetic orator. His death in an airplane accident in 1957 was a tragedy for the Philippines and for all of free Asia.

The most exciting stop on the trip turned out to be Burma. This nation had recently received its independence from Britain, and its gentle, friendly people were having a difficult time combating persistent and skillful Communist infiltration.

On Thanksgiving Day we drove fifty miles into the jungle outside Rangoon to see the famous reclining Buddha in the town of Pegu. A luncheon was held for us at the city hall, and in honor of our American holiday the Burmese had managed to find a turkey that they served as the main course. We were scheduled to walk to the shrine, but during dessert the local police captain told our Secret Service agent that a walk would not be safe because the Communists had organized a demonstration. They had distributed anti-American signs, and a sound truck was whipping up the crowd. The police feared an unpleasant incident with hecklers and scuffling. There was even a real possibility of violence.

We had driven from Rangoon to Pegu with an armed escort because just a week earlier a guerrilla band had ambushed and killed some government officials traveling on the same road. Our Secret Service agent suggested that they bring our car around so that we could avoid the crowd by using the back door.

I said I thought we should go ahead with the walk to the shrine exactly as arranged. No crowd of Communist demonstrators should be allowed to alter the itinerary of the Vice President of the United States. Our local hosts were not keen on the walk, however, so Pat and I started alone out the door of the city hall and toward the temple. The crowd filled the street. I ordered the Secret Service agents and the Burmese security officials not to go in front but to stay behind us and to show no weapons. As we walked into the crowd, it backed away.

I went up to a man carrying a sign that said in English, "Go Back Warmonger." I gave him a friendly smile. "I notice these cards are addressed to Mr. Nixon," I said. "I am Nixon, and I am glad to know you. What's your name?" The man backed away in shocked surprise as I extended my hand to him. I then zeroed in on the man who seemed to be the leader, and said to him, "Your signs here are wrong. America doesn't want aggression. America wants peace. But

160

what do you think about the countries who start aggressions, like the ones in Korea and Indochina?"

He shrugged uncomfortably, and replied in English. "That is different," he said.

"How different?" I asked.

"That is a struggle for national liberation," he replied.

I waited until I felt that the translation of this exchange had spread through the crowd and had a chance to sink in. Then I nodded my head as if he had explained everything perfectly. "Oh, I see, *they* are wars of national liberation," I said. I paused, then smiled and said, "Well, at least tell me how many children you have." Embarrassed, he began to sputter. The crowd laughed at his discomfiture, and one by one they put the signs down and began to move away. I was later told that by backing the leader down I had made him lose face with the people.

This experience bolstered my instinctive belief that the only way to deal with Communists is to stand up to them. Otherwise, they will exploit your politeness as weakness. They will try to make you afraid and then take advantage of your fears. Fear is the primary weapon of Communists.

The least friendly leader I met on this trip was Nehru. I had two private meetings with him in his office in New Delhi, one of them lasting for two hours. While I sat listening to Nehru's softly modulated British English, a uniformed waiter served us tangerine juice and cashews. "We need a generation of peace in order to consolidate our independence," he said. When I was President, I used his phrase "generation of peace" in many of my speeches as an expression of my own foreign policy goals.

Nehru spoke obsessively and interminably about India's relationship with Pakistan. He spent more time railing against India's neighbor than discussing either U.S.-Indian relations or other Asian problems. He strongly opposed the controversial proposal of U.S. aid to Pakistan, and I was convinced that his objection owed much to his personal thirst for influence, if not control, over South Asia, the Middle East, and Africa. Nehru was a great leader who had pulled together a disparate collection of races, states, and religions in a way that no other Indian leader could have done. But having led his nation to independence against great odds, he then forced it into official neutrality and made himself a spokesman for nations that wanted to remain similarly uncommitted. Had he devoted as much of his ability to solving India's internal economic and social ills as he did to playing his self-appointed role as spokesman for the underdeveloped nations of the Third World, Indian democracy might be more secure today.

Nehru's daughter, Indira Gandhi, was his official hostess during our visit. She was intelligent, poised and gracious, and I felt her deep inner strength and determination. Her father clearly adored her, and in every way she was her father's daughter.

I met scores of presidents and princes and prime ministers during this trip, but for me the most memorable meeting was with the leader of the province of Madras, Rajagopalachari, a wizened contemporary of Gandhi. The afternoon I spent with Rajaji, as he was known, had such a dramatic effect on me that I used many of his thoughts in my speeches over the next several years, and to this day I can see in my mind's eye his small body, his large hawk nose, the fringe of wispy white hair around his ears, and his dark, piercing eyes as he sat on a straw mat, wearing just a *dhoti* and sandals.

Paul Hoffman, who had supervised the Marshall Plan before becoming president of the Ford Foundation, had told me he was one of the world's most gifted men. This was an understatement. After Rajaji's name in the three pages of notes I made about our conversation I wrote: "Infinitely wise."

We talked about the nature and appeal of communism. "Communism will never succeed in the long run," he said, "because it is based on a fundamental error. Self-interest is the motivating force for most human action. But by denying man the possibility of belief in God, the communists forfeit the possibility of any altruistic self-interest."

He was interested in learning what Eisenhower was like. "Is he religious?" he asked. "He is a very religious man," I replied, "but not so much in outward form as in inner spirit." Rajaji smiled. "That is typical of a military man," he said. "It's also typical for military men to be pacifists."

He spoke with great simplicity and emotion about the

horror of the atomic bomb. "It was wrong to discover it," he said. "It was wrong to seek the secret of creation of matter. It isn't needed for civilian purposes. It is an evil thing, and it will destroy those who discovered it."

We discussed predestination, and I suggested that perhaps he was meant to lead India and South Asia along the paths of his ideas. He smiled sadly and said, "Oh, no, I am happy here. The world is unhappy, so why should I leave? I am seventy-four years old. In India, that is *very* old. My body is tired. Perhaps my brain is not, but younger men must be found to conduct the fight. Younger men like you," he said as he smiled again.

In Pakistan I met Ayub Khan, who was then commander of Pakistan's armed forces and had not yet assumed political power. I particularly enjoyed talking to him because, unlike most of his countrymen, he was not obsessed by the Pakistan-India problem. He did indicate his total contempt for the Hindus and his distrust of the Indians, but he was more anticommunist than anti-Indian. He was seriously concerned about the communist threat, both ideological and military, and about the danger that the Soviets would use India as a cat's-paw for establishing a major presence in South Asia. At that period in his career he was strongly pro-American and believed that Pakistan and the United States should be allies and friends.

Foster Dulles had not been able to visit Iran during his Middle East trip because of the unsettled conditions there at that time. A few months later a violent coup had taken place and the procommunist regime of Prime Minister Mohammed Mossadegh was overthrown by the military. A government supporting the Shah, Mohammed Riza Pahlevi, was installed under Prime Minister Fazollah Zahedi. Zahedi, whose son later served as ambassador to the United States while I was President, was intelligent and wise, with enormous strength of character. Without his leadership I am convinced Iran would not be an independent nation today.

The Shah was only thirty-four. He had just come through a harrowing experience—an attempt had been made to assassinate him. In our meetings he let Zahedi do most of the talking, but he listened intently and asked penetrating questions. I sensed an inner strength in him, and I felt that in the years ahead he would become a strong leader.

When our plane landed at National Airport on December 14, we drove to the White House, where Eisenhower invited us upstairs to have coffee with him and Mrs. Eisenhower.

The next day I received a two-page handwritten letter that, coming from one who meted out praise in very small and careful doses, I knew to be an extraordinarily warm and personal gesture.

Dear Dick:

Proud as I am of the record you—and Pat—established on your recent visit to a number of Asian Countries, yet I must say I'm glad to have you home.

We, by which I mean all the principal figures in the Administration, have missed your wise counsel, your energetic support and your exemplary dedication to the service of the country.

On the purely personal side it was fine to see you both looking so well after the rigors of a trip that must have taxed the strength of even such young and vigorous people as yourselves. I look forward to some quiet opportunity when I can hear a real recital of your adventures and accomplishments.

With warm personal regards,

Sincerely,
Dwight D. Eisenhower

The 1953 trip had a tremendously important effect on my thinking and on my career. It was an undisputed success in that it accomplished its stated objectives and more. But further, it established my foreign policy experience and expertise in what was to become the most critical and controversial part of the world.

The trip was highly educational for me. I learned much about the people of Asia through contact with hundreds of

164

leaders and hundreds of thousands of ordinary citizens. I also saw three centuries of European colonialism on their deathbed, and I felt that I was able to diagnose the illness. I saw how the leaders and the masses of Asia longed for independence—whether or not they were ready for it, and whether or not they really understood it—because for them it meant dignity and respect. It meant being taken seriously and treated decently, and that was what they wanted.

I found that many people in these countries knew America only as an immensely powerful nation that both Communist propaganda and European snobbery had painted as crass and rapacious. I reassured them that we were not a colonial power, nor did we approve of the lingering colonialism of our European allies. Both Pat and I took every opportunity to let the people, as well as their leaders, know that America was genuinely interested in them, in their opinions, in their problems, and in their friendship. During years of oppression and repression the people had developed efficient underground communications networks, so that word of the little gestures we made quickly reverberated through a whole city or even a whole country.

This novel personal diplomacy made headlines everywhere we went and became, I think, one of the most significant contributions of the trip. In Singapore, for example, a front-page headline proclaimed: *Nixon Chats with Common Man,* and a news account of my arrival began by noting, "The American Vice President, Mr. Richard Nixon, yesterday found time to stretch his arm over a five-foot fence and offer his hand to an ordinary citizen of Malaya."

A columnist in Djakarta's mass-circulation *Abadi* wrote, "Maybe you readers would not believe that Vice President of the United States Richard Nixon yesterday helped fry sweet potatoes in a peasant's home between Bogor and Tjipanas. But that really happened yesterday. . . . Nixon even dropped in at a village coffee shop, and seated on a bamboo chair with Sukarno, had a chat with the proprietor."

Both Pat and I had a tremendous amount of personal contact with the people wherever we went. One day in the Philippines we shook hands with more than five thousand students at a 4-H exhibition. Later, as I walked through heavy crowds at a factory, my Filipino escort touched my arm and said, "That man back there, Mr. Vice President, said, 'He is not afraid to shake my hand even if my shirt is dirty!' " I shall never forget the look of quiet pride in my escort's face.

The New York *Times* surveyed its correspondents in each of the places we had visited and presented their observations in a front-page story on the day we returned home: "According to correspondents of the *Times* along his route, Mr. Nixon has shown that he has a knack for walking into delicate foreign political situations and saying the right things. In summary, the reports were that 'the common man of Asia liked this big, friendly, informal, democratic, serious young American, and got the impression that he likes them.' "

Today it may hardly seem a revelation that the peoples of Asia wanted to be treated with respect; but it was a lesson that the European nations did not learn sufficiently well or sufficiently soon in the years after World War II. In Hong Kong, the best run and most prosperous of the Asian cities I visited, I asked a local Chinese leader how the people would vote if offered independence. Without hesitation he said, "They would vote for independence by ten to one." I asked him why this was so, since the British presence had obviously materially benefited the people. He replied, "There is a saying that when the British establish a colony they build three things, in this order: a church, a racetrack, and a club to which Orientals cannot belong. That is an exaggeration but it is based upon a truth, and that is why we would always choose to be independent."

For better or worse, the colonial empires were disintegrating. The great question in the 1950s was who would fill the vacuum. Japan had the potential but was prohibited from doing so by the postwar treaties. None of the other countries in the region had the military and economic resources to defend itself unaided against Communist infiltration and subversion. It was clear to me that if the United States did not move, the Chinese or the Soviets, acting with or through the local Communist insurgent groups in each country, certainly would. The question, therefore, was not *whether* but *how*.

I learned much on this trip about the theory and practice of communism. In each country I saw how the Communists had carefully targeted their propaganda and aid where it did them the most good, and how they always presented themselves as being on the side of the people against the ruling classes—whether European or native. The Soviets were skillful with their propaganda and lavish with their money. But they, like us, were still interlopers in an Oriental world. The major new and unfathomable factor in Asia and the Pacific was Communist China. It was a giant looming beyond every Asian horizon—475 million people ruled by ruthless, disciplined ideologues. At a time when wishful thinkers in Washington and other Western capitals were saying that Communist China would not be a threat in Asia because it was so backward and underdeveloped, I was able to report firsthand that its influence was already spreading throughout the area.

With some countries, for example, the Chinese Communists had established student exchange programs, and large numbers of students were being sent to Red China for free college training. In Indonesia this amounted to as many as a thousand students a year, and I was shocked to find some of our embassies completely unconcerned about the impact this could have on the next generation of leaders.

I returned home convinced that, since the great battle in Asia was between communism and the free nations, we could not ignore the powerful Communist propaganda. I believed that the best way to undercut the appeal of the Communists was to confront them and show uncommitted observers that representatives of democratic nations were neither afraid of the Communists nor unable to debate them on any question. The most dramatic justification of this belief had come at the Pegu pagoda.

The trip also impressed upon me the tremendous spirit of enterprise and discipline in postwar Japan: it seemed as if everyone we saw—from farmers in the fields to factory hands on the assembly lines— was working feverishly. The country was still pretty much on its back in 1953, but after this trip there was no question in my mind that Japan would recover much more quickly than most Americans had predicted. When I got back to Washington I became a staunch advocate of close American-Japanese ties.

The 1953 trip had two lasting results. During those sixty-nine days I was able to meet not only those in power, but many of the younger up-and-coming generation whose careers developed over the next two decades as did my own. Each time I returned to these countries—as Vice President, as a private citizen, and then as President—I found that I was often dealing with people I had met on this first trip. The relationships that even these few early meetings had established and what I learned through these contacts were tremendously important to the development of my thinking about foreign affairs. It was as a result of this trip, too, that I knew that foreign policy was a field in which I had great interest and at least some ability.

One less significant but equally lasting result of this trip has been that neither Pat nor I has cared for champagne since. I would guess that during those two months we drank at least two cases of it. At every lunch and dinner and at almost every stop along the way, our hosts proudly produced bottles of fine French champagne and proposed toasts, which I then had to return. Before this, Pat and I had always enjoyed champagne as a way to celebrate a special occasion, but neither of us has willingly taken a glass of it since. When I was President, I would sip a little, as required when a toast was offered or returned, but I never actually finished a whole glass of the stuff.

JOE McCARTHY

One of the most serious problems we inherited from Truman was Joe McCarthy. As a Democratic friend put it to me, "Joe has been a snake in the grass for us. If you're not careful he'll become a viper in your bosom."

Both McCarthy and I had come to Washington in 1946. He was elected to the Senate as "the fighting Marine" after a brief career in local Wisconsin politics. I saw very little of him in those early years. He was a senator and I was a congressman, and we moved in different circles.

In February 1950, the month after Hiss was convicted of perjury, McCarthy gave a Lincoln Day speech to a Republican Women's Club in Wheeling, West Virginia. His subject was communist infiltration of government, and he ended by brandishing a paper that he said contained a list of individuals employed by the State Department who were known to the Secretary of State as members of the Communist Party. By the time he reached Salt Lake City the next day the number of names on the list had changed, but the charge remained the same.

Like everyone else in Washington, I read these stories with great interest. I also read them with great trepidation. Joe McCarthy had never been involved in fighting communists before, and I could not help wondering whether he understood the need for absolute accuracy and fairness in going after them. He called me shortly after he returned to Washington from Salt Lake City to ask whether, as a result of my work on the Hiss case, I had any files on communists in the State Department.

I told him that he was welcome to look through whatever files I had. But I urged that he be especially careful about facts. I noted that in his speeches he had talked about "card-carrying Communists." I told him he would be on firmer ground talking about the problems of security risks. He thanked me warmly for my advice and said I had made an important point. As the months went by, however, he continued to strike out indiscriminately.

I had a peculiar encounter with McCarthy in December 1950, at a small dinner-dance at the exclusive Sulgrave Club in Washington. Among the guests was Drew Pearson, who had been attacking McCarthy almost every day in his "Washington Merry-Go-Round" column. Although the two men were not seated near each other at the dinner table, it was clear that McCarthy was spoiling for a fight. Pearson seemed ready to give it to him.

There was dancing between the courses, and at one of the intermissions McCarthy went over to Pearson and said, "You know, I'm going to put you out of business with a speech in the Senate tomorrow. There isn't going to be anything left of you professionally or personally by the time I get finished with you." Pearson looked up impassively and said in a low voice, "Joe, have you paid your income taxes yet?" Pearson had been running articles about McCarthy's

169

personal finances, and the remark infuriated him. He challenged Pearson to step outside, but some of the other guests intervened and got McCarthy to return to his seat.

As the party began to break up, I went downstairs to the cloakroom. There was Joe McCarthy with his big, thick hands around Pearson's neck. Pearson was struggling wildly to get some air. When McCarthy spotted me, he drew his arm back and slapped Pearson so hard that his head snapped back.

"That one was for you, Dick," he said.

I stepped between the two men and pushed them apart. "Let a good Quaker stop this fight," I said. Pearson grabbed his overcoat and ran from the room. McCarthy said, "You shouldn't have stopped me, Dick," and went upstairs to bid his hostess good night.

Relations between McCarthy and Eisenhower had long been strained because of McCarthy's attacks on George Marshall.

After the election, I felt I should try to broker their feud. I began, therefore, to act as a go-between for McCarthy and the administration. I soon learned that the go-between is seldom popular with either side.

Most Republicans in the House and Senate were then still strongly pro-McCarthy and wanted Eisenhower to embrace him, while the predominantly liberal White House staff members opposed McCarthy and wanted Eisenhower to repudiate him. The President himself was torn. He disliked McCarthy personally, not only because of the attacks on Marshall but because of his coarse familiarity, which Eisenhower found distasteful. But he was reluctant to plunge into a bitter personal and partisan wrangle, aware that if he repudiated McCarthy or tried to discipline him, the Republican Party would split right down the middle in Congress and in the country. The unique personal good will that enabled Eisenhower to lead his party even while representing only its minority wing would have been severely damaged. So he hung back from provoking any confrontation.

Almost immediately, I found myself putting out brushfires started by McCarthy.

Two early nominations Eisenhower sent to the Senate were of James Bryant Conant, president of Harvard, as U.S. High Commissioner for Germany and of veteran diplomat Charles E. "Chip" Bohlen as ambassador to the Soviet Union. Conant had stirred up the ire of many anti-communists a few months earlier by flatly asserting that it was inconceivable that any member of the Harvard faculty was a Communist. McCarthy prepared to attack Conant's nomination on the Senate floor. Getting wind of his plan, I managed to talk him out of it. He agreed, instead, just to send a letter to Eisenhower expressing his opposition to the nomination. I was less successful, however, when the Bohlen nomination was debated several weeks later.

In the summer of 1953 McCarthy came across the tantalizing bit of information that William Bundy, one of Allen Dulles's brightest young men at the Central Intelligence Agency, had made a contribution to Alger Hiss's legal defense fund. McCarthy decided to investigate not only Bundy but the whole CIA. Allen Dulles asked me if I could do anything to help prevent a confrontation. He said that he had complete confidence in Bundy, and that his main interest was to keep the CIA out of the newspapers. I told McCarthy that I had seen Bundy's performance in several National Security Council meetings and he seemed to me a loyal American who was rendering vital service to the country.

"But what about his contribution to Hiss?" McCarthy persisted.

"Joe," I said, "you have to understand how those people up in Cambridge think. Bundy graduated from the Harvard Law School, and Hiss was one of its most famous graduates. I think he probably just got on the bandwagon without giving any thought to where the bandwagon was heading."

The next day I had lunch with McCarthy and the other Republicans on his subcommittee, Everett Dirksen, Karl Mundt, and Charles Potter. I enlisted their support, and McCarthy with obvious reluctance agreed to drop his investigation of Bundy and the CIA.

I tried to convince all parties—Eisenhower, the White House staff, the Cabinet, and many congressmen—that, while urging McCarthy to use restraint, we should consider each of his cases on its merits. I thought that until a break was unavoidable we should attack McCarthy only when his facts were wrong, and I hoped that in the meantime the anticommunist cause would not be irreparably damaged by his excesses. In August 1953, for example, he had discovered a Communist working in the Government Printing Office. He stretched the case far beyond its importance, but I argued against opposing him because there was at least some factual basis for his charges.

In his search for new areas of possible communist infiltration, McCarthy began investigations into the Army. The atom spy Julius Rosenberg had worked at an Army base, and McCarthy felt that where there had been one Communist there were likely to be more. At the end of December 1953, I invited him to Key Biscayne, where Bill Rogers, now Deputy Attorney General, and I double-teamed him about the dangers of pushing the Army investigation too hard.

I said that he should continue to go after communists in government. "It doesn't make any difference if they are in this administration or in previous ones," I told him. "If they are there, they should be out. But remember that this is your administration, and the people in it are just as dedicated as you are to cleaning out subversives." I suggested he talk with Robert Stevens, the Secretary of the Army. Rogers and I urged that he should think about moving into some new areas lest he become known as a "one-shot" senator.

McCarthy seemed to understand the good advice we were giving him, and before he left Florida he told some reporters that he planned to broaden his investigations to include questionable income tax settlements that had been made during the Truman administration. But no sooner had he returned to Washington than he was back in furious pursuit of communists and headlines.

In January 1954 McCarthy discovered Irving Peress, the Army dentist who was to lead to his downfall.

Peress had received a routine promotion even after he refused to answer a loyalty questionnaire. An Army investigation revealed that in fact Dr. Peress, by now a major, had not complied with its regulations and they decided to discharge him.

When McCarthy got wind of the incident and learned of Peress's membership in the far left-wing American Labor Party, he decided that he had hit pay dirt. He summoned Peress before a closed session of his subcommittee, where the dentist invoked the Fifth Amendment. A few days later Peress requested and received an honorable discharge from the Army. McCarthy hit the roof.

He subpoenaed General Ralph Zwicker, the commanding general, and three other officers. In a closed session Zwicker tried to explain how Peress had merely slipped through a loophole in Army red tape. As the commanding officer Zwicker accepted full responsibility, but he refused to name any individuals involved in processing Peress's case. McCarthy charged that Zwicker was shielding communists and said he was not fit to wear the uniform of an Army officer. He threatened to humiliate him in a public hearing the following week unless he changed his mind and decided to cooperate.

When Army Secretary Stevens learned of the incident, he ordered Zwicker not to appear at the public session, and announced that he would testify himself.

Once again I seemed to be the only person with enough credibility in both camps to suggest a compromise. Eisenhower was away on a golfing vacation, and I wanted to keep the situation from spilling over into a public brawl. However unconscionable McCarthy's treatment of Zwicker may have been, the fact remained that the Army was on very weak ground as far as the Peress case was concerned. The mistake may have been understandable, but it was a mistake.

Working closely with Jerry Persons, the White House congressional liaison officer, I arranged a meeting in my office in the Capitol. Stevens came with the Army's counsel, John Adams. Also present were Persons, Bill Rogers, Bill Knowland, Everett Dirksen, and Jack Martin, who had been Senator Taft's administrative assistant and was now on the White House staff.

Both Stevens and Adams seemed to have the naive idea that they could go in and finesse the Peress case at the outset by admitting the Army's errors and then move on to the Zwicker incident and talk about how badly McCarthy had behaved. I said that they should certainly try to do that if they could, but I reminded them that it was McCarthy as chairman, not Stevens as witness, who would control the hearing.

We agreed that Dirksen should try to arrange a luncheon meeting with Stevens and McCarthy for the next day.

The luncheon was held in Dirksen's office, next door to mine in the Capitol. The meal consisted of fried chicken, peas, french fried potatoes, and hearts of lettuce. Within a few hours, the press had tagged it the "chicken luncheon," and that bland menu turned into one of the most controversial repasts of the 1950s.

From the beginning the meeting was stormy. In addition to McCarthy and Stevens, only the three Republican senators on McCarthy's subcommittee—Dirksen, Potter, and Mundt—were invited. As soon as the luncheon broke up Mundt filled me in on what had taken place. At first there had appeared to be no ground for compromise, but Mundt finally negotiated a written agreement that Army witnesses would appear and answer questions when called before McCarthy's subcommittee. There was an understanding, not mentioned in the agreement itself, that McCarthy would treat these witnesses respectfully.

Stevens telephoned me as soon as he got back to the Pentagon, and he seemed fairly happy with the way things had worked out. Within an hour, however, McCarthy casually told a reporter that Stevens could not have surrendered more "abjectly if he had gotten down on his knees."

Since the text of the Mundt agreement did not explicitly state that McCarthy would treat the witnesses respectfully, McCarthy's remark made the agreement appear to be a complete capitulation to him. Around 11:30 that night I got a call from Stevens. He was in a highly emotional state. He said that he had decided to issue a statement the following day and then resign. I told him to quit talking about resigning and suggested that in the morning we could talk about what kind of statement could be made.

At that point, Eisenhower returned to Washington. He immediately tried to get the luncheon participants to issue another statement that might resolve the situation. McCarthy proved adamant. The President then asked me to work with Stevens, Sherman Adams, and Jerry Persons in drafting a statement that Stevens could issue from the White House. We worked all afternoon in Persons's East Wing office while Eisenhower, probably to relieve the tremendous anger he felt, practiced chip shots on the South Lawn.

We took the draft to him in the Family Quarters, and he approved it. In the statement, Stevens said that he had received assurances from subcommittee members that there would be no more browbeating or humiliation of his officers and that he would "never accede to the abuse of Army personnel under any circumstances, including committee hearings."

A few days later, Eisenhower decided to issue his own statement on the Peress case. He mentioned his decision at a congressional leadership meeting on March 1, and I made a diary note about it:

Diary

At the conclusion of the meeting, the President on his own initiative brought up the Stevens thing. He said that he was preparing to make the statement on it at his press conference and that one thing he wanted to say was that in fighting communism we could not destroy Americanism.

Saltonstall [Senator Leverett Saltonstall of Massachusetts] said that he thought the Army had made a mistake in not admitting its error in the Peress case. The President reacted sharply and said that the Army had admitted it in a letter to McCarthy and in a public statement.

Saltonstall came back by saying it had not admitted it clearly enough. Knowland very emphatically defended the Senators for the action they took at the luncheon with Stevens. He said that the Army's conduct in this case was inexcusable and that such a hearing on television would have been even worse than the situation with which we are confronted at this time. He tore sheets of paper off his note pad for emphasis. I don't know when I have seen him quite so stirred up on a matter as he was on this one.

At the conclusion of the meeting the President said he was going to have a talk with me about this matter and attempt to get the thing in perspective.

By this time Eisenhower's reaction to the whole incident had become very emotional. As an Army man he was embarrassed by the Army's blunder and annoyed that it had been paraded through the newspapers. As party leader, he was worried about the way the issue was polarizing Republicans and giving the Democrats aid and comfort as the congressional elections approached. As President, he was offended by McCarthy's tactics, techniques, and personality. He wanted his statement to say that those who investigated communism were as great a danger as the communists themselves, and that the methods of investigators were the same as communist methods.

I believed that such a statement at that time would cause Eisenhower and the party more trouble than he or his White House staff and liberal friends who were urging it could imagine. A poll in January 1954 found that 50 percent of the people had a favorable opinion of McCarthy and only 29 percent had an unfavorable opinion.

I was again able to work out a compromise, and on March 3 Eisenhower opened his press conference by reading a long statement that adopted most of my suggestions and some of my language. It said: "In opposing communism, we are defeating ourselves if either by design or through carelessness we use methods that do not conform to the American sense of justice and fair play."

For almost three years the leaders of the Democratic Party had stood on the sidelines, watching the Republicans slug it out over McCarthy. As Lyndon Johnson, the Democratic Leader in the Senate, put it, "I will not commit my party to some high school debate on the subject 'Resolved, that communism is good for the United States,' with my party taking affirmative." But as both parties began to gear up for the 1954 elections, it became clear that the bitterly sensational Peress-Zwicker-Stevens affair had created a target of opportunity: McCarthy and McCarthyism could now safely be exploited by the Democrats.

On March 6, Adlai Stevenson, as titular head of the Democratic Party, fired the first shot of the off-year election campaign. In a televised speech he blasted Eisenhower's leadership and mocked what he portrayed as his weakness in refusing to confront and control McCarthy.

The immediate problem of who should reply to Stevenson was discussed at length during a Republican leadership meeting at the White House on March 8. Finally the President looked straight at me. "I am going to make a suggestion, even though he is present, that I think we probably ought to use Dick more than we have been," he said. "He can sometimes take positions which are more political than it would be expected that I take. The difficulty with the McCarthy problem is that anybody who takes it on runs the risk of being called a pink. Dick has had experience in the communist field, and therefore he would not be subject to criticism."

After the meeting, Eisenhower took me into his small private office next to the Oval Office. He said that he would recommend treating McCarthy and Stevenson with an easy backhand rather than making them the subject of the whole speech. One of the reasons he disliked McCarthy was that he felt McCarthy was drawing too much attention away from the administration's positive programs.

This was not a speech I looked forward to writing or delivering. No matter how it was done, it was bound to alienate large segments of the party and large segments of the public. What it really involved was what Eisenhower himself had purposely avoided for the past two years: determining the administration's policy on McCarthy. But now with the election coming up and the Democrats beginning to stir, it was clear that we could no longer afford the luxury of trying to deal piecemeal and behind the scenes with each new crisis McCarthy created.

The broadcast was set for Saturday night, March 13, so I would have only five days of preparation. I wrote dozens of outlines and drafts, and by Friday morning I felt that I had condensed them into a speech that was the best that could be done in the circumstances.

I had planned to spend Friday in seclusion going over

my notes. I took a room at the Statler Hotel and left word that I was to be disturbed only in case of an emergency.

About 10 A.M., I was informed that I had an urgent call. It was Bill Knowland, furious because someone in the White House had leaked an unflattering item about him to a newspaper columnist. He said he could not put up with such internal sabotage any longer and was going to call a conference of the Senate Republicans to submit his resignation as Majority Leader. I tried to calm him down and convince him that he should wait until after my speech before doing anything.

I had just resumed work on the speech when a call came through from Tom Stephens, Eisenhower's Appointments Secretary, saying that the President had just asked if I could come over to talk to him before he went to Camp David for the weekend. I walked across Lafayette Square to the White House and was immediately ushered into the Oval Office. A few days later I recalled the conversation in my diary:

Diary

He said that first, he didn't think I needed advice on a political speech, and that I had his complete confidence in my ability to handle it.

He said, however, he felt that he knew what lifted people and he was convinced that it was necessary to get across to them that we had a progressive, dynamic program which benefited all the people.

He did advise that I work a smile or two into the program. I told him that that was one of my difficulties and some people had suggested that was one thing I should try to do. He suggested I might work a smile in with regard to my comments on Stevenson. I told him that I planned to stick a few barbs into him, and then he suggested he was perfectly content that I do so but that he thought it was best to laugh at him rather than to hit him meanly.

On Stevenson's attack on his defense program, he said, "What qualification does Stevenson have on this subject? Who is he?"

He pointed out that Lincoln and Washington, our

two greatest Presidents, were men who were subjected to considerable attack and who never indulged in personalities. He said, "Now be sure and don't put me on the same level, but it might be well subtly to work in that fact as you answer Stevenson."

He suggested that I tell of Hiss and my part in that case. He said, "After all, there are great numbers of people who think that McCarthy got Hiss." He said, "I want you to know that I put you on the top of my list in Chicago because you had gotten Hiss and you had done it decently." He said that was also the reason he had selected me to do this broadcast.

He said, "Try to get across to the people that we are working for a program for America, and that the little snapping at our heels isn't going to deter us." He suggested I might get in the fact he had commanded 5 million troops in Europe.

Stevenson's speech had been made before a cheering partisan audience at a Democratic fund-raising dinner; it had been one of his characteristically arch performances. I decided to try to convey the opposite impression, so I spoke in a calm and low-keyed manner in front of a plain backdrop. I purposely chose simple words and graphic examples. During my preparation for the speech, I tried always to bear in mind that my primary audience was the large middle ground of public opinion that believed that, regardless of McCarthy's tactics, there was no gentle way to deal with communists. I tried, therefore, to come up with some idea or some turn of phrase that would make my position memorable and unmistakable.

Now, I can imagine some of you will say, "Why all this hullabaloo about being fair when you are dealing with a gang of traitors?" As a matter of fact, I have heard people say, "After all, we are dealing with a bunch of rats. What we ought to do is go out and shoot them."

Well, I agree they are a bunch of rats. But just remember this. When you go out to shoot rats, you have to shoot straight, because when you shoot wildly, it not only means that the rats may get away more easily—but you make it easier on the rats. Also you might hit someone else who is trying to shoot rats, too. So, we have to be fair—for two very good reasons: one, because it is right; and two, because it is the most effective way of doing the job.

Eisenhower called me from Camp David with his congratulations. "As you know, Dick," he said, "I am not one who likes to use flattery, but I want you to know that I think you did a magnificent job and the very best that could have been done under the circumstances." I said that the speech would not satisfy either extreme of opinion; he replied he thought it would satisfy 85 percent of the people and that was what was important. "The people who are violently pro-McCarthy or anti-McCarthy will never be satisfied with anything except all-out war," he said. He seemed very pleased that I had smiled a couple of times during the speech and said that at one point he had turned to the others in the room with him and said, "There's that smile I told Dick to use."

At the meeting of legislative leaders the following Monday morning, Eisenhower was in the best spirits he had been in for a long time. My speech seemed to have buoyed him by giving voice to his own frustrations over McCarthy and by providing some focus for the administration's efforts.

The March 13 speech marked the beginning of a new phase of the McCarthy episode, a phase that turned out to be the beginning of the end. By the time the Army-McCarthy hearings began five weeks later, those who knew McCarthy said that he seemed to have fallen apart. In my diary for March 22, I recounted a conversation with Len Hall:

Diary
    Len seemed to feel that Joe was beginning to blow up and that he was in no condition whatever to attend a hearing and to participate in it.
    The same view was expressed by Karl Mundt when I talked to him on the phone. He had talked to Joe until two o'clock the night before and he said it was pretty grim with Jean [McCarthy's wife] almost in tears, and him having very little influence due to the

fact that Joe said that he knew his political life was at stake and that he was not going to agree to anything that would make it difficult for him to defend himself.

Len Hall said when he had been in to see Joe a couple of days before, when he came up to the apartment door Joe opened it and had a gun in his hand. Apparently he was carrying one all the time because of the threats that had been made against him.

Major shifts in public opinion now began to appear. A Gallup poll at the end of March showed that a solid 46 percent favored McCarthy and 36 percent disapproved of him. By August a dramatic reversal had occurred: while 36 percent still held firm in their approval, now 51 percent disapproved. As soon as the first cracks appeared in his public support, a startling erosion set in. Just a few months earlier the Republican National Committee had been calling McCarthy an asset to the party. Now there was an effort to write him off as soon as possible.

For almost two months, from April 22 to June 17, the grotesque melodrama of the Army-McCarthy hearings unfolded each day in the Senate Caucus Room. Eisenhower privately called the hearings "a damn shameful spectacle," and he urged that everything possible be done to get them over with as quickly as possible. But there was nothing we could do. The hearings became a national obsession. People stayed home from work to see the key confrontations. The posturing before the cameras on both sides repelled me, and after the first day I did not watch any of them. As I told a reporter, "I just prefer professional actors to amateurs."

On July 30, Vermont Republican Senator Ralph Flanders introduced Senate Resolution 301: "Resolved, That the conduct of the Senator from Wisconsin, Mr. McCarthy, is unbecoming a Member of the United States Senate, is contrary to senatorial traditions, and tends to bring the Senate into disrepute, and such conduct is hereby condemned." On August 2, by a vote of 75 to 12, the Senate adopted a resolution to appoint a select committee to consider the Flanders resolution. The committee was chaired by Senator Arthur V. Watkins, a stern Mormon from Utah. None of them, including the freshman senator from North Carolina, Sam Ervin, had taken a strong public stand on McCarthy.

After almost a month of hearings, the Watkins Committee unanimously recommended that McCarthy be censured on two counts: for contempt of the Senate because he had refused to appear before a subcommittee investigating his finances in 1952, and for his abuse of General Zwicker. The vote was postponed until after the November elections.

I was presiding over a tense Senate chamber when the final debate began on December 2. It was late afternoon by the time the vote was taken. A sudden hush fell over the Chamber as a lone figure came through the swinging doors at the back and walked slowly down the aisle. Joe McCarthy had arrived for the vote on his own censure. His arm was in a sling from an attack of bursitis that had kept him in the hospital for several days.

When the vote was taken, every Democrat voted against McCarthy; the Republicans split right down the middle, 22 for and 22 against. Among those voting against the resolution was Bill Knowland, the Minority Leader. The final vote was 67 to 22, and at 5:03 P.M. on December 2, Joseph R. McCarthy of Wisconsin became the third United States Senator ever to be censured by his colleagues. He sat quietly in his seat, staring at the bare desktop in front of him, surrounded by his supporters.

There was a brief procedural hassle when Styles Bridges of New Hampshire pointed out that as the word *censure* did not appear in the body of the resolution, it should be struck from the title. The parliamentarian advised me that Bridges was technically correct and that the resolution as formally passed was one of condemnation rather than censure. But by this time the rhetoric did not matter. McCarthy had already left the chamber. For him it was all over.

Joseph McCarthy cast his shadow over four critical years of American politics. From the Wheeling speech in February 1950 to his condemnation in December 1954, intense controversy surrounded everything he said and did.

I remember a luncheon at the White House a few days after the chicken luncheon had brought the Stevens episode to fever pitch. As I noted in my diary at the time, everyone was very tense:

Diary

At the luncheon, the President for some reason brought up the story of his old boxing instructor at West Point who he said used to hit him clear across the ring. He said that unless he got up smiling every time the boxing instructor would turn his back and walk out of the room.

Apparently the purpose of the story was to see that everybody did not get too excited about the whole McCarthy incident and the attacks that he made.

The President seems to have been convinced that people in the administration were actually afraid of McCarthy. Another purpose, I think, was the line he had been developing during the past week or so, that he wanted to see smiling faces around him.

My own feelings about Joe McCarthy were mixed. I never shared the disdain with which fashionable Washington treated him because of his lack of polished manners. In fact, I found him personally likable, if irresponsibly impulsive. At the end, I felt sorry for him as a man whose zeal and thirst for publicity were leading him and others to destruction. But it is despicable to make a racket of anticommunism or any other cause—to stir people up and then give them no positive leadership or direction. By the spring of 1954 J. Edgar Hoover was telling Eisenhower that McCarthy had reached a point where he was actually impeding the investigation of communists. As Eisenhower expressed it, "McCarthy is probably Malenkov's best helper in the United States."

I broke with McCarthy when he began to attack the administration openly. For some time he had picked up one of Senator Jenner's lines and been referring to the period before Eisenhower was elected as "twenty years of treason." In 1954, he began talking about "twenty-one years of treason," thus including the first year of Eisenhower's administration.

McCarthy was sincere, and I know from personal investigation that there was real substance to some of his charges. But he could not resist grossly exaggerating his facts. The communists and the compulsive anti-anti-communists, together with many who were as anti-

183

communist as McCarthy himself, ended up discrediting everything the man had to say when McCarthy became the issue instead of communism.

CRISIS IN INDOCHINA: 1954

The names Vietnam and Indochina meant little to most Americans when, in March 1954, the first news stories appeared about the Communist siege of a remote French military outpost called Dien Bien Phu. Within a few weeks, however, we shared the daily agony and valor of its defenders, and we saw the threat of a Communist takeover in Vietnam bring America to the brink of war. After seven years of fighting and 50,000 men killed, there were serious questions in France about whether to continue the fight against Ho Chi Minh's Communist guerrillas.

A French withdrawal from Vietnam would have placed us in a very difficult position because American policy was predicated upon the vital importance of maintaining an independent Vietnam. Early in 1952 Truman's National Security Council had prepared a study of Southeast Asia that set forth what Eisenhower later referred to as the "falling domino" principle: that "the loss of any single country would probably lead to relatively swift submission to or an alignment with communism by the remaining countries of this group." The study described America's vital interests in the natural resources of this area—rubber and tin—and concluded that the French effort to defeat Ho Chi Minh's Communist Vietminh was "essential to the security of the free world, not only in the Far East but in the Middle East and Europe as well."

In February 1954, Eisenhower had sent two hundred Army mechanics as advisers to the French and Vietnamese forces. There was no serious opposition in Congress because the men would be in Vietnam only as technical advisers, and Eisenhower promised that they would not stay longer than June.

As the French and Vietminh settled in for a long siege, the press began to build up Dien Bien Phu as the first test since Korea of the free world's ability to resist Communist aggression. In Washington the Joint Chiefs of Staff, under their Chairman, Admiral Arthur Radford, devised a plan, known as Operation Vulture, for using three small tactical atomic bombs to destroy Vietminh positions and relieve the garrison. Both Eisenhower and Dulles, however, felt that nothing less than overt Chinese Communist aggression would be sufficient provocation for our going into Vietnam in any such a direct and unilateral way.

The Communist Chinese were the Vietminh's patrons and principal source of military supplies. At a congressional leadership meeting at the end of March, Eisenhower said that if the military situation at Dien Bien Phu became desperate he would consider the use of diversionary tactics, possibly a landing by Chiang Kai-shek's Nationalist forces on China's Hainan Island or a naval blockade of the Chinese mainland. Very simply, but dramatically, he said, "I am bringing this up at this time because at any time within the space of forty-eight hours, it might be necessary to move into the battle of Dien Bien Phu in order to keep it from going against us, and in that case I will be calling in the Democrats as well as our Republican leaders to inform them of the actions we're taking."

Reports of the situation in Dien Bien Phu were constantly changing, and our day-to-day attitude frequently reflected the shifting tides of the battle. I made a diary note of an NSC meeting on April 6:

Diary

The President was in a very serious mood in this meeting. Dulles presented his plan about trying to get united action among the allies. I said that such a plan was all right as far as it goes but that, if it were limited to resisting overt aggression alone, it would not meet the real future danger in Asia. I said that we must adopt the principle of uniting together to resist subversive aggression of the Indochina and Chinese Civil War type. I pointed out that we had never yet found a formula to resist this kind of aggression on a united basis.

The President said, "What about Korea?" I answered that Korea was a case of the Communists marching across a line even though it was technically in the same country and that, therefore, the united action principle applied because what was really involved was overt aggression.

I also said that I didn't think the President should underestimate his ability to get the Congress and the country to follow his leadership. I suggested that more technicians could be sent to Indochina if the President asked for them. He asked Wilson to check on this immediately.

From the conversation, however, it was quite apparent that the President had backed down considerably from the strong position he had taken on Indochina the latter part of the previous week. He seemed resigned to doing nothing at all unless we could get the allies and the country to go along with whatever was suggested and he did not seem inclined to put much pressure on to get them to come along.

The challenge we faced in 1954 was to convince the American people of the importance of Dien Bien Phu—that much more was at stake than the defense of some French troops besieged at a colonial outpost. No one, except possibly Admiral Radford, wanted American military intervention. We were all convinced, however, that unless the Communists knew that their so-called wars of liberation would be resisted by military means if necessary, they would not stop until they had taken over Southeast Asia, just as they had Eastern Europe.

Dulles spent several weeks trying to get the British and French to join us in concerted opposition to the Communists. The French government, however, was too much on the psychological defensive to be able to mount or sustain the kind of military and diplomatic offensive required.

Admiral Radford went to London to consult with Churchill, who said bluntly that if his people had not been willing to fight to save India for themselves, he did not think they would be willing to fight to save Indochina for the French. Churchill admitted that the rest of Indochina might fall if Vietnam were lost, but he did not foresee any threat to the rest of Southeast Asia, Japan, or Australia. Both Radford and I were astonished that Churchill, who had understood the communist problem so well as early as 1946, could have made this statement.

It was clear that we could not count on Britain or France for support in resisting communism in Indochina. If we decided to move, we would have to move on our own.

Early in April there was a respite from the crisis; it seemed that the French troops might be able to hold on at Dien Bien Phu. Eisenhower decided to go to Augusta for a few days, and Dulles, exhausted and disheartened by his unsuccessful attempts to promote allied unity, went to Canada. The news from Vietnam continued hopeful, and in order to extend his stay in Georgia, Eisenhower asked me to fill in for him at the American Society of Newspaper Editors' annual convention in Washington on April 16.

The ASNE convention is a prestigious and responsible forum, and I asked that all my remarks be off the record so that I could speak candidly. After delivering a prepared speech I agreed to take questions from the floor. I was asked whether I thought we would send American troops to Indochina if the French decided to withdraw and it was the only way to save Indochina from being taken over by the Communists. I said that I did not believe that "the presumption or the assumption which has been made by the questioner will occur, and I recognize that he has put it as a hypothetical question." Given those major reservations, however, I said that if sending American forces was the only way to avoid further Communist expansion in Asia, particularly in Indochina, "I believe that the executive branch of the government has to take the politically unpopular position of facing up to it and doing it, and I personally would support such a decision."

Two foreign reporters who were not at the meeting heard about my response and sent the story to their papers. By the next morning it was headline news all across America. It was widely interpreted as a trial balloon aimed at reversing the administration's policy, which, so far, had drawn the line at direct American military intervention in Vietnam.

I was concerned that Eisenhower might be upset over the incident, but he told me that if he had been confronted with a hypothetical question under similar circumstances he probably would have answered it the same way.

At a meeting with the Republican congressional leaders

a week later, Eisenhower supported me when the matter was raised. I made a note of the meeting:

Diary

Charlie Halleck, during the course of the discussion, said that the suggestion that American boys might be sent to Indochina "had really hurt," and that he hoped there would be no more talk of that type. The President, however, immediately stepped in and said he felt it was important that we not show a weakness at this critical time and that we not let the Russians think that we might not resist in the event that the Communists attempted to step up their present tactics in Indochina and elsewhere. He said that we had to think of whether it was best to take a strong stand now when we could or wait until later when we could not. He also pointed out that it was not well to tell the Russians everything as to what we would or would not do.

At the end of April the situation at Dien Bien Phu took another turn for the worse, and it did not look as if the French forces could hold on much longer. I made a diary note on April 29:

Diary

The NSC meeting started at ten o'clock and did not end until one. The last hour and three-quarters was spent discussing Indochina.

Radford reported on the military situation and on his conversations with the French and British. Bedell Smith read a message from Dulles which indicated considerable pessimism but that Dulles was going to stand firm for the American position.

The President was extremely serious and seemed to be greatly concerned about what was the right course to take.

After the reports were made, Harold Stassen said that he thought that decision should be to send ground troops if necessary to save Indochina, and to do it on a unilateral basis if that was the only way it could be done.

The President himself said that he could not visualize a ground troop operation in Indochina that would be supported by the people of the United States and which would not in the long run put our defense too far out of balance. He also raised the point that we simply could not go in unilaterally because that was in violation of our whole principle of collective defense against communism in all places in the world.

After Stassen's proposal had been discussed, I said that in my judgment winning the war in Vietnam was not necessarily a question of committing a lot of ground troops to combat. Sending an Air Force contingent representing a unified alliance would have the double effect of letting the Communists know that we were going to resist further expansion in the area, and of bolstering the morale of the French and the Vietnamese troops. I suggested that we explore the possibilities of developing a Pacific coalition without the British, an alliance with Thailand, the Philippines, Indochina, Australia, New Zealand, and whatever other nations would join.

The next morning I met with Eisenhower and General Robert Cutler, his Special Assistant for National Security Affairs. Cutler reported that the NSC planning board had been discussing the possibility of telling our allies that if we went into Indochina, we might use the atom bomb. Eisenhower asked me what I thought about this idea; I said that whatever was decided about using the bomb, I did not think it was necessary to mention it to our allies before we got them to agree on united action. I emphasized, as I had at the NSC meeting, that it might not be necessary to have more than a few conventional air strikes by the united forces to let the Communists see that we were determined to resist. Eisenhower turned to Cutler and said, "First, I certainly do not think that the atom bomb can be used by the United States unilaterally, and second, I agree with Dick that we do not have to mention it to anybody before we get some agreement on united action."

On May 7, after a gallant but utterly hopeless defense of a territory that had been reduced to the size of a baseball field, the French garrison at Dien Bien Phu was overrun by the Vietminh. The almost universal reaction was relief that the crisis had ended without precipitating a major war. But while attempting to put the best face on it publicly, we knew that the defeat at Dien Bien Phu would probably lead to French withdrawal from Vietnam, and that America would either have to take over the burden of stopping Communist aggression in Indochina or abandon the entire region.

On May 20 the NSC discussed the possibility of keeping the two hundred American mechanics in Vietnam past June, but Eisenhower dismissed the idea. First, he said, the French were already going back on their word to keep up the fighting. Second, he said that such an extension would make our future relations with Congress very difficult, because he had given a solemn pledge that the mechanics would come out by June 15, and he intended to honor his pledge.

After the fall of Dien Bien Phu, the heart fell out of the French will to win, and the next several weeks of desultory battle were a holding action until a negotiated settlement could be reached at the Geneva Conference, which had opened eleven days before the fortress fell. Dulles was infuriated and dispirited by the plan to surrender half of Vietnam to the Communists. When the Indochina settlement was made on July 21, the United States did not sign it. I agreed with this decision. In fact, a month earlier, I had urged Dulles not to be part of any settlement that would result in the surrender of any part of Indochina to the Communists.

The press perceived Dulles, Radford, and me as the hawks in the Indochina crisis. To some extent Radford did believe that the early use of tactical nuclear weapons would convince the Communists that we meant business. Dulles and I both believed that if the Communists pushed too far we would have to do whatever was necessary to stop them. Eisenhower fully agreed, although I think that Dulles and I were probably prepared to stand up at an earlier point than he was. We all hoped that by being prepared to fight we would never actually have to do any fighting.

Years later, after Dulles was dead and America was deeply involved in a war in Vietnam under another President, Eisenhower was asked privately whether he and Dulles had agreed on the question of being ready to send troops into Vietnam. "All the way," Eisenhower said.

MEETING CHURCHILL

In June 1954, Prime Minister Winston Churchill and Foreign Secretary Anthony Eden visited the United States for meetings with Eisenhower and Dulles. I dictated an extensive diary note describing the visit, beginning with my first meeting with the great man:

Diary

I met Churchill and Eden at the airport this morning. As he came down the steps of the airplane, he took each step alone by himself although he was very hesitant in his steps when he arrived at the bottom. He shook hands and said that he was very happy to meet me for the first time. Later in the car he said that although this was the first time that he had met me that he had read of some of my statements and that he had admiration for them.

I was supposed to make a speech of introduction which I had spent an hour or so last night preparing even though it was only to be a minute and a half long. However, when Churchill saw the microphones he walked immediately over to them and took out a sheet of paper from which he read his own speech to the people who were at the airport.

We then got into the open car and rode into town. Churchill was rather slow to react to questions or statements but on the other hand after the conversation had gone on for a while his reactions picked up considerably.

He said that there was a period for four months in Roosevelt's last months that there was very little communication or understanding between him and the American government. This was in response to my remarks that I had just read the fourth volume of his memoirs. He said that Roosevelt was not himself at that time and that Truman did not know what was going on. In fact, he said that he was sure Truman had not been taken in on the great decisions that were being made. He felt Roosevelt made a great mistake in not developing his second in command when he knew that he himself was ill and could not be around much longer. I said that I often wondered what would have happened had the allies accepted his judgment with regard to the conduct of World War II, particularly in respect to the southern offensive rather than the Channel crossing. His only remark was, well it would have been very "handy to have Vienna."

The diary described the dinner the Eisenhowers gave that evening:

Diary
    I think this was perhaps the most enjoyable occasion we have ever had at the White House. The crowd was relatively small—approximately 30—and the President, Churchill, et al. were in a relaxed, informal mood.

    The President proposed a toast to General Marshall after he had proposed one to the Queen and Churchill had responded. He pointed out that both Churchill and Marshall had been his immediate superiors during the war and that he knew they would forgive him if he made a protocol exception and proposed a toast to Marshall. I looked at Marshall as the toast was being proposed and it was obvious that he was very deeply moved by this gesture.

    After the guests who were not staying at the White House had gathered in one of the reception rooms downstairs we were all invited to come upstairs.

    Eden was particularly impressed by the reports of our visit to Malaya—the occasion when we went out and met the troops he said made a great impression in Britain.

    After we had finished dinner, we went in for

cigars and after the President sat with Churchill for a little while he asked me to come over and sit by him and said, "This is one of the young men I have been telling you about and I want you to get acquainted with him." I asked Churchill about his writing his memoirs. He pointed out that he had started them in 1946 and that he did it all by dictation. I asked him if he used a machine and he said no; that the Americans had given him one of the best machines but he preferred a pretty girl to talk to rather than a machine.

We went down to the movie room and saw *The Student Prince.* The program was not over until about 12:30 A.M. During the program both Churchill and the President exchanged pleasantries which we could all hear and remarks about the movie. The movie significantly enough came out just the opposite to the way Edward VIII came out with Mrs. Simpson.

Pat sat at Churchill's right during the dinner and she said it was a very enjoyable evening from all standpoints. Mrs. Eisenhower watched over him as his food was being served and when he tried to cut a piece of the meat in half before putting it on his plate she told him the knives weren't sharp and that they had all been received as part of the White House set—this was part of the gold set that had been bought in Paris. Pat remarked how Mamie took things over just as if she were handling any youngster who happened to be visiting or any close friend.

Foster Dulles had his usual highball rather than the wines during dinner. Pat asked Churchill whether or not he would prefer that. He said no, that he usually had his first drink of whiskey at 8:30 in the morning and that in the evening he enjoyed a glass of champagne. I noted that Churchill was much sharper than he had been in the morning and he seemed to thrive on the fact that he was participating in these conferences. As a matter of fact, at the dinner he was just as quick as any person and he had—I learned later—not taken a nap in the afternoon but had played cards after the conference had been completed.

The last evening of Churchill's visit there was a stag dinner at the British Embassy. I attended as Eisenhower's representative and was therefore seated next to him at the table:

Diary

I asked him how the three-day conference had affected him. He said that except for a few blackouts—and I assume he meant by that periods when he took a nap—that he had felt better during this conference than he had for some time. He said, "I always seem to get inspiration and renewed vitality by contact with this great novel land of yours which sticks up out of the Atlantic."

During the course of the evening the conversation turned to General Lee and I asked his appraisal of Lee. He said that he thought he was one of the greatest men in American history and one of the greatest generals at any time. He said that somebody ought to "catch up in a tapestry or a painting the memorable scene of Lee riding back across the Potomac after he had turned down the command of the Union Armies in order to stay with the Southern side." He also said that one of the other great moments in the Civil War was at Appomattox when Lee pointed out to Grant that the officers owned their horses as personal property and asked that they be allowed to retain them. Grant said to have them take all of their horses—the enlisted men and the officers as well. "They will need them to plow their fields." Churchill said, "In the squalor of life and war, what a magnificent act."

He reiterated his press club statement to the effect that we should have a policy of patience and vigilance. He said we could not deal with the Communists on the basis of weakness—that it had to be a policy of strength. He said he didn't like to call it a go-slow policy because that was not really a fair appraisal of the kind of policy he was advocating. He pointed out his record after World War I and also his Fulton, Missouri speech in properly appraising the communist threat and advocating means to meet it. He said, "I think that I have done as much against the Communists as McCarthy has done for them." He grinned and said, "Of course, that is a private statement. I never believe in interfering in the domestic politics of another country." He said that Bevan in England was just as much of a problem to him and to the British as was McCarthy to us. I asked him what it was that the British people didn't like about McCarthy and he said one thing they couldn't understand was why the Senate did not investigate all of the charges about his finances and other irregularities in getting elected and while he was Senator. I pointed out that very possibly Senators did not want to set the precedent of investigating a colleague for fear that it might someday react in a case against themselves.

I saw them off at the airport and Churchill was careful to see that I delivered some farewell remarks. I could tell that his declining health would soon cause him to give up the reins of leadership he had held for so long. While he was obviously not up to his best, he still was better than most leaders half his age. He had enormous experience, intelligence, and understanding of the forces that shape the world. My emotions were mixed as I said good-bye to him. I was honored to have met one of the world's greatest leaders, but I was saddened by the realization that he would soon be passing from the scene.

1954 ELECTIONS

It seemed as if the Eisenhower administration had hardly begun to settle in before it was time to fight the 1954 off-year election campaign. The Republicans' razor-thin majority of one in the Senate was the most obvious target for the Democrats, but they also had their sights set on regaining control of the House of Representatives.

It was clear that Eisenhower planned to remain above the battle. He said he did not want a heavy campaign schedule because he did not think it wise for the President to go on a barnstorming trip, and because at sixty-three he now needed more rest.

If Eisenhower had no taste for this campaign, I had little for it myself. In the eighteen months of his administration Eisenhower had maintained his personal popularity, but the party was as divided as it had been before he was elected. Indeed, the passing of Bob Taft and the ascent of Joe McCarthy had deepened the divisions within Republican ranks. The Democrats were making the most of our problems. Adlai Stevenson led the charge, telling his listeners that the Republican Party had "as many wings as a boardinghouse chicken" and that "caught between contradiction, apathy, and McCarthy, they act as confused as a blind dog in a meathouse." I led the counterattack, but my heart wasn't in the battle. Once again I realized how much the agony of the fund crisis had stripped the fun and excitement from campaigning for me.

Requests for campaign appearances on behalf of Republican congressmen and senators began flooding my office. They were worried about the effect Eisenhower's refusal to campaign would have on our chances. I decided that there was no choice for me but to lead the party in the election, so I threw myself into two full months of intensive campaigning. It was not a decision I made lightly, or enthusiastically.

As I made my first campaign trips into the country I was surprised to find how complacent the Republican organizers were. On September 19 I placed a conference call to Brownell, Summerfield, and Jerry Persons. I told them, "Don't give the President the idea that things are in good shape. They're not. If we don't get moving and get the issues working for us instead of killing us, we're going to lose fifty seats."

After a few weeks of campaigning around the country I decided I had to remove some of the simplistic ideas held by many of the political amateurs in the administration and even by some of the professionals at the Republican National Committee.

I wrote a memorandum to RNC Chairman Len Hall setting out some of my ideas. As far as the issues were concerned, I felt that we should be concentrating on the ones where we were strong and the Democrats were weak. "These are peace, communism, corruption, taxes," I wrote. "They are not unemployment and farm prices. If the voters on election day are thinking of unemployment and/or farm prices primarily, we will lose the election without any question. This is not because our position on these issues is not right and not because it is not salable if we had enough time to talk to each individual personally, but because these two issues are *defensive* from our standpoint while the others are *offensive* for our side and *defensive* for the other side."

I also addressed the McCarthy issue in terms of its impact on the party and the election:

1. Our handling of the issue has gained us no new support. Those people who were against us because they thought we tolerated McCarthy were against us anyway and will continue to vote on the other side because they consider the ADA [Americans for Democratic Action] gang as more anti-McCarthy than we are.

2. We have lost considerable support among Democrats whose reason for voting for us in '46, '50, and '52 was their distrust of the Truman administration on the handling of the domestic communist issue.

3. The greatest damage has been done in splitting the Republicans and causing apathy in our ranks.

We can remedy to an extent the situations mentioned in 2 and 3 by emphasizing vigorously the Administration's anticommunist record and by attacking the other side for its past and present softness on the issue.

In discussing the communist issue during the campaign I emphasized as I had in 1950 and 1952 that the question as far as our opponents were concerned was not one of loyalty but of judgment. On a number of occasions I categorically dissociated the administration from McCarthy's reckless charge that the Democratic Party was the party of treason. I said, "There is only one party of treason in the United States—the Communist Party."

Eisenhower spent the first month of the campaign at the Denver White House. After a few hours of work in the morning he would golf in the afternoon. He followed my travels and activities closely, and at the end of September he wrote me a very warm letter: "Good reports have been reaching me from all parts of the country as a result of your intensive—and I am sure exhaustive—speaking tour. . . . Please don't think that I am not unaware that I have done little to lighten your load. On the contrary, I am, in point of fact, constantly suggesting other places for you to visit. You will have to consider these burdens I impose upon you the penalty for being such an excellent and persuasive speaker. One thing that is coming out of this is that you are constantly becoming better and more favorably known to the American public. This is all to the good."

As Election Day neared, the polls showed that the Democrats and Republicans were almost evenly matched. The campaign became increasingly bitter. As my campaigning seemed to be particularly effective, Stevenson and other Democrats, led by DNC Chairman Stephen Mitchell, zeroed in on me with a barrage of attacks. In a mocking reference to my successful good will tour in the Far East in 1953, Stevenson called my campaigning an "ill will tour." Mitchell, less elegant than Stevenson, called me a liar. The Washington *Post* and half a dozen other Democratic papers charged that I had taken over McCarthy's tactics—Stevenson characterized my campaigning as "McCarthyism in a white collar." I counterattacked hard, accusing Stevenson of trying to dismiss serious charges with quips and adding that he had derisively made a "typically snide and snobbish innuendo toward the millions of Americans who work in our shops and factories."

I continued to campaign right up to the wire. In the seven weeks between September 15 and November 2, I flew nearly 26,000 miles to visit 95 cities in 30 states, campaigning on behalf of 186 House, Senate, and gubernatorial candidates. During the last three weeks of the campaign I slept no more than five hours a night.

A few days before the election, Eisenhower made one of the typically gracious gestures that bound people so closely to him. At a time when I was exhausted and more than a little frustrated that very few of the Republican leaders seemed to be working as hard to win this election as I was, a letter arrived from the White House.

October 27, 1954

Dear Dick:

Whenever my burdens tend to feel unduly heavy, I admire all the more the tremendous job you have done since the opening of the present campaign. You have personally carried a back-breaking load of hard, tedious, day by day and state by state campaigning. And in doing so you have been undismayed by problems of time, distance, and physical effort.

I know we share the urgent hope that there may be returned to the Congress a Republican majority that will work with the Executive Branch in completing the program that we believe is in the best interests of all America. No man could have done more effective work than you to further that hope. Whatever the outcome next Tuesday, I can find no words to express my deep appreciation of the contribution you have made toward that goal.

Please tell Pat, too, that she has aroused my admiration as an able campaigner; there is no question but that she is the most charming of the lot.

With warm regard,

As ever,
D. E.

Pat and I stayed home election night, November 2. We sat together in front of the fireplace, and for a while I got up every few minutes to take calls from the campaign headquarters at the Republican National Committee. The news was mixed, and about what I expected. We lost 16 seats in the House and 2 seats in the Senate. This was substantially less than the usual off-year election loss for the party in power: during the previous fifty years, the average loss had been 40 in the House and 4 in the Senate. However, historical comparisons were small comfort. The Democrats regained control of the House and Senate; and Eisenhower, despite his enormous personal popularity, had to deal with a Democratic Congress for the last six years of his presidency.

At the first Cabinet meeting after the election, most members who were new to politics were downcast. I said that the important thing was to learn from this experience so that we would not repeat our mistakes. I pointed out that while we had fielded many outstanding candidates, we had also put forward some notably unexceptional ones. "There were just too many turkeys running on the Republican ticket," I told the Cabinet.

Then I took a little wind-up toy drummer from my pocket, released the catch, and put it on the Cabinet table. Everyone watched, puzzled, as the little fellow picked out a zigzag course across the polished surface and the sharp sound of his drum filled the room. "Gentlemen," I said, "we should take a lesson from this: this is no time to be depressed, and we have got to keep beating the drum about our achievements." Eisenhower beamed.

The 1954 election raised some disturbing questions for me. It was clear that Eisenhower was going to maintain his President-of-all-the-people posture and that, as long as we were a team, it would be my job to do the hard partisan campaigning. The prospect of having to go through it all again in another two years was depressing. It was also clear that I was going to continue to be the prime target for the Democrats' attacks. Eisenhower's popularity was too great and his above-the-battle strategy too successful to make attacking him worthwhile. But I was out front, a target of opportunity, and the more effective I was as a campaigner, the more determined many of the Democrats and their supporters in the media became to clobber me.

Although the fund crisis had thickened my skin, I still resented being portrayed as a demagogue or a liar or as the sewer-dwelling denizen of Herblock cartoons in the Washington *Post*. As the attacks became more personal, I sometimes wondered where party loyalty left off and masochism began. The girls were reaching an impressionable age, and neither Pat nor I wanted their father to become the perennial bad guy of American politics.

During the last week of the 1954 campaign, when I was so tired that I could hardly remember what it felt like to be rested, I decided that this would be my last campaign. I began to think more and more about what Murray Chotiner had said almost two and a half years earlier at the convention in Chicago: I should pretty much be able to write my own ticket after retiring from the vice presidency at age forty-four. By the time I made a nationally televised broadcast on election eve, I had decided not to run again in 1956 unless exceptional circumstances intervened to change my mind.

On Election Day, as we flew back to Washington, I took out my brief case. A folder on top contained the several pages of handwritten notes I had made for the election-eve broadcast. Chotiner was in the seat next to me, and I handed them to him. "Here's my last campaign speech, Murray," I said to him. "You might like to keep it as a souvenir. It's the last one, because after this I am through with politics."

THE HEART ATTACK

September 24, 1955, was a hot Indian summer day in Washington. Around 5:30, I sat down to look over the *Evening Star*, and I noted a small item from Denver on the front page that the President was suffering from a slight case of indigestion. This was not unusual for him, and I turned to the sports pages without giving it a second thought. I was looking over the baseball scores when the phone rang.

"Dick, this is Jim Hagerty," the familiar voice said. "I have some bad news—the President has had a coronary."

"Are they sure?" I asked.

"We are absolutely sure," Hagerty replied. He had no further information, and we agreed that he would call me again as soon as he learned anything more. At the end of the conversation he said, "Dick, let me know where you can be reached at all times."

For several minutes I sat motionless, absorbing the full impact of the news. Not only was I concerned about Eisenhower's health; I was going to have to think about my own conduct in an unprecedented national crisis.

I called Bill Rogers, who was Acting Attorney General

while Herb Brownell was in Spain, and asked him if he could come over. Rogers arrived just ahead of the reporters and cameramen who had rushed to our house as soon as Eisenhower's heart attack was announced in Denver. We agreed that we should not let them know I was there. I thought it was important that I not be seen or quoted until I had more information from Denver.

Rogers suggested that I spend the night at his home. He called his wife to pick us up and asked her to park on a side street behind my house. Fifteen minutes later Adele Rogers drove up in her Pontiac convertible, and Bill and I slipped out the side door. We walked quickly through my neighbor's backyard and piled into the car.

The Rogers house was well off the main road in Bethesda, Maryland. As soon as we arrived, I put in a call to Denver.

For the first time I learned that the attack had been officially diagnosed as a "mild" coronary thrombosis. Chances for recovery were good, but it was still too early to be sure of anything. After long discussions with Rogers and Jerry Persons and telephone conversations with various Cabinet members, it was decided that we would continue carrying on the nation's business as a united team until Eisenhower was able to return to his duties.

As I lay awake that night, I considered my future course. Assuming the best—that Eisenhower would be back on the job within a few weeks —it would be foolish for me to do anything that the press could in any way interpret as being self-serving. Assuming the worst—that Eisenhower died or was completely incapacitated—there would be no question about my succession to the presidency; and if that happened it would be even more important that my conduct beforehand be above question. In the most likely situation—that Eisenhower would not be able to return for several weeks or months and a determination would have to be made about my taking over some of his responsibilities—it was equally important that nothing I did made it appear that I was seeking his power.

I knew that there would be many attempts to drive a wedge between Sherman Adams and me. Adams, the powerful Assistant to the President who was the White House

Chief of Staff, was known as Eisenhower's most devoted and selfless staff member. The rumor had even spread around Washington that Adams's first words when he arrived back at the White House were: "It's quite a surprise to come back here and suddenly find yourself the President."

By Sunday morning I knew that I could not avoid the press any longer. But a press conference might appear self-serving, so I decided to let the reporters accompany Pat and me to church and then invite some of them home afterward for an informal chat.

We settled down in the living room, and I told them the little I knew about Eisenhower's condition. I described the team system he had created and said that I expected it to function smoothly until his return.

The reporters, of course, were after hard news, not talk about team spirit. They were looking for a statement about the political implications of Eisenhower's illness. There had already been speculation about whether Eisenhower would run again in 1956. A Gallup poll at the beginning of September had shown him preferred by 61 percent of the voters when matched up against Stevenson. Another Gallup poll taken at about the same time indicated that if Eisenhower did not run, I was the first choice among Republicans for the presidential nomination. I politely but firmly refused any questions about the political significance of Eisenhower's illness.

On Monday night Sherman Adams, Len Hall, Jerry Persons, Hall's press aide Lou Guylay, Rogers, and I met at Rogers's house to discuss the political aspects of the situation. Adams sat slightly apart from the rest of us. Whenever a question was addressed to him, he launched into a description of the fishing in Scotland. Finally it became clear that either he was determined not to engage in any substantive discussion until he could get to Denver and see Eisenhower's condition for himself, or else he was in something close to a state of shock.

I said that our main task was to prevent any scramble for the presidential nomination, at least until Eisenhower recovered and had had a chance to express his feelings about running again. Earlier that day Len Hall had flatly told reporters who had cornered him that the 1956 Republican ticket would be the same winning one as in 1952: Ike and Dick. Despite that necessary public show of optimism, I do not think any of us in that room believed that Eisenhower would run again, even if he recovered completely.

During the next two weeks I presided over various meetings in the White House, including the regular Cabinet and National Security Council meetings. I sat in the Vice President's chair, opposite the President's, and I was careful to act more as moderator than director. I signed several ceremonial documents "in behalf of the President," but I continued to work out of my office at the Capitol rather than in the White House. During those weeks I made it a point to visit Cabinet members in their own offices whenever a meeting was necessary, rather than asking them to come to my office. Despite all my precautions along these lines, and despite my determination to have as little to do with the press as I reasonably could, one or two members of the Cabinet seemed to feel that I was seeking publicity.

On October 8, exactly two weeks after Eisenhower's heart attack, I flew to Denver to see him. I was the first official visitor; after my visit the Cabinet members saw him according to rank. I was startled to see how pale and thin he was. But it was immediately clear that his mind was as sharp as ever, and he was able to talk about his heart attack with great detachment, although he had obviously been through an ordeal. "It hurt like hell, Dick," he told me. "I never let Mamie know how much it hurt."

Forty-eight days after his heart attack Eisenhower flew back to Washington. Thousands of cheering people lined the downtown streets in the autumn sunshine to cheer him as he returned to the White House. The country seemed to breathe a sigh of relief. There was no more need to worry—Ike was back.

RUNNING FOR RE-ELECTION: 1956

Since the 1954 campaign I had been considering leaving politics. I knew that Pat wanted to return to California. The only thing that made me hesitate was the unexpected situation created by Eisenhower's heart attack. Whereas before I had assumed that he would run again in 1956, now I was not at all sure. If he did not, I would be the next in line for the presidential nomination. A Gallup presidential preference poll after Eisenhower's heart attack, based on the assumption he would not be a candidate, showed me leading Earl Warren, 28 percent to 24 percent, followed by Dewey and Stassen with 10 percent each.

On December 26, 1955, Eisenhower called me into the Oval Office. He said that he had been giving a lot of thought to the coming election, and he wondered whether I ought to run for Vice President again or whether I might do better to accept a Cabinet post instead. He said that a Cabinet position such as Secretary of Defense would give me the kind of administrative experience, so important for a President, that the vice presidency did not offer. He pointed out that Herbert Hoover had been able to use his position as Secretary of Commerce to build a national reputation and a successful candidacy.

I was taken aback by this suggestion, although he seemed to be making it in a friendly and sincere spirit. He said that he was disappointed that other suitable candidates for the presidency had not emerged from the party during the last few years, and he referred to some of Gallup's trial heats in which Stevenson beat me by a fairly wide margin. He said it was too bad that my popularity had not grown more during the last three years.

For the first time I began to understand what was behind this conversation. Eisenhower's staff or his friends had evidently been sowing doubts in his mind, suggesting not only that I might lose if I ran on my own, but that I might be a drag on the ticket if I were his running mate again. It was hard not to feel that I was being set up, since more recent polls than the ones he was referring to showed me doing considerably better.

A few weeks later we had another conversation which covered the same ground. Eisenhower once again expressed his opinion that my own political future would be better served by taking a Cabinet post than by running again for Vice President. He seemed to be expecting a reply, and for a moment I felt as if the clock had been turned back to the fund crisis, when he had paused on the telephone so that I could offer him my resignation from the ticket. I had the same reaction now: as Vice President, I fully accepted that I was his to choose or his to dismiss. But I did not feel that my getting off the ticket would be the best thing for him or for the party, and I was not going to offer to do so.

As in 1952, my silence put the ball back into Eisenhower's court. Finally I said, "If you believe your own candidacy and your administration would be better served with me off the ticket, you tell me what you want me to do and I'll do it. I want to do what is best for you."

"No, I think we've got to do what's best for you," he replied.

Any doubts about Eisenhower's motives were removed when Foster Dulles independently initiated the same discussion and suggested that I might be named Secretary of Defense or succeed him as Secretary of State when he resigned. I was sure that Dulles had my best interests at heart.

From the point of view of historical experience, there was considerable merit in Eisenhower's and Dulles's suggestion. But neither of them took into account the derogatory way the media would have interpreted such a course or how it would have upset the many Republicans who still considered me Eisenhower's principal link with party orthodoxy.

Eisenhower had made a remarkable physical recovery, and within a short time after his return to Washington he resumed his regular schedule. But, as with many who have suffered heart attacks, his brush with death left him subject to debilitating bouts of depression. He would sit immobile for long periods of time, brooding silently about the future. Mamie Eisenhower was especially insistent that her husband not run for re-election. Her arguments ranged from the highly emotional to the coldly logical.

By the end of January, however, Eisenhower had in fact reached a tentative decision to run, which was strengthened by an excellent medical report on February 14. I think he decided to run again for several reasons. As in 1952 he felt it was his duty to his country. Also, he could not abide the idea that Adlai Stevenson might be his successor, and he was not confident of the election of any other Republican. I believe too that Eisenhower had a desire to finish what he had begun. He had strong feelings about what the Republican Party should be, and he knew that he had not been able to accomplish much in this area during his first term. He would need another four years to leave a lasting imprint on the party and on the nation.

Eisenhower declared his intention to run at a press conference on February 29. He invited a small group to join him in the Oval Office that night for the televised speech he was going to make announcing his decision. Jim Hagerty, Len Hall, Jerry Persons, Milton Eisenhower, and I sat on the sofas in front of the fireplace while Eisenhower sat at the desk facing the camera. When he had finished we all shook hands, and he invited us up to the Family Quarters for a drink. "I'll need some moral support with Mrs. Ike," he said with a sheepish grin.

As we sat in the living room at the end of the West Hall, Eisenhower was in a strangely subdued mood. He was glad that the decision had finally been made and announced, but he did not relish the campaigning that would now begin or even the prospect of four more years of the burdens of the presidency. "At least," he said, "I can say that I have done my duty."

Eisenhower had gone through a difficult period reaching his decision, and he had enjoyed the drama of announcing it. But I think the reaction of the reporters took him by surprise. He immediately had to respond to a barrage of political questions, and the first one had to do with me.

Q: Mr. President, since your answer is affirmative, would you again want Vice President Nixon as your running mate?
A: As a matter of fact, I wouldn't mention the vice presidency in spite of my tremendous admiration for Mr. Nixon, for this reason: I believe it is traditional that the Vice President is not nominated until after a presidential candidate is nominated; so I think that we will have to wait to see who the Republican convention nominates, and then it will be proper to give an expression on that point.

Responding to a follow-up question, he added: "I will say nothing more about it. I have said that my admiration and my respect for Vice President Nixon is unbounded. He has been for me a loyal and dedicated associate, and a successful one. I am very fond of him, but I am going to say no more about it."

I think that once the question was raised, Eisenhower had three basic reactions to having me as his running mate in 1956. First, his rule of thumb for making all political judgments was understandably never to do anything that would adversely affect his own chances of winning.

Second, while Eisenhower believed that he owed me the loyalty due a staunch and hard-working subordinate, and while he knew that I had supported him in situations that had clearly been against my own political interests, he did not feel that this loyalty required any special future commitment as far as the vice presidency was concerned.

Third, Eisenhower was used to the military system, in which men advanced by taking on the next toughest job and doing it well. He did not think in terms of grooming a successor or having a protégé—that was alien to the general-staff concept that everyone should serve the commanding general with equally unselfish fervor. When Eisenhower said that other candidates would be equally acceptable to him, he meant precisely that.

Further evidence of White House staff intrigue came when *Newsweek* reported Eisenhower's suggestion that I take a Cabinet position. I never could positively trace the source of the story, but it had come from a White House insider. It was hard to believe that something so sensitive could leak without Eisenhower's approval. And if Eisenhower had approved the leak, perhaps I had been misreading him all along—perhaps he *was* determined to get me off the ticket and could not understand why I had not taken the hint.

The first question at Eisenhower's next news conference on March 7 concerned this *Newsweek* story.

Q: Mr. President, there have been some published reports that some of your advisers are urging you to dump Vice President Nixon from the Republican ticket this year; and, secondly, that you yourself have suggested to Mr. Nixon that he consider standing aside this time and, perhaps, take a Cabinet post. Can you tell us whether there is anything to those reports?

A: Well, now, as to the first one, I will promise you this much: if anyone ever has the effrontery to come in and urge me to dump somebody that I respect as I do Vice President Nixon, there will be more commotion around my office than you have noticed yet.

Second, I have not presumed to tell the Vice President what he should do with his own future. . . .

The only thing I have asked him to do is to chart out his own course, and tell me what he would like to do. I have never gone beyond that.

"Chart out his own course" immediately became a catchphrase for the columnists during the next several weeks. Everyone had his own interpretation of what Eisenhower meant, but it was generally taken to indicate varying degrees of indifference toward me, or even an attempt to put some distance between us.

By this time my disillusionment with the way Eisenhower was handling the matter and my lack of a burning desire to be Vice President began to affect my own attitude. After Eisenhower's press conference, I took a page of notepaper and drafted an announcement that I would not be a candidate in 1956. I mentioned it to Vic Johnston, the chief of staff of the Senatorial Campaign Committee, when he was in my office later that afternoon. Within a few hours, he was back with Len Hall and Jerry Persons. They said that if I announced I was withdrawing, the Republican Party would be split in two.

I said that it just is not possible in politics for a Vice President to "chart out his own course," and that if Eisenhower did not want me on the ticket I was damned if I was going to fight to stay on it. "It's up to him if he wants me," I said. "I can only assume that if he puts it this way, this must be his way of saying he'd prefer someone else."

Len Hall tried to calm me down. "That's not what he meant at all," he said. "Damn it, Dick, you and I have talked about this a hundred times if we've talked about it once. We all know that if this was anyone else it'd be different. But this is Ike, and you can't apply the kind of politically sophisticated standards to him that you do to anybody else."

I agreed to withhold any announcement for at least a few weeks. I later found out that about this same time Eisenhower himself had become unhappy with the way the story had developed and held several meetings in an effort to decide what he should do. Charlie Jones, president of Richfield Oil, told me about a small stag dinner at the White House during this period at which Eisenhower raised the question of the vice presidency. Some of the guests said that they thought he should make a change. They argued that if there was any possibility that I might lose Eisenhower any votes he should drop me like a hot potato. Jones was Eisenhower's contemporary and had been his friend for many years; he was one of the few who still called him Ike. After my critics had had their say, Jones looked across the table and said, "Ike, what in the hell does a man have to do to get your support? Dick Nixon has done everything you asked him to do. He has taken on the hard jobs that many of your other associates have run away from. For you not to support him now would be the most ungrateful thing that I can possibly think of."

On March 13, the first primary election of the 1956 campaign was held in New Hampshire.

That night Pat and I were having dinner with Alice Longworth. When we arrived at her big Victorian house on Massachusetts Avenue, she met us at the top of the stairs and said, "Have you been listening to the radio? There is a write-in for you in New Hampshire."

Mrs. Longworth could never resist anything political, and we were rushed through dinner. As we sipped coffee and listened to the radio in her drawing room filled with animal skins and photographs and other mementos of her father, I learned that my write-in vote was the big story of the New Hampshire primary.

Eisenhower could be well satisfied with the 56,464 voters who had gone out to mark the box next to his name on the ballot. But the big surprise was that almost 23,000 voters had written in my name on their ballots. I was elated, and I wondered what effect the news would have on the President.

When Eisenhower was asked about the New Hampshire results at his next press conference, he inched as near to an outright endorsement as he possibly could.

> Well, I will make this comment: apparently there are lots of people in New Hampshire that agree with what I have told you about Dick Nixon. . . .
>
> Anyone who attempts to drive a wedge of any kind between Dick Nixon and me has just as much chance as if he tried to drive it between my brother and me. . . .
>
> I want to say again what I said last week or a week before; I will say it in exactly the terms I mean: I am very happy that Dick Nixon is my friend. I am very happy to have him as an associate in government. I would be happy to be on any political ticket in which I was a candidate with him.
>
> Now, if those words aren't plain, then it is merely because people can't understand the plain unvarnished truth.
>
> I have nothing further to add.

Then, midway through a news conference on April 25, Eisenhower was asked, "Some time ago, Mr. President, you told us that you had asked Vice President Nixon to chart his own course and then report back to you. Has he done this?" Eisenhower replied, "Well, he hasn't reported back in the terms in which I used the expression that morning, no."

When I heard about this exchange, I knew the time had come to act. The more I thought about it, the more I was convinced that I could not get off the ticket without hurting Eisenhower more than helping him. I knew there would be no way to explain my leaving the ticket that would convince large numbers of party workers that I had not been dumped. These people were more my constituency than Eisenhower's and if they felt I had been treated badly they might decide to sit out the election.

Eisenhower had learned a great deal about politics since 1952, but he still did not like or understand those he called the "conservative party hacks" in Congress and in local Republican organizations throughout the country. He felt that they had no other place to go. But Eisenhower needed more than just their votes. He needed their whole-hearted organizational support.

I disagreed with the premise that Eisenhower could

pick up substantial votes from Democrats and independents by dropping me. Eisenhower now had a four-year record to run on and, particularly on economic, foreign policy, and internal security issues, that record was basically conservative. Stevenson would be the choice of liberals who preferred a softer line.

Early the next morning, April 26, I called the White House and said that I would like to see the President. That afternoon I sat across the desk from him in the Oval Office. "Mr. President," I said, "I would be honored to continue as Vice President under you. The only reason I waited this long to tell you was that I didn't want to do anything that would make you think I was trying to force my way onto the ticket if you didn't want me on it."

Eisenhower said that he was glad I felt that way and that he had wondered why I had taken so long to say so. He picked up the phone and asked for Jim Hagerty.

"Dick has just told me that he'll stay on the ticket," he told Hagerty. "Why don't you take him out right now and let him tell the reporters himself. And," he added, "you can tell them that I'm delighted by the news."

Eisenhower's imprimatur was enough to silence my potential opposition and bring his own White House staff in line—at least temporarily. Three weeks later, I received another unexpected boost when 32,878 voters wrote in my name on their ballots in the Oregon primary.

With the question of the ticket apparently settled, I expected smooth sailing until the convention. But a few weeks later Eisenhower was in the hospital being operated on for ileitis, and the whole question of his candidacy was superseded by concern about whether he would be able to complete his first term.

Jim Hagerty called me just before the operation began at about 2:30 A.M. on June 8. He told me that the President had just been put under anesthetic. "I know that this is really an unnecessary precaution," he said, "but I knew you would want to be ready in the unlikely case that any crisis arises in the next few hours, or, God forbid, that anything goes wrong with the operation."

Eisenhower recovered from the operation so quickly that there was never much doubt that he could complete his term. But the confidence that had grown up since his recovery from the heart attack was dealt a serious blow, and once again there was speculation about his running in November. Doubt rekindled presidential aspirations in some Republican breasts, and the fact that an eleventh-hour decision by Eisenhower not to run would make me the front-runner for the nomination resurrected the desire to "dump Nixon."

In the summer of 1956 Harold Stassen was at the height of his public stature as Eisenhower's "Secretary of Peace." As the President's Cabinet-level Adviser on Disarmament, Stassen was prominent and popular because of his conduct of the delicate Geneva disarmament talks with the Soviets.

Stassen had been among the first to call me in the days immediately following Eisenhower's heart attack the previous September pledging his support for the presidential nomination. But on July 20, 1956, he told Eisenhower that he had commissioned a private poll that showed I would lose more votes for Eisenhower than many other possible running mates, most particularly Governor Christian Herter of Massachusetts. Stassen thought Herter should be Eisenhower's running mate. Eisenhower later said that he found this proposal "astonishing"—not least because he knew that a week earlier Len Hall and Jim Hagerty had received a tentative agreement from Herter to place *my* name in nomination at the convention.

Eisenhower told Stassen that he was not going to dictate to the convention. Stassen asked if Eisenhower would mind if he tried to convince me to withdraw. "You are an American citizen, Harold," Eisenhower said, "and you are free to follow your own judgment in such matters."

Stassen thanked Eisenhower and left the White House. He called some of his supporters and told them that Eisenhower had said he supported an open convention. He then called Herter and told him that the President had been very interested in what he had to say and had authorized him to talk to Len Hall and me and to give us the benefit of his conclusions about the vice presidency. Stassen was clearly doing his best to edge all of us—Eisenhower, Herter, and me—to a confrontation. Three days later, on Monday, July 23, I received a letter from Stassen. In it he said: "I have concluded that I should do what I can to nominate Governor Chris Herter for Vice President at the coming convention. I sincerely hope that after careful reflection during the coming weeks you will conclude to join in supporting Chris Herter."

That afternoon Stassen called a press conference and announced his support for Herter's candidacy. Many supporters urged me to shrug off Stassen's effort as a clownish and transparent power play. But I knew that Stassen was a clever man and, except when blinded by ambition, a very able one. My concern was that if Stassen managed to raise doubts among the convention delegates in San Francisco about what Eisenhower really wanted, he might be able to create the kind of dangerously fluid situation in which the convention could be stampeded before the delegates realized what was happening. There were several potential vice presidential candidates eagerly waiting in the wings for just such a situation.

Eisenhower had left for an official visit to Panama immediately after his meeting with Stassen. He was furious when Stassen's press conference knocked his trip out of the headlines, and he authorized a curt statement: "The President pointed out to Mr. Stassen that, while he had every right as an individual to make any statement he so desired, it was also equally obvious that he could not make such a statement as a member of the President's official family." A few days later Sherman Adams informed Stassen that he would have to take a leave of absence from the White House staff if he intended to pursue his present course.

When Eisenhower arrived back in Washington things moved quickly. Herter called Sherman Adams to find out Eisenhower's real opinion of what had been happening. Adams told him that Eisenhower held him in very high esteem. If he wished to be a vice presidential candidate, that would be a matter of his own choosing, although Eisenhower had expected that in a second term he might be able to help in the international field and had already talked to Dulles about this possibility. That would not be possible, however, if Herter decided to run for Vice President. Herter said that he thought he would continue with his plans as they had stood prior to Stassen's press conference and arrange to place my name in nomination. He thought that would cut off any further attempts to make him Vice President.

Adams replied, "All right, let's consider it settled that way," and the Stassen bubble was burst less than twenty-four hours after it surfaced.

Herter telephoned Hall to tell him that he would nominate me, and Hall informed me of the news. Stassen was undeterred. He blithely told a press conference that the fact that Herter had been asked to nominate me was itself a confirmation of his very strong standing in the party. The next morning Herter held a press conference in Boston and formally endorsed me for the nomination.

On August 22, the day on which the convention was to select the vice presidential nominee, Stassen arrived at Eisenhower's suite at the St. Francis Hotel for an appointment with the President. He found himself confronted by Len Hall and Sherman Adams. Stassen produced a letter he planned to discuss with Eisenhower. It was an ultimatum addressed to Hall as Republican National Chairman, demanding that the nomination for Vice President be postponed until the next day.

Adams told Stassen that he could see Eisenhower only if he agreed beforehand to second my nomination and limit his conversation to informing the President of his agreement. Stassen finally seemed to get the message and agreed to accept these terms. Immediately after their meeting, Eisenhower held a televised news conference to announce: "Mr. Stassen called to see me a few minutes ago. . . . He said this morning that after several days here, he had become absolutely convinced that the majority of the delegates want Mr. Nixon. . . . He thought in order to get his own position clear before the convention and the American public, he was going to ask the convention chairman for permission this afternoon to second the nomination of the Vice President, Mr. Nixon, for renomination."

215

While Eisenhower was making his announcement in San Francisco, I was four hundred miles away in Whittier. Early that morning I had learned that my father had suffered a ruptured abdominal artery and was not expected to live. He had rallied a little by the time we got to Whittier, and I was able to talk with him even though he was in great pain and in an oxygen tent. He said that he was feeling much better and insisted that I get back to San Francisco. Flashes of his old temper broke through the pain and medication as he said, "You get back there, Dick, and don't let that Stassen pull any more last-minute funny business on you."

That afternoon I watched the convention on TV in my parents' living room and saw Chris Herter place my name in nomination. Half an hour later the curtain finally came down on the "dump Nixon" movement when I was renominated by a vote of 1,323 to 1.

The following morning the doctor said my father was much better; he was certain the thrill that came with my renomination was a major factor in his improvement. When I suggested canceling my acceptance speech to stay with him, he practically blew his top. So Pat and I returned to San Francisco and that afternoon, with some valuable help from my old friend Father John Cronin, I finished my acceptance speech just minutes before we had to leave for the convention hall.

We returned to Washington after the convention, but a few days later I was called back to California because of my father's illness. The doctor told me that it was only his determination to see me defeat Stassen and be renominated that had kept him alive this long. Now his condition was rapidly worsening. He knew that the end was near, so he gave my mother instructions for his funeral and asked to be allowed to die at home rather than in the hospital. He died at 8:25 P.M. on September 4, 1956.

After the drama of the preliminaries, most of the 1956 campaign was relatively tame. Eisenhower invited several hundred party leaders to a picnic at his farm in Gettysburg to kick off the campaign. Stevenson had already opened his with a stinging attack on the Eisenhower administration as a "ruthless" government "with a false front." Eisenhower, always thin-skinned about criticism and especially resentful of Stevenson, was furious and wanted to hit back. He phoned me on the morning of the picnic, and my note of our conversation shows the way he worked when he wanted something political done:

Diary

The President called me this morning and he said, "Look, you are going to speak up there at Gettysburg today."

He said, "Of course, everybody is now noting that you are talking the new high level. However, I think today you ought to take notice of some of these attacks that have been made on the administration and on me." He said, "I think that when Stevenson calls this administration racketeers and rascals, when they say we are heartless in dealing with the problems of the people and the problems of the farmers, when they say we have no peace and no prosperity, I want them to be called on it. I would like for you to do so and if you have to praise me that will be okay. I, of course, will be a little embarrassed by that but I know you have to do it to answer. I suggest something along the lines: Do you want to go back to war in order to have prosperity under the Democrats? After all, there were 9 million unemployed in 1939 before World War II, and also a great number before the Korean war.

I told him I agreed that Stevenson was swinging very wildly. He said, "Of course, it isn't necessary to attack him personally but we should point out that he is wrong."

I then talked to Brownell and he said, "I don't think we could win with a so-called high level campaign. It has to be fair but you have to take the opposition on. It has to be hard-hitting."

There was warm sunshine that afternoon as Eisenhower played host at his farm. Everyone gathered in a big tent set up on the lawn for the speeches. I followed Eisenhower's instructions and sank some solid barbs into Stevenson and the Democrats. Then he got up and began his speech by praising me. He said: "There is no man in the history of America who has had such a careful preparation as has Vice President Nixon for carrying out the duties of the presidency, if that duty should ever fall upon him."

Eisenhower came out to National Airport on the morning of September 18 to see Pat and me off on our first campaign swing. He said that this campaign should be based on the administration's record, and that there was no need to indulge in "the exaggerations of partisan political talk." In 1948 Harry Truman had campaigned to cries of "Give 'em hell." Eisenhower's parting admonition in 1956 was, "Give 'em heaven."

I followed this advice for the first two days of the campaign. The press corps was stupefied, and the Republican audiences disappointed, when I delivered serious, low-key speeches without any of the tough campaign rhetoric both groups looked forward to hearing from me. As Stevenson's attacks on Eisenhower and me grew increasingly shrill and irresponsible, I knew that it was only a matter of time before I would have to go on the offensive against him.

We arrived in Eugene, Oregon, for a big rally, and I gave my "give 'em heaven" speech. Once again I could tell that the audience felt let down. It was midnight before I went to bed, but I couldn't get to sleep. Around 5:30 in the morning I got out of bed and went into the living room of our suite to work on some hard-hitting additions to my basic speech. Suddenly I felt as if a great weight had been lifted from me. I had not realized how frustrating it had been to suppress the normal partisan instincts and campaign with one arm tied behind my back while Stevenson bombarded us with malicious ridicule and wild charges. I went over to the grand piano in one corner of the suite and began playing Brahms's Rhapsody in G. I had just launched into Sinding's "Rustle of Spring" when Pat came in and said, "What on earth are you doing? Dick, you'll wake up the whole hotel—it isn't even 7:30 yet."

My new speech delighted audiences, and for the first time the campaign began to catch fire.

The underlying issue of the campaign was still Eisenhower's health and the fact that if anything happened to him I would become President. From the start I came under intense and bitter fire. Describing the Democratic National Convention in Chicago in August, *Newsweek* stated:

> From the opening crack of the gavel in Chicago until the last lusty cheer echoed and died, Nixon was the target. Speakers pronounced his name with a sneer, as though it were an obscene epithet. He was attacked as "the vice-hatchet man," "the White House pet midget," a traveler of "the low road." . . . In attacking Nixon, the Democrats, in effect, were asking: "Do you want a man like this in the White House? Remember, he'll be President if you re-elect Mr. Eisenhower and Ike dies."

Stevenson had told the delegates: "The American people have the solemn obligation to consider with the utmost care who will be their President if the elected President is prevented by a higher will from serving his full term."

He pointed out that seven of our Presidents had come into office "as a result of such an indirect selection." He pulled out all stops in a speech in Flint, Michigan, on October 17:

> There is no man who can safely say he knows where the Vice President stands. This is a man of many masks. Who can say they have seen his real face? . . .
> In these critical days, America cannot afford the risk of having a President or a Vice President who treats a tragic war as an occasion for political demagoguery, and who spreads ill will instead of good will abroad.

He described the vice presidency as "this nation's life insurance policy," and he concluded that the election of the Eisenhower-Nixon ticket would mean that the nation would "go for four years uninsured."

On October 4, I made a nationwide television broadcast answering questions piped in live from newsmen in eight cities. This experiment proved so successful that I used the televised question-and-answer format in every election campaign until 1972.

Even though television was beginning to come into its own as a campaign tool—by 1956, 73 percent of American homes had a television set—we still mounted an old-fashioned down-to-the-wire effort that was as physically punishing as all the others had been. Pat and I made three cross-country campaign sweeps in a chartered plane. Because I was carrying the main load of campaigning for the administration, and because I myself was an issue in the campaign, I was accompanied by the largest press contingent ever assigned to a vice presidential candidate. I held at least one and sometimes two press conferences every working day. The New York *Times* reported that I was "adroitly . . . running a campaign that has to be seen to be believed."

From the start of the campaign, the polls had fairly consistently shown Eisenhower and me ahead. In the final days and even hours of the campaign, three foreign crises erupted that effectively finished off what few hopes of winning Stevenson might have had. The American people rally around the President in times of international crisis, and this was no exception. On October 19 a brief revolt broke out in Communist Poland, and on October 23 the Hungarian rebellion began in Budapest and quickly spread through the country before Soviet troops rolled in to crush it. I called Nikita Khrushchev the "Butcher of Budapest"—a sobriquet that stuck and was repeated around the world. Then, on October 29, Israel invaded Egypt after several months of dispute over access to the Suez Canal. On November 5, the day before our election, British and French paratroops landed in Egypt to support the Israeli invasion and to protect their own rights there.

Eisenhower and Dulles put heavy public pressure on Britain, France, and Israel to withdraw their forces from Suez. In retrospect I believe that our actions were a serious mistake. Nasser became even more rash and aggressive than before, and the seeds of another Mideast war were planted. The most tragic result was that Britain and France were so humiliated and discouraged by the Suez crisis that they lost the will to play a major role on the world scene. From this time forward the United States would by necessity be forced to "go it alone" in the foreign policy leadership of the free world. I have often felt that if the Suez crisis had not arisen during the heat of a presidential election campaign a different decision would have been made.

Stevenson made a desperate election-eve speech, going even further than he had before, bluntly reminding the voters that, because of Eisenhower's health, his election would probably mean voting me into the White House:

> Distasteful as this matter is, I must say bluntly that every piece of scientific evidence we have, every lesson of history and experience, indicates that a Republican victory tomorrow would mean that Richard M. Nixon probably would be President of this country within the next four years. . . .
>
> Distasteful as it is, this is the truth, the central truth, about the most fateful decision that American people have to make tomorrow.
>
> I have confidence in that decision.

Many considered this a crude and tasteless appeal, and it probably lost Stevenson more support than it gained. When the votes were counted the next night, the Eisenhower-Nixon ticket won 57 percent of the vote, carrying forty-one of the forty-eight states.

On election night Pat and I joined the Eisenhowers at a victory celebration at the Sheraton-Park Hotel. I had rarely seen Eisenhower in higher spirits; he was genuinely elated at what looked like a real landslide from the moment the first fragmentary returns started coming in. By the time the returns from the Midwest were tallied, however, it was clear that Eisenhower's personal victory was not going to spill over into the state or congressional races. Despite one of the biggest landslides in presidential history, Eisenhower was the first President in 108 years who could not carry at least one house of Congress for his party.

Eisenhower simply could not understand how this could happen, just as I found it difficult to understand when it happened to me in 1972. He became more and more subdued as we sat there slowly sipping highballs and watching television for the latest returns. "You know why this is happening, Dick?" he said. "It's all those damned mossbacks and hard-shell conservatives we've got in the party. I think that what we need is a new party."

This was not the first time that Eisenhower had blamed the conservatives for the party's problems. In many cases he was justified in being exasperated and annoyed by the splits within the party; in others, he lacked the tolerance for diversity that someone more schooled in politics would have had. Eisenhower's thoughts turned to the crowd waiting for us in the ballroom below and he said, "You know, I think I will talk to them about Modern Republicanism." "Modern Republicanism" was a popular phrase at that time, particularly in the press, for the kind of liberalism that commentators described as the antithesis of Taftite conservatism.

I thought it would be a mistake for Eisenhower to talk about as controversial a party issue as Modern Republicanism on an occasion like this and risk offending the party regulars downstairs and across the country. But I also knew that Eisenhower would say whatever he wanted.

Stevenson conceded at about 1:30 A.M., and Eisenhower went downstairs and said that his victory was a victory for Modern Republicanism. As I had feared, many party regulars took these words either as a boast that he had won the victory by himself, or as a threat that those within the party who did not share his views would gradually be replaced by those who did. There was just enough truth in both interpretations to start the second term off on a slightly sour note in some Republican circles.

A few days before the end of the year I received a letter from the White House.

Dear Dick:

As both 1956 and our first administration draw to a close, I want to tell you, in a personal letter, what I have so often expressed publicly. In these last four years you have brought to the office of the Vice President a real stature that formerly it had not known; you

222

have proved yourself an able and popular "Ambassador" to our friends in many other parts of the world; and you have worked tirelessly and effectively to interpret to the people of America—and to forward— the policies of the administration. For all of this I am personally indebted to you, and gratified that you have so capably filled all of my expectations.

Also—somewhat to my chagrin—I find that while I have thanked what seem to be thousands of people from Maine to California for their help in the political campaign, I have never expressed my appreciation to you for carrying the brunt of the state-by-state effort. I know you were rewarded as, of course, I could not fail to be, by the verdict of the voters. But I do want to express to you, and to your loyal and overworked staff, my tremendous gratitude for all that you did to bring about the final result.

With affectionate regard to Pat and the children, and, as always, my best to yourself,

As ever,
Dwight Eisenhower

OPERATION MERCY

The Hungarian uprising of 1956 captured the sympathy of the American people. In November and December 1956, after crushing the last flickers of rebellion, the Soviets reimposed their brutal and oppressive control over the Hungarian people. Many tried to escape across the border into Austria, and, to the great embarrassment of the determinedly neutral Austrian government, the number of refugees soon reached several thousand a day.

The Soviets and their Hungarian puppets accused the United States of having provoked the uprising by assuring the Hungarian rebels that we would aid them if they revolted against their government. Much to our dismay and embarrassment some of the freedom fighters seemed to agree. They blamed us for first encouraging them to revolt and then sitting back while the Soviets cut them down.

On December 13, Eisenhower called me back to Washington from a brief pre-Christmas holiday Pat and I were taking in New York and asked me to meet with Dulles to discuss some ideas they had about this problem. Eisenhower had offered asylum to 21,500 of the more than 100,000 refugees who had already escaped to Austria, and more were pouring over the borders each day. This had not been a particularly popular decision. There was considerable opposition in Congress to letting in any refugees at a time of domestic unemployment, and public opinion was not yet strongly committed to the humanitarian aspects of the situation. Because Eisenhower had acted under temporary provisions of the existing law, he wanted more permanent legislation to handle the refugee question. He also hoped more would be permitted to enter the United States.

Dulles said that Eisenhower wanted me to lead an emergency mission to Austria that would focus national attention on the plight of the refugees. Then, when I returned, I could prepare a report that could be used to buttress the case for new legislation. My mission would be called Operation Mercy.

Partly from fear that an embarrassing diplomatic incident might develop and partly because of their characteristic desire for orderliness, the Austrians pretty much sanitized my scheduled visit to the refugee camp at the frontier town of Andau. I met a few refugees, but most of the people I talked to were Austrian or Red Cross officials.

That night the Austrian government gave a dinner in my honor. When we returned to the American Embassy, I told our ambassador, Llewellyn "Tommy" Thompson, that I wanted to go to the border and get a real look at what was happening there. Thompson arranged for a car, and, together with Bill Rogers, Congressman Bob Wilson of California, and Bob King, my administrative assistant, I went back to Andau.

In the bleak refugee center at the border we saw the real agony and the heroism of the Hungarian freedom fighters.

Some of those who had just escaped that night were university students who spoke English, and they told us about the suffering that was still going on in Budapest and throughout Hungary.

"Do you feel that the Voice of America and Radio Free

Europe played a part in encouraging the revolution?" I asked. Looks of surprise came over their faces as my deliberately undiplomatic question was translated. One of them blurted out the answer— "Yes."

I was later told that that simple exchange broke the ice and convinced the refugees that I wasn't going to try to sweep their situation under the carpet.

One of the refugee leaders told me that many people escaped through the deep forests that covered the border for some miles to the north. Once across, the refugees would wait in the barn of some friendly farmer until they could be brought to the refugee center. He asked me if I would like to go along while they picked up that night's "crop," as he called it. I said that I would; he smiled and said, "Well, sir, you will have to travel the way we do."

I climbed into the back of a large hay wagon coupled to a tractor. We left the lights of the refugee center behind, following the winding road that ran between the forest on one side and the farms on the other. At one farm, we picked up a young man who said he had hidden for three days before he had finally made a dash across the border about five hours before.

It was after six o'clock in the morning by the time we got back to the center, and I could only say some hasty farewells before the long drive back to Vienna. After a quick shower and change at the ambassador's residence, I was only a few minutes late for a nine o'clock meeting.

I returned to Washington on Christmas Eve, and by working through the holiday I was able to submit my report to Eisenhower on New Year's Day.

I urged that the McCarran-Walter Act regulating immigration be amended so that we could make a flexible response to this situation. I said that it would not be wise or realistic to tie ourselves down to either a fixed number of refugees or a fixed percentage of the total number. "I believe that the countries which accept these refugees will find that rather than having assumed a liability, they have acquired a valuable national asset," I wrote. I was disappointed by the hardhearted attitude many Americans seemed to have toward the Hungarian refugees. I felt the same way when there was similar resistance to the Cuban refugees in 1959 and to the Vietnamese refugees in 1975.

When I reflect on the Hungarian uprising of 1956, and the Czechoslovakian rebellion of 1968, I still feel an utter hopelessness about what we can do to help the people in the Communist countries of Central and Eastern Europe. The combined realities of their geographic position and the difficulty of arranging the kind of joint military operation with our European allies that would be required to be effective mean that we simply cannot and will not use our armed forces in the event that they engage in open rebellion against their Communist dictators. Consequently, it is irresponsible to urge them to armed rebellion, raising their hopes and encouraging them to risk their lives without any prospect of assistance from us. But I do not feel that it is an acceptable alternative to slam down the Iron Curtain and accept the idea that they are destined to live forever under Communist rule.

Peaceful change is the only practicable answer. Admittedly it is not a very satisfactory one because such change could take a generation, maybe even a century. In the meantime we must seize every opportunity that may arise to increase contact and communication with the people of these countries so that they will know we share their hopes for a better and freer life.

THE PRESIDENT'S STROKE

On November 25, 1957, I received a terse phone call from Sherman Adams, asking me to come to the White House right away.

As soon as the door closed behind us he said, "The President has suffered a stroke."

We were silent for a moment. "How serious is his condition?" I asked.

"We'll know more in the morning," he replied. "Right now he's more confused and disoriented than anything else. It will take a few days before the doctors can assess the damage. This is a terribly, terribly difficult thing to handle," Adams said. "You may be President in twenty-four hours."

In fact, the stroke had been relatively mild. Eisenhower's ability to read, write, and reason had suffered no damage, and the only aftereffect was an occasional hesitancy in finding the right word, an impairment about which he was painfully self-conscious but that was scarcely noticeable to others. He made a point in public of appearing to be in complete control, but those of us who saw him in private caught occasional glimpses of the serious psychological effect the stroke had on him. He was depressed by the fear that he could no longer bring to the presidency the physical or mental qualities it required, and this was a serious blow to his morale. "This is the end," he said when he first heard the diagnosis. "Mamie and I are farmers from now on."

He was deeply disturbed by some of the press coverage of his condition during his recovery, especially references to occasional misspoken words. He did have some difficulty in speaking at times but by iron discipline and will power he overcame it. Some editorial writers and columnists even suggested he should resign or delegate interim powers to me—much as they recoiled at the idea of my succeeding him in office.

One day when he seemed particularly depressed by these attacks, I told him that he should consider the source and ignore them. The most important point, I reminded him, was that there was nothing the matter with his brain. "The trouble with most politicians is that their mouths move faster than their brains. With you it is the other way around."

This broke the tension, and he laughed more heartily than I had heard him laugh for weeks.

I had always felt that Eisenhower could cut down considerably on his workload without neglecting his essential duties. I told him there was no reason that individual Cabinet officers should not make more decisions on their own, particularly domestic ones. Eisenhower agreed, but he was sensitive about taking any step that might be interpreted as an admission that he could no longer handle the full job. Within a few months he was again attending every meeting and allowing the discussions to ramble on as if it were his duty to be bored for his country as well as to lead it.

An important result of his stroke was the procedure that Eisenhower established in case of any future debilitating illness during his term. When Congress took no action to fill the constitutional void with regard to presidential disability, Bill Rogers, Foster Dulles, and I worked with Eisenhower to develop a plan that would suffice at least for the balance of his administration. Eisenhower personally drafted and sent to me a letter setting forth the procedures to be followed. The entire determination of fitness was to be made by the President and Vice President. If during some future illness Eisenhower concluded that he could no longer perform his duties, he would tell me and I would then become acting President with full authority until he decided he was able to resume his duties. If he were incapable of making or expressing a decision, I was to act on my own authority after appropriate consultation and serve as acting President until such time as he decided he was sufficiently recovered to resume. This plan was no substitute for a permanent constitutional solution, but it was a workable arrangement, which, fortunately, never had to be put to the test. Kennedy wrote a similar letter to Lyndon Johnson before his inauguration.

This issue was formally settled by the adoption in 1967 of the Twenty-fifth Amendment to the Constitution.

SOUTH AMERICA: 1958

In the spring of 1958 I could already see the November elections shaping up as a disaster. Secretary of Labor Jim Mitchell and I were desperately—and unsuccessfully—trying to talk our colleagues in the Cabinet into a job-stimulating tax cut that would get the economy moving again and possibly help Republican chances. Therefore I was not enthusiastic when Assistant Secretary of State Roy Rubottom, Jr., asked me in early March if I would consider heading our official delegation to the inauguration of the new President of Argentina, Arturo Frondizi. The dictator Juan Perón had been overthrown in 1955, and Frondizi was the winner of Argentina's first free elections in twenty years.

I said that I could not take on another foreign trip at that time, but in the next few days both Dulles and Eisenhower made it clear that they felt it was important for me to go, and I had little choice but to agree. Rubottom immediately began lobbying for one or two extra stops, and by the end of the week, the itinerary included every country in South America except Brazil, where I had represented Eisenhower at the inauguration of President Kubitschek in 1956, and Chile, whose President was to have been in Washington on a state visit at the time I would have been in Chile.

The CIA had warned that although the Communist Party had been officially suppressed in most South American countries, I might have to face occasional demonstrators; but I expected the trip to be so uneventful that I advised several reporters not to bother coming with us.

In Montevideo, Uruguay, our first stop, the crowds were warm and friendly; only a few hecklers displayed signs as we drove past the University of the Republic. Later in the visit I arranged an unscheduled stop at the University. I walked through the campus, shaking hands and answering questions. When several communist students tried to interrupt me, they were shouted down by the rest, and I left amid cheers.

Ambassador Robert Woodward told me that this brief stop had been a tremendous success. He said that South Americans above all have contempt for fear or timidity and admire courage and the dramatic gesture.

We received warm receptions from the people in Argentina, Paraguay, and Bolivia. By the time we reached Peru, it was clear that the communists would have to resort to more extreme tactics if they were to succeed in spoiling the trip.

They did. When we got back to our Lima hotel after lunch with President Manuel Prado, there was a large crowd in front, obviously less than friendly and more than curious. The whistles and catcalls were loud and menacing. It was clear that the demonstrations were entering a more dangerous phase.

The next day's schedule included a visit to the old and distinguished San Marcos University. The communists had openly boasted that they would prevent me from going there, and both the rector of the university and the chief of police had let it be known that they hoped we would cancel the visit. Most of our embassy officials felt that I should cancel rather than risk an incident that might have a serious effect on our relations with Peru.

I said that I would call it off only if the rector or the chief of police issued a statement requesting me to do so. An embassy staff member made some phone calls and returned to inform us that the rector was afraid the communist students might blame him for depriving them of the incident they were hoping to provoke, and the chief of police did not want to run the risk of being charged with inability to maintain order. We consulted with several Peruvian government leaders. Each wanted the visit canceled, but none would take the responsibility for canceling it.

My administrative assistant, Bill Key, proposed an alternate solution. He suggested that, instead of going to San Marcos, I visit Lima's Catholic University, where the students were much more responsible and disciplined, and where the rector had said he would welcome a visit.

I asked Ambassador Ted Achilles what he thought I should do. He took a long time before he answered me. Finally he said, "I believe from a personal standpoint you should make a decision not to go. But from the standpoint of the United States, I will have to say that your failing to go may lead to some very detrimental publicity reactions throughout the hemisphere."

I slept very little that night. The crowd outside the hotel had grown large and ugly, and around midnight it started chanting anti-American and anti-Nixon slogans.

In the morning, the first thing everyone wanted to know was what I had decided. I said I had not yet made a final decision.

I asked Pat to stay behind at the hotel when I left for my first activity that morning, a wreath-laying ceremony at the statue of José de San Martín, the liberator of Peru. The custom is to place the wreath and then stand at attention for about thirty seconds in silence. That morning, however, I must have stood there for at least two minutes. I knew that as soon as I returned to the car I would have to give the order that would take us either to San Marcos or to Catholic University.

After laying the wreath, I turned and walked over to one of my three Secret Service agents, Jack Sherwood, and said, "San Marcos." Then I walked quickly to my car.

For two blocks before we reached the gates of San Marcos, we could hear the thousands of demonstrators chanting, "*Fuera Nixon! Fuera Nixon!*"—"Go Home Nixon!" Sometimes the chant became "*Muera Nixon! Muera Nixon!*"—"Death to Nixon!" I did not want a provocative retinue of embassy officials or policemen to accompany me onto the campus. Only my interpreter, Colonel Vernon Walters, and Jack Sherwood were with me as I walked toward the solid wall of screaming demonstrators that blocked the gate. I shouted, "I want to talk to you. Why are you afraid of the truth?" Walters shouted the translation.

I shouted a few more sentences, hoping to get them to listen. Suddenly a rock hit Sherwood in the face, breaking a tooth. A shower of rocks rained down on us. I realized that we had no choice but to leave. As we drove away, I stood up in the convertible and shouted, "You are cowards, you are afraid of the truth!" Sherwood held my legs as the car swerved into the street.

We drove directly to Catholic University, and as I entered the auditorium everyone rose in a tremendous ovation. After about thirty minutes, as I was answering a question, Sherwood came over and whispered, "We'd better get out of here; the gang from San Marcos is on its way."

We left just in time. When we got near our hotel, however, we could see that a great part of the San Marcos mob had preceded us. I assumed that the ringleaders were expecting us at the front entrance, so I had the driver let us out a short distance away. We walked as quickly as we could, and we were only about fifty feet from the entrance when the crowd realized who we were, and a shrill, savage cry went up. But surprise was on our side, and, in wedge formation, we were able to cover the rest of the distance in just a few moments.

I was about to go through the door of the hotel when one of the demonstrators blocked my way. I thought he was going to speak to me or shout at me; instead, he spit in my face. When I got upstairs, Pat rushed over and embraced me. She had been watching the mob from our hotel room, and she said, "It wasn't just hate those people had in their eyes. It was a sort of frenzy that frightened me."

For the rest of the day, wherever I went I was hailed as a hero by the citizens of Lima. The incident at San Marcos had shocked and shamed patriotic Peruvians, and cheering crowds tried to erase the memory of the jeering students. Late in the afternoon I held a press conference.

I told the reporters that the greatest danger a non-Communist nation faced was from the handful of activists and infiltrators who could impose their will on the whole society. I said that the story of the San Marcos incident was the story of how some 200 trained agitators had led a demonstration of 2,000 students, bringing disgrace to the whole of Peru.

On the flight from Lima to Quito, Ecuador, we tried to call Tricia and Julie on the plane's radio telephone in order to reassure them that we were all right, but it was impossible to make a connection. We received a message from Eisenhower: "Dear Dick. Your courage, patience, and calmness in the demonstration directed against you by radical agitators have brought you a new respect and admiration in our country." And Clare Boothe Luce sent a one-word wire: "Bully."

In Bogotá, Colombia, we received a disturbing message from the chief of the Secret Service in Washington: "The Central Intelligence Agency advises the Secret Service in Washington that information has been received relating to rumors of a plot to assassinate the Vice President in Venezuela." I cabled ahead to have our ambassador tell the Venezuelan government that if it wanted to cancel my visit I would understand. Right up until our arrival, however, the Venezuelan officials reported that everything was completely under control.

We landed at Maiquetía Airport, just outside Caracas, on the morning of May 13. We could hear yelling and whistling even before the plane's engines had cut off. Pat and I stood at attention at the top of the ramp while the honor guard fired a nineteen-gun salute and a band played the Venezuelan and American national anthems. The landing strip had been cleared except for the official welcoming party. The large crowd of demonstrators stood behind the fences at the edge of the runways and on the observation deck on the roof of the terminal building. A red carpet ran from the foot of the stairs to the terminal building where the motorcade was assembled to take us the twelve miles into Caracas.

As we started to descend the stairs, Walters whispered in my ear, "They aren't friendly." That much was clear from the whistles and catcalls that had kept up a raucous counterpoint to both anthems. As I shook hands, the welcoming party seemed determined to ignore the screams of the crowd. The Venezuelan chief of security assured me, "Oh, they are just kids. They are harmless."

I took Pat's arm and started walking along the red carpet toward the terminal. The others fell in quickly behind us. We had almost reached the terminal door when the band leader suddenly began playing the Venezuelan anthem again. We stopped and stood at attention. For a second it seemed as if it had begun to rain, and then I realized that the crowd on the observation deck just above our heads was showering us with spit. It fell on our faces and our hair. I saw Pat's bright red suit grow dark with tobacco-brown splotches. After we passed through the terminal and walked out in front, we were surrounded by the demonstrators. While we waited for Sherwood and our other agents to clear the way to the car they continued to pelt us. Pat leaned over the barricade toward a young girl who had just spit at her. The girl's face was contorted with hate. When Pat put her hand on the girl's shoulder and smiled at her, it was as if something snapped inside the girl, and she turned her head away and broke into sobs.

Finally our agents were able to clear a path. I got into the first car, along with the Foreign Minister. Pat and the Foreign Minister's wife were in the second car. The embarrassed Foreign Minister kept offering me his handkerchief to wipe some of the spit off my clothes. Finally I snapped at him, "Don't bother. I am going to burn these clothes as soon as I can get out of them."

He tried to explain what had happened. "The Venezuelan people have been without freedom so long that they tend now to express themselves more vigorously perhaps than they should," he said. "In our new government we do not want to do anything which would be interpreted as a suppression of freedom."

"If your new government doesn't have the guts and good sense to control a mob like the one at the airport, there soon will be no freedom for anyone in Venezuela," I replied.

As we entered Caracas, a barrage of rocks flew toward us, and a mob ran out from the side streets and alleys. Our driver pushed the accelerator to the floor and we got through.

About four blocks from the Pantéon Nacional a solid wall of vehicles was strung across the street from the sidewalk to the traffic island in the center. A steady flow of cars in the opposite direction made it impossible to drive over the island. We pulled to a stop. For a moment everything seemed suspended. Then Sherwood said, "Here they come." Hundreds of people suddenly appeared from the streets and alleys, running toward our car. Our Venezuelan motorcycle escort evaporated. Our only protection was our augmented detail of twelve courageous Secret Service agents who did a superhuman job in trying to fend off the mob.

We realized that we were completely alone as the first rock hit the car window, lodging itself in the glass and spraying us with tiny slivers. One sliver hit the Foreign Minister in the eye, and he started to bleed heavily. He tried to stop the blood, moaning over and over, "This is terrible. This is terrible."

I saw a thug with an iron pipe work his way up to the car. He was looking right at me as he began trying to break the window. Once again the glass held, but flying slivers hit Walters in the mouth. Both Sherwood and I caught some in the face. Suddenly the car began to move, and the idea that we had somehow broken free gave me a surge of relief. Then I realized that the crowd was rocking the car back and forth—slower and higher each time. I remembered that it was a common tactic for mobs to turn a car over and then set it on fire.

I believe that at that moment, for the first time, each of us in the car realized we might actually be killed. My first thought was of Pat. I looked through the rear window and was relieved to see that the mob was concentrating on us and ignoring her car.

Suddenly Sherwood pulled out his revolver and said, "Let's get some of these sons of bitches." I told him to hold his fire. Once a gun went off the crowd would go berserk and that would be the end of us.

Finally the press truck in front of us managed to break out of the jam and swerve over the traffic island and into the lane of traffic coming from the opposite direction. Like a blocker leading a running back, the truck cleared a path for us. Our driver gunned the engine and shot around the truck, picking up speed. I was greatly relieved to see Pat's car right behind us.

We had been trapped for only twelve minutes, but it seemed like a lifetime. Our police motorcycle escort suddenly appeared again and started signaling our driver to follow. The Foreign Minister began talking about getting back on schedule, and it dawned on me that the escort was leading us to the Panteón for the wreath-laying ceremony. As we reached the next intersection I called out to the driver to turn quickly, and as he did the motorcycles rode on. The Foreign Minister looked panic-stricken. He cried, "We cannot leave our protection. We've got to follow the police escort!" I looked at him and said, "If that's the kind of protection we are going to get, we are better off going it alone."

I told the driver that the important thing was not to go anyplace where we would be expected. There would certainly be another mob waiting at the Panteón and also at the government guesthouse where we were scheduled to stay. By some miracle Pat's car and the truck carrying the reporters and photographers were following right behind. I asked the driver to pull over, and I walked back to make sure that she was all right. Several reporters ran up. I gave them a brief rundown of the situation and told them that I had decided to go directly to the embassy.

It was an immense relief to drive through the embassy gate and see the American flag flying from the roof. Pat and I showered and changed. By the time I came back downstairs, word had arrived that a bloodthirsty mob of several thousand had been waiting for us at the Panteón plaza, and later investigation revealed a cache of Molotov cocktails ready to be thrown at us during the ceremony. I also learned that the members of the ruling military junta were on their way to the embassy to make an official apology. One of the ambassador's aides wanted to have our battered limousine taken around to the back of the building so that it would not embarrass them. I said, "Leave it where it is. It's time that they see some graphic evidence of what communism really is."

I held a press conference late in the afternoon and made the same point that I had made in Lima: that the men and women who had led the riots could not claim to be loyal to their country because their first loyalty was to the international Communist conspiracy. I said that it would be very dangerous to ascribe the riots to the fact that after ten years of repressive dictatorship the people did not know how to exercise restraint in enjoying their new freedom. Those mobs were communists led by Communists, and they had no devotion to freedom at all.

That night Pat and I had dinner alone in our room at the embassy. Around nine o'clock there was a knock on the door and Rubottom and the ambassador asked if they could have a word with me. I didn't see how I could take another meeting at this point and started to tell them so when Rubottom said that a new crisis had arisen because of a news report that had just been received from Washington. Eisenhower had dispatched two companies of airborne infantry and two companies of Marines to the Caribbean to be "in a position to cooperate with the Venezuelan government if assistance is requested." The Venezuelan radio was apparently reporting this precautionary measure as a full-scale invasion.

I could hardly believe my ears. Why hadn't the White House consulted us before doing such a thing? Only later did we find out that communications between Caracas and Washington had been cut for a critical period immediately after the riot that afternoon. The last message the State Department had received before the cutoff was a flash report that the local security system had completely broken down, that anti-American mobs were on the loose, and that

I was under attack. Eisenhower had acted on the basis of this message. We immediately tried to rectify the situation by issuing a statement that the Venezuelan authorities had the situation well in hand and that we saw no need for outside assistance.

~The next morning I felt that we should leave Venezuela as soon as possible. The junta members were pleading that I attend the luncheon they had planned in my honor that afternoon, and they guaranteed that they would deliver me safely to the airport immediately afterward. I accepted their invitation, even though I still had trepidations about their ability to maintain security.

From the moment they arrived at the embassy to escort me to the luncheon, however, I realized that my fears had been unnecessary. It looked as if they had come to declare war rather than take me to lunch. The courtyard was filled with tanks and jeeps and armored cars. There were twelve truckloads of troops flanking our limousines. The security extended even to the food; they had replaced the caterer lest our food be tampered with.

After the luncheon, we were escorted to our cars. The limousine in which I was riding with the Provisional President was an arsenal on wheels. The floor was piled with submachine guns, revolvers, rifles, tear gas canisters, and ammunition clips; there was hardly room for our feet. I saw that the junta had decided to make a symbolic point by taking me along the same route I had traveled the day before. This time, however, the streets were almost empty and heavily patrolled by armed soldiers. The few civilians I saw were holding handkerchiefs to their faces. At first I thought this was a protest sign, but when I saw the police wearing gas masks I realized that the whole area had been tear-gassed.

The airport was like a ghost town; the terminal was empty and eerily silent. After shaking hands with our hosts, Pat and I went up the steps to our plane. At the top we turned and waved briefly to the small group standing below.

A large crowd came out to greet us when we landed at National Airport in Washington. Eisenhower was there, along with the Cabinet, the leaders of Congress, and the diplomatic corps. Tricia and Julie were waiting for us at the bottom of the stairs, and they could hardly contain their tears of joy.

For several weeks after our return from South America, neither Pat nor I could appear anywhere in public without people standing up to applaud. For the first time I pulled even with Kennedy in the Gallup presidential trial heat polls. The positive reaction to the Caracas incident was naturally satisfying. But I never forgot how lucky we were to get out alive from what I had thought was going to be the most boring trip we had ever taken.

THE RESIGNATION OF SHERMAN ADAMS

Congress was in an ugly mood in the summer of 1958. The Republicans were fighting each other more than they were fighting the Democrats, and the Democrats were frantically digging up every possible issue they could throw at us in the fall elections. I paid little attention in June when charges were brought against Sherman Adams by the Subcommittee on Legislative Oversight of the House Interstate and Foreign Commerce Committee. It appeared that some of Adams's hotel bills had been paid by a New England industrialist named Bernard Goldfine. The Democrats charged that Adams had done favors for Goldfine and claimed they had uncovered a case of influence-peddling in the White House. Goldfine denied the charges, and on June 11 Jim Hagerty, speaking on behalf of the President, characterized the allegations as "completely false."

Stories of Adams's immense influence with Eisenhower and his cold and abrupt personal demeanor were a standard feature of many Washington dinner parties and gossip columns. For the Democrats he was a natural target as the President's Chief of Staff. Two days after Hagerty's flat denial, Adlai Stevenson accused Adams of "hypocrisy." Such criticism was to be expected from the Democrats. But many of Adams's most vocal and unrelenting critics turned out to be Republicans.

The day after Stevenson made his attack, Barry Goldwater, who was running for re-election to the Senate, called

Adams a political liability. Unfortunately for Adams, he was not able to depend on compensating support from liberal Republicans. He had been so successful and so even-handed in his role as Eisenhower's "no man" that he had few friends when he came under serious attack.

The next day, June 15, a story appeared in the New York *Post* that excited public opinion more than the accusations about hotel bills: the *Post* reported that Goldfine had given Adams a vicuña coat. Most people did not have the slightest idea what a vicuña coat was, but it sounded expensive.

With Eisenhower's approval, Adams testified before the subcommittee. He admitted to a lack of prudence in his dealings with Goldfine, and he made a favorable impression as an honest man who would not intentionally use his public influence for private profit. Eisenhower stood by him staunchly. At a press conference the next day, he replied to a question about Adams by saying: "I need him."

But Eisenhower's personal popularity was not as high as it had been, and he was increasingly plagued by his lame-duck status. His defense of Adams had surprisingly little influence on Republican leaders. Bill Knowland, the Minority Leader in the Senate, called for Adams's resignation, and Republican state chairmen around the country clamored for Adams's head.

Meanwhile the story grew more troublesome. It turned out that Goldfine had paid bills for and given presents to several senators and governors; the hotel bills for Adams and his family amounted to over $3,000; and the subcommittee found that Goldfine had deducted some of the money spent on Adams as business expenses.

A temporary respite occurred when it was discovered that Goldfine's hotel room had been bugged by a House committee investigator who had been found listening in an adjoining room, along with Jack Anderson, then an assistant to columnist Drew Pearson. The investigator was forced to resign.

Then the controversy resumed when, on July 10, it was revealed that Goldfine had paid not only Adams's hotel bills but also those of Senator Fred Payne, a Republican coming up for re-election in Maine.

On July 14, in the midst of this political turmoil, the Middle East erupted. King Faisal and other members of the royal family of Iraq were murdered during a successful military takeover. Fearing that Syria would follow suit and cross the frontier into Lebanon, Lebanese President Camille Chamoun asked for American help. On July 15, Eisenhower ordered the Marines into Lebanon. He asked me to come to his office that morning. He was pacing the floor, and for the first time he conveyed to me his frustration with the Adams situation. He said, "Here on a day that I am making a decision that could involve the United States in war, I have to be worried about this damned Goldfine-Adams business." He said nothing to indicate any lack of support for Adams, but I could tell that his patience was wearing thin. He asked me to keep him advised of anything I thought he should know about the situation.

Just before Congress adjourned in late August, Eisenhower and I talked about the Adams case. "Some people have been telling me that the issue has quieted down considerably in the past few weeks," he said.

I felt I had to be completely frank with him about the political implications. I said that the Democrats would inevitably make the Adams case a major campaign issue and Republican candidates would eventually have to take sides. I told him that most of our candidates would probably come out against Adams.

He thought for a moment, then said, "Well, Sherm could use that as a good reason for his resigning—that he did not want his presence in the administration to be an embarrassment to the Republican Party or to me." He then suggested, "Why don't you have a talk with Sherm after Congress adjourns? See how he feels about this, and let him know what he's going to be up against once the campaign begins."

When Congress adjourned on August 24, I kept a long-standing promise to Pat and the girls and took them by train to The Greenbrier in West Virginia. Every vacation we had planned since coming to Congress in 1947 had been cut short, but this time I really thought it would be different.

On the morning we arrived, however, Eisenhower

called from the White House: "I wonder if you could talk to Sherm now that the Congress is out." He had heard that the Adams issue might be brought up at the Republican National Committee meeting in Chicago in a few days and had asked the RNC Chairman, Meade Alcorn, to try to avoid a public discussion of Adams. "I was really hoping," Eisenhower said, "that we could get the matter resolved before then."

I had a brief meeting with Eisenhower the next day, August 26. He asked me to talk bluntly to Adams about the political realities of the situation we faced. He did not authorize me to say that he wanted him to resign, but it was clear that he wanted the result of our conversation to be Adams's resignation.

I gave Adams my straightforward appraisal of the present situation from a political standpoint. I told him that most of the candidates and party leaders across the country believed that he should resign.

"Who will take my place? I've never heard anyone suggested," Adams said bluntly.

I replied that only Eisenhower could answer that question, and I had not discussed it with him. He pressed me further to try to determine whether I was expressing my own views, reporting on the views of others, or actually reflecting the President's position.

Before I left, Adams pinned me down with a direct question: "What do you think is the President's view?" I replied, "He hasn't told me to tell you this, Sherm, so I am only expressing my personal view. But I believe that the President thinks you are a liability and that you should resign."

Adams rather abruptly terminated the conversation by saying, "Well, I will have to talk to the boss myself." From the way he talked about "seeing the boss," it seemed clear that he was not going to take my hints and that he intended to hang on as long as he could.

Sherman Adams had earned the reputation of keeping icy cold no matter how hot the situation. In this case, however, I could see that the strain was beginning to tell. While I was in his office he took a bottle of pills from his desk, poured a couple of the tablets into his hand, and swallowed them with a glass of water. I felt deeply sorry for him.

I went to the Oval Office to report to Eisenhower on our meeting. I told him that I had just talked to Adams as he had asked, but that Adams was clearly not going to budge without first talking directly to him personally.

Adams saw Eisenhower that same afternoon. I was called over to the Oval Office a while later and found the President hitting 5-irons on the South Lawn. He made no mention of Adams, but said, "I'm going to play some golf this afternoon, Dick, and I wonder if you would like to join me."

We drove out to Burning Tree. Ann Whitman, Eisenhower's personal secretary, had warned me that he was in a "sour mood," and it showed up in his golf game. He told me it was the worst round he had had in months.

On the ride home he finally opened up: "Sherm won't take any of the responsibility. He leaves it all to me. Still, I can't fire a man who is sincere just for political reasons. He must resign in a way I can't refuse." He added, "I think Sherm must have misunderstood what you said. You had better write me an aide-mémoire on your conversation."

When I mentioned that Adams had raised the question of his replacement, Eisenhower's face flushed, and he said curtly and coldly, "That's my problem, not his." He looked out the car window for a minute and then said, "He has a heart condition. He might use that as a reason for resigning." Then he told me to ask Meade Alcorn to report the facts to Adams. He said, "I want Alcorn to really lay it on the line with him." He did not make a personal judgment on Adams except to say, "It's incredible, because with all these things that have been coming out one by one in the press, Sherm sees no wrong whatever in anything that he has done."

Later that evening I went back to The Greenbrier to rejoin Pat and the girls. Eisenhower went to his summer White House in Newport, and Adams went to his vacation home in New Brunswick.

Meade Alcorn was able to forestall any public action by the Republican state chairmen and campaign officials when

242

they met in Chicago. He did, however, take a confidential poll, and found the overwhelming majority in favor either of Eisenhower's firing Adams or of Adams's voluntarily submitting his resignation. On September 4, Eisenhower phoned Alcorn from Newport and said that he had received some disturbing messages from party leaders and contributors concerning "the matter we discussed the other day." They had apparently told him that an association between a man like Goldfine and the chief assistant to the President was a reflection upon the White House that Eisenhower should not allow to continue.

Eisenhower was upset. He told Alcorn to work with me to settle the matter as quickly as possible. "I want to solve this as soon as we can after the Maine election so that it isn't hanging around during the campaign," he said. "This is the way I feel. It doesn't seem as if Sherm is going to do anything about it, and I am going to leave this entirely in your hands."

Adams was called back from his vacation in Canada on September 15. At eleven that morning Alcorn came to my office at the Capitol so that we could plan our strategy. The halls were swarming with reporters who sensed a crisis brewing, so I suggested to Alcorn that he meet with Adams alone. If the two of us left my office and went to the White House together, the reporters would follow us and it might become impossible to accomplish our objective of giving Adams a dignified opportunity to resign.

Alcorn met with Adams at two o'clock that afternoon in Adams's White House office. After the meeting Alcorn called to report that it had been a long and difficult session; Adams had hung on, stubborn to the last. Finally, Alcorn convinced him that we were acting at the direct request of the President.

On September 22, Sherman Adams flew to Newport and met with Eisenhower. He officially informed him that he had decided to resign, and Eisenhower said that he would accept the resignation but only with the deepest regret. Adams flew back to Washington, and that night announced his resignation in a nationally televised speech.

I called Adams's resignation a tragic loss to the country. I am convinced that he was personally an honest man who would not in any circumstances have allowed any decision he made to be influenced by his friends or by any gifts he received. Adams had come to Washington as a man of modest means, and as far as I knew he left with less than he had when he arrived. But he had not heeded one of the oldest political maxims: it is not necessary to prove guilt of the men around the President—the appearance of guilt is enough to destroy their usefulness.

Sherman Adams was cold, blunt, abrasive, at times even rude. But I never doubted that he always did what he believed "the boss" wanted and expected him to do, and he kept the complicated wheels of the executive office turning during more than one major crisis.

Why hadn't Eisenhower himself talked to Adams, his closest associate and the top man on his staff? Why did he use Alcorn and me for this painful task? General Walter Bedell Smith, Eisenhower's chief of staff in World War II, provided an important insight into Eisenhower's personality and his technique of leadership one night when he was reminiscing about his years with Eisenhower. He was very tired, and he uncharacteristically began showing his emotions. Tears began to stream down his cheeks, and he blurted out his pent-up feelings. "I was just Ike's prat boy," he said. "Ike always had to have a prat boy, someone who'd do the dirty work for him. He always had to have someone else who could do the firing, or the reprimanding, or give any orders which he knew people would find unpleasant to carry out. Ike always has to be the nice guy. That's the way it is in the White House, and the way it will always be in any kind of an organization that Ike runs."

Over the years a story spread that Adams and I were deadly enemies, the two major rivals for power in the Eisenhower White House. The fact is that we were neither friends nor enemies. We worked together in harness for the President. I was probably not Adams's first choice for Vice President, and certainly Adams was jealously protective of his prerogatives during the time of the President's major illnesses. But Adams was not against me; he was for Eisenhower.

What was it that Eisenhower saw in Sherman Adams that made him choose him in the first place?

I once asked Eisenhower if there was a single quality he

valued above all in selecting a man for a top position on his staff. He thought for a long time—so long that I wondered if he had forgotten my question. Then he looked at me and said, "Selflessness. Selflessness is the most important attribute a member of any organization can have. He must always consider that his first responsibility is to do his job well, regardless of whether it serves his own self-interest or not."

Adams had this quality. He had no political ambitions; he did not seek any other position; unlike many White House aides, he was not trying to advance his own career. All he was interested in was serving "the boss" as best he could. And ironically, it was this interest that made Adams so many enemies. In making the President look good, Adams made himself look bad. But it was also this quality of selflessness that made him—except for his tragic misjudgments in his relationship with Goldfine—such an outstanding and successful chief of the White House staff.

1958 ELECTIONS

Off-year elections for the House, Senate, and state houses are often even more bitter and divisive than presidential elections. This was particularly true in 1958. As the year began, the economy was turning downward. Heated intraparty battles were taking place in a number of key states, including California. In this summer of discontent for the Republican Party, Eisenhower's popularity sank below 50 percent for the only time in his eight years in the White House

Eisenhower, always reluctant to involve himself in partisan politicking, would be able to do even less than in 1954 because of his health. And once again most of the Cabinet members were planning to sit out the campaign.

In the aftermath of Caracas, my popularity was now at its highest point. If I wanted to run for the presidency in 1960, it would be risky to put myself again in the position of Eisenhower's political point-man. Tom Dewey was almost passionately insistent that I not become involved: "I know that Ike won't do it, and I know that all those old party wheelhorses will tell you stories that will pluck your heartstrings, but you're toying with your chance to be President.

Don't do it, Dick. You've already done enough, and 1960 is what counts now."

But I was deluged by appeals from across the country to appear on behalf of Republican candidates. In the end, I took on the task because it had to be done, and because there wasn't anyone else to do it.

In the campaign I traveled all over the country, doing what little I could. Some of the candidates were personal friends and good men who deserved to be elected or re-elected to Congress. But the more I traveled the more I appreciated the truth of Richard Rovere's observation in *The New Yorker* that I was "climbing into harness with a bunch of wheelhorses scarcely capable of drawing their own weight." In the last weeks of the campaign I labored under a feeling of total hopelessness.

The defeat was massive, and November 4, 1958, was one of the most depressing election nights I have ever known. The statistics still make me wince. In the Senate, the Democratic majority increased by 13 seats, bringing the proportion up to 62 to 34. They increased their majority by 47 seats in the House, thus outnumbering the Republicans by a whopping 282 to 153. Republicans won only 8 of 21 gubernatorial contests, and the Democrats now controlled 34 of the 48 state houses. The defeats in crucial states, among them California and Ohio, meant that the party would have to face the formidable task of rebuilding its state organizations if I was to have any hopes of carrying them in 1960. The reasons for the defeat were fairly easy to analyze, but the disappointment was still great. I knew that this defeat would make the campaign coming up in less than two years the most difficult of my career.

The next morning I heard that one television commentator had told his viewers that the big winner of 1958 was Nelson Rockefeller—who had been elected governor of New York by a wide margin—and the big loser was Richard Nixon. It seemed that the worst fears of my friends and advisers had been realized. My campaigning had had little visible effect, had gained me little thanks or credit, and had tarred me with the brush of partisan defeat at a time when my potential rivals for the nomination, Rockefeller and

Barry Goldwater, were basking in the glory of victory. Perhaps Dewey had been right: I should have sat it out.

—————————

After the depressing ordeal of the 1958 disaster, I welcomed the opportunity to represent Eisenhower at the dedication of the American Chapel in St. Paul's Cathedral in London.

My major speech on this trip was to the English-Speaking Union at London's historic Guildhall on November 27.

I said that a new kind of battle was being fought, especially in the countries of Asia, the Middle East, Africa, and Latin America, where the leaders of those countries were struggling to satisfy their peoples' desire for the physical well-being and material comfort advanced nations enjoy. They would prefer to attain these objectives and retain their freedom—but if they believed that was impossible, they would choose progress even without liberty. "No people in the world today," I said, "should be forced to choose between bread and freedom."

I closed by saying that we should speak less of the threat of communism and more of the promise of freedom; that we should adopt as our primary objective not the defeat of communism but the victory of plenty over want, of health over disease, and of freedom over tyranny.

The trip gave me an opportunity to meet with and obtain the views of Britain's major political leaders on foreign policy issues. I was particularly impressed by the high intelligence and common sense that Prime Minister Harold Macmillan displayed in a long discussion we had on what policy we should follow in dealing with the Soviet Union.

While we were in London I met with Winston Churchill at his house in Hyde Park Gate. I was surprised by how old and feeble he had become. As we talked about world affairs, however, he became more animated and by the end of our conversation there were flashes of the old brilliance.

After almost an hour, I said that I would not impose upon him any longer. He insisted on seeing me to the door. I was sad to see that he could not move without the assistance of his aide, who supported him as he walked. As the door swung open, we could see the lights from the movie cameras and all the reporters and photographers standing on the step. With sudden surprising strength, Churchill pushed his aide aside and almost seemed to puff himself up as he stood beside me. The cameras rolled and the flashbulbs popped, and the picture of the scene shows the proud, strong, upright Churchill of people's memory rather than the sad reality of time and age that I had just seen in private in his sitting room.

CASTRO: 1959

On January 1, 1959, Fidel Castro led his rebel army in triumph through the streets of Havana. He had defeated and ousted the repressive Batista regime, and he promised justice and freedom for the people of Cuba.

Castro had received a generally favorable press in the United States as the leader of a successful revolution against a right-wing dictator. Within the Eisenhower administration, however, opinions about him were mixed. Most of the State Department's Latin American experts advocated immediate recognition of Castro's government. But Allen Dulles and others in the CIA and NSC felt that we should delay such action until we had a better fix on Castro: was he an unwitting front man for the Communists, or perhaps even a Communist himself?

Eisenhower had not yet made a decision on this issue when Castro accepted an invitation to speak in Washington at a meeting of the American Society of Newspaper Editors on April 17, 1959. The President refused to see him, but Herter urged that I meet with Castro informally as I might be able to gain for the administration additional information about his background and insight into his views. On Sunday, April 19, we met alone in the Vice President's formal office in the Capitol, and for three hours we discussed his political views, his attitude toward the United States, and other international issues.

After that meeting I dictated a long memorandum for Eisenhower, Herter, and Foster and Allen Dulles summarizing our conversation and describing my impressions. In it I noted Castro's reaction to my urging that he declare himself in favor of elections at the earliest possible time:

> He went into considerable detail as he had in public with regard to the reasons for not holding elections, emphasizing particularly that "the people did not want elections because the elections in the past had produced bad government."
>
> He used the same argument that he was simply reflecting the will of the people in justifying the executions of war criminals and his overruling the acquittal of Batista's aviators. In fact he seemed to be obsessed with the idea that it was his responsibility to carry out the will of the people whatever it might appear to be at a particular time....
>
> It was this almost slavish subservience to prevailing majority opinion—the voice of the mob—rather than his naive attitude toward communism and his obvious lack of understanding of even the most elementary economic principles which concerned me most in evaluating what kind of a leader he might eventually turn out to be. That is the reason why I spent as much time as I could trying to emphasize that he had the great gift of leadership, but that it was the responsibility of a leader not always to follow public opinion but to help to direct it in the proper channels—not to give the people what they think they want at a time of emotional stress but to make them want what they ought to have. I pointed out that it might be very possible that the people of Cuba were completely disillusioned as far as elections and representative government were concerned but that this placed an even greater responsibility on him to see that elections were held at the very earliest date, and thereby to restore the faith of the people in democratic processes. Otherwise, the inevitable result would be the same dictatorship against which he and his followers had fought so gallantly. I used the same argument with regard to freedom of the press, the right to a fair trial before an impartial court, judge, and jury, and on other issues which came up during the course of the conversation. In every instance he justified his departure from democratic principles on the ground that he was following the will of the people. I, in my turn, tried to impress upon him the fact that while we believe in majority rule that even a majority can be tyrannous

and that there are certain individual rights which a majority should never have the power to destroy. . . .

Whatever we may think of him he is going to be a great factor in the development of Cuba and very possibly in Latin American affairs generally. He seems to be sincere. He is either incredibly naive about communism or under Communist discipline—my guess is the former, and as I have already implied his ideas as to how to run a government or an economy are less developed than those of almost any world figure I have met in fifty countries.

But because he has the power to lead to which I have referred, we have no choice but at least to try to orient him in the right direction.

Castro's actions when he returned to Cuba convinced me that he was indeed a Communist, and I sided strongly with Allen Dulles in presenting this view in NSC and other meetings. In early 1960 Eisenhower became convinced we were right and that steps should be taken to support the anti-Castro forces inside and outside Cuba. I was present at the meeting in which Eisenhower authorized the CIA to organize and train Cuban exiles for the eventual purpose of freeing their homeland from the Communists.

The irony, and the tragedy, of Castro's coming to power was that the Cuban people were rid of a right-wing dictator only at the cost of accepting a left-wing dictator who turned out to be far worse. From the U.S. point of view, Batista at least was friendly; Castro turned out to be an implacable and dangerous enemy.

KHRUSHCHEV AND THE "KITCHEN DEBATE"

Early in 1959 Eisenhower approved a recommendation by the United States Information Agency for me to represent the United States at the opening of the American National Exhibition in Moscow in July.

It may be difficult for those who do not remember the late 1950s to understand the nature of the relations between the Communist nations and the free world then. Russia was still shrouded in much of the sinister mystery of the Stalin era. The Iron Curtain was pulled tight across Europe, and Soviet missiles were feared in Bonn, Paris, London—and in Washington.

Nikita Khrushchev, a crude bear of a man who had risen from the ranks, was the leader of the Communist Party. Khrushchev's rough manners, bad grammar, and heavy drinking caused many Western journalists and diplomats to underestimate him. But despite his rough edges, he had a keen mind and a ruthless grasp of power politics.

Bluntly ignoring Western invitations for disarmament and détente, Khrushchev openly continued to stockpile missiles, build submarines, and test nuclear weapons. The bellicose way in which Khrushchev flaunted his new leadership in rocketry made many believe that he would have no qualms about using it to unleash a nuclear war.

Few foreigners had been invited to meet Khrushchev, and those who did were often deeply disturbed by him. At times he was almost seductively charming; at other times he was boorish and obtuse. Some visitors came away swearing that he was the devil incarnate; others came away swearing that he was just a drunk. All thought he was a bully.

For this trip to the Soviet Union, I undertook the most intense preparation I had ever made for a trip or meeting. I read everything I could find about the Soviet Union and its peoples. Pat and I spent several evenings learning Russian words and phrases. I received briefings from the State Department and the CIA and familiarized myself with the backgrounds of the Soviet leaders I would be likely to meet. By the time I left for Moscow on July 22, I was prepared to discuss any of the more than a hundred topics or problems of Soviet-American relations that Khrushchev was likely to bring up.

I asked the few Westerners who had met and talked to Khrushchev what he was like and what I could expect from him. Many said that of prime importance was to leave absolutely no doubt in his mind about the sincerity of our dedication to peace. Khrushchev would be scrutinizing my conduct for any hints of belligerence, they warned, so, as Walter Lippmann put it, I should bend over backward not to rock the boat. Others, equally expert, felt that Khrushchev would fasten on any sign of weakness or appeasement on my part and exploit it to his advantage.

I wanted to get the advice of Foster Dulles, who was then in Walter Reed Hospital with terminal cancer. When I arrived he was sitting in a wheelchair, a red plaid bathrobe covering his shrunken frame. His voice was weak, and between sentences he would suck on an ice cube to dull the burning in his throat.

"What above everything else should I try to get across to Khrushchev?" I asked him.

As usual he took time to consider his answer, and he expressed his thoughts with customary firmness and logic.

"Khrushchev does not need to be convinced of our good intentions," he said. "He knows we are not aggressors and do not threaten the security of the Soviet Union. He understands us. But what he needs to know is that we also understand him. In saying that he is for peaceful competition, he really means competition between his system and ours only in our world, not in his. He must be made to understand that he cannot have it both ways. Point the record out to him, that we have concrete proof of the Kremlin's activities around the world. He should be told that until he puts a stop to such activities, his call for reducing of tensions and for peaceful coexistence will have a completely false and hollow ring."

We chatted a little longer. Then Dulles looked out the window. "It's too fine a day for you to be in here," he said. "You should be out golfing." Those were his last words to me. He died four days later, on May 24, 1959.

Foster Dulles and I were friends. Although there were considerable differences in our ages and backgrounds, we shared a fascination with the world and the same basic outlook on America's role in it. Dulles was by no means politically inexperienced or naive, but as Secretary of State he was frequently traveling and always busy, so he used me as his political eyes and ears to keep him abreast of what was going on in Washington, especially in Congress. Many nights I would have cocktails or dinner with him, and then we would sit for hours talking our way around the world. It was an incomparable opportunity for me to learn from one of the great diplomats of our time.

Most people who did not know Dulles thought him severe, dour, almost ascetic. The press generally presented him as a cold fish, devoid of human emotions, who talked with abstract righteousness about "massive retaliation" and about going to the "brink of war." Dulles was, indeed, a brilliant, disciplined, and deeply religious man who saw many dimensions of principle and logic in every issue he encountered. But he was also a man who thought that the life of each individual on earth was important and precious because it was the gift of God.

Dulles appreciated the considerable leeway Eisenhower gave him in the conduct of foreign affairs, and he was constantly aware of the responsibilities and obligations involved. "I never want to be a burden on the President," he would say to me when a controversy was brewing. "As a friend, I want you to tell me whenever you believe that I have become a burden, either politically or otherwise." He recognized the fundamental truth a public man must never forget—that he loses his usefulness when he, rather than his policy, becomes the issue. In this respect Foster Dulles was perhaps the most conscientious public man I have ever known.

At a time when the political and intellectual climate in the West appeared to be moving slowly but steadily toward advocacy of shortsighted and opportunistic arrangements with the Soviets, Dulles was made to seem and sound like a throwback to cold war rigidity. But he saw his work as a high calling, and a few months before his death he said, "Communism is stubborn for the wrong; let us be steadfast for the right. A capacity to change is indispensable. Equally indispensable is the capacity to hold fast to that which is good."

World leaders and heads of government came to Dulles's funeral, as well as the foreign secretaries and foreign ministers who were his opposite numbers. Few came because they loved him; most had often disagreed with him. But they all respected him for his integrity and for his profound dedication to the principles of peace, freedom, and justice that motivated every decision he made.

Shortly before I left for Moscow, Congress passed the Captive Nations resolution, as it had every year since 1950. Eisenhower issued the proclamation provided for in the resolution urging Americans to "study the plight of the Soviet-dominated nations and to recommit themselves to the support of the just aspirations of those captive nations."

While the fact that Eisenhower issued the proclamation just a week before I left for Moscow was coincidental, I knew that Khrushchev might interpret it as an intentionally belligerent action.

We left Friendship Airport in an Air Force jet on July 22. The reception awaiting us in Moscow was cool and controlled. Deputy Premier Frol Kozlov gave a long welcoming speech while the American and Soviet flags hung limp in the warm afternoon air. But there were no bands, no anthems, and no crowds.

Llewellyn "Tommy" Thompson, whom I had first met in Austria in 1956, was now our ambassador in Moscow. We talked for a long time in the secure room on the second floor of Spaso House, the ambassador's official residence; in every country our embassy has a room that is constantly guarded and swept for listening devices. Thompson told me that the Soviet leaders were furious about the Captive Nations resolution, and the airport reception was probably only the first sign of their disapproval. He said that they were particularly sensitive to such criticism because their relations with some of the satellite countries were strained.

Because of the time change I could scarcely sleep that night, and around 5:30 I woke my Secret Service agent, Jack Sherwood, and told him I wanted to go to the famous Danilovsky market, where farmers bring their vegetables and meat. It would be a good way to get a sense of the city and its people before starting my official schedule. Sherwood and I were joined by a Russian security policeman who served as driver and interpreter.

As I walked through the crowded aisles between the stalls, word of my arrival spread quickly. Soon a crowd had gathered.

For almost an hour I mingled with the crowd, answering questions, caught up in the friendly and spontaneous exchange. As I was about to leave, several people asked if I had any tickets to the American Exhibition. I said I had none but would be delighted to buy some for my new friends there in the market so they could be my guests. I had Sherwood hand the spokesman for the group a hundred ruble note, enough for a hundred tickets. The spokesman handed it back, explaining that the problem was not the cost of the tickets but the fact that the government made them available only to selected persons. We all laughed about the problem, and I shook hands and left. The next day the three largest Soviet newspapers, *Pravda, Izvestia*, and *Trud*, headlined the incident, accusing me of having tried to "bribe" and "degrade" Soviet citizens by offering them money.

Later that morning, I went to the Kremlin for my first meeting with Khrushchev. He was standing at the far corner of his large office, examining a small model of the Soviet rocket that had recently been fired into outer space. We shook hands for the photographers. He was shorter than I expected, but otherwise he looked exactly like his photographs—the girth, the brash smile, the prominent mole on his cheek.

While the reporters and photographers were present Khruchshev chatted amiably about the fine Moscow weather. He praised my London Guildhall speech and said that he too welcomed the kind of peaceful competition I had described in it. Then he waved the photographers out and gestured toward a long conference table with chairs on both sides.

Abruptly the atmosphere changed, and Khrushchev launched into a tirade against the Captive Nations resolution. He called it a stupid and frightening decision and he asked whether war would be the next step. "Heretofore, the Soviet government thought Congress could never adopt a decision to start a war," he said. "But now it appears that, although Senator McCarthy is dead, his spirit still lives. For this reason the Soviet Union has to keep its powder dry."

I tried to explain how the resolution had come about and suggested we go on to other subjects. But he was not to be deterred. Blustering, he tried to twist it into a justification for Soviet arms. Finally I said, "At the White House we have a procedure for breaking off long discussions that seem to get nowhere. President Eisenhower says, 'We have beaten this horse to death; let's change to another.' Perhaps that is what you and I should do now."

Khrushchev's face remained impassive while the translator interpreted my words. "I agree with the President's saying that we should not beat one horse too much," he said, "but I still cannot understand why your Congress would adopt such a resolution on the eve of such an important state visit. It reminds me of a saying among our Russian peasants, that 'people should not go to the toilet where they eat.'" By this time his face was flushed with anger, and he said, "This resolution stinks. It stinks like fresh horse shit, and nothing smells worse than that!"

Khrushchev watched me closely while the translation was made. I decided to call his bluff, and in his own terms. I remembered from some of the briefing materials that Khrushchev had in his youth worked as a herder of pigs. I also remembered from my childhood that horse manure was commonly used as fertilizer—but that a neighbor had once used a load of pig manure, and the stench was overpowering.

Looking straight into Khrushchev's eyes but speaking in a conversational tone, I replied, "I am afraid that the Chairman is mistaken. There is something that smells worse than horse shit—and that is pig shit."

For a split second after the translator had finished, Khrushchev's face hovered on the borderline of rage. Then he suddenly burst into a broad smile. "You are right there," he said, "so perhaps you are right that we should talk about something else now. However, I must warn you that you will hear about this resolution during your visit here." On this subject if on few others, Khrushchev kept his word.

We drove from the Kremlin to take a look at the American Exhibition before it opened officially that evening. One of the first displays we came to was a model television studio, and a young engineer asked if we would like to try out a new color television taping system by recording greetings that could be played back during the Exhibition. Khrushchev seemed suspicious, but when he saw a group of Soviet workmen near the display the actor in him took over. Before I knew what he was doing he had scrambled onto the platform and was talking for the cameras and playing to the gallery.

"How long has America existed?" he asked me. "Three hundred years?"

"One hundred and eighty years," I replied.

Khrushchev was unfazed. "Well, then, we will say

America has been in existence for one hundred and eighty years, and this is the level she has reached," he said, taking in the whole Exhibition hall with a broad wave of his arm. "We have existed not quite forty-two years, and in another seven years we will be on the same level as America." The audience was obviously enjoying his boasting, and he continued. "When we catch up with you, in passing you by, we will wave to you," he said, looking over his shoulder and waving goodbye to an imaginary America.

Pointing to a burly Russian worker standing in the front of the crowd, he asked, "Does this man look like a slave laborer? With men of such spirit, how can we lose?"

I pointed to an American worker and said, "With men like that *we* are strong! But these men, Soviet and American, work together well for peace, even as they have worked together in building this Exhibition. This is the way it should be." I added, "If this competition in which you plan to outstrip us is to do the best for both of our peoples and for peoples everywhere, there must be a free exchange of ideas. You must not be afraid of ideas. After all, you don't know everything."

Khrushchev, furious, jumped in. "If *I* don't know everything, *you* don't know anything about communism," he shouted, "except fear of it!"

Walking through the Exhibition, we soon arrived at its most controversial attraction. This was a full-size model of a middle-class American home, priced at $14,000 and full of conveniences that dazzled the Russians. The Soviet press called it the "Taj Mahal" and insisted that it did not represent the way that an average American family really lived. I told Khrushchev that this was the kind of home that might be owned by an American steelworker, but either he did not believe me or he was unwilling to admit that it was true. We stopped in the model kitchen, and our exchange there turned into a debate that reverberated around the world.

Unlike our encounter in the model television studio, our "kitchen debate" was not televised, but it was widely reported—with a dramatic photograph showing me prodding my finger in Khrushchev's chest for emphasis. He was defensive, declaring that Russian houses, too, would have the modern equipment displayed in the American exhibit;

and he was aggressive, arguing that it was better to have just one model of washing machine than many. When I asked if it wasn't better to be arguing about the relative merits of washing machines than about the relative strengths of rockets, he shouted, "Your generals say we must compete in rockets. Your generals say they are so powerful they can destroy us. We can also show you something so that you will know the Russian spirit. We are strong, we can beat you."

I replied, "No one should ever use his strength to put another in the position where he in effect has an ultimatum. For us to argue who is the stronger misses the point. If war comes we both lose."

Khrushchev tried to turn the tables, accusing me of issuing an ultimatum. "We, too, are giants," he declared. "You want to threaten—we will answer threats with threats."

I told him we would never engage in threats. "You wanted indirectly to threaten me," he shouted. "But we have the means to threaten too."

Finally he was ready to move to less belligerent ground. He said, "We want peace and friendship with all nations, especially with America." I responded, "We want peace, too."

Standing next to me during this heated exchange was one of Khrushchev's chief aides, a party official named Leonid Brezhnev.

We returned to the Kremlin, where Pat and Mrs. Khrushchev joined us for a lavish luncheon. We toasted each other with champagne and, following our host's lead, threw our glasses into the fireplace. Then we were served caviar on silver dishes.

The following night we gave a dinner for Khrushchev at the American Embassy. Midway through the evening he began describing the beauties of the Russian countryside. Suddenly he said that we should not wait to see them, and he insisted that Pat and I spend the night in his dacha outside Moscow: he would join us there the next day for the scheduled meetings. Half an hour later we were in a limousine speeding down deserted roads. Soon we were in the forest, where the air was cooler and the darkness seemed deep and still. Khrushchev's dacha, which had been a Czarist summer home, was almost as large as the White House. It was surrounded by acres of grounds and gardens, and on one side the forest dropped down to the banks of the Moskva River.

Khrushchev and his wife arrived late the next morning. With the gusto of a social director he immediately took everything in hand. "First, let's have pictures taken in front of the house," he said, "and then we can take a ride on the Moskva River so that you can see how the slaves live."

"Oh, yes, the captives," I said, determined not to let him provoke me on that again.

Boats were waiting at the dock, and we followed the winding Moskva upriver for almost an hour. Several times groups of bathers swam out from the shore and surrounded the boat, cheering Khrushchev and clamoring to shake our hands. The first time this happened I was amused by Khrushchev's asking the swimmers, "Do you feel like captive people?" But I soon realized it was a setup. "You never miss a chance to make propaganda, do you?" I asked him. "No, no," he insisted, "I don't make propaganda. I tell the truth."

We had lunch on the lawn under a canopy of magnificent birch trees; the scene could have been out of Chekhov. When we sat down, Khrushchev made some playful verbal jabs. When Anastas Mikoyan started to speak in English to Pat, Khrushchev accused him of trying to be a Romeo when he was too old for the part. Then he told him, "Now look here, you crafty Armenian, Mrs. Nixon belongs to me. You stay on your side of the table." With his finger he drew an imaginary line down the middle of the starched white tablecloth between Pat and Mikoyan. "This is an iron curtain," he said. "And don't you step over it!"

One of the first courses was a Siberian delicacy, raw whitefish sliced very thin and spiced with salt, pepper, and garlic. Khrushchev took a generous portion and smiled approvingly when he saw me do the same. "It was Stalin's favorite dish," he remarked as he took a large mouthful. "He said it put steel in his backbone."

When the plates had been cleared, I expected that Khrushchev and I would excuse ourselves and settle down for serious talk. But he made no move to go. Instead, as we all sat there he began boasting about the power and accuracy of Soviet rockets and missiles. He cast a chill over the table by casually admitting that accidents can happen. A couple of months earlier, for example, he had been worried when a Soviet ICBM malfunctioned and overshot its course by 1,250 miles. At first he had been afraid that it might land in Alaska, but fortunately it fell into the ocean.

I asked him why the Soviets bothered to continue building bombers if they were so far advanced in missile production. Khrushchev answered, "We have almost stopped production of bombers, because missiles are much more accurate and not subject to human failure and human emotions. Humans are frequently incapable of dropping bombs on their assigned targets because of emotional revulsion. That is something you don't have to worry about in missiles."

When I asked him about submarines, Khrushchev said, "We are building as many submarines as we can." Mikoyan shot him a quick glance and said, "The Chairman means we are building as many submarines as we need for our defense."

I asked about the development of solid fuels for powering missiles; Khrushchev replied, "Well, that is a technical subject which I am not capable of discussing."

By this time the atmosphere had become fairly tense. Pat smiled at Khrushchev and said, "I'm surprised that there is a subject that you're not prepared to discuss, Mr. Chairman. I thought that with your one-man government you had to know everything and have everything firmly in your own hands."

Mikoyan came suavely to his leader's rescue. "Even Chairman Khrushchev does not have enough hands for all he has to do, so that is why we are here to help him," he said.

Finally I said quietly that it was largely because of belligerent talk from the Soviet leaders that the world was as fearful of war as it was. "I hope you don't think that you can hold a meeting of Communists from fifty-one countries in Moscow without our knowing what they are up to and what kind of directives they are getting. Just recently in Poland, you openly declared that the Soviet Union supports communist revolutions everywhere."

"We are against terror against individuals," he replied, "but if we go to the support of a communist uprising taking place in another country, that is a different question. If the bourgeoisie doesn't surrender power peacefully, then it is true that force may be necessary."

"In other words, you consider that workers in capitalist states are 'captives' whose liberation is justified?" I asked.

Khrushchev blustered and said that it wasn't interference if the Soviets were supporting a genuine internal uprising.

I asked him about the fact that the Soviet newspapers and radio had openly endorsed the terrorism against Pat and me in Venezuela. The Soviet press had expressed complete sympathy with the mob that had tried to kill us there.

Khrushchev paused for a moment and then leaned across the table toward me. In a low voice, thick with emotion, he said, "We have a saying that 'you are my guest, but truth is my mother,' so I will answer your very serious question. You were the target of the righteous indignation of the people there. Their acts were not directed against you personally, but against American policy—against the failure of your American policy."

"I accept your right to have your own opinion and to have sympathy for these violent acts," I said. "But I want to point out that when great military power like that of the Soviet Union is coupled with such revolutionary opinions and sympathies, there is a grave danger of matters getting out of control. This is why such strong men like Eisenhower and you should meet. But such meetings would have to take place on a basis of give and take. You are one of the most effective spokesmen for your own views that I have ever seen, Mr. Chairman. But you have only one theme. You say that the United States is always wrong, and the Soviet Union is never wrong. Peace cannot be made that way."

This fired him anew and he began another long harangue which lasted almost an hour. As he finally wound down, I said, "My question is whether there is any room for negotiation in your position. Suppose I were the President of the United States sitting here across the table from you instead of the Vice President. Is your position so fixed that you would not even listen to the President?"

Perhaps he was tired by his long monologue. He was

obviously not interested in pursuing the question further, because he answered me with a vague reference to Berlin and soon rose to indicate that the luncheon was at an end.

It had been 3:30 when we sat down; it was almost nine o'clock when we finally rose from the table. Everyone seemed a little dazed. We had been talking for over five hours.

Khrushchev's intention had been to bully us—to overwhelm us with Soviet military strength and his willingness to use it. Like most tyrants, he considered the trapped audience and the interminable monologue important weapons in his personal arsenal. But I had deprived him of their use that afternoon. Tommy Thompson confirmed what I had already guessed: the ordinary instincts of most of the Americans who met Khrushchev were to be pleasant and agreeable with him, and he took this courtesy as a sign of weakness. After that long luncheon at the dacha I knew that my intuition had been right. Khrushchev would respect only those who stood up to him, who resisted him, and who believed as strongly in their own cause as he believed in his.

At the end of my trip I made an unprecedented radio and television address to the Soviet people. Tommy Thompson and Professor William Y. Elliott of Harvard, who had come at my request as a member of my party, helped me prepare my remarks. Thompson suggested that I mention the incident at the market. He said that the Soviet press had made so much of it that it would be on many of my listeners' minds. In my speech I simply described what had happened, but this was the first time anyone could remember that *Pravda* had been criticized publicly, and the incident stirred debate among the Russian people long after I was gone.

Looking to the future, I said that "to me the concept of coexistence is completely inadequate and negative." I went on to explain: "Coexistence implies that the world must be divided into two hostile camps with a wall of hate and fear between. What we need today is not two worlds but one world where different peoples choose the economic and political systems which they want, but where there is free communication among all the peoples living on this earth."

I tried to make clear what lay at the heart of our differences with the Soviet leadership: not which system was better, but whether one nation should seek to impose its system on other nations. Recalling Khrushchev's famous prediction that our grandchildren would live under communism, I said: "Let me say that we do not object to his saying this will happen. We only object if he tries to bring it about....We prefer our system. But the very essence of our belief is that we do not and will not try to impose our system on anybody else. We believe that you and all other peoples on this earth should have the right to choose the kind of economic or political system which best fits your particular problems without any foreign intervention."

After leaving the Soviet Union, we made a brief visit to one of the captive nations—Poland.

The Polish government was extremely sensitive to the fact that Khrushchev had received a noticeably cool reception when he had recently visited Warsaw, and therefore no public announcement had been made of the time of our arrival or the route our motorcade would take. But the people knew, thanks to Radio Free Europe and the underground network that survives even in tightly controlled Communist societies.

It was a Sunday, and many people did not have to be at work. As we left the airport we soon were greeted, first by small clusters, and then by huge throngs of people, waving, clapping, shouting, cheering, many with tears streaming down their faces. Hundreds threw bouquets of flowers into my car, into Pat's car, even into the press buses that followed behind. The government security forces were totally unprepared. Time and again the motorcade was stopped by the surging crowds pressing forward, shouting "*Niech zyje Ameryka*"—"long live America"—and "*Niech zyje Eisenhower*," "*Niech zyje Nixon*." A quarter of a million people turned out that Sunday. Despite the presence of Soviet troops, and the fact that they share a common border with the Soviet Union, on that Sunday the people of Poland demonstrated dramatically not only their friendship for the United States but also their detestation of their Communist rulers and Soviet neighbors.

When we landed in Washington on August 5, we were welcomed by a large and enthusiastic crowd. The Soviet trip had an enormous impact in America. The film clip of my first encounter with Khrushchev at the Exhibition had been shown 'on U.S. television, and the coverage of our other meetings had presented me as the man who stood up to Khrushchev.

There was a disadvantage to this reputation, however. Some press observers suggested that if I became President I might not be able to get along with Khrushchev, and Khrushchev subsequently did everything he could to lend credence to this theory.

1960 CAMPAIGN

Of the five presidential campaigns in which I was a direct participant, none affected me more personally than the campaign of 1960. It was a campaign of unusual intensity. Jack Kennedy and I were both in the peak years of our political energy, and we were contesting great issues in a watershed period of American life and history.

Our differences were distinct. He preached the orthodox Democratic gospel of government activism, making sweeping promises and issuing rhetorical challenges to leap ahead into an era of new leadership and social welfare. I carried the banner of constructive postwar Republicanism, bred of conservative beliefs that a healthy private sector and individual initiative set the best pace for prosperity and progress. But beyond these differences, the way the Kennedys played politics and the way the media let them get away with it left me angry and frustrated.

Kennedy and I entered the 1960 race fairly evenly matched in terms of our personal campaigning strengths and weaknesses. My most formidable asset was that, since Caracas and my confrontation with Krushchev, I was probably the best known political figure in the country after Eisenhower. The polls showed that people thought of me as the more experienced candidate, and I intended to stress my experience in the campaign. Perhaps most important of all, I was physically, mentally, and emotionally ready for this campaign, and I was enthusiastically looking forward to it. I knew it would be an uphill battle, but I felt I could win.

On the other side of the ledger, my most serious liability was the weakness of my Republican Party base. In 1960 there were 50 million Americans of voting age who considered themselves Democrats and only 33 million who considered themselves Republicans. In the disastrous 1958 elections, Republican candidates had won only 43 percent of the total votes cast. The Republican Party was at its lowest ebb since 1936, and 1960 boded to be a bad year for anyone who ran with an (R) after his name on the ballot.

I considered Kennedy's biggest assets to be his wealth and the appeal of his personal style. Some Republican strategists thought that these would weigh against him, but I felt that in the new decade of the sixties, after eight years of Eisenhower's rather grandfatherly manner, people might be ready for an entirely new style of presidential leadership. He would also be able to count on strong party unity. Unlike Republicans, Democrats are usually able to swallow their differences and unite behind their party's nominee.

Kennedy had two principal political liabilities. In my judgment one was only apparent—his Catholicism; the other was real—his lack of experience. The religion issue would cut several ways and would probably end up as an advantage for Kennedy. The pockets of fundamentalist anti-Catholic prejudice that still existed were concentrated in states that I stood to win anyway. But many Catholics would vote for Kennedy because he was Catholic, and some non-Catholics would vote for him just to prove they were not bigoted. The experience issue, however, was one on which Kennedy was vulnerable. He had been an active senator for nearly eight years and had established a reputation for the caliber of his mind and the quality of his staff, but he had not carved out any particular areas of expertise.

Just as I was sure that Kennedy would be the Democratic nominee, I was almost as sure that Lyndon Johnson would be his running mate. Both men were superb campaigners and politicians, and a Kennedy-Johnson ticket would be ideally balanced in age, experience, region, and religion. It might be an uneasy and joyless marriage of convenience, but it was a ticket that would unite the party by assuring Southern conservative support even though the ticket was headed by a Northern liberal.

The obvious Republican equivalent of the Kennedy-

Johnson ticket would have been a Nixon-Rockefeller ticket. I made the gesture of offering him the position when we met in New York on July 22. As I expected, he declined. I was not altogether sorry, because Rockefeller's independent temperament would have made him a much more difficult running mate for me to deal with than Johnson would be for Kennedy. But his refusal left me without the option of the kind of finely balanced ticket the Democrats had achieved.

Kennedy made a strong impression and received a great deal of favorable publicity during the Democratic National Convention, which was held in Los Angeles in mid-July. Before the Republicans convened in Chicago on July 25, my pollster, Claude Robinson, placed the Kennedy-Johnson ticket 55 percent to 45 percent ahead of any ticket the Republicans might field.

Just after 11 P.M. on Wednesday, July 27, the state of Arizona moved to make unanimous my nomination as Republican candidate for President of the United States. I immediately called a meeting of thirty-two Republican Party leaders to confer on the selection of the vice presidential nominee.

Before the convention there had been six names on my list of possible running mates: Ambassador to the United Nations Henry Cabot Lodge of Massachusetts; Senator Thruston Morton of Kentucky; Congressman Walter Judd of Minnesota; Congressman Gerald Ford of Michigan; Secretary of the Interior Fred Seaton of Nebraska; and Secretary of Labor Jim Mitchell of New Jersey.

By the time I met with the leaders in my suite at the Blackstone Hotel, I had narrowed the list to three: Judd, Morton, and Lodge. Both Judd and Morton urged that I select a man with a national reputation who would appeal to wider political constituencies than I might otherwise attract. Morton wanted the position badly, but he magnanimously recommended that I choose Lodge. Eisenhower had also urged me to select him.

Lodge had the greatest support among the assembled party leaders, and overall, I thought he was the right choice. While I was concerned that his domestic views were more liberal than mine, I had no doubt that if the need ever arose he would be able to take over and serve as President with great distinction. At 2:30 A.M. I telephoned him and asked him to be my running mate. He accepted and immediately made plans to come to Chicago.

My next task was the final preparation of my acceptance speech. I wanted to use the speech to break the stolid and unimaginative stereotype of Eisenhower and his administration that had been presented by Kennedy and the Democrats at their convention. I wanted to challenge people with the rather daring idea that a Republican campaign could be exciting and even inspiring. I asked Rockefeller to introduce me to the convention. He understood that the unity of the party would depend largely on his words, and he came through effectively—as did Goldwater, when he spoke.

I declared my intention to wage a campaign unprecedented in scope: "I announce to you tonight—and I pledge to you—that I personally will carry this campaign into every one of the fifty states of this nation between now and November 8." In an election between evenly matched contenders, every vote—and thus every state—would be important.

I believed the key issue of the campaign would be experience, and in my acceptance speech I brought home that message.

I asked all Americans to join in meeting what I believed was to be the exciting challenge we faced in the years ahead:

> We shall build a better America . . . in which we shall see the realization of the dreams of millions of people not only in America but throughout the world—for a fuller, freer, richer life than men have ever known in the history of mankind.

> What we must do is wage the battles for peace and freedom with the same . . . dedication with which we wage battles in war. . . . The only answer to a strategy of victory for the Communist world is a strategy of victory for the free world. Let the victory we seek . . . be the victory of freedom over tyranny, of plenty over hunger, of health over disease, in every country of the world.

The publicity surrounding the Republican convention and my acceptance speech succeeded as I had hoped they would. Gallup reported a decisive switch from the pre-convention results: now Nixon-Lodge led Kennedy-Johnson, 53 percent to 47 percent. But I knew that the immediate impact of the convention and the speech would soon wear off, and the projections about the election itself were that we would be neck and neck until the finish.

An entirely new factor entered American political campaigning in 1960 with the first televised debates between the two presidential candidates.

An incumbent seldom agrees willingly to debate his challenger, and I knew that the debates would benefit Kennedy more than me by giving his views national exposure, which he needed more than I did. Further, he would have the tactical advantage of being on the offensive. As a member of Eisenhower's administration, I would have to defend the administration's record while trying to move the discussion to my own plans and programs. But there was no way I could refuse to debate without having Kennedy and the media turn my refusal into a central campaign issue. The question we faced was not whether to debate, but how to arrange the debates so as to give Kennedy the least possible advantage.

We agreed to a series of four appearances. The second and third were to be, in effect, joint press conferences. The first and fourth would more nearly resemble a debate format: each candidate would make opening and closing statements, and a panel of reporters would ask questions. One of these two programs would be devoted exclusively to domestic issues, the other exclusively to foreign policy. Determining our preferred order of these two broadcasts turned out to be one of my most important decisions of the campaign—and one of my biggest mistakes.

Since there was no precedent for this kind of televised debate, we could only guess which program would have the larger audience. Foreign affairs was my strong suit, and I wanted the larger audience for that debate. I thought more people would watch the first one, and that interest would diminish as the novelty of the confrontation wore off. Most of my advisers believed that interest would build as the campaign progressed, and that the last program, nearest

Election Day, would be the most important one. I yielded to their judgment and agreed that in the negotiations to set up the debates I would agree to scheduling the domestic policy debate first and the foreign policy debate last.

I began my fifty-state campaign with two trips into the South in mid-August. The first was to North Carolina, my home for three years when I had been at Duke. We received a warm welcome, and the successful visit was marred only by a seemingly small incident: I bumped my knee getting into a car in Greensboro. The immediate pain soon passed, and I thought no more about it. But twelve days later the knee became intensely painful, and tests showed it was badly infected. I required massive doses of penicillin and other antibiotics—and two weeks in bed at Walter Reed Hospital.

All the plans I had made for seizing the initiative by extensive early campaigning were now useless. It was painful when my knee was injected with antibiotics, but it was even more painful to know that each day I was falling behind Kennedy and losing precious time in the campaign.

I was finally able to leave the hospital on Friday, September 9. After only a weekend at home I began an intensive two-week tour covering 15,000 miles and twenty-five states. The first day of that tour was representative of the entire schedule. We took an early morning flight from Baltimore to appear at a rally in Indianapolis, from Indianapolis we flew to Dallas for a motorcade and rally, and from Dallas to San Francisco for a rally at the airport and one downtown in Union Square. I got to bed at 2 A.M. Eastern time.

This pace was bound to tell. Within three days I was running a fever of over 103 degrees, but I continued to keep my schedule. I can now see that I should have accepted the advice of my campaign manager, Bob Finch, my chief scheduler, Jim Bassett, and other members of my staff who urged that my hospital stay was a compelling and legitimate reason to abandon the pledge I had made to carry my campaign to all fifty states of the Union. But having made the pledge, I was stubborn and determined to carry it through. I felt that I had to move decisively to catch up with Kennedy. While I was in the hospital he had regained the lead in the Gallup poll by a slender 51 percent to 49 percent. So instead of lightening my campaign load, I intensified it to make up for lost time.

In the first week after leaving the hospital, I covered fourteen states. In the second week, I covered eleven states. After less than a day at home in Washington, I took a night flight to Chicago, where a crowd of 5,000 was waiting at the airport. After making a short speech and shaking some hands, we moved on to the street rallies that had been planned in each of the five election wards we were to drive through. It was after 1 A.M. before I got to bed. The first debate with Kennedy was set for that evening, September 26.

In the morning I was scheduled to make a speech to the annual convention of the carpenters' union, so I had only the afternoon for an uninterrupted review of my notes for the debate. When I arrived at the studio I was mentally alert but I was physically worn out, and I looked it. Between illness and schedule, I was ten pounds underweight. My collar was now a full size too large, and it hung loosely around my neck.

Kennedy arrived a few minutes later, looking tanned, rested, and fit. My television adviser, Ted Rogers, recommended that I use television makeup, but unwisely I refused, permitting only a little "beard stick" on my perpetual five o'clock shadow.

During the debate Kennedy was continually on the offensive, attacking Eisenhower's policies and calling them ineffective. His solution was a more active and interventionist federal government. I did not disagree with many of the goals he outlined, but I sharply attacked the means he advocated to achieve them.

While most of the questions dealt with substantive issues, it was a question of no real substance that hurt me. One of the reporters referred to a response Eisenhower had made a month earlier at the end of a press conference when asked what major ideas I had contributed as Vice President: "If you give me a week, I might think of one." Eisenhower had meant, "Ask me at next week's conference"—but he immediately knew that it had come out wrong, and he called me that afternoon to express his regret. The Democrats leaped on Eisenhower's slip to undercut my emphasis on experience and to imply that Eisenhower was less than enthusiastic about my candidacy.

Most of the editorial writers who based their opinions on substance rather than image, even in the pro-Kennedy Washington *Post* and St. Louis *Post-Dispatch*, called the debate a draw, but postdebate polls of the television audience gave the edge to Kennedy. Ralph McGill of the Atlanta *Constitution*, who supported Kennedy, observed that those listening to the debate on radio reported that I had had the better of it. This was small comfort, since the television audience had been five to six times larger than the radio audience.

It is a devastating commentary on the nature of television as a political medium that what hurt me the most in the first debate was not the substance of the encounter between Kennedy and me, but the disadvantageous contrast in our physical appearances. After the program ended, callers, including my mother, wanted to know if anything was wrong, because I did not look well.

The second debate was scheduled for October 7, eleven days later, in Washington. I knew I had to counter the visual impression of the first debate. A four-a-day regimen of rich milkshakes helped me put on weight, and this time I agreed to use makeup.

I immediately took the offensive, hitting at Kennedy's vulnerabilities. In May he had made a rash statement after the Soviets had shot down one of our U-2 spy planes, suggesting that Eisenhower should apologize to Khrushchev. I argued that an American President should never apologize for action taken to defend America's security. I also hammered hard on Kennedy's shortsighted unwillingness to defend the offshore islands of Quemoy and Matsu, occupied by Chiang Kai-shek's forces.

After the second debate, the consensus was that I had had the better of it. The New York *Times* reported that I "clearly made a comeback, came out ahead." A New York *Herald Tribune* editorial stated that I had "clearly won the second round." But 20 million fewer people had watched this debate than had watched the first one.

In the third debate, on October 13, I appeared in a studio in Los Angeles while Kennedy spoke from New York. I continued on the offensive throughout. Once again I hit hard on the Quemoy-Matsu issue, stating that Kennedy's willingness to surrender the islands to the Communists under threat of war was no different from submitting to blackmail. Shortly after the third debate I learned that one of Kennedy's top foreign policy advisers had telephoned Secretary of State Herter to say that Kennedy did not want to give the Communists the impression that America would not stand united against aggression and was therefore prepared to revise his position in order not to appear to oppose the administration on this issue. I saw this as Kennedy's way of trying to slide away from an unpopular position, and my immediate inclination was not to let him get away with it. But the Quemoy-Matsu situation was so tense, and the importance of America's role in discouraging Communist aggression was so great, that I decided not to press the point if Kennedy modified his stand. I pointed out how his changed attitude reflected his lack of experience, and then let the issue drop.

The fourth and final debate took place in New York on October 21. This was the foreign policy debate, which we had hoped would have the largest audience. Instead, the number of viewers stubbornly remained 20 million fewer than for the first.

The day before, afternoon newspaper headlines had proclaimed: *Kennedy Advocates U.S. Intervention in Cuba; Calls for Aid to Rebel Forces in Cuba.* I knew that Kennedy had received a CIA briefing on the administration's Cuban policy and assumed that he knew, as I did, that a plan to aid the Cuban exiles was already under way on a top-secret basis. His statement jeopardized the project, which could succeed only if it were supported and implemented secretly.

I knew that this matter would be raised in our debate. In order to protect the secrecy of the planning and the safety of the thousands of men and women involved in the operation, I had no choice but to take a completely opposite stand and attack Kennedy's advocacy of open intervention in Cuba. This was the most uncomfortable and ironic duty I have had to perform in any political campaign. I shocked and disappointed many of my own supporters and received support from all the wrong places for what I considered to be all the wrong reasons. I was praised in the Washington *Post* for my restraint. Within a few days Kennedy modified his position; but only a fraction of the debate audience ever was aware of that. In that debate, Kennedy conveyed the image—to 60 million people—that he was tougher on Castro and communism than I was.

Those who claim that the "great debates" were the decisive turning point in the 1960 campaign overstate the case. To ascribe defeat or victory to a single factor in such a close contest is at best guesswork and oversimplification.

The public opinion polls seem to indicate that the debates had little significant effect on the outcome of the election. Before the first debate, Gallup had shown Kennedy ahead, 51 percent to 49 percent. Seven weeks later, after all debates and intensive nationwide campaigning, Gallup showed Kennedy with 50.5 and me with 49.5. On Election Day the polls were virtually even: 49.7 percent for Kennedy, 49.6 percent for me.

As for television debates in general, I doubt that they can ever serve a responsible role in defining the issues of a presidential campaign. Because of the nature of the medium, there will inevitably be a greater premium on showmanship than on statesmanship.

After the last debate, with just over two weeks left before the election, I intensified my efforts even more. The polls showed me slightly behind, but I could sense a momentum beginning to develop, and I felt that with a final push we could go over the top.

I continued the killing pace of the rally speeches and in the last week added several fifteen-minute television talks on the major issues. I tried to draw even more sharply my major differences wtih Kennedy over domestic issues, primarily the economy. The government spending programs he was proposing would raise the federal budget some $15 billion and set off rounds of higher prices. I wanted to reach as many voters as I could in these last days, and television would have been the ideal way. But television time costs money, and our campaign had run short. We could afford only one telethon, which we scheduled for the day before the election.

From the earliest days of the campaign I had planned to keep Eisenhower in reserve as a political weapon that would be the more powerful for having been sparingly used. We felt that his appearances in the last two weeks of the campaign might tip the balance to me in some close areas in key states. Eisenhower fully agreed with my strategy at the outset. But as Kennedy began to attack the record of his administration—especially on the phony issue of the alleged "missile gap," which insulted Eisenhower's intelligence as well as his competence—he began to bridle under his self-imposed restraint.

I was to have lunch with Eisenhower at the White House on October 31 to discuss a specially expanded campaign schedule, which he had suggested undertaking. The night before the luncheon Pat received a phone call from Mamie Eisenhower. She was distraught and said that Eisenhower was not up to the strain campaigning might put on his heart. But he was so determined to get out and answer the attacks on his record that she could not dissuade him. She begged Pat to have me make him change his mind without letting him know that she had intervened. "Ike must never know I called you," she said.

The next morning I received an urgent call from the White House physician, Major General Howard Snyder. He told me he could not approve a heavy campaign schedule for the President. Eisenhower's dander was up because of Kennedy's attacks, but the strain of intense campaigning might be too much for his limited cardiac reserves. "I know what he *wants* to do, and he usually won't take my advice," Snyder said. "Please, either talk him out of it or just don't let him do it—for the sake of his health."

I had rarely seen Eisenhower more animated than he was when I arrived at the White House that afternoon. An expanded itinerary had been worked out that included several additional stops in the crucial areas of downstate Illinois, upstate New York, and Michigan, where the race was believed to be particularly close. He was confused—to put it mildly—when I opened the discussion with half a dozen rather lame reasons for his not carrying out the expanded itinerary. At first he was hurt and then he was angry. But I stood my ground and insisted that he should limit himself to the original schedule and to the election eve telecast with

Lodge and me. He finally acquiesced. His pride prevented him from saying anything, but I knew that he was puzzled and frustrated by my conduct.

Those who traveled with Eisenhower for his few appearances during that final week said that they had never seen him show such partisan fervor, not even in his own campaigns. In retrospect, it seems possible that if he had been able to carry out his expanded campaign schedule, he might have had a decisive impact on the outcome of the election. For example, his appearance in southern Illinois, which would have had extensive coverage in eastern Missouri as well, might have tipped the balance in those states that Kennedy won by razor-thin margins.

Under the circumstances, however, I could make no other decision than to discourage him and limit his participation. It was not until years later that Mrs. Eisenhower told him the real reason for my sudden change of mind regarding his campaigning.

After one last frenetic week, it was over. Since the convention in August I had traveled over 65,000 miles and visited all fifty states. I had made 180 scheduled speeches and delivered scores of impromptu talks and informal press conferences. There was nothing more I could have done. I did not let up once, nor did my staff. The campaign had an intensity of spirit that was at once exhausting and uplifting.

We flew to California to vote and wait for the results, which would begin coming in around six o'clock, after the polls closed in the East. To make the long afternoon pass more quickly, Pat took Tricia and Julie to Beverly Hills to have their hair done. I eased the tension of the wait by driving south on the Pacific Coast Highway with Don Hughes, Jack Sherwood, and a Los Angeles police driver. Hughes remarked that he had never been to Tijuana, so we continued all the way to Mexico. We were back in Los Angeles by the time the first results were coming in.

Any election night is an emotional roller coaster ride, but election night in 1960 was the most tantalizing and frustrating I have ever experienced. The Texas results went back and forth; Ohio leaned my way; but Pennsylvania was going to Kennedy. The Daley machine was holding back the Chicago results until the downstate Republican counties had reported and it was known how many votes the Democrats would need to carry the state. The overall trend seemed to favor Kennedy, but at midnight I was fast closing the gap of 1.7 million votes that had opened up between us early in the evening. It was problematical whether I could overtake him, but the race was still not over. Even so, most of the press had already predicted a substantial Kennedy victory, and there was tremendous pressure from reporters and commentators for me to concede. I decided to make a brief statement acknowledging the apparent trend of the returns thus far.

Pat, fierce with pride, adamantly opposed making any statement and said that she would not join me. A few minutes later, as I tried to jot down notes on what to say, she came into my room and said, "I think we should go down together." I do not know which quality I loved more—the fight or the warmth. It is at such moments, when you see the effect it has on your family, that the ache of losing is the greatest.

At 12:15 A.M. we went downstairs to the ballroom of the Ambassador Hotel. I said, "If the present trend continues, Senator Kennedy will be the next President of the United States." Our loyal supporters in the ballroom were yelling, "Don't give up!" and "You're still going to win!" Pat could barely manage to keep back the tears. I wanted only to get away to the solitude of our suite.

Julie shook me awake at six the next morning. Kennedy's lead had narrowed to 500,000 votes, and there were stories of massive vote frauds in Chicago and Texas. Everett Dirksen urged me to request a recount and demanded that I not concede. He warned that once I had conceded, voting records would be destroyed or otherwise disappear, and a recount would be impossible. After his call I sat alone for a few minutes reviewing the situation.

We had made a serious mistake in not having taken precautions against such a situation, and it was too late now. A presidential recount would require up to half a year, during which time the legitimacy of Kennedy's election would be in question. The effect could be devastating to America's foreign relations. I could not subject the country to such a situation. And what if I demanded a recount and it turned out that despite the vote fraud Kennedy had still won? Charges of "sore loser" would follow me through history and remove any possibility of a further political career. After considering these and many other factors, I made my decision and sent Kennedy a telegram conceding the election.

I had planned to sleep on the long flight back to Washington, but I found I could not. Instead, I thought about how close we had come and what we should have done differently.

The 1960 election was the closest presidential contest since Harrison-Cleveland in 1888. Kennedy received 34,221,000 votes and I received 34,108,000: a difference of only 113,000. The shift of one-half vote per precinct could have changed the outcome.

We found Washington astir with talk of election fraud. Many Republican leaders were still urging me to contest the results and demand recounts. Eisenhower himself urged that course, offering to help raise the money needed for recounts in Illinois and Texas.

There is no doubt that there was substantial vote fraud in the 1960 election. Texas and Illinois produced the most damaging, as well as the most flagrant, examples. In one county in Texas, for example, where only 4,895 voters were registered, 6,138 votes were counted. In Chicago a voting machine recorded 121 votes after only 43 people had voted; I lost this precinct, 408–79. The Washington journalist and editor Benjamin Bradlee, a close friend of Kennedy's, has written in his book, *Conversations with Kennedy,* that Kennedy called Mayor Daley on election night to find out how things were shaping up in Chicago. "Mr. President," Daley reportedly said, "with a little bit of luck and the help of a few close friends, you're going to carry Illinois."

Several years after Kennedy's death, New York *Times* columnist Tom Wicker wrote in the foreword of Neal Peirce's *The People's President:* "Nobody knows to this day, or ever will, whom the American people really elected President in 1960. Under the prevailing system, John F. Kennedy was inaugurated, but it is not at all clear that this was really the will of the people or, if so, by what means and margin that will was expressed."

As experienced as I was in politics by 1960, I encountered several new and unexpected factors, each of which had a strong influence on the outcome of the election.

First, there was the substantial and influential power that the emergence of television as the primary news medium gave the reporters, commentators, and producers. It was largely they who decided what the public would hear and see of the campaign.

Another new political phenomenon was the way so many reporters in 1960 became caught up in the excitement of Kennedy's campaign and infected with his personal sense of mission. This bred an unusual mutuality of interests that replaced the more traditional skepticism of the press toward politicians. Theodore H. White described this in his book *The Making of the President 1960*:

> By the last weeks of the campaign, those forty or fifty national correspondents who had followed Kennedy since the beginning of his electoral exertions into the November days had become more than a press corps—they had become his friends and, some of them, his most devoted admirers. When the bus or the plane rolled or flew through the night, they sang songs of their own composition about Mr. Nixon and the Republicans in chorus with the Kennedy staff and felt that they, too, were marching like soldiers of the Lord to the New Frontier.

Writing to me after the election, Willard Edwards, the Chicago *Tribune*'s veteran political analyst, put it more bluntly. He referred to the "staggering extent of . . . slanted reporting" as "one of the most, if not the most, shameful chapters of the American press in history."

The other unique aspect of this campaign was the Kennedy organization and technique. I had been through some pretty rough campaigns in the past, but compared to the others, going into the 1960 campaign was like moving from the minor to the major leagues. I had an efficient, totally dedicated, well-financed, and highly motivated organization. But we were faced by an organization that had equal dedication and unlimited money that was led by the most ruthless group of political operators ever mobilized for a presidential campaign.

Kennedy's organization approached campaign dirty tricks with a roguish relish and carried them off with an insouciance that captivated many politicians and overcame the critical faculties of many reporters. I should have anticipated what was coming as I observed some of what went on in Kennedy's brilliant but coldly mechanical destruction of Hubert Humphrey in the primaries. In his autobiography, *The Education of a Public Man*, published sixteen years later, Humphrey wrote that the Kennedy organization was undeniably impressive and successful. "But underneath the beautiful exterior," he added, "there was an element of ruthlessness and toughness that I had trouble either accepting or forgetting."

Finally, I was not prepared for the blatant and highly successful way the Kennedys repeatedly made religion an issue in the campaign even as they professed that it should not be one. Led by Robert Kennedy, they managed to turn the election partially into a referendum on tolerance versus bigotry. From this point on I had the wisdom and wariness of someone who had been burned by the power of the Kennedys and their money and by the license they were given by the media. I vowed that I would never again enter an election at a disadvantage by being vulnerable to them—or anyone—on the level of political tactics.

During the 1972 campaign, in the diary I was keeping at the time, I reflected on what might have happened if I had won the presidency in 1960:

Diary

If we had known then as much about how to campaign, etc., as we know now we would have probably won in 1960. Whether that would have been a good thing or a bad thing I am not sure. I am speaking now not personally but so far as the country was concerned. It might have been that we would have continued the establishment types in office too long and would not have done the job we should have done as far as the country was concerned. On the other hand, had we won in 1960 we would have handled the Cuban Bay of Pigs crisis much differently, and would probably have faced down the Russians and saved Cuba from Castro, with all the implications that might have had for the future. I think also that we would have handled Vietnam quite differently, and would have used our power effectively very early in the war if we had found it necessary to use it at all. In any event, history was certainly kind to us by arranging for the Cuban missile confrontation to come in 1962, which sealed the fate as far as the gubernatorial election was concerned. Had we won the gubernatorial election, as I have often pointed out, I would have inevitably been nominated in 1964 and would have lost. Of course, you could write the script a different way—had we won [in 1962] Kennedy might not have been going to Texas and Oswald might never have shot him and under the circumstances we might have had a re-run of the '60 campaign with a better chance to win than was the case after the Kennedy assassination and the martyr halo which Johnson was able to clutch to his brow as against Goldwater.

Within a few days after the election I was already thinking about what we would do next after my fourteen years in public life came to an end on January 20, 1961.

Pat and I went directly from the inaugural ceremony to the F Street Club, where Admiral and Mrs. Lewis Strauss were the hosts at a farewell luncheon for President and Mrs. Eisenhower.

When I said goodbye to Eisenhower, he held my hand for a long time as he shook it. For a moment I thought he was going to become emotional, but he said simply, "I want you and Pat to come up and visit us in Gettysburg very soon." I said that we would.

That night Pat and I had a quiet dinner at home with Tricia and Julie. They were very subdued. Both said that if I had not been cheated in Chicago and a couple of other places, we would be having this dinner at the White House. Despite the way I felt I told them that this was no time for bitterness and that one benefit of losing the election was that I would be home for dinner more often. When school was out we could do some traveling together.

My Secret Service protection had ended at noon, but I had my official car and chauffeur until midnight. John Wardlaw had been my driver for almost eight years, and I asked him if he would mind coming back after dinner for one last ride through the city.

The streets were snarled with traffic, made worse by the snow and ice. Hundreds of cars and rented limousines were lined up outside the hotels, waiting to pick up men in tails and women in long gowns on their way to the inaugural balls. No one noticed us as we drove past the White House and headed through the streets toward Capitol Hill.

I asked John to park in the space reserved for the Vice President's car, and I got out and walked up the broad stone stairs. A surprised guard let me in, and I walked past the entrance to the Senate Chamber and down the long corridor to the Rotunda, the dome of the Capitol rising above it. The only sound was the echo of my heels on the bare stone floor.

I opened a door and went onto the balcony that looks out across the west grounds of the Capitol. I had stood there many times before. It is one of the most magnificent vistas in the world, and it never seemed more beautiful than at this moment. The mall was covered with fresh snow. The Washington Monument stood out stark and clear against the luminous gray sky, and in the distance I could see the Lincoln Memorial. I stood looking at the scene for at least five minutes. I thought about the great experiences of the past fourteen years. Now all that was over, and I would be leaving Washington, which had been my home since I arrived as a young congressman in 1947.

As I turned to go inside, I suddenly stopped short, struck by the thought that this was not the end—that someday I would be back here. I walked as fast as I could back to the car.

Private Citizen
1961-1967

The day after Kennedy's inauguration, Pat and I flew to Eleuthera in the Bahamas to spend a few days with friends, trying to relax while we discussed our plans for the immediate future.

During my fourteen years of public service, we had lived a comfortable but simple life. After we paid the costs of moving from Washington to Los Angeles, our sole asset other than personal effects was a $48,000 equity in our house in Washington. I felt that I owed it to Pat to take a job that would pay well enough to support a reasonably comfortable life and send our daughters to good colleges, and also give me time with them to make up for the long hours and days I had had to spend away from home during the vice presidency. I also wanted a job that would allow me to stay at least a little involved in politics.

Pat and I wanted to move back to California, so I decided to accept an offer from the Los Angeles law firm of Adams, Duque, and Hazeltine. In 1946, when I was running against Voorhis, Earl Adams had offered me a job with the firm in the event I lost the election. As I told him jokingly, 'it had taken me only fourteen years to get the right qualification. We did not want to take Tricia and Julie out of school in the middle of the year, so we decided that Pat would stay with them in Washington and I would live in Los Angeles until June.

It was not an easy time. Relatives and friends wanted me to stay with them, but I preferred to be alone, so I rented a small bachelor apartment on Wilshire Boulevard not far from the office. I learned to fix my own meals. Fortunately, I have never been fussy about food and I actually learned to enjoy heating a TV dinner and eating it alone while reading a book or magazine.

I had thought that I could move right into the work of the law firm, just as I had done with every other challenging new job. For several weeks, however, I found it difficult to concentrate and almost impossible to work up much enthusiasm. I realized I was experiencing the letdown of defeat.

In 1968 I had a different and completely unexpected experience: the fatigue and letdown of victory. But then there was the challenge of setting up a new administration. In 1961 I found that virtually everything I did seemed unexciting and unimportant by comparison with national office. When you win, you are driven by the challenges you have to meet; when you lose, you must drive yourself to do whatever is required.

The last thing I wanted to do was talk to people about the election. But many of those who called or wrote had supported me so loyally over the years that I felt an obligation to see them or at least to talk to them by phone. Requests for public appearances and speeches continued to pour in. But aside from the fact that I was simply "talked out" from the campaign, I believed that the new administration should have the traditional honeymoon of freedom from partisan criticism.

As time went on I began to adjust to my new life and even to enjoy it. In the spring Pat and the girls came out, and we spent Easter vacation by the ocean in Santa Monica. The girls loved the beach and the warm weather, and their enthusiasm about California began to rub off on me.

THE BAY OF PIGS

I became increasingly interested in taking up my role as titular leader of the Republican Party. I was disturbed by some of Kennedy's early foreign policy actions. During his first weeks in office he was confronted with a crisis involving Communist aggression in Laos. After an initial show of strength in one of his first press conferences, he pulled back and ended up accepting a supposedly neutral government that everyone knew would be heavily influenced by the Communists. I decided that it was time for the administration's honeymoon to end, and I agreed to give a speech before the Executives Club of Chicago on May 5, 1961.

Because my speech was to deal with foreign policy, I asked the White House to allow Allen Dulles to give me a CIA briefing. My request was approved, and we arranged to meet at my house in Washington at six o'clock on April 19.

Two days earlier, while I was still in California, I heard the news that anti-Castro rebel forces had landed in Cuba at a spot unhappily known as the Bay of Pigs. During the next few days the news reports were frustratingly sketchy and incomplete, but it was clear that the invaders had met with considerable resistance and had not been able to achieve much initial success.

While I was waiting for Dulles on April 19, I picked up the afternoon Washington *Star,* and read more pessimistic—but still inconclusive—reports about the invasion. Dulles sent word that he would be late, and when he finally arrived shortly after 7:30, he looked nervous and shaken.

I asked him if he would like a drink, and Dulles replied, "I certainly would—I really need one. This is the worst day of my life!"

"What's wrong?" I asked.

He shook his head. "Everything is lost," he said dejectedly. "The Cuban invasion is a total failure."

Dulles explained that after his election Kennedy had given his go-ahead to the invasion plans formulated under Eisenhower, and the CIA had continued to train the Cuban exiles. However, some of Kennedy's advisers urged him to call off the action on the ground that if our support became known, America's prestige in the world would be badly damaged. They held out the specter of World War III if the

Soviet Union decided to intervene, and they painted grim pictures of the repercussions if the invasion failed.

The invasion had been planned for February, but Kennedy postponed it while internal debate raged within the administration. Finally on April 15 Kennedy decided to go ahead. There was sad admiration in Dulles's voice when he said, "It took great courage for the President to overrule some of his advisers and order the invasion to proceed." But the nervous aides made a final attempt to dissuade Kennedy, and he tried to keep both sides happy by making last-minute compromises. He canceled two of the three air strikes that were intended to knock out Castro's air force and to provide air cover for the invasion forces. The Free Cuban forces landing in the Bay of Pigs found themselves sitting ducks for Castro's Soviet-made bombers. By holding back the air support, Kennedy had doomed the operation.

At first the White House and Adlai Stevenson, our ambassador to the United Nations, completely denied any American involvement in the invasion. Then Kennedy had to deny the denials. Our international prestige suffered a double blow—first for having mounted an unsuccessful invasion and then for trying to deny it.

Dulles stared at the floor. "I should have told him that we must not fail," he said. "And I came very close to doing so, but I didn't. It was the greatest mistake of my life."

I spent the morning of April 20 on Capitol Hill conferring with the Republican leaders. We agreed that the situation was too serious for partisanship. We all had to stand behind the President until the crisis was over. When I got home early that afternoon, I found a note from Tricia next to the telephone in the hall: "JFK called. I knew it! It wouldn't be long before he would get into trouble and have to call on you for help." I dialed the familiar White House number. The operator immediately put my call through to the President. Sounding tense and tired, he wasted no time on small talk. He said, "Dick, could you drop by to see me?"

Kennedy was standing at his desk in the Oval Office talking to Lyndon Johnson. We greeted each other with solemn handshakes. The atmosphere was tense.

After Johnson left the room, Kennedy motioned me to

one of the small sofas near the fireplace; he sat in his rocking chair. "I had a meeting with the members of the Cuban Revolutionary Council," he said. "Several of those who were there had lost their sons, brothers, or other close relatives or friends in this action. Talking to them and seeing the tragic expressions on their faces was the worst experience of my life."

I asked about the Cubans' morale. He said, "Last night they were really mad at us. But today they have calmed down a lot and, believe it or not, they are ready to go out and fight again if we will give them the word and the support."

With that he jumped up from his chair and began pacing back and forth in front of his desk. His anger and frustration poured out in a profane barrage. Over and over he cursed everyone who had advised him: the CIA, the Chairman of the Joint Chiefs of Staff, members of his White House staff. "I was assured by every son of a bitch I checked with—all the military experts and the CIA—that the plan would succeed," he said.

Everything had been going so well for him; a few days earlier he stood high in the polls, and his press was overwhelmingly favorable. Now he was in deep trouble, and he felt that he was the innocent victim of bad advice from men whom he had trusted. He paced up and down with his fists clenched tightly.

After he had blown off some steam, he returned to his rocking chair. For a moment the room was silent. It suddenly struck me how alone he must feel—how wronged yet how responsible.

He looked over at me and said, "What would you do now in Cuba?" Without any hesitation I replied, "I would find a proper legal cover and I would go in. There are several justifications that could be used, like protecting American citizens living in Cuba and defending our base at Guantánamo. I believe that the most important thing at this point is that we do whatever is necessary to get Castro and communism out of Cuba."

He seemed to think about what I said, and then he shook his head. "Both Walter Lippmann and Chip Bohlen have reported that Khrushchev is in a very cocky mood at this time. This means that there is a good chance that, if we move on Cuba, Khrushchev will move on Berlin. I just don't think we can take the risk, in the event their appraisal is correct."

I explained that I looked at Cuba in the larger context of Communist ambitions around the world. Khrushchev would probe and prod in several places at the same time, and as soon as we showed any weakness, he would create a crisis to take advantage of us. I said that we should take some action in both Cuba and Laos, including if necessary a commitment of American air power.

"I just don't think we ought to get involved in Laos," Kennedy said, "particularly where we might find ourselves fighting millions of Chinese troops in the jungles." This was a complete reversal of what he had said on television in March about the vital importance of defending Laos. "In any event," he continued, "I don't see how we can make any move in Laos, which is thousands of miles away, if we don't make a move in Cuba, which is only ninety miles away."

I was surprised and disappointed that he did not make the logical connection between his own statements: that the Communist threat was indivisible, and unless it was resisted everywhere there was really no point in resisting it anywhere. But I knew that this was no time to try to convince him of that; this was a crisis—he wanted and needed my support.

I said, "I will publicly support you to the hilt if you make such a decision in regard to either Laos or Cuba, and I will urge all other Republicans to do likewise. I realize that some political observers say you might risk political defeat in 1964 if either the Cuban or Far East crisis involves an American armed forces commitment. I want you to know that I am one who will never make that a political issue if such action becomes necessary."

For a moment he seemed lost in thought, weighing what I had said. Then he gave a slight shrug of his shoulders and said, "The way things are going and with all the problems we have, if I do the right kind of job, I don't know whether I am going to be here four years from now."

We had been talking for almost an hour, and I felt that I had at least lightened his burden by listening to him and by assuring him that I would not turn this crisis into a partisan exercise.

"It really is true that foreign affairs is the only important issue for a President to handle, isn't it?" he said. "I mean, who gives a shit if the minimum wage is $1.15 or $1.25, in comparison to something like this?"

We walked out to the covered porch alongside the Oval Office. The spring flowers in the Rose Garden were in full bloom. A White House car was waiting for me in the driveway.

As he walked to the car with me, he said that Pat Brown was concerned because a poll showed him running behind me for governor of California. Although supporters had suggested I run, I didn't have the slightest intention of doing so, and I was very surprised that Kennedy and Brown were discussing that possibility.

We shook hands, and he turned and walked back up the path to his office. His hands were thrust in his jacket pockets, but his head was bowed and his usually jaunty walk seemed slow. At that moment I felt empathy for a man who had to face up to a bitter tragedy that was not entirely his fault but was nonetheless his inescapable responsibility.

I flew to Chicago on May 5 to make the Executives Club address.

I began by stressing that as far as I was concerned, criticism of the new administration should be responsible and constructive, and focus only on issues of substance. Still, I was concerned about the way Kennedy had handled the Bay of Pigs, and I wanted to make my concerns known. I said, "Those who talk constantly of our prestige would seem to believe that we are in a popularity contest with other countries to see who was most liked and admired. What we must remember is that we are in a fight for our lives."

My greatest concern was that Kennedy, having been burned in Cuba, would be reluctant to stand up to the Communists in the other places like Laos, Vietnam, or Berlin. I said that "the worst thing that could flow from our failure in Cuba is not the temporary drop in prestige which seems to obsess too many observers but that this failure may discourage American policymakers from taking decisive steps in the future because there is a risk of failure."

There was a long round of applause when I said that we

should learn at least one lesson from the Cuban invasion: "Whenever American prestige is to be committed on a major scale we must be willing to commit enough power to obtain our objective even if all of our intelligence estimates prove wrong. Putting it bluntly, we should not start things in the world unless we are prepared to finish them."

After this speech I found that I was back in the national limelight as leader of the "loyal opposition." Any concerns I might have had that time would hang heavy in private life were soon dispelled. With the demands of the law firm, my personal and political correspondence, unavoidable travel, routine office work, preparation of the columns I was writing for the Times-Mirror syndicate, and planning for a book I had agreed to write, this was one of the busiest periods of my life. As usual, the ones who suffered most, and most silently, were my family. One of my reasons for moving to California was to have more time with Pat and the girls, but I think I saw them even less that year than I had when we were in Washington.

By December 1961, I was more tired than I had been at the end of the 1960 campaign. I was almost ten pounds underweight from strain and fatigue, and I became short-tempered at home and at the office.

It was ironic that while I was writing a book about handling crises, I had let myself get so run-down that I was not in good shape for making a decision which created a major new crisis for me and my family.

RUNNING FOR GOVERNOR: 1962

The pressures to run for governor began almost from the day I arrived back in California.

Friends, old supporters, and business and party leaders from all over the state approached me by letter, phone, or in person, urging me to run. I replied that I wasn't interested in running for anything so soon after the 1960 presidential election, and urged that they look elsewhere for a candidate.

But the pressure continued and by the beginning of the summer I began for the first time to consider seriously the possibility of running. My intuition was unchanged—I still thought it would be a case of running for the wrong office at the wrong time.

I had a long talk with Eisenhower at the El Dorado Country Club near Palm Springs. He thought that I should run for governor in 1962 and then run for the presidency again in 1964. He said, "It has been my experience that when a man is asked by a majority of the leaders of his party to take on an assignment, he must do so or risk losing their support in the future. If you don't run and the Republican candidate loses, you will be blamed for it, and you will be through as a national political leader."

A few weeks later I wrote a long letter to Eisenhower outlining the pros and cons of running. In this letter I expressed the deepest underlying reason for my apparent indecisiveness and lack of enthusiasm:

> Another argument which is made against my running is that from the time I started the campaign in January through the period I served in office, I would have to devote my attention almost exclusively to the problems of California. It is true that Rockefeller has been able to comment at times on national and international issues but my own belief is that our problems here are so complex and also we are, frankly, physically so far away from the centers of national and international news media that I simply do not believe it would be possible for me to continue to speak at all constructively on national and international issues if I decided to run for governor.

The polls were then indicating that I could defeat Brown fairly easily; one had me beating him 5 to 3. I am not sure that Eisenhower's advice would have been the same had he thought there was a considerable risk of my losing.

Rose Woods had come to California to be my secretary at the law firm. She called me at home on the afternoon of July 11 to tell me that Whittaker Chambers had died. The news hit me hard. I knew that Chambers had not been well, but he had survived so much in his life that I suppose I had come to think of him as indestructible. Now he was dead.

That night I reread the last letter he had written to me, shortly after I had returned to California in February 1961:

It seems possible that we may not meet again—I mean at all. So forgive me if I say here a few things which, otherwise, I should not presume to say.

You have decades ahead of you. Almost from the first day we met (think, it is already 12 years ago) I sensed in you some quality, deep-going, difficult to identify in the world's glib way, but good, and meaningful for you and multitudes of others. I do not believe for a moment that because you have been cruelly checked in the employment of what is best in you, what is most yourself, that that check is final. It cannot be. . . .

You have years in which to serve. Service is your life. You must serve. You must, therefore, have a base from which to serve.

Some tell me that there are reasons why you should not presently run for governor of California. Others tell me that you would almost certainly carry the state. I simply do not know the facts. But if it is at all feasible, I, for what it is worth, strongly urge you to consider this.

Friends whose political judgment I respected were sharply divided as to what I should do. Eisenhower, Tom Dewey, and J. Edgar Hoover urged me to run for governor so that I could have a new political base. Herbert Hoover and General Douglas MacArthur advised me to run for Congress so that I would have a forum from which I could address national and international issues. MacArthur put it in his characteristically oracular way: "California is a great state but it is too parochial. You should be in Washington, not Sacramento."

Early in August I had a long talk with Bob Finch. We discussed some of the political forces that would be arrayed against me if I ran.

First, there would be the all-out opposition of the Kennedy administration. They would do everything they could to stop me from getting a new political lease on life by winning the governorship. Nor could I count on the support of the many California Republicans who favored Rockefeller or Goldwater for President in 1964. The two men would be opposing each other as the convention neared, but they would join in opposing me now.

Joe Shell, the Republican leader in the state assembly,

had already begun to campaign for the gubernatorial nomination, and had picked up considerable conservative support and money. Finally, there was Pat Brown himself. Although generally considered something of a bumbler, he was in the enviable political position of being a man whom no one particularly disliked.

By the end of the conversation I was more convinced than ever that my first intuition was right: I should not run for governor in 1962. The word found its way back to Washington, and within a couple of days I received a call from Len Hall and Cliff Folger urgently requesting to talk with me before I announced my decision. The next afternoon they were on a plane for California.

Hall said, "Either you run or you're finished in national politics. In 1962 you'll have Rockefeller running in New York, another strong candidate for governor in Pennsylvania, another in Michigan. Who will remember Dick Nixon? You can only win in '64 if you run and win for governor now." They both stressed how much Eisenhower was counting on me to run and win.

My own political judgment at that point told me that Kennedy would be almost unbeatable in 1964. If I ran for governor I felt I would have to pledge to spend the full term in Sacramento. That would leave someone else to square off in 1964 against Kennedy, his money, and his tactics.

The real problem was that I had no great desire to be governor of California. Equally compelling was my knowledge of how strongly Pat felt against my running. She thought that we owed it to ourselves as well as to Tricia and Julie to spend more time with them during their adolescent years.

My inclination was against making the race. But Eisenhower's advice and the pressures brought to bear by Hall and Folger, by Whittaker Chambers's letter, and by the importunings of many close friends began to tip the balance in favor of a decision to run.

I dreaded bringing up the subject with Pat and Tricia and Julie, so I left it until the last possible moment. I had asked Bob Finch to arrange a press conference on September 27, when I would announce my decision. On September 25, as we all sat around the table after dinner, I described some of the factors and the conflicting advice I had been receiving and weighing. I said that I was now thinking of running, but I wanted to know their feelings before I made up my mind.

Pat, as I expected, took a strong stand against it. Many women would give everything they have to be a celebrity, but Pat has always been one of those rare individuals whose ego does not depend on public attention. Her deepest feelings have always been private, and she shares them only with her family and loved ones. She had been by my side through all the invective and controversy of the congressional campaigns; she had endured nobly and silently the agony of the fund crisis; and during the vice presidency she had constantly balanced the requirements of national office with the importance of maintaining a normal and loving home for Tricia and Julie. But there had been so many campaigns and dinners and trips that after the 1960 defeat she had looked forward to building a new and private life in California for ourselves and the girls. She said, "If you run this time, I'm not going to be out campaigning with you as I have in the past." Tricia and Julie at fifteen and thirteen were still too young to exert a major influence on my decision, but I wanted to hear their views. When Julie saw that Pat and I had such a strong difference of opinion, she said that she would approve whatever I decided. Tricia was the only one who took a positive line: "I am not sure whether you should run," she said, "but I kind of have the feeling that you should just to show them you aren't finished because of the election that was stolen from us in 1960!"

We talked about it for almost an hour. Finally I went upstairs to my study. I sat at my desk and started to make some notes for the press conference, announcing that I had decided not to run for governor.

Half an hour later Pat came in. She sat down on the sofa, outside the pool of light cast by my desk lamp. Her face was in the shadows, but I could tell from her voice that she was fighting not to show her tremendous disappointment. "I have thought about it some more," she said, "and I am more convinced than ever that if you run it will be a terrible mistake. But if you weigh everything and still decide to run, I will support your decision. I'll be there campaigning with you just as I always have."

"I'm making notes to announce that I won't be running," I said, pointing to the yellow pad before me on the desk.

"No," she said firmly, "you must do whatever you think is right. If you think this is right for you, then you must do it."

We sat for some time in silence. Then she came over to me, put her hand on my shoulder, kissed me, and left the room. After she had gone, I tore off the top sheet of paper and threw it into the wastebasket. On a fresh page I began making notes for an announcement that I had decided to run.

On September 27 I held a press conference at the Statler Hilton Hotel in Los Angeles.

I said I had two decisions to announce. The first was that I would not be a candidate for President of the United States in 1964. The second was that I would be a candidate for governor of California in 1962.

This wasn't enough for many of the reporters, who demanded more. One of them referred to General William Tecumseh Sherman's famous statement, "If nominated I will not run and if elected I will not serve." I told him, "I think General Sherman's statement meant that he wasn't a candidate. Calvin Coolidge's statement was that he did not choose to run. The Nixon statement is that I shall not be a candidate in 1964."

Pat Brown greeted my announcement by immediately stating that despite my claim to the contrary, I would be a candidate for President in 1964: "He sees the governorship of this state only as a stepping-stone for his own presidential ambitions."

Instead of beginning to plan strategy and plot the campaign, I now had to spend the next three months writing and editing the final draft of my book, *Six Crises*. I had undertaken to write it a few months after Kennedy's inauguration, when the prospect of running for anything in 1962 had seemed unthinkable. Now I was up against a publisher's deadline at the very time that I had to make vital decisions about the campaign.

As I traveled through the state before the June primary, I met with a lot of heckling—but it was different from the heckling in 1950. Then I had been heckled by the far left; now I was being heckled by the far right. Members of the ultra right-wing John Birch Society had infiltrated a considerable number of Republican organizations. One of the costliest and most difficult decisions I made was to disavow support for or from any Republican candidate who was a member of the John Birch Society and who would not repudiate the extremist statements of the society's founder, Robert Welch, namely that President Eisenhower was "a dedicated, conscious agent of the Communist conspiracy," and that Foster Dulles was "a Communist agent."

Congressmen John Rousselot and Edgar Hiestand were two of my closest personal and political friends. But both were members of the John Birch Society. Whether or not they personally believed any or all of Welch's accusations, neither would repudiate them. Thus I lost not only their support but the support of their friends in two heavily Republican districts. Politically it was a no-win proposition, but as a matter of conscience I had no choice. I could not accept support from an extremist group whose leader had defamed Eisenhower and Dulles.

The primary was held on June 5. Although I won easily, Shell got over a third of the vote. I took that as a portent of the kind of Republican defections I might have to expect in November.

Fortunately my campaign organization was excellent and already was functioning smoothly; some of those who participated gained valuable experience that served us well six years later in my campaign for the presidency. Bob Haldeman was campaign manager; Maurice Stans was finance chairman. Herb Klein was my major press adviser, and a young man named Ron Ziegler worked on his staff.

Immediately after the primary, pressure began for a candidates' debate. Brown was now running ahead in the polls, so I felt that a debate would be in my interest. Brown tried to avoid a debate for just that reason, and the closest we got was a joint appearance before a group of newspaper

298

editors and publishers in San Francisco on October 1. The Los Angeles *Times* ran a front-page account of the session under the headline: *Brown and Nixon in Violent Clash.*

After Brown and I made brief opening statements, one of the first to ask a question was Tom Braden, publisher of the Oceanside *Blade Tribune.* Braden was a liberal columnist whom Pat Brown had appointed to the State Board of Education.

"I wanted to ask you whether you as Vice President, or as a candidate for governor, think it proper for a candidate for governor, morally and ethically, to permit his family to receive a secret loan from a major defense contractor in the United States?" he said.

The chairman of the meeting jumped in immediately. "Mr. Nixon, you don't need to answer that question if you don't want to. I would rule it out on the basis that it is outside the issues of this campaign."

"As a matter of fact, Dr. Robinson, I insist on answering it," I replied. "I welcome the opportunity of answering it. Six years ago, my brother was in deep financial trouble. He borrowed $205,000 from the Hughes Tool Company. My mother put up as security for that loan practically everything she had—a piece of property, which, to her, was fabulously wealthy, and which now is producing an income of $10,000 a year to the creditor.

"My brother went bankrupt six years ago. My mother turned over the property to the Hughes Tool Company. Two years ago in the presidential election, President Kennedy refused to make a political issue out of my brother's difficulties and out of my mother's problems, just as I refused to make a political issue out of any of the charges made against the members of his family.

"I had no part or interest in my brother's business. I had no part whatever in the negotiation of this loan. I was never asked to do anything by the Hughes Tool Company and never did anything for them. And yet, despite President Kennedy's refusing to use this as an issue, Mr. Brown, privately, in talking to some of the newsmen here in this audience, and his hatchetmen have been constantly saying that I must have gotten some of the money—that I did something wrong.

"Now it is time to have this out. I was in government

for fourteen years as a congressman, as a senator, as Vice President. I went to Washington with a car and a house and a mortgage. I came back with a car and a house and a bigger mortgage.

"I have made mistakes, but I am an honest man. And if the Governor of this state has any evidence pointing up that I did anything wrong in this case, that I did anything for the Hughes Tool Company, that I asked them for this loan, then instead of doing it privately, doing it slyly, the way he has—and he cannot deny it, because newsmen in this audience have told me that he has said, 'We are going to make a big issue out of the Hughes Tool Company loan'—now, he has a chance.

"All the people of California are listening on television. The people of this audience are listening. Governor Brown has a chance to stand up as a man and charge me with misconduct. Do it, sir!"

Brown was taken completely off guard by the way I had turned the issue around, and he made an unsuccessful attempt to deny that he and his staff had been raising it in the campaign. In fact, they continued to raise it throughout the campaign. The media loved the story and played it up big—both because it made such tantalizing copy and because it was so damaging to me.

I felt that I came out considerably ahead of Brown in this meeting; apparently he agreed, because he refused to participate in other joint appearances when I challenged him to do so.

Aside from the Hughes loan and my repudiation of the John Birch Society, my biggest problem in the campaign was the question of my actual interest in being governor of California. Despite my constant disclaimers of any plans to run for presidency in 1964, I was simply not able to convince many people. A poll taken during the campaign showed the extent of the difficulty: 36 percent thought I was interested in serving as governor, 64 percent thought I was interested in running for President.

Looking back, I recognize that there was a measure of truth in what the polls showed the public perceived. I thought that Kennedy would be unbeatable, so my disclaimers of any interest in running for President were absolutely honest. But I was really not all that eager to be governor of California.

Despite my efforts to campaign on the issues, every press conference brought questions about the personal attacks being made against me—I must have answered the question about the Hughes loan at least a hundred times. Reporters never tired of asking if I had repudiated the John Birch Society, or of having me reiterate my refusal to support Rousselot and Hiestand. There was no morning, afternoon, or evening that I did not deny that I was planning to use the governorship as a stepping-stone to a presidential candidacy in 1964. Most reporters showed little interest in the many detailed proposals I made on the cost of state government, crime, education, or the necessity for creating a better business climate in California.

On the evening of October 22 President Kennedy reported in a dramatic television address that the Soviets had moved medium-range nuclear missiles into Cuba. He announced a U.S. naval blockade of Cuba and demanded that the Soviets dismantle and remove the missiles immediately. The world waited tensely for Khrushchev's response to this direct challenge. For almost two days, America seemed to be tottering on the brink of nuclear war. As always in time of international crisis, the nation rallied behind the President. I strongly supported Kennedy's actions in a statement I made in Oakland and a statewide television address in San Diego.

The Cuban missile crisis completely dominated the news for the last days of the 1962 campaign. Now I knew how Stevenson must have felt when Suez and the Hungarian rebellion flared up in the last days before the election in 1956. I knew that any chance I might have had of narrowing Brown's lead in the polls was now gone.

We had to play the dreary drama through to its conclusion on election night. I left for the hotel early in the afternoon, telling my family that I would call as soon as I had an idea how it was going.

It was all over before midnight even though the numerical vote was still close. I knew the state well enough to know that votes in districts not yet reported would not be enough to carry me over. I went to bed around three o'clock, and when I got up four hours later, the worst was confirmed. I had lost to Brown by 297,000 out of nearly 6 million votes cast.

Herb Klein went downstairs to read my concession statement. I watched on the television in my room as the reporters harassed him, demanding that I come down and make a personal appearance. They were so persistent that Klein finally came up to my room and asked if I would consider meeting them. The anger and frustration, the disappointment and fatigue struggling inside me burst out. I said, "Screw them. I'm not going to do it. I don't have to, and I'm not going to. You read them my concession message to Brown, Herb, and if they want to know where I am you can tell them that I've gone home to be with my family."

Klein went back downstairs. Just as I was leaving, I looked at the television for a moment and heard the insulting tone of the reporters still asking, "Where's Nixon?"—as if I had some obligation to appear before them.

I said, "I'm going down there," and started toward the elevator. I walked into the press room and went up to the platform where Herb was talking at the microphone. I had not had time to shave. I felt terrible, and I looked worse.

I began, "Good morning, gentlemen. Now that Mr. Klein has made his statement, and now that all the members of the press are so delighted that I have lost, I'd like to make a statement of my own."

I could see many of the reporters exchanging glances. This didn't sound like the abject performance they had been hoping for.

I thanked my staff and the many volunteer workers in my campaign, and I assessed the Republican victories in New York, Pennsylvania, Ohio, and Michigan. I congratulated Brown on his victory.

Then I returned to my main theme: "At the outset I

said a couple of things with regard to the press that I noticed some of you looked a little irritated about. And my philosophy with regard to the press has never really gotten through. And I want it to get through.

"This cannot be said for any other American political figure today, I guess. Never in my sixteen years of campaigning have I complained to a publisher, to an editor, about the coverage of a reporter. I believe a reporter has got a right to write it as he feels it. I believe if a reporter believes that one man ought to win rather than the other, whether it's on television or radio or the like, he ought to say so. I will say to the reporters sometimes that I think, well, look, I wish you'd give my opponent the same going over that you give me.

"And as I leave the press, all I can say is this: for sixteen years, ever since the Hiss case, you've had a lot of—a lot of fun—that you've had an opportunity to attack me, and I think I've given as good as I've taken."

I continued, "I leave you gentlemen now and you will now write it. You will interpret it. That's your right. But as I leave you I want you to know—just think how much you're going to be missing.

"You won't have Nixon to kick around anymore, because, gentlemen, this is my last press conference, and it will be one in which I have welcomed the opportunity to test wits with you. I have always respected you. I have sometimes disagreed with you. But unlike some people, I've never canceled a subscription to a paper, and also I never will.

"I believe in reading what my opponents say, and I hope that what I have said today will at least make television, radio, and the press first recognize the great responsibility they have to report all the news and, second, recognize that they have a right and a responsibility, if they're against a candidate, to give him the shaft, but also recognize if they give him the shaft, put one lonely reporter on the campaign who will report what the candidate says now and then.

"Thank you, gentlemen, and good day."

The people in the room were stunned into silence. I know that Herb was shocked and disappointed. I turned to him and said, "Herb, I did that for you. These guys deserved it, and I'm glad I did it."

To the great majority of my supporters and virtually all of the press, my so-called last press conference was a personal and political disaster. Maury Stans told me that he thought it would cost me $100,000 a year in new legal clients. My critics and opponents exulted in what they interpreted as the ultimate, self-inflicted blow. Columnist Mary McGrory called it "Richard Nixon's Last Hurrah" and reported: "Nixon carried on for fifteen minutes in a finale of intemperance and incoherence perhaps unmatched in American political annals. He pulled the havoc down around his ears, while his staff looked on aghast."

The reaction was not all negative. I received thousands of letters and wires from friends and supporters across the country who said they were glad that someone finally had the guts to tell the press off.

I have never regretted what I said at the "last press conference." I believe that it gave the media a warning that I would not sit back and take whatever biased coverage was dished out to me. In that respect, I think that the episode was partially responsible for the much fairer treatment I received from the press during the next few years. From that point of view alone, it was worth it.

On the Sunday night following the election, Howard K. Smith appeared on ABC television with a half-hour special program called "The Political Obituary of Richard Nixon." His four guests were intended to represent a cross section of my friends and foes over the years: Murray Chotiner and Jerry Ford spoke as longtime friends, lamenting that my defeat and my press conference seemed to mark the end of my political career. Jerry Voorhis talked bitterly about the 1946 campaign. The fourth participant was Alger Hiss. Smith matter-of-factly asked him how he felt about my conduct during the Hiss-Chambers case. In an arrogantly tolerant tone of voice, Hiss said, "He was less interested in developing the facts objectively than in seeking ways of making a preconceived plan appear plausible. I regard his actions as motivated by ambition, by personal self-serving."

The immediate uproar that followed this remark helped to turn me from the sore loser of the "last press conference" into something of an injured party. The ABC switchboard lit up with hundreds of calls even before the program was finished. Eighty thousand letters and telegrams protesting Hiss's appearance poured in over the next several days. President Eisenhower called Jim Hagerty, then an executive at ABC, to tell him that he was astonished at the incredibly bad taste of putting Hiss on the air to comment on my defeat.

If ABC was prepared to write my political obituary, those within the Kennedy administration were not inclined to leave anything to chance. They did everything possible to drive a final nail into the coffin. Three months after I lost the governor's race, my income tax returns were subjected to an exhaustive audit. Years later, in 1973, the IRS supervisor in charge wrote to Rose Woods to explain that although he had informed his Washington superiors of "no change" in the original audit, they sent the case back to him three separate times—persistently citing articles in newspapers and magazines as reasons for assessing me further taxes. Each time, this auditor courageously resisted, acidly noting: "We don't work cases by what the news media and magazines say; we base our findings on facts."

It was hard for me to believe that such tactics would persist even after I had been defeated for a second time and marked by political observers everywhere as a man without a political future.

Department of Justice files leaked to the New York *Times* in 1972 showed that within months of his brother's inauguration, Attorney General Robert Kennedy used the Justice Department to try to develop evidence that would justify bringing criminal charges against my mother and brother over the matter of the Hughes loan. The probe, according to this report, cleared members of my family of any wrongdoing. The political motivation behind this use of a federal agency was manifest. I especially resented the attempt to get at me through my family. These instances of abuse of the Internal Revenue Service and the Justice Department for political purposes were typical of the partisan vindictiveness that pervaded the Kennedy administration.

NEW YORK LAWYER: 1963

Shortly after the election I took a vacation in Florida

with Bebe Rebozo, whom I had first met there in 1951. We had become close friends over the years. After a few days in Miami, we flew to Nassau, and as soon as school let out Pat and the girls joined us there for the Thanksgiving holidays.

During this trip I had a long talk with my old friend Elmer Bobst, chairman of the board of the Warner-Lambert Pharmaceutical Company. He strongly urged me to leave California and move to New York. He pointed out that now that I had lost the election nothing tied me to California; that business opportunities would be much greater in New York; and that I would find life there much more interesting and stimulating.

The more I thought about the move, the more evenly balanced the arguments seemed. I was reluctant to uproot Pat and the girls again, but since the election California held much less charm for them, and I found they were quite excited by the prospect of living in New York.

A move to New York would of course have a major impact on my political status. Despite my defeat by Brown, I could still play an important, if not uncontested, leadership role in the Republican Party in California. But leaving my political base and moving to a state in which all political power was firmly held by Nelson Rockefeller, my principal rival, would be an announcement that I was ruling myself out as an active political figure for the foreseeable future.

A move to New York would mean giving up any thought of becoming a candidate for President in 1964, and running for any office in New York was out of the question. I think this factor influenced Pat as much as any other. She felt strongly that now was the time for me to get out of the political arena once and for all. Having in effect overruled the family when I ran for governor in 1962, I thought that now it was their turn. We would move to New York as soon as I could find the right job and make the necessary arrangements.

A few months later I joined the Wall Street law firm of Mudge, Stern, Baldwin, and Todd, which became Nixon, Mudge, Rose, Guthrie, and Alexander. We bought a ten-room cooperative apartment that was, coincidentally, in the same building in which Nelson Rockefeller lived.

Before beginning my new job, I was determined to keep

a long-standing promise to Pat and the girls. On June 12 we set out on a six-week vacation in Europe and the Middle East with our friends Jack and Helene Drown and their daughter, Maureen.

From our welcome abroad, no one would have guessed that I had lost two elections in the past three years and that my prospects for any political comeback seemed extremely remote. Everywhere we went we were received as if I were still Vice President.

Our schedule was full: in addition to the rigorous sightseeing involved in traveling with three teenaged girls, I had a number of meetings and talks with foreign leaders. Generalissimo Francisco Franco received me at his summer residence in Barcelona. I had never met him before, and I expected to find the rigid and unpleasant dictator pictured in the press. Instead, I found a subtle, pragmatic leader whose primary interest was maintaining the internal stability necessary to Spain's progress.

President de Gaulle invited Pat and me to have lunch with him in Paris. The luncheon—a simple meal, elegantly prepared and served—was held outdoors on a patio behind the Elysée Palace. After lunch de Gaulle rose and proposed a warm and typically eloquent toast. He said that he knew I had suffered some difficult defeats, but he predicted that at some time in the future I would be serving my nation in a very high capacity.

Perhaps the most indelible memory I have of this trip is my first sight of the Berlin Wall. We were taken on a tour of the drab city of East Berlin, but the oppressive number of Communist police who unsubtly accompanied us meant we had hardly any chance to talk to the people. That night I decided to go back. We walked through Checkpoint Charlie and stood waiting for a taxi. A man dressed in work clothes came up and whispered in my ear, "We are glad you came to East Berlin. Don't let us down. The Americans are our only hope." Then he quickly walked away.

We found a taxi and went to a restaurant where an excellent Hungarian orchestra played gypsy music. I was recognized, and after dinner I went up to the bandstand and banged out the "Missouri Waltz" on the piano.

While we were in Cairo, President Nasser arranged a special trip for us to the site of the Aswan dam. When we arrived around midnight, the temperature was still over 100 degrees. Huge Soviet cranes and bulldozers were working around the clock. When our Egyptian hosts showed us the plans for the dam, they proudly proclaimed that there were very few Russians working on the project. I could tell from the appearance of the drivers, however, that a substantial number of them were Russian.

Nasser invited Pat and me to his surprisingly modest house in Cairo. He was a man of superior intelligence and great charisma. Despite the bombast of his public utterances, I was impressed by his dignity and quiet manner in private. He was eager to have my assessment of the current attitudes and intentions of the Soviet leaders. He ventured some criticisms of President Kennedy's policy toward Israel, but I gave him no encouragement, and he quickly caught the hint and changed the subject. Several times he expressed his warm feeling for Eisenhower.

I emphasized as politely as I could that I thought his first priority should be the welfare and progress of his own people. This was a course that Nasser could not bring himself to follow. Like Sukarno and Nkrumah, Nasser had devoted the best of his energies to revolution. Now he was more interested in a grandiose crusade for Arab unity than he was in the vital but less glamorous tasks of managing and improving Egypt's economic, political, and social structure. His attitude toward Israel served his political purpose, beyond his blind intolerance of the Jews; if Israel had not existed, Nasser would have had to invent something to take its place. Arab unity needed a common cause, and the destruction of Israel filled the bill.

We were awed by the Pyramids and by the Valley of the Kings at Luxor, but equally impressive to me was what I learned about modern Egypt and its ruler. I could see that, despite its terrible poverty, the country was moving ahead and would eventually exert enormous influence throughout the Middle East. I could also see that, despite Israel's superior technology and training, the Egyptians and the Arabs would in the end submerge the Israelis and defeat them by sheer weight of numbers unless some accommodation were reached. Closer relations between the United States and Israel's Middle Eastern enemies were going to be of the utmost importance, not only to Israel itself but also to the prevention of a confrontation between the great powers in the Middle East.

President Kennedy was in Rome on a state visit while we were there. One afternoon the phone rang in our hotel room and the operator informed me that the President was calling. Sounding happy and relaxed, he said that he had heard we were in Rome and just wanted to say hello. We exchanged brief pleasantries. This was to be the last time I talked to him; five months later he was dead.

For Pat, Tricia, Julie, and me, this trip was one of the happiest times of our lives. What made it so special was that it gave us a chance to be together as a family. We walked through castles and cathedrals in Spain; we explored the ruins of the Parthenon in Athens and of the Forum in Rome; we rode in gondolas in Venice and went to the top of the Eiffel Tower in Paris; we sailed down the Rhine and listened to Big Ben chime the hours at London's Houses of Parliament.

Nevertheless, it was a thrill to see the Statue of Liberty below us as our plane came in to New York. Vacation time was over, and I immediately devoted my full energies to my new responsibilities as a Wall Street lawyer.

From the first day at my new job I was sure that I had made the right decision in moving to New York. New business came to Nixon, Mudge, and the firm expanded as we had hoped it would.

The chance to see old friends in the New York area and to make new ones gave our family the stimulation and the revitalized outlook on life that we needed after the California campaign. One night less than two weeks after we had moved into our new apartment, Pat looked across the dinner table and said to me, "I hope we never move again."

By the summer of 1963, although I was barely settled into my New York law practice, I was already getting calls and letters from friends and party leaders across the country urging me to run again for the presidency in 1964. Goldwater, they said, would drive off almost everyone except the party's most conservative fringe; and Rockefeller would split the party down the middle. I could sympathize with their concerns, but my instinct was to stay completely out of it.

I strongly felt that I should not seek the nomination in 1964. Despite Kennedy's recent slippage in the polls, his lackluster domestic record, and his crisis-prone foreign policy, I felt that he was almost certainly going to be re-elected. With party unity and a favorable press added to the advantages of being an incumbent, Kennedy would be virtually unbeatable. I could not idly consider the thought of subjecting Pat, the girls, or myself to the tension and disappointment of another losing campaign against Kennedy. I was also well aware that after my defeats in 1960 and 1962, another defeat in 1964 might so brand me with a loser image that I could never recover.

I also had to consider the motives of those who were urging me to run. Many of them were opposed to Goldwater's candidacy for reasons I did not share. I liked Goldwater personally. He was direct and sincere and deeply patriotic. He had a tendency to be impulsive and to shoot from the hip, but I knew that he was also well intentioned and open to advice. Even though Goldwater was farther to the right of my centrist position than Rockefeller was to the left of it, I felt that Goldwater's deviation from midstream at least put him deeper into Republican territory, while Rockefeller's made him practically a liberal Democrat on many issues.

I received a call from our upstairs neighbor on the morning of September 3, inviting me for cocktails that afternoon. When I arrived Rockefeller greeted me warmly, and after an exchange of small talk, we quickly settled down to a serious discussion.

"I'm going to go for the nomination," he said. "I am not going to back out this time. If I did, I would appear to be unstable. In my opinion, Kennedy will be a one-termer. He has messed up on all issues—Vietnam, the international monetary situation, the Atlantic alliance, civil rights."

He continued, "I have nothing to lose. I would worry if Barry won, because he's just too shallow. He only went to college for one year. He doesn't have a good staff, and he has a very superficial approach to problems. I will take on the task of stopping Barry. If I don't he's going to get it by default."

He turned to his other rivals. "Romney wants to run," he said, "but the regular Republicans don't like his independent attitude toward the party. His greatest weakness is that he knows too little of the world and is too sure of what he doesn't know. Bill Scranton wants to run, but only if he's drafted, and there just isn't a draft around with Bill Scranton's name on it."

He paused, then leaned closer to me. "Dick, you can't run actively. You *could,* but it would be a big mistake, and you don't make that kind of mistake. What we both have to recognize is that you and I are the only ones qualified on both foreign and national issues to serve as President. Despite some differences, we have generally agreed on basic policies."

I kept silent and tried to look noncommittal. Finally he said, "What I want to suggest is that, if you will support me now, if there is a deadlock at the convention, I will support you."

I thanked him for his candor but said that I planned not to participate personally in the campaign, except to support whoever was nominated. I did not respond to his suggestion that we make a deal.

As Thanksgiving approached, I held firm to my plan that unless something completely unexpected happened, I would not become a candidate in 1964; I would not endorse anyone before the convention; and I would try to remain on good terms with all the potential candidates so that I could play the role of party unifier regardless of who won.

I flew to Dallas on November 20 to attend a board meeting of the Pepsi-Cola Company, one of our firm's clients. Several local reporters asked for an interview, and the next day I met with them briefly at my hotel. I had read that demonstrations were planned against Kennedy and Johnson, who were to visit Dallas the next day. I told the reporters that, however strongly people felt about particular issues or personalities, the President and Vice President

311

deserved to be treated with respect wherever they appeared.

Early on the morning of November 22 on the way to the Dallas airport I saw the flags displayed along the motorcade route for the presidential visit. Arriving in New York, I hailed a cab home. We drove through Queens toward the 59th Street Bridge, and as we stopped at a traffic light, a man rushed over from the curb and started talking to the driver. I heard him say, "Do you have a radio in your cab? I just heard that Kennedy was shot." We had no radio, and as we continued into Manhattan a hundred thoughts rushed through my mind. The man could have been crazy or a macabre prankster. He could have been mistaken about what he had heard; or perhaps a gunman might have shot at Kennedy but missed or only wounded him. I refused to believe that he could have been killed.

As the cab drew up in front of my building, the doorman ran out. Tears were streaming down his cheeks. "Oh, Mr. Nixon, have you heard, sir?" he asked. "It's just terrible. They've killed President Kennedy."

Later in the day I called Edgar Hoover in Washington. He came right on the line and without wasting words I asked, "What happened? Was it one of the right-wing nuts?"

"No," he replied, "it was a Communist." Months later Hoover told me that Oswald's wife had disclosed that Oswald had been planning to kill me when I visited Dallas and that only with great difficulty had she managed to keep him in the house to prevent him from doing so.

I never felt the "there but for the grace of God go I" reaction to Kennedy's death that many people seemed to imagine I would. After eight years as Vice President I had become fatalistic about the danger of assassination. I knew that given the number of people who, for whatever reasons, want to kill a President, it takes a combination of luck and the law of averages to keep him alive. I did not think of Kennedy and myself as interchangeable: I did not think that if I had won in 1960 it would have been I rather than he riding through Dealey Plaza in Dallas at that time, on that day.

Since the 1960 election there had been no love lost between Kennedy and me; I had been critical of his performance as President. But I admired his ambition and his competitiveness, and I could feel the terrible impact this tragedy would have on his closely knit family. I remembered how I had felt when first Arthur and then Harold had died, and I wished that there was something that I could do to ease the Kennedys' grief.

That night I sat up late in my library. Long after the fire had gone out I wrote a letter to Jacqueline Kennedy.

Richard M. Nixon
810 Fifth Avenue
New York, N.Y. 10021

November 23

Dear Jackie,

In this tragic hour Pat and I want you to know that our thoughts and prayers are with you.

While the hand of fate made Jack and me political opponents I always cherished the fact that we were personal friends from the time we came to the Congress together in 1947. That friendship evidenced itself in many ways including the invitation we received to attend your wedding.

Nothing I could say now could add to the splendid tributes which have come from throughout the world to him.

But I want you to know that the nation will also be forever grateful for your service as First Lady. You brought to the White House charm, beauty and elegance as the official hostess for America, and the mystique of the young in heart which was uniquely yours made an indelible impression on the American consciousness.

If in the days ahead we could be helpful in any way we shall be honored to be at your command.

Sincerely,
Dick Nixon

A few weeks later I received her reply:

Dear Mr. Vice President —
    I do thank you for your
most thoughtful letter —
    You two young men — colleagues in Congress —
adversaries in 1960 — and now look
what has happened — Whoever thought such a
hideous thing could happen in this country —
    I know how you must feel — so long on the
path — so closely missing the greatest prize —
and now for you, all the question comes up again —
and you must commit all you and your family's
hopes and efforts again — Just one thing I
would say to you — if it does not work out
as you have hoped for so long — please be
consoled by what you already have — your life
and your family —

We never value life enough when we have it —

and I would not have had Jack live his life any other way — Though I know his death could have been prevented, and I will never cease to torture myself with that —

But if you do not win — please think of all that you have — With my appreciation — and my regards to your family   I hope your daughters love Chapin School as much as I did — Sincerely

Jacqueline Kennedy

The three most significant political developments in the period after Kennedy's death were the enormous strength that Goldwater began to pick up among party workers and organizers across the country, the consummate skill with which Lyndon Johnson conducted himself during his first weeks and months in the White House, and the emergence of Henry Cabot Lodge as a serious contender for the Republican presidential nomination. Johnson was able to consolidate the nation's grief over Kennedy's death, and by the first weeks of 1964 it was widely believed by objective observers in both parties that no one could beat him in November. The March 10 New Hampshire presidential primary surprised most political professionals when, as the result of a well-organized write-in campaign, Lodge came in first.

One advantage of my New York law practice was that it allowed me to travel extensively abroad to see some of the firm's international clients. In this way I was also able to visit old friends from my vice presidential days and make new ones. As a private citizen, I was able to meet with opposition leaders as well as government officials, and my business and legal contacts gave me a much more rounded view of local issues and attitudes than I had gained as an official visitor.

I took the first of these trips immediately after the New Hampshire primary, visiting Lebanon, Pakistan, Malaysia, Thailand, Vietnam, the Philippines, Hong Kong, Taiwan, and Japan. Everywhere I went I heard about America's declining prestige, and I heard expressions of dismay that the world's strongest nation was showing so little positive leadership. Perhaps most disturbing of all, I saw for myself how dangerously different the reality of the situation in Vietnam was from the version of it being presented to the American people at home.

The Asian leaders I talked with looked at Laos, where we had suffered an unqualified disaster because of Kennedy's naïve willingness to accept a "neutralist" coalition regime that was known to be a convenient cover for the Communist Pathet Lao guerrillas. They looked at Cuba, where our indecisiveness during the Bay of Pigs had given the Communists their greatest propaganda victory in many years. And now they were looking at Vietnam, where after years of encouraging and building up the anticommunist Saigon government, we seemed reluctant to support the measures needed to defeat the Communists. To our Asian friends and allies it looked as if a combination of political expediency, public apathy, distorted reporting in the media, and partisan politics was undermining America's will to fight against communism in Asia.

In Pakistan I saw my old friend, President Ayub Khan. He spoke sadly about what he believed had been American collusion in the murder of President Ngo Dinh Diem in Vietnam on November 1, 1963, three weeks before Kennedy's assassination. "I cannot say—perhaps you should never have supported Diem in the first place. But you did support him for a long time, and everyone in Asia knew it. Whether they approved or disapproved, they knew it. And then, suddenly, you didn't support him anymore—and Diem was dead." He shook his head and continued, "Diem's murder meant three things to many Asian leaders: that it is dangerous to be a friend of the United States; that it pays to be neutral; and that sometimes it helps to be an enemy! Trust is like a thin thread, and when it is broken it is very hard to put together again."

In Bangkok, Prime Minister Thanom Kittikachorn warned against any relaxation of the war against the Vietcong. If Vietnam were to fall, he said, Communist influence would have a green light in Southeast Asia. Pote Sarasin, the distinguished scholar-diplomat who had been Thailand's ambassador in Washington when I was Vice President, said that Johnson's eagerness to begin talks with the Vietcong would only encourage them to hold out for better terms. "What America should do," he said, "is convince the Vietcong that they cannot win their struggle either in South Vietnam or in Washington. Then you should present them with a final offer that they can accept or reject. If they reject it, then you should prosecute the war relentlessly."

I arrived at Saigon's Tan Son Nhut Airport on a hot rainy afternoon. Sandbags were piled up around the hangars, and armed soldiers patrolled the runways.

The Vietnamese military leaders I met fully understood the nature of their enemy. One told me, "It is the same as when they were the Vietminh. They will stop at nothing, and they will settle for nothing short of winning everything. We cannot compromise with them, and we cannot negotiate with them. This has to be a fight to the finish. With your help and support, we are ready to fight them and beat them."

Both the Americans and the Vietnamese military leaders were distressed that Washington was holding them back from launching air raids into North Vietnam as well as ground raids into Laos to cut off the pipeline of Vietcong arms and supplies known as the Ho Chi Minh trail. Many American officers I talked to thought they were being restrained because of the election year at home, and some of them blamed the highly distorted reports in the American media.

During a long conversation over dinner with Cabot Lodge, who was then U.S. ambassador to South Vietnam, I described my concerns. He listened attentively and took a long time before he replied. "I know that a lot of people are impatient with the way things are going here," he said, "and I know that the military men don't like being held back. But there's a bigger and broader problem that can't be settled by fighting over it. The problem in South Vietnam is less military than economic. The Vietcong draw their strength from hungry peasants, and if we want to wean them from communism we shouldn't shoot at them—we should distribute food to them."

Lodge argued against pursuing the Vietcong forces into Laos or Cambodia. Even more surprising to me, he said American troops should avoid fighting the Vietcong except to retaliate when Americans were killed. I could hardly believe that I was hearing this from one as versed as Cabot Lodge in the tactics and techniques of international communism. I wondered whether he felt it was his duty to defend the administration's policy regardless of his own feelings, or whether he had actually been converted by the academic theorists around Johnson who thought that the problem of communism in Southeast Asia could be solved by economic development.

What I saw and heard on this trip convinced me that Johnson's Vietnam policy would not succeed.

In our discussions in Saigon, Lodge was eager to have my reading of the political situation at home. He thought that Johnson was highly vulnerable and could be beaten. Reversing Goldwater's "Southern strategy," he argued that a moderate Republican concentrating on the Northern cities could do very well. It was clear that he was thinking of himself as that Republican. Several years later, in fact, he told me that if he had won the Oregon primary in May he had planned to resign and return home to campaign for the nomination.

In Taiwan I was the houseguest of Chiang Kai-shek, who was predictably critical of our Vietnam policy. He said that we could never win without invading North Vietnam, and he laughed at the Strategic Hamlet Program then being pursued. "It is the familiar fallacy that economic development will defeat the Communists," he said. He leaned closer to me and almost whispered, "But only bullets will really defeat them!"

I met with Japanese Prime Minister Ikeda in Tokyo; like the other leaders I had seen he was concerned by America's apparent crisis of confidence over its policy in Vietnam. Minister of State Sato and former Prime Minister Kishi felt that the key to victory in Vietnam lay with China and Russia, and they suggested that American policy on Vietnam be formulated in terms of the great-power interests involved there.

When I returned home from this trip on April 15 I found that Vietnam was not nearly of as much interest in Washington as the race developing among Lodge, Goldwater, and Rockefeller, and by the battle of wills shaping up over whether Johnson would allow Bobby Kennedy a place on the ticket as his running mate. Asia seemed far away, and attention was focused on the Oregon primary, in which many expected Lodge to repeat his New Hampshire victory.

During April and May the polls continued to show Rockefeller doing well with voters; but in the area that counted—getting convention delegates—Goldwater was on the way to winning the nomination by a landslide. Some of my supporters still refused to give up, and they mounted a write-in effort for me in the Nebraska primary on May 12. The 42,800 votes I received there represented an astonishingly strong showing, but I had no illusions that this would slow the Goldwater bandwagon, let alone stop it. Rockefeller won a surprise victory in the Oregon primary, thus eliminating Lodge. But Goldwater's victory in the all-important California primary on June 2 eliminated Rockefeller. Last-ditch efforts to launch campaigns for Governor William Scranton of Pennsylvania and Governor George Romney of Michigan proved too little and too late. Goldwater had the nomination locked up long before the convention began in San Francisco.

THE GOLDWATER CAMPAIGN: 1964

Goldwater was nominated on the first ballot. I had asked that as the former standard-bearer I be given the honor of presenting the nominee to the convention before his acceptance speech; I looked upon this as the first and best chance to begin the ministry of party unity that I expected to preach right through Election Day in November. I singled out Scranton, Romney, Lodge, and Rockefeller by name as men of whom the Republican Party could be proud as we entered the campaign of 1964—just as in my acceptance speech in 1952 I had named Bridges, Martin, and Taft for the same reasons of party unity. I said, "Before this convention we were Goldwater Republicans, Rockefeller Republicans, Scranton Republicans, Lodge Republicans, but now that this convention has met and made its decision, we are Republicans, period, working for Barry Goldwater for President of the United States. And to those few, if there are some, who say that they are going to sit it out or take a walk, or even go on a boat ride, I have an answer: in the words of Barry Goldwater in 1960, 'Let's grow up, Republicans, let's go to work'—and we shall win in November."

I tried to stress Goldwater's Republicanism and to place him in the historical tradition of other Republican nominees. In an attempt to build drama around his first appearance before the convention as its nominee, and to go over the heads of the reporters and ask the American people to listen and judge for themselves, I concluded: "I ask you tonight, look at this man. Listen to him for the next thirty minutes. Forget the too harsh criticisms of his critics and forget even perhaps the too complimentary compliments of his friends. Remember, this is the moment of truth. Judge him as he is. Make this decision yours, not as someone else tells you to make it."

I had worked hard to find the right turn of phrase to close the speech, and I had finally found one that satisfied me: "He is the man who earned and proudly carries the title of Mr. Conservative. He is the man who, by the action of this convention, is now Mr. Republican. And he is the man who, after the greatest campaign in history, will be Mr. President—Barry Goldwater."

The speech seemed to have the desired effect of pleasing the different party factions. As Goldwater strode to the rostrum he was greeted by a long ovation. Here was the best opportunity he would have to heal the party's wounds and unite it behind him for the campaign ahead.

To my dismay, Goldwater proceeded to deliver a strident, divisive speech. He said, "Anyone who joins us in all sincerity we welcome. Though those who don't care for our cause, we don't expect to enter our ranks in any case." Half of those in the crammed Cow Palace cheered wildly. The other half sat in stunned silence: they had just been read out of the Goldwater campaign and out of the party. And he was not yet finished. He said, "Extremism in the defense of liberty is no vice! . . . Moderation in the pursuit of justice is no virtue!" This was the statement that, more than any other, enabled Johnson and the Democrats to put the skids under his campaign.

Goldwater had won the nomination, but if he had ever had any chance to win the presidency, he lost it that night with that speech.

I felt almost physically sick as I sat there on the platform. Not only did Goldwater fail to close the rifts in the party and heal its wounds; he opened new wounds and then rubbed salt in them. It was terribly sad to see a man throw away his chance for something he wanted and had worked very hard to get. But my major concern was for the thousands of Republican candidates across the country who would now be doomed to spend their campaigns trying to explain away the man at the top of the ticket.

From Goldwater's point of view, his speech was an unforgivable folly. It should have been his aim to unify the party while moving it to the right. Losing to Johnson, who was running as Kennedy's successor, need not have been ruinous. If Goldwater could have minimized congressional and state losses in 1964 and then picked up a few seats by campaigning in 1966, he would have been in a very strong position to reclaim the nomination in 1968, when the odds would favor a Republican.

Unless someone got to Goldwater and toned him down, the Republican nomination in 1968 might not be worth anything to anyone.

I knew Goldwater's speech had greatly disturbed Eisenhower. I waited until he had been back in Gettysburg for a few days before I called him to suggest two ideas.

"General," I said, "you are the only person Barry will

listen to, and you are the only person who can do something that will at least give Republican candidates a fighting chance."

"Well," he asked hesitantly, "what do you think I could do?" I suggested that he meet with Goldwater. "I know you have your doubts," I said, "but I know that Barry can be very reasonable. I am sure that he would respond to any advice you gave him about the campaign."

Eisenhower agreed to a meeting on the condition I be present. He also agreed to my second suggestion, that a Republican "summit conference" of party leaders be held a few days after our meeting with Goldwater. With Goldwater's cooperation we could turn this summit meeting into a highly publicized display of party unity. It would give Goldwater a chance to start his campaign anew, on a basis of moderation and unity.

To set the stage, I suggested to Goldwater that we take steps to quiet the controversy still raging over his acceptance speech. I offered to write a letter asking for clarification, and then to make public both my letter and his reply. He agreed, and in his letter he substantially modified his controversial "extremism" statement. He wrote: "If I were to paraphrase the two sentences in question in the context in which I uttered them I would do it by saying that wholehearted devotion to liberty is unassailable and that halfhearted devotion to justice is indefensible."

When I read this I breathed a sigh of relief. At least he had not used the codeword *extremism*. Rockefeller had hung the extremist tag around Goldwater's neck in the primaries, and Goldwater's acceptance speech had turned it into a noose. I hoped this letter would loosen it a bit, but my hopes were soon dashed. The master political operator of our time, Lyndon B. Johnson, knew that he had a devastatingly good issue, and with invaluable assistance from Goldwater's numerous gaffes in the campaign, he tied the extremist tag so tight on Goldwater that it choked the political life out of him.

Goldwater came to Gettysburg on August 6. Eisenhower did not want us at his farm so we crowded into his small office in town. He began the meeting with some straight talk. In fact I had seldom, if ever, heard Eisenhower lay it on the line the way he did on this occasion. He told Goldwater that he ought to stop shooting from the hip. He suggested that Goldwater give a speech discussing the charges of extremism that had been made against him and admit that he may have encouraged them by the language of his acceptance speech.

Goldwater responded just as candidly. He said that it was not in his nature to be cautious. He could understand that Eisenhower was particularly sensitive about those of his comments that were taken to be critical of the Eisenhower administration, but he had not meant anything personal by them. On the whole, however, Goldwater took a conciliatory line. This, and the impending publication of our exchange of letters, seemed to bode well for the success of the upcoming summit meeting.

The summit meeting of party leaders, candidates, governors, and aides met at the rambling old Hotel Hershey in Hershey, Pennsylvania, on August 12.

The main session was held behind closed doors. Goldwater made a speech in which he considerably modified some of his most extreme positions. Then Goldwater, Rockefeller, Romney, Scranton, Eisenhower, and I engaged in a rambling and falsely optimistic discussion of how the campaign should be run. Of course, the real purpose of the exercise was to make effective use of the press conference to be held at the end. This was to be Goldwater's chance to emerge as the leader and spokesman of a united party.

The press conference was crammed with reporters and TV cameras. Eisenhower, Scranton, and I sat flanking Goldwater and his running mate, New York Congressman Bill Miller, as the flashbulbs popped and the cameras whirred. To my amazement and disappointment, after all our planning Goldwater did not grasp the opportunity the meeting had given him. Instead he stated that he did not consider his speech earlier in the day to have been conciliatory, and he would not agree that he had made any concessions on issues of substance. The rest of the press conference was a typical Goldwater performance. He himself brought up his controversial statement that he would consider giving military commanders in the field control over the use of tactical nuclear weapons and, under intense questioning, refused to back away from it. When one reporter asked about his policy toward Germany, I saw Eisenhower wince when Goldwater replied, "I think that Germany originated the modern concept of peace through strength."

Eisenhower was infuriated by Goldwater's performance. I learned later that on the drive back to Gettysburg he said, "You know, before we had this meeting I thought that Goldwater was just stubborn. Now I am convinced that he is just plain dumb."

While the "Spirit of Hershey" may have fooled some of the press and the public, the politicians weren't taken in for a minute. A sense of doom enveloped the Goldwater campaign, and very few national leaders wanted any part of it. Nelson Rockefeller and most of his major supporters sat it out. George Romney concentrated on his own gubernatorial campaign in Michigan. Scranton was a good soldier and tried to help, but his efforts had little effect even with his own supporters; and Eisenhower played hardly any role.

My office in New York was swamped with speaking invitations from candidates all over the country. Many were old friends and supporters; others were promising new candidates who had the ill fortune to be running their first races in a year of dismal presidential prospects. I decided to devote five solid weeks to campaigning.

It was frustrating for me to see as inept a candidate as Goldwater running for President. It was especially heartbreaking because Republican voters seemed to be interested in the campaign that year; everywhere I went I found the audiences big and enthusiastic. But time after time the senatorial or congressional candidate on whose behalf I was to speak begged me to avoid associating his candidacy with Goldwater. It was a difficult tightrope to walk, but I usually found some way to praise the local candidates independently of expressing, as I did in every speech I gave, my personal support for Goldwater. I made over 150 appearances in thirty-six states. But it was a hopeless task. From the time the campaign began I knew that we were going to lose heavily.

Election Day was November 3. By eight o'clock in New York all three networks were projecting a Johnson landslide. The next morning I got up early to check the final reports on the campaigns for House and Senate. It was a

Republican disaster: we had lost 37 seats in the House, 2 in the Senate, and over 500 in state legislatures. Most of the new young candidates Eisenhower and I had tried to encourage failed in their first bids for public office.

One Republican winner was not on the ballot. The week before the end of the campaign, Ronald Reagan made a nationwide television broadcast on Goldwater's behalf. Reagan's views were as conservative as Goldwater's, but he had what Goldwater lacked: the ability to present his views in a reasonable and eloquent manner. The broadcast started a ground swell of support that swept Reagan into the California governor's office in 1966 and into the race for the presidential nomination in 1968.

Goldwater took his defeat with grace, and Johnson resisted what must have been a great temptation to crow over his landslide. It was Nelson Rockefeller who tried to turn the disaster to his own advantage. The day after the election, he issued a statement aimed at reading Goldwater and his followers—and, by indirection, those like me who had supported Goldwater—out of the party. I had intended to make no comment on the results until after a "cooling-off" period, but Rockefeller's attack changed my mind.

On November 5, I held a press conference. I complimented Goldwater, saying that he had fought courageously against great odds. I said that those who had divided the party in the past could not now expect to unite it in the future. At the end, I pulled out all stops and said that Rockefeller was a spoilsport and a divider, and that there now was so much antipathy to him among Republicans throughout the country that he could no longer be regarded as a party leader anywhere outside New York.

As I expected, this press conference stirred up a furor. But I had said what needed to be said in order to avert an irreconcilable split between conservatives and liberals within the party. At first timidly and then in larger numbers, other party leaders joined me in calling for a cooling-off period and for renouncing recriminations over 1964, so that the party could be united for a comeback in 1966.

REVIEWING THE SITUATION: 1965

While I did not have any illusions about the extreme

state of disarray in which the 1964 defeat left the Republican Party, I did not completely share the widespread pessimism about the future. Within just a few months after the election I could see developing in the Democratic Party the political climate that would bring Lyndon Johnson down from his pinnacle of popularity and force him to decide not to run for re-election in 1968. Soon Johnson would have to deal with the fact that the left wing of his own party was as extreme and self-righteous as the Republican right wing. Johnson's magic seemed to be wearing thin even at the height of his power. The Eastern media had been contemptuous of his Texas ways when he was Vice President, and now that he was no longer Kennedy's legatee but had been elected on his own, a newly critical tone began to appear in some of his coverage.

I saw no reason that the Republican Party could not make a comeback in 1966—if only we could keep it from falling apart in the meantime.

I felt that two things would be necessary to keep the party together: we would have to be on constant guard against attempts by leaders of the left or the right to take over the party; and we would have to convince the party rank and file that there were better times ahead. I knew from experience that this would be hard, boring, and sometimes thankless work. But this was the job that I increasingly saw as my own. It was pragmatism more than altruism that led me to take it on, because I believed that whoever did would gain a significant advantage in the race for the 1968 presidential nomination. This enabled me to reconcile the paradox of having to help my Republican competitors—Rockefeller, Romney, and Reagan. I felt that if the base of the party were not expanded, the 1968 nomination would be worthless. If the party were expanded by the victories of others, I thought I had a good chance of benefiting from its greater strength.

I did not reveal to my family or anyone else that this was what I had in mind. I knew that Pat and the girls would again be disappointed. But I had finally come to the realization that there was no other life for me but politics and public service. Even when my legal work was at its most interesting I never found it truly fulfilling. I told some friends at this time that if all I had was my legal work, I would be mentally dead in two years and physically dead in four. I knew that they thought I was exaggerating; but I was telling the truth about the way I thought and felt.

On January 9, 1965, after a small family party to celebrate my fifty-second birthday, I sat in my study to look back on the past year and look ahead into the future.

I reflected on the fact that Winston Churchill had been in his mid-fifties when he lost his position of leadership in the House of Commons in 1929, and most of his contemporaries had then written him off as a political leader. But Churchill refused to write himself off. I took heart from the example of his refusal to give up just because people thought he was finished. I wrote down some "New Year's Resolutions for 1965":
- —Set great goals.
- —Daily rest.
- —Brief vacations.
- —Knowledge of all weaknesses.
- —Better use of time.
- —Begin writing book.
- —Golf or some other kind of daily exercise.
- —Articles or speeches on provocative new international and national issues.

I put down my yellow pad, turned out the light, and stared into the fire. For the first time in seven years, I started not only to think seriously about running for the presidency again but to think about where I should begin.

It was still much too early to make any final decision, much less any announcement, about running for President again. Besides, I was convinced that any attempt at presidential politics before the party had had a chance to rebuild itself for 1966 would be self-defeating. The party's best interests and my own dovetailed on this point: until the organization had been restored to the point that the nomination would be worth something to whoever won it, I would be foolish to make any commitment. But if I was interested in running, it would be equally foolish not to begin laying plans and harnessing some of the good will I had built up in the 1964 campaign. Barry Goldwater was a vocal adherent of this view. At the Republican National Committee meeting in Chicago on January 22 he introduced me as the man "who worked harder than any one person for the ticket." He turned to me and said, "Dick, I will never forget it. I know that you did it in the interests of the Republican Party and not for any selfish reasons. But if there ever comes a time I can turn those into selfish reasons, I am going to do all I can to see that it comes about."

I began making lists of the odds for and against my nomination in 1968. There was no denying that the odds against were formidable. After 1960 and 1962, I had what every politician dreads most, a loser image. In fact, after the "last press conference," I had a *sore* loser image.

Almost equally serious was my lack of political funds. For the first time in my life I was making a solid six-figure income from the law firm and from my book royalties and writing fees. But we had an expensive apartment, and one daughter in private school and the other in college. After all the frugal years in Washington, I felt that Pat and the girls deserved the best, and I would not have them stint in order to bankroll another candidacy.

Another serious problem was the lack of a political base. By leaving California I had become in political terms a man without a country. It was almost unprecedented for a major candidate to build a serious presidential campaign without having the party machinery in his home state working for him. New York, however, was Rockefeller turf, and the New York Republican organization would actually be working against me. Rockefeller had made this clear from the beginning, and I was effectively frozen out of any major role in New York Republican politics.

Although the odds against me were heavy, there were also some points in my favor. One was my position as front-runner for the presidential nomination in polls of Republican voters. In the summer of 1966, for example, the Gallup poll gave me a lead of almost 2 to 1 over my nearest competitor, Henry Cabot Lodge. My many years of labor in the Republican vineyards were being rewarded by the support of the party organization in most of the country.

Another advantage was that, like me or not, the press

seemed to consider me the most consistently newsworthy of the potential presidential candidates. Even though I did not hold an office, I could count on overflow attendance any time I called a press conference, and wherever I traveled local television usually covered my speeches and appearances.

In my judgment, however, the most important thing in my favor was less tangible and more substantive than polls or press coverage. I was confident that because of my background and experience, particularly in the field of foreign policy, I had the best grasp of the issues and trends that would determine the campaign and the election. Whether this was in fact true, I believed it was true, and the confidence that belief gave me was itself a tremendous advantage.

Since the best way to prepare for 1968 was to do well in 1966, I decided to begin some rudimentary planning for the coming year's election campaign. In the middle of 1965, Maurice Stans, Al Cole, and Peter Flanigan began raising money for my travels on behalf of the party and its candidates in the 1966 elections.

The issues that were to dominate the political dialogue of the latter part of the 1960s were already taking shape by the middle of the decade. In May 1964 President Johnson had told the graduating class of the University of Michigan that "in your time we have the opportunity to move not only toward the rich society and the powerful society, but upward to the Great Society." Johnson observed quite correctly that "the solution to these problems does not rest on a massive program in Washington," but the fatal flaw of his Great Society was precisely its inclination to establish massive federal programs. The price tag was astronomical. In five years, Johnson's spending for the poor doubled, from $12.5 billion to $24.6 billion. Federal funds for health and education jumped by over $18 billion.

As I read the legislative messages that poured out of the White House during the first few months of 1965, I could see that Johnson had fallen into the trap that snares so many believers in big government: he was promising far more than ever could be achieved. Even allowing for a healthy dose of oratorical overstatement, the Great Society promised so much to so many that, instead of inspiring people to work hard to attain its goals, it made people impatient and angry when the goals were not immediately achieved without effort on their part.

I knew that Johnson would soon be bitterly disappointed by the ingratitude of those he tried to help. His Great Society programs spawned a new constituency of government dependents who would always demand more than he could give. Johnson was a man who needed praise, but he would get precious little of it from them.

I also anticipated the breakdown of performance of the Great Society programs themselves. The Great Society was created by liberal academics and bureaucrats steeped in the myths of the New Deal. When its theoretical high-mindedness ran up against the self-interested tough-mindedness of the people it was intended to serve, there was certain to be conflict.

The philosophical distinction between the Republican and Democratic parties was never clearer than in the middle 1960s. It was therefore the perfect time for Republicans to lead an active opposition. I fully recognized, however, that one of our biggest problems lay in our public image as a "negative" party. Goldwater's rhetoric had much to answer for in this regard. Republicans had always been tagged as reactionary, but after his campaign we were portrayed as reckless and racist.

Republicans needed to leapfrog the Democrats on the Great Society issues and get ahead of them. The Democrats were the majority party, but it seemed to me that the great strength of the Republicans lay in our ability to lead effectively on the local level, much as the great strength of the Democrats rested on their ability to mobilize the resources of Washington.

In a number of speeches during 1965, I urged my audiences to be Lincoln Republicans: liberal in their concern for people and conservative in their respect for the rule of law. I deliberately used the terms *liberal* and *conservative,* which in 1964 had been the sorrow of the party, to show how they had been abused and distorted almost beyond recognition. I said, "If being a liberal means federalizing everything, then I'm no liberal. If being a conservative means turning back the clock, denying problems that exist, then I'm no conservative."

I stressed that the Republican Party must have no room for racism. I made it clear that contrary to what some conservatives might have thought, George Wallace did not belong in the Republican Party. I was equally critical of the black activists and the extremists in the civil rights movement. When the Watts district of Los Angeles was swept by black rioters, arsonists, and looters in the summer of 1965, I refused to accept that such outbursts were the inevitable result of any systematic racism of American society. In my judgment, the real culprits in the race riots of the 1960s were neither society nor the police, but the extremists of both races who encouraged the idea that people need obey only the laws with which they agree.

Another widespread concern during this period was the general tone of American society and the growth of permissiveness. Psychologists, preachers, and parents worried as traditional standards of social and sexual behavior were flouted or abandoned. I felt that to a large degree these excesses reflected the malaise of affluence. In some cases, however, they represented a real change in American culture, and I felt that rather than just bemoaning them Republicans should try to understand them.

Increasingly in the forefront in 1965 was the war in Vietnam. I had become deeply concerned about the contrast between the actual situation I found when I visited Vietnam in 1964 and what the Johnson administration was telling the American people. I concluded that Johnson hoped to achieve a quick negotiated settlement before antiwar dissent within the Democratic Party and media criticism began undercutting his Great Society legislation.

Johnson had not leveled with the American people and told them why we were fighting in Vietnam or how deeply American troops were actually involved. To some extent he was trapped by his own words in the campaign. He had said: "We are not about to send American boys 9,000 or 10,000 miles away from home to do what Asian boys ought to be doing for themselves." He was expanding the war, and it would be difficult to explain why he considered it necessary without arousing the ire of the antiwar forces and the skepticism of the average citizen.

The price of Johnson's dissembling was high, and I was to inherit that debt: the "credibility gap." The government lost the confidence of the people, which I believe it could have kept had Johnson taken the risk and fully explained the war and patiently educated the people about it.

This was Johnson's strategic mistake—and it was a serious one. It was compounded by a no less serious tactical mistake.

By limiting the military effort to retaliation and small-scale operations, he forfeited the military initiative to the Communists. Johnson seemed to believe that restraint on his part—partly an effort to placate the left wing of his party—would be interpreted by the Communists as proof of his sincerity in seeking a negotiated settlement. He did not see how they could refuse to come to the conference table when faced with anyone as reasonable as he was determined to be.

Successful negotiation requires the creation of conditions that make it advantageous for the other party to do what you want. For a favorable outcome in Vietnam, it would have been necessary for the United States to employ its great economic and military power to demonstrate convincingly to the Communists that aggression would not pay and that it would be more desirable for them to negotiate a settlement. The Johnson administration pursued a policy of only the most gradual escalation of the air and ground war. What this policy actually accomplished was to convince the Communists that the United States lacked the will to win in Vietnam and could be worn down with propaganda directed against both our domestic front and our allies around the world.

As I saw it, Johnson should have told the American people about our role in Vietnam frankly and without any rosy predictions. The country should have been informed how difficult and costly the struggle would be. He also should have portrayed the stakes more convincingly. The United States was not just fighting to maintain an independent South Vietnam, but also to defeat the indirect aggression of China and the Soviet Union under the guise of a "war of national liberation." General Vo Nguyen Giap, the North

Vietnamese military commander, had stated that the war against South Vietnam was a model for the Communist movement around the world: if such a style of aggression could succeed there, it could work elsewhere.

After the Munich Conference in 1937, Winston Churchill warned the House of Commons that "the idea that safety can be purchased by throwing a small state to the wolves is a fatal delusion." What had been true of the betrayal of Czechoslovakia to Hitler in 1938 was no less true of the betrayal of South Vietnam to the Communists advocated by many in 1965. The fall of free Vietnam to outside aggression would have sent shock waves throughout Asia. As I put it in many of my speeches, "If America gives up on Vietnam, Asia will give up on America."

To me the choice lay not, as many doves thought, between *this war* and *no war*—but between *this war* and a *bigger war later* when the Communists would be stronger and more confident.

In my speeches in 1965 I sought to justify and explain the American commitment in Southeast Asia. I pointed out that we were not like the French colonialists, who had been fighting to stay in Vietnam. We were fighting to get out once aggression had been defeated.

On January 26, 1965, in a speech to the Sales Executives Club of New York I stated bluntly that we were losing the war in Vietnam. I urged that we take the war to North Vietnam by naval and air bombing of the Communists' supply routes in South Vietnam and by destroying the Vietcong staging areas in North Vietnam and Laos. "It is dangerous and foolhardy to try to gloss over the truth as to what the war in Vietnam really involves," I said. "The war in Vietnam is not about Vietnam but about Southeast Asia." I warned that we must not delude ourselves with schemes for coalition governments or neutralization. "Neutrality where the Communists are concerned means three things: we get out; they stay in; they take over." Any negotiated settlement would inevitably lead only to further Communist demands. "We finally get back to the very difficult decision we have to make," I said. "We must realize that there is no easy way out. We either get out, surrender on the installment plan through neutralization, or we find a way to win."

Unlike some of the extremist "hawks," I did not think

that we should use nuclear weapons in Vietnam. Nor did I think that we should rely on a strategy of committing increasing numbers of American troops to land battles. I said that we should instead "quarantine" the war in Vietnam by using our air and sea power to close off the outside interference from Laos and North Vietnam that made it possible for the Vietcong to practice their guerrilla terrorism. "If that were accomplished," I said, "the South Vietnamese would have a fair chance to defeat the Vietcong in battle."

I was aware that this policy would risk involving Red China, so I added: "There are risks, yes. But the risks of waiting are much greater. This becomes apparent when we look ahead and realize that if South Vietnam is lost, and Southeast Asia is lost, and the Pacific becomes a Red Sea, we could be confronted with a world war where the odds against us would be far greater."

At the end of the speech I acknowledged that "the course of action I advocate is one that is not popular in America and would probably not get a vote of confidence in Congress or by a Gallup or Harris poll." But I felt that what I had proposed was the right way, in fact the only way, to deal with the problem of Vietnam.

Two weeks later, on February 6, the Vietcong began a new stage in the escalation of the war by shelling the Army barracks at our air base near Pleiku; Johnson responded with a statement that since Hanoi had embarked upon a more aggressive course of action, "We have no choice now but to clear the decks and make absolutely clear our continued determination to back South Vietnam in its fight to maintain its independence." He ordered retaliatory air raids in North Vietnam.

I spent another four days in Saigon in September 1965. I found the situation a bit improved from eighteen months before, particularly in terms of the morale among the South Vietnamese. But American and Vietnamese military officials still seemed frustrated. They felt they were being held back because Washington thought this would encourage negotiations, while the enemy was making advances. When I appeared on *Meet the Press* after my return from Vietnam, for example, I said: "I don't know what President Johnson presently thinks with regard to negotiations, but certainly I think continued talk on his part . . . suggesting that we only want peace, that we want to negotiate, has the effect of prolonging the war rather than bringing it to a close. I think President Johnson has got to make it clear to the world and to the people of South Vietnam that our objective is a free and independent South Vietnam with no reward and no appeasement of aggressors." I repeated my call for more air and sea power against North Vietnam.

During 1965 the volume of political mail, phone calls, and speaking requests coming into my office took a quantum leap. Rose was working twelve and fourteen hours a day. Pat came down to pitch in. By the end of the year it was clear that I would have to begin building a personal staff—not just for the 1966 campaign but with an eye to being ready for 1968. In January 1966, Pat Buchanan, a young editorial writer for the St. Louis *Globe-Democrat,* joined my staff as a researcher and speech-writer.

1966 ELECTIONS

As the 1966 elections neared, I began carefully assessing the opportunities they presented and the risks they entailed for me. The risks were obvious. If the party went down to defeat or even failed to make a reasonable comeback, my adversaries in the press and my political competitors in the party would say that Nixon, the perennial loser, had once again dragged the party down to defeat, and that we needed new faces to win in 1968. However, Republicans had good reason to be optimistic about the 1966 elections, and if I had a hand in a sweeping party victory, it would not go unnoticed in the party ranks.

Between the end of the 1964 debacle and the beginning of the 1966 campaign, I had logged 127,000 miles visiting forty states to speak before more than 400 groups. I helped to raise more than $4 million in contributions to the party.

Early in 1966 I began to concentrate specifically on the fall campaign. My speaking schedule intensified. Tom Evans and Len Garment, both lawyers with our firm, were often in my office talking more politics than law. John P. Sears, a twenty-five-year-old associate in the firm, volunteered after-hours work. The fund-raising efforts of Cole, Stans, and Flanigan were stepped up and formalized in three committees, the major one of which was called Congress '66. RNC Chairman Ray Bliss refused our request for committee funds to rent a plane on the ground that this would be showing favoritism for me over other potential presidential candidates. So we raised the money on our own. It was a political miracle that we were able to do it all by ourselves.

On March 12 I attended the Gridiron Dinner of the press in Washington. Johnson had sent his regrets, and Hubert Humphrey was sitting in for him. Later in the evening, however, after many of the speeches and skits were completed, Johnson burst into the room, followed by the presidential entourage.

As he was being escorted from the dais after the toasts he greeted me and said that he would like me to stop by to have coffee with him the next morning.

As I got off the elevator on the second floor of the White House, a butler greeted me and escorted me to Johnson's room. He was sitting in bed in his pajamas. "Hello, Dick," he said. His voice was extremely hoarse, and he looked tired, almost to the point of exhaustion.

We discussed the situation in Vietnam. I told him my views regarding the need to take stronger actions to bring the North Vietnamese to the conference table. I said that I had defended the administration's policy in all the foreign countries I visited. He nodded. "I am receiving the benefit from the support I gave you and Ike in the foreign policy field in the eight years you were here," he said.

He then turned to my recommendations regarding a harder line in Vietnam. "China's the problem there," he said. "We can bomb the hell out of Hanoi and the rest of that damned country, but they've got China right behind them, and that's a different story."

I had not been in the room long when the door opened and Mrs. Johnson walked in, wearing a dressing gown. She greeted me warmly, got into bed beside her husband, and joined us for the remainder of our conversation.

He shifted gears and in muted tones began talking like a man arriving at the end of his term, rather than a President in full control of events. "When I leave this office, Bobby, Hubert, or you will have the problem of China on your hands," he said. I urged a diplomatic communication with China as soon as possible. "Mr. President," I said, "time is on their side. Now is the time to confront them on the diplomatic front." Johnson did not respond, but I sensed he agreed with me.

I said that since it was an election year, I would be out campaigning and making speeches for Republican candidates just as he had done for Democrats in 1954 and 1958 when the Republicans were in office. "I know you will understand and not take any criticism I make on issues as being directed personally at you," I said.

"I know, Dick," he replied. "We politicians are just like lawyers who get together for a drink after fighting each other like hell in the courtroom."

Johnson got up and walked to his dressing room closet, where he chose a pair of presidential cufflinks from his jewelry box and gave them to me. We shook hands and I said goodbye.

The 1966 campaign was one that I thoroughly enjoyed. With very few exceptions I was able to give my enthusiastic endorsement to the Republican candidates. I personally picked the districts and states in which I felt I could be effective, and I was pretty much on my own because the other big guns on the national scene were tied up with their own campaigns. The polls indicated that the Democrats were going to take a fairly substantial beating, and I could feel a tremendous confidence and enthusiasm in the crowds I met and spoke to. But rumors began to circulate that Johnson was planning a last-minute grandstand play that would restore public confidence right before the election. I knew him well enough to know that such a move would be entirely in character for him, so I assumed a position of watchful waiting.

At the end of September Johnson made a surprise announcement that he was going to meet with President Nguyen Van Thieu of South Vietnam and other Vietnamese and allied leaders in Manila in late October, just two weeks before the election. In the newspaper column I was writing at this time I bluntly noted the widespread skepticism that greeted this announcement. I wrote, "From diplomats in Tokyo to members of the President's own party in Washington, the question is being posed: Is this a quest for peace or a quest for votes?"

At the conclusion of their Manila meetings on October 25, Johnson, Thieu, and the leaders of Australia, Korea, New Zealand, the Philippines, and Thailand issued a joint communiqué. It offered an American and allied troop withdrawal from South Vietnam within six months, contingent upon a North Vietnamese withdrawal of forces, cessation of their support of Vietcong infiltration, and a general lessening of the levels of violence in the war.

I was on a campaign trip when we received a copy of the Manila Communiqué, and I stayed up a good part of the night analyzing it. I called in Rose Woods and Pat Buchanan and dictated several pages of notes. I asked them to travel ahead to the next stop so that Buchanan could begin incorporating my thoughts into a working draft.

By the time I got back to New York, I had a long, point-by-point analysis of what Johnson had agreed to at Manila, which I issued to the press on November 3, five days before the election. It began by pointing out that the apparently promising offer of mutual U.S. and North Vietnamese troop withdrawals was far more illusory than real.

I stated that "the effect of this mutual withdrawal would be to leave the fate of South Vietnam to the Vietcong and the South Vietnamese Army. . . . The South Vietnamese Army could not prevail for any length of time over the Communist guerrillas without American advisers, air support, and logistical backing. Communist victory would most certainly be the result of 'mutual withdrawal' if the North Vietnamese continued their own logistical support of the Communist guerrillas. . . ." The situation in 1966, when the South Vietnamese were totally untrained and unprepared to defend themselves, was very different from that in 1969, when in my presidency we were able to propose a mutual withdrawal with the assurance that our Vietnamization policies would prepare the South Vietnamese to defend themselves. I said that if I understood the Manila Communiqué correctly, it offered to tie American withdrawals to the level

The Nixon family in Yorba Linda in 1916. From left: Harold, Frank, Donald, Hannah, Richard.

The Nixon brothers in Yorba Linda in 1922. From left: Donald, seven, in the tire; Richard, nine; Harold, thirteen, already sick with tuberculosis, wearing a bathrobe; and Arthur, four.

RN in East Whittier in 1927.

Fullerton High School orchestra,
sophomore year, 1928

The last photograph
of Harold, who died
in 1933, and RN.

Number 23 on the Whittier College football team, October 1933.

RN in front of "Nick's Hamburger Stand" on Bougainville in the South Pacific in 1944.

The photograph of Pat that RN carried with him during the war.

Tricia and her parents in the yard of their house in Whittier in 1946.

AMERICA NEEDS
NEW LEADERSHIP NOW!
ELECT
RICHARD M.

NIXON

YOUR CONGRESSMAN

World War II Navy Combat Veteran
A vote for NIXON is a vote for new,
progressive and EFFECTIVE leadership—
for a change!

4

The first political campaign: opposing Jerry Voorhis for the House of Representatives from California's Twelfth District.

RN and John F. Kennedy (back row at right) in a radio interview with other freshman members of the Eightieth Congress in January 1947.

The Hiss case: examining the "pumpkin papers" microfilm with Robert Stripling.

Campaigning for the U.S. Senate in California's San Joaquin Valley in 1950.

Photo from 1950 Senate election campaign poster.

Rose Mary Woods became RN's secretary in 1951.

Receiving the nomination for Vice President at the 1952 Republican National Convention in Chicago.

Letter from John F. Kennedy after receiving the Republican vice presidential nomination. Text of the letter appears on page 112.

The Fund Speech: September 23, 1952.

RN discloses, Stevenson refuses. The front page of
The New York Times after RN and Eisenhower met in
Wheeling, West Virginia, following the Fund Speech.

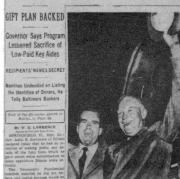

© 1952 BY THE NEW YORK TIMES COMPANY.
REPRINTED BY PERMISSION.

Inauguration Day 1953. From left: Presidents Truman, Eisenhower, and Hoover.

THIS wire fence was no barrier as the U.S. Vice-President, Mr. Richard M. Nixon reached over it to shake hands with peons, clerks and people of all walks of life, as they crowded round to meet him while he was leaving the V.I.P. room at Kallang airport yesterday. — Standard photo.

NIXON CHATS WITH COMMON MAN

Standard Staff Reporter

WITHIN 15 minutes of his arrival in Singapore yesterday Mr. Richard Nixon, America's youngest Vice-President and President Eisenhower's personal ambassador, got down to meeting the ordinary people of Singapore's varied communities.

The Vice-President turned away from the pomp and ceremony of an official reception at Kallang Airport to shake hands with 20 or more of the hundreds of ordinary Singapore working men and boys who had stood for several hours under a broiling sun to see America's second most important man.

To the chagrin of hundreds of security men and high police officers who guarded the disembarkation apron, Mr. Nixon leaned over a wire fence and shook hands with a tiny Malay boy.

Broad grins of approval spread over the faces of the crowd and they surged forward wanting to shake the hand of one of America's most popular politicians.

1953 trip: front page of the Singapore *Standard*, October 25, 1953.

1953 trip: with Generalissimo and Madame Chiang Kai-shek in Taipei.

1953 trip: while I was in meetings, Pat insisted on having her own schedule of activities. Here she visits the Shwedagon Pagoda in Burma. Her guide (left) is U Thant, later secretary-general of the United Nations.

1953 trip: with President Syngman Rhee in Seoul.

1953 trip: with Prime Minister Nehru and his daughter Indira Gandhi.

Letter from President Eisenhower following the 1953 trip. Text of the letter appears on page 164.

Inauguration Day 1957. President Eisenhower stands with two of his grandchildren, Anne and David Eisenhower; RN with Tricia and Julie. This was the first meeting between David and Julie, who were to be married twelve years later.

RN's first and only White House news conference as Vice President, in November 1957, following President Eisenhower's stroke.

Frank Nixon in Whittier in 1952.　　RN with Hannah Nixon in 1952.

Caracas: RN's limousine after the mob attack on May 13, 1958.

With Queen Elizabeth II in London, November 1958.

Sir Winston Churchill pushed aside his aide to stand alone before the cameras at his door in Hyde Park Gate, London, November 1958.

Making a point with Khrushchev in the "kitchen debate" at the American Exhibition in Moscow in 1959. Leonid Brezhnev is at right.

With Fidel Castro in RN's office at the U.S. Capitol, April 19, 1959.

With President Eisenhower at Washington's Griffith Stadium for the first baseball game of the season on April 18, 1960.

With vice presidential running mate Henry Cabot Lodge at the 1960 Republican National Convention.

Democratic vice presidential candidate Lyndon Johnson and Senate Minority Leader Everett Dirksen visit RN when an infected knee forced him into the hospital during the 1960 campaign.

The Nixon–Kennedy debates: the first was on September 26, 1960, in Chicago.

Election Night 1960: conceding that if the trend continues, John F. Kennedy will be elected President.

One of the Nixon family's favorite photographs, taken on their arrival in California in 1961. Checkers is in the foreground.

The "last press conference" following the 1962 election for governor of California. Herb Klein is standing in the background.

With Checkers in Central Park after the move to New York in 1963.

A grainy wire service photo from South Vietnam during the Asian trip in September 1965.

UNITED PRESS INTERNATIONAL

Relaxing in Key Biscayne before the 1968 campaign.

The Nixons and the Agnews at the Republican National Convention at Miami Beach, August 1968.

Campaigning in 1968 in Philadelphia.

A candid photo taken by Dwight Chapin in RN's hotel suite after his election as President on November 6, 1968. The TV screen shows the Illinois returns that clinched the victory. John Mitchell looks on as RN holds Julie's victory gift—the Great Seal of the United States in crewelwork.

Meeting with Vice President Hubert Humphrey two days after the 1968 election, at the airport at Opa-Locka, Florida.

Escorting Julie on December 22, 1968, the day of her wedding to David Eisenhower.

Inauguration Day, January 20, 1969. Chief Justice Earl Warren administers the oath. Pat holds two Milhous family Bibles.

The last photo of RN and General Eisenhower.

With President Charles de Gaulle in Paris in February 1969. Behind RN are (left) National Security Adviser Henry Kissinger and Secretary of State William Rogers.

The telephone conversation between the earth and the moon: talking to the Apollo XI astronauts from the Oval Office in July 1969.

RN with former President Johnson and John McCormack in May 1970, at a White House luncheon honoring McCormack when he retired as Speaker of the House of Representatives.

In the Oval Office in 1970 with staff aides John Ehrlichman, Henry Kissinger, and Bob Haldeman (seated).

In the Lincoln Sitting Room with Henry Kissinger.

RN at the picture window of Aspen Lodge at Camp David.

Visiting with U.S. troops
in Vietnam in July 1969.

Hats of construction union leaders on the table in the Roosevelt room at the White House after the Cambodian operation in May 1970.

"Working the fence" at the airport at Bangor, Maine, in 1971.

RN with Michael Newton, poster child for Better Hearing and Speech Month Campaign, 1971.

Pat practicing her personal diplomacy at an orphanage in Ivory Coast during her African trip in January 1972.

One of the Nixon family's favorite photographs of the White House years, taken in the Blue Room during the Christmas holidays in 1971.

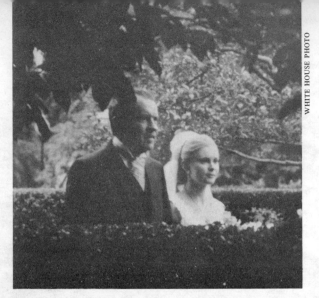

Escorting Tricia in the Rose Garden on June 12, 1971, the day of her wedding to Edward Cox.

Dancing at Tricia's wedding reception in the East Room.

of fighting indulged in by the Vietcong. "If this inference is accurate," I continued, "then we have offered to surrender a decisive military advantage at the Manila Conference."

My statement was printed in full in the New York *Times* and was widely reviewed and discussed. It was treated as major news, particularly because up to that time I had consistently supported our goals in Vietnam, even while I raised questions about the tactics being used to achieve them.

If the Manila meeting had been intended to help the Democrats in the election, it backfired completely. The press was almost insultingly cynical about Johnson's motives. The doves attacked the Manila Communiqué as bellicose, and the hawks attacked it as amounting to surrender on the installment plan.

My criticism of the Manila Communiqué apparently hit a particularly raw nerve in the White House. Johnson's press conference on November 4 opened with some questions that revealed the cynical attitude of the press toward him. Johnson was tired and testy, and when a reporter asked him for a comment on my statement, something inside him seemed to break.

"I do not want to get into a debate on a foreign policy meeting in Manila with a chronic campaigner like Mr. Nixon," he replied. "It is his problem to find fault with his country and with his government during a period of October every two years. If you will look back over his record, you will find that to be true. He never did really recognize and realize what was going on when he had an official position in the government. You remember what President Eisenhower said, that if you would give him a week or so he would figure out what he was doing.

"Since then he has made a temporary stand in California, and you saw what action the people took out there. Then he crossed the country to New York. Then he went back to San Francisco, hoping that he would be in the wings, available if Goldwater stumbled. But Goldwater didn't stumble. Now he is out talking about a conference that obviously he is not well prepared on or informed about."

Reporters stole glances at one another to make sure that they were hearing correctly. Lady Bird Johnson was seated behind her husband. She was trying to smile, but shaking her head slightly.

Johnson began defending the terms of the Manila Communiqué against the charges in my statement. He said that the Communists should have no doubts about our determination to leave Vietnam as soon as the conditions of mutual withdrawal, suspension of infiltration, and a decrease in fighting were met. "They know that," he said, "and we ought not try to confuse it here and we ought not try to get it mixed up in a political campaign here. Attempts to do that will cause people to lose votes instead of gaining them. And we ought not have men killed because we try to fuzz up something. When the aggression, infiltration, and violence cease, not a nation there wants to keep occupying troops in South Vietnam. Mr. Nixon doesn't serve his country well by trying to leave that kind of impression in the hope that he can pick up a precinct or two, or a ward or two."

While Johnson was holding this press conference in Washington, I was at La Guardia Airport in New York, about to board a plane for a campaign appearance in Waterville, Maine. As soon as we were strapped into our seats, Pat Buchanan leaned over and said, "You remember that you asked me to listen to Johnson's press conference just in case he said something about your statement on the Manila Communiqué. Well, I listened, and you're not going to believe what he did."

When Buchanan told me what had happened I realized for the first time how worried Johnson was beneath his booming exterior. He had spoken in desperation, not in malice. I knew that if I handled myself well, this could turn into both a Republican and a personal windfall. When I returned to the airport after my speech at Waterville, a reporter asked me what I thought and how I felt about being personally attacked by the President of the United States. I said, "Now President Johnson and I can disagree about that, but let's disagree as gentlemen. Let's disagree as men who are trying to find the right way. Let me say that the best way is not a one-man way, not just LBJ's way but the two-party way. We need a bipartisan program for Vietnam in which both participate, rather than just a one-party program in which he says, 'I know best and all of the rest of you, if you ever take me on, then I'll hit you personally.' That's all I'm asking him to do. Let's be gentlemen about this and have our discussions in a reasonable way."

With just a few days left before the election, I suddenly found myself the center of national attention. Editorialists and columnists who had had little use for me in the past defended my integrity against Johnson's intemperate attack. Eisenhower called me from Gettysburg and said, "Dick, I could kick myself every time some jackass brings up that goddamn 'give me a week' business. Johnson has gone too far on this, and there will be a very strong backlash in your favor. I just wanted you to know that I'm issuing a statement down here." Eisenhower's statement, which was widely reported, said that I was "one of the best informed, most capable, and most industrious Vice Presidents in the history of the United States."

The Republican Congressional Campaign Committee offered me a half-hour of the network television time that had been allotted to it by NBC.

I opened the broadcast by getting right to the point. I said:

As you have no doubt gathered from that introduction, I was subjected last week to one of the most savage personal assaults ever leveled by the President of the United States against one of his political opponents. . . .

I shall answer it not for myself but because of a great principle that is at stake. It is the principle of the right to disagree, the right to dissent. That means the right to disagree with any government official, even the President of the United States.

I used most of the speech to make the case for a Republican Congress, but at the end I returned to Johnson's attack. I said:

I understand that the President of the United States may be listening to this program tonight. I want to direct these comments to him personally. Mr. President: For fourteen years I had the privilege of serving with you in Washington. I respected you then, I respect you now. I respect you for the great office you hold—an office that we both sought and that you won. I respect you for the great energies you devote to that office, and my respect has not changed because of the personal attack you made on me. You see, I think I understand how a man can be very, very tired and how his temper then can be very short. And if a Vice President or a former Vice President can be bone weary and tired, how much more tired would a President be after a journey like yours?"

I closed the broadcast by offering Johnson my continued support in his search for peace and freedom abroad and progress at home.

The speech was a success, it renewed my credentials as a national spokesman and a fighting campaigner. It also served to identify me with the Republican victory that now seemed almost certain in the election two days hence.

I enjoyed listening to the 1966 election returns. By the end of the night, Republicans had won a net of 47 House seats, 3 Senate seats, 8 governorships and 540 seats in state legislatures. My predictions—that we would win 40 House seats, 3 Senate seats, 6 governorships and 700 state legislature seats—which had seemed so unrealistically optimistic when I made them six months earlier were vindicated with a vengeance.

The election was personally satisfying to me in that the Republicans made gains in the South, defeating Democratic backlash candidates in Arkansas, where Winthrop Rockefeller won, and in Maryland, where Spiro Agnew defeated a Democrat who was running on a subtly racist line. I had specifically predicted that Rockefeller and Agnew would win.

After the last returns were in and our victory was confirmed, I rounded up a small party to go to El Morocco for a victory supper of spaghetti and red wine. There was a lot for me to celebrate. The first major hurdle had been met, faced, and surmounted in style. There were more hurdles ahead, but this was an auspicious start. It was gratifying to know that I had played a major part in this Republican victory—a prerequisite for my own comeback.

"A HOLIDAY FROM POLITICS"

I fully realized that my efforts in the campaign had been only one of many factors in the Republican triumph.

We had been the recipients of a massive anti-Johnson windfall. But no matter what the reasons, I had indisputably played a central part, and for the first time in ten years I was identified with a smashing victory.

The campaign of 1966 had another important effect: it softened the remaining jagged memories of the "last press conference." For one of the few times in my political career, Johnson's attack made me the wounded party. He had not, in fact, been far off. I *was* something of a chronic campaigner, always out on the stump raising partisan hell. But my years in the "wilderness" and the simple process of growing older had probably rounded off some of the hard edges of the younger Nixon. I emerged from the campaign of 1966 as a seasoned senior Republican statesman who could still deliver some effective political licks.

On the day after the election I issued a statement of my belief that the results represented a repudiation of Johnson's policies. I also underscored the message for Hanoi and Peking that the new House of Representatives would be much stronger than its predecessor in supporting a U.S. policy of "no reward for aggression."

Throughout the campaign many of my friends, advisers, and supporters had urged me to gear up my own organization to be ready to go public with my presidential candidacy as soon as the election—and, we hoped, the great Republican victory—had taken place. Such advice made perfect sense in traditional terms, but I had already decided to try a highly unconventional idea: instead of plunging into the arena, I was going to bide my political time. When I had appeared on *Issues and Answers* two days before the election, I announced: "I am going to take a holiday from politics for at least six months with no political speeches scheduled whatever. What the future holds I don't know."

I wanted to run for President in 1968, but I wanted to leave open, until the last possible moment, the option of deciding *not* to run.

Our family spent a relaxed holiday in Key Biscayne. We went sailing with Bebe Rebozo on his boat, the *Coco Lobo,* and spent hours on the beach reading, swimming, and talking about everything except politics. I knew that Pat and

343

the girls were secretly hoping that the moratorium on politics would go on and on.

Shortly after we got back to New York, Peter Flanigan and Maury Stans came to see me. It was the day before Thanksgiving. They said that the time had come to make a move if I had any intention of being a candidate in 1968. Romney was off and running, and Reagan's supporters were talking about renewing the Goldwater conservative movement. There was even talk of another Goldwater candidacy. Nelson Rockefeller was in the wings, ready to pick up the ball if others stumbled. Each hopeful was trying to get party leaders and workers committed to him, and unless I could give my personal supporters some reason to hold out, I might one day find that they had been snatched up by my rivals. Flanigan and Stans wanted to organize a Nixon for President Club and begin some preliminary low-key organizing and fund-raising. I told them that I considered the ability to remain officially undecided for as long as possible to be one of my greatest advantages. Not only would this allow me more independence, but the speculation about my intentions guaranteed far more media attention than I would have if I announced. Therefore, I would publicly neither approve nor disapprove their activity. But I assured them that I agreed completely with their analysis of the need to begin organizing.

A few months later, about the time I was emerging from a meeting with Willy Brandt in Bonn, the formation of the first Nixon for President Committee was announced in Washington.

On January 7 and 8, 1967, I held planning meetings at the Waldorf Towers. I said: "I'm not going to be coy with my oldest friends and closest advisers. I want you to proceed with plans for winning the Republican presidential nomination next year."

I made it clear that my six-month moratorium, while admittedly a risk, was carefully calculated. George Romney could be out front taking the heat from the press and the pundits while I continued my quiet planning and foreign travel. "But make no mistake," I said, "while I am lying back I want you to work your tails off getting the job done.

We will have to work harder and better than the other candidates to win."

I decided to begin building a personal political staff so that I could be ready to plunge into the battle as soon as my moratorium ended. I enlisted Raymond K. Price, Jr., a former chief editorial writer for the New York *Herald Tribune*, to be my principal idea man and speechwriter; he would also work on a book I was considering along the lines of Wendell Willkie's *One World*. In addition to Price, Dwight Chapin, a young advertising executive, joined the staff to serve as a personal aide.

On January 1, 1967, my law firm had merged with the firm of Caldwell, Trimble, and Mitchell, which specialized in municipal bonds. I struck up an immediate friendship with the husky, outwardly gruff senior partner, John Mitchell. Although he had never been involved in a campaign, I felt from our conversations that he had an instinctive talent for politics. As a result of his extensive work with state and local governments in providing legal advice on bond issues, he had an exceptionally wide network of political contacts. Within a few months I was beginning to turn increasingly to him for advice and counsel on political matters.

I decided to use the time during my moratorium on active politics to make a series of foreign study trips. I wanted to bring my impressions up to date and to renew my contacts and refine my ideas about current conditions in the world. By undertaking these trips I was building on my political strong suit, my knowledge of foreign affairs. I also believed this was the best possible way to ensure that I would be able to frame foreign policy issues in a way that would be both effective and responsible, and, if I became President, to ensure that I could get a head start on what to me were the most important decisions a President faces.

I scheduled four trips: to Europe and the Soviet Union in March, to Asia in April, to Latin America in May, and to Africa and the Middle East in June. By this time Robert Ellsworth, an exceptionally able former congressman from Kansas then practicing law in Washington, had arranged to spend approximately half his time helping with my campaign-that-was-not-yet-a-campaign. Ellsworth had a special interest in foreign and defense matters, and he helped make arrangements for the trips through the State Department and the embassies of the countries I would visit. He accompanied me on the first trip and on part of another; Ray Price was on the second; my friend Bebe was on the third to Latin America; and Pat Buchanan on the fourth.

In these 1967 worldwide trips I met the leaders, met the people, and saw at first hand the problems, opportunities, and dangers confronting the United States. The result was to reinforce some views I already strongly held and to modify others.

The trip to Europe and the Soviet Union was to begin on March 5. As usual I requested a CIA briefing before departure; and for the first time since I had left office it was refused. Since such briefings are a privilege—not a right—for a private citizen, no official explanation was given. Unofficially I was told that Johnson was still furious over the Manila Communiqué incident and that he had expressly forbidden the CIA to give me any help or guidance.

This was a very disturbing trip for me. I had not made a systematic tour of the NATO nations since 1963, and I was shocked by the extent to which our relations with them had deteriorated. The Europeans were deeply offended by our failures to consult with them, or even to inform them of decisions we made that touched on their defenses and their destinies. Everywhere I heard the same story: under Kennedy and Johnson, we had shown in a variety of ways how little we valued our allies and how little we appreciated the importance of NATO.

I saw Konrad Adenauer, for the last time. As I entered his room, he embraced me with almost embarrassing warmth. Standing back, his hands still on my shoulders, he said, "Thank God you are here. Your visit is like manna from heaven." This great architect of postwar Europe was depressed about Europe's future. "I am worried, my friend," he said. He predicted that when de Gaulle left the scene, the Communist Party in France, and then in Italy, would gain strength. He completely discounted the Soviet Union's alleged interest in hastening peace in Vietnam, and the popular speculation that the Soviets would turn toward the West out of fear of China. "Make no mistake about it," he said, "they want the world. The whole world. Most of all they want Europe, and to get Europe they know they must destroy Germany. We need you to keep us strong and free. But you also need us." Adenauer urged—as had de Gaulle four years before—that we tilt our policy toward Communist China to counterbalance the growing Soviet threat.

I was surprised to find a similar concern about Soviet strategy expressed by almost everyone I talked with on this trip. In Rome President Saragat and Foreign Minister Fanfani agreed that the Soviets were determined to keep the war going in Vietnam. Like Adenauer, however, they felt that the primary threat from communism was in Europe rather than in Asia. Fanfani said, "NATO is what really counts, but too many people in your country take it for granted and think that Vietnam is the most important thing because that is where you are fighting the Communists. America is like the man confronted with a small fire in his barn when his house is falling apart for want of repairs."

My old friend Manlio Brosio, the Italian diplomat who was then Secretary General of NATO after having served in Washington for six years and in Moscow for five, emotionally and emphatically expressed his doubts about Soviet intentions. "I know the Russians," he said. "They are great liars, clever cheaters, and magnificent actors. They cannot be trusted. They consider it their duty to cheat and lie." A Belgian I talked with pithily expressed his own skeptical view of détente: "It is like the Virgin Birth. I accept it, but I don't believe it."

I had been refused a visa to visit Poland on this trip and was therefore surprised to receive one from Romania. Even so, I assumed that I would get one of the cold-shoulder receptions that Communist governments are particularly good at. But from the moment Ellsworth and I stepped off the plane in Bucharest, it was clear that this was going to be a remarkable visit. Everywhere we were greeted with outbursts of friendship from the people.

I called on the Romanian Communist Party's Secretary General, Nicolae Ceauşescu, at the Central Committee Building. We had a long talk, ranging over the spectrum of East-West relations. I doubted that any true détente with the Soviets could be achieved until some kind of rapprochement could be reached with Communist China. If its 800 million people remained isolated, within twenty years China could pose a grave threat to world peace. I said that I thought the United States could do little to establish effective communications with China until the Vietnam war was ended. After that, however, I thought we could take steps to normalize relations with Peking. Ceauşescu was guarded in his reaction, but I could tell that he was interested to hear me talking in this way, and that he agreed with what I said.

On my trip to Asia in April I wanted to evaluate the situation in Vietnam and the importance of the conflict to Vietnam's neighbors. I also particularly wanted to learn how Asian leaders were viewing China and its future relationship with the rest of Asia and the world.

Many Americans were primarily Europeanists in their approach to foreign affairs, dismissing Asia as relatively unimportant. But the United States is a Pacific power, and rapid changes were taking place in Asia—where more than half the human race lived—that might well determine the world's future. Japan would soon be the world's third-ranking industrial power, behind the United States and the Soviet Union. Some of the most rapid rates of economic progress anywhere were being achieved by the nations of non-Communist Asia. And mainland China potentially posed the greatest threat to peace during the final third of the twentieth century.

I met with Prime Minister Sato, former Prime Minister Kishi, and a number of other Japanese political officials. The Japanese leaders felt strongly that the United States must remain in Asia, and that it was vital that we continue to help defend South Vietnam. They were keenly aware that, because of memories of World War II, there were limits to the leadership Japan could exercise. Nonetheless, they acknowledged the need for regional cooperation to contain the Communist challenge.

I visited Chiang Kai-shek at a lake resort on Taiwan. Chiang still dreamed of returning to the mainland, and once again he urged that America support such an effort. He argued that the Chinese on the mainland were disenchanted with their leaders and ready to rally to another force. A Nationalist invasion of the mainland, he said, would end the threat of a Red Chinese atomic bomb, end Chinese support of the Vietnam war, and end the chance of a Sino-Soviet rapprochement.

Chiang was a friend and unquestionably one of the giants of the twentieth century. I wondered whether he might be right, but my pragmatic analysis told me that he was wrong. His burning desire to return to the mainland was understandable and admirable. But it was totally unrealistic in view of the massive power the Communists had developed.

In Vietnam, despite the military's optimistic prediction, I became further convinced that continuation of the administration's policy of fighting a defensive war of attrition would inevitably lead to defeat. It was small comfort to learn the enemy was losing more men than we were. It had become America's war, and the South Vietnamese were not being adequately trained and equipped to defend themselves. The Communists were willing to continue fighting regardless of losses. They had a total commitment to victory. We had, at most, a partial commitment to avoid defeat. If this situation continued, in the end they would win.

Every leader I talked to in Asia expressed support for a strong American position in Vietnam. But I also found on this trip a growing concern about Communist China. Some who had adamantly opposed any change of American policy toward China had come around to the view that some new and direct relationship between the two nations was essential if there were to be any chance at all after the Vietnam war was over to build a lasting peace in Asia in which free nations would have a chance to survive.

In Latin America in May I found that Kennedy's Alliance for Progress had raised expectations too high. The leaders I met with expressed their disappointment and urged that the United States develop a new approach to attract the private investment from both the United States and Europe that the Latin American economies desperately needed in order to make any meaningful progress.

In Africa in June the leaders emphasized their desire to have more aid from the United States rather than depend on their former colonial masters. But I was discouraged by the fact that, with a few exceptions, the new black African nations simply did not have the trained leadership to achieve their goals in any forseeable future.

I visited Israel just after that country's victory in the June war. In a long conversation with General Yitzhak Rabin I pointed out that Israel had a stake in the outcome of the war in Vietnam. He was obviously interested in my analysis that if the United States were defeated or humiliated in Vietnam, the American people could well turn isolationist and be unwilling to come to the aid of other small nations, like Israel, who depended on us for survival.

I was impressed by the courage and toughness of the Israeli leaders and people. But I was disturbed by the fact that their swift and overwhelming victory over the Arabs had created a feeling of overconfidence about their ability to win any war in the future, and an attitude of total intransigence on negotiating any peace agreement that would involve return of any of the territories they had occupied. Their victory had been too great. It left a residue of hatred among their neighbors that I felt could only result in another war, particularly if the Russians were to step up military aid to their defeated Arab clients.

I summarized my conclusions from these trips first in a speech at the Bohemian Grove and then in an article for the quarterly *Foreign Affairs.*

If I were to choose the speech that gave me the most pleasure and satisfaction in my political career, it would be my Lakeside Speech at the Bohemian Grove in July 1967. Because this speech traditionally was off the record it received no publicity at the time. But in many important ways it marked the first milestone on my road to the presidency.

The setting is possibly the most dramatic and beautiful I have ever seen. A natural amphitheatre has been built up around a platform on the shore of a small lake. Redwoods tower above the scene, and the weather in July is usually warm and clear. Herbert Hoover had always delivered the Lakeside Speech, but he had died in 1964, and I was asked if I would deliver the 1967 speech in his honor. It was an emotional assignment for me and also an unparalleled opportunity to reach some of the most important and influential men, not just from California but from across the country.

In the speech I pointed out that we live in a new world—"never in human history have more changes taken place in the world in one generation"—and that this is a world of new leaders, of new people, of new ideas.

I led the audience on a tour of the world, tracing the changes and examining the conflicts, finding both danger and opportunity as the United States entered the final third of the twentieth century. I urged the need for strong alliances and continued aid to the developing nations; but I also urged that we should provide our aid more selectively, rewarding our friends and discouraging our enemies and encouraging private rather than government enterprise.

Turning to the Soviet Union, I noted that even as the Soviet leaders talked peace they continued to stir up trouble, to encourage aggression, and to build missiles. I urged that we encourage trade with the Soviet Union and Eastern Europe, and that "diplomatically we should have discussions with the Soviet leaders at all levels to reduce the possibility of miscalculation and to explore the areas where bilateral agreements would reduce tensions." But we should insist on reciprocity: "I believe in building bridges but we should build only our end of the bridge." And in negotiations we must always remember "that our goal is different from theirs. We seek peace as an end in itself. They seek victory, with peace being at this time a means toward that end."

Looking ahead, I said:

> As we enter this last third of the twentieth century the hopes of the world rest with America. Whether peace and freedom survive in the world depends on American leadership.
>
> Never has a nation had more advantages to lead. Our economic superiority is enormous; our military superiority can be whatever we choose to make it. Most important, it happens that we are on the right side—the side of freedom and peace and progress against the forces of totalitarianism, reaction, and war.
>
> There is only one area where there is any question—that is whether America has the national character and moral stamina to see us through this long and difficult struggle.

To me, that would be the central question at issue in 1968.

The subject of my October 1967 *Foreign Affairs* article was "Asia After Vietnam." In it I stressed the importance of Asia to the United States and the world, and concluded with a section on U.S. policy toward China:

> Some counsel conceding to China a "sphere of influence" embracing much of the Asian mainland and extending even to the island nations beyond; others urge that we eliminate the threat by pre-emptive war. Clearly, neither of these courses would be acceptable to the United States or to its Asian allies. Others argue that we should seek an anti-Chinese alliance with European powers, even including the Soviet Union. Quite apart from the obvious problems involved in Soviet participation, such a course would inevitably carry connotations of Europe vs. Asia, white vs. non-white, which could have catastrophic repercussions throughout the rest of the non-white world in general and Asia in particular. . . . Only as the nations of non-Communist Asia become so strong—economically, politically, and militarily—that they no longer furnish tempting targets for Chinese aggression, will the leaders in Peking be persuaded to turn their energies inward rather than outward. And that will be the time when the dialogue with mainland China can begin.
>
> For the short run, then, this means a policy of firm restraint, of no reward, of a creative counterpressure designed to persuade Peking that its interests can be served only by accepting the basic rules of international civility. For the long run, it means pulling China back into the world community—but as a great and progressing nation, not as the epicenter of world revolution.

Soon after I got back to New York on June 24 I began checking to find out how the political situation had developed during my absence. Things were moving so fast that even the few months I was away had produced an almost completely different political landscape.

I found that sentiment was beginning to turn very decisively in my favor. But everyone was still asking the big question: after two defeats, could I shake my "loser image"?

It appeared more and more that the presidential primaries offered the only way to show that I could win.

Ronald Reagan was one of the potential presidential candidates who denied any interest in the nomination. I had seen him at the Bohemian Grove in July where Senator George Murphy, he, and I had a candid discussion of the political situation as we sat outdoors on a bench under one of the giant redwoods. I told him about my tentative plans to enter the primaries. I assured him that it was my intention to do everything possible to unite the party and to campaign only against Johnson and his administration, and not against any fellow Republicans.

Reagan said that he had been surprised, flattered, and somewhat concerned about all the presidential speculation surrounding him. He did not want to be a favorite son, he said, but he would probably have to allow it in order to assure party unity in California. He said that he would not be a candidate in the primaries.

On July 17, I flew to Gettysburg to see Eisenhower. I looked forward, as usual, to discussing politics and world affairs with him, but now we had another subject of mutual interest. Julie and his grandson David had been seeing a great deal of each other while at college. Actually, though it was not known to the respective families, they had already decided to marry.

We ate lunch alone on the screened-in porch overlooking the farm. We had chicken with noodles and a salad garnished with pickled watermelon rind, which he proudly said he had helped to make. "The rind wasn't thick enough," he said as he helped himself to more.

Eisenhower had been quite animated at lunch, but afterward he looked tired and had to grope for words. He was particularly fatigued after we took a short walk to the barn, but he was firm in the advice he gave me. He advised me against making Vietnam a political issue because many Republicans supported Johnson's goals, although questioning the means he was using to achieve them. He agreed with my long-held view that Johnson's greatest error in prosecuting the war was not having used more power at the outset. He said he knew from his own military experience that gradual escalation did not work. He said, "If an enemy battalion is defending a hill, you give me two battalions and I'll take the hill—but at a terrible cost in casualties. Give me a division and I'll take it without a fight."

Eisenhower asked if Goldwater was still writing a newspaper column. "Barry is the least qualified man I know to write on foreign policy," he said. "He has charm and he is very likable, but he is just not smart." He felt that Scranton was the best qualified of any of the men who had not held national office.

He also talked about Johnson. "Lyndon is too poll-conscious and too sensitive about press criticism," he said. "I told him that directly. I said, 'You are the President, don't worry about jackasses like Fulbright and Morse.'" He added, "The difficulty with Johnson is that he is only interested in what people will approve, and that makes it difficult to get people to believe him."

That fall of 1967 I visited most of the Republican governors and party leaders in their home states. They all wanted to know my plans, but I said only that I was considering entering the primaries and would be grateful for any advice they had. While this position did not commit me or call for any commitments from them, it reinforced their determination to see how I would do in the primaries before deciding whom to support.

In fact, it looked as if many Republicans were using my possible candidacy as an excuse for remaining uncommitted to anyone else. Many Southern leaders, particularly, were holding back on these grounds. In their hearts they would have preferred Reagan, but they had been burned by Goldwater and had learned a lesson of political pragmatism. If they thought I was the man who could win, they would support me.

I was in my law office in New York on Saturday, September 30, 1967, when Rose came in to tell me that my brother Don was on the telephone. I was in a conference, so I asked Rose to tell him I would return the call. She began to cry and said, "No, you should talk to him. Your mother just died."

My mother had suffered a stroke two years before, and we had reluctantly put her in a nursing home in Whittier.

Whenever I was in the Los Angeles area I drove out to see her. She never gave any signs of awareness and could speak only in monosyllables, but I felt sure that in the deep recesses of her mind she recognized me.

She had always hated the idea of being in a rest home, but she needed constant attention from nurses and doctors that would have been impossible to provide either at Don's house or in our New York apartment. There were times when I regretted that we did not do whatever was necessary to keep her in one of our homes. There was no doubt, however, that it was better for her to be where she could receive proper care. I also knew that she would have wanted it that way, because she never wanted to be a burden to her family.

Perhaps because I was prepared intellectually for the idea of her death, it took some time before the emotional impact of it hit me. By the time I got home about an hour later, Pat had told the girls. They were in tears; they loved their grandmother very much, although it would not have been possible for them to love her as much as she loved them. Her love was all-encompassing and totally unselfish—never expecting or wanting anything in return. I did not cry when I heard the news, nor when I talked with Pat and the girls in the apartment, nor on the plane to California for the funeral. My principal thought was a feeling of deep regret that I had not done as much for her as I might have if I had not been so busy with my own career and concerns.

My mother had been a great admirer of Billy Graham, even before he became famous. She had attended one of his first crusades in Southern California and spoken to him afterward, and he never forgot her in the years that followed. As soon as he heard of her death, he called me from his home in North Carolina and said that he wanted to come to the funeral. The service was held in the same Friends Church in East Whittier where as a child I had played the piano for Sunday School and sung in the choir. It was in this church that my father's funeral service had been held eleven years earlier.

The church was full, and many of my mother's Whittier friends and acquaintances had to stand outside because of the great number of reporters, whose presence I deeply resented, who filled the back and side aisles. At the end of the service the family were the first to leave the church and walk by the open casket. My mother was not pretty, but she was beautiful, and she looked as beautiful in death as she had in life.

The local minister and Billy were standing at the door as we left. I shook hands with the minister and then, as I shook hands with Billy, our eyes met. I could no longer control my pent-up emotions. I broke into tears. He threw his arms around me and said, "Let it all out."

We walked out into the sunlight and rode from the church to Rose Hills Memorial Park. My mother was buried in the family plot, alongside my father, my brothers Arthur and Harold, her mother and father, and her sister Elizabeth, who died of cancer. Only one reporter had the bad manners to stick a microphone in my face and ask how I felt. I just walked past him. I did not want to stay around the places that reminded me so painfully of my mother, so Pat and I went directly to the airport from the cemetery and were soon on our way back to New York.

While Pat slept, I closed my eyes and thought back on my mother's life. She had worked so hard and given so much of herself to others. I remembered the last time we had talked before she had her stroke. She had just had an operation, and although she was in terrible pain she never once complained about it.

I knew that her chances of recovery were very small. Words were utterly inadequate, so all I could say was, "Mother, don't give up."

She pulled herself up in the bed, and with sudden strength in her voice she said, "Richard, don't *you* give up. Don't let anybody tell you you are through."

Only later did I find out that just before her operation she had read a column in the Los Angeles *Times* speculating that I was through as far as any chances of regaining national office were concerned.

"*Richard, don't you give up. Don't let anybody tell you you are through.*" What a typical sentiment, I thought as the plane flew eastward into nightfall. What a marvelous legacy.

The Republican front-runner during the preprimary period was George Romney. I knew that Romney had a head start, but I also suspected that his lack of experience might make him politically accident-prone. Reports from his campaign organization confirmed this suspicion. His statement that he had been successfully "brainwashed" by his official hosts during his study tour of Vietnam was his worst, but by no means his only, gaffe during this period.

From my point of view, the most interesting question about Romney was whether Nelson Rockefeller was using him as a stalking horse for his own candidacy.

I saw Eisenhower again on October 17. By now the political situation was beginning to develop very quickly, and he was outspoken in analyzing the various political personalities who might play a role in 1968.

I told him of my high regard for Jerry Ford. He agreed but was afraid that Ford was not exciting enough. "We need someone who can charge up the troops," he said. He called Mel Laird "the smartest of the lot, but he is too devious." In December 1968, after I had selected Laird as Secretary of Defense, Eisenhower expressed the same doubts. After the two men had a meeting in January, however, Eisenhower told me he thought I had made a good choice. Flashing his famous grin, he said, "Of course Laird is devious, but for anyone who has to run the Pentagon and get along with Congress, that is a valuable asset."

We discussed Rockefeller's intentions and his chances. Eisenhower said, "His major liability is that his becoming a candidate would resurrect all the hard feelings of 1964 at a time when it is imperative to get the party together."

As usual we talked about the situation in Vietnam. I said that I thought we should quarantine North Vietnam by mining its harbors. Eisenhower said that he thought we would need a declaration of war in order to justify such action under international law. He took a hard line, however, regarding the proposals to stop the bombing of North Vietnam. He said, "Who wants to stop it? The Communists want to stop it because it is hurting them. Therefore, we should continue it."

He thought that Johnson's hesitations at crucial occasions had been damaging. He thought he had made a serious mistake in restricting the bombing of North Vietnam, and that Johnson had been about a year and a half too late at every stage: in committing U.S. troops, in initiating the bombing, and in building up public support for the war.

I asked him what he thought of the idea of switching to a volunteer army when the war ended. He strongly opposed it and said that he had written a thesis on the topic at the War College. He had investigated all the options and concluded that universal military training was a good idea. "Besides," he added, "it would be good for the hippie generation."

He looked up suddenly. "Look at that beautiful bluejay," he said. We watched the bird for a few moments. Eisenhower's brow furrowed as he tried to pick up his train of thought, and it was painful for me to watch him struggling to remember. Finally he sighed and said, "If only the time would come when men would sit down and rationally settle their differences in peace."

By the end of 1967 I knew that I had to make a final decision about running. The Nixon for President organization was ready to shift into high gear as soon as I gave the signal. Johnson's personal and political insecurity had become obvious; his party was ready to split apart under pressure from Eugene McCarthy and Bobby Kennedy on the left and from George Wallace on the right. The chances for a Republican to be elected President in 1968 looked better all the time. My chances of being that Republican had also improved over the year. I was the first choice of Republicans for the nomination in almost every Gallup poll taken in 1967; most of the party's organizational leaders either wanted to support me or, at least, felt that I had earned a shot at the nomination by the hard labor I had done for the party during the dark times after Goldwater's defeat. However, many of my strongest supporters were still not sure that I could throw off my "loser image" and lead the party to victory. As I had foreseen, everything was going to depend on the primaries.

In October 1967 the Gallup poll's presidential trial heat had shown me running ahead of Johnson for the first time, 49 percent to 45 percent. Even though he regained the lead in November, this showing did much to improve my chances.

In all the conversations that I had in the latter part of 1967, seeking advice about what to do, I did not reveal to anyone my inner doubts about becoming a candidate. Late on the night of December 22, 1967, I committed some of them to paper.

It had been a long day—lunch with my law partners, an afternoon meeting with key campaign advisers, and in the evening our annual Christmas party at our apartment, at which I played Christmas carols on the piano and Tom Dewey led the singing in his rich baritone. After the party, Pat and I went to the kitchen to thank Manolo and Fina Sanchez for the splendid job they had done in serving over a hundred guests. We realized again, as we had so many times before, how fortunate we were to have had the loyal and efficient services of this remarkable Spanish couple who had come to us as refugees from Cuba in 1961. Then I retreated to the quiet of my library. Manolo had laid a fire, and the room had a comforting, familiar warmth.

I sat in my easy chair and took a fresh yellow pad. I wrote: "I have decided personally against becoming a candidate." Then I summarized my thoughts:

—Unlike some of the political newcomers, I did not want the presidency in order to *be* someone.

—Losing again could be an emotional disaster for the family. The memories of 1960 and 1962 were still painful.

—Perhaps I had lost the spirit and zeal essential to survive the ordeal of a long presidential campaign—particularly one that begins on the tortuous primary route. I wrote, "Combat is the essence of politics." Yet I really did not relish the combat and had to force myself to develop the fighting spirit necessary to inspire others.

—I was tired of having to ask for support from political and business leaders and even from old friends.

—There would be no draft at the convention. People were still hesitating about their support, and I continued to hear the message that the party needed a winner.

—I was bored by the charade of trying to romance the media. They were being relatively courteous at this period, but I knew the majority opposed my views and would strongly oppose my candidacy.

"Personally, I have had it. I want nothing else." Even

as I wrote the words I was surprised by my ambivalence regarding the presidency. As if to restore some balance I noted that neither was the practice of law what I wanted for the rest of my life.

—A good candidate must have five qualities: brains, heart, judgment, guts, and experience. I felt that I measured up to four of them. But I was not sure whether I still had the heart—whether I had not reached the time in life when I lacked the zeal to continue a political career.

—Many of my friends did not want my place in history to be determined by the defeats of 1960 and 1962. They argued that defeat should not be my epitaph. That argument never had much appeal to me because I had a fatalistic, almost deterministic, view of history—that history makes the man more than the man makes history.

Finally, I startled myself again by writing at the bottom of the page a thought that I had never expected to have: "I don't give a damn."

I put down my pen and just sat looking into the fire and thinking. I had somehow always known that if everything worked out right, I could have another presidential candidacy. The road had been tiring and at times unbearably lonely. Had I come all this way to avoid the clash? I *did* want to run. Every instinct said yes. But now, on the brink of that decision, I was surprised to find myself procrastinating.

On Christmas Day, I had a long discussion with Pat, Tricia, and Julie. Pat said that she was completely happy with our life in New York, but whatever I decided, she was resigned to helping out. Tricia and Julie were now grown up, and I gave great weight to their opinions. Julie was a sophomore at Smith College. She had never really accepted the loss in 1960. She said, "You have to do it for the country." Tricia, a senior at Finch College, spoke in more personal terms. "If you don't run, Daddy, you really will have nothing to live for."

With the New Hampshire primary less than three months away, I could not prolong the final decision much longer. It was clear that in the busy holiday atmosphere at home, I would not be able to do any concentrated thinking.

360

I decided therefore to go to Florida for a few days to relax and think in solitude.

As I left on December 28, Pat took my arm and kissed me. "Whatever you do, we'll be proud of you," she said. "You know we love you."

Bebe Rebozo met me at the airport, and we went directly to a villa at the Key Biscayne Hotel. I had telephoned Billy Graham and asked if he could come down and join us. For the next three days I walked on the beach and thought about the most important decision of my life. On the first night we sat up late talking about theology and politics and sports. Billy read aloud the first and second chapters of Romans. The next afternoon I invited him to join me for a walk along the beach. He had been very sick with pneumonia and was still recuperating, so we decided not to tax his strength by walking too far. I told him that I was genuinely torn on the question of whether to run. One part of me wanted to more than anything else, but another part of me rebelled at the thought of all it would entail. It was far from certain that I could win the nomination; even if I did, that would be only the prelude to an even more arduous campaign. Ten months of campaigning would mean great stress and strain on me and on my family, especially Pat.

We had become so involved in our conversation that we walked more than a mile—all the way to the old Spanish lighthouse at the tip of Key Biscayne. By the time we got back, Billy was weak and exhausted. He went upstairs to rest while Rebozo and I watched the Green Bay Packers defeat the Dallas Cowboys 21–17 in subfreezing weather in Green Bay. That night, New Year's Eve, we had dinner at the Jamaica Inn, where I had reserved my favorite table beside a small waterfall.

As Billy was getting ready to leave the next day, I went to his room and sat looking out at the ocean while he finished packing. "Well, what is your conclusion?" I asked. "What should I do?" Billy closed his suitcase and turned toward me. "Dick, I think you should run," he said. "If you don't you will always wonder whether you should have run and whether you could have won or not. You are the best prepared man in the United States to be President." He talked about the problems facing America and how much greater and more serious they were now than in 1960. He said that I had been denied the chance to provide leadership in 1960, but now, providentially, I had another chance. "I think it is your destiny to be President," he said.

I stayed in Florida for another week. One morning when I went to the hotel from my villa to pick up my mail, I found a letter from David Eisenhower.

Dear Mr. Nixon,
During my past visit, Julie told me of the difficult decisions you were facing and of the strong possibility that you might not run for President. I hoped that an appropriate moment would arise to say something about it to you in person, but the subject seemed so delicate that the words and the moment eluded me. . . .

The most discouraging aspect of politics, when I rationally consider my ambitions in life, is its thanklessness. My Grandad is now regarded as a simple country bumpkin and a sweet old General. The liberal element, since it does control educational and journalistic media to a vast degree, has distorted his personal and public image possibly forever. Yet I feel his efforts were, for himself and many others, the source of genuine satisfaction since he served his country to the best of his ability and touched the lives of millions.

Everything I say must be a tremendous understatement since I have never endured a political campaign or political life in its most taxing form. Politics is a sacrifice, in terms of one's family, privacy, and countless other aspects of a man's life. This I have seen. It is rare when someone possesses such wisdom and insight that he should be called upon to sacrifice himself and to serve. But I sincerely feel that you have it and that America needs the guidance you could render. I also feel that America will come to realize this in due time, if it doesn't already. . . .

Only you can determine whether to run is worth the effort and the hardships or not. I simply hoped to tell you a little of how I felt on the matter. . . .

Sincerely,
David

By January 9, my fifty-fifth birthday, I was back in New York. My mind was made up, but I decided to wait until Julie could come home from school for a weekend so that I could tell the whole family at the same time.

On January 15, we were all together for dinner. I asked Rose Woods to join us—she had been through so much with us that she was virtually a part of the family. I felt she should be present at this moment. I waited until dinner was over, and then I asked Manolo and Fina to join us.

I said that, as they probably guessed, I had reached a decision. I knew that Pat was not in favor of my running, and that was the one factor that finally weighed most heavily in my mind against it. But I had increasingly come to understand that politics was not just an alternative occupation for me. It was my life. Although it would be a long, hard road, I felt that this time I could win. Finally, I said, "I have decided to go. I have decided to run again."

There was a brief pause. Then Pat said, "I know what you are asking us to do, and what you are asking of yourself. Now that the decision is made, I will go along with it."

Tricia picked up her water glass and proposed a toast. She said, "Whatever happens, we will win either way!" Fina, standing next to Manolo, said, "You are the man to lead the country! This was determined before you were born!"

1968 Campaign
and Election

I began my second campaign for the presidency with a press conference on the afternoon of February 2, 1968, in the Holiday Inn at Manchester, New Hampshire. I came to the microphones and announced, "Gentlemen, this is *not* my last press conference."

Anticipating the central question, I said at the outset that I had considered the "he can't win" problem and had decided to enter all the primaries to prove that I *could* win. As a challenge to Nelson Rockefeller—who was, I was convinced, behind George Romney's candidacy—I said that the next Republican nominee must be selected not in smoke-filled rooms but in the "fires of the primaries."

I had some reasons for confidence about the chances for success of my primary strategy. The most recent nation-wide Gallup poll of Republicans gave me a commanding 40 percent lead over Romney, and I led Rockefeller by a comfortable 14 percent. Given these generally reassuring figures, I had three major concerns about the New Hampshire primary. First, there was always the danger of an upset; no candidate can be confident of an election when 32 percent of the voters are undecided. I had to show that I could be a winner, but I could not let the proud and independent voters of New Hampshire think me arrogant or start regarding Romney as an underdog. Second, there was always the danger of making a mistake. I knew that the media would analyze and examine everything I did and said, and I would have to be extraordinarily careful of the image and tone my campaign projected. Third, there was the danger of allowing the primary campaign to split the Republican ranks so deeply that whoever won would inherit a dispirited and disunited party. Johnson's popularity ratings were low because of North Korea's seizure of the intelligence ship *Pueblo* in January, the Tet offensive in Vietnam in February, and the bitter disunity being stirred up among the Democrats by Minnesota Senator Eugene McCarthy's antiwar candidacy. Even considering these factors, it would still be very difficult for any Republican to challenge Lyndon Johnson, a resourceful politician armed with the powers of incumbency.

The Vietnam war was the dominant issue in New Hampshire, as it was throughout the campaign. I wanted the war to end, but in a manner that would save the South Vietnamese people from military defeat and subjection to the domination of the North Vietnamese Communist regime.

I felt that there were a number of unexplored avenues to probe in finding a way to end the war. I believed that we could use our armed strength more effectively to convince the North Vietnamese that a military victory was not possible. We also needed to step up our programs for training and equipping the South Vietnamese so that they could develop the capability of defending themselves. Most important, I believed that we were not making adequate use of our vast diplomatic resources and powers. The heart of the problem lay more in Peking and Moscow than in Hanoi.

As a candidate it would have been foolhardy, and as a prospective President, improper, for me to outline specific plans in detail. I did not have the full range of information or the intelligence resources available to Johnson. And even if I had been able to formulate specific "plans," it would have been absurd to make them public. In the field of diplomacy, premature disclosure can often doom even the best-laid plans.

To some extent, then, I was asking the voters to take on faith my ability to end the war. A regular part of my campaign speech was the pledge: "New leadership will end the war and win the peace in the Pacific."

I never said that I had a "plan," much less a "secret plan," to end the war; I was deliberately straightforward about the difficulty of finding a solution. As I told the AP on March 14, 1968, there was "no magic formula, no gimmick. If I had a gimmick I would tell Lyndon Johnson."

Although Romney campaigned vigorously and spent large sums of money —much of which was rumored to have come from Rockefeller—the polls continued to move against him.

I was in the middle of a campaign swing through a number of small towns when Pat Buchanan came up after a speech and said that he had to talk to me alone. He guided me to a nearby men's room and said that he had just heard from a reporter that Romney was going to hold a press conference and pull out of the race. I was utterly astonished, and I asked my staff to watch Romney's press conference and fill me in. Their report was in the broad grins they wore when they walked into my room after the broadcast. Personally I was disappointed by Romney's withdrawal. Even though I had knocked him out of the ring, now I would win without having actually defeated an opponent in the election—and the test of the election was, after all, the reason I had decided to enter the primaries in the first place.

Despite Romney's withdrawal, we continued publicly to forecast my vote at only 45 percent to 50 percent of the total. While I hoped and expected to win more, I believed it was better to understate the prospects than to overstate them.

On the night of March 12, Pat and I went to a victory celebration at national Nixon headquarters in New York. I was pleasantly surprised when I polled 78 percent of the vote. Even without Romney in the race, my win was hailed as significant, and it dwarfed the handful of write-in votes that had been solicited by some of Rockefeller's unofficial supporters.

The New Hampshire results changed the political picture for both parties. On the Democratic side, Johnson won with 49.5 percent of the vote, but Senator Eugene McCarthy's unorthodox antiwar candidacy received a phenomenal 42.4 percent. The media attention and analysis concentrated so heavily on McCarthy that many people got the impression he had actually won—and, for all practical purposes, he had. Four days after McCarthy had shown that Johnson might be defeated, Senator Robert Kennedy of New York announced his candidacy for the nomination. Many of the conscientious antiwar liberals felt that Kennedy was cynically moving in to usurp the fruits of McCarthy's labors. Liberal New York *Post* columnist Murray Kempton charged that Kennedy had merely waited until Johnson was "bloodied in New Hampshire," and that Kennedy was a coward for coming "down the hills to shoot the wounded."

On the Republican side, Romney's withdrawal and my victory put pressure on Rockefeller, and on March 21 he called a press conference. I fully expected him to declare his candidacy. Instead he announced, "I have decided today to reiterate unequivocally that I am not a candidate campaigning directly or indirectly for the presidency of the United States." He said he would "do nothing in the future by word or deed to encourage" a presidential draft and that he had signed an affidavit taking his name out of the Oregon primary. For emphasis he added, "The terms of the affidavit are precise. They plainly declare that I am not, and will not be, a candidate for the presidency."

Rockefeller talked about the need for party unity, and admitted, "Quite frankly, I find it clear at this time that a considerable majority of the party's leaders want the candidacy of former Vice President Richard Nixon, and it appears equally clear that they are keenly concerned and anxious to avoid any such divisive challenge within the party as marked the 1964 campaign."

Governor Spiro T. Agnew of Maryland was watching the broadcast in his office in Annapolis with a group of friends and reporters. Agnew was a sponsor of the National Draft Rockefeller Committee, which had been formed in

Annapolis just three days before, and he fully expected Rockefeller to announce his candidacy. Agnew told the reporters that he was "tremendously surprised and greatly disappointed" by Rockefeller's decision.

The next week I met with Agnew for two hours, and I was impressed by his intelligence and poise. After that meeting he told reporters that he still liked Rockefeller and was not yet ready to announce his support for me. But in speaking of me, he said, "I have high regard for him. He's the front-runner."

I had scheduled a nationwide radio speech for Sunday evening, March 31, to outline my views on the Vietnam war. I intended to propose that America vigorously try to convince the Soviet Union to reduce its military support for North Vietnam. I also planned to deliver a sharp critique of the Johnson policy of gradualism on the military front.

On Saturday afternoon, as I was putting the final touches on my speech before the taping, I received word that Johnson had asked the television networks for time the next night. I had no alternative but to postpone my speech.

I spent most of Sunday campaigning in Milwaukee. Because I would be airborne during Johnson's speech, I asked Pat Buchanan to listen to it and to meet me at La Guardia Airport with a report when I landed.

When Buchanan gave me his report, I was stunned. Johnson had described his latest attempts at de-escalating the war and stressed his personal dedication to obtaining peace. Then he made one of the most unexpected announcements in American political history. He said that he did not believe that he should devote even an hour of his day to any personal partisan causes. "Accordingly," he continued, "I shall not seek, and I will not accept, the nomination of my party for another term as your President."

When reporters clamored for my statement, I flippantly said that this was "the year of the dropouts": Romney, Rockefeller, and now Johnson. While the dropout label might have been apt for the first two, I was justifiably criticized for thus characterizing Johnson's action.

The upshot of these events was that the next primary, held in Wisconsin on April 2, was rendered almost meaningless. I won 79.4 percent of the Republican vote, and McCarthy swamped noncandidate Johnson, 56 percent to 34 percent.

Two days after the Wisconsin primary Martin Luther King, Jr., was assassinated in Memphis, Tennessee. The uproar set off by Johnson's announcement had not yet subsided, and now the nation was about to go through brief but intense agony as shock turned to disillusion, disillusion to despair, and despair to hatred and violence. Within an hour after King's death, looting and vandalism broke out in Washington, within six blocks of the White House. That same evening scattered and sporadic fighting and looting occurred in New York's Harlem and Bedford-Stuyvesant. Soon disorders were breaking out across the nation. The next day, the rioting and vandalism became arson and death. Seven were killed and over 350 arrested in Chicago as rioters pillaged a long stretch of downtown stores. The National Guard was called out there, as well as in Detroit, Boston, and elsewhere.

On Sunday, April 7, I flew to Atlanta to pay my respects to the King family. I went to their home and met his four children, still dazed over their father's murder. I saw Mrs. King in her room, where she was resting; I was moved by her poise and serenity. She thanked me for coming, and we talked about my first meeting with her husband, on the occasion of the independence of Ghana in 1957. I told her how impressed I had been by his insistence that the realization of his dream of equal opportunity for all should be accomplished by peaceful rather than violent means. Two days later I returned to Atlanta for the funeral.

The idealism of Martin Luther King, Jr., expressed in his words and actions, was his unique contribution to the civil rights cause. He worked to resist the extremists in the movement, those who wished to resort to violence to reach their goals. Perhaps their pressure sometimes caused him to be more extreme in his public views than he otherwise would have been. Yet one could reason with him. Like his colleagues, he did not enjoy hearing that patience would be required to achieve his goals; but as a practical man, he realized that this was the case. His death left black America without a nationally recognized leader who combined responsibility with charisma. Others were reasonably effective, but none could match his mystique and his ability to inspire people—white as well as black—and to move them.

I canceled all political activity for two weeks after Dr. King's death. Then I flew to Washington for an April 19 appearance before the American Society of Newspaper Editors. My speech and the lively question-and-answer session that followed went over well, and a few days later I received a letter from Eisenhower.

Dear Dick:

My morning's paper carried excerpts from your speech before the Nation's Editors. I think it was superb. Moreover, I applaud your Q. and A. format—it gives you opportunity for spontaneity, humor, and hard-hitting observations.

Casual word-of-mouth reports coming to me about your campaign's progress are far brighter than a few weeks ago. At first all the self-appointed experts were still saying, "Dick is well prepared for the presidency, but he cannot be elected." Now, by and large—and my reports come not only from locals but from visitors throughout the country—the refrain has changed to "Of course, Nixon is well prepared for the presidency, now we must see if we can elect him." This is real progress and if the trend continues it will not be long before doubt has become conviction. . . .

Devotedly,
Ike E

The cheer I received from Eisenhower's letter was particularly welcome—and timely; within a week Nelson Rockefeller was back in the race against me.

On April 30 Rockefeller convened a press conference in Albany and announced a complete turnaround. He explained that the "dramatic and unprecedented events of the past weeks have revealed in most serious terms the gravity of the crisis that we face as a people," and declared his candidacy.

Rockefeller made his announcement on the day of the Massachusetts primary. Governor John Volpe, one of my early supporters, had insisted on running as a favorite son candidate. Thanks to write-in votes, Rockefeller managed to squeeze out a half percentage-point victory over Volpe. The victory was embarrassing to Volpe, irritating to me, and a great boost to Rockefeller. All thirty-four Massachusetts delegates went to him, and his campaign got a good send-off.

Rockefeller entered the race too late to have his name on the ballot in any of the remaining primaries. I was certain that his late entry was calculated to spare himself the risk of losing.

With Rockefeller back in the race, I began listening for the faint hoofbeats of another aspiring candidate. Ronald Reagan could not win a two-man contest with me at the convention; but with Rockefeller to chip away at me from the left, Reagan would very likely begin seeing visions of a greater role than favorite son of the California delegation.

Therefore, I was not surprised that Reagan had assented to his name's being placed on the ballot by Nebraska state officials for its May 14 primary. He disavowed any personal encouragement of the effort, but his supporters mounted a substantial effort on his behalf, including several statewide prime-time showings of a very effective half-hour television documentary. Rockefeller's supporters launched a write-in campaign and bought 247 television spots and 564 newspaper ads. Despite their efforts, I topped Reagan 70 percent to 22 percent, while Rockefeller limped in at only 5 percent. This was the most competitive Republican primary so far, and I was gratified by the results.

The key primary was now Oregon, the last one I would enter; the June 4 contest in California was Reagan's—I had decided not to risk dividing the party by challenging his favorite son status. For the time being at least, Rockefeller and Reagan shared a common strategy: to slow me down, brake my momentum, and buy time for a final attack at the convention in Miami Beach. I was worried about Oregon because Reagan's people were spending heavily in an attempt to make a last-minute sweep. They eventually spent several hundred thousand dollars in the state, and Rockefeller's forces, seeking write-in votes, did the same.

I doubled my efforts in Oregon, and, unlike Reagan and Rockefeller, I went to the state to campaign. Reagan could not go because he was professing not to be a candidate, and Rockefeller apparently felt he could not afford to because a defeat would look even worse if he had campaigned there.

So Reagan showed his documentary and Rockefeller ran hundreds of ads, but my strategy paid off. I received more than 73 percent of the vote in this final primary test, with Reagan trailing at 23 percent and Rockefeller at 4 percent.

That night in my suite in the Benson Hotel in Portland I had some of the same sense of satisfaction that I had had on election night 1966. It was far from over, but things were falling into place.

In June 1967 Bob Haldeman gave me a memorandum on the use of media in a modern presidential campaign. He stressed that creative thought had to be given to developing ways to use television. "The time has come," he wrote, "for political campaigning—its techniques and strategies—to move out of the dark ages and into the brave new world of the omnipresent eye." Haldeman correctly argued that a candidate could make hundreds of speeches during a campaign and still only meet directly with a few hundred thousand potential new supporters. Such a frenetic pace, in the meantime, causes a candidate to "become punchy, mauled by his admirers, jeered and deflated by his opponent's supporters (and paid troublemakers), misled by the super-stimulation of one frenzied rally after another. He has no time to think, to study his opponent's strategy and statements, to develop his own strategy and statements. No wonder the almost inevitable campaign dialogue borders so near the idiot level."

The most important recommendation in the Haldeman memo was to develop new ways to use television.

A group of my advisers spent an afternoon in New York, watching old television news clips from over the years that showed me in a wide variety of formal and informal situations. The goal was to match the candidate with the medium, to determine exactly what manner of presentation would be the most effective. They analyzed each performance and decided that the more spontaneous the situation, the better I came across. This insight led to the decision that I would use the question-and-answer technique extensively, not only in press conferences and public question sessions with student audiences but also in my paid political programming.

In the campaign this evolved into the "man in the arena" concept, in which I stood alone, with no podium, in the center of a stage surrounded by an audience in bleacherlike tiers. In this setting I was asked questions by a panel of private citizens, sometimes joined by local reporters.

In 1968 the South was to be one of the most important regions in terms of winning both the nomination and the election. In 1964 Governor George Wallace of Alabama had mounted an essentially racist campaign in three Democratic Party primaries, and his strong showing embarrassed party leaders. In 1968 Wallace decided to expand his appeal along more generally conservative lines and make his bid via a third party. He was working to get his name on the general election ballot in as many states as possible.

On the Republican side, it was Ronald Reagan who set the hearts of many Southern Republicans aflutter. He spoke their conservative language articulately and with great passion, and there was always a possibility that Southern delegates could be lured at the last minute by his ideological siren song. Until I had the nomination, therefore, I had to pay careful attention to the dangers of a sudden resurgence on the right. Equally dangerous would be a serious intraparty split that would deliver the Reaganites into Wallace's camp.

On May 31, I flew to Atlanta for one of the most important conferences of the pre-convention period. The Southern Republican state chairmen were meeting, and I spent several hours over two days with these officials individually and in various groups. There was no pretense about the purpose of my visit: I was doing serious courting and hard counting.

I had invited Senator Strom Thurmond to Atlanta, and he sat in on one of the meetings. Thurmond was a former governor of South Carolina and Dixiecrat candidate for President in 1948 on the States' Rights ticket. In 1964 he had switched from the Democratic to the Republican Party and supported Barry Goldwater. Now he was among the strongest Republican leaders in the South, and his support was essential to me.

I had been consulting privately with Thurmond for several months, and I was convinced that he would join my campaign if he were satisfied on the two issues of paramount concern to him. The more important of these was national defense. As a member of the Senate Armed Services Committee he believed that America should be unquestionably first in the world in military power; I agreed with him completely. The second issue was parochial: Thurmond wanted tariffs against textile imports to protect South Carolina's position in the industry. I reluctantly went along with him on this issue because of political realities, but I told him that we should try first to get Japan and other countries to agree voluntarily to reduce their exports to the United States before we took the tariff route. On civil rights, Thurmond knew my position was very different from his. I was for the Civil Rights Act of 1964; he was against it. Although he disagreed with me, he respected my sincerity and candor. He knew that I would enforce the law, but that I would not make the South the whipping boy.

I emerged from this meeting with Thurmond's pledge of support, which would become a valuable element in my ability to thwart any moves by Reagan on my right.

I watched the California primary returns on television in our New York apartment with Pat, Tricia, Julie, and David Eisenhower. Because of the time difference, I stayed up only long enough to get a sense of the trend. It was clear that Bobby Kennedy was gaining back the initiative he had lost to McCarthy in Oregon. I believed that Hubert Humphrey had waited too long before declaring his candidacy, and I saw no way a Kennedy juggernaut could be stopped once it had acquired the momentum of a California victory. As I went to bed, I said, "It sure looks like we'll be going against Bobby." David and Julie said they would stay up watching and give me a report in the morning.

It was not long before I dimly heard David's voice calling my name over and over. "Mr. Nixon. Excuse me, sir. Mr. Nixon." I finally opened my eyes and saw David standing in my room. "What is it?" I asked. "They shot Kennedy," he said. "He's still alive, but he's unconscious. He was shot right after his victory speech."

With millions of other Americans I thought, how could such ghastly tragedy be revisited on the Kennedy family? Who had done it, and why? When would this madness come to an end?

The next day I was working in my study when Pat came in, tears in her eyes. She said, "Dick, that poor boy just died. It's on the radio."

Bobby Kennedy and I were political antagonists, representing wholly different constituencies and philosophies. There was nothing similar about our beliefs or styles. But we shared, as all politicians do, membership in an unchartered club of those who devote their energies and themselves to public life and public service. I was, as I had always been, fatalistic about danger. But I was saddened and appalled by such tragic human waste.

Pat and I attended the funeral mass at St. Patrick's Cathedral in New York, and we were deeply moved by the eloquent eulogy delivered by his brother, Teddy.

All the candidates observed a moratorium on campaigning in the weeks following the funeral. President Johnson ordered round-the-clock Secret Service protection for all presidential candidates and their families.

I renewed my campaigning at the end of June, and except for occasional periods of rest there was no stopping until Election Day, November 5.

As the convention neared, I kept my lead despite formidable efforts by the Rockefeller and Reagan forces to dislodge and attract delegates. Because Rockefeller had declined to fight me in the primaries, he had only one card left to play: the "loser" issue. He would try to demonstrate that he had a better chance to win in November than I did.

To this end he launched a ludicrous "battle of the polls." In a formal telegram sent to me and made public on July 9, Rockefeller proposed, first, that I meet him in a

On July 26 I went to Washington for the intelligence briefing President Johnson had offered to all presidential candidates. He had briefed George Wallace earlier that day, and when I got to the White House, Johnson, Secretary of State Dean Rusk, and Walt Rostow, the President's National Security Adviser, were waiting for me.

The central issue of the briefing was Vietnam. On the question of whether we should unilaterally stop the bombing in North Vietnam, Johnson spoke feelingly of the men who were serving in South Vietnam and the letters he had to write to the next of kin of those who had died. "Do I tell that boy that we'll stop bombing and let 30 percent more trucks filled with ammunition and guns come south so that they will have a better chance to kill him?" he asked.

Rusk, one of the ablest and most honorable men ever to serve as Secretary of State, made the point that the rest of Asia would be in a "panic" if the United States were to withdraw from Vietnam without an honorable peace settlement. He said that he held this view completely apart from

maintained a heavy schedule ... ...
gate support I already had and at collecting additional
delegates to ensure a first-ballot victory. To this end, I felt it
was essential to obtain Eisenhower's endorsement.

Eisenhower was reluctant to become involved in
pre-convention fight. I knew that he would prefer to best
his endorsement after the convention, when it would hav
symbolic unifying effect on the party. But I knew that
wanted me to get the nomination, and I asked Bryce F
low, one of his former top aides now supporting me, to v
to Eisenhower urging him to endorse me before the con
tion.

I visited Eisenhower at Walter Reed Hospital in V
ington on July 15. His smile had not dimmed, but the
wrinkles in his face showed that age and illness had
their toll. After some small talk, he brought up the qu
of the endorsement. Our importunings had apparentl
effective; without any hesitation or qualifications h
"Dick, I don't want there to be any more question

debate, and second, that I join him in commissioning a poll to test our relative strengths in areas of large electoral votes. The results of these polls would be given to the delegates at the convention, who could use them to decide upon their nominee. I had never heard of such a ridiculous way to determine a party's nominee. This was clearly a last-ditch effort, born of desperation.

Although I rejected the offer of a joint poll, Rockefeller went ahead on his own. He hired a polling firm—and then spent millions of dollars on a massive national advertising campaign in an obvious attempt to affect public opinion at the time his polls were being made. Just before the convention, Rockefeller began releasing the results of the polls, which showed him ahead of me in the key electoral states.

My strategy was to wait it out. My own polls showed me doing as well as, or even better than, Rockefeller in the same key states. I was sorely tempted to fire back, but I didn't. I felt certain of defeating Rockefeller, and I didn't want to let him draw me into internecine warfare that could only hurt my chances in the fall.

While Rockefeller continued his charade of the polls, I maintained a heavy schedule aimed at solidifying the delegate support I already had and at collecting additional delegates to ensure a first-ballot victory. To this end, I felt it was essential to obtain Eisenhower's endorsement.

Eisenhower was reluctant to become involved in a pre-convention fight. I knew that he would prefer to bestow his endorsement after the convention, when it would have a symbolic unifying effect on the party. But I knew that he wanted me to get the nomination, and I asked Bryce Harlow, one of his former top aides now supporting me, to write to Eisenhower urging him to endorse me before the convention.

I visited Eisenhower at Walter Reed Hospital in Washington on July 15. His smile had not dimmed, but the deep wrinkles in his face showed that age and illness had taken their toll. After some small talk, he brought up the question of the endorsement. Our importunings had apparently been effective; without any hesitation or qualifications he said, "Dick, I don't want there to be any more question about this. You're my choice, period." He agreed to release his endorsement on July 18. His statement was strong and straightforward, and it meant a great deal to me:

> The issues are so great, the times so confusing, that I have decided to break personal precedent and speak out to endorse a presidential candidate prior to the national convention. . . .
>
> I support Richard M. Nixon as my party's nominee for the presidency of the United States. I do so not only because of my appreciation of the distinguished services he performed for this nation during my own administration but even more because of my admiration of his personal qualities: his intellect, acuity, decisiveness, warmth, and above all, his integrity. I feel that the security, prosperity, and solvency of the United States and the cause of world peace will best be served by placing Dick Nixon in the White House in January 1969.

After the announcement was released, he sent me a copy with a handwritten note across the top: "Dear Dick—This was something I truly enjoyed doing—DE."

On July 26 I went to Washington for the intelligence briefing President Johnson had offered to all presidential candidates. He had briefed George Wallace earlier that day, and when I got to the White House, Johnson, Secretary of State Dean Rusk, and Walt Rostow, the President's National Security Adviser, were waiting for me.

The central issue of the briefing was Vietnam. On the question of whether we should unilaterally stop the bombing in North Vietnam, Johnson spoke feelingly of the men who were serving in South Vietnam and the letters he had to write to the next of kin of those who had died. "Do I tell that boy that we'll stop bombing and let 30 percent more trucks filled with ammunition and guns come south so that they will have a better chance to kill him?" he asked.

Rusk, one of the ablest and most honorable men ever to serve as Secretary of State, made the point that the rest of Asia would be in a "panic" if the United States were to withdraw from Vietnam without an honorable peace settlement. He said that he held this view completely apart from the domino theory, which he considered simplistic. He believed that American withdrawal from Vietnam would leave the Chinese Communists as the only major power on the Asian mainland, thus creating the panic.

The critical part of the briefing concerned the bombing halt. Johnson returned to this point several times. He said he had, in fact, made an offer involving a halt, which both the Soviets and the North Vietnamese were seriously considering. He said bitterly that, as far as we were concerned, previous halts had produced nothing. He was also firm that he would insist on a quid pro quo: "We must get something from them if we halt the bombing," he said. He assured me that no halt was planned at that moment. He was prepared to wait as long as the North Vietnamese and their Soviet sponsors took to come to reasonable terms. I said that I would continue to support our goals in Vietnam even though I would be critical of some of the tactics that had been used. I also pledged not to undercut our negotiating position just in case the Communists came around and agreed to the conditions Johnson would insist upon in return for a bombing halt.

When the briefing was over and the others had left, Johnson seemed almost to deflate before my eyes. He looked old and terribly tired. His voice sounded hollow as he detailed at considerable length his decision not to run again. He gave many reasons and explained the many clues that he said he had been dropping since August 1967. At no point, however, did he mention Eugene McCarthy or Bobby Kennedy, or the pressures their candidates were causing.

By the time he walked me to the door, he was his old self again, fully in command. He praised J. Edgar Hoover; he told me of his gratitude for Eisenhower's support; he complimented me on my family; he said that he had just received a letter from David Eisenhower supporting his position on Vietnam.

As we shook hands he said, "You know, Dick, all the talk about me being obsessed with power is just hogwash. I never cared about having any goddamn power. The only thing that appeals to me about being President is the opportunity it provides to do some good for the country. That's all."

While Johnson was telling me about his use of power, I was thinking of ways to keep power out of the hands of Nelson Rockefeller. He was far from giving up. He continued his frantic polling up to the eve of the convention, and he arrived in Miami Beach with armloads of statistics to distribute to the delegates. His efforts seemed to have minimal effect.

While Rockefeller was working openly, Reagan continued to be coy about his candidacy. But there was no doubt about his intentions. Before the convention Reagan had been flying Southern delegates to California to meet with him, making ideological appeals that were difficult for them to resist. Three weeks before the convention he had set off on a tour of the South with Clifton White, his chief delegate-hunter, in tow.

When Reagan arrived at the convention, he immediately began "dropping in" at delegation meetings, charming the delegates with his personality and speaking ability. Finally, on Monday, August 5, he moved into the open. Bill Knowland emerged from a California delegation caucus to announce it had passed a resolution recognizing that "Governor Reagan in fact is a leading and bona fide candidate for President."

It was not long before a new catchword began making the rounds in Miami Beach: *erosion.* Both Rockefeller and Reagan had an interest in convincing delegates that I had not yet sewn up the nomination, and they joined forces to attempt to show that my strength was eroding and that I was losing delegates.

Lieutenants of both candidates buttonholed delegates arriving in Miami, begging them to believe that I had not yet locked up the nomination. While this frantic activity was going on in Miami, I spent the last few days before the convention at Montauk Point on the eastern tip of Long Island working on my acceptance speech.

On the day Reagan's candidacy was announced, Pat and I flew to Miami Beach. We were welcomed by large and enthusiastic crowds. As soon as we reached the penthouse suite of the Hilton Plaza Hotel, I called John Mitchell.

"John, what's the count?" I asked. He chuckled and answered with characteristic coolness and confidence, "I told you that you didn't need to worry, Dick. We've got everything under control." When I put the same question to Dick Kleindienst, who with Mitchell had responsibility for our delegate operation, he was equally confident. Still, the marriage of convenience between Rockefeller and Reagan was now operating at full force. Rockefeller worked on the Northern and Midwestern states while Reagan tried to breach my Southern flank.

But the months of arduous labor were paying off. Strom Thurmond and Senator John Tower of Texas went to work, visiting or telephoning each delegation personally. Tirelessly they shored the Southern dike against Reagan's rising waters. Tower called it "the thin gray line which never broke."

Holding the South was not our only problem; there were other trouble spots. Governor James Rhodes of Ohio, for example, insisted on remaining a favorite son, thus tying up all the Ohio votes, most of which would have gone to me, on the crucial first ballot. George Romney also refused to cede his favorite son status, although the majority of his delegates supported me.

But by Wednesday night, August 7, I was satisfied that I had the votes to win. After checking and double-checking I saw no way that Reagan or Rockefeller could pull it off. Their talk of "erosion" was pure political gamesmanship, and nothing short of a miracle could bring either of them a victory even on a later ballot.

Some observers claimed that I was smug and complacent about winning the nomination. Any idea that the convention was a boring coronation ceremony ignored the months of backbreaking work that had laid the foundation for my success. What truly galled the critics and commentators who did not favor my candidacy was that they could not honestly maintain that the party bosses had arranged my victory. As the only candidate who ran the primary gauntlet from beginning to end, it could hardly be argued that I was not the choice of the people of my party.

As the nominations began, I invited a small group of friends and staff to join my family in our suite. Pat, Tricia and her guest Ed Cox, and Julie and David were there, as well as Rose Woods, Bob Haldeman, Pat Buchanan, Dwight Chapin, Ray Price, and Len Garment. John Mitchell was in constant touch from his communications trailer command post outside the convention hall. Rogers Morton was my floor manager, helping put out fires and giving last-minute pep talks to wavering delegates. Dick Kleindienst roamed the convention floor, keeping a close watch on his charges until the last vote was counted.

Ted Agnew placed my name in nomination. Mitchell had asked him if he would like to have the assignment and had suggested that, if he did a good job, he would be among those considered for the second spot on the ticket. To that extent, at least, Agnew's speech was an audition.

The balloting began. First, Alabama. We had been able to hold the line against the Reagan inroads, and I won 14 votes to his 12. Wally Hickel delivered all but 1 of Alaska's 12 votes, and Barry Goldwater kept all Arizona's votes in the Nixon column. The first problem state on the roll call was Florida. When I got 32 out of the state's 34 votes, the initial danger point had passed.

In Illinois, despite Chuck Percy's last-minute switch to Rockefeller, I won 50 of the 58 delegates.

There were no surprises in any of the states from Massachusetts through Nevada. The second critical point was coming: New Jersey. Just before the balloting reached that state, John Mitchell called me from his command post trailer. "Dick," he said, "I think you're going to have a pleasant surprise in New Jersey. But Cliff Case may never let you cross the Hudson River again." To counter liberal Senator Clifford Case's recalcitrance, Mitchell had enlisted the help of Frank "Hap" Farley, a Republican stalwart from Atlantic City, and broken open the New Jersey delegation. Case's ego was involved, since he had decided at the last minute to run as a favorite son. But his candidacy was patently a front for Rockefeller, and we had to try to persuade the Nixon supporters in the delegation to assert their independence. Outflanked and defeated, Case did not give up easily or gracefully. The internal fight was bitter, and he finally demanded that the delegation be polled. Each member was thus called upon to declare his choice publicly. The strategy failed; as each name was read, and as each delegate called out, "Nixon," the television screen showed Case sulking in his chair, humiliated and hurt. As I watched him on the screen, I thought of the work we had done together in the House and how my campaigning for him in 1954 had helped to win him his Senate seat by a bare 3,000 votes. Those bonds were loosened that night, and our relationship would never again be the same. I had 18 of New Jersey's 40 delegates.

When the roll call reached New York, I managed to pick up four votes on Rockefeller's home ground. I was a little surprised when Jim Rhodes refused to yield his favorite son status and held the Ohio delegation. Pennsylvania Governor Ray Shafer, like Chuck Percy, had gone over to Rockefeller at the last minute. By breaking his neutrality he made his delegation fair game, however, and we raided it with considerable success: I got 22 of the state's 64 votes.

There were no surprises left. Wisconsin put me over the top. I was pleased that the deciding vote came from a primary state.

The final count gave me 692 votes, 25 more than needed. Ronald Reagan, in a unifying gesture in keeping with his posture of being a strong party man, moved that the nomination be made unanimous by acclamation.

We had come halfway up the mountain. I knew from the experiences of 1960 and 1962 that the next half would be by far more difficult to climb.

Rockefeller called a few minutes later to congratulate me. When I told him that I understood his disappointment, he laughed and said, "Ronnie didn't come through for us as well as we expected." He complimented me on my successful strategy and pledged his total support for the final drive in November.

Now I had to make my decision on a running mate. Two weeks earlier John Mitchell and I had tentatively—and very privately—concluded that the nod should go to Agnew. But like most important decisions, this one would not be final until it was announced. I still wanted to test it, to weigh alternatives, to hear other views. It was a tentative choice, and still reversible.

In talking with Agnew I had been impressed by him as a man who seemed to have a great deal of inner strength. Though he had no foreign policy experience, his instincts in this area appeared to parallel mine. He had a good record as a moderate, progressive, effective governor. He took a forward-looking stance on civil rights, but he had firmly opposed those who resorted to violence in promoting their cause. As a former county executive of Baltimore County, he had a keen interest in local as well as state government. He expressed deep concern about the plight of the nation's urban areas. He appeared to have presence, poise, and dignity, which would contribute greatly to his effectiveness both as a candidate and, if we should win, as Vice President.

From a strictly political standpoint, Agnew fit perfectly with the strategy we had devised for the November election. With George Wallace in the race, I could not hope to sweep the South. It was absolutely necessary, therefore, to win the entire rimland of the South—the border states—as well as the major states of the Midwest and West. Agnew fit the bill geographically, and as a political moderate he fit it philosophically.

In my two meetings with him before the convention I never raised the possibility that he might be considered for the vice presidential spot. When I asked him what he might want to do if we won in November, he said he would not be interested in a Cabinet position but would like to be considered for a federal court appointment if an opening occurred.

In the series of meetings I held that night after the nomination, lasting into the early morning hours, I purposely gave no clue to my tentative choice—or even that I had one. The names most mentioned by those attending were the familiar ones: Romney, Reagan, John Lindsay, Percy, Mark Hatfield, John Tower, George Bush, John Volpe, Rockefeller—with only an occasional mention of Agnew, sometimes along with Governors John Love of Colorado and Daniel Evans of Washington.

The meetings produced no strong consensus for any candidate, but they did gradually tend to eliminate all except Agnew. Before finally deciding, I asked each of two close friends and long-time associates: would he himself be my running mate?

The first was Bob Finch. Bob was probably my closest friend in politics, and after winning the lieutenant governorship of California in 1966 he had become a rising star in the party. I was sure of his answer, but I told him, "You have many of Lindsay's best attributes. You have youth and freshness, and you would have great appeal to the party and to independent voters." He was deeply moved by my suggestion, but he strongly rejected it, arguing that the leap from lieutenant governor to Vice President would be perceived as too great. Besides, he was my former aide and a long-time personal friend, and there would be charges of cronyism. Also, he and Reagan had already developed a rivalry in California, and Reagan's supporters would be extremely irritated if he were chosen.

Next, I took Rogers Morton aside. I had immense respect for Morton, and we saw eye to eye on nearly all issues. As a congressman from Maryland, he knew Agnew well. I asked him for a totally honest, candid appraisal of him. Morton stretched his giant frame and paused for a moment to collect his thoughts. Agnew, he said, was potentially a very good candidate, though he had a tendency to be "lazy." He hastened to add that he did not mean this in a derogatory way, but only as a warning that if Agnew were placed on the ticket, he would have to be given a heavy schedule. I then surprised Morton by saying, "Rog, maybe you would be the better choice for me."

Morton smiled for a moment and then became completely serious. He said that as a member of the House he lacked the credentials for the job—or at least credibility as a candidate. "If you want to know the truth," he said, "if it's between me and Ted Agnew, Ted would be the stronger candidate."

That pretty well clinched it for me. Had Morton said that he wanted it, even at that late moment I might well have picked him. Politically he had the same border-state advantages as Agnew. I knew him far better than I knew Agnew, and I considered him one of the best campaigners, one of the ablest individuals, and one of the most astute politicians in the party.

Finally, after a last review with Mitchell, I decided: it would be Agnew. I asked Morton to telephone him.

About an hour later I went downstairs to tell the waiting press corps. Absolute shock and surprise greeted my announcement. Soon after I announced my choice, Agnew met with the press and acquitted himself well under a barrage of subtly hostile rapid-fire questions. Admitting that his name was not exactly a household word, he assured everybody that he would work to change that situation.

I turned immediately to putting the final touches on my acceptance speech. No other campaign speech would be as important, because none would have a larger or more attentive audience.

As I was getting ready to leave for the convention hall, a minor revolt developed over my selection of Agnew. Some of the party's liberal elements, led by New York Congressman Charles Goodell and Rhode Island Governor John Chafee, sought to enlist John Lindsay to carry their banner in a floor challenge to Agnew. When Lindsay declined—in fact, with Brownell acting as intermediary, Lindsay agreed to place Agnew's name in nomination—the dissidents got George Romney to lead the challenge.

My first reaction was that the politicking was a harmless way to let the delegates blow off steam. But as I thought more about this challenge, it began to make me angry. Nothing was more important this year than Republican unity. We could not afford a replay of 1964. I asked Mitchell for suggestions. He was unconcerned: "Ah, screw 'em, Dick. It'll blow over." Mitchell was a superb manager, but he lacked the political experience to foresee the effect of an apparently unimportant episode like this. I told him, "John, we've got to look past the exigencies of the moment. I'm not going to stand for this kind of revolt. If the sore losers get away with something like this now, they'll do the same damn thing during my presidency. It's a test of my leadership, and I'm going to stand firm. I don't want Agnew's first national exposure to be humiliation."

I told him that I expected him to impose whatever discipline he could on the delegates because I wanted to lose as few votes as possible on this challenge.

The revolt was cut short when Agnew received 1,128 votes to Romney's 186. A few days after the convention Romney wrote to me: "I assume you received my note of August 9 and the attached press release on the vice presidency insurrection. As someone said afterwards, it was like a good big burp! It relieved the tension and united your support."

As Pat and I approached the podium in the convention hall, the roar was deafening. Except for winning the election, very few things are more satisfying to a political candidate than the moment of accepting a presidential nomination.

In 1960 I had had to defend Eisenhower's record: now in 1968 I was the challenger against an incumbent administration, and I felt that a tougher approach was called for. I described the problems America faced exactly as I saw them:

> America is in trouble today not because her people have failed but because her leaders have failed.
>
> When the strongest nation in the world can be tied down for four years in a war in Vietnam with no end in sight;
>
> When the richest nation in the world can't manage its own economy;
>
> When the nation with the greatest tradition of the rule of law is plagued by unprecedented lawlessness;
>
> When a nation that has been known for a century for equality of opportunity is torn by unprecedented racial violence;
>
> And when the President of the United States cannot travel abroad or to any major city at home without fear of a hostile demonstration—then it's time for new leadership for the United States of America.
>
> My fellow Americans, tonight I accept the challenge and the commitment to provide that new leadership for America.

I had written the conclusion of the speech as a personal testimony to the political and social opportunity we have in the United States. It was intentionally dramatic, and it was completely true.

> Tonight, I see the face of a child.
>
> He lives in a great city. He is black, or he is white. He is Mexican, Italian, Polish. None of that matters. What matters, he's an American child.
>
> That child in that great city is more important than any politician's promise. He is America. He is a poet. He is a scientist, he is a great teacher, he is a proud craftsman. He is everything we ever hoped to be and everything we dare to dream to be.
>
> He sleeps the sleep of a child and he dreams the dreams of a child.
>
> And yet when he awakens, he awakens to a living nightmare of poverty, neglect, and despair.

389

He fails in school.

He ends up on welfare.

For him the American system is one that feeds his stomach and starves his soul. It breaks his heart. And in the end it may take his life on some distant battlefield.

To millions of children in this rich land, this is their prospect of the future.

But this is only part of what I see in America.

I see another child tonight.

He hears a train go by at night and he dreams of far away places where he'd like to go.

It seems like an impossible dream.

But he is helped on his journey through life.

A father who had to go to work before he finished the sixth grade, sacrificed everything he had so that his sons could go to college.

A gentle, Quaker mother, with a passionate concern for peace, quietly wept when he went to war but she understood why he had to go.

A great teacher, a remarkable football coach, an inspirational minister encouraged him on his way.

A courageous wife and loyal children stood by him in victory and also defeat.

And in his chosen profession of politics, first there were scores, then hundreds, then thousands, and finally millions who worked for his success.

And tonight he stands before you—nominated for President of the United States of America.

On the whole the convention came off very well. It looked good on television, and the first post-convention Gallup poll showed me leading Humphrey 45 percent to 29 percent—a 16 percent margin.

Immediately after the convention, our entourage flew to California. On the way, Agnew and I stopped in Texas to meet with President Johnson, Secretary of State Rusk, Deputy Defense Secretary Cyrus Vance, and CIA Director Richard Helms. They gave us a full-scale intelligence briefing, ordered by Johnson for each of the nominees.

Johnson and Rusk came out to meet the presidential helicopter that flew us to the LBJ Ranch. It was a very hot day, and we soon had our coats off. Johnson was expansive and cordial, and I could see that he was already enjoying his role as a noncandidate in this election year.

After our meeting we had a delicious lunch of steak and fresh corn on the cob, followed by Lady Bird's home-made toll-house cookies. Johnson drove me from the ranch house to the helicopter pad. On the way he went by the little house where he was born and showed me the plot of land where his parents were buried. After seeing Johnson at his ranch, I understood what Billy Graham had meant when he said that Johnson "loved the land" and always wanted to go back to it.

As I started to board the helicopter, Johnson's dog darted past my legs into the cabin. There was a great deal of laughter, and I practically had to pick the animal up and carry him down the steps. Johnson shouted in mock anger, "Dick, here you've got my helicopter, you're after my job, and now you're gonna take my dog."

There were going to be seven key states in the 1968 presidential campaign: New York, California, Illinois, Ohio, Pennsylvania, Texas, and Michigan. Of these I had won only California and Ohio in 1960. This time I had to win at least three in order to have a chance of winning the election.

The Deep South had to be virtually conceded to George Wallace. I could not match him there without compromising on the civil rights issue, which I would not do. But I would not concede the Carolinas, Florida, Virginia, or any of the states on the rim of the South. These states became the foundation of my strategy; added to the states that I expected to win in the Midwest, the Great Plains, the Rocky Mountains, and the Far West, they would put me over the top and into the White House.

Because of the Wallace candidacy I expected the race to be very close. My polls showed that Wallace's vote was overwhelmingly Democratic but that when his name was not included in the poll sampling, his votes came to me on more than a two-to-one basis, especially in the South. Therefore it was essential that I keep the Wallace vote as low as possible. A major theme that we used very effectively in key states such as Florida, North Carolina, South Carolina, Tennessee, Kentucky, and Virginia was that Wallace couldn't win. Our message to would-be Wallace voters was: "Don't waste your vote."

While the Democrats gathered in Chicago for their convention, I went to Key Biscayne to rest and think. With Bobby Kennedy gone, I knew that Humphrey would get the nomination. Eugene McCarthy nonetheless continued his quixotic candidacy. Although the outcome of such a contest was a foregone conclusion, most of the media sympathized with McCarthy and the coverage given his challenge would have national impact, regardless of its actual influence on the convention's choice.

Thousands of young people had converged on Chicago for the Democratic convention. Many were sincere protesters against the Vietnam war, but some were little more than semiprofessional agitators and educated hoodlums. A series of clashes with the Chicago police finally erupted into a pitched battle on the night of Humphrey's nomination.

Like millions of other Americans watching television that night, I did not want to believe my eyes. It seemed as if the Democrats' convention was confirming every indictment of their leadership that I had made in my campaign speeches. Television magnified the agony of Chicago into a national debacle. I knew, of course, that the impact of Humphrey's nomination would now be seriously undermined. He would have to spend his entire campaign trying to patch up the divisions in his party. Even before the confrontation with the police, McCarthy and his zealous followers had been embittered by the convention because their efforts to pass a peace plank in the platform were defeated.

Humphrey chose Senator Edmund S. Muskie of Maine as his running mate. A former governor who had shown great political skill in getting re-elected in a traditionally Republican state, Muskie was a strong addition to the ticket.

My first scheduled stop in the 1968 presidential campaign was a motorcade through downtown Chicago on September 4. In some respects this was a risk because the city was still tense and reeling from the Democratic convention and from the criticism being leveled against Mayor

Richard Daley and the Chicago police force. The risk paid off. As our motorcade passed through Chicago's Loop at noontime, an estimated half million people turned out in genuine good cheer, with frequent outbursts of enthusiastic support. The contrast with the bitter confrontation that Humphrey was now tied to could not have been greater.

I knew that Humphrey would not remain in his slump forever. His was the majority party, and as Tom Wicker of the New York *Times* put it, "No Republican, as has often been said, unites the Democrats the way Nixon does." Humphrey would soon begin to recover his early losses. The only questions were when and by how much?

The first Gallup poll after the Democratic convention showed that I still had a substantial lead:

Nixon	43%
Humphrey	31%
Wallace	19%
Undecided	7%

But the problem with being the front-runner is that you are the target for everyone behind you.

Though painted as an underdog, Humphrey was not alone in his battle. In addition to his designated partisans, he had in his corner the giant combine of American organized labor. Although intellectuals, upper-middle-class liberals, and young people had temporarily deserted Humphrey, the union bosses never wavered. Under George Meany's orders, labor unions across the country provided Humphrey with millions of dollars, tens of thousands of marching feet, sophisticated direct mail and data processing, and other costly facilities. Although the union leadership was solidly behind Humphrey, the rank and file was far from united. Hundreds of thousands of blue-collar Democrats had voted for George Wallace in the primaries, and Humphrey would not necessarily inherit their support.

The anti-Nixon and anti-Wallace union propaganda eventually began paying off for Humphrey, but he needed more. The stigma of Chicago was not so easily erased. Lyndon Johnson stayed home in the White House, and Humphrey became a handy target for everyone on the left who hated the Johnson administration and the Vietnam war. During Humphrey's first weeks of campaign appearances, he was subjected to persistent heckling; the chant "Dump the Hump" dogged his steps. At one point he was driven almost to tears in front of the television cameras when he could not finish a speech before a derisive audience.

In an attempt to separate himself from Johnson on the war issue, Humphrey delivered a nationally televised speech from Salt Lake City on September 30. He said that his first priority as President would be to end the war and obtain an honorable peace. Although he continued to oppose a unilateral withdrawal of forces, he said that he would stop the bombing of North Vietnam "as an acceptable risk for peace because I believe it could lead to success in the negotiations and thereby shorten the war."

Humphrey's speech was shrewd. While it scarcely differed from Johnson's position, he made it sound like a major new departure. As antiwar columnist Joseph Kraft put it, the speech "has to be judged more by the music than the words. . . . The important thing is that the Humphrey campaign may finally be getting off the ground." The New York *Times* also concluded that Humphrey's proposal "may be a frail straw for doves to clutch at, but it is more hopeful than anything the administration or the Republican candidate has so far offered." By this point the doves *were* clutching at straws; they were beginning to realize that, however disappointed they were with Humphrey, and however disillusioned by Chicago, unless something were done to knock down my commanding lead in the polls, I was going to be elected President on November 5.

Liberal support and money started pouring back into Humphrey's campaign. Humphrey's problems with hecklers considerably abated; they began instead to focus their efforts on disrupting my campaign. These were not the hecklers of the American and British campaign tradition who press candidates with barbed questions and comments. These were anarchistic mobs. As soon as the speeches began they would start shouting, chanting simplistic and often obscene slogans, less to be heard themselves than to prevent the speaker from being heard. It was not an exercise in debate but a descent into hate.

Waving fists, carrying signs, shouting filth and obscenities, demonstrators made life miserable for me as well as for Pat, Tricia, and Julie when they made campaign appearances on my behalf.

These episodes were the saddest aspect of the 1968 campaign. They were symbolic of the things that were wrong with America that year. To this day I cannot understand the twisted logic that escalates the right of free speech into a license for hysteria and mob violence.

Encouraged by the reaction to his Salt Lake City speech, Humphrey began issuing challenges to me to debate him. I was determined not to be lured into a confrontation, since Humphrey was still far behind me in the polls, and would therefore be the beneficiary of any debate. Besides, as Humphrey knew, there was no way that he and I could have a debate without including George Wallace. Wallace's candidacy was depriving me of a substantial number of votes, and anything I did to elevate Wallace would be self-destructive. It was not fear but self-interest that determined my decision on the debates. Naturally my unwillingness to debate gave Humphrey a major campaign issue. On October 15, he told an audience that I was "Richard the Silent" and "Richard the Chicken-Hearted."

Polls taken after the election indicated that if George Wallace had not run for President in 1968, I might have received the same overwhelming mandate then that Eisenhower had received in 1952. But Wallace was a spoiler. He would siphon off the protest votes of people who were fed up with the policies of the Great Society. I had to try my best to hold down the Wallace vote, but I had to do it in a responsible manner. Humphrey and his advisers saw that Wallace could be used as a blockade against me. As Tom Wicker put it, "As for Wallace, without his heavy-breathing presence in the race Humphrey might as well go home to Waverly and raise turkeys."

If Humphrey could not get enough electoral votes to become President, he could still end up in the White House by making sure that I didn't get enough either. Under the Constitution, if no candidate received a majority of electoral votes, the election would be decided in the House of Representatives. Since the Democrats controlled the House, it was almost certain that Humphrey would make a deal with Wallace and thus emerge as the thirty-seventh President. Toward the end of the campaign I challenged Humphrey to agree that the winner of the popular vote should get the support of the loser, but he avoided the issue and refused to agree.

Having failed to make measurable inroads on my lead, Humphrey—and the media—began concentrating on Agnew. Because of his total lack of previous experience in national campaigning, it did not take long to catch him in a slip and magnify it into a cause célèbre. He naïvely used inflammatory codewords when he referred to Humphrey as "soft on crime" and "soft on communism," and he jokingly called reporter Gene Oishi "the fat Jap."

No one felt worse than Agnew about such embarrassing misjudgments, and I admired him for the way he stood up to the vicious onslaught of national political exposure—the cruel cartoons, the slashing attacks, the stinging commentaries. I tried to reassure him, telling him that these efforts were mainly a way of using him to get at me.

In contrast to their treatment of Agnew, the news media gave Muskie such encomiums as James Reston's "The most refreshing figure in the American campaign is Ed Muskie of Maine." A headline proclaimed in the Washington *Post*: *"Abe Lincoln Quality" Seen as Muskie Campaign Surges.* Muskie emerged from the campaign the favorite of the media—clearly presidential timber for 1972. This infatuation with Muskie could not have pleased Humphrey, but he had to acknowledge and use it. By the end of September he was telling audiences, "If you have any doubts about the top of the ticket, please settle it on the basis of No. 2."

During the two weeks before Election Day I was campaigning eighteen and twenty hours a day. At each appearance I tried to have some new ammunition to fire at Humphrey. In Cincinnati I quoted a statement he had made two years earlier, when riots were convulsing the country: that if he were living in a slum, he could "lead a mighty good revolt" himself. I said that this kind of talk was "adult delinquency" and "not worthy of a Vice President."

At Springfield, Ohio, I hit another key issue, loss of respect for America. "We must gain respect for America in the world. A burned American library, a desecrated flag, a ship captured by international outlaws on the high seas—these are the events which in effect squeeze the trigger which fires the rifle which kills young Americans." One reporter wrote, "There was speculation that the 'old Nixon' had broken through—the slashing campaigner of earlier campaigns who eventually hurt his reputation by his tough attacks." But I felt it was essential to take the battle to Humphrey after his weeks of much harsher rhetorical assaults.

I was especially intent on getting across my stark differences with Humphrey on the issues of crime and justice. His statement about leading a "revolt" was the kind of rationalization many liberals produced to justify the riotous disorders of the 1960s. I charged that Humphrey had exaggerated and overemphasized poverty as a cause of crime and that contrary to what the administration believed and preached, the war on poverty was not a war on crime, and it was no substitute for a war on crime.

Though inflation was on the rise in 1968 and the economic storm signals were clear, the actual detrimental effects of Johnson's guns-and-butter policy were not apparent until after I entered the White House. Consequently, Humphrey was able to campaign on a platform of prosperity while making the classic Democratic charge that every Republican since Herbert Hoover had a compulsion to make people unemployed.

For his part, Humphrey attacked me with characteristic gusto. He charged that I was "joining forces with the most reactionary elements in American society." Variously, he characterized me as someone likely to "weasel" and as one who "has sacrificed national interest for political demagogy."

On October 28 Humphrey claimed that I was about to unleash a "vicious final week of campaigning." He warned: "Batten down the hatches for the most desperate and cynical display of political irresponsibility ever seen in America." In the very same speech without missing a beat, Humphrey expressed *his* sense of political responsibility by charging that I was "urging a mad escalation of the nuclear arms race and advocating an increasing militarization of American life and American foreign policy."

In fact, despite what Humphrey and other Democratic spokesmen were saying, both my rhetoric and actions were restrained in the 1968 campaign. Because of my lead, there was no need for overkill. And because national unity was so fragile that year, I didn't want to enter the White House after a bitterly divisive campaign.

After the Democratic convention, I led Humphrey 43 percent to 31 percent, and a few weeks later 46 percent to 31 percent. During the last few weeks of the campaign, however, the gap narrowed dramatically, and the election turned out to be a cliff-hanger. The trend was reversed as traditional Democrats returned to the party of their fathers, and as the effects of George Wallace's spoiler candidacy were felt. Additionally, toward the end of the campaign the antiwar liberals decided to bury the hatchet and vote for Humphrey. Less than two weeks before Election Day, Eugene McCarthy finally endorsed Humphrey.

More than anything else, Humphrey had Lyndon Johnson to thank for the eleventh-hour masterstroke that almost won him the election.

On October 31 I was to address a nationally televised rally at Madison Square Garden in New York. I set aside a couple of quiet hours in the afternoon, and I was sitting in my study at home making notes for the speech later that evening when the telephone rang. It was a White House operator: the President was placing a conference call to Humphrey, Wallace, and me. A moment later Lyndon Johnson was on the line.

He got right to the point. There had been a breakthrough in Paris, he said, and after wide consultations among his advisers, he had decided to call a total bombing halt over North Vietnam. He would make the announcement on television in two hours. As Johnson went on, I thought to myself that whatever this meant to North Vietnam, he had just dropped a pretty good bomb in the middle of my campaign.

Johnson said, rather defensively, "I'm *not* concerned

with an election. *You* all *are* concerned with an election. *I* don't think this concerns an election. I think all of you want the same thing. So I thought if I laid it on the line that way, and presented it to you, you would at least have a complete, full understanding of all the facts."

Johnson explained that he had not been able to persuade Saigon to agree to the provisions of the bombing halt, so that South Vietnam would not be joining in the announcement.

When Johnson finished and we had asked some perfunctory questions, George Wallace said, "I'm praying for you."

Humphrey said, "We'll back you up, Mr. President."

I thanked Johnson for making the call and seconded Humphrey's pledge of support.

The telephone call over, I could feel my anger and frustration welling up. Johnson was making the one move that I thought could determine the outcome of the election. Had I done all this work and come all this way only to be undermined by the powers of an incumbent who had decided against seeking re-election?

I remembered how categorical Johnson had been at our briefing earlier that summer. Then he had been contemptuous of those who wanted a bombing halt, and his arms had sliced the air as he insisted that he was not going to let one ammunition truck pass freely into South Vietnam carrying the weapons to kill American boys.

In fact, the bombing halt came as no real surprise to me. I had known for several weeks that plans were being made for such an action; the announcement was the other shoe that I had been waiting for Johnson to drop. What I found difficult to accept was the timing. Announcing the halt so close to the election was utterly callous if politically calculated, and utterly naïve if sincere.

I had learned of the plan through a highly unusual channel. It began on September 12, when Haldeman brought me a report from John Mitchell that Rockefeller's foreign policy adviser, Henry Kissinger, was available to assist us with advice. In 1967 Kissinger had served Johnson as a secret emissary, passing Johnson's offers for a bombing halt to the North Vietnamese via French intermediaries. At one point Johnson even recommended a direct meeting, but the North Vietnamese were recalcitrant, and the "Kissinger channel" came to an end in October 1967. Kissinger, however, retained the respect of Johnson and his national security advisers, and he continued to have entrée into the administration's foreign policy inner circles.

I knew that Rockefeller had been offering Kissinger's assistance and urging that I make use of it ever since the convention. I told Haldeman that Mitchell should continue as liaison with Kissinger and that we should honor his desire to keep his role completely confidential.

Two weeks after his first meeting with Mitchell, Kissinger called again. He said that he had just returned from Paris, where he had picked up word that something big was afoot regarding Vietnam. He advised that if I had to say anything about Vietnam during the following week, I should avoid any new ideas or proposals. Kissinger was completely circumspect in the advice he gave us during the campaign. If he *was* privy to the details of negotiations, he did not reveal them to us. He considered it proper and responsible, however, to warn me against making any statements that might be undercut by negotiations I was not aware of.

I asked Haldeman to have Bryce Harlow call the Republican Senate Minority Leader, Everett Dirksen. "Have Ev tell Lyndon that I have a message from Paris," I suggested. "Leave the hint that I know what's going on, and tell Ev to nail Lyndon hard to find out what's happening." I also told Haldeman to have Agnew ask Dean Rusk whether there was anything to "rumors" we had heard.

That same day I sent a memo to my key staff thinkers and writers ordering them to put the Vietnam monkey on Humphrey's back, *not* Johnson's. I wanted to make it clear that I thought it was Humphrey rather than the President who was playing politics with the war.

A few days later Haldeman sent me a memorandum with more information from Kissinger via Mitchell.

> Our source feels that there is a better than even chance that Johnson will order a bombing halt at approximately mid-October. This will be tied in with a big flurry of diplomatic activity in Paris which will have no meaning but will be made to look important.

After covering other diplomatic matters, the memo continued:

> Our source does not believe that it is practical to oppose a bombing halt but does feel thought should be given to the fact that it may happen—that we may want to anticipate it—and that we certainly will want to be ready at the time it does happen. . . .
> Our source is *extremely* concerned about the moves Johnson may take and expects that he will take some action before the election.

That same day I learned that Dean Rusk had reassured Agnew that there were no new developments and that the administration would not "cut our legs off" with an announcement in October. If there were any change, he said, Johnson would call me right away. Rusk did say, however, that although there was nothing currently planned, the situation was "fast-changing."

On October 9, the North Vietnamese in Paris publicly called on Johnson to stop the bombing while he still had the power to do so. Johnson, of course, knew what the public did not know: secret negotiations for a bombing halt were already taking place.

Three days later we received another secret report from Kissinger saying that there was a strong possibility that the administration would move before October 23. Kissinger strongly recommended that I avoid making any statements about Humphrey's hurting the prospects of peace. Rather cryptically, Kissinger reported that there was "more to this than meets the eye." I thought that this report from Kissinger was uncomfortably vague. Why was he trying to get me to avoid making statements about Vietnam and why was he so insistent about laying off Humphrey? One factor that had most convinced me of Kissinger's credibility was the length to which he went to protect his secrecy. But what if Johnson's people knew that he was passing information to me and were feeding him phony stories? In such a tense political and diplomatic atmosphere, I was no longer sure of anything.

Over the next few days rumors became rampant that something big was about to happen in Paris. Reporters demanded to know what was happening, and in response to their questions, the White House press office released a statement that there were no breakthroughs in Paris and no change in the situation.

I was campaigning in Missouri on October 16 when word arrived from the White House that Johnson wanted to clarify matters with a conference call to all three candidates. When the call came, I was in Kansas City's Union Station, about to address a large rally in the main waiting room. I took his call in a tiny room behind the platform. The "room" was like a telephone booth with a glass door. Throughout our conversation people wandered by, staring quizzically at me jammed into this closet.

We had a bad connection, so that I had to strain to make out Johnson's words. He told us to read his Press Secretary's statement. There was no breakthrough in Paris. The rumors were wrong. He urged us not to say anything. He said that there had in fact been some movement by Hanoi, but that anything might jeopardize it. I asked for some assurance that he was still insisting on reciprocity from the Communists for any concessions on our part, and Johnson replied that he was maintaining that three points had to be met: (1) Prompt and serious talks must follow any bombing halt; (2) Hanoi must not violate the Demilitarized Zone; and (3) the Vietcong or the North Vietnamese would not carry out large-scale rocket or artillery attacks against South Vietnam's major cities. If these conditions were fulfilled, of course, I would support whatever arrangements Johnson could work out.

When I saw Johnson that night at the annual Al Smith Dinner in New York, he gave me further assurances that he would not accept any arrangement without reciprocity, and again requested that I be careful about what I had to say on Vietnam. After the dinner I instructed Haldeman to pass the word that, in view of Johnson's request, I would not be making any major speeches criticizing the conduct of the war.

Speaking in Rochester the next day, I said, "If a bombing pause can be agreed to in Vietnam . . . one which will not endanger American lives, and one which will increase the chances for bringing a peaceful and honorable solution to the war, then we are for it." I added, "We do not want to play politics with peace." But, of course, that was inevitably what was happening.

Vietnam was becoming the hottest national issue no matter how much the candidates soft-pedaled it. If there was nothing I could do about Johnson's motivations in this matter, I was determined to make absolutely sure that, if he did stop the bombing, it would at least be done according to the minimum safeguards that I insisted be met.

I was asked the next day about the rumors during a regionally broadcast question-and-answer session televised live from Boston. For the first time, while reiterating my position I suggested that something might be taking place. "There seems to be some movement," I said. "We can't be sure. I have been thoroughly briefed on this, but I won't disclose those briefings." It was a weak answer, but I didn't know what more I could say.

On October 22, Bryce Harlow received information from a source whose credibility was beyond question. It was from someone in Johnson's innermost circle, and, as events turned out, it was entirely accurate. I read Harlow's memorandum several times, and with each reading I became angrier and more frustrated:

> The President is driving exceedingly hard for a deal with North Vietnam. Expectation is that he is becoming almost pathologically eager for an excuse to order a bombing halt and will accept almost any arrangement. . . .
> Clark Clifford, [Joseph] Califano, and Llewellyn Thompson are the main participants in this effort. [George] Ball is in also, though somewhat on the fringe.
> Careful plans are being made to help HHH exploit whatever happens. White House staff liaison with HHH is close. Plan is for LBJ to make a nationwide TV announcement as quickly as possible after agreement; the object is to get this done as long before November 5 as they can. . . .
> White Housers still think they can pull the election out for HHH with this ploy; that's what is being attempted.

I fired off a battery of orders: have Mitchell check with Kissinger; have Dirksen and Tower blast the moves by the

White House; have Dirksen call Johnson and let him know we were on to his plans. I even considered having Harlow fly to Vietnam to talk to General Andrew Goodpaster to get a firsthand military view of the situation there. But I was simply venting my frustration; no matter what I did, Johnson continued to hold the whip hand.

The initial results of my orders raised some doubts about Harlow's secret source. Kissinger had not heard anything about Johnson's plan, and when Ev Dirksen confronted Johnson with the rumor, he denied it with a vehemence that convinced even his skeptical old friend. He said that there was nothing new to report from Paris, and he chided Dirksen for being taken in by such obvious rumors at this stage of his life.

The next day, October 24, Harlow reported from his source that an agreement had been reached with the North Vietnamese the day before, and that it would be announced shortly. I found this hard to believe, but Harlow emphasized that considering his source, there could be no doubt about the accuracy of the report. If it were true, it meant that the settlement had already been reached when Johnson had told Dirksen that no settlement was even being contemplated.

In retrospect I cannot fault Johnson for his secrecy, but I was angry at his lack of candor with me. I felt that he should at least have dropped the pretense that he would keep me fully informed. I would not have used this information if our sources had been opposed to Johnson's policies and were trying to undermine them by talking to us. But they felt that Johnson was using the war to help Humphrey, and that was politics, not policy.

I immediately decided that the only way to prevent Johnson from totally undercutting my candidacy at the eleventh hour was for me to make public the fact that a bombing halt was imminent. In addition I wanted to plant the impression—which I believed to be true—that his motives and his timing were not dictated by diplomacy alone.

I knew that Johnson wanted nothing more than to be able to set peace in motion before he left the presidency. If he waited until after the election, the Communists might decide to hold out in order to deal with the new administration. The next ten days might be Johnson's last chance to redeem his record, and I could not begrudge him the effort. Vietnam had consumed him politically and personally, and negotiating a peace would help him regain much of what he had lost to that conflict.

I was also convinced, however, that Johnson had additional motives. I knew him well enough to know that everything he did was weighed a second time on a strictly political scale. Moreover, Harlow's source had made it clear that, contrary to popular impression, the political liaison between Humphrey and the White House was very active. Adept and dedicated partisans such as Clark Clifford and George Ball would see to it that any political benefits to be gained for Humphrey would not be overlooked. I knew that I would be walking a fine line between political necessity and personal responsibility, but I believed that the actions of Johnson and many of those around him were sufficiently political to permit my taking at least some action.

On October 26, therefore, I issued a statement concerning the peace talks:

> In the last thirty-six hours I have been advised of a flurry of meetings in the White House and elsewhere on Vietnam. I am told that top officials in the administration have been driving very hard for an agreement on a bombing halt, accompanied possibly by a cease-fire, in the immediate future. I have since learned these reports are true.
>
> I am . . . told that this spurt of activity is a cynical, last-minute attempt by President Johnson to salvage the candidacy of Mr. Humphrey. This I do not believe.
>
> At no time in the campaign have I found the President anything but impartial and candid in his dealings with the major presidential contenders about Vietnam. . . .
>
> In every conversation I have had with him he has made it clear that he will not play politics with this war.

While I believed that Johnson would not go out of his way to help Humphrey unless he were forced to meet a clear-cut partisan challenge, the last thing I wanted to do was to give the President an excuse to get angry with me in public. I hoped to avoid Johnson's going all out for Humphrey with every resource at the command of the White House.

There was nothing more I could do. Even though I knew what was coming—had known about it for weeks—the timing and impact were completely in Johnson's hands.

At the Madison Square Garden rally on October 31 I responded to the bombing halt announcement in what I considered the only responsible way: "I will say that as a presidential candidate, and my vice presidential candidate joins me in this, that neither he nor I will say anything that might destroy the chance to have peace." One reporter wrote, "President Johnson gave Richard M. Nixon a trick and Vice President Humphrey a treat for Halloween when he announced a complete halt to the bombing of North Vietnam last night." The bombing halt unquestionably resulted in a last-minute surge of support for Humphrey. The militant liberals came back to the fold. Even those McCarthy zealots who had pledged never to support Humphrey now had an excuse to vote for him. The bombing halt also undercut one of my most effective campaign issues—the inability of the Democratic leadership to win a permanent peace. Studies made after the election showed that public opinion had been particularly volatile during this period, and the hope that the halt might lead to a peace settlement resulted in massive voter shifts to Humphrey.

The Democrats' euphoria was dampened on November 2, when President Thieu announced that his government would not participate in the negotiations Johnson was proposing.

Thieu's reaction was totally predictable. He watched American politics no less carefully than did the leaders in Hanoi. Given his disapproval of any bombing halt, and the fact that Humphrey was now talking like a dove, it was scarcely in Thieu's interest to acquiesce in a bad bargain. By holding back his support, Thieu fostered the impression that Johnson's plan had been too quickly conceived and too shakily executed.

On the heels of Thieu's recalcitrance, I asked Bob Finch to put the word out to newsmen that the prospects for peace were not as advanced as Johnson's announcement might have made them seem. Providing background in his capacity as an "aide to Richard Nixon," Finch explained,

"We had the impression that all the diplomatic ducks were in position." Then for the record he said, "I think this will boomerang. It was hastily contrived."

Johnson saw the news story with Finch's comments. He was furious, and he made his displeasure known. Bryce Harlow urged me to call Johnson to calm him down—and I did so Sunday morning, November 3.

"Who's this guy Fink?" Johnson asked. "Why is he taking out after me?"

I said, "Mr. President, that's Finch, not Fink."

He ignored my correction and continued to refer to Finch as "Fink."

I pointed out that my public statements on the issue were responsible, but that I had to respond to developments as I saw them. He calmed down, and the rest of our conversation was relatively cordial.

On the day of Thieu's announcement, I told a Texas rally: "In view of the early reports that we've had this morning, the prospects for peace are not as bright as they looked only a few days ago." It was Saturday, November 2, less than three days before the election. Bombing halt or no, the campaign had to continue. I decided to treat Johnson's announcement as a potentially beneficial diplomatic move botched by lack of planning rather than as a straight political ploy. I told my staff to get our spokesmen asking why we didn't have the agreement worked out with our allies.

I knew the gap was closing. With the help of hundreds of thousands of dollars in last-minute campaign contributions and loans, Humphrey appeared to be outspending us in television commercials in the week before the election.

I scheduled a four-hour telethon—two hours for the eastern United States and two for the West—the day before the election. Bud Wilkinson acted as moderator, reading the questions to me as they were phoned in from across the country. Some of my advisers had thought such a costly and tiring effort was not needed, but I overruled them. I remembered 1960 and felt I should do everything possible that might make the difference in a close election. It was my best campaign decision. Had we not had that last telethon, I believe Humphrey would have squeaked through with a close win on Election Day.

I felt we could not afford to do anything that would

augment the advantage that Humphrey was getting from sympathetic treatment in the national media. Whatever the reason—sympathy for his temporary underdog status; preference for his liberal views; or simply his likability—Humphrey benefited from favorable press coverage.

Though I had sensed this instinctively during the campaign, I had no idea that the favoritism toward Humphrey was so strong until Edith Efron's carefully researched book, *The News Twisters,* was released in 1971. In it she documented the number of words spoken "for" and "against" me by reporters on the three networks. She found that the ratios were 11 to 1, 67 to 1, and 65 to 1—all "against." She did the same thing for Humphrey and found that only one of the three networks showed a larger ratio of "against" than "for," and that was by a much smaller margin of 6 to 1. She concluded:

> If Richard Nixon is President of the United States today, it is in spite of ABC-TV, CBS-TV, and NBC-TV. Together they broadcast the quantitative equivalent of a New York *Times* lead editorial against him every day—for five days a week for the seven weeks of his campaign period. And every editorial technique was employed on three networks to render the pro-Nixon side less "forceful" than the anti-Nixon side. Indeed, to speak of "forceful" pro-Nixon opinion is impossible. It does not exist.

Pat and I voted by absentee ballot in 1968; for once we did not have to get up early to be photographed voting. We got to the airport in Los Angeles before ten o'clock that morning to board our campaign plane, the *Tricia*. The cabin was decorated with campaign posters and balloons. As I passed by a poster with our campaign slogan, "Nixon's the One," I said aloud to no one in particular, "I hope it's right."

As the plane taxied toward the runway, I sank into the chair in my private compartment. I was tired but I felt confident. I knew that the wide gap of the early campaign had closed and that all the polls showed the race was too close to call. But somehow I believed that this year would be different from 1960.

Although I felt instinctively confident this time, I took

the precaution of preparing my family for the worst. I asked Pat, Tricia, Julie, and David to come to my private office compartment. I told them how proud I was of their tireless campaigning. I said that it would be almost impossible for me to lose this election by popular vote. But it *could* happen, and I wanted them to be prepared just in case. What I really wanted them to be ready for was an electoral stalemate. "If that happens," I told them, "there won't be any winner or loser tonight. The election would be thrown into the House of Representatives, and I can't even guess how we would handle that situation."

I was sure that each of them wondered whether I knew something or had seen some poll that had led me to prepare them for losing. In fact, that afternoon a reporter had asked me for a comment on a Harris poll showing Humphrey winning by three points, approximately two million votes. I felt that Harris might have weighted his sample in the metropolitan areas and that Gallup, whose last poll showed me still leading by two points, was more accurate. "Even though it will be extremely close, we can win," I said. "In fact, I think we probably will. If we don't win, we'll simply go on to other projects which, from a personal viewpoint, may give us more satisfaction. And we won't have the spotlight of the world on us and on every movement that we make."

The *Tricia* touched down at Newark Airport just after six o'clock, and an hour later we were settled into our suite on the thirty-fifth floor of the Waldorf Towers in New York, where we would await the returns. Before I left Pat and the girls in their room, I said jokingly that at least this time we would not have to endure a twenty-four-hour ordeal as we had in 1960. I felt that by midnight or one o'clock Eastern time, when there were sufficient California returns to indicate a trend, we would know for sure.

While the polls were closing in the East and Midwest, I treated myself to a long hot soak in the huge bathtub. I took my time shaving and dressing, and then I called Haldeman to find out what was happening.

The first meaningful results were in by 8:45 P.M.. They ran roughly 41 percent to 36 percent in my favor. For the next half hour my percentage remained the same, and Humphrey's moved up to 38 percent.

Then returns began pouring in. At 9:15 I had a 5 percent lead in New Jersey and a slight lead in Pennsylvania, but I was behind by 2 percent in Texas. Humphrey was walking away with Massachusetts, which was no surprise, but I had fallen hopelessly behind in Connecticut, a state I had hopes of winning. I kept reminding everyone that it was still too early to see any shape in the numbers or percentages.

When I checked the national returns again at 9:30, Humphrey had moved up another point while I remained at 41 percent. In Maryland I held a 12-point lead. In Pennsylvania, with the cities still out, I was leading by 5 points. With 10 percent of the Texas vote in, I trailed Humphrey by 8 points. I asked Haldeman to check our contacts in New Jersey. He reported: "It's tight, but we'll win it."

Just after 10 P.M. Humphrey pulled even with me in the national returns. I was shaken by the early returns from Illinois, which gave me 35 percent to Humphrey's 56 percent and Wallace's 8 percent. Since I knew that Mayor Daley would, as usual, hold back dozens of Cook County precincts, these figures were doubly disturbing. The news from Ohio was not encouraging either. With 27 percent of the vote in, I trailed Humphrey by three points.

The network commentators had begun playing with the numbers and speculating about a possible Humphrey upset.

At 10:15, however, my lead was holding in New Jersey and Pennsylvania, and I was reported ahead by 6 points in South Carolina. Ohio had improved: with 30 percent of the votes in, I had gained on Humphrey and trailed him there by only 1 point. The momentum there was in my direction, and since the late votes would be from the rural areas and small towns, I was fairly confident of Ohio.

At 10:25 I started playing with some possibilities on my notepad. If I won California, Ohio, Illinois, Missouri, and Maryland, and added them to my other states, I would have 288 electoral votes—18 more than I needed. Losing Missouri and Maryland, however, would leave me 4 votes shy of winning. These figures did not include the crucial toss-ups in Texas, New Jersey, Pennsylvania, New Mexico, South Carolina, Hawaii, or Washington. My estimate was conservative; but no matter how the numbers were arranged, it was close.

I thought back to what I had told Pat, the girls, and David earlier in the evening. I had been wrong—once again it was going to be an all-night vigil. I was glad that they were staying in a different room. I had decided to put them in a separate suite and not to meet with them until after I was relatively sure of the outcome. I knew how worried they would be until the winner had been decided, and I did not want to make them feel that they had to keep up a cheerful front for my sake.

At 10:30 the national results were still the same—Humphrey and I were running neck and neck, while Wallace had 18 percent. I was behind in Missouri, Pennsylvania, Delaware, and Ohio and ahead in New Jersey and Maryland, all with 41 percent or less of their votes in.

At 11 P.M. word arrived that something had gone wrong with the voting tabulation in Dallas and the votes could not be counted until the next day. That was alarming news. I feared that Texas Democrats were fully as capable of stealing votes in 1968 as they had been in 1960, and I told Haldeman to find out what the hell was happening and what we could do about it.

At 11:30 I asked Murray Chotiner to come in. He had been following the results as closely as I had, and we had arrived at the same figures. So far I had 231 solid electoral votes. But there were disturbing intimations that the momentum was with Humphrey. By midnight he had moved ahead in the popular vote. A half hour later, NBC showed him leading by about 600,000.

In 1968, as in 1960, the election was apparently going to be determined by the same key states: Illinois, California, Ohio, Missouri, and Texas. All were close. I was counting on Ohio and California. I had high hopes for Texas, but I knew that Johnson and Governor John Connally had fired up the recalcitrant state Democratic organization to get behind Humphrey, and that made Texas a question mark. Missouri was also going to be a seesaw. Mitchell was confident that Missouri would come through and I had learned to trust his confidence.

As Ohio and California moved more solidly into my column, the balance seemed to hang on Illinois, where I now had a substantial lead of almost 100,000 votes. But a number of Cook County precincts were still unreported.

In those early hours of November 6, confident that I had won Illinois and thus the election, I became irritated with Daley's stubbornness in not releasing the count in Cook County. I called Bryce Harlow and told him to get Larry O'Brien, Humphrey's campaign manager, on the phone. "Bryce, lay it on the line. Don't fool around. Tell O'Brien to tell Hubbert to quit playing games. We've won Illinois, so let's get this thing over with." Harlow reached O'Brien's suite, but either he was not there or would not take the call.

Just before 3 A.M., for the first time in that long night, I allowed myself the luxury of self-assurance.

I had won the presidency.

I called in Bob Finch, Murray Chotiner, John Mitchell, and Bob Haldeman. We reviewed the totals. I told them that I was sure of all the big ones, including California, Illinois, Ohio, and Missouri.

"Any objections?" I asked.

There were no objections.

I placed calls to Ted Agnew and Nelson Rockefeller. They agreed that victory was just a matter of time. Then I called in my senior staff. We sat and talked for almost two hours while we waited for the reported results to confirm our predictions. Several times I asked Mitchell or Haldeman to call our people in the key states to break loose better information than the TV commentators seemed able to supply. They always came back with the same message: Don't worry—things are going well —we're almost there. *Almost.* I had been *almost* there in 1960. Finally, around five o'clock, Mitchell and Haldeman persuaded me to try to nap. It was clear that the outcome would not be definite until the morning, and at this point I had been up for almost twenty-two hours. I couldn't get to sleep, and after half an hour I got up again.

Just before 8 A.M. Haldeman brought in word that both NBC and ABC had declared me the winner in California and Ohio. But there was still no movement in Illinois, and that was what I needed to confirm victory. One more state. At 8:30 the door burst open and Dwight Chapin rushed in.

"ABC just declared you the winner!" he shouted. "They've projected Illinois. You got it. You've won."

We hurried into the sitting room where the television set was on, and we watched as ABC continued to survey the electoral vote count. After we had watched for a few moments, I put a hand on John Mitchell's shoulder and said, "Well, John, we had better get down to Florida and get this thing planned out." Before Mitchell could respond, tears welled up in his eyes. He said very quietly, "Mr. President, I think I'd better go up to be with Martha." This was a doubly moving moment for us both. It was the first time that anyone addressed me by the title I had just won. It was also the first time that Mitchell had directly referred to his wife's problems, which I knew had been an immense emotional strain on him. Martha had been in a rest home during the last weeks of the campaign, and I fully understood his desire to be with her now.

I went down the hall to the suite where Pat and the girls were waiting. They were so physically and emotionally exhausted that there wasn't the elation one would normally expect. We all kissed and embraced. Julie went to her room and then called me in. She opened her briefcase and pulled out a piece of crewelwork she had done during campaign flights around the country. It was the Great Seal of the United States, with the inscription "To RN—JN" stitched at the bottom. "Daddy, I never had any doubt you would win," she said as she hugged me. "I just wanted something to be ready right away to prove it."

I sat alone with Pat, and she told me that it had been a terribly difficult night for her. The speculation by the commentators about Illinois had driven her to tears. Waves of nausea had swept over her as she feared that we would have to experience a repeat of the outrageous frauds of 1960. When I told her it was all over, she asked emotionally, "But Dick, are we sure of Illinois? Are we completely sure?" I answered, very firmly, "Absolutely. The votes are in, and there is no way that it can be turned around at this point." Then I held her, and she burst into tears of relief and joy.

I returned to my room and took an hour's nap. I got up at ten o'clock and shaved and dressed. There was still no word from Humphrey, and I could not do anything until he conceded. At 10:35 Haldeman came in with the news that NBC had finally projected my victory. A few minutes later CBS did the same.

At about 11:30 Hubert Humphrey called. His voice, usually so cheerful and confident, was full of fatigue and disappointment. But he was as gracious in defeat as he had been tenacious in combat. When I saw his wife Muriel and the other members of his family standing with him when he appeared on television a little while later, I felt sorrier for them than for him. After all, politics was *his* chosen profession. But I knew from experience how bitter and crushing defeat is for the people one loves.

As soon as Humphrey had finished his concession, Pat, Tricia, Julie, David, and I went down to the ballroom of the Waldorf-Astoria, where hundreds of supporters had remained, keeping the all-night vigil with us. The applause was thunderous. Although I had often thought about what I would say if this occasion came, what I finally said was spontaneous.

I told about receiving Humphrey's phone call, and of how I had told him I knew what it was like to lose a close one. The audience erupted in cheers when I said: "Having lost a close one eight years ago and having won a close one this year, I can say this—winning's a lot more fun."

I philosophized a moment about defeat: "A great philosophy is never one without defeat. It is always one without fear. What is important is that a man or a woman engage in battle, be in the arena."

I referred to an incident during our whistle-stop trip through Ohio:

> I saw many signs in this campaign. Some of them were not friendly and some were very friendly. But the one that touched me the most was the one that I saw in Deshler, Ohio, at the end of a long day of whistle-stopping. A little town, I suppose five times the population was there in the dusk, almost impossible to see—but a teenager held up a sign, "Bring Us Together."
>
> And that will be the great objective of this administration at the outset, to bring the American people together.

When we arrived back at our Fifth Avenue apartment, early in the afternoon, Manolo and Fina were not there, so I suggested to Pat that we all go out for lunch. Then I realized that we could no longer just casually "go out for lunch." She and the girls went into the kitchen and fixed bacon and eggs, and we all sat in my library for this postelection feast.

When Manolo and Fina came back a little later, they reminded me of the reason for their absence. Never imagining that the election would spill over into the following day, they had arranged to take their oaths of citizenship that afternoon. Manolo said, "Mr. President, next time *we* will be able to vote for you. We are now United States citizens."

When the others had left the library, I went to the record player and selected one of my favorites, the musical score from *Victory at Sea* by Richard Rodgers. I put it on and turned the volume up high. My thoughts meshed with the music. The battle had been long and arduous. We had suffered reverses and won victories. The struggle had been hard fought. But now we had won the final victory. The music captured the moment for me better than anything I could say or think or write.

PRESIDENT-ELECT

On November 6 we flew aboard an Air Force jet to Key Biscayne for a postelection rest. On the way we stopped in Washington so that I could visit Eisenhower at Walter Reed Hospital. Few moments in my life have been more satisfying than entering his room as the President-elect. When he saw me, his face brightened and he said, "Congratulations, Mr. President!"

I think Eisenhower had wanted me to win the election as much as I did. He urged me to describe for him every detail of the long election night and morning, and he beamed with pleasure all the while.

Our flight south was happy. Election night had been too draining for celebration, and this was the first time we were really able to relax and savor the joy of having finally reached the top of the mountain after a long and arduous journey.

I drove from Key Biscayne to Opa-Locka Airport to meet with Humphrey and Muskie and their families, who were on their way to a vacation in the Virgin Islands. I asked Humphrey if he would consider becoming ambassador to the United Nations. He asked for time to think about the offer. At the end of the meeting, Humphrey told reporters that the election was over and the national interest must prevail over partisan interest. "He's going to be our President," Humphrey said, "and I'm going to be one of his fellow citizens."

Thus, on the sunny tarmac in Florida, a familiar and moving moment in American political tradition took place: a symbolic message of non-partisan reassurance was sent to our countrymen and to a watching world.

After a five-day rest in Key Biscayne we returned to New York to begin putting together an administration. Once again we stopped in Washington, this time for luncheon at the White House with President and Mrs. Johnson.

After a gracious meal Lady Bird and Pat began a room-by-room inspection of the entire mansion while Johnson had scheduled a series of briefings for me. On our way to the West Wing we stopped in his bedroom. The room was dominated by a canopied four-poster bed. There were a large closet and dressing room, in addition to a white-tiled bathroom. "I wanted you to know about this," Johnson said as he showed me how to open a small safe concealed in the wall.

When we entered the Cabinet Room, the briefers were already waiting for us: Secretary of State Dean Rusk, Secretary of Defense Clark Clifford, Chairman of the Joint Chiefs of Staff General Earle Wheeler, Director of Central Intelligence Richard Helms, and National Security Adviser Walt Rostow.

The main subject was Vietnam. The travail of the long war was etched on the faces around me. These were all able and intelligent men. They had wanted desperately to end the war before leaving office, but they had not succeeded. They seemed very nearly worn out. They had no new approaches to recommend to me. I sensed that, despite the disappointment of defeat, they were relieved to be able to turn this morass over to someone else.

They all emphasized that the United States must see the war through to a successful conclusion—with negotiations if possible, but with continued fighting if necessary.

They agreed that an American bug-out, or a negotiated settlement that could be interpreted as a defeat, would have a devastatingly detrimental effect on our allies and friends in Asia and around the world. Clark Clifford, who during my administration became one of the most outspoken critics of the war, was an ardent supporter of Johnson's policies that afternoon.

When Johnson and I returned to the Oval Office after the briefing, he talked with a sense of urgency. "There may be times when we disagree, and, if such time comes, I will let you know privately," he said. "But you can be sure that I won't criticize you publicly. Eisenhower did the same for me. I know what an enormous burden you will be carrying." He said that he wanted to do everything he could to help me succeed. "The problems at home and abroad are probably greater than any President has ever confronted since the time of Lincoln," he said. Johnson and I had been adversaries for many years, but on that day our political and personal differences melted away. As we stood together in the Oval Office, he welcomed me into a club of very exclusive membership, and he made a promise to adhere to the cardinal rule of that membership: stand behind those who succeed you.

My first staff appointment was Rose Mary Woods as my personal secretary. Rose had been part of my political life since 1951. She combined professional skill with unexcelled personal charm. And she had total dedication. Her faith about my future had never wavered, even when my own sometimes did.

I asked Bob Haldeman to be my Chief of Staff. His role, as we envisaged it, would be administrative rather than substantive. He would examine the paperwork to ensure that opposing views were included and then bring the material to me for my decision; he would be a funnel rather than a filter. His intelligence and his capacity for detaching his personal prejudices from the examination of issues made him the ideal man for the job. He would also be the gatekeeper of the Oval Office. This would place him in the unenviable position of having to say no to a lot of people who felt they needed to see me personally and often, but I knew that his strong ego would be able to handle the jealousy and unpopularity such a role inevitably engenders.

I had strong opinions, many of them derived from my experiences and observations during the Eisenhower years, about the way a President should work. In my view, then and now, the key to a successful presidency is in the decision-making process. I felt that the matters brought before a President for decisions should be only those that cannot or should not be made at a lower level on the White House staff, or by the Cabinet member responsible for them. This was a lesson I had learned directly from Eisenhower, whose staff had too often cluttered his schedule with unimportant events and bothered him with minor problems that drained his time and energy. I knew that I could absorb far more material by reading it than by talking about it, and I have invariably found that staff members will present problems more concisely and incisively in writing than they will in meetings.

I had attended hundreds of Cabinet meetings as Vice President, and I felt that most of them were unnecessary and boring. On the few issues that cut across all departments, such as the economy, group discussions would sometimes be informative. But the day had long since passed when it was useful to take an hour and a half to have the Secretary of Defense and the Secretary of State discuss the Secretary of Transportation's new highway proposal. Therefore I wanted to keep the Cabinet meetings in my administration to a minimum. I felt that the better each Cabinet member performed his job, the less time I should have to spend discussing it with him except for major questions of politics or policy. If we were going to run government with a clear eye for efficiency and a tough approach to wastefulness, we would have to have good managers who could immerse themselves in detail and learn the job. I was willing to trade flamboyance for competence. I had also seen the hazards of appointing Cabinet members who were too strong-willed to act as part of a team. I wanted people who would fight to the finish in private for what they thought was right but would support my decision once it was made.

I was fully conscious that I had won the presidency

with a narrow plurality of the popular vote. I knew that some of my choices for Cabinet posts would have to serve, even if only symbolically, to unite the country, and "bring us together." I wanted to have some Democrats in the Cabinet or in Cabinet-level posts, but Humphrey turned down the UN ambassadorship, and Senator Henry Jackson of Washington turned down an offer to be Secretary of Defense.

For the UN post we approached President Kennedy's brother-in-law Sargent Shriver, whom Johnson had appointed ambassador to France. Shriver expressed great interest and sent me a message stating the conditions for his acceptance. Among other things he required a pledge that the federal poverty programs would not be cut. It was intolerable to have a prospective ambassadorial appointee making demands relating to domestic policy, so I told Bill Rogers to inform Shriver that I had decided against him and to let him know why. Rogers reported that Shriver realized that he had overstepped himself and had tried to backpedal, claiming that he had not meant his message to set forth conditions but to make suggestions. I told Rogers to say that my decision remained unchanged.

In addition to some Democrats, I had hoped to bring some black leaders into my Cabinet. I offered the UN post to Ed Brooke, but he felt he could make a greater contribution by staying in the Senate. I urged the Executive Director of the Urban League, Whitney Young, to be Secretary of Housing and Urban Development, but he declined, saying that he felt he could do more for his cause working outside the government. What he meant, of course, was that serving in a Republican Cabinet would be the political kiss of death for anyone who wanted a role of real leadership in the black community.

In this respect I was reaping the harvest of the Goldwater campaign. In 1960 I had received 32 percent of the black vote; in 1964 Goldwater received only 6 percent. I was able to increase the Republican share of the black vote to 12 percent in 1968, but the false impression that Goldwater was a racist was still too prevalent for an easy relationship to exist between the black community and a Republican administration. I regretted this fact, but I knew that there was nothing I could say that would change it. I would have to show by my actions in office that I was indeed President of all the American people.

The Cabinet gradually began to take shape. As a group, its members were less conservative than Eisenhower's Cabinet, and in fact somewhat to the left of my own centrist positions. But each man knew his subject and each brought both competence and imagination to his job.

Bill Rogers, a strong administrator, would have the formidable job of managing the recalcitrant bureaucracy of the State Department. He was a resourceful negotiator, and as a personal friend I knew that I could trust him to work with me on the most sensitive assignments in domestic as well as foreign policy. During his service as Attorney General in the Eisenhower years he had demonstrated that he could get along with Congress. I felt that the almost institutionalized enmity between Senator Fulbright's Foreign Relations Committee and the White House had become damaging to the national interest, and I thought Rogers could thaw that freeze.

For the Defense Department I chose Melvin Laird of Wisconsin, a veteran of seventeen years in the House of Representatives and an expert on defense appropriations. Mel Laird was respected by his congressional colleagues as a strong man and a shrewd politician.

Even as John Mitchell was helping me develop a list of candidates for Attorney General, I decided that I would try to persuade him to accept the position himself. I wanted someone who shared my concern about permissiveness in the courts and even in many law enforcement agencies. Mitchell was tough, intelligent, and fair. Moreover, I counted him my most trusted friend and adviser and I wanted to have his advice available, not just on legal matters but on the whole range of presidential decision-making.

David Kennedy, head of the Continental Illinois National Bank and Trust Company in Chicago, brought to the Treasury Department his experience and expertise in international finance. He also met my requirement that my Secretary of the Treasury not be part of the New York–Boston banking establishment that had dominated the department for too long. Winton "Red" Blount for Postmaster General, Walter Hickel for Interior, Clifford Hardin for Agriculture, Maurice Stans for Commerce, George Shultz for Labor, Bob Finch for Health, Education, and Welfare, George Romney for Housing and Urban Development, and John Volpe for Transportation rounded out the Cabinet.

I had invited Ted Agnew and his wife, Judy, to Key Biscayne right after the election to begin making plans for his role in the administration. I told Agnew that I wanted him to assume policy-making responsibilities, and I suggested that he have an office in the West Wing of the White House, the first time in history that a Vice President would do so. I asked him to draw on his experience as a state official by taking the major responsibility for federal-state relations. I urged him to start immediately to use his role as President of the Senate to get to know Congress and its members, to work with them, and to serve as their primary liaison with the White House.

When Eisenhower selected Foster Dulles as his Secretary of State, he wanted him to be his chief foreign policy adviser, a role Dulles was uniquely qualified to fill. From the outset of my administration, however, I planned to direct foreign policy from the White House. Therefore I regarded my choice of a National Security Adviser as crucial. Considering the importance I placed on the post, I made my choice in an uncharacteristically impulsive way.

I knew that Henry Kissinger had served for many years as a foreign policy adviser to Nelson Rockefeller. I had also heard that in the period before the 1968 Republican convention, while Rockefeller and I were rivals for the nomination, Kissinger had privately made a number of disparaging comments about my competence in the field. But I expected this from a Rockefeller associate, and I chalked it up to politics. During the last days of the campaign, when Kissinger was providing us with information about the bombing halt, I became more aware of both his knowledge and his influence.

John Mitchell arranged for Kissinger and me to meet on November 25 in my transition office in the Hotel Pierre in New York. Since neither of us was interested in small talk, I proceeded to outline for him some of the plans I had for my administration's foreign policy. I had read his book *Nuclear Weapons and Foreign Policy* when it first appeared in 1957, and I knew that we were very much alike in our general outlook in that we shared a belief in the importance of isolating and influencing the factors affecting worldwide balances of power. We also agreed that whatever else a foreign policy might be, it must be strong to be credible —and it must be credible to be successful. I was not hopeful about the prospects of settling the Vietnam war through the Paris talks and felt that we needed to rethink our whole diplomatic and military policy on Vietnam. Kissinger agreed, although he was less pessimistic about the negotiations than I was. I said that I was determined to avoid the trap Johnson had fallen into, of devoting virtually all my foreign policy time and energy to Vietnam, which was really a short-term problem. I felt that failing to deal with the longer-term problems could be devastating to America's security and survival, and in this regard I talked about restoring the vitality of the NATO alliance, and about the Middle East, the Soviet Union, and Japan. Finally I mentioned my concern about the need to re-evaluate our policy toward Communist China, and I urged him to read the *Foreign Affairs* article in which I had first raised this idea as a possibility and a necessity.

Kissinger said he was delighted that I was thinking in such terms. He said that if I intended to operate on such a wide-ranging basis, I was going to need the best possible system for getting advice. Kennedy had replaced NSC strategic planning with tactical crisis management; and Johnson, largely because of his concern with leaks, had reduced NSC decision-making to informal weekly luncheon sessions with only a few advisers. Kissinger recommended that I structure a national security apparatus within the White House that, in addition to coordinating foreign and defense policy, could also develop policy options for me to consider before making decisions.

I had a strong intuition about Henry Kissinger, and I decided on the spot that he should be my National Security Adviser. I did not make a specific offer to him then, but I made it clear that I was interested in having him serve in my administration. I guessed that he would want to think about our conversation, and also that he would feel an obligation to discuss it with Rockefeller.

I met with Kissinger again two days later and asked him if he would like to head the NSC. He replied that he would be honored to accept. He immediately began assembling a staff and analyzing the policy choices that I would have to address as soon as I took office. From the beginning he worked with the intensity and stamina that were to characterize his performance over the years.

The combination was unlikely—the grocer's son from Whittier and the refugee from Hitler's Germany, the politician and the academic. But our differences helped make the partnership work.

Daniel Patrick Moynihan had one of the most innovative minds for domestic policy in the country. Like Kissinger a Harvard professor, he had served as Assistant Secretary of Labor in the Kennedy and Johnson administrations. I had read several of his articles before the 1968 campaign, and I found his thinking refreshing and stimulating. Unlike so many liberal academics, Moynihan was free of professional jargon and ideological cant. He had helped design the Great Society poverty programs, but he was not afraid to acknowledge that many of them had failed, and he was ready to apply the lessons learned from that failure to devising new programs that might work.

I met with Moynihan to explore his views and to sound him out about coming to the White House. Although he quickly made known his opposition to the Vietnam war, he was clearly interested by the opportunity. Our shared conviction that the current welfare system had to be totally reformed helped to cement the rapport I immediately felt with him. I told Moynihan about my intention to establish an Urban Affairs Council, describing it as the domestic policy equivalent of the National Security Council in foreign affairs. "That's a capital idea!" he exclaimed. Then I asked him if he would like to head it. He accepted immediately. Even when I thought Pat Moynihan was wrong about a particular issue or problem, I found his intellect scintillating and challenging. As I said after he had left the administration and returned to Harvard, "I disagreed with a lot of what he said—but he certainly did light up the place!"

I created a new Cabinet-level position, Counsellor to

the President, for my old friend and adviser Arthur Burns. I thought that his conservatism would be a useful and creative counterweight to Moynihan's liberalism.

I could remember as if it were only yesterday sitting in Eisenhower's suite in the Blackstone Hotel in 1952 and wondering whether he knew what he was getting himself in for as I watched him sign his letter of resignation from the Army. He had not been in politics very long and was bound to be surprised by many of the things that happened. But I had been involved in presidential politics for almost two decades, and I was determined to be as prepared as anyone ever had been for the power and position I was about to assume. Therefore, despite the demands of daily events during this transition period, I set aside time to think about the condition of the nation and the world I would be inheriting from Johnson and about how I wanted my presidency to change and improve things.

Like Eisenhower, I was about to assume four different hats: as head of state I would have to deal with foreign affairs; as head of government I would have to provide domestic leadership and legislative programs; as Commander in Chief I would have the ultimate authority and responsibility for America's armed forces; and as leader of the Republican Party I would have to do something to breathe new life into the national, state, and local party organizations.

As I looked at America's foreign policy during the 1960s, I felt that it had been held hostage, first under Kennedy to the cold war and then under Johnson to the Vietnam war. Our tendency to become preoccupied with only one or two problems at a time had led to a deterioration of policy on all fronts. I did not feel that there should be any single foreign policy priority. There were many priorities, moving in tandem, each affecting the others. To the extent that I would have to start somewhere, I felt that I had to put Europe at the top of the list. Only when we had secured our Western alliance would we be on sufficiently solid footing to begin talks with the Communists. NATO was in disarray, largely because of the failure of the United States to consult adequately with our European allies.

In the Far East, Japan, now the second most productive nation in the free world, was beginning to have doubts about the credibility of America's defense commitments. Our control of the island of Okinawa was a constant irritant in our relations.

In the Middle East the truce that followed the June war of 1967 was continually interrupted by intermittent fighting. The United States seemed to be unable to do anything more than arm Israel against the next Arab onslaught. Egypt and Syria, Israel's two major potential enemies, were receiving Soviet arms, and this turned the already explosive area into an international powder keg, that, when it exploded, might lead not only to another war between Israel and its neighbors, but also to a direct confrontation between the United States and the Soviet Union.

From Communist China there was only ominous silence. Except for sterile and sporadic talks between the American and Chinese ambassadors in Warsaw, a gulf of twenty years of noncommunication separated the world's most populous nation from the world's most powerful nation.

As I looked at America's position in the world and examined our relations with other nations, I could see that the central factor in 1968 on the eve of my presidency was the same as it had been in 1947 when I first went to Europe with the Herter Committee: America now, as then, was the main defender of the free world against the encroachment and aggression of the Communist world.

For twenty-five years, I had watched the changing face of communism. I had seen prewar communism, luring workers and intellectuals with its siren call of equality and justice, reveal itself as an aggressive imperialistic ideology during the postwar period of the Marshall Plan. Despite the most nobly ringing rhetoric, the pattern was tragically the same: as soon as the Communists came to power, they destroyed all opposition. I had watched the Soviets' phenomenal recovery from the devastation of war and their costly but successful struggle to achieve for communism the

425

selling point of potential prosperity. At home I had seen the face of underground subversive communism when it surfaced in the Hiss case, reminding people not only that it existed, but that its purpose was deadly serious.

In the late 1940s and during the 1950s I had seen communism spread to China and other parts of Asia, and to Africa and South America, under the camouflage of parties of socialist revolution, or under the guise of wars of national liberation. And, finally, during the 1960s I had watched as Peking and Moscow became rivals for the role of leadership in the Communist world.

Never once in my career have I doubted that the Communists mean it when they say that their goal is to bring the world under Communist control. Nor have I ever forgotten Whittaker Chambers's chilling comment that when he left communism, he had the feeling he was leaving the winning side. But unlike some anticommunists who think we should refuse to recognize or deal with the Communists lest in doing so we imply or extend an ideological respectability to their philosophy and their system, I have always believed that we can and must communicate and, when possible, negotiate with Communist nations. They are too powerful to ignore. We must always remember that they will never act out of altruism, but only out of self-interest. Once this is understood, it is more sensible—and also safer—to communicate with the Communists than it is to live in icy cold-war isolation or confrontation. In fact, in January 1969 I felt that the relationship between the United States and the Soviet Union would probably be the single most important factor in determining whether the world would live at peace during and after my administration.

I felt that we had allowed ourselves to get in a disadvantageous position vis-à-vis the Soviets. They had a major presence in the Arab states of the Middle East, while we had none; they had Castro in Cuba; since the mid-1960s they had supplanted the Chinese as the principal military suppliers of North Vietnam; and except for Tito's Yugoslavia they still totally controlled Eastern Europe and threatened the stability and security of Western Europe.

There were, however, a few things in our favor. The most important and interesting was the Soviet split with China. There was also some evidence of growing, albeit limited, independence in some of the satellite nations. There were indications that the Soviet leaders were becoming interested in reaching an agreement on strategic arms limitation. They also appeared to be ready to hold serious talks on the anomalous situation in Berlin, which, almost a quarter century after the war had ended, was still a divided city and a constant source of tension, not just between the Soviets and the United States, but also between the Soviets and Western Europe. We sensed that they were looking for a face-saving formula that would lessen the risk of confrontation in the Mideast. And we had some solid evidence that they were anxious for an expansion of trade.

It was often said that the key to a Vietnam settlement lay in Moscow and Peking rather than in Hanoi. Without continuous and massive aid from either or both of the Communist giants, the leaders of North Vietnam would not have been able to carry on the war for more than a few months. Thanks to the Sino-Soviet split, however, the North Vietnamese had been extremely successful in playing off the Soviets and the Chinese against each other by turning support for their war effort into a touch-stone of Communist orthodoxy and a requisite for keeping North Vietnam from settling into the opposing camp in the struggle for domination within the Communist world. This situation became a strain, particularly for the Soviets. Aside from wanting to keep Hanoi from going over to Peking, Moscow had little stake in the outcome of the North Vietnamese cause, especially as it increasingly worked against Moscow's own major interests vis-à-vis the United States. While I understood that the Soviets were not entirely free agents where their support for North Vietnam was concerned, I nonetheless planned to bring maximum pressure to bear on them in this area.

I was sure that Brezhnev and Kosygin had been no more anxious for me to win in 1968 than Khrushchev had been in 1960. The prospect of having to deal with a Republican administration—and a Nixon administration at that—undoubtedly caused anxiety in Moscow. In fact, I suspected that the Soviets might have counseled the North Vietnamese to offer to begin the Paris talks in the hope that the bombing halt would tip the balance to Humphrey in the election—and if that was their strategy, it had almost worked.

427

After the election Johnson proposed that as President and President-elect he and I attend a summit meeting with the Soviets in the period before my inauguration. I understood his desire to make one last dramatic demonstration of his dedication to peace, but I saw no solid basis for concluding that the Soviet leaders were prepared to negotiate seriously on any critical issue. Nor did I want to be boxed in by any decisions that were made before I took office.

The most that might come from such a last-minute summit would be a "spirit," like the "Spirit of Glassboro" that followed Johnson's meeting with Kosygin in New Jersey in 1967 or the "Spirit of Camp David" that followed Eisenhower's meeting with Khrushchev in 1959. It was my feeling that such "spirits" were almost entirely spurious and that they actually worked heavily to the Soviets' advantage. Since public opinion played no role whatever in the Communist system, such summit "spirit" was a one-way street in their direction, because the optimistic attitudes that characterized American public opinion after a summit made it harder for us to assume a tough line in our postsummit dealings with the Soviets.

During the transition period Kissinger and I developed a new policy for dealing with the Soviets. Since U.S.–Soviet interests as the world's two competing nuclear superpowers were so widespread and overlapping, it was unrealistic to separate or compartmentalize areas of concern. Therefore we decided to link progress in such areas of Soviet concern as strategic arms limitation and increased trade with progress in areas that were important to us—Vietnam, the Mideast, and Berlin. This concept became known as linkage.

Lest there be any doubt of my seriousness in pursuing this policy, I purposely announced it at my first press conference when asked a question about starting SALT talks. I said, "What I want to do is to see to it that we have strategic arms talks in a way and at a time that will promote, if possible, progress on outstanding political problems at the same time—for example, on the problem of the Mideast and on other outstanding problems in which the United States and the Soviet Union acting together can serve the cause of peace."

Linkage was something uncomfortably new and different for the Soviets, and I was not surprised when they bridled at the restraints it imposed on our relationship. It would take almost two years of patient and hard-nosed determination on our part before they would accept that linkage with what we wanted from them was the price they would have to pay for getting any of the things they wanted from us.

We made our first contacts with the Soviets during the transition period. In mid-December Kissinger met with a Soviet UN diplomat who was, as we knew, actually an intelligence officer. I wanted it made clear that I was not taken in by any of the optimistic rhetoric that had characterized so much of recent Soviet-American relations. Kissinger therefore stated that while the tendency during the last few years had been to emphasize how much our two nations supposedly had in common, the Nixon administration felt that there were real and substantial differences between us and that an effort to lessen the tension created by these differences should be the central focus of our relationship. Kissinger also said that I did not want a pre-inauguration summit meeting and that if they held one with Johnson I would have to state publicly that I would not be bound by it. Nothing more was heard about this summit project.

We received a prompt reply from Moscow. Our UN contact reported that the Soviet leadership was "not pessimistic" because of the election of a Republican President. He said that the Soviet leadership had expressed an interest in knowing if I desired to "open channels of communication." It was with this in mind that I said in my inaugural address, "After a period of confrontation, we are entering an era of negotiation. Let all nations know that during this administration our lines of communication will be open."

The most pressing foreign problem I would have to deal with as soon as I became President was the war in Vietnam. During the transition Kissinger began a review of all possible policies toward Vietnam, distilling them into specific options that ran the gamut from massive military escalation to immediate unilateral withdrawal. A strong case could be made for each option.

For example, it could be argued that military victory was still possible if I would remove the restrictions Johnson had placed on our commanders in the field and allow them to use our massive power to defeat the enemy. The most serious of these constraints was the bombing halt; because of it the Communists had been able to regroup their forces and amass supplies for a new offensive. Those who favored the escalation option argued that just the threat of an invasion of North Vietnam would tie down North Vietnamese troops along the DMZ; that mining Haiphong Harbor would cripple the enemy's supply lines; and that free pursuit of the Communist forces into Laos and Cambodia would blunt their ability to continue making hit-and-run attacks against our forces in South Vietnam. Renewed bombing would reinforce these other moves. That, in essence, was the escalation option. It was an option we ruled out very early.

The opinion polls showed a significant percentage of the public favored a military victory in Vietnam. But most people thought of a "military victory" in terms of gearing up to administer a knockout blow that would both end the war and win it. The problem was that there were only two such knockout blows available to me. One would have been to bomb the elaborate systems of irrigation dikes in North Vietnam. The resulting floods would have killed hundreds of thousands of civilians. The other possible knockout blow would have involved the use of tactical nuclear weapons. Short of one of these methods, escalation would probably have required up to six months of highly intensified fighting and significantly increased casualties before the Communists would finally be forced to give up and accept a peace settlement. The domestic and international uproar that would have accompanied the use of either of these knockout blows would have got my administration off to the worst possible start. And as far as escalating the conventional fighting was concerned, there was no way that I could hold the country together for that period of time in view of the numbers of casualties we would be sustaining. Resorting to the escalation option would also delay or even destroy any chance we might have to develop a new relationship with the Soviet Union and Communist China.

At the other end of the spectrum from escalation was the case for ending the war simply by announcing a quick and orderly withdrawal of all American forces. If that were done, the argument went, the Communists would probably respond by returning our POWs after the last American had departed.

There were some undeniably compelling political arguments to recommend this particular course. As one of my friends in Congress put it, "You didn't get us into this war, so even if you end it with a bad peace, by doing it quickly you can put the blame on Kennedy and Johnson and the Democrats. Just go on TV and remind people that it was Kennedy who sent the 16,000 Americans in there, and that it was Johnson who escalated it to 540,000. Then announce that you're bringing them all home, and you'll be a hero."

As I saw it, however, this option had long since been foreclosed. A precipitate withdrawal would abandon 17 million South Vietnamese, many of whom had worked for us and supported us, to Communist atrocities and domination. When the Communists had taken over North Vietnam in 1954, 50,000 people had been murdered, and hundreds of thousands more died in labor camps. In 1968, during their brief control of Hué, they had shot or clubbed to death or buried alive more than 3,000 civilians whose only crime was to have supported the Saigon government. We simply could not sacrifice an ally in such a way. If we suddenly reneged on our earlier pledges of support, because they had become difficult or costly to carry out, or because they had become unpopular at home, we would not be worthy of the trust of other nations and we certainly would not receive it.

As far as I was concerned, almost everything involving a Vietnam settlement was negotiable except two things: I would not agree to anything that did not include the return of all our POWs and an accounting for our missing in action; and I would not agree to any terms that required or amounted to our overthrow of President Thieu.

I was aware that many Americans considered Thieu a petty and corrupt dictator unworthy of our support. I was not personally attached to Thieu, but I looked at the situation in practical terms. As I saw it, the alternative to Thieu was not someone more enlightened or tolerant or democratic but someone weaker who would not be able to hold together the contentious factions in South Vietnam. The South Vietnamese needed a strong and stable government to carry on the fight against the efforts of the Vietcong terrorists, who were supported by the North Vietnamese Army in their efforts to impose a Communist dictatorship on the 17 million people of South Vietnam. My determination to honor our commitment to Thieu was a commitment to stability, and that is exactly why the Communists were so insistent upon securing his downfall as part of a settlement. For three and a half years, until the fall of 1972, the North Vietnamese insisted upon our willingness to overthrow or sacrifice Thieu as a sine qua non for a settlement. Once they dropped this demand serious negotiations began.

I began my presidency with three fundamental premises regarding Vietnam. First, I would have to prepare public opinion for the fact that total military victory was no longer possible. Second, I would have to act on what my conscience, my experience, and my analysis told me was true about the need to keep our commitment. To abandon South Vietnam to the Communists now would cost us inestimably in our search for a stable, structured, and lasting peace. Third, I would have to end the war as quickly as was honorably possible.

Since I had ruled out a quick military victory, the only possible course was to try for a fair negotiated settlement that would preserve the independence of South Vietnam. Ideally the war could be over in a matter of months if the North Vietnamese truly wanted peace. Realistically, however, I was prepared to take most of my first year in office to arrive at a negotiated agreement.

In mid-December I told Kissinger that I wanted to send a message to North Vietnam. We decided to use Jean Sainteny as an intermediary. Sainteny was a French businessman who had spent many years in Indochina and who still knew personally many of the leaders in both North and South Vietnam, including Ho Chi Minh. I had first met Sainteny in the South of France in 1965, and Kissinger knew him as well.

My first message, which Sainteny gave to the North Vietnamese in Paris, set forth in conciliatory terms our proposals for a negotiated settlement. Eleven days later we received a reply charging that Saigon was holding up the opening of the Paris peace talks and that we supported the "absurd demands" of the South Vietnamese leaders. "If the U.S. wishes," their note concluded, "it may communicate its general ideas, and its specific ideas for making more precise points than are already known, for our serious examination." When he handed this reply to Sainteny, Mai Van Bo, Hanoi's representative in Paris, commented, "At the beginning, I believe that the question is to know if the U.S. wants peace, if it really wishes to withdraw its troops from South Vietnam, or if it only talks of this to make it possible to do nothing."

I waited only two days to reply, sending word through Sainteny that "the Nixon administration is willing to negotiate seriously and in good faith." The North Vietnamese reply to this message still took a hard line, but I was neither surprised nor discouraged; I had never expected to end the long war quickly or easily. In my inaugural address I reiterated my desire to reach a peaceful settlement if possible, but I left no doubts about my determination to see through to an honorable conclusion the commitment we had undertaken. I said: "To all those who would be tempted by weakness, let us leave no doubt that we will be as strong as we need to be for as long as we need to be."

The Vietnam war was complicated by factors that had never occurred before in America's conduct of a war. Many of the most prominent liberals of both parties in Congress, having supported our involvement in Vietnam under Kennedy and Johnson, were now trying to back off from their commitment. Senators and congressmen, Cabinet members and columnists who had formerly supported the war were now swelling the ranks of the antiwar forces. In 1969 I still had a congressional majority on war-related votes and questions, but it was a bare one at best, and I could not be sure how long it would hold. Another unusual aspect of this war was that the American news media had come to dominate domestic opinion about its purpose and conduct and also about the nature of the enemy. The North Vietnamese were a particularly ruthless and cruel enemy, but the American media concentrated primarily on the failings and frailties of the South Vietnamese or of our own forces. In each night's

TV news and in each morning's paper the war was reported battle by battle, but little or no sense of the underlying purpose of the fighting was conveyed. Eventually this contributed to the impression that we were fighting in military and moral quicksand, rather than toward an important and worthwhile objective.

More than ever before, television showed the terrible human suffering and sacrifice of war. Whatever the intention behind such relentless and literal reporting of the war, the result was a serious demoralization of the home front, raising the question whether America would ever again be able to fight an enemy abroad with unity and strength of purpose at home. As *Newsweek* columnist Kenneth Crawford wrote, this was the first war in our history when the media was more friendly to our enemies than to our allies. I felt that by the time I had become President the way the Vietnam war had been conducted and reported had worn down America's spirit and sense of confidence.

As I prepared to enter the presidency, I regarded the antiwar protesters and demonstrators with alternating feelings of appreciation for their concerns, anger at their excesses, and, primarily, frustration at their apparent unwillingness to credit me even with a genuine desire for peace. But whatever my estimation of the demonstrators' motives—and whatever their estimate of mine—I considered that the practical effect of their activity was to give encouragement to the enemy and thus prolong the war. They wanted to end the war in Vietnam. So did I. But they wanted to end it immediately, and in order to do so they were prepared to abandon South Vietnam. That was something I would not permit.

The final returns of the 1968 presidential election showed that I had defeated Humphrey by only 500,000 votes—43.3 percent to 42.6 percent. But George Wallace had received 13.5 percent, nearly 10 million votes. My votes and Wallace's totaled 56.8 percent, and together they represented a clear mandate: after almost four decades in which the federal government had insatiably drawn power to itself, the American voters wanted a change of direction away from Washington paternalism. As I considered the situation that could confront me when I assumed responsibility as head of government, the major question as I saw it was: given an opposition Congress and an essentially liberal bureaucracy, how far would I be able to go toward carrying out this mandate?

I was the first newly elected President since Zachary Taylor 120 years earlier to take office with both houses of Congress controlled by the opposition party. If I were to get legislation passed, I would need a coalition of bipartisan support.

Throughout my presidency my strongest and most dependable support in foreign affairs came from conservatives in both parties. I came to depend particularly on a group of Southern Democrats including Sonny Montgomery of Mississippi, George Mahon of Texas, William Colmer of Mississippi, and Joe Waggonner, Eddie Hébert, and Otto Passman of Louisiana in the House, and Dick Russell of Georgia, John Stennis of Mississippi, and John McClellan of Arkansas in the Senate.

Unfortunately, there was no similar coalition I could tap for support on domestic policy. In that area I knew that the different interests of different groups would coincide on some issues and diverge on others. Liberals would seldom think that I had gone far enough, and conservatives would often think I had gone too far. On every issue I would have to gather enough borderline members of each persuasion to pass my legislation. To get my programs through Congress I would have to devise complex political strategies. To prevent things I opposed from being enacted I would have to be prepared to bear the political and public relations consequences of vetoing large amounts of legislation.

I won the 1968 election as a Washington insider, but with an outsider's prejudices. The behind-the-scenes power structure in Washington is often called the "iron triangle": a three-sided set of relationships composed of congressional lobbyists, congressional committee and subcommittee members and their staffs, and the bureaucrats in the various federal departments and agencies. These people tend to work with each other year after year regardless of changes in administrations; they form personal and professional associations and generally act in concert.

I felt that one of the reasons I had been elected was my

promise to break the hammerlock Washington holds over the money and decisions that affect American lives. I wanted to break open the iron triangle and start turning money and power back to the states and cities, and I wanted to throw the red tape out the window. But Washington is a city run primarily by Democrats and liberals, dominated by like-minded newspapers and other media, convinced of its superiority to other cities and other points of view; from the beginning I knew my chances of succeeding with the kinds of domestic reforms I had in mind were slim.

I urged the new Cabinet members to move quickly to replace holdover bureaucrats with people who believed in what we were trying to do. I warned that if they did not act quickly, they would become captives of the bureaucracy they were trying to change. "In effect, we want to reverse the whole trend of government over the last eight years. We may only have four years in which to do it, so we can't waste a minute," I said. I urged them to resist the Washington habit of recruiting their staffs solely from Eastern schools and companies and instead to branch out and get new blood from the South, the West, and the Midwest. "We can't depend on people who believe in another philosophy of government to give us their undivided loyalty or their best work," I concluded. "For some reason this is something that the supposedly idealistic Democrats have always been better at recognizing than the supposedly hard-nosed Republicans. If we don't get rid of those people, they will either sabotage us from within, or they'll just sit back on their well-paid asses and wait for the next election to bring back their old bosses."

As I saw it, America in the 1960s had undergone a misguided crash program aimed at using the power of the presidency and the federal government to right past wrongs by trying to legislate social progress. This was the idea behind Kennedy's New Frontier and Johnson's Great Society. The problems were real and the intention worthy, but the method was foredoomed. By the end of the decade its costs had become almost prohibitively high in terms of the way it had undermined fundamental relationships within our federal system, created confusion about our national values, and corroded American belief in ourselves as a people and as a nation.

The 1960s had been a decade of great restlessness and change. Prodded by the emotional power of Kennedy's liberal rhetoric, new sensitivities—some sincere, some merely fashionable—developed regarding the black, the poor, and the young in our society.

This was the period of what social critic Henry Fairlie has called "the politics of expectation," when the President held out the promise of solutions by means of federal programs to the problems of poverty and racial discrimination, thereby raising the expectations of millions of people—and, of course, securing the support of millions of voters. From 1960 to 1969 the cost of welfare benefits for families with dependent children nearly tripled. More than a quarter of a trillion federal dollars was spent between 1964 and 1969 in an attempt to eradicate poverty and inequality. But instead of solving problems, these programs themselves became part of the problem, by raising hopes they proved unable to fulfill.

Billions of dollars were poured into new federally sponsored programs and agencies to help the poor, but the poor frequently did not see much of this money because it went to pay the salaries of the social workers and the overhead of the vast new poverty bureaucracy, much of it composed of middle-class whites, that administered the programs and agencies. Housing and education services were tied up in red tape and foundered on the fundamentally mistaken notion that the poor can be talked or taught out of their poverty.

In 1961 John Kennedy had challenged people to "ask not what your country can do for you ask what you can do for your country." By the end of the decade, however, many people were asking why the federal government had not done all the things it had promised and undertaken to do for them.

Perhaps most demoralizing of all, the working poor watched while the nonworking poor made as much money—and in some cases even more money—by collecting welfare payments and other unemployment benefits. This began a bitter cycle of frustration, anger, and hostility.

I wanted to be an activist President in domestic policy,

but I wanted to be certain that the things we did had a chance of working. "Don't promise more than we can do," I told the Cabinet. "But do more than we can promise."

I had watched the sixties from outside the arena of leadership, but I had strong feelings about what I had seen happen. I saw the mass demonstrations grow remote from the wellsprings of sensitivity and feeling that had originally prompted them, and become a cultural fad. And the new sensitivity to social inequities that was awakened at the beginning of the decade had, by the middle of the sixties, spawned an intolerance for the rights and opinions of those who disagreed with the vocal minority. I had no patience with the mindless rioters and professional malcontents, and I was appalled by the response of most of the nation's political and academic leaders to them. The political leadership seemed unable to make the distinction between a wrong that needed to be set right and the use of such a wrong as a justification for violating the privileges of democracy. The young demonstrators held firmly to their beliefs, while the adults seemed stricken with ambivalence about their own guilt and doubts about their own values. By proving themselves vulnerable to mob rule, the political and academic leaders encouraged its spread. Contemptuous of most of their professors, encouraged by others on the faculty and in the political arena, and spotlighted by the rapt gaze of television cameras, the demonstrators and their demonstrations continued and grew, and so did the often rationalized or romanticized violence connected with them.

I was ready to take a stand on these social and cultural issues; I was anxious to defend the "square" virtues. In some cases—such as opposing the legalization of marijuana and the provision of federal funds for abortions, and in identifying myself with unabashed patriotism—I knew I would be standing against the prevailing social winds, and that would cause tension. But I thought that at least someone in high office would be standing up for what he believed.

Since the advent of television as our primary means of communication and source of information modern Presidents must have specialized talents at once more superficial and more complicated than those of their predecessors. They must try to master the art of manipulating the media not only to win in politics but in order to further the programs and causes they believe in; at the same time they must avoid at all costs the charge of trying to manipulate the media. In the modern presidency, concern for image must rank with concern for substance—there is no guarantee that good programs will automatically triumph. "Elections are not won or lost by programs," I once reminded Haldeman in a memo. "They are won or lost by how these programs are presented to the country and how the political and public relations considerations are handled." I do not like this situation; I can remember a time in American politics when it was not the case. But today it is a fact of life, and anyone who seeks a position of influence in politics must cope with it; anyone who seeks a position of leadership must master it.

I knew that as President my relations with the media would be at best an uneasy truce. Some of the problems were simply institutional. The media see themselves as adversaries of government, and consider it their obligation to be skeptical. The government knows that there is no such thing as a perfect program, and searches for ways to mitigate criticism sufficiently well and long enough to get something accomplished. Often the tension between the two results from nothing more than this. But in my case the problems were more than just institutional. The majority of New York and Washington newspaper and television reporters, news executives, columnists, and opinion-makers are liberals. I am not, and for many years we had looked at each other across an ideological chasm that Vietnam only deepened further. After the press treatment I received during the Hiss case and the fund episode, and after the flagrant media favoritism for Kennedy in 1960, I considered the influential majority of the news media to be part of my political opposition. Whatever the reasons—institutional, ideological, or simply those based on personality—my relationship with them was somehow different even from that of other political figures whom they disliked or with whom they disagreed. I knew that I must expect no generosity, even for mistakes; I knew that my conduct and that of my family would be held up to the most severe scrutiny; and I felt that if anything ever went seriously wrong, the media would jump in and give me a fight for my political life.

I was prepared to have to do combat with the media in order to get my views and my programs to the people, and despite all the power and public visibility I would enjoy as President, I did not believe that this combat would be between equals. The media are far more powerful than the President in creating public awareness and shaping public opinion, for the simple reason that the media always have the last word.

I also felt that it would be important to establish a more direct relationship with the media outside New York and Washington. I did not want all the views and opinions reaching me filtered through the *Times*, the *Post*, and the three television networks. Therefore I asked for a daily summary of the main ideas and opinions expressed across the country in news reports, editorials, columns, and articles from fifty newspapers, thirty magazines, and the two major wire services.

Within the White House I created the post of Director of Communications for the executive branch. Herb Klein, who had served as my press spokesman in 1960 and 1962, headed this new office. One of his tasks was to stay in touch with the media in the rest of the country, bring their reports to me, and get my ideas out to them. I named Ron Ziegler, my twenty-nine-year-old campaign press assistant, as Press Secretary.

As I assembled my Cabinet and senior staff during this transition period, I thought that one of our most important tasks would be to place our stamp on the federal bureaucracy as quickly and as firmly as we possibly could. Ever since Andrew Jackson and the era of "To the victor belong the spoils," the Democrats had understood and excelled at acting on this premise. I could remember my concern when Eisenhower, upon entering office after twenty years of uninterrupted Democratic power, failed to press his Cabinet members and other appointees to Republicanize their agencies and departments. After the eight Kennedy-Johnson years the need was hardly less great, and at every meeting during the transition and the first months of my administration I urged, exhorted, and finally pleaded with my Cabinet and other appointed officials to replace holdover Democrats with Republicans who would be loyal to the administration and support my programs.

Week after week I watched and listened while even the Cabinet members who had been in politics long enough to know better justified retaining Democrats in important positions in their departments for reasons of "morale" or in order to avoid controversy or unfavorable publicity. Looking back, I think that Eisenhower, because of his many years of experience with the Army, understood that the combination of human nature and the inertia of institutions will generally override even the most determined attempts to change them. Once the opportunity had passed, it was too late to correct this failure during my first term. I could only console myself with the determination that, if I were reelected in 1972, I would not make the same mistake of leaving the initiative to individual Cabinet members.

I knew that I was assuming the role of Commander in Chief at what was perhaps the most troubled time in the history of our armed forces. Never before had our fighting men been subjected to such criticism—and never to such obloquy—during wartime. Among the most serious effects of the antiwar movement in America was its effect on the morale and discipline of our armed forces both at home and on the battlefield, and the problem became worse as the expanded monthly draft calls began bringing in more young men who had been infected by antiwar attitudes. As I looked ahead to the end of the Vietnam war, I saw that we could end the recruitment of our armed forces through universal conscription and create an all-volunteer force. In 1969 I introduced this plan, and by 1973 the civilian draft had been completely eliminated.

I addressed the problems of the military in a speech I gave a few months later at the Air Force Academy commencement exercises in June 1969. I said, "It is open season on the armed forces. . . . The military profession is derided in some of the so-called best circles of America. Patriotism is considered by some to be a backward fetish of the uneducated and unsophisticated." While it was undeniably important to keep the power of the military firmly under civilian control and to check wastefulness in military programs, I also considered it important to let our armed forces know that their Commander in Chief stood behind them. I told the cadets in Colorado Springs, "The American defense establishment should never be a sacred cow, but on the other hand, the American military should never be anybody's scapegoat."

By 1968 I had been dedicated to the Republican Party and its electoral fortunes for twenty-two years. Unfortunately the party had not emerged much strengthened from the 1968 election despite our victory at the top of the ticket. Perhaps the problems were too deep-seated for any easy solution. The fact was that the Democrats had controlled both houses of Congress for all but two of the past thirty years. From the outset of my administration, I decided that I would use the power of incumbency to help the Republican Party and to enhance its electoral prospects. I took it as a serious responsibility as leader of the party to inject some much-needed old-time partisan fire and spirit into Republican veins. Although off-year elections almost always go against the party in the White House, I hoped that we could at least hold our own in 1970. By 1972 I hoped to have restored vitality to the Republican organization and to have identified and encouraged a new generation of winning Republican candidates.

In the meantime I would also have to keep an eye on my own political position. The victory over Humphrey had been far too close for comfort. If it had not been for the debacle of the Chicago convention and the burden of Johnson's unpopularity, Humphrey might have won. There was no reason to expect that the Democrats would be so obliging as to provide me with similar advantages in 1972. If they were able to unite around Teddy Kennedy or Muskie or even Humphrey again, they would be very hard to beat. Therefore I decided that we must begin immediately keeping track of everything the leading Democrats did. Information would be our first line of defense.

I met with President Johnson again on December 12. I sat on one of the sofas in front of the fireplace in the Oval

Office while he sat in the king-size rocking chair that he had brought in to replace Kennedy's smaller one. He began by stressing the need for maintaining secrecy on all matters involving national security. This comment was prompted by my recent announcement that I planned to revive the moribund National Security Council. Johnson was dubious about this decision, and as he warmed to his subject he sat on the edge of his rocker and leaned forward until his face was just inches from mine.

Jabbing his finger at my chest, his voice raised, he said, "Let me tell you, Dick, I would have been a damn fool to have discussed major decisions with the full Cabinet present, because I knew that if I said something in the morning, you could sure as hell bet it would appear in the afternoon papers. It's the same thing with the National Security Council. Everybody there's got their damned deputies and note-takers with them sitting along the wall. I will warn you now, the leaks can kill you. I don't even let Hubert sit in on some of those meetings for fear his staff might let something out. And even with all the precautions I take, things still leak."

Johnson shifted his massive frame to one side of the chair and rocked toward me again. "If it hadn't been for Edgar Hoover," he said, "I couldn't have carried out my responsibilities as Commander in Chief. Period. Dick, you will come to depend on Edgar. He is a pillar of strength in a city of weak men. You will rely on him time and time again to maintain security. He's the only one you can put your complete trust in."

I told Johnson that I knew one of his greatest disappointments was that he had not been able to end the war before leaving office. I assured him that we would do everything possible to bring the war to an early and honorable conclusion, and that when the goal was accomplished I would see to it that he received the credit due him. I told him he could be proud of having stood up to his critics, particularly those in his own party.

Johnson mentioned, as he had at our meeting during the summer, the letter of support that David Eisenhower had written to him. He said, "That was a time when I wasn't receiving a whole lot of letters like that from college students." He looked over his shoulder at the Rose Garden.

His eyes moistened and his voice softened. "I am mighty proud of my family and particularly proud of my two sons-in-law, who are fighting in Vietnam," he said. "You can be equally proud of your family."

My daughter Julie first met David Eisenhower at his grandfather's second inauguration in 1957, when they were both eight years old. They did not see each other at all during the early 1960s; it was a geographical coincidence that brought them together again. In 1966 David began his freshman year at Amherst College and Julie began her freshman year at Smith College, only a few miles away. One day he called her on an impulse and asked if he could come over to see her. They met, they fell in love, and just before the start of their sophomore year they told Pat and me that they planned to marry.

On the night their engagement was announced I wrote a note for Julie and left it on her bed table.

The wedding was set for December 22. I told Julie that she should give serious consideration to waiting until after the inauguration and being married in the White House. That was a unique privilege, and I wanted to be sure that she did not renounce it lightly. But both she and David felt that they wanted their wedding ceremony to be as personal and non-political as it possibly could.

Dr. Norman Vincent Peale's Marble Collegiate Church in New York had played such an important and happy part in our family's life since we moved to New York that Julie felt very deeply about being married there and about having all reporters and cameramen excluded from the ceremony.

Just as the preparations had reached their height on the evening of the rehearsal and the wedding party dinner, I came down with the flu and had to be given medication to lower my fever. I was determined, however, not to miss any of the events and not to let Julie or David know that I was not feeling well.

The church was beautifully decorated for Christmas with fresh pine boughs and red bows draped over the balco-

November 22, 1967

Dear Julie —

I suppose no father believes any boy is good enough for his daughter.

But I believe both David and you are lucky to have found each other —

Fina often says — "Miss Julie always brings life into the home"

In the many years ahead you will have ups and downs but I know you will always "bring life into your home" wherever it is — love

Daddy

nies and a large wreath behind the altar. Red and white poinsettias banked the entire front of the church and surrounded the small white prie-dieu on which David and Julie knelt during the ceremony.

The most memorable moment for me was when I gave Julie away at the altar. She suddenly turned and kissed me. This impulsive, spontaneous gesture brought tears to the eyes of many in the church—including mine.

It was not until I had joined Pat in our pew that the reality of what was happening hit me. Until now I had always thought of our family as a complete unit. Now it would be larger, but it would also be different. I could not help thinking back to one of my first conversations with Paul Douglas, the senator from Illinois, shortly after I had entered the Senate in 1950. One day we had lunch together and he asked me about my family. I told him about Tricia and Julie, and suddenly he became very pensive. He said, "I've got a little girl that all of a sudden became a teenager without my realizing it. It wasn't long ago she was just a tiny girl. Now she's a young lady, and I was so caught up in my work that I missed the years in between. Don't let that happen to you."

Pat and I had always been careful to set aside time each day to spend with the girls. But there were all the times when we were away campaigning or on official trips or when we would suddenly be called on to fill in for the Eisenhowers and would not be able to have dinner at home.

Our family time together in California before I embarked on the governor's race had been far too brief. I knew that Pat and the girls thought that the move to New York would finally put an end to politics. But here we were, almost six years later, and I was the President-elect. I felt tremendous joy and pride watching my daughter get married but I couldn't help wondering if it would not have been possible to have spent even a little more time with her, and regretting that I had not tried harder to do so.

Mamie Eisenhower had been hospitalized a week earlier with a respiratory infection, so she as well as General Eisenhower saw the wedding from Walter Reed Hospital on a closed-circuit television hookup. Eisenhower had been unhappy about the length of David's hair, and he told me

446

that he had offered him a hundred dollars if he would have it cut short. David usually respected his grandfather's wishes, but he got only a light trim. I could not help noticing at the ceremony that despite Eisenhower's concern, David's hair was considerably shorter than any of his college friends' in the wedding party, and I thought that at least in comparative terms he might have put in a claim for the reward, but he never did—and Eisenhower never paid.

The reception after the ceremony was held at the Plaza Hotel. David and Julie chose "Edelweiss" from *The Sound of Music* as their first dance. I do not think I have ever felt lighter on my feet than when I tapped David's shoulder and cut in for my dance with the bride. In my toast I mentioned the joyous things that had happened that day: the Apollo VIII astronauts had gone into the first manned moon orbit; the North Koreans had released the crew of the *Pueblo*; and the wedding.

When they were ready to leave for their honeymoon in Florida, Julie threw her bridal bouquet—into Tricia's waiting hands. During the wedding Julie had worn the same thin blue garter that Mamie Doud had worn on July 1, 1916, when she married Lieutenant Dwight Eisenhower. Julie had therefore given David a different garter to throw to the waiting groomsmen.

That night Pat and I sat in front of the fire in our apartment and talked about the day and how beautiful Julie had looked and about how perfect the ceremony had been. But I know that we were both thinking about time: about how fast it goes, and about how little of it there is to do the important things with the people who really matter to you.

As I anticipated becoming President, I found that I was awed by the prospect but not fearful of it. I felt prepared. I had the advantage of experience and of the detachment that comes from being out of office. The "wilderness years" had been years of education and growth.

I had no illusions about either the difficulty of the challenge or about my ability to meet it. I felt I knew what would *not* work. On the other hand, I was less sure what *would* work. I did not have all the answers. But I did have definite ideas about the changes I felt were needed.

As 1968 came to a close, I was a happy man. At Key Biscayne a wreath hung on the front door and a beautifully trimmed Christmas tree stood in the living room. David and Julie came over from their honeymoon retreat in Palm Beach to join Pat and Tricia and me for Christmas dinner. Far out in space Apollo VIII orbited the moon while astronaut Frank Borman read the story of the Creation from the Book of Genesis. Those were days rich with happiness and full of anticipation and hope.

On Sunday morning, January 19, 1969, Pat and I attended Norman Vincent Peale's morning service at Marble Collegiate Church, and in the afternoon we boarded the plane Johnson had sent to bring us to Washington.

I spent my last evening as a private citizen putting the final touches on my inaugural address. At about eight o'clock Eisenhower called me from Walter Reed.

"Hi, Dick!" he said. "I want to wish you the best on what I am sure will be a great day tomorrow." He paused for a moment. "I have only one regret. This is the last time that I can call you Dick. From now on it will always be Mr. President."

The Presidency
1969-1971

On inauguration day, January 20, 1969, I woke at 7:45
A.M. and had breakfast with Pat in our suite. Then we
attended a prayer service in the State Department Auditorium before driving to the White House. As our car slowly
turned into the driveway, we could see the Johnsons waiting
for us on the porch under the North Portico.

We went in for the traditional coffee and rolls in the
Red Room. "I think maybe you should deliver my address
today, Hubert," I said to Humphrey in an attempt to keep
the mood light.

"That's what I had planned to do, Dick," he replied
with a smile.

I remembered from 1961 how painful this ceremony
could be for a man who had lost a close election, and I was
touched by Humphrey's graceful show of good humor.

During the short ride to the Capitol, Johnson waved to
the crowds lining the route and carried on a lively conversation all the way. That night I dictated a note about what he
said:

Riding down to the Capitol, Johnson spoke with very strong feeling with regard to Muskie and Agnew.

He said that at a dinner the night before, a group of people were talking about how much Muskie had contributed to the campaign. He, Johnson, had replied that all the press had slobbered over Muskie, but when it came down to votes Muskie had delivered Maine with four votes, whereas Agnew could take credit or at least a great deal of the credit on South Carolina, North Carolina, Virginia, Tennessee, and Kentucky. Obviously, he liked Agnew and had very little use for Muskie.

For the swearing in, Pat held the same two Milhous family Bibles that she had held in 1953 and 1957. I had requested that they be opened to Isaiah 2:4: "They shall beat their swords into plowshares, and their spears into pruning hooks: nation shall not lift up sword against nation, neither shall they learn war any more."

After Chief Justice Earl Warren administered the oath, I delivered my inaugural address.

My major theme was peace. I said: "The greatest honor history can bestow is the title of peacemaker. This honor now beckons America. . . . If we succeed, generations to come will say of us now living that we mastered our moment, that we helped make the world safe for mankind. This is our summons to greatness."

When we were ready to begin the inaugural parade from the Capitol back to the White House, I saw that the Secret Service had put the top on the presidential limousine. The agent in charge explained that there were several hundred demonstrators along the route and there had already been some skirmishes with the police and the other spectators.

For the first few blocks the cheering crowds were friendly. Around 12th Street I could see protest signs waving above a double line of police struggling to keep the crowd back. Suddenly a barrage of sticks, stones, beer cans, and what looked like firecrackers began sailing through the air toward us. Some of them hit the side of the car and fell into the street. I could hear the protesters' shrill chant: "Ho,

Ho, Ho Chi Minh, the NLF is going to win." A Vietcong flag was lifted, and there was a brief scuffle as some in the crowd tried to tear it down. Seconds later we rounded the corner onto 15th Street, and the atmosphere changed completely. A loud cheer rose from the crowds on the sidewalks in front of the Washington Hotel and the Treasury Building. I was angered that a group of protesters carrying a Vietcong flag had made us captives inside the car. I told the driver to open the sun roof and to let the other agents know that Pat and I were going to stand up so the people could see us.

That night we attended each of the six inaugural balls. It was about 1:30 A.M. when we returned to the White House. Tricia and Julie found the refrigerator stocked with butter brickle ice cream and Dr Pepper, left by the Johnson girls.

I sat down at the grand piano in the center hall of the Family Quarters and played "Rustle of Spring" and a song I had composed for Pat before we were married.

When we had all gathered on the sofas in the West Hall Pat said with a happy sigh, "It's good to be home." Everyone looked up. The White House was now our home.

The White House is both a national museum and a home. The great historical rooms are primarily on the ground and first floors—the East Room, the Green, Blue, and Red Rooms, and the State Dining Room. The private rooms on the second and third floors are known as the Residence or the Family Quarters. Their personality changes with every administration.

In decorating our Family Quarters Pat chose yellows, blues, and golds—sunny, California colors. Tricia, who lived with us until her marriage in 1971, took Lynda Bird Johnson's room, which looked out over Pennsylvania Avenue and Lafayette Park. The bright and airy third-floor Solarium, which had been a schoolroom for the Kennedy children and then a no-adults-admitted teenage party room for Luci and Lynda Johnson, became our family room.

Yet even in the Family Quarters, history surrounds you. When I asked for a regular bed rather than the large canopied four-poster used by Johnson, the bed that was brought out of storage for me turned out to have been first Truman's and then Eisenhower's. I could not help thinking that here was a case in which politics had literally bred strange bedfellows.

From John Adams to Theodore Roosevelt the President and his staff worked in the White House itself. But TR's family of six children and their menagerie of cats, dogs, raccoons, snakes, a pony, and a bear proved too much and he requested the addition of a West Wing.

The West Wing is actually a small three-story office building. On the ground floor are the Oval Office, the Cabinet Room, and another meeting room, which we called the Roosevelt Room. During World War II an East Wing was added to provide additional offices for the President's staff and the staff of the First Lady.

Even after Pat had warmed the Oval Office with a rich blue and gold rug and vibrant gold sofas and curtains, it was still undeniably formal. I decided, therefore, to have a second and more comfortable office in the old Executive Office Building, which is next to the White House, separated from it by a narrow closed-off street. Reporters usually referred to the EOB office as my "small hideaway office," but it was almost as large as the Oval Office. Pat filled the shelves with my favorite books and decorated it with some of the mementos I had collected over the years. There were many family photographs, but the one that meant the most to me was a picture of Pat, Tricia, Julie, and me, taken on the day we moved back to California after I lost the 1960 presidential election. Julie once wrote to me, "I like to think that the reason you kept it on your desk was that it symbolized the happiness that we felt as a family in the midst of a difficult defeat and a difficult new start for you in private life after serving so many years as congressman, senator, and Vice President." I preferred working and thinking surrounded by these personal things rather than by the formal atmosphere of the Oval Office.

From the first days, I also used the Lincoln Sitting Room on the second floor of the White House for the work I did at night after dinner. It is a small room that was used as an office by Lincoln's secretaries, John Hay and John Nicolay. Pat added a few special touches to the decoration, including my favorite old brown velvet easy chair and footstool that I had brought from my study in our New York apartment.

For the Oval Office I requested the antique desk that I had used in my ceremonial office in the Capitol when I was Vice President. For the EOB office we brought in the desk and chair Eisenhower had used in the Oval Office. It had been in storage since Kennedy decided to replace it with a desk Franklin D. Roosevelt had used during his presidency.

Above the mantel in the Oval Office, Johnson had a portrait of FDR holding the Atlantic Charter. I replaced it with a Gilbert Stuart portrait of George Washington. Following White House tradition, I personally selected portraits of three predecessors for the Cabinet Room. I chose Eisenhower, Woodrow Wilson, and Theodore Roosevelt.

Lyndon Johnson had been captivated by gadgets and electronic equipment and he felt a constant need to know what was being said about him in the press and on television. Standing against the wall of the Oval Office to the left of his desk was a large specially constructed cabinet with insulated sides and a thick glass top, housing two constantly clattering wire service news tickers. Next to it, a long low cabinet concealed three large-screen color TV sets arranged side by side. Using a special remote control device, Johnson could watch the three networks simultaneously while switching back and forth among them for the sound. There was a similar three-set console in the small office adjacent to the Oval Office, and still another in the President's bedroom. I told Haldeman that I would like a single set put in the small office, and that all the others were to be removed, along with the wire service machines.

I discovered a mass of wires and cables underneath Johnson's bed. I was told that some were for his telephones, some were remote control wires for the TV sets, and some were for tape recording equipment connected to the phones. I asked that they all be removed.

One other piece of Johnsonian paraphernalia was the shower in the President's private bathroom in the Residence. It consisted of half a dozen different jets and showerheads, controlled by a complicated panel of knobs. My first few attempts at using it nearly flung me out of the stall, so I asked that it be replaced with a regular overhead fixture.

I slept only about four hours my first night in the White House, and was up at 6:45 A.M. While I was shaving, I remembered the hidden safe that Johnson had shown me during our visit in November. When I opened it, the safe looked empty. Then I saw a thin folder on the top shelf. It contained the daily Vietnam Situation Report from the intelligence services for the previous day, Johnson's last day in office.

I quickly read through it. The last page contained the latest casualty figures. During the week ending January 18, 185 Americans had been killed and 1,237 wounded. From January 1, 1968 to January 18, 1969, 14,958 men had been killed and 95,798 had been wounded. I closed the folder and put it back in the safe and left it there until the war was over, a constant reminder of its tragic cost.

On February 17 Soviet Ambassador Anatoly Dobrynin came to the White House to pay his first official call.

I told him that I wanted to have completely open communications with him and with the leaders of his government.

"Both you and I, Mr. Ambassador, recognize the very fundamental differences that exist between us," I said. "We may or may not be able to settle them. I hope that we will. But you and I must at least make sure that no differences arise between us because of lack of communication."

Kissinger had suggested that we develop a private channel between Dobrynin and him. I agreed that Dobrynin might be more forthcoming in strictly private and unpublicized meetings and we arranged for him to arrive unseen through a seldom-used East Wing door so that no one need know they had met. Within a short time they were meeting weekly, often over lunch.

When Dobrynin said that his government wanted to

begin talks in the area of arms limitation, I expressed my feeling that progress in one area must logically be linked to progress in other areas.

"History makes it clear that wars result not so much from arms, or even from arms races, as they do from underlying political differences and political problems," I said. "So I think it is incumbent on us, when we begin strategic arms talks, to do what we can in a parallel way to defuse critical political situations like the Middle East and Vietnam and Berlin, where there is a danger that arms might be put to use."

Before Dobrynin left, he handed me an official seven-page note from Moscow which indicated that the Soviets were prepared to move forward on a whole range of topics, including the Middle East, Central Europe, Vietnam, and arms control.

This note seemed to augur well for our policy of linkage. The major question, of course, was whether the Soviets would follow up on their words with action.

EUROPE AND de GAULLE

On February 23 I left Washington for an eight-day working visit to Europe. I wanted this trip, my first abroad as President, to establish the principle that we would consult with our allies before negotiating with our potential adversaries. I also wanted to show the world that the new American President was not completely obsessed with Vietnam, and to dramatize for Americans at home that, despite opposition to the war, their President could still be received abroad with respect and even enthusiasm.

Most important, I felt that President de Gaulle's cooperation would be vital to ending the Vietnam war and to my plans for beginning a new relationship with Communist China. France had diplomatic relations with Hanoi and Peking, and Paris would be the best place to open secret channels of communication between us and them. But de Gaulle had become seriously alienated from America during the last several years. In 1966 he had NATO headquarters removed from France. Whether we would be able to use Paris as a site for our diplomatic overtures would depend on my ability to overcome the estrangement that had grown up between us and to establish a relationship of trust and confidence with de Gaulle.

The first stop was Brussels, where I set the tone for the trip when I told the North Atlantic Council, "I have come for work, not for ceremony; to inquire, not to insist; to consult, not to convince; to listen and learn, and to begin what I hope will be a continuing interchange of ideas and insight."

In London I had a luncheon with Queen Elizabeth, and a long informal conversation with nineteen prominent British citizens. I had a private talk with Prime Minister Wilson in a comfortable room at 10 Downing Street. A warm fire cast a glow over the room and after a few minutes Wilson leaned back in his chair and put his feet up on the table. He was wearing carpet slippers. Our conversation ranged from America's position in Vietnam to Britain's role in Europe. Wilson had met the Soviet leaders when he visited Moscow, and he offered his impressions of their different personalities. He said that if Brezhnev had been born in Britain he probably would have ended up Secretary General of the Trades Union Council, and if Kosygin had been an Englishman he would likely have become Chairman of Imperial Chemical Industries.

A potentially awkward situation arose when Wilson gave a small dinner party for me at 10 Downing Street. In 1962 the British magazine *New Statesman* had described my defeat by Pat Brown as "a victory for decency in public life." John Freeman, who had then been the magazine's editor, had recently been appointed British ambassador in Washington. That evening at Downing Street would be the first time that he and I would be in the same room in an intimate social setting.

I decided to relieve the tension by addressing it directly. In my toast after dinner I said that American journalists had written far worse things about me than had appeared in Freeman's magazine. It was now a part of the past and best forgotten. "After all," I said, "he's the new diplomat, and I'm the new statesman."

The men thumped the table and called, "Hear, hear."

That was one of the kindest and most generous acts I have known in ... politics.

Just power my proud.

You can't guarantee being born a lord. It is possible — you can choose it — whether born a gentleman.

H.

DINNER

in honour of

The President of the

United States of America

10 Downing Street,
25th February, 1969

The Rt. Hon.
The Prime Minister

When I sat down, Wilson slid his menu to me. On the back of it he had written: "That was one of the kindest and most generous acts I have known in a quarter of a century in politics. Just proves my point. You can't guarantee being born a lord. It is possible—you've shown it—to be born a gentleman."

We had feared antiwar demonstrations, and a few took place during this trip, but none could mar the overwhelmingly friendly reaction of the large crowds that greeted us everywhere we went in London, Paris, Bonn, Brussels, Berlin, and Rome. Whenever possible, I took impromptu walks or plunged into the crowds to shake hands and meet people.

The high point of this trip personally and substantively was my series of meetings with de Gaulle. When *Air Force One* taxied to the terminal at Orly Airport, I could see him standing coatless at the foot of the ramp. I had been told that the temperature was just above freezing, but I immediately took off my overcoat. As we shook hands, de Gaulle greeted me in English—a virtually unprecedented personal gesture for him.

When we met privately that afternoon at the Elysée Palace, the first topic of discussion was the Soviet Union.

He said that the central fact of life for postwar Europe was the Soviet threat, but he believed that the Soviets themselves had become preoccupied with China. He said, "They are thinking in terms of a possible clash with China, and they know they can't fight the West at the same time. Thus I believe that they may end up opting for a policy of rapprochement with the West." He thought that the Russians' traditional fear of German armies would give added impetus to whatever inclination they already had toward détente.

"As far as the West is concerned," he continued, "what choice do we have? Unless you are prepared to go to war or to break down the Berlin Wall, then there is no alternative policy that is acceptable. To work toward détente is a matter of good sense: if you are not ready to make war, make peace."

"If the Russians made a move," I asked, "do you think

they believe that the United States would react with strategic weapons? And do the Europeans have confidence that we would move in answer to a Soviet attack, or the threat of an attack, by massive conventional ground forces?"

"I can only answer for the French," he replied. "We believe that the Russians know that the United States could not allow them to conquer Europe. But we also believe that if the Russians marched, you would not use nuclear weapons right away, since it would imply a total effort to kill everyone on the other side. If both the Russians and the United States were to use tactical nuclear weapons, Europe would be destroyed. Western Europe and the United Kingdom would be destroyed by Soviet tactical weapons, and East Germany, Poland, Czechoslovakia, and Hungary would be destroyed by American tactical weapons. Meanwhile, the United States and the Soviet Union would not be harmed."

That night there was a state dinner at the Elysée. I talked with Madame de Gaulle, a woman of great strength and character. Her main concerns were her husband and her family. She observed, "The presidency is temporary—but the family is permanent."

The next day de Gaulle and I met in the Grand Trianon Palace at Versailles. "Louis XIV ruled Europe from this room," he said as we stood at one of the huge windows looking out over acres of formal gardens.

We talked about the tragic effect World War II had had on the great nations of Europe. He compressed volumes of history into a single sentence when he said, "In the Second World War, all the nations of Europe lost. Two were defeated."

I turned our conversation to China. As we talked, I could see that his thinking paralleled my own. "I have no illusions about their ideology," he said, "but I do not feel that we should leave them isolated in their rage. The West should try to get to know China, to have contacts, and to penetrate it."

"In looking down the road," I said, "as I pursue my talks with the Soviets, I too might want to keep an anchor to windward with respect to China. In ten years, when China has made significant nuclear progress, we will have no choice. It is vital that we have more communications with them than we have today."

"It would be better for you to recognize China before you are obliged to do so by the growth of China," he agreed.

We returned to Paris from Versailles late in the afternoon, and that night I was host for a return dinner in de Gaulle's honor. He confirmed his acceptance of my invitation to visit the United States, and we agreed that a working visit similar to this one would be the most useful. We settled on January or February 1970 as the best time.

In his toast that night de Gaulle said, "As I am learning to know you better—and by this visit you have given me that opportunity which I consider historic—I appreciate more the statesman and the man that you are."

I felt that the new entente cordiale between the Presidents of France and the United States expressed by his words would alone have made the European trip worthwhile.

We discussed Vietnam at our meeting on my last day in France. America had become deeply involved in Vietnam despite de Gaulle's warnings and without seeking his advice, so I opened the session by asking, "Mr. President, what would you do regarding Vietnam?"

He paused for a long time before he spoke. "What is it you expect me to do, Mr. President?" he asked. "Do you want me to tell you what I would do if I were in your place? But I am not in your place!"

He said that he believed the only way to end the war was by conducting negotiations on political and military issues simultaneously and by establishing a calendar for the departure of our troops. "I do not believe that you should depart with undue haste."

He leaned forward and placed his large hands flat on the table and said, "I recognize that France had some part in this as she did not give the Vietnamese freedom early enough and thus enabled the Communists to pose as the champions of national independence, first against us and then against you. But you Americans can make this kind of settlement because your power and wealth are so great that you can do it with dignity."

When he suggested that direct conversations with the

North Vietnamese would be the best way to make progress, I indicated great interest in attempting this. De Gaulle said nothing more and our meetings drew to a close, but I felt confident that the message would be passed to the North Vietnamese Embassy.

Our last stop was at the Vatican, where I met with Pope Paul VI. We discussed the whole range of world issues and problems, but he was particularly interested to learn about my plans concerning Vietnam. He talked about the importance of resisting the spread of communism in Southeast Asia. He recalled how the Communists had murdered Christians and suppressed religion after they took over North Vietnam in 1954, and with emotion in his voice he agreed that America should continue to hold the line against the Communists in South Vietnam.

I felt that the European trip had accomplished all the goals we set for it. It showed the NATO leaders that a new and interested administration which respected their views had come to power in Washington. It served warning on the Soviets that they could no longer take for granted—nor take advantage of—Western disunity. And the TV and press coverage had a positive impact at home, instilling, however briefly, some much needed pride into our sagging national morale.

EISENHOWER

President Eisenhower's rapidly failing health cast a sad shadow over the early days of my presidency. He had been in Walter Reed Hospital since April 1968, and there was little hope that he would ever leave it.

When I visited him before my trip, he had asked me to extend his regards to some of his old friends, particularly de Gaulle. "I don't think we handled him right, now that I look back on it," he had said. "Roosevelt and Churchill were too inconsiderate of him. They treated his pride as if it were just vanity, and they never saw that a few gestures of recognition might have made him less antagonistic toward us."

When I went to see him after I returned from Europe, I

was so shocked at the deterioration of his condition that later I made a note, "Looked like a corpse—waxen face." As soon as he saw me, however, he brightened, raised his hand, and called out, "Hi!"

Even though it was visibly painful for him to talk, he insisted on having a conversation. "You know, the doctors say I'm getting better," he said. Always the optimist, perhaps he believed it.

I told him that the leaders of Europe had sent their regards to him, and I said, "You were absolutely right about de Gaulle." I told him that the Pope had said he was praying for him and hoping that a miracle might occur and bring about his complete recovery.

Shortly after noon on Friday, March 28, I had walked back from an NSC meeting to the Oval Office with Haldeman, Kissinger, and Mel Laird. While we were talking, Dr. Walter Tkach, the White House physician, entered the room. Standing near the door he said, "Mr. President, President Eisenhower just died." I knew that he had been sinking fast, but the news hit me so hard that I could not speak. A wave of sadness swept over me, and I could not hold back tears.

Mamie met us at the door of the presidential suite when we arrived at Walter Reed. I embraced her and told her how we all shared her loss. Julie and David had been there when he died. David was pale and shaken, and I could see that Julie had been crying.

When I got back to the White House, I decided to go to Camp David to write the eulogy I would deliver in the Capitol Rotunda on Sunday.

I talked with Mamie briefly on the telephone about plans for the funeral service, and then she said, "Maybe you would like to know the last thing Ike said to me before he died. You know how weak he was, but he was wide awake. He knew I was sitting there, and he said, 'I have always loved my wife. I have always loved my children. I have always loved my grandchildren. And I have always loved my country.'" I wrote down the words because I knew that I would want to use them in the eulogy.

Perhaps the best description I can give of Dwight Eisenhower is that he had a warm smile and icy blue eyes. It was not a case of being outwardly warm and inwardly cold. Rather, beneath his captivating personal appearance was a lot of finely tempered hard steel. He had exceptional warmth; but there was always a reserve, even an aloofness, that balanced it. Masses of people all over the world thought they knew him, but the people closest to him, his friends and colleagues who loved or admired him, understood that even they did not really know him well.

While most people probably remember him for his engaging, outgoing personality, I remember him for his decisive leadership. He was at his best in times of crisis and when he had to deal with great issues. It has become popular to think of the 1950s in nostalgic terms as a time of domestic apathy and international stability. But in fact, Eisenhower became President just as America and the world had reached a turning point in history, when the proliferation of nuclear weapons and the rise of Soviet militancy had forever changed the nature of international relations.

One of the questions Eisenhower had to address was whether we would utilize our nuclear advantage and fight a total war or confine ourselves to applying only limited military strength. I made a diary dictation describing Eisenhower's decisive approach to this question at an NSC meeting on March 25, 1954:

At the NSC meeting this morning there was a discussion of what the strategy of the United States should be in the event of a major war with the Soviet Union. The Joint Chiefs of Staff had a division on this point. The President took over in as emphatic a manner as I have ever seen him use. He stated that he felt this was a problem for the Commander in Chief primarily. He said that the only policy we could follow once war was started against us was to win victory. That under no circumstances could we hold back punches because of some feeling that total victory might bring greater problems than if victory were obtained through limited war. He said, in effect, that there was no possibility of a limited-war concept in view of the type of enemy we had and the type of weapons with which we have to reckon. He said we are talking about sizes of bombs and potential destructive power in fantastic amounts and that the casualties would reach 7 million one day, 8 million another possibly. He said in other words they would be in "Amos and Andy" figures.

He softened it to an extent by suggesting that the Joint Chiefs talk to him about it privately at any time to attempt to convince him, if they wanted, that his view was wrong. At the present time, he was convinced that this is the only sound position to take.

The only qualification he made was that we might consider not using our strongest weapon if we felt from a military standpoint the reaction would be so great as to make that use unadvisable. For example, he told of how the allies had discovered thousands of tons of much more deadly gas than anybody had believed existed when they overran the German positions in World War II. The Germans had not used it because they realized they were more vulnerable to gas in their constricted positions than were the Allies.

He also objected to a paragraph which said that we should insist on countries in effect being free and democratic after the war. He pointed out that in the next war every country would come out a dictatorship inevitably and would have to remain a dictatorship for some time. He, of course, said they would try in the United States to return to a free economy as soon as possible but that it would be more difficult in the future than it had been in the past wars.

While he had an engaging, outgoing personality, he also had a very definite sense of dignity. He was not the kind of man who appreciated undue familiarity. I remember the chilling looks he gave to those who tugged at his sleeve or slapped him on the back. In this respect he could not have been more different from Lyndon Johnson, who seemed unable to carry on a conversation without nudging or poking or even shaking the other person. General Jerry Persons, who had been with Eisenhower during the war years and then served as his Director of Congressional Relations before succeeding Adams as chief of the White House staff in 1958, told me of an occasion in 1959 when Eisenhower called him in shortly before Johnson was due to arrive for a meeting. "I want you to stand between Lyndon and me," Eisenhower told him. "My bursitis is kicking up, and I don't want him to grab me by the arm."

What seemed most characteristic of Eisenhower was his determined optimism. He was constantly waging a battle for high spirits on his staff. Hardly a meeting went by without some exhortation to cheerfulness. "Long faces don't win hard battles," he once told the Cabinet. "Why can't our people have a grin on their face instead of always a frown?" he asked during a meeting with legislative leaders. Yet though he enjoyed a good joke, he saw little humor in the weighty problems of his office, and he did not particularly like it when others introduced humor into serious discussions.

One afternoon early in his administration, a legislative leadership meeting debated whether to prepare the public for the horrors of nuclear war. Eisenhower strongly felt that something had to be done to develop civil defense and national preparedness. At one point, Senator Eugene Millikin, a conservative Republican from Colorado, recalled what a Colorado governor once said when confronted with some excessively dire predictions regarding his policies: "Well, if things are so bad maybe what we ought to do is paint our asses white and run with the antelope." Everyone laughed, but Eisenhower's laughter was not very enthusiastic. As we returned to the discussion, he said, rather shortly, "Well, maybe we won't even have time to paint our asses white if they begin to drop the bombs and we are not prepared for it."

Eisenhower often said that he himself never read newspaper editorial columns or looked at the political cartoons; in fact he was extremely sensitive about them, as evidenced in a diary note I made in June 1954, when Eisenhower gave vigorous expression to his views about press criticism:

At the legislative leaders meeting on Monday morning, June 21, Jerry Persons brought up an article which had been written by Drew Pearson to the effect that the President was not going to support Bridges and several other senators.

The President blew his top and said that he

wished that everybody in his whole organization would quit reading the columnists and quit reporting such incidents to him.

Eisenhower was not used to being criticized, and he found criticism hard to take. He never forgave Truman for his widely quoted quips about his lack of political experience during the 1952 campaign. "Why, this fellow don't know any more about politics than a pig knows about Sunday," Truman once said.

At one point during the administration we were planning a big bipartisan rally to build support for the mutual security program. I suggested that Truman, who supported the program, be invited to appear on the platform. A cold, hard look came over Eisenhower's face, and he said that he would not appear on the same platform with Truman no matter what was at stake.

As a political leader, Eisenhower knew that he was much stronger than his party. He felt that by doing a good job he could pull his party up; and he did not want his party to drag him down. The serious erosion of Republican strength during the years of his presidency was in some measure the result of this hands-off, arm's-length attitude. Yet he knew better than most politicians how to move people, how to rally the nation to his support, and how to inspire their faith and win their trust—and these are the essence of politics.

Contrary to the generally held view that Eisenhower was a staid standpatter, he actually welcomed and encouraged new and even unorthodox ideas.

Early in 1954 I made a diary note of a conversation I had with Persons in which I was especially struck by his description of Eisenhower's style:

He said that the difficulty with some of the people around the President is that every word that the President spoke they took as gospel. Jerry said that those who worked with him before knew that they should not do this and that the President many times would take a very forward position and finally settle upon one which was not so far out front.

"Yep," he said, "Ike sure likes to hit those fun-goes out there and see what happens to them!"

To many, Dwight Eisenhower seemed a rather kindly and benign grandfather, but his own view of himself and his conception of the presidency were quite different. He saw himself in very active terms as the man responsible for doing the right thing for America.

The last time I saw Eisenhower was two days before his death. His doctor greeted me outside the entrance to the presidential suite. "How's he doing?" I asked.

"I'm afraid there's not much hope, Mr. President," he replied.

I talked with Eisenhower for about fifteen minutes before the doctor came in to indicate that I should leave. Eisenhower obviously did not want me to go. But I could see that he was tiring fast, so I shook hands with him and walked quickly to the door.

It struck me that this was probably the last time I would see him alive. I turned impulsively and tried to keep the emotion out of my voice as I said: "General, I just want you to know how all the free people of Europe and millions of others in the world will forever be in your debt for the leadership you provided in war and peace. You can always take great pride in the fact that no man in our history has done more to make America and the world a better and safer place in which to live."

His eyes were closed as I spoke, but after a brief moment he opened them and lifted his head from the pillow. With an unusual formality he said, "Mr. President, you do me great honor in what you have just said."

Then he slowly raised his hand to his forehead in a final salute.

OPERATION BREAKFAST

We had wondered whether a new President and a serious new peace overture would produce a breakthrough that would end the Vietnam war. The North Vietnamese gave us the answer in February when they launched a small-scale but savage offensive into South Vietnam. It was a deliberate test, clearly designed to take the measure of me and my administration at the outset.

My immediate instinct was to retaliate. Kissinger and I agreed that if we let the Communists manipulate us at this early stage, we might never be able to negotiate with them from a position of equality, much less one of strength. Johnson had made this mistake and had never been able to recover the initiative.

This view was shared by General Creighton Abrams, the U.S. Commander in Vietnam, and by Ambassador Ellsworth Bunker in Saigon. When the Communists stepped up their offensive, both Abrams and Bunker recommended B-52 bombing runs against their supply lines in the Cambodian sanctuaries.

Bill Rogers and Mel Laird opposed this recommendation. They feared the fury of Congress and the media if I expanded the war into Cambodia. But Kissinger argued, "What do we care if the New York *Times* clobbers us now if it helps us end the war sooner?" I agreed with him, but I decided to postpone a final decision about the bombing until I returned from the European trip, because a leak of plans to bomb Cambodia might have triggered serious antiwar demonstrations abroad. I directed that a cable be sent to Bunker through regular channels saying that all discussions of bombing should be suspended. I simultaneously sent a top secret "back-channel" message—a routing outside the official system—to General Abrams telling him to ignore the message to Bunker and to continue planning the B-52 strikes on a contingency basis even though I would have to withhold approval until after my trip.

While I was in Europe, the Communist offensive intensified. At a press conference two days after my return I was asked what our reaction would be. "We have not moved in a precipitate fashion," I said, "but the fact that we have shown patience and forbearance should not be considered as a sign of weakness. . . . An appropriate response to these attacks will be made if they continue."

Ten days later, on the morning of my next press conference, the North Vietnamese mounted a new attack across the DMZ. In reply to a question about whether my patience was growing thin with this kind of provocation, I said, "You may recall that on March 4, when I received a similar question, at an earlier stage in the attacks, I issued what was interpreted widely as a warning. It will be my policy as President to issue a warning only once, and I will not repeat it now. Anything in the future that is done will be done."

On Sunday, March 16, I met for two hours with Rogers, Laird, Kissinger, and General Earle Wheeler, the Chairman of the Joint Chiefs, to review the military and diplomatic situation in Vietnam.

I asked for the latest casualty figures. Because of the Communist offensive, they were high. Three hundred fifty-one Americans had died during the past week, 453 the week before, and 336 the week before that.

Our intelligence reports indicated that over 40,000 Communist troops had secretly been amassed in a zone ten to fifteen miles wide just inside the Cambodian border. Cambodia was a neutral country. We respected that neutrality, but the Communists were blatantly violating it by launching raids across the Cambodian border into South Vietnam and then retreating to the safety of their jungle sanctuaries.

"Gentlemen," I said, "we have reached the point where a decision is required: to bomb or not to bomb."

I assured everyone that I understood the problems and recognized the risks involved in bombing the sanctuaries, no matter how justified such action might be.

"But we have to look at what we're up against," I continued. "The state of play in Paris is completely sterile. I am convinced that the only way to move the negotiations off dead center is to do something on the military front. That is something they will understand."

I said that short of resuming the bombing of North Vietnam, this was the only military action we could take that might succeed in saving American lives and getting the peace negotiations moving.

I concluded, "I have decided to order the bombing to begin as soon as possible. Tomorrow, if the weather is good enough."

The weather was good, and on March 17, B-52 bombers struck the Communist sanctuaries inside the Cambodian border. The Pentagon gave the secret bombing the code-name Menu, and the various target areas were designated by different mealtimes. The attack on the first area was called Operation Breakfast. It was the first turning point in my administration's conduct of the Vietnam war.

Maximum precautions were taken to keep the bombing secret, for several reasons. We knew that Prince Sihanouk, the head of the Cambodian government, strongly objected to the presence of the North Vietnamese army in his country. As early as 1968, he had asked the United States to retaliate against the North Vietnamese, either with "hot pursuit" on the ground or by bombing the sanctuaries. We also knew that because of Cambodia's neutral status, Sihanouk could not afford to endorse our actions officially. Therefore, as long as we bombed secretly, we knew that Sihanouk would be silent; if the bombing became known publicly, however, he would be forced to protest it publicly.

We also anticipated that as long as the bombing remained secret, the North Vietnamese would find it difficult to protest since they were officially denying that they had any troops in Cambodia.

Another reason for secrecy was the problem of domestic antiwar protest. My administration was only two months old, and I wanted to provoke as little public outcry as possible at the outset.

In order to preserve the secrecy of the bombing, we informed only Richard Russell and John Stennis, the Chairman and the ranking member of the Senate Armed Services Committee. Although Russell was beginning to have doubts about the war in general, both men thought that the bombing was the right decision, and both said that they would back me up in the event that it became public.

Soon after Operation Breakfast began, there was a steady decline in American casualties in South Vietnam.

EC-121

Less than a month after the secret bombing of the Communist sanctuaries in Cambodia began, we were suddenly confronted with a major crisis from a completely unexpected quarter of the Communist world.

Just before seven in the morning on April 15, my

472

bedside phone began ringing. It was Kissinger. He informed me of reliable but as yet unconfirmed reports that North Korean jets had shot down one of our Navy reconnaissance planes with thirty-one men aboard.

As soon as I got to the Oval Office, I read the fragmentary intelligence reports. The North Koreans had shot down a four-engine propeller-driven EC-121 Navy aircraft which was on a regular reconnaissance mission off the North Korean coast. Such flights had been made for almost twenty years under standing orders that the aircraft not approach closer than forty nautical miles to the coast of North Korea, well outside the international territorial limit.

It was remotely possible that the men aboard the EC-121 had been taken captive in North Korea as the *Pueblo* crew had been fifteen months earlier. All during the day we assumed the worst—that the men were dead—but hoped for the best.

I reacted in the same way and with the same instincts that I had felt when the North Vietnamese offensive began: we were being tested, and therefore force must be met with force.

At ten the next morning, Washington time, I met with the NSC in the Cabinet Room to consider how we would respond to our first international crisis.

Both Rogers and Laird urged restraint. They reasoned that this might be a completely isolated incident, and thought we should stay our hand until we were completely sure what had happened and why. Ted Agnew disagreed. With obvious frustration he asked, "Why do we always take the other guy's position?"

Nothing was decided that morning, but two serious options emerged. Option One involved retaliation by sending a military strike against a North Korean airfield. Option Two involved continuing the EC-121 reconnaissance flights but sending combat escorts with them to ward off any future incidents.

Neither option was ideal. The North Koreans were well armed, and if we chose Option One we would have to be prepared to suffer further losses and to confront the possibility of reopening the fighting in Korea. And Option Two, while it would clearly establish the principle of our right to fly reconnaissance missions in international airspace, was admittedly a very weak protest against what appeared to be the murder of thirty-one men and a deliberate affront to American honor. Americans would rightly wonder about the value of our costly overseas commitments if we could not adequately protect our men and our honor in a situation that was as clear-cut as this one.

In midafternoon we received word that two bodies had been recovered from the water, along with some of the debris of the plane, ninety miles from the coast. There could be no more hope that there had been any survivors nor could there be any doubt that the incident was a calculated and cold-blooded challenge.

Intelligence reports indicated that shooting down the EC-121 was an isolated provocation like the seizure of the *Pueblo*. One of them pointed out that April 14 was the birthday of North Korea's leader, Kim Il-sung, and it was even possible that this was his macabre birthday present to himself. The case against retaliation was strongly supported in an urgent cable from Ambassador William Porter in Seoul, warning that any major military action we took would end up playing into the hands of North Korea's extremist leadership.

On the other hand, Kissinger and I continued to feel that retaliation was important. As he put it, a strong reaction from the United States would be a signal that for the first time in years the United States was sure of itself. It would shore up the morale of our allies and give pause to our enemies. We discussed the possibility that the North Koreans would respond with an attack on South Korea. Kissinger said that he did not believe that would happen, but, if it did, we had to be prepared to take whatever steps were necessary to bring the North Koreans to their knees.

I said that plans should be initiated for Option One. And since Option Two, the immediate resumption of the intelligence flights with fighter escorts, did not preclude the subsequent use of Option One, I decided to go ahead and announce its implementation at a press conference the next morning.

At the press conference, on April 18, I announced: "I have today ordered that these flights be continued. They will be protected. This is not a threat; it is simply a statement of fact."

In the meantime, we began to discuss a third possibility: Option Two backed up with a second round of bombing of the North Vietnamese sanctuaries in Cambodia. This would avoid the risks of a direct retaliation against North Korea, and still would be an effective way to impress the Communist leaders of both North Korea and North Vietnam with our resolve to support our allies and resist aggression.

Before we reached the go stage of the Option One bombing plan, I decided to call it off and adopt this combination of Option Two and a renewal of the secret Menu bombing in Cambodia. This second round, aimed at the next target area, would be called Operation Lunch.

Kissinger still felt that our credibility vis-à-vis the Communist world was at stake in our response to this deliberate challenge. The Soviets, the North Vietnamese, and the Chinese would all be watching. "If we strike back, even though it's risky," he said, "they will say, 'This guy is becoming irrational—we'd better settle with him.' But if we back down, they'll say, 'This guy is the same as his predecessor, and if we wait he'll come to the same end.'"

I still agreed that we had to act boldly; I was just not convinced that this was the time to do it. It was a calculated risk that the North Koreans would not escalate the situation any further if we retaliated with a single strike against one of their airfields. But what if they did and we suddenly found ourselves at war in Korea? As long as we were involved in Vietnam, we simply did not have the resources or public support for another war in another place.

I also had to consider the fact that except for Agnew and Mitchell, most of my top national security advisers, particularly Rogers and Laird, were strongly opposed to Option One. Kissinger agreed that we could ill afford a Cabinet insurrection at such an early date in the administration. He also agreed that congressional and public opinion were not ready for the shock of a strong retaliation against the Communists in North Korea.

Making my decision in favor of Option Two turned out to be easier than getting it carried out. Despite my April 18 directive—and the public announcement of it—we were faced with a series of postponements, excuses, and delays from the Pentagon, and it was nearly three weeks before my order was implemented. Even worse, we discovered that without informing the White House, the Pentagon had also canceled reconnaissance flights in the Mediterranean. Thus from April 14 to May 8, the United States had not conducted its scheduled aerial reconnaissance in the Mediterranean and the North Pacific—two of the most sensitive areas of the globe.

I was surprised and angered by this situation. The North Koreans would undoubtedly think that they had succeeded in making us back off the reconnaissance flights. Thanks to this incident I learned early in my administration that a President must keep a constant check not just on the way his orders are being followed, but on whether they are being followed at all.

Before long, other issues absorbed us and the EC-121 incident was largely forgotten. Yet I remained troubled by the response we had made—or, as I saw it, that we had failed to make. I told Kissinger, "They got away with it this time, but they'll never get away with it again."

On April 28, de Gaulle resigned as President of France. He had staked his political future on the outcome of a plebiscite involving Senate and regional reforms.

In addition to the public statement wishing de Gaulle well, I wrote him a personal letter. I said, "The message I sent to you through official channels could not convey adequately my deep sense of personal loss when you announced your retirement," and that "I believe history will record that your resignation was a great loss to France and to the cause of freedom and decency in the world."

I extended an open invitation to him and Madame de Gaulle to visit the United States, and at the end I wrote, "Putting it in blunt terms—in this age of mediocre leaders in most of the world—America's spirit needs your presence."

When this letter was personally delivered to him at Colombey, de Gaulle read it and said, "He is a true comrade." Then he sat down at his desk and wrote a reply to be sent back the same day:

Dear Mr. President:

Your gracious official message and your very warm personal letter touched me deeply. Not only because you occupy the high office of President of the United States, but also because they are from you, Richard Nixon, and I have for you—with good reason—esteem, confidence, and friendship as great and as sincere as it is possible to have.

Perhaps one day I will have the occasion and the honor to see you again; in the meantime, I send you from the bottom of my heart all my best wishes for the successful accomplishment of your immense national and international task.

Would you please give Mrs. Nixon my most respectful regards, to which my wife adds her warm wishes. For you, my dear Mr. President, the assurance of my feeling of faithful and devoted friendship.

Charles de Gaulle

De Gaulle died a year and a half later. I went to Paris for the funeral service in Notre Dame Cathedral, and afterward paid my respects to Georges Pompidou, once de Gaulle's deputy, and now his successor.

Pompidou was rightly known as a rather unemotional man, and he had had his differences with de Gaulle over the years. But after waiting a moment for him to begin the conversation, I looked over and saw that he was choked up and could not speak.

Remembering how I felt after Eisenhower's death, I waited silently until he had composed himself. The two of us had lived and worked for so many of our public years in the shadows of two giants, Eisenhower and de Gaulle. Now both were dead.

Pompidou sighed, and looking at me, said, *"Enfin seuls."* He too must have been thinking about this bond we had shared; now we were alone.

Leaks about the Vietnam war had plagued Lyndon Johnson during the last years of his presidency. At first he was frustrated, then angered, and, finally, nearly obsessed by the need to stop them. He tried to circumvent leaks by working with fewer and fewer people, until he was making national security policy in private Tuesday afternoon luncheon meetings with a tight circle of trusted advisers. I have already described how, when he heard that I had decided to reactivate the NSC system, he told me about his experiences with leaks and predicted that it would be a decision I would regret.

I soon learned that his concerns were fully justified. The leaks began almost with the start of my administration, and before long I experienced firsthand the anger, worry, and frustration that Johnson had described. In the first five months of my presidency, at least twenty-one major stories based on leaks from materials in the NSC files appeared in New York and Washington newspapers. A CIA report listed forty-five newspaper articles in 1969 that contained serious breaches of secrecy.

Within a matter of days after the NSC held its first meeting on the Middle East on February 1, the details of the discussion that had taken place were leaked to the press. Eisenhower, whom I had personally briefed on this meeting, considered any leak of classified foreign policy information whether in war or peace, treasonable. When he saw the news story he telephoned Kissinger and warned him in no uncertain terms. "Tighten your shop," he said. "Get rid of people if you have to, but don't let this go on."

On April 4 the New York *Times* carried a story about Soviet missile deployment based on highly classified information gathered in secret intelligence surveys.

On April 1 an NSC directive was issued that called for a comprehensive new study of alternative policies for Vietnam, including, for the sake of completeness, the radical option of unilateral withdrawal. On April 6, five days after the study was submitted, the New York *Times* reported that the United States was considering a unilateral withdrawal.

This came as a shock to our allies and undoubtedly gave encouragement to our enemies.

On April 22 the *Times* ran a story based on our planning sessions for the coming disarmament talks with the Soviets. Two days later the *Times* had a detailed report of our deliberations on whether to post an intelligence ship off North Korea. The next day the *Times* reported a leak from "reliable sources" on our negotiations for arms sales to King Hussein.

I talked with Edgar Hoover and John Mitchell about this problem. Hoover's three suggestions were to conduct background checks on those suspected as possible sources of leaked information, to have them tailed, or to place wiretaps on their telephones. Tapping, he said was the only really effective means of uncovering leakers. He told me that tapping had been authorized by every President starting with FDR.

It was decided that when leaks occurred Kissinger would supply Hoover with the names of individuals who had had access to the leaked materials and whom he had any cause to suspect. I authorized Hoover to take the necessary steps—including wiretapping—to investigate the leaks and find the leakers.

On May 1 the New York *Times* ran a leak from an administration study of the U.S. strategic force posture, including options for improvement ranging from antiballistic missiles to offensive systems and the cost estimates for each. On May 6 the same reporter had an inside story of our deliberations during the EC-121 crisis.

I was in Key Biscayne on May 9, when the early edition of the New York *Times* carried on its front page a disclosure we had been fearing for months. The secret bombing was no longer secret. The headline read: *Raids in Cambodia by U.S. Unprotested.* The story was filed from Washington, and the reporter attributed his information to Nixon administration sources.

The Cambodian bombing policy had worked well. It had saved American lives, the enemy was suffering, and the pressure to negotiate was building. The *Times* leak threatened everything.

Kissinger was enraged, and I was as well. He immediately speculated that the leak must have come from State or Defense. We knew that State Department bureaucrats routinely leaked. But in this particular case, Rogers was the only person at State who had been told about the bombing, and I was certain that he would never leak secret information.

Nor were we naïve about the Pentagon's proclivity for leaking whatever would make the Pentagon look good or advance its positions. But this leak would embarrass Mel Laird and was likely to cause him some uncomfortable moments at coming Capitol Hill hearings.

As I had when several of the earlier leaks had appeared, I suggested that Kissinger take a hard and objective look at his own staff: if there were any leakers in the NSC, better to find out now. Kissinger agreed and during the day he talked by phone with Hoover.

According to Hoover's memo of the conversations, Kissinger expressed our shared feeling that the leaks were more than just damaging; they were potentially dangerous to national security. Kissinger sent Hoover the names of four individuals who had access to the leaked materials. The FBI immediately installed four wiretaps.

I wanted maximum secrecy on this wiretap project and I also instructed that the taps be taken off as soon as possible. I knew that a leak about the wiretaps would be a blow to the morale of the White House staff, and provide a potent issue for the domestic antiwar groups and a propaganda weapon for the North Vietnamese. In fact the average number of warrantless wiretaps per year during my presidency was less than in any administration since Franklin D. Roosevelt's. But I felt that what previous Presidents had done in this regard would matter little if the press and the antiwar activists found out about what Nixon was doing.

Meanwhile, the leaks continued. On May 20 the Washington *Post* carried a leak of my plans to meet with President Thieu. On May 22 the New York *Times* reported sensitive details of an administration debate over whether to test a new missile warhead before the SALT talks began. On June 3 the *Times* published an article based on an NSC memo, issued only a week earlier, outlining our fallback position for the negotiations with the Japanese on Okinawa. Its premature revelation seriously undermined our bargaining position; even before the negotiations began, the Japanese side knew how far we were willing to compromise.

That same day the Washington *Star* published a story about the administration's decision to begin troop withdrawals from Vietnam. This leak undercut Thieu, whom we had assured that we would make the announcement jointly lest the Communists interpret it as a sign that we had begun to abandon South Vietnam.

From 1969 to early 1971, seventeen individuals were wiretapped by the FBI in an effort to find the source of national security leaks. The group included four newsmen and thirteen White House, State, and Defense Department aides. I was only asked to approve the program itself and not each individual tap. Today, nine years later, I cannot reconstruct the particular events that precipitated each of them.

There was an eighteenth national security tap, one on syndicated columnist Joseph Kraft. I remember being disturbed that Kraft, who had very good sources in the White House and NSC staffs and at the State and Defense Departments, was in direct contact with the North Vietnamese. I know that I told Ehrlichman on at least one occasion that Kraft's contacts with the North Vietnamese were all that we were interested in.

I cannot recall specifically, however, what made me decide to act. I authorized a tap on Kraft's home phone in Washington, but the FBI was reluctant to place a tap at that location. Consequently I authorized a plan to install a tap without using the FBI, but we abandoned this effort when the FBI arranged for a tap on Kraft during one of his trips to Paris to see the North Vietnamese.

Unfortunately none of these wiretaps turned up any proof linking anyone in the government to a specific national security leak.

For at least twenty-five years, every President and Attorney General authorized wiretaps to obtain intelligence in both foreign and domestic security matters. It was not until 1972—over a year after the last of our national security taps had been removed—that the Supreme Court ruled that national security taps on American citizens must be authorized by a court-ordered warrant if the subject had no "significant connection with a foreign power, its agents or agencies."

In the early years of my administration I saw the government's ability to function effectively in international affairs being undermined by leaks which I felt were a violation of law as well as of the code of honorable behavior. Particularly where leaks involving Vietnam were concerned, as long as Americans were fighting and dying there I had no patience with the argument that the people who leaked information did so because they opposed the war on moral grounds. So even though I disliked wiretapping and felt that it was at best a technique of only limited usefulness, it seemed to be our only chance to find out who was behind the leaks, and to stop them.

When our efforts to discover the source of the leaks failed, we began conducting our foreign policy planning in smaller groups. It is an ironic consequence of leaking that instead of producing more open government, it invariably forces the government to operate in more confined and secret ways. So it was that the widely reported impression of a Nixon administration "paranoia" about secrecy developed. Secrecy unquestionably exacts a high price in the form of a less free and creative interchange of ideas within the government. But I can say unequivocally that without secrecy there would have been no opening to China, no SALT agreement with the Soviet Union, and no peace agreement ending the Vietnam war.

VIETNAM: PUBLIC OFFERS AND SECRET OVERTURES

During the first months of the administration, despite the Communist offensive in February and despite the stalemate at the Paris talks, I remained convinced that the combined effect of the military pressure from the secret bombing and the public pressure from my repeated invitations to negotiate would force the Communists to respond. In March I confidently told the Cabinet that I expected the war to be over in a year. We had taken the initiative in Paris and proposed the restoration of the DMZ as a boundary between North and South Vietnam and advanced the possibility of a simultaneous withdrawal of American and North Vietnamese troops from the South. For his part, President Thieu offered to begin talks with the North Vietnamese on the question of a political settlement, and to permit free elections.

But the North Vietnamese yielded nothing. They insisted that political and military issues were inseparable, that American troops must be withdrawn unilaterally, and that Thieu must be deposed as a precondition to serious talks.

In mid-April we increased the diplomatic pressure. Kissinger showed Dobrynin a page of three points that I had initialed. In diplomatic usage, this was a sign that I considered them to be extremely important. Their message was unmistakable:

1. The President wishes to reiterate his conviction that a just peace is achievable.

2. The President is willing to explore avenues other than the existing negotiating framework. For example, it might be desirable for American and North Vietnamese negotiators to meet separately from the Paris framework to discuss general principles of a settlement. If the special US and DRV negotiators can achieve an agreement in principle, the final technical negotiations can shift back to Paris.

3. The USG is convinced that all parties are at a crossroads and that extraordinary measures are called for to reverse the tide of war.

Kissinger told Dobrynin that U.S.-Soviet relations were involved because, while we might talk about progress in other areas, a settlement in Vietnam was the key to everything.

Dobrynin said that we had to understand the limitations of Soviet influence on Hanoi, and he added that the Soviet Union would never threaten to cut off supplies to their allies in North Vietnam. He promised, however, that our proposals would be forwarded to Hanoi within twenty-four hours.

After weeks passed with no response, we decided to take the initiative once again. In a televised speech on May 14 I offered our first comprehensive peace plan for Vietnam. I proposed that the major part of all foreign troops—both U.S. and North Vietnamese—withdraw from South Vietnam within one year after an agreement had been signed. An international body would monitor the withdrawals and supervise free elections in South Vietnam. I warned the enemy not to confuse our flexibility with weakness. I said, "Reports from Hanoi indicate that the enemy has given up hope for a military victory in South Vietnam, but is counting on a collapse of will in the United States. There could be no greater error in judgment."

There was no serious response from the North Vietnamese, either in Hanoi or Paris, to my May 14 proposals. I had never thought that peace in Vietnam would come easily; for the first time I had to consider the possibility that it might not come at all. Nonetheless, I decided to continue on the course we had planned, in the hope that the enemy would decide to take up our proposals and join us in the search for a settlement.

Early in the administration we had decided that withdrawing a number of American combat troops from Vietnam would demonstrate to Hanoi that we were serious in seeking a diplomatic settlement; it might also calm domestic public opinion by graphically demonstrating that we were beginning to wind down the war.

Mel Laird had long felt that the United States could "Vietnamize" the war—that we could train, equip, and inspire the South Vietnamese to fill the gaps left by departing American forces. In March Laird returned from a visit to South Vietnam with an optimistic report about the potential of the South Vietnamese to be trained to defend themselves. It was largely on the basis of Laird's enthusiastic advocacy that we undertook the policy of Vietnamization.

This decision was another turning point in my administration's Vietnam strategy.

President Thieu was among those who objected to the proposed plan for American withdrawals from South Vietnam. I privately assured him through Ambassador Bunker that our support for him was steadfast. In order to dramatize this pledge, I proposed that we meet on Midway Island in the Pacific. Thieu readily accepted, and we met there on June 8.

After our meeting we both made brief statements to reporters. I announced that, as a consequence of Thieu's recommendation and the assessment of our own commander in the field, I had decided to order the immediate redeployment from Vietnam of approximately 25,000 men. This involved some diplomatic exaggeration, because both Thieu and Abrams had privately raised objections to the withdrawals.

I said that in the months ahead I would consider further troop withdrawals, based on three criteria: the progress in training and equipping the South Vietnamese armed forces; the progress of the Paris talks; and the level of enemy activity.

Although Thieu was somewhat mollified by the Midway meeting, he was still deeply troubled. He knew that the first American withdrawals would begin an irreversible process, the conclusion of which would be the departure of all Americans from Vietnam.

To make sure the message of Midway was not lost on Hanoi, I spelled it out when we arrived back at the White House. I told the people gathered on the South Lawn to welcome us that the combination of my May 14 peace plan and the Midway troop withdrawal left the door to peace wide open. "And now we invite the leaders of North Vietnam to walk with us through that door," I said.

At the end of June it looked as if we might be getting a response of sorts from Hanoi. There seemed to be a lull in the fighting, and our intelligence indicated that some North Vietnamese units were being withdrawn from South Vietnam. Le Duc Tho, the Politburo member who was the Special Adviser to the North Vietnamese delegation at the Paris talks, suddenly returned to Hanoi, and there was speculation that he had been called back to receive new negotiating instructions.

This military lull continued through early July. Although the evidence was still entirely circumstantial, and although the dangers of appearing overeager were as great as ever, I decided to try once again to cut through whatever genuine doubts or misunderstandings might still be holding Hanoi back. I decided to "go for broke" in the sense that I would attempt to end the war one way or the other—either by negotiated agreement or by an increased use of force.

One reason for making this decision at this time was my feeling that unless I could build some momentum behind our peace efforts over the next several weeks, they might be doomed to failure by the calendar. Once the summer was over and Congress and the colleges returned from vacation in September, a massive new antiwar tide would sweep the country during the fall and winter. Then, with the approaching dry season in Vietnam, there was almost sure to be a renewed Communist offensive during the Tet holiday period in February. By early spring the pressures of the November 1970 elections would make congressional demands for more troop withdrawals impossible to stop and difficult to ignore.

After half a year of sending peaceful signals to the Communists, I was ready to use whatever military pressure was necessary to prevent them from taking over South Vietnam by force. During several long sessions, Kissinger and I developed an elaborate orchestration of diplomatic, military, and publicity pressures we would bring to bear on Hanoi.

I decided to set November 1, 1969—the first anniversary of Johnson's bombing halt—as the deadline for what would in effect be an ultimatum to North Vietnam.

Since November 1 was only three and a half months away, there was no time to waste. On July 15 I wrote a personal letter to Ho Chi Minh. Once again Jean Sainteny acted as our courier. I met with him at the White House so that he would be able to talk at firsthand about my strong desire for peace. But I also told him to say that, unless some serious breakthrough had been achieved by the November 1 deadline, I would regretfully find myself obliged to have recourse "to measures of great consequence and force."

My letter to Ho Chi Minh was sent to Sainteny by secret courier and on July 16 he delivered it to Xuan Thuy, head of the regular North Vietnamese delegation in Paris, for transmittal to Hanoi. In it I tried to convey both the sincerity and the urgency of our desire for a settlement:

> I realize that it is difficult to communicate meaningfully across the gulf of four years of war. But precisely because of this gulf, I wanted to take this opportunity to reaffirm in all solemnity my desire to work for a just peace. . . .
> As I have said repeatedly, there is nothing to be gained by waiting. . . .
> You will find us forthcoming and open-minded in a common effort to bring the blessings of peace to the brave people of Vietnam. Let history record that at this critical juncture, both sides turned their face toward peace rather than toward conflict and war.

With this letter I felt that I had gone as far as I could until the North Vietnamese indicated that they too were interested in an agreement. Now we would have to wait to see how Ho Chi Minh responded. As far as I was concerned, my letter put the choice between war and peace in his hands.

In a few days word was flashed to us that the North Vietnamese were proposing a secret meeting between Kissinger and Xuan Thuy.

On July 23, I flew to the South Pacific for the splashdown of Apollo XI. This was to be the first leg of an around-the-world trip that included stops in Guam, the Philippines, Indonesia, Thailand, South Vietnam, India, Pakistan, Romania, and Britain. In honor of Apollo's accomplishment, we gave the trip the codename Moonglow.

The trip provided the perfect camouflage for Kissinger's first secret meeting with the North Vietnamese. It was arranged that Kissinger would go to Paris, ostensibly to brief French officials on the results of my meetings. While there he would meet secretly with Thuy.

The first stop after the Apollo splashdown was on the

island of Guam. Shortly after we arrived I conducted an informal press conference with the reporters covering the trip. It was there that I enunciated what at first was called the Guam Doctrine and has since become known as the Nixon Doctrine.

I stated that the United States is a Pacific power and should remain so. But I felt that once the Vietnam war was settled, we would need a new Asian policy to ensure that there were no more Vietnams in the future. I began with the proposition that we would keep all our existing treaty commitments, but that we would not make any more commitments unless they were required by our own vital interests.

In the past our policy had been to furnish the arms, men, and matériel to help other nations defend themselves against aggression. That was what we had done in Korea, and that was how we had started out in Vietnam. But from now on, I said, we would furnish only the matériel and the military and economic assistance to those nations willing to accept the responsibility of supplying the manpower to defend themselves. I made only one exception: in case a major nuclear power engaged in aggression against one of our allies or friends, I said that we would respond with nuclear weapons.

The Nixon Doctrine announced on Guam was misinterpreted by some as signaling a new policy that would lead to total American withdrawal from Asia and from other parts of the world as well. In one of our regular breakfast meetings after I returned from the trip Senate Majority Leader Mike Mansfield articulated this misunderstanding. I emphasized to him, as I had to our friends in the Asian countries, that the Nixon Doctrine was not a formula for getting America *out* of Asia, but one that provided the only sound basis for America's staying *in* and continuing to play a responsible role in helping the non-Communist nations and neutrals as well as our Asian allies to defend their independence.

When we landed in Bucharest, Romania, on August 2, I became the first American President to make a state visit to a Communist satellite country.

President Nicolae Ceauşescu is a strong, independent leader who had cultivated good relations with the Chinese in spite of the fact that he had to walk a very fine line lest the Soviets decide to intervene in Romania as they had in Hungary in 1956 and in Czechoslovakia in 1968. So far he had walked that line with consummate skill.

I had been briefed to expect a courteous reception, but the size and spontaneous enthusiasm of the crowds exceeded all our expectations. At one point Ceauşescu and I were literally swept up by the dancing in the streets.

Romania had good diplomatic relations with the North Vietnamese, and I knew that anything I said would be repeated to them, so I used one of my meetings with Ceauşescu to reinforce my message to Hanoi. I said, "We cannot indefinitely continue to have two hundred deaths a week in Vietnam and no progress in Paris. On November 1 this year—one year after the halt of the bombing, and after the withdrawal of some of our troops and several reasonable offers for peaceful negotiations—if there is no progress, we must re-evaluate our policy."

I told him that in order to get peace we might have to open another channel of communications between the two sides. Ceauşescu said he would do everything he could to be helpful in furthering negotiations.

The story of Kissinger's secret meetings with the North Vietnamese, which began on August 4, 1969, and extended over the next three years, is an extraordinary one, full of classic cloak-and-dagger episodes, with Kissinger riding slouched down in the back seats of speeding Citroëns, eluding inquisitive reporters, and putting curious embassy officials off the scent.

The first conversation took place in Jean Sainteny's Paris apartment in the fashionable Rue de Rivoli, where Kissinger met with Xuan Thuy and Mai Van Bo.

Kissinger opened by saying that he wanted to convey a message from me personally. He reminded them that November 1 would be the first anniversary of the bombing halt. During this time the United States had made what we considered significant moves: we had ended troop reinforcements, we had observed a partial bombing halt and then a total bombing halt, and we had already withdrawn 25,000 combat troops and offered to accept the result of free elections. As far as we could see, there had been no significant response. Now, in order to expedite negotiations, I was ready to open another channel of contact with them. "But at the same time," Kissinger added, "I have been asked to tell you in all solemnity, that if by November 1 no major progress has been made toward a solution, we will be compelled—with great reluctance—to take measures of the greatest consequences." He pointed out that in their propaganda and in the Paris discussions, the North Vietnamese were attempting to make this "Mr. Nixon's war." "We do not believe that this is in your interest," he said, "because if it is Mr. Nixon's war, then he cannot afford not to win it."

Xuan Thuy replied with a relatively restrained restatement of Hanoi's most extreme position: he called for the complete withdrawal of all American forces and observance of the National Liberation Front's ten points, which in effect provided for total Communist domination over South Vietnam. He insisted on maintaining the patent fiction that there were no North Vietnamese troops in South Vietnam. He also continued to demand that we overthrow President Thieu before any agreement could be reached.

Finally Kissinger decided that he had said all he could to representatives who were not actually empowered to negotiate. Exercising his tremendous skill, he brought the conversation around to a mellower tone, saying, "We would prefer to have the Vietnamese as friends rather than as enemies. I believe that we must make an effort to find a solution between now and November 1."

The three men shook hands and departed separately to avoid attracting any attention.

Having put the Nixon Doctrine on record and having begun to put pressure on Hanoi, I decided it was time to assume the offensive in the public forum of the Paris peace talks. The diplomats and reporters who had become accustomed to Cabot Lodge's usually complacent demeanor were surprised when he rose from his chair on August 7, looked directly at the Communist delegates, and said, "We have done all that we can do by ourselves to bring a negotiated peace in Vietnam. Now it is time for you to respond." The press called it his toughest talk since taking over in January as chief U.S. negotiator.

Ho Chi Minh's reply to my July letter arrived dated August 25. In it, he referred to "the war of aggression of the United States against our people" and said that he was "deeply touched at the rising toll of death of young Americans who have fallen in Vietnam by reason of the policy of American governing circles."

In response to my statement that we would be willing to discuss any proposal or program that might lead to a negotiated settlement, he said that the ten-point program of the NLF had "earned the sympathy and support of the peoples of the world." He concluded:

> In your letter you have expressed the desire to act for a just peace. For this the United States must cease the war of aggression and withdraw their troops from South Vietnam, respect the right of the population of the South and of the Vietnamese nation to dispose of themselves, without foreign influence.

Considering the tone of my letter to him, and even taking into account the stridency of communist jargon, there was no doubt that Ho's reply was a cold rebuff.

After receiving this unpromising reply, I knew that I had to prepare myself for the tremendous criticism and pressure that would come with stepping up the war.

On September 3, Ho Chi Minh died. There were rumors of a struggle over the succession for several days before Premier Pham Van Dong emerged as the Hanoi Politburo's leading figure. Veteran Vietnam-watchers were at a loss to predict what effect this would have on the war.

In the middle of September I announced the withdrawal of another 35,000 troops by December 15. In my statement I pointed out that the withdrawal of 60,000 troops was a significant step and that "the time for meaningful negotiations has therefore arrived." This announcement was intended to let the new leaders of North Vietnam know that I was not assuming that they were bound by Ho's reply to my letter.

Two days later, in a speech at the opening of the UN General Assembly, I said that "the time has come for peace.

And in the name of peace, I urge all of you here—representing 126 nations—to use your best diplomatic efforts to persuade Hanoi to move seriously into the negotiations which could end this war."

On September 20 Kissinger received a letter from Sainteny, who had been in Hanoi for Ho Chi Minh's funeral and, while he was there, had had a long conversation with Pham Van Dong. The new Premier was notably unvituperative in his references to the United States. When Sainteny stressed that he knew how eager I was for peace from his own conversation with me, Dong said, "I see that they have convinced you. But we, we are not able to take them at their words: only acts will convince us."

Since this conversation had taken place before my mid-September troop withdrawal, I felt that I had supplied the deed to prove our words. Once again the choice lay with Hanoi.

In the weeks remaining before November 1, I wanted to orchestrate the maximum possible pressure on Hanoi. I was confident that we could bring sufficient pressure to bear on the diplomatic front. But the only chance for my ultimatum to succeed was to convince the Communists that I could depend on solid support at home if they decided to call my bluff. However, the chances I would actually have that support were becoming increasingly slim.

There had been serious riots and disorders on more than a score of college campuses during the winter and spring of 1969, the causes of which covered a wide spectrum of frustrations of which Vietnam was by no means the predominant one. Students at Berkeley demanded an autonomous College for Ethnic Studies. Black students seized the administration building at Duke and demanded a nongraded black education program and money for a black student union. One hundred black students, armed with rifles and shotguns, held the student union at Cornell University and demanded that disciplinary reprimands to three black students be revoked. The faculty first refused and then capitulated on the issue. The University of Pennsylvania administration decided to avoid a confrontation with student war protesters by taking down American flags and putting them in storage.

I was disgusted—and I said so—by the capitulation of professors and administrators to students using force. I praised those who held firm—like San Francisco State College's Dr. S. I. Hayakawa, who ripped out the wires of a public address system set up by radicals in violation of campus regulations, and Rev. Theodore Hesburgh of Notre Dame, who announced he would give protesters who substituted "force for rational persuasion" fifteen minutes, and then suspend them from the university; five minutes after that, if they continued the disturbance, they would be expelled.

During the first months of my presidency Vietnam was not the primary issue in campus demonstrations largely because Johnson's bombing halt had suspended the most actively controversial aspect of the war, and my announced plans to establish an all-volunteer Army and our reform of the draft, which made it less threateningly disruptive, also helped in this regard.

I knew that this situation was bound to change. As the fall term began on college campuses, and as Congress returned from its summer recess, newspapers and television began reflecting signs of a new level of intensity in the antiwar movement. There was talk of holding a "Moratorium," a nationwide day of protest, on October 15, right in the period most crucial to the success of my November 1 ultimatum.

In a press conference on September 26, in answer to a question about the Moratorium and other public protests against the war, I said, "Now, I understand that there has been and continues to be opposition to the war in Vietnam on the campuses, and also in the nation. As far as this kind of activity is concerned, we expect it. However, under no circumstances will I be affected whatever by it."

I was fully aware of the furore that this statement would cause. But having initiated a policy of pressure on North Vietnam that now involved not only our government but foreign governments as well, I felt that I had no choice but to carry it through. Faced with the prospect of demonstrations at home that I could not prevent, my only alternative was to try to make it clear to the enemy that the protests would have no effect on my decisions. Otherwise my ultimatum would appear empty.

We continued to keep up the diplomatic pressure on the Soviets. On September 27, Kissinger told Dobrynin that the apparent failure of all our requests for Soviet help toward ending the war made it very difficult for us to carry on more than basic diplomatic relations between our two countries.

I telephoned Kissinger in the middle of this discussion, and we talked for a few minutes. When they resumed their conversation, Kissinger said, "The President just told me in that call that as far as Vietnam is concerned, the train has just left the station and is now headed down the track."

Dobrynin tried to ease the atmosphere with a diplomatic turn of phrase. "I hope it's an airplane rather than a train," he said, "because an airplane can still change its course in flight."

Kissinger replied, "The President chooses his words very carefully, and I am sure he meant what he said. He said, 'train.'"

As another part of our efforts to apply pressure on Hanoi, I ordered a survey of non-Communist nations shipping to North Vietnam. We found that Cyprus, Malta, Singapore, and Somalia were among the countries with registered ships going to Hanoi. When the first two governments refused to cooperate with us, I ordered their foreign aid programs cut off. Singapore and Somalia agreed to cut down the shipping under their flags.

I met with the Republican congressional leadership and told them that the next sixty days would be of the utmost importance for the ending of the war. "We are going to need unity more than we have ever needed it before," I said. "I can't tell you everything that will be going on, because if there is to be any chance of success, it will have to be done in secret. All I can tell you is this: I am doing my damnedest to end the war. I am approaching the whole question with only two operating principles: I won't make it hard for the North Vietnamese if they genuinely want a settlement; but I will not be the first President of the United States to lose a war."

Later the same day I moved the pressure on Hanoi up a notch when I met with nine Republican senators and planted a story that I knew would leak. I did not have to wait long. In eight days Rowland Evans and Robert Novak ran a column saying that I was considering blockading Haiphong and invading North Vietnam. I wanted this rumor to attract some attention in Hanoi. Although I never knew for sure that it did, I do know that it attracted the attention of Mel Laird. He and Bill Rogers immediately urged that before taking any drastic action I consider the very low American casualty rates over the last few months and the improved performance of the South Vietnamese as a result of our stepped-up Vietnamization program.

VIETNAM MORATORIUM

The antiwar forces on the campuses, in Congress, and in the media had coalesced around the Vietnam Moratorium scheduled for October 15 in Washington. The plan was to hold similar demonstrations in different cities on the fifteenth of each month until the war was over.

By the first week of October, the pent-up fury reached full force. There were antiwar speeches, teach-ins, and rallies. The controversy over my Supreme Court nomination of Judge Clement Haynsworth, the debate over welfare reform, the defeat of a Republican incumbent by an antiwar Democrat in a special election in Massachusetts, the vocal impatience of some civil rights leaders with the pace of our integration policy—all prominently in the news—created the impression of an administration reeling under siege. These factors were lumped together in the media and labeled a crisis of leadership. The headline in *Newsweek* was *Mr. Nixon in Trouble,* and *Time* devoted its National Affairs section to describing *Nixon's Worst Week*: "It did not take an alarmist of Chicken Little proportions to discern that bits of sky were falling on the Nixon administration."

Pronouncements of no-confidence and predictions of political paralysis were widespread. On October 7 David Broder wrote in the Washington *Post* that "it is becoming more obvious with every passing day that the men and the movement that broke Lyndon Johnson's authority in 1968 are out to break Richard Nixon in 1969. The likelihood is great that they will succeed again." A few days later Dean Acheson warned against "the attempt being made from so many sources to destroy Nixon." In an exclusive interview in the New York *Times* he said, "I think we're going to have a major constitutional crisis if we make a habit of destroying Presidents."

My deliberate refusal to acknowledge these dire predictions itself became an element of the supposed crisis. *Time* reported, "Nixon seemed unconcerned and aloof from it all," and the magazine's Washington bureau chief, Hugh Sidey, found my attitude "perhaps as alarming as the events themselves in the most trying time Nixon has yet had in office."

My real concern was that these highly publicized efforts aimed at forcing me to end the war were seriously undermining my behind-the-scenes attempts to do just that. Weeks later, in a meeting with Cabot Lodge, the North Vietnamese ambassador recited statements made by leading Senate doves. The New York *Times* reported that Le Duc Tho, "with a wide grin," told an American visitor about Senator Fulbright's accusation that I was trying to prolong the war with Vietnamization. Although publicly I continued to ignore the raging antiwar controversy, I had to face the fact that it had probably destroyed the credibility of my ultimatum to Hanoi.

On October 13 Ron Ziegler announced that I would make a major address to the nation concerning Vietnam on Monday, November 3.

This announcement was generally interpreted as either an attempt to undercut the October 15 Moratorium, then only two days away, or as a sign that the Moratorium had already been successful in forcing me to reconsider my Vietnam policy. In fact, I hoped that the announcement of a major speech for two days after the November 1 deadline would give Hanoi second thoughts about fishing in our troubled domestic waters.

On October 14, I knew for sure that my ultimatum had failed when Kissinger informed me that Radio Hanoi had just broadcast a letter from Premier Pham Van Dong to the American people. In it Dong declared:

> This fall large sectors of the U.S. people, encouraged and supported by many peace- and justice-loving American personages, are launching a broad and powerful offensive throughout the United States to demand that the Nixon administration put an end to the Vietnam aggressive war and immediately bring all American troops home. . . .
>
> We are firmly confident that with the solidarity and bravery of the peoples of our two countries and with the approval and support of peace-loving people in the world, the struggle of the Vietnamese people and U.S. progressive people against U.S. aggression will certainly be crowned with total victory.
>
> May your fall offensive succeed splendidly.

To indicate the seriousness with which I viewed this blatant intervention in our domestic affairs, I asked Agnew to hold a press conference at the White House. He called Dong's letter an "incredible message" and read excerpts of it for the cameras. He said, "The leaders and sponsors of tomorrow's Moratorium, public officials, and others leading these demonstrations should openly repudiate the support of the totalitarian government which has on its hands the blood of 40,000 Americans."

I considered the question period that followed Agnew's remarks a disgraceful performance on the part of the White House press corps. As if it were our fault that Dong had written this letter, one reporter asked, "Mr. Vice President, let us take the bull by the horns. Isn't seizing upon this letter a last-minute attempt to dampen down the Moratorium by the administration?"

The media generally either played down the Dong letter or indicated that the administration had unreasonably fastened upon it as an excuse for the repression of legitimate dissent.

I had to decide what to do about the ultimatum. I knew that unless I had some indisputably good reason for not carrying out my threat of using increased force when the ultimatum expired on November 1, the Communists would become contemptuous of us and even more difficult to deal with. I knew, however, that after all the protests and the Moratorium, American public opinion would be seriously divided by any military escalation of the war.

A quarter of a million people came to Washington for the October 15 Moratorium. Despite widespread rumors that some of the more radical left-wing organizations would provoke violent confrontations with police, the demonstrations were generally peaceful.

Opinion within the administration was divided over how to respond. Kissinger urged that I do nothing at all and let the protest run its course, lest I upset our foreign policy strategy. John Ehrlichman, however, was upset by our apparent indifference to the sincere fervor of many of the protesters and urged that I declare a National Day of Prayer on October 15 as a show of tacit support for the underlying goal of peace.

The Washington *Post* praised the protesters and said that the Moratorium was "a deeply meaningful statement" of the anguish they felt about the war. Elsewhere, however, reservations were expressed. The Washington *Star,* for example, said, "What counts is whether the demonstration, regardless of intention, does in fact give encouragement to Hanoi and thereby presumably prolongs the war." As if in answer to that point, the Vietcong Radio said that the Communists had gained "strong encouragement" from the Moratorium.

The Vietnam Moratorium raised, for the first but by no means the last time in my administration, a basic and important question about the nature of leadership in a democracy: should the President or Congress or any responsible elected official let public demonstrations influence his decisions?

I had strong opinions about this question, and I decided to address it head on. I asked that one letter be selected from all those we had received criticizing my press conference statement that I would not be affected by the protests and that a reply be prepared to it.

The letter the staff chose was from a student at Georgetown University. In it, he stated, "It has been my impression that it is not unwise for the President of the United States to take note of the will of the people; after all, these people elected you, you are their President, and your office bears certain obligations. Might I respectfully suggest that the President reconsider his pre-judgment."

I replied, "If a President—any President—allowed his course to be set by those who demonstrate, he would betray the trust of all the rest. Whatever the issue, to allow government policy to be made in the streets would destroy the democratic process. It would give the decision, not to the majority, and not to those with the strongest arguments, but to those with the loudest voices. . . . It would allow every group to test its strength not at the ballot box but through confrontation in the streets."

On the night of October 15 I thought about the irony of this protest for peace. It had, I believed, destroyed whatever small possibility may still have existed of ending the war in 1969. But there was nothing I could do about that now. I would have to adjust my plans accordingly and carry on as best I could. At the top of the page of preliminary notes I was making for my November 3 speech, I wrote: "Don't get rattled—don't waver—don't react."

THE SILENT MAJORITY

After the Moratorium attention immediately began to focus on my speech. Most doves in the media and Congress assumed that I had been so impressed—or so frightened—by the Moratorium that I had decided to announce major new troop withdrawals in order to blunt the impact of the next Moratorium scheduled for November 15. An AP wire story on October 20 stated that I might offer a cease-fire in the speech, and some papers reported this in front-page headlines. Flora Lewis, writing in the Boston *Globe,* stated categorically that I would announce the withdrawal of 300,000 men during 1970 and that I had ordered the Pentagon to work out the necessary schedules. Dan Rather, on a special CBS news report on the Moratorium, claimed that I was considering stepped-up troop withdrawals, fewer B-52 raids, a reduction in fighting, and perhaps even a cease-fire before the end of the year. In the Senate, Hugh Scott called for a unilateral cease-fire. Since he was

Minority Leader, his statement was widely interpreted as a White House trial balloon. Hubert Humphrey predicted that I would announce a major program for the "systematical and accelerated withdrawal of U.S. forces" from Vietnam.

How far off the mark these predictions and expectations were can be seen in notes I made for the November 3 speech in the early morning hours of October 22:

> They can't defeat us militarily in Vietnam.
> They can't break South Vietnam.
> Include a paragraph on *why* we are there.
> They cannot break us.

As the November 1 deadline approached, three factors strongly influenced my thinking about the ultimatum. The first was that American casualty figures in Vietnam had been reaching new lows. I knew that these reductions might be a ploy on the part of the Communists to make escalating the fighting that much more difficult for me.

The second factor was the possibility that the death of Ho Chi Minh might have created new opportunities for reaching a settlement that deserved a chance to develop.

The third factor was a conversation I had on October 17 with Sir Robert Thompson, the British expert on guerrilla warfare.

"What do you think of the 'option to the right'?" I asked. "What would you think if we decided to escalate?"

Thompson was clearly not in favor of escalation because it would risk a major American and worldwide furore and still not address the central problem of whether the South Vietnamese were sufficiently confident and prepared to defend themselves against a renewed Communist offensive at some time in the future. His estimate was that, continuing the current U.S. policy and assuming South Vietnamese confidence that we would not pull out, victory could be won within two years. He thought that our only chance for a negotiated settlement in the meantime would be if it were clear to Hanoi that we were there for the duration. I asked if he would go to Vietnam and make a personal study of the situation there for me and report as soon as possible.

When I asked Thompson whether he thought it was important for us to see it through in Vietnam, he said, "Absolutely. In my opinion the future of Western civilization is at stake in the way you handle yourselves in Vietnam."

In view of these three factors, and recognizing that the Moratorium had undercut the credibility of the ultimatum, I began to think more in terms of stepping up Vietnamization while continuing the fighting at its present level rather than of trying to increase it. In many respects Vietnamization would be far more damaging to the Communists than an escalation that, as Thompson had pointed out, would not solve the basic problem of South Vietnamese preparedness, and that would stir up serious domestic problems in America.

It was important that the Communists not mistake as weakness the lack of dramatic action on my part in carrying out the ultimatum. We would be able to demonstrate our continuing resolve to the North Vietnamese on the battlefield, but I thought that the Soviets would need a special reminder. Therefore when Ambassador Dobrynin came to the White House for a private meeting on the afternoon of October 20, I decided to use the encounter to make our position absolutely clear to the Soviet leadership.

Kissinger accompanied Dobrynin to the Oval Office, and after greetings were exchanged the ambassador said that he had received an aide-mémoire from his government, with instructions to read it to me.

"Go ahead, Mr. Ambassador," I said.

"I am instructed to frankly inform the President that Moscow is not satisfied with the present state of relations between the U.S.S.R. and the U.S.," he began. "Moscow feels that the President should be frankly told that the method of solving the Vietnam question through the use of military force is not only without perspective, but also extremely dangerous. . . . If someone in the United States is tempted to make profit from Soviet-Chinese relations at the Soviet Union's expense, and there are some signs of that, then we would like to frankly warn in advance that such line of conduct, if pursued, can lead to a very grave miscalculation and is in no way consistent with the goal of better relations between the U.S. and the U.S.S.R."

Dobrynin seemed a little uncomfortable with my silence when he had finished reading from the paper. After a moment I leaned back in my chair and opened the center drawer of my desk. I took out a yellow pad and slid it across toward him.

"You'd better take some notes," I said.

He took the pad and put it on his lap.

"You have been candid, Mr. Ambassador, and I will be equally so. I, too, am disappointed in U.S.-Soviet relations. As of today, I have been in this office for nine months. The babies should have been born by now. Instead, there have been several miscarriages."

Taking some of the major issues—the Middle East, trade, European security, Berlin—I analyzed point by point the problems with each. Most arose from Soviet intransigence or jockeying for position.

Turning to China, I said, "Anything we have done or are doing with respect to China is in no sense designed to embarrass the Soviet Union. On the contrary, China and the United States cannot tolerate having a situation develop in which we are enemies, any more than we want to be permanent enemies of the Soviet Union. Therefore, we expect to make moves in trade and exchanges of persons and eventually in diplomacy. I want to repeat that this is not directed against the Soviet Union. Within ten years, China will be a nuclear power, capable of terrorizing many other countries. The time is running out when the Soviet Union and the United States can build a different kind of world."

Having put in the hook this far, I pulled it hard. "The only beneficiary of U.S.-Soviet disagreement over Vietnam is China," I said, "and therefore this is the last opportunity to settle these disputes."

Before Dobrynin could interrupt, I moved on to Vietnam. "Prior to the bombing halt, which, as you are aware, will be one year old on November 1, Ambassador Bohlen and Ambassador Thompson and Ambassador Harriman pointed out to President Johnson that the Soviet Union could not do anything as long as we were bombing a fellow socialist country. They said that the Soviet Union would be very active with its help if we stopped. The bombing halt was then agreed to, but the Soviet Union has done nothing to help."

At this Dobrynin raised his hand as if to be called on, but I waved it down. "Of course, we now have an oblong table at the talks in Paris, and I know the Soviet Union contributed something to that, but we do not consider that a great achievement. All the conciliatory moves for the past year have been made by us."

I said that I had concluded that perhaps the Soviet Union did not want to end the war in Vietnam. "You may think that you can break me," I said. "You may believe that the American domestic situation is unmanageable. Or you may think that the war in Vietnam costs the Soviet Union only a small amount of money while it costs us a great many lives. I do not propose to argue with this kind of assessment. On the other hand, Mr. Ambassador, I want you to understand that the Soviet Union is going to be stuck with me for the next three years and three months, and during all that time I will keep in mind what is being done right now, today. If the Soviet Union will not help us get peace, then we will have to pursue our own methods for bringing the war to an end. We cannot allow a talk-fight strategy to continue without taking action.

"Let us be frank, Mr. Ambassador," I continued. "All you have done is repeat the same tired old slogans that the North Vietnamese used six months ago. You know very well they can lead nowhere. It is time to get discussions started, because, I can assure you, the humiliation of a defeat is absolutely unacceptable to my country. I recognize that the Soviet leaders are tough and courageous. But so are we."

I stopped only a moment and then went on. "I hope that you will not mind this serious talk," I said. "If the Soviet Union found it possible to do something in Vietnam, and the Vietnam war ended, then we might do something dramatic to improve our relations, indeed, something more dramatic than could now be imagined. But until then, I have to say that real progress will be very difficult."

Dobrynin waited to see if I would go on. This time I did not.

"Does this mean that there can be no progress?" he asked.

"Progress is possible," I replied, "but it would have to be confined essentially to what is attainable in diplomatic channels. The war can drag on, in which case we will find our own way to bring it to an end. There is no sense in just repeating the proposals of the last six months."

I wanted no reply to this, so I brought the meeting to a close by saying, "The whole world wants us to get together. I, too, want nothing so much as to have my administration remembered as a watershed in American and Soviet relations. But let me repeat that we will not hold still for being diddled to death in Vietnam."

With that I rose, shook his hand, and escorted him to the door.

Kissinger came back in after he had seen Dobrynin to his car. "I wager that no one has ever talked to him that way in his entire career!" he said. "It was extraordinary! No President has ever laid it on the line to them like that."

"We shouldn't have any illusions that it will do any good or make any difference," I said, "but it is good to let them know that we're not as big fools as the requirements of diplomacy may sometimes make us seem."

I received much conflicting advice concerning what I should say on November 3. Rogers and Laird urged me to concentrate on the hopes for peace, Rogers emphasizing the Paris talks and Laird stressing the prospects of Vietnamization. The majority of the White House staff, the Cabinet members, and the congressional leaders I consulted advocated that I use the speech to establish beyond any doubt my sincere desire for peace.

Kissinger was advocating a very hard line. He felt that if we backed off, the Communists would become totally convinced that they could control our foreign policy through public opinion. And Dean Acheson sent word that any announcement of withdrawal schedules would put us at a disadvantage in negotiations.

Speculation about the speech reached fever pitch as the date approached. I welcomed this because I knew that the more it was talked about, the bigger the audience would be.

I kept my own counsel, and very few people knew the way my thinking was really going or the surprise I was planning for the antiwar agitators who thought that their street marches could force me to make foreign policy the way they wanted.

I went to Camp David for a long weekend on October

24 and worked twelve to fourteen hours a day writing and rewriting different sections of the speech. Haldeman cleared most of my schedule during the following week so that I could continue the work uninterrupted.

By Friday the speech had gone through twelve drafts, and I was ready to take it to Camp David for a final review. Senate Majority Leader Mike Mansfield had written down his thoughts in a memorandum, and he asked that I read it before I made any final decisions about what I would say.

I read Mansfield's memorandum later that night. He began by stating: "The continuance of the war in Vietnam, in my judgment, endangers the future of this nation." He said that it was more than just the loss of lives or the waste of money and resources that concerned him. "Most serious," he wrote, "are the deep divisions within our society to which this conflict of dubious origin and purpose is contributing."

He said that he would give articulate public support to "any or all of the following decisions if in your responsibility you decide that they are necessary, as well they may be, to a rapid termination of the war in Vietnam." He then listed actions that amounted to a unilateral cease-fire and withdrawal. "I know that a settlement arrived at in this fashion is not pleasant to contemplate," he wrote, "especially in view of the dug-in diplomatic and military positions which, unfortunately, were assumed over the past few years." The memo was signed, "With the greatest respect."

I realized that with this memorandum Mansfield was offering what would be the last chance for me to end "Johnson's and Kennedy's war." I interpreted his references to it as a "conflict of dubious origin" and to the military positions "unfortunately" assumed over the past few years as signals that he would even allow me to claim that I was making the best possible end of a bad war my Democratic predecessors had begun. I knew that the opponents of the war would irrevocably become my opponents if my speech took a hard line. But I could not escape the fact that I felt it would be wrong to end the Vietnam war on any terms I believed to be less than honorable.

I worked through the night. About 4 A.M. I wrote a paragraph calling for the support of "the great silent majority of Americans." I went to bed, but after two hours of restless sleep I was wide awake, so I got up and began work again. By 8 A.M. the speech was finished. I called Haldeman, and when he answered, I said, "The baby's just been born!"

The message of my November 3 speech was that we were going to keep our commitment in Vietnam. We were going to continue fighting until the Communists agreed to negotiate a fair and honorable peace or until the South Vietnamese were able to defend themselves on their own —whichever came first. At the same time we would continue our disengagement based on the principles of the Nixon Doctrine: the pace of withdrawal would be linked to the progress of Vietnamization, the level of enemy activity, and developments on the negotiating front. I emphasized that our policy would not be affected by demonstrations in the streets.

At least in part because of the very different expectations that had been built up around this speech, my strongly expressed determination to stand and fight came as a surprise to many people and therefore had a greatly increased impact. I called on the American people for their support:

I have chosen a plan for peace. I believe it will succeed. If it does succeed, what the critics say now won't matter. If it does not succeed, anything I say then won't matter. . . .

And so tonight—to you, the great silent majority of my fellow Americans—I ask for your support.

I pledged in my campaign for the presidency to end the war in a way that we could win the peace. I have initiated a plan of action which will enable me to keep that pledge.

The more support I can have from the American people, the sooner that pledge can be redeemed; for the more divided we are at home, the less likely the enemy is to negotiate at Paris.

Let us be united for peace. Let us also be united against defeat. Because let us understand: North Vietnam cannot defeat or humiliate the United States. Only Americans can do that.

Very few speeches actually influence the course of history. The November 3 speech was one of them. Its impact came as a surprise to me; it was one thing to make a rhetorical appeal to the Silent Majority—it was another actually to hear from them.

After the speech I had dinner by myself in the Lincoln Sitting Room. I did not listen to the TV commentators, but the rest of the family did, and they were livid with anger. They said that the comment and analyses broadcast by the network news correspondents criticized both my words and my motives. Instead of presenting impartial summaries of what I had said and cross sections of political and public reaction, most of the reporters talked about the speech they thought I should have given. Tricia came in and said, "They talked as if they had been listening to a different speech than the one you made."

But there were signs that the critics and the commentators were unrepresentative of public opinion. The White House switchboard had been lighted up from the minute I left the air. The calls continued for hours, and soon the first waves of telegrams began to arrive. After I took calls from Cabinet officers, staff, and others—including Dean Acheson—I began to realize that the reaction to the speech was exceeding my most optimistic hopes.

I was too keyed up to sleep very well that night. The various reports of the public response to the speech excited me; the reports of the television coverage rankled me. Later I made a note: "Before November 3 a majority of the press expected RN to cave, and those who did not expected him to have a violent reaction to the demonstrations. He surprised them by doing neither. The RN policy is to talk softly and to carry a big stick. That was the theme of November 3."

By morning the public reaction was confirmed. The White House mail room reported the biggest response ever to any presidential speech. More than 50,000 telegrams and 30,000 letters had poured in, and the percentage of critical messages among them was low. A Gallup telephone poll taken immediately after the speech showed 77 percent approval.

There was no mistaking that the Silent Majority speech had hit a responsive chord in the country. In fact, for the first time, the Silent Majority had made itself heard.

The outpouring of popular support had a direct impact on congressional opinion. By November 12, 300 members of the House of Representatives—119 Democrats and 181 Republicans—had cosponsored a resolution of support for my Vietnam policies. Fifty-eight senators—21 Democrats and 37 Republicans—had signed letters expressing similar sentiments.

The November 3 speech was both a milestone and a turning point for my administration. Now, for a time at least, the enemy could no longer count on dissent in America to give them the victory they could not win on the battlefield. I had the public support I needed to continue a policy of waging war in Vietnam and negotiating for peace in Paris until we could bring the war to an honorable and successful conclusion.

During the weeks after November 3 my Gallup overall-approval rating soared to 68 percent, the highest it had been since I took office. Congressional reaction was so positive that I took the unprecedented step of personally appearing before both the House and Senate and addressing them separately to thank them for their support.

At the same time I was under no illusions that this wave of Silent Majority support could be maintained for very long. My speech had not proposed any new initiatives; its purpose had been to gain support for the course we were already following. I knew that under the constant pounding from the media and our critics in Congress, people would soon be demanding that new actions be taken to produce progress and end the war.

One result of the unexpected success of the November 3 speech was the decision to take on the TV network news organizations for their biased and distorted "instant analysis" and coverage. Unless the practice were challenged, it would make it impossible for a President to appeal directly to the people, something I considered to be of the essence of democracy.

A few days after the speech, Pat Buchanan sent me a memorandum urging a direct attack on the network commentators and a few days later he submitted a speech draft that did so in very direct and articulate language. Ted Agnew's hard-hitting speeches had attracted a great deal of attention during the fall, and I decided that he was the right man to deliver this one. I toned down some of Buchanan's rhetoric and gave it to Agnew. We further moderated some sections that Agnew thought sounded strident, and then he edited it himself so that the final version would be his words. He decided to deliver the speech in Des Moines, Iowa, on November 13.

When the advance text arrived at the networks, there was pandemonium; all three decided to carry the speech live. For thirty minutes, Agnew tore into the unaccountable power in the hands of the "unelected elite" of network newsmen. He said, "A small group of men, numbering perhaps no more than a dozen anchormen, commentators, and executive producers, settle upon the film and commentary that is to reach the public. They decide what 40 to 50 million Americans will learn of the day's events in the nation and in the world." Referring to my November 3 speech, he said that my words had been unfairly subjected to "instant analysis and querulous criticism."

The national impact of Agnew's Des Moines speech was second only to that of my November 3 speech. Within a few hours telegrams began arriving at the White House; the switchboards were tied up all night by people calling to express their relief that someone had finally spoken up, and within a few days thousands of letters began pouring in from all over the country.

The networks purposely ignored the widespread public support Agnew's words received and tried to label the speech as an attempt at government "repression." The president of CBS, Frank Stanton, called it "an unprecedented attempt by the Vice President of the United States to intimidate a news medium which depends for its existence upon government licenses." The president of NBC, Julian Goodman, said that Agnew's "attack on television news is an appeal to prejudice." George McGovern reflected left-wing and liberal congressional reaction when he said, "I feel that the speech was perhaps the most frightening single statement ever to come from a high government official in my public career."

Some voices were raised on Agnew's side. Jerry Ford said that if the media distorted the news, they should be called to account: "I don't know why they should have a

509

halo over their heads," he said. George Christian, President Johnson's last Press Secretary, said that LBJ had been concerned about the very questions Agnew raised, but he had been afraid to make a speech about them because he knew it would be interpreted as an attack on freedom of the press.

Even some of our severest critics admitted that Agnew's complaints were not unfounded. Writing in the *Saturday Review*, for example, British journalist Henry Brandon stated, "The Vice President made a few telling points. Instant commentary based on a hasty reading of a speech without much time for contemplation is hazardous and can lead to rash conclusions or unfair criticism."

After the tremendous success of my November 3 speech, an element of desperation entered into the planning of the November Vietnam Moratorium, known as the New Mobe. We received alarming reports that several militant groups involved in the New Mobe now felt that only a violent confrontation could adequately dramatize their concerns. Because of the radical background of some of the New Mobe organizers, many congressmen who had supported the October Moratorium managed to be unavailable for comment before the New Mobe began and out of town while it was going on.

On November 15 the New Mobe arrived. In San Francisco, while some of the crowd of 125,000 yelled "Peace!" Black Panther leader David Hilliard insisted, "We will kill Richard Nixon. We will kill any [one] that stands in the way of our freedom."

In Washington, 250,000 demonstrators surged into the city, causing the Washington *Post* to rhapsodize: "To dig beneath the rhetoric is to discover something extraordinary, and quite beautiful. Those who were here . . . are here in support of what is best about this country." At the Washington Monument, Dick Gregory brought the crowd to its feet when he said, "The President says nothing you kids do will have any effect on him. Well, I suggest he make one long distance call to the LBJ Ranch." And later in the day came scattered episodes of violence. A group of protesters battled with police as they made their way through the streets knocking out windows. At the Justice Department protesters shouting "Smash the state!" stormed the building, tore down the American flag, burned it, and raised the Vietcong flag in its place.

I had never imagined that at the end of my first year as President I would be contemplating two more years of fighting in Vietnam. But the unexpected success of the November 3 speech had bought me more time, and, bolstered by Sir Robert Thompson's optimistic estimate that within two years we would be able to achieve a victory—either in the sense of an acceptable negotiated settlement or of having prepared the South Vietnamese to carry the burden of the fighting on their own—I was prepared to continue the war despite the serious strains that would be involved on the home front. Two years would bring us to the end of 1971 and the beginning of the 1972 campaign, and if I could hold the domestic front together until then, winning an honorable peace would redeem the interim difficulties.

As 1970 began, I envisioned a year of limited and even diminishing battlefield activity. I also envisioned the continuation of Kissinger's activity in the secret channel. I was rather less optimistic than Kissinger regarding the prospect of a breakthrough in the secret negotiations but I agreed that we must continue to pursue them as long as there was even a possibility they would be successful. Kissinger and I agreed that at the very least they would provide an indisputable record of our desire for peace and our efforts to achieve it.

I was disappointed but not surprised by the apparent ineffectiveness of our attempts in 1969 to get the Soviets to apply pressure on North Vietnam. But I understood the pressures placed on Moscow by the rivalry with Peking for ascendancy in the Communist world, and I felt that the important thing was to keep the Soviets aware that while we might recognize their inability to decrease their support of Hanoi or to apply pressure on the North Vietnamese to negotiate a settlement, we would not tolerate any major increase in aid or belligerent encouragement. Not surprisingly, the greatest incentive for Soviet cooperation in Vietnam was our new relationship with the Chinese, but that would not become a major factor until the middle of 1971.

I do not know whether or how I would have acted differently if at the end of 1969 I had known that within less than four months I would be forced to order an attack on the Communist sanctuaries in Cambodia, or that the next two years would once again bring America to the brink of internal disruption over Vietnam. At the same time I would have to walk a constantly higher tightrope trying to support our allies and our fighting men while not pushing the increasingly powerful antiwar forces in Congress into passing legislation that would cut off funds for the war or require our withdrawal.

All this lay ahead. As I sat in my study in San Clemente on New Year's Day thinking about these problems, I actually allowed myself a feeling of cautious optimism that we had weathered the worst blows from Vietnam and had only to hold firm until time began to work in our favor. I suppose that in some respects the Vietnam story is one of mutual miscalculation. But if I underestimated the willingness of the North Vietnamese to hang on and resist a negotiated settlement on any other than their own terms, they also underestimated my willingness to hold on despite the domestic and international pressures that would be ranged against me.

1969: PRESIDENT AND CONGRESS

I was determined to be an activist President in domestic affairs. I had a definite agenda in mind, and I was prepared to use the first year of the presidency to knock heads together in order to get things done. "The country recognizes the need for change," I told the first meeting of my new Urban Affairs Council, "and we don't want the record written that we were too cautious."

But it didn't take long to discover that enthusiasm and determination could not overcome the reality that I was still the first President in 120 years to begin his term with both houses of Congress controlled by the opposition party. I sent over forty domestic proposals to Congress that first year, including the first major tax reform package since Eisenhower's first term, a proposal to reorganize foreign aid, a message on electoral reform, the first presidential message in our history dealing with the explosive problems of population growth, and some twenty proposals dealing with crime and drug and pornography control. Only two of these proposals were passed: draft reform and our tax bill. Legislation that would take the Post Office Department out of politics and turn it into a non-partisan corporation soon followed. We won some tactical legislative victories over the Democratic opposition, but it soon became clear that my attempts to get Congress to approve creative and comprehensive proposals were going to be resisted.

Three major congressional battles that first year illustrated the kind of problems I would face in my dealings with Congress throughout my first term. There was the cliff-hanging one-vote margin of victory on my request for an anti-ballistic missile (ABM) system, underscoring the uncomfortably narrow bipartisan coalition I had to depend on when it came to foreign policy and defense issues. Then there were the battles over the Supreme Court vacancies: with the Haynsworth nomination at the end of 1969 and the Carswell nomination at the beginning of 1970, Congress, in an unprecedented partisan display, refused to confirm two successive presidential Supreme Court nominees. Finally, our bold attempt to reform the federal welfare system—the Family Assistance Plan—illustrated the problem of the Senate's tendency to fracture into special interest groups. As George Shultz later summed it up. "He who walks in the middle of the road gets hit from both sides."

It was clear to me by 1969 that there could never be absolute parity between the U.S. and the U.S.S.R. in the area of nuclear and conventional armaments. For one thing, the Soviets are a land power and we are a sea power. For another, while our nuclear weapons were better, theirs were bigger. Furthermore, absolute superiority in every area of armaments would have been meaningless, because there is a point in arms development at which each nation has the capacity to destroy the other. Beyond that point the most important consideration is not continued escalation of the number of arms but maintenance of the strategic equilibrium while making it clear to the adversary that a nuclear attack, even if successful, would be suicidal.

Consequently, at the beginning of the administration I began to talk in terms of *sufficiency* rather than *superiority* to describe my goals for our nuclear arsenal. Putting an end to the arms race meant working out trade-offs with the Soviets, and I wanted us to have the most bargaining chips from the outset in order to get the best deal. I said that Congress must not send me to the negotiating table as the head of the second strongest nation in the world.

This is where the ABM came in. The Soviets had indicated that they were willing to reach agreement on defensive arms limitation. Most of the liberals in Congress, the media, and the academic community tended to take them at face value in this regard and feared that a congressional vote for an ABM system would destabilize the existing arms balance and compel the Soviets to increase their own construction programs, thus losing a precious opportunity and moving the arms race up another notch.

I thought they were wrong. I thought the Soviets' primary interest in opening arms negotiations at that point was that without an ABM we would be in a disadvantageous negotiating position. Our intelligence reports indicated that in 1969 the Soviets spent the equivalent of $25 billion on nuclear weapons. They deployed more than a hundred intercontinental ballistic missiles (ICBMs) while we deployed none; they added several nuclear missile-firing submarines to their Navy while we added none; and they deployed forty new ABMs around Moscow. We knew that even as the debate in Congress over an American ABM was raging, the Soviets had initiated work on more ICBMs and ABMs, as well as major new radar systems in conjunction with their deployment; they were also building additional submarine missiles. I felt that tactically we needed the ABM as a bargaining chip for negotiations with the Soviets: they already had an ABM system, so if we went into negotiations without one we might have to give up something else, perhaps something more vital. In that sense, we had to have it in order to be able to agree to forgo it. I tried to persuade Congress that what the ABM vote represented was really a philosophical turning point in America's strategic credibility.

I knew that the vote on ABM would reverberate around the world as a measure of America's resolve. The minute the Europeans or the Japanese decided that we could not be depended upon to keep our commitments and stand up to the Soviets, the American position in Europe and the Far East would be severely damaged. But as I saw it, the ABM vote involved the much deeper question of whether Americans still believed that we stood for something in the world and that we must be willing to bear the burden of resisting aggression against our allies and friends. I believed that the majority of Americans felt this way; but as long as there was any doubt about it among our enemies, the temptations to test us would be that much stronger. The ABM vote would be the first significant congressional vote on defense measures in my administration, and I wanted the signal to go out that we had not lost our national sense of purpose and resolve—because I did not think we had.

Unfortunately, Vietnam soured the debate. It had convinced the liberals that America suffered from too belligerent a posture and made them determined to curb our military spending. As Stewart Alsop wrote in his column, "There are, of course, perfectly rational arguments against the ABM. But a great deal of the opposition to ABM is essentially emotional—it is the liberals' way of getting back at the generals for Vietnam." The liberals hated the war and they thought our best solution was just to get out. I hated the war too, but I thought we had to end it in a way that would keep our commitment to South Vietnam. I thought the liberals had deluded themselves: America would not make the world safer by acting dishonorably.

One good argument against the ABM was that many people—Eisenhower, incidentally, among them—doubted the efficacy of defensive weapons systems and preferred to put our money into building our offensive capability. There were also technical objections involving the cost of the system measured against the increased levels of defense it would actually produce. These arguments lost me support among some responsible conservatives and moderates whose votes I might otherwise have had, and made the tension even greater as we headed into the final vote.

The ABM vote actually involved a request for additional appropriations to carry on a building program that had begun under President Johnson. The system of extensive ABM coverage he had proposed in 1967 was called Sentinel. The reduced version I decided to propose in 1969 was called Safeguard.

Once I had made the decision, we faced the biggest congressional battle of the first term. We would be fairly sure of carrying the House; but in the Senate, where the powerful liberal forces were headed by Teddy Kennedy, it was clearly going to be very close. Democratic Senator Henry Jackson, a strong proponent of national defense, led the fight for us. He said that it was just like war, and we were going to have to fight it like war if we wanted to win.

We blanketed Capitol Hill with White House staff members. This was our first major attempt to use the delicate technique of persuasion without pressure, and we were constantly having to adjust our strategy as the daily reports indicated that we were not pushing hard enough with one congressman or that we were coming on too strong with another. I started out with a heavy schedule of calls and meetings with congressmen, but after the initial contacts had been made and the arguments presented I concluded that I was squandering presidential prestige that might be needed later. Some legislators tried to use the ABM vote as a bargaining chip of their own. In one case a powerful committee chairman hinted that I could have his support in exchange for approving a major federal installation in his district.

I felt we were fighting with one hand tied behind our back because we could not publicly explain the bargaining chip rationale for the ABM, nor could we reveal the intelligence reports of Soviet arms. Kissinger and I used these arguments in congressional briefings and meetings, but the liberal forces were well organized and were largely able to control the public debate.

The Senate would cast the first vote on ABM, and from the outset it was clear that the vote would be close. One of the key figures was the independent Republican senator, Margaret Chase Smith. Both sides sought to win her support; Mike Mansfield said he'd never seen so many men publicly woo one woman. Seemingly unrelated issues and events were weighed for the import they might have for the ABM vote. Thus, one of the arguments raised against retaliation when the North Koreans shot down our EC-121 in April was that the resulting furore would strengthen the anti-ABM forces. And when Teddy Kennedy's car went off a bridge at Chappaquiddick in July, the effectiveness of his leadership against the ABM was significantly reduced. As the time of the vote neared, I told Bryce Harlow, "Make sure that all our guys are there all the time. Don't let anyone get sick. Don't even let anyone go to the bathroom until it's all over."

When the vote was taken on August 6 it was in the form of three separate amendments to the bill that, if they had been adopted, would have halted construction of the ABM. All three were defeated. On the first and most important amendment—which would have prohibited all spending for Safeguard deployment, the Senate divided 50-50. Under Senate rules a tie vote would have defeated the amendment anyway, but Agnew cast his tie-breaking vote and the final tally read 51-50.

Even though the margin of victory was razor thin, the vote established that America was still prepared to maintain its military strength. I am absolutely convinced that had we lost the ABM battle in the Senate, we would not have been able to negotiate the first nuclear arms control agreement in Moscow in 1972. But the one-vote margin was undeniably a nerve-racking one, and it confirmed my resolve to pour every possible resource of money and manpower into the congressional elections of 1970 in order to shore up our position in Congress and make our margin more secure.

The Supreme Court is always keenly aware of political and social trends. During the 1950s and 1960s, under the leadership of Chief Justice Earl Warren, the Court had become unprecedentedly politically active. Like many legal and political moderate conservatives, I felt that some Supreme Court Justices were too often using their interpretation of the law to remake American society according to their own social, political, and ideological precepts.

By the time of the 1968 political campaign Warren was seventy-seven years old. It was unlikely that he would be able to lead the Court through the next four—or possibly eight—years of what might become the Nixon administration. On June 13, 1968, he sent his resignation to Lyndon Johnson "effective at your pleasure."

On June 26, Johnson nominated Abe Fortas to be Chief Justice. Fortas had been an Associate Justice since Johnson appointed him to the Court in 1965. Shortly after his nomination as Chief Justice was announced, it came to light that while on the Court, Fortas, a close friend of Johnson's, had performed a number of personal and political chores for him. This was a clear violation of the principle of separation of powers. It was also discovered that Fortas had accepted a $15,000 fee for a lecture series at American University. One of Fortas's former law partners had raised the money from influential business and financial leaders—men who might have interests in cases coming before the Supreme Court.

On October 2 Fortas asked Johnson to withdraw his nomination. By then it was then too close to the election for Johnson to make another nomination without seeming blatantly political. Thus whoever won the election would have the opportunity of selecting a Chief Justice at the beginning of his presidency.

Shortly after I was elected, I asked Bill Rogers to approach Chief Justice Warren and work out an understanding with regard to the timing of his resignation. Warren agreed to stay on until the end of the Court's session in June, and I asked John Mitchell to begin looking for a candidate to replace him. I was the thirty-seventh President, but the man I nominated would be only the fifteenth Chief Justice in our history. It was not a selection to be made lightly or hastily.

My first choice was former Attorney General Herb Brownell. There was only one drawback: he had been Eisenhower's Attorney General in 1957 at the time of the Little Rock school crisis, and I knew that many Southerners were still deeply embittered by his role in the use of federal troops to enforce integration. After getting negative reactions from key Southern senators, Mitchell told Brownell that his confirmation fight would be messy. Brownell said that such a controversy would not be in the interests of the nation or of the new administration, and he asked to be removed from consideration.

I asked Mitchell to sound out Tom Dewey, but as I expected, he ruled himself out because of his age. He was already sixty-six, and he felt strongly that any Chief Justice should serve for at least ten years.

I also considered Associate Justice Potter Stewart, an articulate dissenter from many of the Warren Court's activist decisions. On April 30, however, he came to the White House and said he wanted me to know that, in terms of the morale of the other Justices, he did not believe it was in the best interests of the Court to have one of the Associate Justices elevated to Chief Justice.

As the search continued, I developed five criteria for the selection process. The next Chief Justice must have a top-flight legal mind; he must be young enough to serve at least ten years; he should, if possible, have experience both as a practicing lawyer and as an appeals court judge; he must generally share my view that the Court should interpret the Constitution rather than amend it by judicial fiat; and he must have a special quality of leadership that would enable him to resolve differences among his colleagues so that, as often as possible, the Court would speak decisively on major cases with one voice or at least with a strong voice for the majority opinion.

I reviewed the list of appeals court judges Mitchell prepared for me and began looking particularly into the record of Judge Warren E. Burger of the District of Columbia Court of Appeals. I had been impressed by excerpts from one of Burger's speeches on the role of law and order in society that I read in 1967 in *U.S. News & World Report*. I had used several ideas from it in my speeches during the 1968 campaign. Mitchell gave me some of Burger's opinions to read, and I was impressed by their forcefulness and clarity. I knew Warren Burger to be philosophically a moderate conservative and personally an impressive man. On May 21 I nominated him as Chief Justice of the United States. He was confirmed readily and sworn in on June 23.

As I was nearing my decision on a new Chief Justice, I unexpectedly had the opportunity to fill another seat on the

Supreme Court when Abe Fortas suddenly submitted his resignation.

Life magazine had recently disclosed further improprieties involving Fortas's finances and potential conflicts of interest, and I had told Mitchell that as a courtesy and on a completely confidential basis, we should keep Chief Justice Warren informed about the new charges emerging from the Justice Department's ongoing investigation. Warren was grateful because he felt that the new information represented a serious threat to the reputation of the Court; he was convinced that Fortas had no choice but to step down.

It was a difficult time for Fortas. I felt that the press had to some extent singled him out for criticism as a belated way of getting at Johnson, and I called him the day he announced his resignation and expressed my sympathy. Still, there was no question that he had been astonishingly indiscreet, and that it was important for the Court that he resign.

Once again I asked John Mitchell to direct the search for a Supreme Court Justice. We selected Judge Clement F. Haynsworth of South Carolina and announced his nomination on August 18, 1969. Haynsworth came from a distinguished legal family, was fifty-six years old, and had served with great distinction for twelve years on the Fourth Circuit Court of Appeals.

Harsh criticism began as soon as I announced the nomination. Civil rights organizations immediately called Haynsworth a racist; one group said he was a "laundered segregationist." George Meany claimed that his record was antilabor. The press picked up these themes and played daily variations on them. Soon the pack mentality took hold in Washington. Organized interest groups went to work, and letter and phone campaigns began putting pressure on the Senate.

Senator Birch Bayh of Indiana became the leader of the anti-Haynsworth forces. During Haynsworth's confirmation hearings, Bayh charged him with conflict of interest, claiming that he should have disqualified himself in several cases involving litigants who were customers of a company in which he owned stock. These disclosures had been investigated several years earlier by then Attorney General Robert Kennedy and by Judge Simon Sobeloff of the Fourth Circuit, who both found no conflict of interest. John Frank, the leading legal authority on disqualification of judges, testified at the time that not only did Haynsworth have no obligation to disqualify himself, he had an affirmative responsibility to rule on the cases in question. But the truth never caught up with Bayh's charges as he and other liberal Democrats on the Senate Judiciary Committee worked with a cooperative press corps to discredit Haynsworth.

Bayh and his supporters ended up maintaining that it was no longer sufficient that a nominee had not engaged in any impropriety; now there must be no "appearance" of impropriety. Thus opponents of a nominee could raise an "appearance" of impropriety by false charges and thereby defeat him. It was a vicious circle: the nominee would not be condemned for what he had done but for what he had been accused of having done by his detractors.

Few senators were candid enough to admit on the record the real grounds for their opposition to Haynsworth, but one anonymously told a reporter, "Conflict of interest is so much jazz; we are against him for what he believes."

In the middle of the furore, a delegation of Republican senators led by the Minority Whip, Robert Griffin of Michigan, came to the White House to ask me to withdraw the Haynsworth nomination. They explained the pressure they were under and the political leverage that was being brought to bear on them by labor and the press.

I refused. In fact, I went further and said that I would not withdraw Haynsworth's name even if he himself asked me to. There was a basic constitutional principle involved, the right of a President to choose his nominees for the Supreme Court. There was also a human element. To withdraw Haynsworth's name while he was under such bitter partisan fire might destroy his reputation, driving him from the bench and from public service. I made it clear that I planned to see the nomination through to the end.

On November 21 the Senate had rejected the Haynsworth nomination, 55 to 45, with seventeen Republicans joining the liberal Democrats in opposition.

On December 4 Haynsworth came to the White House, and we talked for an hour in the Oval Office. He seemed confused and dazed by what had happened. He is a quiet, refined, and extraordinarily kind man. When he said that the ordeal had been harder on his wife than on him, I thought about how Pat had felt during the fund crisis, and I hoped that the private hell they must have endured would not leave them scarred for life as ours had done. That night I wrote a note: "Haynsworth was the victim of forces he probably did not understand."

On January 19, 1970, two months after the Haynsworth vote, I nominated Judge G. Harrold Carswell of the Fifth Circuit Court of Appeals in Florida. I had told Mitchell to make sure that our second nominee was absolutely above personal or professional reproach; the fact that Carswell owned no stocks or securities seemed to put him beyond even the "appearance" of impropriety that had contributed to Haynsworth's defeat.

It did not take long for the liberal opposition to Carswell to start. As if on cue, the ritual charges of "racist" were made in the media and in Congress. Any conservative Southern judge would have to expect this kind of attack, and I was not surprised by it. Unfortunately, we had missed one statement from Carswell's distant past. In 1948, as a Democratic candidate for the Georgia legislature, he had said, "Segregation of the races is proper and the only practical and correct way of life in our states. I have always so believed and I shall always so act." Carswell had renounced his twenty-two-year-old views, but the damage was irreparable. I was distressed that we had overlooked this unfortunate statement, but I did not believe that youthful indiscretions that had been recanted and redeemed should be held against an individual in later years.

Carswell had looked highly qualified on paper; the exceptionally rigorous scrutiny to which he was subjected, with various senators and their staffs determined to dig out anything bad they could find and then present it in the worst possible light, revealed that he was not as highly qualified as we had thought. I still believe that Carswell would have passed muster by the standards of other times. But the post-Haynsworth partisan fallout was too intense. The word *mediocre* was increasingly used to describe him and his career. His defenders were placed in the position of having to prove a negative—that he was not mediocre.

When the vote was taken on April 8, the Carswell nomination was rejected, 51 to 45. It was cold and reasoned anger that impelled me to make a statement the next day commenting on the Senate's action. If the Northern liberals had tasted victory in defeating my second nominee, I was determined that they would at least pay a political price for it in the South. I said:

> I have reluctantly concluded that it is not possible to get confirmation for a Judge on the Supreme Court of any man who believes in the strict construction of the Constitution, as I do, if he happens to come from the South. . . .
>
> When you strip away all the hypocrisy, the real reason for their rejection was their legal philosophy, a philosophy that I share, of strict construction of the Constitution, and also the accident of their birth, the fact that they were born in the South. . . .
>
> And I have concluded, therefore, that the next nominee must come from outside the South, since this Senate, as it is presently constituted, will not approve a man from the South who shares my views of strict construction of the Constitution.

Looking back I have no quarrel with some of those senators who voted against Carswell because of their belief that he lacked the superior intellectual and judicial qualities to be a Supreme Court Justice. But I still believe that many of the senators who voted against him used the issue of his competence as camouflage for their real reason, which was their disapproval of his constitutional philosophy.

On April 14, 1970, I nominated Federal Circuit Court of Appeals Judge Harry A. Blackmun. An Eisenhower appointee who had practiced law for twenty years prior to ten and a half years of distinguished service on the federal bench, Blackmun was a Northerner, from Minnesota. He was unanimously confirmed by the Senate on May 12.

Within a week in September 1971, Supreme Court Justices Hugo Black and John Harlan both submitted letters of retirement to me for reasons of health.

After my experience with the Carswell and Haynsworth appointments, I did not intend to make the same mistakes again. I was still determined, however, that those appointed be strict constructionists, and I still wanted to find a qualified Southerner. This time I also wanted to find a qualified woman. Above all, I wanted to be sure that my nominees would be confirmed.

Now I decided that while John Mitchell would once again play the leading role in recommending possible candidates, I would try to elicit some independent evaluations.

Our search for a woman nominee was serious and intense, and accompanied, I might add, by Pat's cogent and determined lobbying on every available occasion. But we found that in general the women judges and lawyers qualified to be nominated for the Supreme Court were too liberal to meet the strict constructionist criterion I had established.

On October 19, 1971, I asked Mitchell to extend to Lewis Powell, a Virginia attorney and a former president of the American Bar Association, an offer to fill one of the vacancies. Powell was reluctant because he was sixty-four years old, but that night I telephoned him and urged him to take it. The next afternoon he called Mitchell and accepted the nomination.

My friend and White House Special Counsel Dick Moore suggested that I consider Assistant Attorney General William Rehnquist for the other vacancy. Rehnquist had been first in his class at Stanford Law School and then served as a clerk to Supreme Court Justice Robert Jackson. Apart from his unquestioned legal qualifications and his moderately conservative philosophy, Rehnquist's most attractive attribute was his age: he was only forty-seven and could probably serve on the Court for twenty-five years. Mitchell shared Moore's high opinion of Rehnquist and enthusiastically endorsed him.

When I announced Powell and Rehnquist as my nominees on national television on October 21, there were the predictable charges that I was packing the Court with ultra-conservatives, and the Senate dragged its feet in order to give the critics time to try to knock down the new nominees. But they were so obviously highly qualified that only the most partisan opposition could be raised. Both men were confirmed, Powell on December 6 and Rehnquist on December 10, by overwhelming votes.

I consider my four appointments to the Supreme Court to have been among the most constructive and far-reaching actions of my presidency. Some critics have characterized my appointments as an effort to create a "Nixon Court." It is true that the men I appointed shared my conservative judicial philosophy and significantly affected the balances of power that had developed in the Warren Court. But as individuals they were each dedicated and able constitutional lawyers who often disagreed on major cases. When I appointed them, I told each that I would never try to influence his judgment and that his only loyalty should be to the law and not to me. Their decisions in cases that affected me politically or personally reflected the fact that they accepted my admonition.

———————

From the first days of my administration I wanted to get rid of the costly failures of the Great Society—and I wanted to do it immediately. I wanted the people who had elected me to see that I was going to follow through on my campaign promises. The worst offender was the welfare system, and welfare reform was my highest domestic priority.

It was Pat Moynihan who made an uncharacteristic plea for caution. In several long sessions in the Oval Office he paced back and forth in front of my desk, waving his arms to punctuate his argument. "All the Great Society activist constituencies are lying out there in wait," he said, "poised to get you if you try to come after them: the professional welfarists, the urban planners, the day-carers, the social workers, the public housers. Frankly, I'm terrified at the thought of cutting back too fast. Just take Model Cities. The urban ghettos will go up in flames if you cut it out."

Moynihan wanted to take a year to consolidate our domestic situation before proposing any domestic legislation. But a year was simply too long, so I pushed the

Cabinet and staff to develop a program of creative and innovative social legislation as soon as possible.

The current welfare system was a mess. It was inefficient and inconsistent. Payment for equivalent families could range from as high as $263 a month in one state to $39 a month in another. In most states higher payments were made to fatherless families; not surprisingly, families split up in order to collect more money. From 1961 to 1967, 93 percent of the families added to the welfare rolls had absent fathers. There was a rise in illegitimacy; by 1969 over 69 percent of welfare births in New York City were out of wedlock. There were loopholes that meant an individual could earn more on welfare than working for the minimum wage and that a woman earning over $12,000 a year might still be eligible for welfare benefits. There were also flagrant problems of fraud, along with the graft that plagues any big system with a multitude of different regulations and large amounts of money.

Seething beneath the surface of the welfare problem was a disturbing undercurrent of racial friction. Moynihan summarized this in a memo to me on May 17, 1969: "In the present time the service-dispensing groups in the society—teachers, welfare workers, urban planners, nutrition experts, etc., etc.—are preoccupied with the black problem and almost at times seem to resent hearing there are whites who are in difficulty or marginally so." Moynihan pointed out that the current services strategy for welfare tended not only to exclude working-class whites—and 60 percent of low income workers were white—but to create a group of middle-class whites and blacks who were in what he called the "resentment business":

> They earn very good livings making the black poor feel put upon, when they are, which is often the case, and also when they are not. . . .

> On average, I would suppose for example, that the white women who teach Head Start children earn about three times as much per hour as the black men who fathered the children. And for all this the results are really rather marginal so far as the children are concerned. In the meantime the black poor *seem* to be favored over the white near poor, the loud mouths get louder and temperatures rise.

The result of this situation was that, as one magazine writer described it, we were on the brink of "The Revolt of the White Lower Middle Classes."

After several months of study and discussion of every aspect of the problem, we devised the Family Assistance Plan, which I announced in a televised address on domestic legislation on August 8, 1969.

The Great Society programs had poured billions of dollars into supplying a formidable range of social services for the poor; if you could prove that your income was below a certain level you could qualify for any number of free or subsidized goods and services. I felt that this kind of approach encouraged a feeling of dependence and discouraged the kind of self-reliance that is needed to get people on their feet. I thought that people should have the responsibility for spending carefully and taking care of themselves. I abhorred snoopy, patronizing surveillance by social workers which made children and adults on welfare feel stigmatized and separate. The basic premise of the Family Assistance Plan was simple: what the poor need to help them rise out of poverty is money.

The answer we came up with was also simple, but revolutionary: we decided to provide federal financial aid not just to the unemployed poor, but to the working poor. Payments would go not just to families with fatherless children but to families in which the fathers lived at home. By providing a federal income floor we would ease the financial burden on the states; by setting nationwide standards and establishing automated payment procedures we hoped to cut down on red tape, and before long to eliminate social services, social workers and the stigma of welfare.

But there was something else that was revolutionary about FAP. It was not a simple guaranteed income. The plan required that everyone who accepted benefits must either accept work or training for work if suitable jobs were available within a reasonable distance. The bottom line was—no work, no welfare. The only exceptions would be the aged, the infirm, and mothers of pre-school children.

FAP was a risk. I knew that. We would be making thirteen million more people eligible for federal help than were currently eligible in an effort to reward work and not punish the poor for holding jobs. We would be incurring a first-year cost increase of $4 billion on the speculation that once people were not penalized for work—once they were certain they could earn more in jobs than solely on welfare—they would prefer to work. We hoped that the stability that the increased money would provide would be an incentive to get better and better paying jobs, ultimately taking people off the welfare rolls. It was a speculation that no one was certain would work. For these reasons FAP had a rocky passage through my own staff and Cabinet, where Moynihan, Finch, Ehrlichman and Secretary of Labor George Shultz defended it against the criticisms of the opposing conservative faction led by Arthur Burns, Ted Agnew, and Budget Director Robert Mayo.

I knew that we were taking a chance with FAP. But I also knew that the current system was a disaster that deteriorated faster every year. And FAP was the only plan with any chance of changing that.

In many respects I was in a very peculiar situation: less than eight months after my inauguration as the first Republican President in eight years, I was proposing a piece of almost revolutionary domestic legislation that required me to seek a legislative alliance with Democrats and liberals; my own conservative friends and allies were bound to oppose it. I thought the biggest danger would be the attack from the right. I was in for a surprise.

Predictably, conservatives denounced the plan as a "megadole" and a leftist scheme. But then, after a brief round of praise from columnists, editorialists, and academics, the liberals turned on the plan and practically pummeled it to death. They complained that the dollar amounts were not enough and the work requirements were repressive. In fact, FAP would have immediately lifted 60 percent of the people then living in poverty to incomes above that level. This was a real war on poverty, but the liberals could not accept it. Liberal senators immediately began to introduce extravagant bills of their own that had no hope of passage. As Moynihan observed, it was as if they could not tolerate the notion that a conservative Republican President had done what his liberal Democratic predecessors had not been bold enough to do.

The interest groups reacted no more admirably. The National Welfare Rights Organization, purportedly representing the interests of welfare recipients, formed an alliance with the social workers who were threatened with extinction, and denounced the plan. NWRO called it an "act of political repression" and accused the administration of conspiring to starve children. The plan was even called "racist," despite the fact that immediately upon passage it would have provided roughly 40 percent more money to blacks living in fourteen Southern states—and in 1969 slightly more than half the black population lived in the South. NWRO held noisy hearings at which welfare recipients testified, "We only want the kind of jobs that will pay $10,000 or $20,000" and "You'd better give me something better than I'm getting on welfare." NWRO proposed its own plan, which was introduced in the Senate by George McGovern, to guarantee a $6,500 income to every family of four. Such a plan would have put about half of America on welfare.

We fought hard. On April 16, 1970, thanks in large part to the leadership of Jerry Ford with help from Wilbur Mills, FAP passed the House. But the Senate Finance Committee, with Southern conservatives in key positions and no coordinated endorsement from the liberals, kept the plan on ice. On July 1, 1970, Moynihan wrote to me: "I fear the chances are now less than even that Family Assistance will be passed this year, and if not this year, not this decade." He said that no Republican was resisting efforts to kill the measure and that "increasingly the Democrats see an opportunity to deny you this epic victory and at the same time blame you for the defeat."

During the fall I put pressure on the Senate Finance Committee, but my efforts failed. On November 20 the committee voted the measure down, 10-6. In 1971 the House again passed the bill and again the Senate Finance Committee bottled it up. Ultimately only the sections of FAP providing guaranteed incomes for the aged and disabled passed the full Congress.

By 1971 the momentum for FAP had passed and I knew it. I still believed in the validity of the idea, but I no longer believed in the political timing. In 1969 the American people had been ready for change; in 1971 they were thinking of other things—of Vietnam and the economy. By 1971 there was also the prospect of the 1972 election; I did not want to be in a losing fight with the conservatives over FAP in an election year. Therefore, in the summer of 1972 when I was given a choice either to endorse a more costly version of the bill proposed by Senator Ribicoff or to stay with our original FAP even though it would surely fail, I decided on the latter. FAP finally died in the Senate Finance Committee in 1972—an idea ahead of its time.

APOLLO XI

For me the most exciting event of the first year of my presidency came in July 1969 when an American became the first man to walk on the moon. The moon landing was the culmination of a program begun a dozen years earlier after the Soviets launched Sputnik, the first man-made orbiting satellite. American public opinion was jolted at the thought of the Soviets in control of outer space, but Eisenhower and most of his advisers were not so disturbed. Sherman Adams, for example, told a predominantly Republican audience that the so-called satellite race was just "an outer space basketball game." I believed that this flippant remark was wrong in substance and disastrous in terms of public opinion. The next night I told an audience in San Francisco, "We could make no greater mistake than to brush off this event as a scientific stunt of more significance to the man in the moon than to men on earth."

In Cabinet and NSC meetings during this time I strongly advocated a sharp increase in our missile and space programs. Eisenhower finally came around to this view and approved a proposal for manned space vehicles. While he justified this decision on military grounds, I felt that something far more basic was involved. I believe that when a great nation drops out of the race to explore the unknown, that nation ceases to be great.

The manned space program was already well under way when President Kennedy captured the national imagination in 1961 by setting the goal of a moon landing by the end of the decade. President Johnson was an enthusiastic

530

supporter of NASA, and under his administration the Apollo program made great strides.

I decided that when the Apollo XI astronauts actually landed on the moon, the occasion should be well and widely marked. Working with NASA officials, we made plans for a televised phone conversation from the White House to the moon. In addition to planting an American flag on the lunar surface, the astronauts would leave behind a plaque bearing our signatures and a message that read:

HERE MEN FROM THE PLANET EARTH
FIRST SET FOOT UPON THE MOON
JULY, 1969 A.D.
WE CAME IN PEACE FOR ALL MANKIND

On Sunday night, July 20, Apollo VIII astronaut Frank Borman, Bob Haldeman, and I stood around the TV set in the private office and watched Neil Armstrong step onto the moon. Then I went into the Oval Office next door where TV cameras had been set up for my split-screen phone call to the moon.

Armstrong's voice came through loud and clear. I said, "Because of what you have done the heavens have become a part of man's world. And as you talk to us from the Sea of Tranquillity, it inspires us to redouble our efforts to bring peace and tranquillity to earth."

After a journey of almost half a million miles to the moon and back, Apollo XI landed less than two miles from the prearranged target about a thousand miles southwest of Hawaii in the Pacific Ocean. I was there to welcome the astronauts home. Because the mission's command module was named *Columbia,* I had asked the Navy band to play "Columbia, the Gem of the Ocean" as the astronauts stepped from the helicopter onto the aircraft carrier *Hornet*'s deck.

When I talked with them through the window of their quarantine chamber, it was hard to contain my enthusiasm or my awe at the thought that the three men on the other side of that glass had just returned from the moon. I said impulsively, "This is the greatest week in the history of the world since the Creation." When I talked to Billy Graham a few days later, he said, "Mr. President, I know exactly how you felt, and I understand exactly what you meant, but, even so, I think you may have been a little excessive."

The Apollo program ended on December 19, 1972, with the splashdown of Apollo XVII. By then, the public had become blasé about the ever-present hazards of space as well as the excitement of its challenge. The program had also begun to fall victim to the introverted attitude that threatened so much new technology in the 1970s. This contributed to the congressional refusal to support my proposal to continue our supersonic jet transport program, which I considered essential if America were to retain its lead in the field of commercial aviation. The argument went, as long as one person on earth is poor, not a dollar should be spent on space. In my opinion, however, exploration of space is one of the last of the great challenges to the American spirit. Space is perhaps the last frontier truly commensurate with America's capacity for wonder.

LYNDON JOHNSON: DECEMBER 1969

On Thursday, December 11, 1969, Lyndon Johnson was in Washington, and I invited him to the White House for breakfast. I met him in the Red Room and we went right into the first-floor family dining room, where I had arranged the table so that he could look into the fire. Without his asking, a bottle of liquid saccharin had been placed by his plate and the waiter brought him very light coffee.

He was extremely agitated about charges that while he was President he had used his influence to get his friends special deals for land acquisition and federal loans for their geriatrics center in Texas. Several times during breakfast he returned to this subject. But he also had some fascinating afterthoughts on the Vietnam bombing halt and on his dealings with the Soviets.

Late that night I dictated some recollections of our meeting; this was one of the handful of detailed dictations I made before I began keeping an almost daily dictated diary in November 1971.

Lyndon Johnson was such an intensely physical man that it is probably impossible for words to convey what being with him was like. I think this dictation gives at least some sense of the range of impressions and emotions a conversation with him might generate:

He seemed to have gotten considerably heavier, and I noted that when he got excited he breathed very hard and on the [geriatrics center] point even seemed to have tears in his eyes.

He reviewed in detail his attitude on Vietnam negotiations and his relations with the Russians. He again told me, as he had in California, that his major mistake as President was in "trusting the Russians" too much. He said that he thought that Eisenhower got along well with the Russians for the first six or seven years of his term due to the fact that "they feared Ike" because of what Dulles had threatened to do in Korea [use the A-Bomb]. He thought the reason Ike had difficulties in the last year was because some of the fear had been dissipated. He thought the same thing had happened to Kennedy when he tried to placate the Russians up until the time of the Cuban missile crisis. He thought that he had gone through the same experience during his years in office.

He recounted that Kosygin at Glassboro had indicated that the Russians would be willing to help out on Vietnam and had set out a proposition which Johnson said he would like to consider. Johnson suggested that they meet again in New York. When they met Johnson had studied the Kosygin proposition with Rusk and McNamara and made a counterproposal which Kosygin said was "different from his but in the ball park." Johnson confidently expected that something would happen. Two weeks went by without result. Rusk called Dobrynin in and was stonewalled on the matter. Two weeks later Thompson [U.S. ambassador in Moscow] called on Gromyko and got a cold shoulder. Nothing at all came from this initiative.

He said at the time of the bombing halt Harriman told him "at least twelve times" that they had assurances from the North Vietnamese that if the bombing were halted, the "understanding" with regard to shelling cities would be carried out. He felt that the Russians had given a similar assurance along these lines.

He said that all the bombing pauses were a mistake and he had accomplished nothing. Each one of them was undertaken only because of some assurance that he received, either through Russian or other sources, that there would be a positive reaction from the other side. He said that he did not want to call a bombing halt late in the campaign unless he was absolutely convinced he had a "deal." He knew he would be charged with having done it for political reasons.

He spoke with considerable bitterness about *Look*'s article on his brother. He told the story of one of his big financial supporters, who also had a brother who got into lots of trouble; [the man's] mother insisted on his doing something for the brother and he finally gave him a job driving a truckload of dynamite across the state. "He stopped at a roadside stand, had a couple of beers, propositioned the waitress to marry him, and went off down the road, and then a tree moved in front of him."

He spoke warmly of Agnew and said that he had a high opinion of him when he had been governor of Maryland. Agnew apparently had given him strong support on his foreign policy.

He felt that newspapermen are just naturally vicious and are not happy unless they are attacking somebody. He felt that he was free from such attacks during his first year in office only because Goldwater was his opponent and that as soon as Goldwater was out of the way it was inevitable that they would take him on. "The press just isn't happy unless they are attacking who happens to be President" was his conclusion.

He gave me at least a twenty-minute monologue on the geriatric center, referring very movingly to his having determined to build such a center due to the fact that the mayor of his home town had spent the last years of his life in a rest home which was just like a "hawg pen" and that his mother also spent some time in such a place.

He told the story about his going on the ticket [in 1960] and said he did so because Sam Rayburn insisted that he had to stop Nixon since Nixon had "called him a traitor." Johnson recalled that while I was Vice President, I had called him up to the rostrum in the Senate one day and shown him the speech which they were referring to. Johnson had shown it to Rayburn later, and Rayburn simply brushed it aside and said that I had said it another time. In any event Rayburn believed that was the case until he died.

As we were leaving he spoke very warmly of the courtesies we had extended him and to his girls and to Lady Bird.

THE FIRST YEAR

By the end of 1969, after almost a year in the White House, I felt that the administration was operating as an effective team.

Bob Haldeman had proved that, contrary to accepted belief, it is possible to make the White House run efficiently, to get the most out of people, and to prepare for decisions with sufficient information in sufficient time. Haldeman should get the credit for this, because he was made to pay the price for it. From the outset there were conflicts between the Cabinet and the White House staff, as there are in every presidency. Stories spread about Haldeman's alleged rudeness to Cabinet members and party leaders. Most of the stories were apocryphal, although I am sure that some were not. Haldeman was a quick, cogent thinker with limited tolerance for those whose decisiveness and dedication did not match his own. He had great expectations, and he drove the White House staff to meet them.

There were conflicts of viewpoint and clashes of personality in the Nixon administration, but no human organization ever has been or ever will be free of them. The most important of these conflicts—because of its potential effect on policy—involved Bill Rogers, Henry Kissinger, and Mel Laird. When three such distinctive personalities and temperaments were added to the already volatile institutional mix of the State Department, the NSC, and the Pentagon, it was inevitable that there would be fireworks. To Rogers's credit, it must be said that in many cases his primary concern was simply to be kept informed of what was going on. He had to testify before several congressional committees, and the secrecy with which our decisions customarily—and usually necessarily—were surrounded often placed him in an embarrassing position. I once jokingly remarked that Laird did not have this problem because he would answer questions and state his views whether he was informed or not.

Rogers and Laird occasionally carried on sensitive dealings and negotiations without coordinating them with the White House. In some cases this was inadvertent, when they lacked information about our secret diplomacy; sometimes it was done to preclude Kissinger's or my own disapproval; and sometimes, I think, it was done just to show themselves, their departments, and the press that they were capable of independent action. In some cases the results were harmless or even positive, but in a few cases the outcome threatened to undercut our policy and credibility with foreign countries.

Eventually the relationship between Kissinger and Rogers took on a fairly combative aspect. Kissinger bridled at my assignment in 1969 and 1970 of all Middle Eastern problems to Rogers. He felt that Rogers was overly influenced by the pro-Arab elements of the State Department, and that he did not have the necessary skill or subtlety or a sense of broad foreign policy strategy. Kissinger also worried when foreign policy power seemed to become dispersed, and he was concerned by Rogers's direct access to the Oval Office. Rogers felt that Kissinger was Machiavellian, deceitful, egotistical, arrogant, and insulting. Kissinger felt that Rogers was vain, uninformed, unable to keep a secret, and hopelessly dominated by the State Department bureaucracy. The problems became increasingly serious as the years passed. Kissinger suggested repeatedly that he might have to resign unless Rogers was restrained or replaced.

Since I valued both men for their different views and qualities, I tried to keep out of the personal fireworks that usually accompanied anything in which they were both involved. In this regard, Haldeman rendered valiant service since he ended up as a sort of DMZ between the two, and between them and me. Finally, even Haldeman had difficulties mediating the strongly held views of these proud and powerful men, and by the end of 1969 I was beginning to include John Mitchell in many foreign policy decisions so that he could provide a stabilizing personal influence.

The clashes between my liberal and conservative domestic advisers were perhaps more cerebral but no less dramatic or deeply felt. During the summer and fall I had gradually moved John Ehrlichman into the position of coordinating all domestic programs and issues. He had a strong creative streak and a refreshingly acerbic sense of humor, and I considered him to be the ideal choice to bring to domestic policy the same intellectually wide-ranging but organizationally disciplined approach that Kissinger had brought so successfully to foreign policy.

On the personal side, the biggest surprise of the first year for Pat and me was that we had not been prepared for the paradoxical combination of loss of privacy and sense of isolation that we experienced in the White House. When I was Vice President we had had many official obligations, but at the end of the day we went home to our family in a residential area of Washington where we did our shopping in the local markets, and had a large circle of friends with whom we could unwind and relax. But the President and First Lady soon discover that everything they do or say is potentially news. They are surrounded by Secret Service agents, staff members, communications teams, medics and doctors, transportation aides, and scores of reporters and photographers whose only job is to try to get a word with them or a picture of them. Any moments of real privacy suddenly seem especially precious, and increasingly Pat and I liked to spend time at Camp David, in Key Biscayne, and at our home in San Clemente, California.

At the same time I discovered how isolated from the reality of American life a President can feel in the White House. For all its cosmopolitan self-confidence, Washington is a parochial city preoccupied by politics and gossip—which at times in Washington are the same thing. Like other Presidents before and after me, I felt a need to get out of the White House and out of Washington in order to keep some sense of perspective.

Looking back over 1969, I saw it as a beginning—a solid beginning. We had held our own. The new year would begin a new decade, and I looked forward to the opportunity to leave the turbulent 1960s behind and begin a new era of creative and peaceful progress for America and the world.

1970

From a political standpoint, my approach to the question of civil rights for black Americans was similar to my approach to the question of Israel. In each case, I was in the unique position of being politically unbeholden to the major pressure group involved, and this meant that I was more readily trusted by opposing or competing groups; this, in turn, meant that I had more flexibility and freedom to do solely what I thought was the right thing.

During the 1960s, particularly under President Johnson, there had been great strides in making the laws ensure the guaranteed rights of every American. With the passage of the Civil Rights Act of 1964 and the Voting Rights Act of 1965, almost every legislative roadblock to equality of opportunity for education, jobs, and voting had been removed. But passing legislation in Washington was one thing; enforcing it throughout the country was another. Expectations had been raised too high, and some black extremists now advocated and engaged in violent action in their efforts to pressure the federal government to hasten the rate of real progress.

Two weeks after the 1964 Civil Rights Act was passed, the first new outbreaks of racial violence occurred. The Harlem riots of 1964 were followed by the 1965 Watts riot, in which arson, looting, sniping, even killing suddenly became the preferred tools of many of the new activists of both races. George Wallace used the inevitable white backlash to build a formidable third party candidacy in 1968.

When I came into office in 1969, the black extremists

were still riding high. Despite the laws, the money spent on the problem, and the significant progress that had in fact been made, black Americans appeared to be more dissatisfied with their lot at the end of the 1960s than they were at the beginning, and tensions between black and white had never been higher. I felt that as a Republican and a moderate conservative I had a better chance of achieving an accommodation between the races than a Democrat or a liberal who was publicly committed to one particular constituency. In formulating my policies I tried to strike a moderate balance. Inevitably I dissatisfied the people on both extremes. As I told members of my staff at one of our early meetings, "I could deliver the Sermon on the Mount and the NAACP would criticize the rhetoric. And the diehard segregationists would criticize it on the grounds that I was being motivated solely by public pressure rather than by conscience. So let's just tackle the problems instead of talking about them. We will be judged by what we do rather than what we say on this issue."

Finally, I knew that we had to attack the problem on a number of fronts. I felt that while education would be the most difficult and the most important, there were also questions of jobs, of welfare reform, of encouraging minority business enterprise, and of housing.

A few weeks after the inauguration, Pat Moynihan brought Rev. Ralph Abernathy, president of the Southern Christian Leadership Conference, and several of his associates to the White House. I had first met Abernathy in 1957 when he was Martin Luther King's chief lieutenant. While he may have been a good lieutenant, I could see that he had not developed into a good general; he lacked the vision and the wisdom that King had had in such a remarkable degree. Most of the Cabinet and key members of the White House staff assembled in the Roosevelt Room to meet with Abernathy, but the long session was a shambles because he was either unprepared or unwilling, or both, to have a serious discussion. Instead he postured and made speeches. He began by reading a list of demands and spent the rest of the time restating them in more colorful ways. Nonetheless he seemed pleased that we had made this effort and at the end he thanked me profusely for taking the time to meet with them. When he left the Cabinet Room he walked into the briefing room and told reporters that he had just sat through "the most disappointing, the most fruitless of all the meetings we had had up to this time."

Moynihan was embarrassed and outraged. He came into the Oval Office and paced the floor and said, "After the way you and the rest of us listened and indicated our sincere desire to find solutions to the problems, he goes into the press room and pisses on the President of the United States. It was unconscionable and I promise you it will never happen again."

Moynihan had been surprised by Abernathy's conduct, but I wasn't. I said, "The problem as I see it, is that they don't think that I care. We must demonstrate to them that we *do* care by our actions and not just by our words."

It was ironic that Moynihan, who was among the strongest advocates of civil rights programs in my administration, provided the very words over which we were subsequently accused of being reactionaries in a memo he wrote to me early in 1970. In it he set forth a number of positive initiatives he felt we should undertake. In a section clearly referring to the desirability of cooling inflated rhetoric, he wrote:

> The time may have come when the issue of race could benefit from a period of "benign neglect." The subject has been too much talked about. The forum has been too much taken over by hysterics, paranoids, and boodlers on all sides. We may need a period in which Negro progress continues and racial rhetoric fades.

The phrase *benign neglect* was seized upon out of context to characterize the administration's attitude toward blacks and other minorities. It was a term that caught on and was played back to us every time we tried to do something constructive in the civil rights area. Moynihan was deeply distressed by this incident and offered to resign. Of course, I refused his offer.

A good job is as basic and important a civil right as a good education, and many blacks and members of other minorities were being prevented from getting good jobs because of the policies of the major labor unions which excluded them from membership or discriminated against them in hiring and promotion. Therefore the first problem we addressed was unemployment. I asked Secretary of Labor George Shultz to see what could be done. He proposed a plan which would require all contractors working on federally funded construction projects to pledge a good faith effort toward the goal of hiring a representative number of minority workers.

Shultz pointed out that of the 1.3 million construction workers in the United States, only 106,000 were black, and 80 percent of those were in the lowest paid category of laborers; of the 130,000 building apprentices in the country, only 5,000 were black.

As Vice President I had been chairman of Eisenhower's Committee on Government Contracts, which made substantial progress in using persuasion and publicity to encourage companies with government contracts to hire more minority workers. I felt that the plan Shultz devised, which would require such action by law, was both necessary and right. We would not fix quotas, but would require federal contractors to show "affirmative action" to meet the goals of increasing minority employment. For example, in Philadelphia the goal would be to increase it from 4 percent to 26 percent between 1969 and 1973. Other cities would have other goals.

Congressional conservatives joined organized labor in vehemently opposing this plan. They considered it heretical for a Republican President to propose such a thing—and heresy is rarely politically popular. Right up to his death in September 1969, Everett Dirksen urged me to abandon it. In a meeting in the Cabinet Room with the legislative leaders he said, in his characteristically colorful way, "As your leader in the Senate of the United States, it is my bounden duty to tell you that this thing is about as popular as a crab in a whorehouse. You will split your own party if you insist on pursuing it. And, Mr. President, I do not think that I myself will be able to support you on this ill-conceived scheme."

By the end of October 1969, a contract was awarded that put the plan into effect for six construction unions working on a federally funded hospital in Philadelphia. What became known as the Philadelphia Plan was soon extended to building trades unions in New York, Pittsburgh, Seattle, Los Angeles, St. Louis, San Francisco, Boston, Chicago, and Detroit.

George Meany hit the roof, charging that the administration was making the unions a whipping boy and trying to score "brownie points" with civil rights groups. Union lobbyists applied tremendous political power and pressure to members of Congress, and damaging amendments were adopted by the Senate. We carried the battle to the floor of both houses. Eventually, due in large part to the leadership of Jerry Ford and Hugh Scott, our efforts paid off. Both the Senate and House rejected the amendments, which would have gutted the Philadelphia Plan.

Getting the plan written into law turned out to be easier than implementing the law. There were some initial successes, but I was disappointed that we received only lukewarm support from most of the national black leaders, who tended either to minimize the results we had achieved, or to complain that we had not gone far enough. Once again I had to wonder whether the black leadership was not more interested in dramatic tokenism than in the hard fight for actual progress.

An important area where we were able to make a considerable impact was in the field of minority business enterprise. During the 1968 campaign I had delivered a radio address entitled "Bridges to Human Dignity" in which I urged new efforts to bring members of minority groups into the economic mainstream. Unless they were to be a permanent inferior economic class apart from other Americans, we had to find ways to give qualified blacks and other minorities a stake in the American private enterprise system. During the transition period I delegated this responsibility to Secretary of Commerce Maurice Stans and told him that I considered it to be of the highest priority. The statistics demonstrate that while we did not attain all the goals we set for ourselves, we made substantial progress in this area.

When I entered office in 1969, minority enterprises were getting only $8 million of business through government contracts. By 1972 they were getting $242 million. In the same period the total of all government grants, loans, and guarantees directed toward helping minority business enterprises had jumped from $200 million to $472 million. Of the 100 largest black-owned businesses in 1975, more than two-thirds had been formed since 1968. Most important, all of this activity was reflected at the cash register, where receipts of black-owned businesses jumped from $4.5 billion in 1968 to $7.2 billion in 1972.

The most explosive of the civil rights issues during my presidency were the questions of school desegregation and busing. Fifteen years had passed since the Supreme Court handed down its landmark decision that laws requiring segregated schools were unconstitutional in *Brown* v. *Board of Education.* After the *Brown* decision, segregation by law—de jure segregation—was illegal as well as wrong; where it could be proved to exist, the law could be used to stop it. It was more difficult to deal with the problem of unequal education for black and white students because of segregation which existed, not as a result of conscious discrimination by law, but as the natural outgrowth of economic and social patterns within individual communities and neighborhoods—de facto segregation.

Despite a great deal of rhetoric and a few highly publicized symbolic confrontations during the Kennedy and Johnson administrations, very little progress was made in ending the dual school system in the South. When I came into office in January 1969, 68 percent of black children in the South were still going to all-black schools and 78.8 percent were going to schools that were 80 percent or more black.

The question in 1969 was whether the courts should try to correct the remnants of de jure segregation, which existed primarily in the South, by forcibly mixing the races in the schools. The principal tool by which this was to be accomplished was busing, whereby schoolchildren would be put on buses and driven to different schools within the district until the racial balance in each school reflected the racial balance in the community as a whole. One alternative to busing was for Congress to provide money to upgrade inferior education wherever it existed and thereby remedy the problem without disrupting the neighborhood school.

I wanted to eliminate the last vestiges of segregation by law, and I wanted to do it in a way that treated all parts of the nation equally. I was determined that the South would not continue to be a scapegoat for Northern liberals. I was not willing, however, to impose wholesale busing, because I believe strongly in the neighborhood school. Even more important, I do not believe that schoolchildren should be torn from their home environments and, solely because of their race, be forced to go to distant schools where they might not be welcome or even safe. Compulsory segregation was wrong; but compulsory racial balancing was also wrong.

I believed that with the right approach we could persuade people in the South and elsewhere not just to obey the law because it was the law, but gradually to bring them to an understanding and acceptance of the wisdom and humanity that lay behind it. In the meantime, I felt that as long as the law was not being deliberately disobeyed, the federal government should be an instrument of persuasion rather than an engine of coercion; the President should be the conciliator rather than the divider.

I felt that, to the greatest extent possible, plans for desegregation should be made by school boards, local communities, and the courts in each area or region, rather than by bureaucrats in HEW in Washington.

Many school districts decided not to forestall the inevitable and simply complied with the desegregation deadlines which had been laid down by the Supreme Court in 1968. Some districts decided to resist any change and submitted proposals for delays that were patently obstructionist. We rejected a number of these proposals and cut off federal funds. Others, however, tried to find solutions in responsible and responsive ways, and we planned to grant these districts limited and supervised delays.

But on October 29, 1969, just as the school year was getting under way, the Supreme Court handed down a unanimous decision that required every school district to terminate segregated school systems *at once*. I felt that the

Court had set a deadline that was unrealistic and would be impossible to meet, but I had no choice other than to enforce the ruling.

At my next press conference I was asked about my policy on school desegregation. I replied that it was "to carry out what the Supreme Court has laid down. I believe in carrying out the law even though I may have disagreed as I did in this instance with the decree."

I felt obliged to uphold the law; but I did not feel obliged to do any more than the minimum the law required, while hoping that the Court would eventually see how its well-intentioned ruling was both legally and socially counterproductive. One thing I was determined to ensure was that the many young liberal lawyers in HEW and in the Justice Department's Civil Rights Division would not treat this decision as a carte blanche for them to run wild through the South enforcing compliance with extreme or punitive requirements they had formulated in Washington.

The Court's February deadline for immediate desegregation passed without incident. Some of the remaining segregated schools complied; some closed down; others ignored it and waited to see what would happen. Even before that, George Wallace had urged the South to defy the federal government and talked about running for President in 1972. A national Gallup poll found that more than half of those responding felt that school integration was going too fast.

I appointed a Cabinet Committee on Education to consider the problem at the highest level. I told them, "First of all I want everyone, but especially the Negro leaders, to know that our motto around here is 'I care.' The President cares about the situation and he plans to do something about it. The important thing, however, is to keep things in their proper perspective. Once we have made it clear that the law is being upheld and no segregation is legal anywhere in the country, I think we should take into account the possibility that local communities, black and white, might want to keep a certain degree of separation. That's why I want to put our federal money into the best possible education in each school. We've got to stop using the classrooms and the kids as the cutting edges for social and economic problems that will have to be solved elsewhere. Our goal should be education, not litigation."

A week later, Senator Richard Russell of Georgia came to the White House to transmit the views of four Southern governors that HEW bureaucrats were going around the South stirring up trouble and inciting suits. "I don't know what I'd do in your place, Mr. President," my ailing friend said. "I only know you've got a problem that won't go away and will get worse unless you do something about it. The people of Georgia are more worked up over this problem than anything I've seen in all of my years in politics."

I decided that the time had come to issue a major policy statement from the White House. On March 24 I released an 8,000-word statement covering every aspect of the civil rights issue. I reaffirmed my support for desegregation and my opposition to busing; I also indicated that the primary reliance should be on cooperation with local authorities and on voluntary compliance with the law rather than on federal involvement and enforcement. I said that my first priority would be maintaining and improving the quality of public education, and I announced that I would request $1.5 billion over two years for helping school districts desegregate. Reaction to this statement split between those who wanted to coerce the South to comply with the Court's ruling and those who were willing to take a chance on persuasion.

I was convinced that involvement on the part of local leaders and officials was the first prerequisite for a successful policy of persuasion. At the suggestion of my Cabinet Committee, seven of the Southern states which were still in various degrees of noncompliance with the Court's ruling formed State Advisory Committees on school desegregation. On June 24 I met with the Mississippi State Advisory Committee in the White House; there were fifteen members, nine whites and six blacks. One of the black members said to me, "The day before yesterday I was in jail for going to the wrong beach. Today, Mr. President, I am meeting you. If that's possible anything can happen."

Over the next few weeks I met with all of the other state committees, and with each of them I stressed the same points. First, I condemned the hypocrisy in much of the North about the segregation problem. I affirmed my belief that the South should be treated with understanding and patience, but I also stressed the need to solve the problem through peaceful compliance. Second, I emphasized my commitment to the principle of local leadership to solve local problems. I got across subtly but unmistakably the point that if they did not act to solve the problem I would be forced to act to carry out my responsibility to enforce the law of the land.

Most of the whites who attended these meetings believed that the Court's decision was wrong; and some of the blacks entered the meetings with a skeptical view because they thought that only strong federal intervention would bring about compliance with the law. The meetings showed that it was possible for both sides to meet and talk about their concerns.

I knew that I was walking a fine line between the instant integrationists and the segregation-forever extremists, but I felt that the risk would be well worth it if we could solve the problem without getting the federal government involved.

At the end of July, I received a long memorandum from Harry Dent, my Southern political liaison man. He wrote that there was "a dangerous, growing concern in the Southern and conservative political communities—a concern that the administration is heading left in an effort to quiet those who have been against the administration." He said there was a feeling that " 'the squeaky wheel gets the grease' " and that at a recent meeting most of the Southern Republican chairmen had expressed the feeling that "We've been good guys too long and have gotten nothing but rhetoric while the bad guys have been in the streets getting all the attention and action."

On August 6, the same day that the Georgia State Advisory Committee came to the White House, I met with the leading conservative senators and Southern Republicans, including Ed Gurney of Florida, Barry Goldwater, Strom Thurmond, and John Tower. They complained bitterly that the administration had turned sharply to the left on the civil rights issue. Demands were made that I fire Jerris Leonard, Assistant Attorney General for the Civil Rights Division, and others who had been working to implement my policies. I listened to them and told them I was actually restraining bureaucrats from HEW and the Justice

Department who wanted to move more aggressively, and in my opinion irresponsibly, on the South. At the same time I emphasized that I had a responsibility to carry out the law of the land and that I was determined to meet that responsibility.

On August 14 I flew to New Orleans to join the Louisiana State Advisory Committee, which was holding its first meeting. Before I arrived the members had become hopelessly deadlocked. After talking to each one individually, I was able to convince them of the need for progress and they agreed to make another try.

As the beginning of the new school year approached, tension began to mount. Would my faith in the power of persuasion be justified? Or would federal troops have to be called out to enforce integration?

At the end of August I personally asked Billy Graham to record some TV appeals in support of voluntary compliance. He made a videotape that was shown in all the Southern states, and I am convinced it had a very positive and powerful influence.

To my great relief, the policy worked. Schools in the South and all across the country opened in the fall of 1970 without violence and in compliance with the Supreme Court's order. The dramatic success of our Southern school desegregation program is eloquently told by the statistics. By 1974 only 8 percent of black children in the South were attending all-black schools, down from 68 percent in the fall of 1968.

My personal philosophy regarding the problem of busing and civil rights issues generally was set forth in detail in a memorandum I wrote to John Ehrlichman on January 28, 1972:

I begin with the proposition that freedom of choice in housing, education, and jobs must be the right of every American. My support for family assistance, even though I have serious doubts as to whether it will work, is primarily based on the conclusion that only by such a program does freedom of choice have any chance to become a reality for millions of families who live below the poverty line. By freedom of choice of course I mean in the deepest philosophical sense and not in the narrow obstructionist sense that the term was used in fighting the school cases in the South in 1966-67 and 68. Legally segregated education, legally segregated housing, legal obstructions to equal employment must be totally removed.

On the other hand I am convinced that while legal segregation is totally wrong, forced integration of housing or education is just as wrong.

I realize that this position will lead us to a situation in which blacks will continue to live for the most part in black neighborhoods and where there will be predominantly black schools and predominantly white schools in the metropolitan areas. While I cannot go as far as Scammon in contending that those who insist on forced integrated education are really practicing white supremacy there is unfortunately a grain of truth in it. . . .

In any event I believe there may be some doubt as to the validity of the Brown philosophy that integrating education will pull up the blacks and not pull down the whites. But while there may be some doubt as to whether segregated education is inferior there is no doubt whatever on another point—that education requiring excessive transportation for students is definitely inferior. I come down hard and unequivocally against busing for the purpose of racial balance. . . .

Having made all these points I come down hard on another point which I think is absolutely overriding. This country is not ready at this time for either forcibly integrated housing or forcibly integrated education. . . .

We simply have to face the hard fact the law cannot go beyond what the people are willing to support. This is true insofar as Prohibition is concerned. It is far more true with regard to education and even more true with regard to housing where economic considerations enter the picture. . . .

We cannot sweep this issue under the rug. It is going to explode all over the landscape during this next year. . . . My feelings on race as you know are if anything ultraliberal. But I cannot duck the responsibility for coming down on the side which is right. . . . Even if I should become convinced—and I don't think it would be possible to convince me—that forced integration of education and housing was in the best interests of blacks and not too detrimental to whites I could not possibly support it in good conscience. What I am saying through this memorandum, is that as a matter of conscience I have reached a conclusion motivated not by politics but by my considered evaluation of all the issues involved, that I must speak to these two controversial issues now firmly without equivocation and if necessary through the advocacy of a constitutional amendment.

Although I considered the idea of a constitutional amendment at that time, I now believe that it would have exacerbated the already volatile issues of integrated education and housing with which we were confronted.

Personally I had always felt that the real issue in school desegregation was that of quality education. In my opinion, the *Brown* decision was based on the principle that the dual school system in the South was wrong not because segregation was wrong per se, but because in practice it produced Negro schools that were educationally inferior. To my mind, subsequent Court decisions have muddied the waters by assuming, incorrectly, that the issue involved race rather than education. I simply do not believe that education is the great leveler of social barriers that it was thought to be by the framers of the Great Society programs. I feel that home environment has more to do with success in life than has any amount of integrated education; busing black children from poor families to richer white schools will have little effect on how they learn.

During the years I was President I placed primary emphasis on better education in neighborhood schools. In a message to Congress on March 16, 1972, I proposed directing over $2.5 billion mainly toward improving the education of children from poor families. I hoped by doing this that we could retrieve a lost generation of children who had been doomed to inferior education in the central cities.

Controversy continued to rage over the interpretation of the Supreme Court's decisions on busing. Some lower courts ordered or approved busing plans that went much further than the Supreme Court had intended, and in 1972 Chief Justice Burger issued a memorandum for the guidance of courts across the country, making it clear that the high Court did not *require* busing for the purpose of achieving racial balance.

Just before I resigned in 1974, the Supreme Court further endorsed my position by holding that unless school districts were gerrymandered for the purpose, or with the intent, of segregating blacks from whites, the law did not require busing to ensure racial balance. In his opinion, Chief Justice Burger wrote that "no single tradition in public education is more deeply rooted than local control."

As far as my administration's overall record on civil rights is concerned, I believe we can point with justifiable pride to what was accomplished in the area of peacefully desegregating schools in the South. As Pat Moynihan put it in a memo shortly after the school year began in 1970, "There has been more change in the structure of American public school education in the past month than in the past 100 years."

CAMBODIA AND KENT STATE

As 1970 began, our intelligence indicated that Communist infiltration from North into South Vietnam was increasing substantially. The North Vietnamese had also begun moving large numbers of troops and equipment into Cambodia and Laos.

In view of this enemy activity I felt that we had to think about initiatives we could undertake to show the enemy that we were still serious about our commitment in Vietnam.

On February 21 Kissinger had his second secret meeting in Paris with the North Vietnamese. The situation had changed dramatically since the first meeting in August, largely because my November 3 speech had strengthened my position at home. A Gallup poll at the end of January found that 65 percent of the nation approved of my handling of Vietnam. Even more disturbing for the North Vietnamese must have been the knowledge that we were now talking to their two major military patrons: the Soviets had recently proposed four-power discussions on the Berlin question in Bonn, and the Chinese Communists had agreed to resume the ambassadorial talks with us in Warsaw.

This time Le Duc Tho joined Xuan Thuy in participating in the talks with Kissinger. Tho was a member of the Hanoi Politburo, which meant that the talks now had at least reached the decision-making level.

Trying to capitalize on the reaction to my speech, Kissinger emphatically warned them not to underestimate the strong support I had for my Vietnam policy. "I know that here in Paris you see many Americans who are extremely sympathetic to your position. But in the last election the big bloc of votes was not on the left but on the right. President Nixon can appeal to people whom President Johnson could not reach," he told them. Le Duc Tho countered suavely that it was his impression that since August the antiwar movement in the United States had surged higher than ever. He said that he had seen many statements by the Senate Foreign Relations Committee, by the Democratic Party, and by Clark Clifford demanding the total withdrawal of American forces and the change of the Thieu government. Tho bluntly told Kissinger, "The present administration of Thieu-Ky-Khiem is opposed by the people and the press of the U.S., as by the great majority of the people of South Vietnam."

Kissinger had felt from the start that Tho's bombast concealed genuine North Vietnamese doubts and worries. This appraisal seemed to be borne out later in the meeting when the North Vietnamese became more conciliatory. In fact, it appeared that they were ready to begin serious negotiations in the private channel. They suggested another meeting for March 16.

When Kissinger returned to Washington he reported that "this has been an important meeting, certainly the most important since the beginning of your administration and even since the beginning of the talks in 1968."

At the end of Kissinger's memo proposing our strategy for the next secret meeting, I wrote a short note about the way I thought he should deal with the North Vietnamese at their next session. "Don't haggle so much over 'what did they mean by this or that,' " I wrote. "They thrive on this kind of discussion. Come directly to the hard decisions on the two major issues and say 'we will leave details to subordinates'—otherwise you will spend two days on details and make no progress on substance. We need a breakthrough on principle—and substance. Tell them we want to go immediately to the core of the problem."

When they met again on March 16, Kissinger told the North Vietnamese that if a settlement could be reached, we would have all our troops out of Vietnam within sixteen months. They appeared interested but remained noncommittal. Kissinger's conclusion was that "two more meetings should tell the story."

A few days later an unexpected event completely altered the situation. On March 18, while the Cambodian head of state Prince Sihanouk was visiting Moscow, he was overthrown by a bloodless military coup that brought to power General Lon Nol, a strong anti-Communist.

Lon Nol's coup came as a complete surprise. The CIA had received no indication that the opposition to Sihanouk had gone so far. "What the hell do those clowns do out there in Langley?" I asked Bill Rogers impatiently.

My immediate inclination was to do everything possible to help Lon Nol, but Rogers and Laird strongly recommended that we hold back. They pointed out that Moscow, Peking, and Hanoi would be in great turmoil and suspect us of having financed and staged the coup. If we provided economic and military aid now, they argued, we would confirm such suspicions and possibly even supply the North Vietnamese with a pretext for abandoning their official facade of noninvolvement and thereby unleash a full-scale invasion of Cambodia. Helms also urged restraint. He reported that the Lon Nol government was unlikely to survive. It would put us in a very bad light, he said, to rush aid to a government that might be overthrown even before our aid arrived.

I decided to withhold any aid for at least a week, during which time Lon Nol, whose troops fought surprisingly well against the highly trained Communist Khmer Rouge and North Vietnamese, proceeded on his own to cut off a major source of Communist supplies by closing the Cambodian port of Sihanoukville.

Against this background Kissinger prepared for another meeting with the North Vietnamese in Paris. Before he left, he sent me a memo requesting approval for the strategy he wanted to follow. He felt that the time had come for our side to be very firm and find out whether the Communists really meant to negotiate. I approved this strategy and even strengthened it. "Put a time limit on it," I wrote on his memo.

The meeting lasted almost five hours. The North Vietnamese were not forthcoming. Kissinger felt that they had been confused by the events in Cambodia, which they charged us with having engineered. Following my instructions, he proposed that a time limit be set for reaching an agreement in the secret talks. When they would not agree to this, he suggested that the channel be closed down until one side or the other had something new to discuss.

The whole situation over Cambodia and Vietnam was becoming so tense that I felt I had to make a very painful personal decision. Although I knew how much Pat and Julie were counting on it, I canceled our plans to attend David's graduation from Amherst and Julie's graduation from Smith later in the spring. Pat had never known the joy of having a parent attend any of her graduations, and I knew that she had been looking forward to Julie's. Julie was also terribly disappointed. She tried to hold back her tears, and she pointed out that only a few small radical groups were involved, and that everyone she knew—including students who opposed the war and my administration—felt that I should be able to attend the ceremony.

Ted Agnew felt particularly strongly about this. "Don't let them intimidate you, Mr. President," he said, barely restraining his indignation. "You may be President, but you're her father, and a father should be able to attend his daughter's graduation." The Secret Service, however, had received reports of several protest demonstrations that were already being planned against me, and the possibility of an ugly incident that would mar the graduation, not just for us but for all the other students and parents, was too great to risk.

Despite the impasse in the secret talks and the worsening military situation in Cambodia, I decided to go ahead with the troop withdrawal scheduled for April 20. I discussed the issue at length with Kissinger, and we agreed that the time had come to drop a bombshell on the gathering spring storm of antiwar protest.

554

Vietnamization had progressed to the point that, for the first time, we felt we could project our troop withdrawals over the next year. We decided, therefore, that instead of announcing a smaller number over a shorter period, I would announce the withdrawal of 150,000 men over the next year.

The withdrawal figure came as a dramatic surprise when I revealed it in a speech on April 20. The only Communist reaction was an escalation of the fighting.

By the end of April, the Communists had a quarter of Cambodia under control and were closing in on Phnom Penh. It was clear that Lon Nol needed help to survive. If the Communists succeeded in overthrowing him, South Vietnam would be threatened from the west as well as the north. This situation would jeopardize our troop withdrawal program and would also virtually assure a Communist invasion of South Vietnam as soon as the last American had left.

Support for Lon Nol was to be discussed at an NSC meeting on April 22. I woke up early that morning and dictated a memorandum to Kissinger:

Assuming that I feel the way today at our meeting as I feel this morning (it is 5 A.M., April 22), I think we need a bold move in Cambodia to show that we stand with Lon Nol.

I do not believe he is going to survive. There is, however, some chance that he might, and in any event we must do something symbolic to help him survive.

We have really dropped the ball on this one due to the fact that we were taken in with the line that by helping him we would destroy his "neutrality" and give the North Vietnamese an excuse to come in. Over and over again we fail to learn that the Communists never need an excuse to come in.

They didn't need one in Hungary in 1956 when the same argument was made by the career State people and when Dulles bought it because he was tired and it was during the campaign.

They didn't need one in Czechoslovakia when the same argument was made by the State people. And they didn't need one in Laos where we lost a precious day by failing to make the strike that might have blunted the whole offensive before it got started, and in Cambodia, where we have taken a completely hands-off attitude by protesting to the Senate that we have only a delegation of seven State Department jerks in the embassy, and would not provide any aid of any kind because we were fearful that if we did so it would give them a "provocation" to come in.

They are romping in there, and the only government in Cambodia in the last twenty-five years that had the guts to take a pro-Western and pro-American stand is ready to fall . . .

I will talk to you about this after the NSC meeting.

The Communist sanctuaries in Cambodia were in two main areas. The Parrot's Beak is a sliver of land that pushes into South Vietnam and reaches within thirty-three miles of Saigon. A particularly strong ARVN [South Vietnamese Army] force was stationed on the border in this area. Our intelligence reports indicated that the heaviest Communist concentration was in another border area, the Fishhook, a thin, curving piece of Cambodian territory jutting right into the heart of South Vietnam, about fifty miles northwest of Saigon. This was the primary area of operation for what intelligence referred to as COSVN—the Central Office of South Vietnam. COSVN was the Communists' floating command post of military headquarters, supplies, food, and medical facilities. The Fishhook was thus the nerve center of the Communist forces in the sanctuaries, and it would be strongly defended. The initial intelligence estimates projected that the heavy fortifications and the concentration of Communist troops in the area might result in very high casualties in the first week of the operation.

I began to consider letting the ARVN go into the Parrot's Beak and sending a mixed force of American and South Vietnamese troops into the Fishhook. Giving the South Vietnamese an operation of their own would be a major boost to their morale as well as provide a practical demonstration of the success of Vietnamization. It would also be a good diversionary cover for the more important and more difficult Fishhook operation.

I never had any illusions about the shattering effect a decision to go into Cambodia would have on public opinion at home. I knew that opinions among my major foreign policy advisers were deeply divided over the issue of widening the war, and I recognized that it could mean personal and political catastrophe for me and my administration.

On Sunday night, April 26, I reached my decision. We would go for broke. The ARVN would go into the Parrot's Beak and a joint ARVN-U.S. force would go into the Fishhook.

On Monday morning I met with Rogers, Laird, and Kissinger. It was a tense meeting, because even though Rogers and Laird had by now given up hope of dissuading me from taking some action in Cambodia, they still thought they could convince me not to involve American troops. Rogers said, "It will cost us great casualties with very little gain. And I just don't believe it will be a crippling blow to the enemy." Laird said, "I'm not really opposed to going after the COSVN, but I'm not happy with the way this is being implemented." He was more upset, it seemed, with an apparent snub of the Pentagon in our decision-making process. He also suggested that General Abrams might not approve of the COSVN operation, but backed away when Kissinger contradicted him. Nevertheless, immediately after our meeting I sent a back-channel cable to Abrams, ordering him to send me the "unvarnished truth" about the way he felt.

A joint response from Abrams and U.S. Ambassador Ellsworth Bunker indicated full support on their part. Speaking specifically of the attack on the Fishhook, they wrote: "We both agree that attack on this area should have maximum unsettling effect on the enemy, who has considered until now his sanctuaries immune to ground attack." Abrams added his personal views in a separate paragraph: "It is my independent view that these attacks into the enemy's sanctuaries in Cambodia are the military move to make at this time in support of our mission in South Vietnam both in terms of security of our own forces and for advancement of the Vietnamization program."

That night I sat alone going over the decision one last time. It was still not too late to call the operation off: the Parrot's Beak action would not begin until the next morning, and the Fishhook not until two days after that. I took a pad and began to make a list of the pluses and minuses of both operations. The risk and danger involved were undeniably great; there was no assurance of success on the battlefield and there was the certainty of an uproar at home. But there was also no question that the continued existence of the Cambodian sanctuaries would threaten the safety of the remaining American troops in South Vietnam and almost guarantee a Communist invasion as soon as we had pulled out.

Early the next morning I showed Kissinger my notes. He blinked his eyes as he took a piece of paper from the folder he was carrying and handed it to me. It was a list almost identical to mine. "I did the same thing, Mr. President," he said, "and it looks like we're both able to make a good case both ways on it."

I said that as far as I was concerned, the simple fact of showing the Communists that we intended to protect ourselves and our allies put all the weight on one side. "Now that we have made the decision there must be no recriminations among us," I said. "Not even if the whole thing goes wrong. In fact, *especially* if the whole thing goes wrong."

South Vietnam's announcement of the Parrot's Beak operation came over the wires on Wednesday, April 29. Within minutes the leading Senate doves were in front of the TV cameras, demanding that I disavow Thieu's offensive and not send any American troops into Cambodia. All during the day I continued to work on the speech I would deliver the next night announcing the operation. I asked Rose to call Julie for me. "I don't want to get her upset, but it's possible that the campuses are really going to blow up after this speech," I said, "so could you just say I asked if she and David could come down from school to be with us."

That night I found it difficult to get to sleep. After tossing fitfully for an hour or so, I got up and sat in the Lincoln Sitting Room until 5:30. At nine o'clock I walked over to my EOB office to go over the first pages of the typed speech. That afternoon I had Haldeman and Kissinger come over so I could read the announcement to them. I asked Kissinger to brief George Meany, because I knew that labor support would be vital. A little later he reported that Meany supported my decision whole-heartedly. Kissinger had less success with his own NSC staff. Three of his top assistants decided to resign in protest over my decision.

Shortly before delivering the speech from the Oval Office, I went to the White House Theatre to brief the bipartisan congressional leadership. I said I understood that many of them would oppose the decision I had made. I knew how they felt about it, and I respected their feelings. "I just want you to know that whether you think it's right or wrong, the reason I have decided to do this is that I have decided it's the best way to end the war and save the lives of our soldiers," I told them.

I looked around the room. The faces were intent and strained. Some of the strongest doves were there: Fulbright, Mansfield, Aiken, Kennedy. The sincerity of my words must have reached them, even though they remained opposed to the decision I had made. As I left the room, everyone stood and applauded.

I began the speech by describing how the Communists had responded to my recently announced troop withdrawal by stepping up their attacks throughout Indochina. "To protect our men who are in Vietnam and to guarantee the continued success of our withdrawal and Vietnamization programs," I said, "I have concluded that the time has come for action."

I used a map to explain the geographic and strategic importance of the Cambodian sanctuaries and to describe the South Vietnamese operation in the Parrot's Beak. Then I announced that a joint U.S.-Vietnamese force would go into the Fishhook.

I stressed that this was not an invasion of Cambodia. The sanctuaries were completely occupied and controlled by North Vietnamese forces. We would withdraw once they had been driven out and once their military supplies were destroyed. The purpose, I said, was not to expand the war into Cambodia, but to end the war in Vietnam by making peace possible.

Setting my decision in its widest context, I continued, "If, when the chips are down, the world's most powerful nation, the United States of America, acts like a pitiful, helpless giant, the forces of totalitarianism and anarchy will threaten free nations and free institutions throughout the world."

For an hour after the speech I sat with my family in the

Solarium while they discussed the speech and tried to gauge the reactions to it. Then I went to the Lincoln Sitting Room and began returning calls that had come in after the speech.

Just after 10:30 I was informed that Chief Justice Warren Burger was at the gate with a letter for me. I instructed the Secret Service agent on duty to have him shown up immediately.

"I didn't want to disturb you, Mr. President," Burger said, "but I wanted you to know that I think your speech tonight had a sense of history and destiny about it."

I said that the critics had already begun denouncing the speech and the decision, but he said that he was sure it would be supported by the people. "I think anyone who really listened to what you said will appreciate the guts it took to make the decision," he added. He also pointed out that anyone who thought about it would realize that, as a shrewd politician, I would obviously not do anything that might damage Republican chances in the November elections unless I felt that it was absolutely necessary for national security.

"Speaking in the greatest confidence, Mr. Chief Justice," I said, using his formal title as I always did when addressing him, "I am realist enough to know that if this operation doesn't succeed—or if anything else happens that forces my public support below a point where I feel I can't be re-elected—I would like you to be ready to be in the running for the nomination in 1972."

When I finally went to my bedroom around three o'clock, I found a note from Julie.

Dear Daddy,

I was very proud of you tonight. You explained the situation in Vietnam perfectly—I am sure the American people will realize why you made your decision. I especially want to tell you how effective—and heartfelt—your final message to the people of South and North Vietnam, the Soviet Union, and the United States was. I feel that the strongest message which resulted from your speech was: We cannot abandon 17 million people to a living death, and we cannot jeopardize the chances for future world peace by an unqualified pull-out of Vietnam.

I know you are right and, again, I am so proud.

Love,
Julie

Reactions to the speech were along predictable lines. Senator Muskie said, "This speech confirms a judgment that I've been reluctant to reach: the President has decided to seek a military method of ending this war rather than a negotiated method." Senator Walter Mondale of Minnesota said, "This is not only a tragic escalation, which will broaden the war and increase American casualties, but is outright admission of the failure of Vietnamization."

The New Republic began a front-cover editorial with the sentence: "Richard Nixon is going down in history, all right, but not soon enough," and said my speech was "insensitive," "phony," "a fraud," "indifferent," and "dangerous." The New York *Times* said I was "out of touch" with the nation.

In Britain, *The Economist* took a different point of view: "It is not the Americans who have brought the war to Cambodia, but the Communists. For years, North Vietnam has violated the neutrality of this country—with barely a chirp of protest from the rest of the world. . . . To condemn the United States for 'invading' neutral Cambodia is about as rational as to condemn Britain for 'invading' formally neutral Holland in 1944."

Despite very little sleep, I was up early on the morning after the speech. I went to the Pentagon for a firsthand briefing on the Cambodian operation from the Joint Chiefs and their top advisers. As I walked through the halls to the briefing room, I was mobbed by people cheering and trying to shake my hand. "God bless you!" "Right on!" "We should have done this years ago!" they shouted.

The atmosphere in the briefing room was generally positive if some-what more restrained. A huge map of the battle area almost covered one wall. Different colored pins indicated the positions and movements of the various forces. As the briefers described the initial success of the operation,

I found myself studying the map more and more intently. I noted that in addition to the Parrot's Beak and the Fishhook, four other areas were marked as occupied by Communist forces.

Suddenly I asked, "Between the ARVN and ourselves, would we be able to mount offensives in all of those other areas? Could we take out *all* the sanctuaries?"

The reply to my question emphasized the very negative reaction any such action would receive in the media and Congress.

"Let me be the judge as far as the political reactions are concerned," I said. "The fact is that we have already taken the political heat for this particular operation. If we can substantially reduce the threat to our forces by wiping out the rest of the sanctuaries, now is the time to do it."

Everyone seemed to be waiting for someone else to speak. Usually I like to mull things over, but I made a very uncharacteristic on-the-spot decision. I said, "I want to take out all of those sanctuaries. Make whatever plans are necessary, and then just do it. Knock them all out so that they can't be used against us again. Ever."

As I left the Pentagon after the briefing, once again employees rushed into the halls. By the time I reached the lobby, I was surrounded by a friendly, cheering crowd. One woman was particularly emotional as she thanked me on behalf of her husband, who was serving in Vietnam. As I thought of these men and women with loved ones fighting in Vietnam, I could not help thinking about those students who took advantage of their draft deferments and their privileged status in our society to bomb campuses, set fires, and tyrannize their institutions.

"I have seen them," I said about our soldiers in Vietnam. "They're the greatest. You see these bums, you know, blowing up the campuses. Listen, the boys that are on the college campuses today are the luckiest people in the world, going to the greatest universities, and here they are burning up the books, storming around about this issue. . . . Then out there, we have kids who are just doing their duty. And I have seen them. They stand tall, and they are proud."

That afternoon, while the tempest of reaction over Cambodia continued to build, I decided to get my family away from the White House for at least a few hours of relaxation after the great tension we had all experienced. It was a warm, clear day, so I suggested that we sail down the Potomac to Mount Vernon on the *Sequoia.*

It is the custom for all naval vessels passing Mount Vernon to honor George Washington, who is buried there. When we neared the spot, I had everyone move onto the deck and face the shore. Pat was next to me, then David, Julie, and Bebe Rebozo. As we passed by the first President's tomb, over the *Sequoia*'s loudspeaker came "The Star-Spangled Banner." We all stood at attention until the last note died away.

By the time the *Sequoia* had returned to Washington, the indignant reaction to my "bums" statement that morning at the Pentagon had almost overwhelmed the response to the Cambodia speech itself.

All through the spring of 1970 the country had faced wave after wave of violent campus unrest. As with the disturbances at the beginning of 1969, the issues were largely campus-oriented, dealing with disciplinary regulations, campus administration, and minority admissions.

What distinguished many of the 1970 campus disturbances from all earlier ones was the increase in bombings and violence connected with them. Radical groups openly encouraged the bombing of institutions of which they disapproved.

In the academic year 1969-70 there were 1,800 demonstrations, 7,500 arrests, 462 injuries—two-thirds of them were to police—and 247 arsons and 8 deaths.

April 1970 had been a particularly violent month. For the second time, a bank near the University of California at Santa Barbara was set on fire. A fire was set at the University of Kansas that destroyed buildings worth $2 million. At Ohio State University protesters demanding the admission of more black students and the abolition of ROTC on campus engaged in a six-hour battle with police. There were 600 arrests and 20 wounded. Governor James Rhodes finally had to call in 1,200 national guardsmen and impose a curfew to quiet the campus.

It was criminal and barbarous to burn banks as a

protest against capitalism or to burn ROTC buildings as a protest against militarism. But to me the most shocking incidents were those that I considered to be directed at the very quality of intellectual life that should characterize a university community. In March, an arsonist caused $320,000 damage to the University of California library at Berkeley. At the end of April as part of a demonstration in support of Black Panthers charged with murder in New Haven, $2,500 worth of books were set on fire in the basement of the Yale Law School.

The most shameful incident occurred at Stanford University. On April 24 an anti-ROTC group set a fire at the university's center for behavioral studies. One of the offices that was completely gutted belonged to a visiting Indian anthropologist, Professor M. N. Srinivas. His personal notes, files, and manuscripts went up in flames.

When Pat Moynihan told me about this tragedy, I wrote to Professor Srinivas:

> As did countless other Americans, I responded with disbelief at the news that your study at the Center for Advanced Studies in the Behavioral Sciences had been fire-bombed, and that much of the work of a lifetime had been destroyed.
>
> It can be small consolation for you to know that the overwhelming proportion of the American people, and of the American academic community, utterly reject the tactics of the person or persons who did this. To say that they are deranged, does not excuse them. To say, what is more probably the case, that they are simply evil, does not make them go away.
>
> I hope that the great insights of social anthropology that you have brought to your studies might serve in this moment to help you understand this tragedy. Please at all events know that you are an honored and welcome guest, whose work is appreciated and valued in this nation as indeed throughout the world.

I do not think that anyone who heard my comments at the Pentagon or who heard the tape recording of it, had any doubt that when I talked about "bums" burning up the books and blowing up the campuses, I was referring to the arsonists at Berkeley and Yale and the Stanford firebombers and others like them. The Washington *Post* headline the next morning accurately reflected my meaning: *Nixon Denounces Campus "Bums" Who Burn Books, Set Off Bombs.*

But the front-page headline in the New York *Times* conveyed a slightly different meaning: *Nixon Puts "Bums" Label on Some College Radicals*; and the inside continuation of the story was headlined: *Nixon Denounces "Bums" on Campus.*

Within a few days, it was the widespread impression that I had referred to all student protesters as "bums."

The media coverage and interpretation of the "bums" statement added fuel to the fires of dissent that were already getting out of control on many campuses. The National Student Association called for my impeachment, and editors of eleven Eastern colleges, including most of the Ivy League schools, ran a common editorial in their campus newspapers calling for a nationwide academic strike.

At the University of Maryland, just outside Washington, fifty people were injured when students ransacked the ROTC building and skirmished with police. In Kent, Ohio, a crowd of hundreds of demonstrators watched as two young men threw lighted flares into the Army ROTC building on the campus of Kent State University, and burned it to the ground. Governor Rhodes called in the National Guard. He said that 99 percent of the Kent State students wanted the school to remain open, and that the rest were "worse than the brownshirts."

On Monday, May 4, I asked Haldeman to come to the EOB office to go over trip schedules with me. He looked agitated. "Something just came over the wires about a demonstration at Kent State," he said. "The National Guard opened fire, and some students were shot."

I was stunned. "Are they dead?" I asked.

"I'm afraid so. No one knows why it happened."

It appeared that an uneasy confrontation had begun brewing around noon. Finally, a large crowd of students began throwing rocks and chunks of concrete at the guardsmen, forcing them up a small hill. At the top the soldiers turned, and someone started shooting.

In the newspaper the next day I saw the pictures of the

four young people who had been killed. Two had been bystanders; the other two had been protesting a decision they felt was wrong. Now all four were dead, and a call was going out for nationwide demonstrations and student strikes. Would this tragedy become the cause of scores of others? I could not get the photographs out of my mind. I could not help thinking about the families, suddenly receiving the news that their children were dead because they had been shot in a campus demonstration. I wrote personal letters to each of the parents, even though I knew that words could not help.

Those few days after Kent State were among the darkest of my presidency. I felt utterly dejected when I read that the father of one of the dead girls had told a reporter, "My child was not a bum."

Kent State also took a heavy toll on Henry Kissinger's morale. Members of his staff had resigned because of Cambodia, and former Harvard colleagues whom he had considered among his most loyal friends wrote bitter letters to him demanding that he make his professed moral position credible by resigning.

On a day several of these letters arrived, he came into my office and sat staring disconsolately out the window. Finally he said, "I still think you made the right decision as far as foreign policy considerations were involved. But in view of what has happened I fear I may have failed to advise you adequately of the domestic dangers."

I told him that I had been fully aware of both the military and the political risks. I had made the decision myself, and I assumed full responsibility for it. Finally I said, "Henry, remember Lot's wife. Never turn back. Don't waste time rehashing things we can't do anything about."

I was shocked and disappointed when an apparently intentional leak to the press revealed that Bill Rogers and Mel Laird had been opposed to my Cambodian decision. The operation was still in a critical stage, and I called Rogers and told him that I felt the Cabinet should get behind a decision once it had been made by the President.

Walter Hickel, the Secretary of the Interior, chose a more public way to express his conviction that I should listen to the students and spend more time with the Cabinet.

566

In what he later explained as a mishap, a copy of a letter he had written to me raising these points was already going out over the AP wire before it had been delivered to the White House. Several other Cabinet and administration members also took public positions of less than full support.

In the midst of all the furore, it meant a great deal to me when one of the two living Americans who could really know what I was going through wrote to me.

I received a note from Johnson City: "Dear Mr. President," it read, "I hope you have a chance to read this. My best always. LBJ." Attached to it was a recent column by one of Johnson's former assistants, John P. Roche, entitled "The President Makes the Decisions." It began: "What distinguishes the Republican regime from that of Lyndon Johnson is that Mr. Nixon announced an 'open administration,' with the consequence that everyone above the rank of GS-15 feels free to comment on the wisdom of the President's actions." After noting examples of Cabinet members dissociating themselves from my Cambodian decision, Roche concluded by making the point that "Nixon was elected to make a choice and he made it. One can attack it on the merits if he so chooses, that is, say it was mistaken. Or one can support his actions (as I do). But under the Constitution no one has the right to impeach his decision because he did not consult Senator Fulbright, Secretary Finch, Pat Moynihan or the International Security Affairs section of the Pentagon."

Kent State triggered a nationwide wave of campus protests. The daily news reports conveyed a sense of turmoil bordering on insurrection. Hundreds of college campuses went through a paroxysm of rage, riot, and arson. By the end of the first week after the killings, 450 colleges and universities were closed by student or faculty protest strikes. Before the month was over, the National Guard had been called out twenty-four times at twenty-one campuses in sixteen states.

A national day of protest was hastily called to take place in Washington on Saturday, May 9. I felt that we should do everything possible to make sure that this event was nonviolent and that we did not appear insensitive to it.

Ehrlichman urged that we make whatever gestures of communication were possible. Kissinger, however, took a particularly hard line on the demonstrators. He was appalled at the violence they provoked and at the ignorance of the real issues they displayed. He felt strongly that I should not appear more flexible until after the Cambodian operation was successfully completed. As he put it, we had to make it clear that our foreign policy was not made by street protests.

I decided to try to defuse the tension by holding a press conference. The risks were high, and my staff was deeply divided about the wisdom of having one at this time. Most of the reporters and commentators were bound to be bitterly critical, and it was highly possible that an acrimonious session would only make things worse. Nonetheless I decided to go ahead, and the conference was announced for prime time on Friday evening, May 8.

I could feel the emotions seething beneath the hot TV lights as I entered the East Room at ten o'clock Friday night. Almost all the questions were about the Cambodian operation and Kent State.

The first question was whether I had been surprised by the intensity of the protests and whether they would affect my policy in any way. I replied that I had not been surprised by the intensity of the protests. I knew that those who protested did so because they felt that my decision would expand the war, our involvement in it, and our casualties. "I made the decision, however, for the very reasons that they are protesting," I said. "I am concerned because I know how deeply they feel. But I know that what I have done will accomplish the goals that they want. It will shorten this war. It will reduce American casualties. It will allow us to go forward with our withdrawal program. The 150,000 Americans that I announced for withdrawal in the next year will come home on schedule. It will, in my opinion, serve the cause of a just peace in Vietnam."

One reporter asked what I thought the students were trying to say in the demonstration that was about to take place in Washington. I wanted my answer to this question to be compassionate but not weak. I said, "They are trying to say that they want peace. They are trying to say that they want to stop the killing. They are trying to say that they want to end the draft. They are trying to say that we ought to get out of Vietnam. I agree with everything that they are trying to accomplish. I believe, however, that the decisions that I have made, and particularly this last terribly difficult decision of going into the Cambodian sanctuaries which were completely occupied by the enemy—I believe that that decision will serve that purpose, because you can be sure that everything that I stand for is what they want."

Immediately after the press conference I began returning some of the dozens of phone calls that had come in and placing calls to others. I was agitated and uneasy as the events of the last few weeks raced through my mind.

I slept for a few hours and then went to the Lincoln Sitting Room. I put on a record of Rachmaninoff's Second Piano Concerto and sat listening to the music. Manolo heard that I was up and came in to see if I would like some tea or coffee. Looking out the windows I could see small groups of young people beginning to gather on the Ellipse between the White House and the Washington Monument. I mentioned that I considered the Lincoln Memorial at night to be the most beautiful sight in Washington, and Manolo said that he had never seen it. Impulsively I said, "Let's go look at it now."

This event was spontaneous on my part and I purposely did not take any staff members along or alert any reporters to accompany me. Thus it was especially frustrating when the newspapers reported that I had been unable to communicate with the young people I met, and that I had shown my insensitivity to their concerns by talking about inconsequential subjects like sports and surfing. Some of this mistaken impression apparently came from the students themselves. One of them told a reporter, "He wasn't really concerned with why we were here." Another said that I had been tired and dull and rambled aimlessly from subject to subject.

In a meeting a few days later John Ehrlichman referred to the problems that I had created by talking about sports to students who had traveled hundreds of miles to protest my war policies. I was tired and tense, and I snapped at him about the problems a President has when even his own staff believes the false stories that are spread about him.

That night I dictated a long memorandum describing

what had actually taken place, and I sent it to Haldeman with another memo analyzing my frustrations about this incident:

The attached is a memorandum of what actually took place at the Lincoln Memorial.

After you read it, I think you will share my complete frustration with regard to coverage of my activities. I can understand why John Ehrlichman got the idea from the news reports that I was tired and all I talked about was surfing and nonsensical things. . . .

As I evaluated the situation, this was the one time this group of students—most of whom perhaps were middle class or lower middle class—most of whom were about as poor as I was when I was in college and who had driven all this long distance to Washington—this was the only time they had ever talked to a President of the United States. They will see me many times discuss these heated, angry subjects that they would hear about later at the Monument, and that they hear in their classrooms. Perhaps the major contribution I could make to them was to try to lift them a bit out of the miserable intellectual wasteland in which they now wander aimlessly around.

I do not write this memorandum to you critically of our staff, because I think it is the best staff any President has had by far in terms of loyalty, willingness to work, etc.

The only problem is that we seem to lack on the staff any one individual who really understands or appreciates what I am trying to get across in terms of what a President should mean to the people. Not news; not gimmicks like rushing out to that Negro junior college with a covey of newsreels following. All of this seems to be big stuff and I realize makes big news—perhaps it is.

But on the other hand, I really wonder in the long run if this is all the legacy we want to leave.

If it is, then perhaps we should do our job as easily as we can, as expeditiously as we can, and get out and leave the responsibilities of the government to the true materialists—the socialists, the totalitarians who talk idealism but rule ruthlessly without any regard to the individual considerations—the respect for personality that I tried to emphasize in my dialogue with the students.

I dictated this long diary-like memorandum describing

the visit to the Lincoln Memorial because I wanted to make a record of what was for me a memorable event, and because I wanted to knock down the idea that I would have engaged in the kind of inane conversations the news reports had indicated.

Manolo and I got out of the car at approximately 4:40 and walked up the steps to the Lincoln statue. . . .

By this time a few small groups of students had begun to congregate in the rotunda of the Memorial. I walked over to a group of them . . . and shook hands. They were not unfriendly. As a matter of fact, they seemed somewhat overawed, and, of course, quite surprised.

When I first started to speak to the group there were approximately eight in it. I asked each of them where they were from and found that over half were from upper New York State. At this point, all of them were men. There were no women. To get the conversation going I asked them how old they were, what they were studying, the usual questions. . . .

Two or three of them volunteered that they had not been able to hear the press conference because they had been driving all night in order to get here. I said I was sorry they had missed it because I had tried to explain in the press conference that my goals in Vietnam were the same as theirs—to stop the killing and end the war—to bring peace. Our goal was not to get into Cambodia by what we were doing, but to get out of Vietnam.

They did not respond, so I took it from there by saying that I realized that most of them would not agree with my position, but I hoped that they would not allow their disagreement on this issue to lead them to fail to give us a hearing on some other issues where we might agree. And also particularly I hoped that their hatred of the war, which I could well understand, would not turn into a bitter hatred of our whole system, our country, and everything that it stood for.

I said, I know that probably most of you think I'm an SOB, but I want you to know that I understand just how you feel. I recall that when I was just a little older than you, right out of law school and ready to get married, how excited I was when Chamberlain came home from Munich and made his famous statement about peace in our time. I had heard it on the radio. I had so little in those days that the prospect of going into the service was almost unbearable and I felt that the United States staying out of any kind of conflict was worth paying any price whatever. I pointed out, too, the fact that I came from a Quaker background. I was as close to being a pacifist as anybody could be in those times. As a result I thought at that time, that Chamberlain was the greatest man alive, and when I read Churchill's all-out criticism of Chamberlain I thought Churchill was a madman.

In retrospect, I now realize I was wrong. I think now that Chamberlain was a good man, but that Churchill was a wiser man and that we in the world are better off than we would be because Churchill had not only the wisdom but the courage to carry out the policies that he believed were right even though there was a time when both in England and all over the world he was extremely unpopular because of his "anti-peace" stand.

I then tried to move the conversation into areas where I could draw them out. I said that since some of them had come to Washington for the first time I hoped that while they were young that they would never miss an opportunity to travel. One of them said that he didn't know whether he could afford it, and I said I didn't think I could afford it either when I was young but my wife and I borrowed the money for a trip we took to Mexico and then one to Central America. The fact is, you must travel when you are young. If you wait until you can afford it you will be too old to enjoy it. When you're young, you can enjoy it. . . .

At that time a girl joined the group and since I had been discussing California I asked if anybody there was from California. She spoke up and said she was from Los Altos and I said that was one of my favorite towns in Northern California and I hoped it was as beautiful as I remembered it. She did not respond.

572

In trying to draw her out, I told the rest of the group that when they went to California that they would see there what massive strides we could take to deal with the problem of the environment which I knew they were all interested in. I said that right below where I live in California there was the greatest surfing beach in the world, that it was completely denied to the public due to the fact that it was Marine Corps property, and that I had taken steps to release some of this property for a public beach so that the terribly overcrowded beaches further north could be unburdened, and so that the people could have a chance to enjoy the natural beauty which was there. I said that one of the thrusts of our whole "quality of life" environmental program was to take our government property and put it to better uses and not simply to continue to use it for military or other purposes because it had been used for that way from time immemorial.

Most of them seemed to nod in agreement when I made this point.

I then spoke of how I hoped that they would have the opportunity to know not only the United States but the whole world. I said most people will tell you to go to Europe. I said Europe was fine, but it's really an older version of America. It is worth seeing, but the place that I felt they would particularly enjoy visiting would be Asia.

I told them my great hopes that during my administration, and certainly during their lifetime, that the great mainland of China would be opened up so that we could know the 700 million people who live in China who are one of the most remarkable people on earth. Most of them seemed to nod in agreement when I made this point. . . .

I then moved on to the Soviet Union. Then one of them asked me what Moscow was like, and I said "gray." It's very important if you go to Russia, of course, to see Moscow because of the historical and governmental operations that are there, but if you really want to know Russia, its exciting variety and history, you must go to Leningrad. I said that in

Russia Leningrad was really a more interesting place to visit. The people were really more outgoing there since they were not so much under control and domination of the central government.

I also said that in terms of beautiful cities, they would find Prague and Warsaw of much more architectural beauty than Moscow. I made this point because I was speaking directly to one of the students who said he was a student of architecture. In fact, there were two who said they were studying architecture and I thought that they would be interested. But the most important point I made about Russia was that they should go to places like Novosibirsk, a raw, new city in the heart of Siberia, and Samarkand in Asian Russia where the people were Asians rather than Russians.

One of them asked whether it would be possible to get a visa to such cities, and I said I was sure they could and if any of them took a trip to Russia and wanted to contact my office I would help out. This seemed to get a little chuckle from them.

I then moved back to the problem and my thrust then that what really mattered in the world was people rather than cities and air and water and all other things that were material. I said, for example, of all the countries I have visited in Latin America, Haiti is probably the poorest . . . but that the Haitians, as I recalled from 1955, while they were poor, had a dignity and a grace which was very moving, and that I always had wanted to return, not because there was anything in Haiti worth seeing in terms of cities or good food, etc., but because the people had such character.

I then made this same point again with regard to the people I had seen in Asia and India and returned again to the United States, where I again emphasized the importance of their not becoming alienated from the people of this country, its great variety.

I expressed distress that on the college campuses the blacks and whites, while they now go to school together, have less contact with each other than they had when they weren't. . . . This seemed to get through, although none of them had much to say and none of them responded specifically.

By this time the group around me had begun to get considerably larger. I would say that the original group of approximately eight to ten had now become perhaps thirty and some of those who seemed to be more leader types and older began to take part in the conversation.

One spoke up and said, "I hope you realize that we are willing to die for what we believe in."

I said, I certainly realize that. Do you realize that many of us when we were your age were also willing to die for what we believed in and were willing to do so today? The point is that we were trying to build a world in which you will not have to die for what you believe in, in which you are able to live for it.

I put in one brief comment with regard to the point I had made in the press conference, that while we had great differences with the Russians we had to find a way to limit nuclear arms and I had hoped that we could make some progress in that direction. They seemed to have very little interest in that subject. Perhaps it was because we moved through so fast and perhaps because they were overawed by the whole incident.

Then another spoke up and said, "We are not interested in what Prague looks like. We are interested in what kind of life we build in the United States."

I said the whole purpose of my discussing Prague and other places was not to discuss the city but the people. For the next twenty-five years the world is going to get much smaller. We are going to be living in all parts of the world and it is vitally important that you know and appreciate and understand people every place, wherever they are, and particularly understand the people in your own country.

I said, I know that the great emphasis that is currently being put on the environment—the necessity to have clean air, clean water, clean streets—that, as you know, we have a very bold program going further than any has ever gone before to deal with some of these subjects. But I want to leave just one thought with you. Cleaning up the air and the water and the streets is not going to solve the deepest problems that concern us all. Those are material problems. They must be solved. They are terribly important. . . . But you must remember that something that is completely clean can also be completely sterile and without spirit.

What we all must think about is why we are here—what are those elements of the spirit which really matter. And, here again, I returned to my theme of thinking about people rather than about places and about things. I said candidly and honestly that I didn't have the answer, but I knew that young people today were searching, as I was searching forty years ago, for an answer to this problem. I just wanted to be sure that all of them realized that ending the war, and cleaning up the streets and the air and the water, was not going to solve spiritual hunger which all of us have and which, of course, has been the great mystery of life from the beginning of time. . . .

By this time the dawn was upon us, the first rays of the sun began to show, and they began to climb up over the Washington Monument and I said I had to go, and shook hands with those nearest to me, and walked down the steps.

A bearded fellow from Detroit was taking a picture as I began to get in the car. I asked him if he wouldn't like to get in the picture. He stepped over with me and I said, Look, I'll have the President's doctor take the picture, and Tkach took the picture. He seemed to be quite delighted—it was, in fact, the broadest smile that I saw on the entire visit. As I left him I said . . . that I knew he had come a long way for this event and I knew, too, that he and his colleagues were terribly frustrated and angry about our policy and opposed to it. I said, I just hope your opposition doesn't turn into a blind hatred of the country, but remember this is a great country, with all of its faults. I said, If you have any doubt about it, go down to the passport office. You won't see many people lining up to get out of the country. Abroad, you will see a number lining up to get in.

He smiled and took it all in good humor. We shook hands, and I got into the car and drove away.

I knew that those days in April and May were as hard for my staff as they were for me. Haldeman, Ehrlichman, and Kissinger, in particular, had borne the brunt of the Cambodian crisis. I wanted to do something to show how much I appreciated their strength and support. While we were in Key Biscayne over the weekend of May 15, I asked Bebe if his girl friend, Jane Lucke, would mind doing a little sewing for me.

On the plane back to Washington I asked Haldeman, Ehrlichman, and Kissinger to come to my cabin. When they arrived, I thanked them for all that they had done. "In fact," I said, "you deserve something like the Purple Heart for all the wounds you have sustained in the line of duty over the past few weeks."

They all laughed and said that they had only done their jobs.

"No," I continued, "you have done more than your jobs, and I have devised a new award—a Blue Heart, for those who are true blue."

I gave them each a small heart made from blue cloth. "This will be our secret," I said, "but I wanted you to know how much I appreciate what you have done."

Public opinion seemed to rally during the weeks after Kent State, when the military success of the Cambodian operation became increasingly apparent.

On May 20 the New York Building and Construction Trades Council sponsored a parade to City Hall in support of the President. There had already been scattered incidents of scuffling between the hardhats and various groups of antiwar demonstrators, especially after Mayor John Lindsay had ordered the flag on City Hall to be flown at half-staff as part of a "Day of Reflection" about the Kent State tragedy. The hardhats decided to show their support for our war aims, and more than 100,000 people came out to march with them.

I invited the leaders of the construction workers'

unions to come to the White House. A photograph was taken of their hard hats on the Cabinet table. I gave a short briefing about the background of the Cambodian operation, and as I shook hands with them, one man said, "Mr. President, if someone would have had the courage to go into Cambodia sooner, they might have captured the bullet that took my son's life."

In the middle of May, *Newsweek* published a remarkable Gallup poll. It showed that 65 percent approved of my handling of the presidency; 30 percent of these described themselves as "very satisfied." Fifty percent approved of my decision to send troops into Cambodia; 39 percent disapproved; and 11 percent had no opinion. In response to the question, "Who do you think was primarily responsible for the deaths of four students at Kent State?" 58 percent blamed "demonstrating students" while only 11 percent blamed the National Guard.

On May 30, one month after the Cambodian operation began, I made a televised report to the nation on the progress to date. After conferring with General Abrams, I could state that this had been the most successful operation of the Vietnam war. We had already captured almost as much in enemy arms, equipment, ammunition, and food during the past month in Cambodia alone as we had captured in all of Vietnam during all of 1969.

On June 30, exactly on schedule and exactly as I had promised, we announced the departure of the last American troops from Cambodia. The operation had been a complete success. We had captured enough individual weapons to equip seventy-four full strength North Vietnamese infantry battalions; enough rice to feed all the Communist combat battalions estimated to be in South Vietnam for about four months; 143,000 rockets, mortars, and recoilless rifle rounds—equivalent to the amount used in about 14 months of fighting; 199,552 antiaircraft rounds, 5,482 mines, 62,022 grenades, and 83,000 pounds of explosives; 435 vehicles were captured and 11,688 bunkers and other military structures were destroyed.

Most important, the Cambodian operation had destroyed the Communists' capability of launching a spring offensive against our forces in South Vietnam. Our casualties had dropped from 93 a week in the six months before the operation to 51 per week in the six months after; and the performance of the ARVN had demonstrated that Vietnamization was working. The 150,000-man troop withdrawal I had announced on April 20 could go forward on schedule. And, finally, the pressure against Lon Nol had been reduced, and he was now expected to be able to survive. That would mean that Sihanoukville, the major port of entry for Soviet and Chinese heavy weapons into the Cambodian sanctuaries, would remain closed.

On the day of the previously announced departure from Cambodia the Senate passed the Cooper-Church amendment, the first restrictive vote ever cast on a President in wartime. In essence it demanded that I remove all American troops from Cambodia by July 1. The symbolism of the timing was as serious as the action itself was meaningless, since all Americans had already left Cambodia.

Kissinger's first secret meeting with the North Vietnamese since the Cambodian operation took place on September 7. Instead of the propaganda and vituperation he had expected, he found the friendliest atmosphere of any of the sessions so far. Summing up the meeting for me, he wrote, "Not only did they change their tone, but they also indicated a readiness to move on substance. They in effect dropped their demand for a six-month 'unconditional' withdrawal schedule, made no mention of the ten points, and indicated that they would reconsider their political proposals. They are very anxious to continue this channel, coming back repeatedly with proposals to meet again when I insisted that this channel required major progress."

I was somewhat skeptical about his optimism, because beneath the friendly atmosphere and the new elements of accommodation, the North Vietnamese still insisted that a settlement could be reached only if we deposed President Thieu. On Kissinger's memo, next to the reference to Thieu, I wrote, "This is probably the breaking point unless we can find a formula"—and it was hard to see how even Kissinger's negotiating skill could find a middle ground on that particular issue.

A follow-up meeting was scheduled for September 27. On Kissinger's memo describing the approach he planned, I wrote: "I would only suggest that I would try to get sooner at the heart of the question. Do they mean business—or is this just another rehash?"

The meeting of September 27 dashed all hopes of a breakthrough. The North Vietnamese were argumentative and repetitive. They made it clear that their tactic would be to isolate Thieu as the man who stood in the way of peace. Kissinger broke off the meeting without setting a date for another one.

Since it seemed unlikely that the secret talks were going to produce any solid progress, I decided to present publicly a significant new peace plan.

Because of the success of the Cambodian operation, I felt that now, for the first time, we could consider agreeing to a cease-fire in place in South Vietnam without first requiring that the North Vietnamese agree to withdraw their forces. As long as the Communist troops in South Vietnam could not depend on the Cambodian sanctuaries for supplies, ammunition, and reinforcements, I felt that the ARVN forces, which had been greatly improved and strengthened by more than a year of Vietnamization, would soon be able to defend themselves and their country.

In addition to a cease-fire in place throughout Indochina, the other key points of my new plan were an all-Indochina peace conference to be followed by a negotiated timetable for the withdrawal of all U.S. troops, a political settlement which reflected "the existing relationship of political forces in South Vietnam," and immediate release of all prisoners on both sides.

I presented this plan on television on October 7. Five days later I announced that 40,000 more troops would be withdrawn by Christmas. These two moves went so far toward removing the obstacles to a settlement that they effectively silenced the domestic antiwar movement by placing the burden squarely on the North Vietnamese to begin serious negotiations. But Hanoi stayed silent, and the secret channel in Paris remained closed.

THE HUSTON PLAN

By 1970 the evolutionary cycle of violent dissent spawned an ugly offshoot: the urban underground of political terrorists urging murder and bombing.

The most prominent of these groups were the Black Panthers and the Weathermen. The Black Panthers was founded in 1966 by Bobby Seale and Huey Newton while they were working for the Office of Economic Opportunity. Newton said they would exert power not through political channels but through a capacity for destruction. Eldridge Cleaver, the Panther "Minister of Communication," urged that the masses be spurred toward "revolutionary temptation to kidnap American ambassadors, hijack American airplanes, blow up American pipelines and buildings and to shoot anyone who uses guns and other weapons in the bloodstained service of imperialism against the people."

The Black Panthers had bases in urban areas all around the country. Because their organization was small and highly disciplined, it was extremely difficult to obtain advance information about their plans or the places they intended to strike. In 1969 and 1970 two members pleaded guilty to the murder of a suspected informant.

In 1969 police said they found a cache of Panther weapons that included a submachine gun, thirteen rifles, a handmade grenade, and thirty firebombs. Five policemen were wounded in a Chicago gun battle in July; in November, again in Chicago, two policemen were killed and six wounded, and one Black Panther was killed in another shoot-out. In December, Los Angeles police and Panthers engaged in a four-hour gun battle. In 1969 alone, 348 Panthers were arrested for serious crimes, including murder, armed robbery, rape, and burglary. "Off the Pig" was the Black Panther slogan.

The Weathermen were a terrorist offshoot of the Students for a Democratic Society. At their National Council meeting in 1969, the Weathermen decided to begin a new campaign of underground warfare, police murder, and bombing. "Revolutionary violence is the only way," they stated subsequently in their first public communiqué. With as many as a thousand estimated members, the Weather

Underground separated into secret floating commando-type units. As with the Black Panthers, there was no way of knowing where or how they were going to strike.

Terrorists caused no fewer than 174 major bombings and bombing attempts on campus in the school year 1969-70. Cities were now targets as well. On March 6 a large townhouse in Greenwich Village exploded. Three bodies were found in the wreckage, along with fifty-seven sticks of dynamite, plumbing pipes stuffed with dynamite and roofing nails, and fragmentation bombs. It was a Weatherman bomb factory. There was evidence of Weatherman involvement in the planting of two bombs that same day in police facilities in Detroit. On March 12 explosions in three midtown Manhattan buildings caused the evacuation of some 15,000 people. A terrorist group calling itself Revolutionary Force 9 took the credit. In one twenty-four-hour period, there were more than 400 bomb scares in New York City. On March 30 police found dynamite in a Weatherman bomb factory in Chicago.

Fear was increasingly generated throughout the country. It was accompanied by demands for effective government action. A New York *Times* editorial stated, "The actual and threatened bombings of the past few days must not be glossed over as the action of idealistic if misguided revolutionaries; they are the criminal acts of potential murderers. . . . The mad criminals who threaten and bomb must be recognized for what they are and prosecuted with the full force not only of the law but of the community they would rule and ruin."

J. Edgar Hoover informed me that FBI agents had begun to pick up rumors of a calculated nationwide terrorist offensive by radical student groups using arson, bombing, and kidnaping of university and government officials. Violence was increasing in the high schools. Plane hijackings were up from 17 in 1968 to 33 in 1969.

From January 1969 through April 1970 there were, by conservative count, over 40,000 bombings, attempted bombings, and bomb threats—an average of over eighty a day. Over $21 million in property was destroyed. Forty-three people were killed. Of these 40,000 incidents, 64 percent were by bombers whose identity and motive were unknown.

On March 25 I sent Congress a message asking for urgent legislation to mete out the death penalty in cases where bombs caused the death of others. But weeks passed, and nothing had been done.

On May 25 the New York *Times* published excerpts from a "Declaration of War" issued by the Weathermen: "Within the next 14 days," it said, "we will attack a symbol or institution of Amerikan injustice." Two weeks and one day later a dynamite time bomb exploded in New York police headquarters. A handwritten communication signed "Weatherman" was sent to the Associated Press claiming that they had planted the bomb because "the pigs in this country are our enemies."

The Black Panthers were closely affiliated with North Korean groups and with radical Arab terrorists. We knew that Weathermen identified with North Vietnam, Cuba, and North Korea. I was eager to learn whether the foreign support went beyond ideological sympathy. I was sure that it did; the patterns were too clear. But the intelligence community never had a conclusive answer. Not until 1977 would the New York *Times* report that the FBI had developed evidence of direct support for the Weathermen from both Cuba and North Vietnam. Cuban and North Vietnamese agents counseled them, and the Cuban intelligence agency guided and paid for their escape from the FBI. Cuban military officers instructed them in "practical weaponry."

Now that this season of mindless terror has fortunately passed, it is difficult—perhaps impossible—to convey a sense of the pressures that were influencing my actions and reactions during this period, but it was this epidemic of unprecedented domestic terrorism that prompted our efforts to discover the best means by which to deal with this new phenomenon of highly organized and highly skilled revolutionaries dedicated to the violent destruction of our democratic system.

I turned for assistance in this effort to the various intelligence agencies. Working together, they developed a program to counter revolutionary violence. Three years later this program would be publicly revealed and labeled the Huston Plan. It was attacked as an authorization of Gestapo tactics bent on violating personal liberties. In the light of more recent revelations, we now know that this program did not involve the use of any measures not previously employed by federal law enforcement and intelligence agencies.

J. Edgar Hoover had become director of the Bureau of Investigation in 1924 and over the next forty years was hailed as a national hero. In the mid-sixties, however, he sensed that the temper of the times was turning against him. A new liberalism was fashionable, in which there appeared to be more concern for the rights of the accused than for the protection of the innocent. Now that his career was nearing its end he was determined not to give anyone ammunition in his last years to damage him or his organization. He had always been rigidly territorial when it came to the functions and prerogatives of the FBI. He totally distrusted the other intelligence agencies—especially the CIA—and, whenever possible, resisted attempts to work in concert with them. He was sensibly reluctant to go out on a limb for anyone, lest he find himself suddenly alone.

For more than twenty years, FBI agents had, when necessary, gathered foreign intelligence and evidence of foreign subversion and intelligence about domestic violence by secret break-ins. Between 1942 and 1968, apart from the foreign targets, domestic groups suspected of subversive or violent illegal activities were the targets of over 200 of these break-ins, which were known as "black bag" jobs.

In 1966, threatened with a congressional investigation and liberals in control of the Justice Department, Hoover summarily canceled all FBI black bag jobs and secret mail-opening operations. He also drastically decreased the use of room bugs since they, too, required surreptitious entry, and in 1967 he also cut back the recruitment of student and campus informants.

Just as Hoover cut back on these practices, domestic violence began increasing at an alarming rate. The Johnson administration reacted with great concern. Top administration officials put pressure on the FBI to obtain information about the potential rioters and their activities and even developed extraordinary additional programs of their own.

For example, whereas his predecessor restricted the role of the FBI in racial demonstrations exclusively to investigating "subversive involvement," in 1967 the new Attorney General, Ramsey Clark, ordered the FBI to "use the maximum resources, investigative and intelligence, to collect and report all facts bearing upon the question as to whether there has been or is a scheme or conspiracy by any group of whatever size, effectiveness, or affiliation to plan, promote, or aggravate riot activity." Clark's Assistant Attorney General for the Civil Rights Division, John Doar, went even further: he expressed concern that the FBI was not taking a "broad spectrum approach" to intelligence collection and evaluation, and was instead focusing too narrowly on "traditional subversive groups" and on persons suspected of specific statutory violations.

Clark and Doar set up a central unit for coordinating riot intelligence from informants in the Great Society poverty, community relations, and legal services programs. By 1968 they had over 3,000 people reporting on their neighbors.

In the late 1960s, under pressure from the White House and from Ramsey Clark at the Justice Department, the small domestic intelligence division at the Pentagon, which had been created in 1963, was dramatically expanded. By 1968, 1,500 Army intelligence agents were monitoring various civilian groups, ranging from the Poor People's March and the Mobilization Committee to protests by welfare mothers and classes in black studies. Later, in 1971, Mel Laird, with my approval, abolished the military intelligence program. By that time it had amassed files on more than 100,000 people.

In 1970 the already uneasy relationship between the CIA and FBI was exacerbated when the CIA refused to give Hoover the name of an FBI agent who had assisted them on a case without first having sought Hoover's permission. Hoover retaliated by cutting off all liaison between the FBI and the CIA. I received reports that Hoover's action, coupled with the general lack of coordination among the various intelligence agencies, had left us with an insufficient intelligence capability at a time when terrorist violence was at fever pitch. Weeks later, reportedly irritated further by criticism within the intelligence community, he proceeded to cut off all liaison with all other intelligence agencies, retaining communication only with the White House.

On June 5, 1970, I called a meeting with Hoover, Helms of the CIA, Lieutenant General D. V. Bennett of the Defense Intelligence Agency, and Vice Admiral Noel Gayler, Director of the National Security Agency. Haldeman, Ehrlichman, Bob Finch, and Tom Huston were also present. Huston was a young lawyer and former Defense Intelligence Agency aide whose assignments on the White House staff included the problem of violence from radicals. He was seriously concerned about the inadequacies of the U.S. intelligence apparatus, both in the face of domestic violence and in comparison to the intelligence capabilities of Communist-bloc countries.

I told the group that I wanted to know what the problems were in intelligence-gathering and what had to be done to solve them. I wanted their report submitted to me jointly, and I asked Hoover to act as chairman for this purpose.

The committee formed a study group to evaluate the situation and draw up alternatives. A report was drafted that was approved by the heads of the CIA, DIA, and NSA. Then it went to Hoover, who added, as footnotes to the body of the document, his personal objections to several of the sections.

The report was completed on June 25, 1970. It was officially called "Special Report Interagency Committee on Intelligence (Ad Hoc)."

The report opened with a brief analysis of the problems confronting us, ranging from the Black Panthers and the Weathermen to Communist infiltrators. It differentiated radical terrorist groups from those that merely indulged in incendiary rhetoric. It gave a summary of the available intelligence techniques, the current restrictions on them, and the advantages and disadvantages of lifting those restrictions.

There was only one technique which Hoover had no objection to seeing expanded—the National Security Agen-

586

cy's coverage of overseas telephone and telegraph communications. He had strong objections to the four central possibilities discussed: resumption of covert mail-opening, resumption of black bag jobs, increased electronic surveillance, and an increase in campus—therefore young—informants.

In a separate memo recommending the two most controversial methods, covert mail-opening and surreptitious entry, Huston indicated that the former would be primarily targeted at foreign intelligence and cases of suspected espionage, and the latter would be resumed against foreign targets when they might provide information that could break a code, and possibly against other "urgent and high priority internal security targets," namely, "the Weathermen and Black Panthers."

The final technique discussed in the plan was military intelligence. Hoover objected to an increase in military undercover agents. The group also requested budget increases for each agency—which Hoover approved—and recommended the creation of an intelligence coordinating committee which would ensure that coordination existed between the disparate intelligence-gathering activities of the government. Hoover objected to this.

When I learned of Hoover's dissent from the committee's otherwise unanimous approval of the report, I felt that it was primarily a case of his inability to overcome his natural resistance to cooperating with the CIA or the other intelligence agencies. Beyond that, I thought he was afraid that if he agreed to cooperate, and was on record as having done so, the other agencies might use this to undercut him through leaks.

On July 14, following Huston's recommendations, I turned down an increase in military intelligence activities and approved relaxation of restrictions on the other techniques. I felt they were necessary and justified by the violence we faced. I was satisfied that none of the special techniques would be used indiscriminately, and that none of them represented any threat to legitimate dissent. The express domestic targets—the Black Panthers and the Weathermen—had announced their intentions to kidnap and assassinate and were already building an arsenal of weapons to carry out their threat.

On July 23 Huston sent a memo to the heads of the intelligence agencies notifying them of my decision.

When Hoover learned about this, he appealed to John Mitchell. He said he thought the possibility of public exposure was too great to justify the risks. Mitchell conveyed Hoover's arguments to me, adding that he agreed with Hoover. I knew that if Hoover had decided not to cooperate, it would matter little what I had decided or approved. Even if I issued a direct order to him, while he would undoubtedly carry it out, he would soon see to it that I had cause to reverse myself. There was even the remote possibility that he would resign in protest.

On July 28, five days later, before the plan could be implemented, I withdrew my approval.

The irony of the controversy over the Huston Plan did not become apparent until a 1975 investigation revealed that the investigative techniques it would have involved had not only been carried out long before I approved the plan but continued to be carried out after I had rescinded my approval of it.

It is clear that when a nation confronts dire situations someone is going to act. People will not stand by and let criminals destroy life and property. If the President does not decide how to meet the emergency, someone at a lower level will. I would rather it be the President exercising his judgment than the FBI agent in the field. As Senator Frank Church said in hearings on intelligence agency activities, the Huston Plan "was limited to techniques far more restrictive than the far-reaching methods that were employed by the FBI during the years that we have reviewed."

The bombing and violence continued unabated, and more than once I wondered whether the Huston Plan, if it had been in operation, might have detected and prevented the death and destruction. In August a policeman was killed and six others were wounded in a series of gun battles with the Black Panthers and another black militant group in Philadelphia. That same month, a bomb planted in a research center at the University of Wisconsin took the life of a graduate student working there; four other people were injured. On October 8 there were several bomb explosions—reportedly the work of the Weathermen—at the University of Washington and in two northern California towns. Five buildings were hit by dynamite blasts in Rochester, New York, on October 12; a research center in Irvine, California, was demolished by a bomb on October 18. On March 1, 1971, the U.S. Capitol was bombed by the Weather Underground.

I believe today as I believed then that in view of the crisis of terrorism and violence visited upon countless innocent people, the recommendations made to me by the interagency intelligence group in its 1970 report were justified and responsible. Critics who later contended that the recommendations were repressive and unlawful had the luxury of a calmer environment. They did not face the exigencies of a critical period in which the President, whose paramount responsibility is to ensure the safety of all citizens, was forced to consider measures that would undoubtedly be unacceptable in more tranquil times.

In the 1960s an FBI official report claimed that the results of just one surreptitious entry helped bring about the "near disintegration" of the Ku Klux Klan. Was the FBI right or wrong in taking that action? Did the threat of murder and violence by Klan members warrant an infringement on its members' liberties?

My decision to approve the recommendations of the Huston Plan, like the decisions of President Roosevelt to incarcerate thousands of Japanese-Americans and of President Lincoln to suspend the constitutional guarantee of habeas corpus, will always be debated. In the 1970s did the threatened and actual bombings of the Weathermen, and the brutal assaults of the Black Panthers, justify an intrusion on their liberties? When the issue juxtaposes the lives of innocent citizens against the possible curtailment of personal liberties we all cherish, the answers are never easy.

Sometimes the letter of one law will conflict with the spirit of another, and that is when the President must choose. He cannot throw up his hands in dismay, because inaction may be as devastating as wrong action. The question is: What is the law, and how is it to be applied with respect to the President in fulfilling the duties of his office? Precedents over the years have sanctioned some degree of latitude in the use by Presidents of emergency measures to meet emergency situations. I believe such latitude is necessary, and at times vital, to defend the nation and to protect innocent people whose lives are threatened by criminal forces. Jefferson was talking about this problem in 1810 when he noted:

> A strict observance of the written laws is doubtless one of the high duties of a good citizen, but it is not the highest. The laws of necessity, of self-preservation, of saving our country when in danger, are of a higher obligation. ... To lose our country by a scrupulous adherence to written law, would be to lose the law itself, with life, liberty, property and all those who are enjoying them with us; thus absurdly sacrificing the end to the means.

I think it would be disastrous if, in an excess of prohibitory zeal, we were to tie the President's hands now and in the future, limiting him to the mechanical functions of executing the precise letter of the law, because laws cannot foresee every circumstance. We have to place faith in his judgment; we have to weigh the potential for abuse of power if we allow him reasonable latitude to act, against the potential harm that may result if we too narrowly restrict that latitude.

WAR IN JORDAN

America's Middle Eastern policy under Presidents Kennedy and Johnson was aimed primarily at supplying the arms and money to enable Israel to defend itself against its potential enemies.

This policy seemed to be successful. In 1967 the numerically inferior Israeli forces were able to defeat and humiliate the Soviet-armed Egyptians and Syrians in less than a week of fighting. As a result of this Six-Day War, the Israelis expanded their territory by occupying several areas along the banks of the Suez Canal, on the Sinai Peninsula, on the west bank of the Jordan River, in Jerusalem, and in the Golan Heights along the Israeli-Syrian border. The victory was overwhelming—so overwhelming that it was inevitable that further wars would be fought by Israel's neighbors for repossession of these conquered and occupied territories.

After the war high-level visits between Moscow and

Cairo, Damascus, and Baghdad produced a massive new infusion of Soviet money, men, and matériel. The Soviets wanted to maintain their presence in the Middle East, not because of ideological support for the cause of Arab unity but because it was through Egypt and the other Arab countries that the Soviets could gain access to what the Russians had always wanted—land, oil, power, and the warm waters of the Mediterranean. As I commented to Bill Rogers, "The difference between our goal and the Soviet goal in the Middle East is very simple but fundamental. *We* want peace. *They* want the Middle East."

The potential for a confrontation between the United States and the U.S.S.R. loomed large. If the Soviets were committed to Arab victories, and we were committed to Israeli victories, it did not require much imagination to see how we both might be drawn in even against our wills —and almost certainly against our national interests.

At the beginning of my administration, I assigned the Middle East exclusively to Bill Rogers and his Assistant Secretary of State for Near Eastern and South Asian Affairs, Joseph Sisco. I did this partly because I felt that Kissinger's Jewish background would put him at a disadvantage during the delicate initial negotiations for the reopening of diplomatic relations with the Arab states. Primarily, however, I felt that the Middle East required full time and expert attention. As I told Kissinger, "You and I will have more than enough on our plate with Vietnam, SALT, the Soviets, Japan, and Europe."

It was clearly in America's interests to halt the Soviet domination of the Arab Mideast. To do so would require broadening American relations with the Arab countries. Within the first few months of my administration I began taking the first steps in this direction.

At the beginning of April 1969, King Hussein of Jordan made a state visit to the United States. In our last meeting before he left I told him that I was deeply troubled because the absence of diplomatic relations with some of the governments in the Middle East precluded our playing a constructive role in the region. Although he made no reply at the time, I knew that Hussein would carry this message back to the other Arab leaders.

591

The next day, I met with Mahmoud Fawzi, who had come to Washington as a personal emissary of President Nasser of Egypt. I told him that we regretted the United States did not have formal relations with Egypt. I said that I did not believe there would ever be a settlement that would fully satisfy either side, but I was confident that a mutually acceptable compromise could be achieved if the United States could establish a new relationship with Egypt and the Arab nations. "Of course, this will require trust between the parties, and I know that trust has to be deserved and earned," I said.

The key to peace in the Middle East lay as much in Moscow as it did in Cairo or Damascus. Therefore when our new ambassador to the Soviet Union, Jacob Beam, presented his credentials in April 1969, I had him deliver a personal letter from me to Premier Kosygin. In it I said that it was essential that both our countries exert a calming influence in the Middle East, and that no outside power seek any advantage in the area at the expense of any other.

On September 25, 1969, Golda Meir came to Washington for a state visit. In Israeli terms she was a "hawk," and a hard-liner opposed to surrendering even an inch of the occupied territory Israel had won in the 1967 war. Mrs. Meir conveyed simultaneously the qualities of extreme toughness and extreme warmth; when the survival of her country was involved, the toughness was predominant. She requested twenty-five Phantom jets and eighty Skyhawk fighters and complained about the delays in delivery of planes that had already been approved. She also asked for low-interest loans of $200 million a year for periods up to five years. I reassured her that our commitments would be met.

At the state dinner in her honor she expressed concern regarding our moves toward détente with the Soviets. I told her that we had no illusions about their motives. I said, "Our Golden Rule as far as international diplomacy is concerned is: 'Do unto others as they do unto you.'"

"Plus ten percent," Kissinger quickly added.

Mrs. Meir smiled. "As long as you approach things that way, we have no fears," she said.

In December 1969, Bill Rogers gave a speech in which he outlined what became known as the "Rogers Plan" for peace in the Middle East. This plan was based on the principle of the return of the occupied Arab territories in exchange for Arab assurances of Israel's territorial integrity. In strictly practical terms, the provision for return of occupied territories meant that the Rogers Plan had absolutely no chance of being accepted by Israel.

Rogers and the State Department argued that the plan offered the best hope for peace, since the return of the occupied territories would at least remove for the Arabs the hated reminder of their humiliating defeat. Kissinger countered that the plan encouraged the extremist elements among the Arabs, gratuitously offended the Israelis, and earned the contempt of the Soviets, who saw it as playing naïvely into their hands. As Kissinger predicted, the Rogers Plan drew fierce criticism from the Israelis and made Rogers, as Kissinger frequently reminded me, "the most unpopular man in Israel."

I knew that the Rogers Plan could never be implemented, but I believed that it was important to let the Arab world know that the United States did not automatically dismiss its case regarding the occupied territories or rule out a compromise settlement of the conflicting claims. With the Rogers Plan on the record, I thought it would be easier for the Arab leaders to propose reopening relations with the United States without coming under attack from the hawks and pro-Soviet elements in their own countries.

On January 31, 1970, I received what Kissinger termed the first Soviet threat of my administration. Significantly, it involved the Middle East. It came in the form of a letter from Premier Kosygin that stated: "We would like to tell you in all frankness that if Israel continues its adventurism, to bomb the territory of U.A.R. and of other Arab states, the Soviet Union will be forced to see to it that the Arab states have means at their disposal, with the help of which a due rebuff to the arrogant aggressor could be made."

My reply was carefully low-keyed: I urged a more positive Soviet response to the Rogers Plan and proposed discussions on limiting arms supplies to the Middle East.

In the meantime a different kind of diplomatic problem had arisen closer to home. Many members of the American

Jewish community and its political friends had decided to boycott the state visit of President Georges Pompidou of France as a protest against his recent sale to Libya of more than a hundred Mirage jet fighters.

Shortly before Pompidou's arrival, I received word that neither Governor Rockefeller nor Mayor Lindsay would officially greet him in New York nor attend the dinner in his honor at the Waldorf-Astoria Hotel on the last night of his visit. I fully understood the importance of the Jewish vote in New York, but, as I said to Haldeman, "It's completely hypocritical to treat Pompidou this way when they slobbered all over Kosygin when he was there—and *he's* the direct cause of the whole damn problem." I told Kissinger, "I consider this unconscionable conduct towards an official guest of the United States of America, and I will not tolerate it. Nor will I lead people to believe that it has any effect whatsoever on me."

After four days in Washington, the Pompidous visited Cape Kennedy and San Francisco before flying to Chicago. There, obscenity-screaming demonstrators broke through police lines and jostled the Pompidou party. Madame Pompidou was shaken by the incident, and Bus Mosbacher, our Chief of Protocol, informed me that she was going to fly home to Paris the next morning.

I told Mosbacher, "I don't care what you have to do, but I don't want her to leave."

I decided to fly to New York and attend the Waldorf-Astoria dinner that Rockefeller and Lindsay were boycotting. My appearance at the dinner came as a dramatic surprise, and nothing I said in our many talks over the years on substantive matters did as much to win Pompidou's friendship and cooperation as this gesture.

At the beginning of March I decided to postpone our delivery of Phantom jets to Israel. I had heard that the Soviets were coming under renewed pressures from their Arab clients to surpass the new American deliveries to Israel, and I hoped that since Israel was already in a strong military position, I could slow down the arms race without tipping the fragile military balance in the region. I also believed that American influence in the Middle East increasingly depended on our renewing diplomatic relationships with Egypt and Syria, and this decision would help promote that goal.

On March 12 I received a personal letter from Mrs. Meir. She said, "It is true that our pilots are very good, but they can be good only when they have planes. Lately some rumors have reached me that your decision may be negative or at best postponed. I absolutely refuse to believe it. If, God forbid, this were true, then we would feel really forsaken."

Israel had survived only because its people were ready to fight and die for it. I could understand their reluctance to accept our assurances instead of our jet fighters at a time when they faced a possible attack.

As I had told Pompidou, "If you put yourself in the position of Dayan, Rabin, Eban, or Mrs. Meir, who are intelligent and tough people, you must admire them: there they sit, a very few people, surrounded by enemies, and the fact is, they aren't prepared to take advice even from the President of the United States." I tried to reassure Mrs. Meir that if it ever came to the test of a crisis—as it did in September 1970 and again in October 1973—then we would be found fully and firmly on Israel's side. In the meantime, I realized that my new policy would cause much pain and many problems. I also realized that it would be misunderstood and denounced by many on both sides. What I was trying to do, however, was to construct a completely new set of power relationships in the Middle East—not only between Israel and the Arabs, but also among the United States, Western Europe, and the Soviet Union.

One of the main problems I faced in this regard was the unyielding and shortsighted pro-Israeli attitude prevalent in large and influential segments of the American Jewish community, Congress, the media, and in intellectual and cultural circles. In the quarter century since the end of World War II this attitude had become so deeply ingrained that many saw the corollary of not being pro-Israeli as being anti-Israeli, or even anti-Semitic. I tried unsuccessfully to convince them that this was not the case.

There was a wave of criticism in the media and in Congress when my decision to postpone the Phantom deliveries was announced. Israeli Ambassador Rabin knew the decision was coming and complained to Kissinger that we were failing to meet our responsibilities. I was annoyed that a number of the senators who were urging that we send more military aid to save Israel were opposing our efforts to save South Vietnam from Communist domination. I dictated a memorandum to Kissinger describing my feelings and pointing out the danger for Israel of relying on the prominent liberal and dove senators of both parties to come through in the event a crisis arose in which Israel was attacked by the Arabs or was even threatened directly by Soviet power:

> What they must realize is that these people are very weak reeds. They will give Israel a lot of lip service, but they are peace at any price people. When the chips are down they will cut and run, not only as they are presently cutting and running in Vietnam, but also when any conflict in the Mideast stares them straight in the face.
>
> On the other hand, their real friends (to their great surprise) are people like Goldwater, Buckley, RN et al., who are considered to be hawks on Vietnam but who, in the broader aspects, are basically not cut-and-run people whether it is in Vietnam, the Mideast, Korea, or any place else in the world. . . .
>
> They must recognize that our interests are basically pro-freedom and not just pro-Israel because of the Jewish vote. We are *for* Israel because Israel in our view is the only state in the Mideast which is *pro*-freedom and an effective opponent to Soviet expansion. We will oppose a cut-and-run policy either in Vietnam or Cuba or the Mideast or NATO or anyplace else in the world. This is the kind of friend that Israel needs and will continue to need, particularly when the going gets very tough in the next five years. . . .
>
> What all this adds up to is that Mrs. Meir, Rabin, et al., must trust RN completely. He does not want to see Israel go down the drain and makes an absolute commitment that he will see to it that Israel always has "an edge." On the other hand, he must carry with him not just the Jewish constituency in New York and Pennsylvania and California and possibly Illinois which voted 95 percent against him, but he must carry with him the 60 percent of the American people who are in what is called the silent majority, and who must be depended upon in the event that we have to take a strong stand against Soviet expansionism in the Mideast. Only when the Israeli leaders realize this fact are they going to have any kind of security which will be reliable. . . .

We are going to stand up in Vietnam and in NATO and in the Mideast, but it is a question of all or none. This is it cold turkey, and it is time that our friends in Israel understood this.

We are going to be in power for at least the next three years and this is going to be the policy of this country. Unless they understand it and act as if they understood it beginning now, they are down the tubes.

Throughout the spring there were sporadic but bitter outbreaks of fighting between Israel and Egypt and Syria. At the beginning of June 1970, Rogers sent me a memorandum proposing a U.S. peace initiative, and on June 25 he announced that we would encourage the parties "to stop shooting and start talking."

On August 7, an uneasy cease-fire was declared. It was a major accomplishment for Rogers and Sisco. Even though the cease-fire was violated by Egypt almost before the ink was dry, it established the United States as the honest broker accepted by both sides.

On August 17 Kissinger and I met with Ambassador Rabin. He said emotionally that Mrs. Meir and the Israeli government were unsettled because the United States did not seem to accept the evidence that serious Egyptian cease-fire violations were taking place. He said that Soviet surface-to-air missiles had been moved into the forward area along the Suez Canal, changing the entire balance of power in the area. Unless something were done, it would be just a matter of time before the Egyptians attacked. The Israelis therefore wanted to send air strikes against these missile complexes. The attrition of their aircraft would be very high, however, unless we gave them the special electronic jamming equipment and missiles they were requesting.

"Israel must understand that I have no illusions about Soviet motives," I said. "Perhaps I even understand them better than Israel itself. We have launched our cease-fire initiative with no preconceived notions as to Soviet good will. On the other hand, it was important that the initiative be made so that it is on the record."

I pointed out that American public opinion would be very important if another war began in the Middle East. This was why I had wanted America to be the prime mover of the cease-fire proposal, and why I wanted Israel to be scrupulously careful in observing it. "If our peace initiative fails, everyone should be able to recognize who is at fault," I said. "And I hope that it will not be Israel."

I said that I would approach the Soviets through special channels concerning their involvement in the current crisis. "I completely agree with you," I said, "that the Soviets are the main cause of Middle East tensions, and that if they were removed from the situation Israel would be able to handle matters without difficulty."

A month later our policy of building a new balance of power in the Middle East was put to the test of war.

At the beginning of September, the extremist Palestinian guerrillas became increasingly active. One group of them hijacked four commercial airliners and blew them up after holding the hundreds of passengers, most of them Americans, hostage for several days. It seemed likely that a serious showdown was going to be unavoidable, so I decided to revoke my earlier order and to send more military aid and more Phantom jets to Israel.

On September 15 a full-blown crisis erupted in Jordan. The Palestinian extremist leaders, backed by Syrian arms and aid, had stirred up the Palestinian refugees living in Jordan and threatened to provoke a civil war against Hussein's regime. When Kissinger reported this news to me, he said, "It looks like the Soviets are pushing the Syrians and the Syrians are pushing the Palestinians. The Palestinians don't need much pushing."

The situation was confused, and until we had reliable information or intelligence about what was really going on, I felt it was important to keep as cool as possible. I was scheduled to leave on a two-day trip to Kansas City and Chicago, and I decided to keep to the schedule.

However, one thing was clear. We could not allow Hussein to be overthrown by a Soviet-inspired insurrection. If it succeeded, the entire Middle East might erupt in war: the Israelis would almost certainly take pre-emptive measures against a Syrian-dominated radical government in Jordan; the Egyptians were tied to Syria by military alliances; and Soviet prestige was on the line with both the Syrians and the Egyptians. Since the United States could not stand idly by and watch Israel being driven into the sea, the possibility of a direct U.S.-Soviet confrontation was uncomfortably high. It was like a ghastly game of dominoes, with a nuclear war waiting at the end.

The next morning the phone rang at 8:00 in my Chicago hotel suite. It was Kissinger, calling with the news that civil war had broken out in Jordan. Palestinian rebel forces were fighting Hussein's troops, and Syrian tanks were poised and ready on the border. That afternoon, I talked to a group of reporters and editors and told them that we might have to intervene if Syrian tanks or troops or any of the Arab League Iraqi troops already encamped in Jordan moved against Hussein. When the afternoon newspapers appeared, headlines announced: *Nixon Warns Reds: Keep Out.*

The next day, September 18, we received a note from the Kremlin stating that the Soviets had no intention of intervening in Jordan, urging us not to intervene, and suggesting that we discourage others—in other words, Israel—from doing so.

I had one of my regular breakfast meetings with Mike Mansfield that morning. Mansfield strongly opposed any American military involvement in the Mideast, and I was able to tell him that, based on the Soviet note, I was optimistic that we could work things out without a confrontation. He raised his hands over his head and slowly brought them down to the table as he closed his eyes and said: "Praise Allah!"

At eleven o'clock that same morning I had an appointment with Golda Meir, who was in the United States on an unofficial visit.

When Mrs. Meir was ushered into the Oval Office, I could see from her fixed smile that she was in a very stern mood. I opened by saying that I was not naïve about Soviet intentions and that I was aware of the difficulties that cease-fire violations had caused Israel.

"In my view, Mr. President," she replied, "the American response to our reports about cease-fire cheating was slow, and your initial acquiescence encouraged additional violations." She asked Rabin to explain, and on the rug he spread out three large Israeli intelligence maps pinpointing the specific violations.

Mrs. Meir said that Israel's problems were not caused

primarily by the Arabs. They were the direct result of the Soviet presence and Soviet military equipment. The Egyptians did not even know how to operate the surface-to-air missiles the Soviets had given them, and Soviet personnel had had to be interspersed at all levels within the Egyptian military. She said that Israeli pilots had already met Soviet pilots in air-to-air combat over the Suez Canal.

Mrs. Meir continued. "Now, in my opinion, I think you should go to the Soviets directly and demand an adjustment of the situation if the negotiations are to continue."

I assured Mrs. Meir that we had already sent several strong notes to the Soviets through diplomatic channels. I said that I wanted her to understand the major principles underlying American policy in the Mideast. We were under no illusions concerning the Soviet intent and involvement in the region, and we recognized that something had to be done about Egyptian cease-fire violations. We did not intend to permit the military balance in the Middle East to be disturbed, and we were prepared to work with her in developing a military aid program that would be appropriate for the strategy the Israelis adopted.

Mrs. Meir said that Israel would not move precipitately into Jordan; she agreed that it was preferable to have Hussein solve the problem himself.

Reports from Jordan indicated hard fighting throughout the country, with Hussein's troops holding their own or better. Then, on September 18 word was flashed to the White House Situation Room that Syrian tanks had crossed the border into northern Jordan. The next day we learned that the invasion force had numbered at least a hundred tanks. We moved quickly and decisively on the diplomatic front. Kissinger drafted a very stern note and delivered it to the Soviets; Rogers issued a strong public statement calling on Syria to halt its invasion. By early evening it appeared that about half the Syrian tanks had returned to Syria.

"They're testing us," I said to Kissinger, "and the test may not be over yet."

On the night of September 21 at around ten o'clock another message was received in the Situation Room: about three hundred Syrian tanks had crossed the Jordanian border. They had broken through the Jordanian defenses and were rumbling almost unopposed along the roads toward Amman. By the next morning, however, most of these tanks had also been pulled back. The testing was continuing, moving a few notches higher each time. We would have to decide what to do very soon, or it might be too late to do anything.

We decided to pursue a very hard but very quiet line. I authorized Kissinger to call Ambassador Rabin and suggest that he inform his government that we would be fully in support of Israeli air strikes on Syrian forces in Jordan if this became necessary to avoid a Jordanian defeat. I decided to put 20,000 American troops on alert and moved additional naval forces into the Mediterranean.

In the end Jordan under Hussein's courageous leadership saved itself. By the morning of September 22, the Syrian tanks were once again heading back toward the border. Rabin called early in the afternoon to confirm that the tanks had left Jordan and that the rebel forces were in disarray. He ascribed Hussein's victory to the tough American position, the Israeli threat, and the superb fighting by Hussein's troops.

CRISIS IN CUBA

On Friday, September 18, while I was waiting for Golda Meir to arrive for her meeting in the Oval Office, I received an urgent memo from Kissinger. It was headed "TOP SECRET/SENSITIVE/EYES ONLY." Its first sentence stated: "Analysis of reconnaissance flight photography over Cuba has this morning confirmed the construction of a probable submarine deployment base in Cienfuegos Bay." If the intelligence was correct, it meant that the Soviets were building a nuclear submarine base on Cuba.

So far the details were very sketchy. On August 4 Yuli Vorontsov, the Minister Counselor of the Soviet Embassy and Chargé in Dobrynin's absence, had delivered a note to Kissinger expressing concern over alleged anti-Castro activity by Cuban revolutionary groups in the United States. The note stressed that the Soviets were adhering to the understanding President Kennedy had agreed to in 1962, which included a provision that the Soviets would not put nuclear weapons on Cuban territory in return for our assurance that we would not undertake or support military action to overthrow Castro.

Regular U-2 reconnaissance flights over Cuba in August showed nothing unusual. In September, however, the photographs revealed that construction had begun on the shores of Alcatraz Island, a tiny dot of land off Cuba's southern coast in the middle of Cienfuegos Bay. A submarine tender was anchored to four buoys in the deep-water basin, and submarine nets were strung across the harbor. A large complex of barracks, administrative buildings, and recreation facilities was almost completed on Alcatraz Island.

When a U-2 had discovered Soviet missile sites in Cuba in October 1962, President Kennedy revealed their presence in a nationwide television speech and had Adlai Stevenson display the enlarged photographs at the UN General Assembly. These actions placed Khrushchev in an almost impossible situation in terms of his international prestige. He was able, however, to use the universal fear of war to put pressure on Kennedy, thus making himself appear responsible for resolving the crisis and reaching a peaceful settlement. So instead of dealing with Khrushchev from the position of immense nuclear superiority that we still held in 1962, Kennedy ended up by agreeing to refrain from any anti-Castro activities in return for Khrushchev's removal of the Soviet missiles from Cuba.

In view of what had happened in the 1962 crisis, I decided that I would not force a public confrontation unless I had no other choice, and I would not deal with the Soviets from anything less than a position of unyielding strength.

I wrote a note to Kissinger: "I want a report on a crash basis on: (1) What CIA can do to support *any* kind of action which will irritate Castro; (2) What actions we can take which we have not yet taken to boycott nations dealing with Castro; (3) Most important, what actions we can take, covert or overt, to put missiles in Turkey—or a sub base in the Black Sea—anything which will give us some trading stock."

During the next few days further U-2 flights confirmed our worst fears. The construction was proceeding at a rapid pace, and unless we acted quickly and decisively, we would wake up one morning to find a fully functioning nuclear-equipped Soviet submarine base ninety miles from our shores.

Not all my advisers agreed on the need for immediate action. Bill Rogers was particularly forceful in an NSC meeting on September 23, urging that we keep the situation completely quiet until after the November elections. I did not feel, however, that the crisis would keep that long, and I directed the NSC to work on a contingency plan.

On September 24 Dobrynin requested an appointment with me to deliver the Kremlin's reply concerning proposals we had made recently regarding a possible summit meeting. I was surprised by the boldness of this request. The Soviets apparently thought we were still unaware of what they were doing in Cuba, and were clearly planning to take us by surprise with a fait accompli, just as they had in 1962. Kissinger and I agreed that he should meet with Dobrynin and see what the Soviets were up to.

The next morning, the New York *Times* ran a story by its distinguished foreign correspondent C. L. Sulzberger that "initial information" suggested that a naval installation for nuclear submarines was being built in Cienfuegos. Because the information was vague and unconfirmed and because Sulzberger's column appeared on the paper's editorial pages, there was a chance that the story might not be picked up for several days. When Kissinger and Dobrynin met in the Map Room that morning, neither mentioned the column nor the alleged base. Dobrynin, in fact, reported that the Soviet leaders were interested in holding a summit, and he even proposed dates. Kissinger suggested that he return to the White House later that afternoon for a reply.

However, at a press briefing across the river in the Pentagon, a Deputy Assistant Secretary inadvertently revealed that there was evidence that a Soviet submarine facility was possibly being constructed in Cuba. Confronted with this leak, Kissinger had to meet with reporters. He tried to finesse the situation as much as possible, but the story was in the news that evening.

Kissinger told me that when Dobrynin came back to the White House at 5:30 that afternoon his face was ashen.

To Dobrynin's surprise and then to his discomfort, Kissinger studiously ignored the afternoon's events and began by stating calmly that he had my answer concerning the proposed summit. In principle, he said, I would agree to a meeting in Moscow in either June or September 1971. Finally he said that he wanted to talk about the press statements that had come out of the Pentagon and his own press conference earlier that afternoon. He had implied to the reporters that we did not yet know whether there actually was a submarine base in Cuba. He told Dobrynin that he had done this deliberately in order to give the Soviets an opportunity to withdraw without a public confrontation.

"I want you to know, however, that we have no illusions about this matter," Kissinger added. "We know there is a base in Cuba, and we will view it with the utmost gravity if construction continues and the base remains."

Dobrynin tried to minimize the problem, but Kissinger persisted. We were giving the Soviets an opportunity to pull out because we did not want a public confrontation. But we would not shrink from other measures, including public ones, if we were forced into them.

Dobrynin asked whether we considered that the 1962 understandings on Cuba had been violated. Kissinger replied that we did. Cuba was a place of extreme sensitivity for us, and we considered that the installation of the submarine base had been carried out with maximum deception. Dobrynin said that he would immediately inform the Kremlin of what Kissinger had said.

I gave orders that absolutely no further news leaks about the submarine base were to occur until we received the Soviet reply. The entire success of our strategy of keeping the crisis low key depended on keeping a tight lid on the story. I knew from the 1962 experience that a serious war scare would sweep the country if the real story of Cienfuegos hit the headlines.

We were able to keep the secret so well that during the next few days several prominent political leaders and journalists dismissed Cienfuegos as a trumped-up crisis. Senator Fulbright, the Chairman of the Senate Foreign Relations Committee, charged the administration with "hoodwinking the American people" and said that stories of nuclear submarine bases in Cuba were aimed at getting Congress to approve generous appropriations for the Pentagon. I did nothing to discourage such mistaken opinions; in fact, I did everything possible to carry on business as usual. The most recent U-2 flights indicated a slowing of activity at Cienfuegos, so on September 27 I left for a week-long trip to Europe.

On October 6, our first morning back in Washington, Dobrynin called to arrange an appointment with Kissinger. He handed Kissinger a note in which the Soviet government reaffirmed the 1962 understanding about Cuba and stated that it was not doing anything in Cuba that would contradict that understanding. When Kissinger showed me the note, I was tremendously relieved. Our strategy had worked. The Soviets had decided to take advantage of the maneuverability a low profile afforded. They were backing away from the crisis by denying that it had ever existed.

We could not, however, accept Dobrynin's vague declaration as the definitive settlement of such a serious incident. A few days later Kissinger handed him a note from me that welcomed the Soviet reply but specifically outlined our interpretation of the 1962 understanding. I wrote, "The U.S. government understands that the U.S.S.R. will not establish, utilize, or permit the establishment of any facility in Cuba that can be employed to support or repair Soviet naval ships capable of carrying offensive weapons, i.e. submarines or surface ships armed with nuclear-capable, surface-to-surface missiles." To nail down the details so that there would be no further "misunderstandings," I listed five specific actions that we would consider violations of the 1962 agreement.

Dobrynin objected to the bluntness of some of the language, but he hinted that the question would soon be put to rest. A few days later TASS, the Soviet government news agency, issued a statement that no submarine base existed, thus putting the Soviets officially on record.

The crisis was over. After some face-saving delays, the Soviets abandoned Cienfuegos. Through strong but quiet diplomacy we had averted what would have been known as the Cuban Nuclear Submarine Crisis of 1970 and which, like its predecessor, might have taken us to the brink of nuclear confrontation with the Soviet Union.

————————

The events at Cienfuegos Bay convinced me that I had chosen the right course in dealing with another Communist threat in Latin America—this one in Chile.

In Chile's presidential elections of September 4, 1970, a pro-Castro Marxist, Salvador Allende, came in first with a 36.3 percent plurality. Under Chilean law Allende's slim plurality was insufficient for election, and the Chilean Congress would choose the new President on October 24. The CIA estimated that Cuba had pumped about $350,000 into the Allende campaign. Allende's own intentions, stated in a campaign speech, were clear: "Cuba in the Caribbean and a Socialist Chile in the Southern Cone will make the revolution in Latin America."

Allende had run for President three times before and been defeated each time. In the Chilean elections of 1962 and 1964 Presidents Kennedy and Johnson had authorized CIA expenditures of almost $4 million to avert a Communist takeover in Chile. Knowing this, and knowing that nearly two-thirds of Chile's voters had rejected Allende, I directed the CIA to provide support for Allende's opponents in order to prevent his election by the Chilean Congress.

We live in a far from ideal world. As long as the Communists supply external funds to support political parties, factions, or individuals in other countries, I believe that the United States can and should do the same and do it secretly so that it can be effective. Under Communist standards of morality, governments are meant to be subverted and elections influenced. To me it would have been the height of immorality to allow the Soviets, the Cubans, and other Communist nations to interfere with impunity in free elections while America stayed its hand. It is a peculiar double standard that would require us alone to stand abjectly aside as democracies are undermined by countries less constrained by conscience. In Chile we sought to help non-Communist parties have at least the same resources as the lavishly financed pro-Allende forces.

606

In mid-October I was informed that our efforts were probably not going to be successful; therefore I instructed the CIA to abandon the operation. Allende was inaugurated President of Chile on November 3.

I was extremely troubled by this. I believed, as had my two predecessors, that a Communist regime in Cuba exporting violence, terrorism, and revolution throughout Latin America was dangerous enough. An Italian businessman who called on me before the Chilean election had cautioned, "If Allende should win, and with Castro in Cuba, you will have in Latin America a red sandwich. And, eventually, it will all be red." Such fears were realized when, soon after Allende came to power, Cuban intelligence agents began operating from a base in Chile, exporting revolution to Bolivia, Argentina, Brazil, and Uruguay.

After three years of inefficient administration, during which the Chilean economy suffered from a series of crippling strikes, Allende was overthrown by the Chilean military in September 1973, and according to conflicting reports, was either killed or committed suicide during the coup.

America was being tested in the fall of 1970—by war in Vietnam; by the threat of war in the Middle East; by the introduction of threatening nuclear capabilities in Cuba. In Chile the test was just as real, although much subtler.

Communist leaders believe in Lenin's precept: Probe with bayonets. If you encounter mush, proceed; if you encounter steel, withdraw. I had feared that in our handling of the EC-121 incident in 1969 the Communists may have thought they had encountered mush. While our effort to prevent Allende from coming to power failed, at least in 1970 in Jordan and in Cuba, their probing had encountered our unmistakable steel.

1970 ELECTIONS

Shortly before the 1970 congressional campaign began, Pat Buchanan sent me an eleven-page memorandum analyzing *The Real Majority,* a new book which claimed that the elections in 1970 and 1972 would be decided by what the authors, Richard Scammon, Kennedy's Director of the Census Bureau, and Ben Wattenberg, a former Johnson speechwriter, called the "Social Issue."

In what became a highly publicized formulation, Scammon and Wattenberg described the average American voter in the next election as a forty-seven-year-old housewife from the outskirts of Dayton, Ohio, whose husband was a machinist. "To know that the lady in Dayton is afraid to walk the streets alone at night," they wrote, "to know that she has a mixed view about blacks and civil rights because before moving to the suburbs she lived in a neighborhood that became all black, to know that her brother-in-law is a policeman, to know that she does not have the money to move if her new neighborhood deteriorates, to know that she is deeply distressed that her son is going to a community junior college where LSD was found on the campus—to know all this is the beginning of contemporary political wisdom."

The purpose of *The Real Majority* was to persuade Democrats to stop playing so heavily to the fashionable but unrepresentative constituencies of the young, the poor, the racial minorities, and the students. Once the Democrats got on the right side of the Social Issue, the book argued, they could win the election by taking the offensive on the economy, which was the Republicans' weak point.

If this analysis was right, and I agreed with Buchanan that it was, then the Republican counterstrategy was clear: we should preempt the Social Issue in order to get the Democrats on the defensive. We should aim our strategy primarily at disaffected Democrats, at blue-collar workers, and at working-class white ethnics. We should set out to capture the vote of the forty-seven-year-old Dayton housewife.

I had decided not to do any active campaigning in 1970. I felt confident that I would not be needed because in Ted Agnew we had the perfect spokesman to reach the silent majority on the Social Issue. Our strategy worked brilliantly at first. The Social Issue had liberals on the run everywhere, with Agnew in hot rhetorical pursuit. He stirred up predictable emotions—Hubert Humphrey called him the "brass knuckles of the administration"—but in fact his salvos were remarkably restrained for campaign rhetoric and hit right on target.

When the campaign began to heat up around the middle of September, I was deeply involved in preparations for my second European trip, which lasted from September 27 to October 5. When I left, it seemed as if we actually had a chance to pull off an upset victory and pick up some seats. When I returned, I discovered that we were in serious trouble in almost every major race.

The problem was that we had peaked too early on the Social Issue. Democrats know how to read too, and they had obviously taken the lessons of *The Real Majority* to heart. Adlai Stevenson III, running for the Senate in Illinois, responded to attacks on his ultraliberal record with a highly emotional invocation of his war record. *Newsweek* dryly called it "the most improbable speech" in his political career and noted that the Illinois Senate race "was offering final proof that this is the year when even the proudest liberals feel they had better pay major attention to the flag and to all the traditional values, yearnings, and fears of Richard Nixon's silent majority." Running for the Senate in California, Ted Kennedy's liberal protégé John Tunney used TV commercials that showed him riding around in a police car.

As the campaign progressed and the Democrats successfully blunted the Social Issue, they unleashed a full-scale attack on us about the economy, which was undeniably having problems. They hammered at the fact that unemployment had climbed to 5.5 percent and insisted it was going to go higher still.

We commissioned a quick private poll that indicated that as things stood we were going to lose thirty House seats and possibly all but one of the key Senate seats. I decided to reverse my earlier decision and announced that I would campaign personally for our candidates in a number of key races. During the three weeks before the election I devoted seven full days to campaigning for candidates in twenty-two states.

Almost everywhere I went during the campaign there were bands of demonstrators. As I was entering a hall in New Jersey, a young man reached out and as he shook my hand shouted a few obscenities at me. I motioned the Secret

Service back, and I stood looking at him while he screamed, "You're guilty of murder every day you fight this war." I said to him, very quietly, so that he had to lean a little bit forward to hear me, "Have you been to Vietnam?" He seemed surprised, and hesitated before he said, "No." I looked at him again for a moment before I said, "Our men are fighting there so you won't have to fight there or anyplace else in your lifetime." By this time he had released his grip on my arm, and I walked directly into the hall.

I would not have wanted Pat or the girls to see some of the things the demonstrators did or hear some of the things they shouted, and I was concerned about the vast majority of individuals and families who had come out in high spirits for a presidential rally and suddenly found themselves in the midst of an ugly confrontation.

While I was talking to a crowd of about 5,000 supporters at California's San Jose Municipal Auditorium, a crowd of about 2,000 demonstrators beat on the doors all around the building. As I walked the few steps to my car after the speech, I could see protesters gathered on the other side of the police barricades just a hundred feet away. They were chanting their favorite slogans, including "One, two, three, four—we don't want your fucking war," and I could not resist showing them how little respect I had for their juvenile and mindless ranting.

I stood on the hood of the car and gave them the V-sign that had become my political trademark. It had a predictable effect, and a chorus of jeers and boos began. Then I saw something coming toward me. When it hit the roof of the car, I realized that it was a rock. Suddenly rocks and eggs and vegetables were flying everywhere. Within seconds I was inside the car and Secret Service agents were following emergency evacuation procedures. Unfortunately one of the cars in the motorcade behind us stalled, and its windows and windows in the press bus were broken by rocks. Several people, including Secret Service agents, were hit by rocks and flying glass.

The local police chief may have exaggerated when he said it was an act of God that I got out safely. But the dents in the presidential limousine and the broken glass from the bus were real enough, and the possibility of a more serious incident having developed was very disturbing. The orga-

610

nizer of the demonstration proudly claimed credit for the mêlée, saying that the Peace and Freedom Party and other antiwar groups had staged the demonstration to call attention to their claim that I was a "war criminal" who was not welcome in California. He said, "After dropping that many bombs on the Vietnamese people how can anyone associated with the government claim to be upset about people throwing some eggs and rocks at Nixon? What's so precious about Nixon that he can't take a few eggs when he can dish out so many bombs?"

We flew to San Clemente from San Jose, and that night I sat in my study for over an hour, thinking about what had happened and about how I should respond. As far as I knew this was the first time in our history that a mob had physically attacked the President of the United States. I did not care what these demonstrators or their leaders thought about me personally, but if they did not respect the office of the presidency, I thought that people should be made to recognize that fact and take sides on it.

Two days later, at a rally at Sky Harbor Airport in Phoenix, I discussed the San Jose incident.

I wanted to cut through the fashionable notion that all our troubles were the result of the supposedly immoral war in Vietnam. It was time to brand this alibi for violence as the pure nonsense it was. "Those who carry a 'peace' sign in one hand and throw a bomb or a brick with the other are the super hypocrites of our time," I said. "Violence in America today is not caused by the war; it is not caused by repression. There is no romantic ideal involved. Let's recognize these people for what they are. They are not romantic revolutionaries. They are the same thugs and hoodlums that have always plagued the good people."

The speech was interrupted many times by loud cheers from the noontime audience. One of the loudest came when I said, "And now could I add a personal note? The terrorists, the far left, would like nothing better than to make the President of the United States a prisoner in the White House. Well, let me just set them straight. As long as I am President, no band of violent thugs is going to keep me from going out and speaking with the American people wherever they want to hear me and wherever I want to go. This is a free country, and I fully intend to share that freedom with

611

my fellow Americans. This President is not going to be cooped up in the White House."

I told Haldeman that I wanted to have the film of this speech rebroadcast as my election night address to the nation.

What happened next was one of those mistakes that it is hard to believe could actually have been made. The film we had of the Phoenix speech turned out to be a poor quality black-and-white videotape. The picture was grainy, and the sound, bouncing from the walls of the huge airport hangar, was shrill and occasionally slightly garbled. Everyone who worked on it remarked that it was terrible; some of the TV technicians wondered whether it was even of minimum broadcast quality. But election eve was two days away, there was no time for lengthy debates, and no one wanted to assume the responsibility for saying that we should not use it. The editing was completed just in time for the tape to be rushed to the studios for broadcast.

The result was a disaster. The quality was so bad that many TV stations received calls from outraged Republicans who were convinced that the program must have been sabotaged by the Democrats. Even worse, it was followed immediately by Senator Muskie's election eve broadcast on behalf of the Democratic candidates. In contrast to the harsh tone of my Phoenix speech, Muskie sounded calm and measured as he spoke from the homey setting of his summer house in Cape Elizabeth, Maine. What should have been a comparison based on substance thus became a comparison based on tone, and there was no doubt that Muskie emerged the winner. As John Mitchell put it, the Phoenix speech made me sound as if I were running for District Attorney of Phoenix, rather than the President of the United States addressing the American people at the end of an important national campaign.

In a postelection memo I dictated to Haldeman dissecting our performance in the 1970 election, I talked about the ill-fated Phoenix broadcast:

> There is a good lesson out of this. . . . It is that in this age of television, technical quality is probably more important than the content of what is said. We learned this from the first debate with Kennedy, and now we have had to relearn it in

fortunately a less decisive forum in our handling of this particular matter. The important thing is for us not to brush it off as something that "wasn't all that bad" but to recognize that it was a mistake and to be sure that kind of mistake is not made again.

Election Day was November 3. We lost nine House seats and gained two in the Senate. In fact this was an excellent showing because in past election years in which unemployment was on the rise the average loss of seats by the party controlling the White House was forty-six. In that respect we had defied overwhelming historical trends. It was also particularly gratifying to me that some extreme liberals were among those senators retired by the voters. The greatest disappointment was the drubbing we took in the gubernatorial contests, where we lost eleven state houses and ended up with only twenty-one Republican governors in the fifty states.

The most important result of the 1970 election was that the shaky coalition of support we had to rely on in the Senate was now replaced by a slim but more dependable majority on foreign policy and national defense issues.

Despite this fact and despite the fact that our losses in the House were substantially smaller than the off-year defeats of previous administrations, the postelection media analysis, led by the TV networks and the news magazines, treated the election as a significant political failure for me and a serious setback to my chances for being re-elected. *Newsweek*'s cover featured Senator Muskie and the story inside reported that the Democrats now dared to dream that I might be "retired" in 1972.

Although our first efforts to consolidate a constituency based on the Social Issue had met with only mixed success, I still felt that the basic strategy was right.

In the lengthy post-mortem I dictated for Haldeman, I turned my sights toward 1972. I said that we should start now to weed out lackluster Republican House, Senate, and gubernatorial candidates, help them get other jobs, and replace them with candidates who could win.

At least two major candidates had been defeated in 1970 because of their involvement in political scandals, and I urged that we take precautions against this particular hazard. The personal ethics and conduct of our candidates had to be above suspicion or reproach. I wrote: "We cannot afford to have anybody on our ticket in 1972 who will pose this problem to us. We must be absolutely ruthless in bringing such matters to the attention of candidates and getting them cleaned up, or getting the candidate off the ticket if he has such a problem and cannot clean it up."

I said that I thought it was imperative that we get politics out of the White House either by introducing dynamic campaign management into the Republican National Committee or by setting up a special presidential re-election committee. I wrote, "I want to be in the position where I can honestly say the White House does not have its hand in the political maneuvering that is going to begin the moment the new Congress comes in session."

Agnew, I said, should "de-escalate the rhetoric without de-escalating the substance of his message." He should be shown fighting for something, rather than just railing against everything.

I wrote that I hoped we could get some enthusiasm into the RNC, and I urged that people be "upbeat and act as if they were having some fun in carrying out assignments." This extended to my own schedule, where I wanted more spontaneity and less gimmickry. Somehow we weren't getting across to people all the activities at the White House—the social evenings, the worship services, the special parties. I added, "This must be done, incidentally, without trying to make the President a laughing boy, and without having Martha Mitchell appear to be the only one who seems to enjoy being in Washington!"

Finally I wrote that I was going to take the advice of nearly all those around me and firmly and flatly keep out of my re-election campaign until as late as possible in 1972.

In fact my determination to keep politics out of the White House was short-lived. I should have known that the attempt would be futile. As each day brought the election closer, and as the competition heightened, the need for action and information became irresistible. Democratic Presidents since FDR had excelled—and reveled—in flexing the formidable political muscle that goes with being the party in the White House. I planned to take no less advantage of it myself. So I ended up keeping the pressure on the people around me to get organized, to get tough, and to get information about what the other side was doing. Sometimes I ordered a tail on a front-running Democrat; sometimes I urged that department and agency files be checked for any indications of suspicious or illegal activities involving prominent Democrats. I told my staff that we should come up with the kind of imaginative dirty tricks that our Democratic opponents used against us and others so effectively in previous campaigns.

John Mitchell was going to be my campaign manager, but he would have his hands full organizing and running the Committee to Re-elect the President. Increasingly I turned to Chuck Colson to act as my political point-man. Colson had joined the administration in late 1969 in the role of White House liaison with special interest groups. He worked on policy matters with energy and devotion. He spent hours with labor groups, veterans' organizations, ethnic minorities, and religious groups. He was positive, persuasive, smart, and aggressively partisan. His instinct for the political jugular and his ability to get things done made him a lightning rod for my own frustrations at the timidity of most Republicans in responding to attacks from the Democrats and the media. When I complained to Colson I felt confident that something would be done, and I was rarely disappointed.

I was confident that I could win re-election in a contest on the issues in 1972. That only reinforced my determination not to let the other side be politically tougher than we were.

1971

The first months of 1971 were the lowest point of my first term as President. The problems we confronted were so overwhelming and so apparently impervious to anything we could do to change them that it seemed possible that I might not even be nominated for re-election in 1972. Early in January it was announced that unemployment had reached 6 percent—the highest point since 1961. In February we became involved in the Laotian operation, which turned out to be a military success but a public relations disaster. In May 200,000 antiwar demonstrators converged on Washington and, led by hard-core agitators who had been openly encouraged by the North Vietnamese, mounted a violent but unsuccessful attempt to close down the government for a day. In June the publication of the Pentagon Papers assaulted the principle of government control over classified documents. The economy was in bad shape and did not look like it was going to get better very soon. On the foreign exchange markets the dollar hit its lowest point since 1949. As the opinion polls registered my losses, they marked Muskie's gains. The Soviets had set back détente by their adventurism in Cuba and the Middle East, and the likelihood of a breakthrough in SALT or the other outstanding issues between us seemed remote. Similarly our tentative approaches to Communist China appeared to have fallen on deaf ears. Without these levers to bring pressure to bear on Hanoi it looked as if the war could drag on indefinitely, although the increasing strength and confidence of the antiwar forces in Congress might mean a sudden termination vote or cutoff of funds at almost any time.

Having hit the lowest of low points in 1971, we suddenly rebounded with a series of stunning successes, among them the announcement of the China trip, a breakthrough in the SALT negotiations, an extremely popular and apparently effective economic program including a freeze of wages and prices, and the scheduling of a Soviet summit. These and other things gave us a momentum that carried right into the presidential election year of 1972.

The year 1971 proved the political maxim that one should never despair until the votes have been cast and counted. Something can always turn up, often from an unexpected source or quarter, that utterly transforms one's situation and one's prospects.

LAM SON

Before our successful Cambodian operation in 1970, it was estimated that 85 percent of the heavy arms used by the Communists in South Vietnam had come by sea through the port of Sihanoukville. Once we closed that route, everything had to come overland through Laos down the Ho Chi Minh trail. By mid-December 1970, Laos was clogged with men and supplies, the bulk of which would be moved into Cambodia for a 1971 spring offensive.

On January 18, 1971, in a meeting with Laird, Rogers, Helms, Kissinger, Colonel Alexander Haig, Kissinger's deputy, and Admiral Thomas H. Moorer, Chairman of the Joint Chiefs of Staff, I authorized a major military operation to cut the Ho Chi Minh trail by attacking enemy forces in Laos. Because of the problem of American domestic opinion and because the South Vietnamese wanted to prove how successful Vietnamization had been, we decided that the operation would be an ARVN exercise; the United States would supply only air cover and artillery support. The principal American contribution would be ferrying troops and supplies by helicopter, gunship support, and B-52 raids. Even the operation's codename was Vietnamese: Lam Son 719.

On February 8, a 5,000-man ARVN force crossed the border into Laos. The Communists put up stronger resistance than had been anticipated, and the American military command in Saigon failed to respond to this unexpectedly intense level of combat with the necessary increase in air cover for the invading forces. The resulting ARVN casualties were heavy, but they continued to fight courageously.

The South Vietnamese forces quickly recovered from these initial setbacks, and most of the military purposes of Lam Son were achieved within the first few weeks as the Communists were deprived of the capacity to launch an offensive against our forces in South Vietnam in 1971.

In view of the operation's substantial success and because of signs that the Communists were trying to prepare a major counteroffensive, the ARVN commanders decided to withdraw early. On March 18 they began what was to have been a strategic retreat. Our air support was inadequate, however, and under severe enemy pounding some of the ARVN soldiers panicked. It took only a few televised films of ARVN soldiers clinging to the skids of our evacuation helicopters to reinforce the widespread misconception of the ARVN forces as incompetent and cowardly.

The net result was a military success but a psychological defeat, both in South Vietnam, where morale was shaken by media reports of the retreat, and in America, where suspicions about the possibility of escalation had been aroused and where news pictures undercut confidence in the success of Vietnamization and the prospect of ending the war.

Sir Robert Thompson wrote to Kissinger from Vietnam shortly after Lam Son ended. He praised its military success and stated that the major factor in the war was now the question of South Vietnamese psychology and confidence. Thanks to Lam Son there was no Communist offensive in 1971 despite the largest influx of matériel in the history of the war. American and South Vietnamese casualties were reduced, and Vietnamization continued at a steady pace.

I still agree with Kissinger's assessment of Lam Son at the end of March 1971 when he said, "If I had known before it started that it was going to come out exactly the way it did, I would still have gone ahead with it."

———————

On March 29, 1971, just days after the withdrawal of ARVN troops from Laos, First Lieutenant William Calley,

Jr., was found guilty by an Army court-martial of the premeditated murder of twenty-two South Vietnamese civilians. The public furore over Lam Son had just begun to settle down, and now we were faced with still another Vietnam-related controversy. This one had been simmering since the fall of 1969, when the murders were first revealed.

It was in March 1968, ten months before I became President, that Calley led his platoon into My Lai, a small hamlet about 100 miles northeast of Saigon. The village had been a Vietcong stronghold and our forces had suffered many casualties trying to clear it out. Calley had his men round up the villagers and then ordered that they be shot; many were left sprawled lifeless in a drainage ditch.

Calley's crime was inexcusable. But I felt that many of the commentators and congressmen who professed outrage about My Lai were not really as interested in the moral questions raised by the Calley case as they were interested in using it to make political attacks against the Vietnam war. For one thing, they had been noticeably uncritical of North Vietnamese atrocities. In fact, the calculated and continual role that terror, murder, and massacre played in the Vietcong strategy was one of the most underreported aspects of the entire Vietnam war. Much to the discredit of the media and the antiwar activists, this side of the story was only rarely included in descriptions of Vietcong policy and practices.

On March 31 the court-martial sentenced Calley to life in prison at hard labor. Public reaction to this announcement was emotional and sharply divided. More than 5,000 telegrams arrived at the White House, running 100 to 1 in favor of clemency.

John Connally and Jerry Ford recommended in strong terms that I use my powers as Commander in Chief to reduce Calley's prison time. Connally said that justice had been served by the sentence, and that now the reality of maintaining public support for the armed services and for the war had to be given primary consideration. I talked to Carl Albert and other congressional leaders. All of them agreed that emotions in Congress were running high in favor of presidential intervention.

I called Admiral Moorer on April 1 and ordered that,

pending Calley's appeal, he should be released from the stockade and confined instead to his quarters on the base. When this was announced to the House of Representatives, there was a spontaneous round of applause on the floor. Reaction was particularly strong and positive in the South. George Wallace, after a visit with Calley, said that I had done the right thing. Governor Jimmy Carter of Georgia said that I had made a wise decision. Two days later I had Ehrlichman announce that I would personally review the Calley case before any final sentence was carried out.

By April 1974, Calley's sentence had been reduced to ten years, with eligibility for parole as early as the end of that year. I reviewed the case as I had said I would but decided not to intervene. Three months after I resigned, the Secretary of the Army decided to parole Calley.

I think most Americans understood that the My Lai massacre was not representative of our people, of the war we were fighting, or of our men who were fighting it; but from the time it first became public the whole tragic episode was used by the media and the antiwar forces to chip away at our efforts to build public support for our Vietnam objectives and policies.

THE WHITE HOUSE TAPES

From the very beginning I had decided that my administration would be the best chronicled in history. I wanted a record of every major meeting I held, ranging from verbatim transcripts of important national security sessions to "color reports" of ceremonial events. Unfortunately the system proved cumbersome, because it was not always convenient or appropriate to have someone in the room taking notes. In many cases it inhibited conversation. We also found that the quality of prose varied as much as the quality of perception, and too many of the reports ended up more hagiography than history. Finally, during the period that Lam Son was being planned and discussed, I decided to reinstall a tape recording system.

The existence of the tapes was never meant to be made public—at least not during my presidency. I thought that afterward I could consult the tapes in preparing whatever books or memoirs I might write. Such an objective record might also be useful to the extent that any President feels vulnerable to revisionist histories—whether from within or without his administration—and particularly so when the issues are as controversial and the personalities as volatile as they were in my first term.

The first President known to record his conversations was Franklin Roosevelt, who reportedly had a microphone placed in a lamp in the Oval Office. There is evidence that Eisenhower taped some of his conversations. President Kennedy taped some of his office conversations and phone calls, and more than 180 such recordings are now in the Kennedy Library kept under the restrictions imposed by the Kennedy family.

Lyndon Johnson had a taping system for his office phone, his bedroom phone, the phone at Camp David, the phone at his ranch in Johnson City, and the phone at his office in Austin. In addition to the phone equipment, he had room microphones placed in the Cabinet Room and in the private office next to the Oval Office. At one point there was also a recording device that could pick up conversations in the room outside the Oval Office where Johnson's visitors would wait before being ushered in to see him. The Johnson system was operated manually, which permitted him to decide which conversations to record. In the Cabinet Room buttons were attached to the underside of the table in front of his chair, and I have been told that in the private office the system was activated by buttons concealed behind the television console in the Oval Office.

Johnson frequently had the tapes transcribed as soon as the conversation had ended. According to the White House grapevine, Johnson taped the conversation when he met privately with Bobby Kennedy to inform him that he would not be the 1964 vice presidential nominee. Immediately after their meeting Johnson asked to have the tape transcribed. When the typist played the tape, however, she found that the entire conversation was inaudible. A tape technician concluded that Kennedy must have carried a small scrambling device with him as a precaution.

Johnson thought that my decision to remove his taping system was a mistake; he felt his tapes were invaluable in writing his memoirs.

Although I was not comfortable with the idea of taping people without their knowledge, I was at least confident that the secrecy of the system would protect their privacy. I thought that recording only selected conversations would completely undercut the purpose of having the taping system; if our tapes were going to be an objective record of my presidency, they could not have such an obviously self-serving bias. I did not want to have to calculate whom or what or when I would tape. Therefore, a system was installed that was voice-activated; talking would trigger the tape machines. Beginning in February recording devices were placed in the Oval Office, the Cabinet Room, and the EOB office. I rejected the suggestion that recording equipment be placed on phones in the Family Quarters and in Key Biscayne and San Clemente; I wanted to record only the official business of the presidency. Recorders were installed on phones in the Oval and EOB offices, the Lincoln Sitting Room, and on the office phone at Camp David.

Initially, I was conscious of the taping, but before long I accepted it as part of the surroundings.

I never listened to a tape until June 4, 1973, when I had to do so because of the Watergate investigation. None of the tapes was transcribed until September 1973, when I was faced with the subpoenas of the Ervin Committee and the Special Prosecutor.

THE KENNEDY PORTRAITS

In February 1971, Pat invited Jacqueline Kennedy Onassis and her children to have dinner with our family and see the official portraits of President Kennedy and herself before the public unveiling ceremony. It was a particularly moving occasion for us because none of them had been inside the White House since the agonizing days immediately after President Kennedy's assassination.

Pat gave explicit orders that the visit be kept secret until it was over so that no reporters or cameramen would intrude on their privacy. We welcomed them in the Diplomatic Reception Room and then took them to see the portraits, which had been painted by a New York artist Jackie had personally chosen.

John Kennedy, Jr., who was ten, and his sister, Caroline, who was thirteen, were very enthusiastic about each of the portraits. Jackie, however, did not make any comments about them. I thought that this might be because she was embroiled in a controversy with the artist who had sold a reproduction of the painting and sketches of her to a national magazine. Pat later told me that when she invited Rose Kennedy to see the portraits, Mrs. Kennedy had stood silently in front of her son's bowed figure for a long time. Finally she said, "I never saw Jack look like that."

Later I made some notes about our dinner:

We had drinks in the West Hall before going in to dinner. The butler, Allen, had been in the White House while the Kennedys were here, and he greeted Jackie warmly. I noticed that he put ice in her white wine at dinner, and she explained that it had been her custom to have this when she was here.

The children were served milk at Jackie's request, and John, Jr., said, "Milk is so bad in foreign countries. It's icky!"

Jackie was very bright and talkative. As we went into the second-floor Dining Room, which she had had converted from Margaret Truman's bedroom, we talked about how Alice Longworth had her appendix out in it. She said that Jack and she practically suffocated when the room was being renovated because of the paint smell. In fact, they had moved to the other end of the floor until the painting was completed.

I recalled that one of the problems of campaigning was that in many hotels, and particularly in the smaller cities, the rooms were often freshly painted before we arrived. It is difficult enough to sleep on the road, but the smell of paint makes it impossible.

She recalled that once when Jack was in the Senate, she had "peeked into your office just across the hall." She also recalled the picture that was taken in Chicago when the three of us arrived on the same plane early in 1960. I reminded her that she had been reading Allen Drury's *Advise and Consent* on the plane. "I never finished it," was her response.

We talked in very general terms about all the changes that had taken place in the years since she had been in the White House. Of course I was determined to keep the conversation away from anything that would distress her or make the visit sad. At one point she looked at me and said, "I always live in a dream world."

623

Tricia first met Ed Cox at a high school dance in 1963. A year later, when she was a freshman at Finch College and he was a freshman at Princeton, he was her escort at the International Debutante Ball, an annual charity event held in New York. They began to date but found themselves at times falling into disagreements about politics. Ed was a Republican, but in the Eastern liberal tradition; during the summer of 1968 he worked for Ralph Nader.

One day late in 1969 Tricia told me that they were becoming serious about each other, but she was concerned about their continuing political differences. Since both of them were extremely strong-willed and articulate, these discussions were often heated. I said that the important thing was the way they felt about each other; if they were truly in love, I said, that was all that mattered and political problems would work themselves out. As time went on, their political differences virtually evaporated as their affection for each other grew steadily stronger.

One November weekend in 1970, Ed Cox came into my study at Camp David and said rather formally, "Mr. President, as I'm sure you know, I am very much in love with Tricia. I would like your permission to ask her to marry me."

I had known Ed for several years, and I told him that what was important was what Tricia wanted and that I was sure she would say yes.

We announced their engagement on Pat's birthday, March 16, after a dinner in honor of Prime Minister John Lynch of Ireland. We asked Tricia if she would like to have a White House wedding. It was entirely up to her and Ed, but we felt it would be something they would remember all their lives. Pat suggested that, since they had chosen June 12, we could have it outdoors in the Rose Garden.

The night before the wedding I wrote a short note to Tricia and slipped it under her door after she had gone to bed.

The day of the wedding dawned cloudy. Intermittent light drizzle was predicted until around four—just when the ceremony was scheduled to begin. I called Tricia and asked her how she felt about taking the risk and counting on the weather clearing as forecast.

"I would prefer to have it in the Rose Garden as we planned," she said.

"Then that's the way we'll do it," I replied.

When I left for the Residence around three, the rain had tapered off slightly, but the sky was still a threatening, sullen gray.

Tricia has described the scene in the Family Quarters when she emerged from her room, dressed in her wedding gown and veil, to join Pat and Julie, who were waiting for her in the West Hall.

> Mama and Julie looked so beautiful that suddenly I felt the event would be beautiful too. They exclaimed over the wedding gown and the fact that the diamond pendant necklace Edward had given me was the perfect length for the V-neck gown. Daddy appeared from the elevator, and said that everyone looked lovely. He went into his room and reappeared shortly in morning coat and striped pants which suited him well because he has the height to do it justice.

By 4:15 the young military officers who serve as White House social aides had gathered the 400 guests into the long ground-floor corridor and were waiting to learn whether to usher them outside into the Rose Garden or upstairs into the East Room. I called for the latest Air Force weather report. Now a clearing front that would last for about fifteen minutes was expected to move into the area at about 4:30. I told Haldeman to pass the word along: we would begin at 4:30.

The rain stopped, the plastic covers were removed from the chairs, and the guests were ushered to their places. At 4:30 Julie and the bridesmaids began the procession down the long curving white staircase into the garden. Tricia described the scene:

> Along the green carpeted path Daddy and I smiled at each other as if to say, "No rain yet!" The Army Strings sounded glorious as we approached the garden entrance. Lucy Winchester smiled from ear to ear like the Cheshire Cat as we walked through the entrance. Julie was ahead of us in her

June 12, 1971
12:10 AM

Dear Trisia —

Well Today is the
day you begin a
long and exciting
journey —

I want you to know
how proud I have been
of you through the years —
some of them — pretty difficult
for you I'm sure.

The years ahead
will be happy ones
because you will make them so.

Your strength of
Character will see you
through whatever comes —
    You have made
the right choice and
I am sure Callie + you
will look back on
this time and be able
to say —
    "The day indeed was
    splendid" —
        love —
        Daddy

ephemeral-looking palest of mint gown, walking in a stately manner into the most breathtaking sight I had ever seen in the United States.

The Rose Garden was a crown of natural beauty, with the gazebo the most spectacular jewel of the crown. Flowers which were exquisite in their own right were intertwined with one another, and out of this composition emerged a creation of beauty that surpassed the beauty of the individual flowers. For once, mankind had improved on nature.

When Julie had almost reached the steps leading to the platform where the minister stood waiting, Lucy whispered, "Go," to us. I released my train which Lucy quickly bent to arrange. Then I turned to Daddy and said, "All right."

We proceeded slowly down the aisle. I recall smiling generally but seeing no specific face. The crowd was one blur until we reached the first row and I saw Mama and gave her a special smile. Eddie and I exchanged little happy smiles as Daddy and I ascended the steps.

The marriage ceremony, which Tricia and Ed had written themselves, was beautiful. When it was over and the groom had kissed the bride, instead of walking immediately up the aisle they went over first to Pat and me and then to the Coxes, to embrace us and to thank us for this day.

There was dancing at the reception in the East Room afterward. Ed and Tricia had chosen "Lara's Theme" from *Dr. Zhivago* for the first waltz. When the band began playing "Thank Heaven for Little Girls," I broke in to dance with Tricia while Ed danced with Pat. This was the first time I danced in the White House. After dancing with Tricia, I cut in and danced with Pat. She is an excellent dancer, and the guests broke into delighted applause as she steered me around the floor. Then I danced with Julie. I knew that she missed David, who was now in the Navy and had been assigned to sea duty in the Mediterranean. I whispered in her ear that I would never forget how beautiful she was on her wedding day two and a half years before.

I saw Lynda Bird Johnson, standing alone, and I asked her to dance and told her how impressed I had been by her beauty and grace when I saw her on television when she and Chuck Robb had been married in the White House in 1967.

After the newlyweds had left for a honeymoon at Camp

David, Pat, Julie, Bebe Rebozo, and I sat in the Residence watching the TV specials.

It had been a wonderful day. Even the weather had turned out to be a friend. It was a day that all of us will always remember, because all of us were beautifully, and simply, happy.

THE PENTAGON PAPERS

On Sunday morning, June 13, I picked up the New York *Times*. In the top left-hand corner there was a picture of me standing with Tricia in the Rose Garden. *Tricia Nixon Takes Vows* was the headline. Next to the picture was another headline: *Vietnam Archive: Pentagon Study Traces 3 Decades of Growing U.S. Involvement.*

The story described a 7,000-page study of American involvement in Southeast Asia from World War II through 1968, which had been commissioned by Robert McNamara, Johnson's Secretary of Defense. It contained verbatim documents from the Defense Department, the State Department, the CIA, the White House, and the Joint Chiefs of Staff. The *Times* announced that it planned to publish not only portions of the study but many of the original documents as well. The newspaper did not say that all these materials were still officially classified "Secret" and "Top Secret." In fact, this was the most massive leak of classified documents in American history.

The McNamara study had been officially titled "The History of U.S. Decision-Making Process on Vietnam." Before long, however, the media had created a more dramatic label: "The Pentagon Papers."

The documents had been illegally turned over to the *Times,* and I believed that the paper acted irresponsibly in publishing them. The *Times* admitted having been in possession of them for more than three months before publishing them, but had never once sought comment from anyone in the government, or inquired whether publication of any of the classified material might threaten national security or endanger the lives of our men in Vietnam.

The defense and intelligence agencies raced to obtain copies of the study in order to assess the impact of its disclosure. The National Security Agency was immediately worried that some of the more recent documents could provide code-breaking clues. They feared that information about signal and electronic intelligence capabilities would be spotted by the trained eyes of enemy experts. The State Department was alarmed because the study would expose Southeast Asia Treaty Organization contingency war plans that were still in effect. The CIA was worried that past or current informants would be exposed; they said that the study would contain specific references to the names and activities of CIA agents still active in Southeast Asia. In fact, one secret contact dried up almost immediately. A tremor shook the international community because the study contained material relating to the role of other governments as diplomatic go-betweens; several of them made official protests. Dean Rusk issued a statement that the documents would be valuable to the North Vietnamese and the Soviets.

On consideration, we had only two choices: we could do nothing, or we could move for an injunction that would prevent the New York *Times* from continuing publication. Policy argued for moving against the *Times*; politics argued against it.

The McNamara study was primarily a critique of the way Kennedy and Johnson had led the nation into war in Vietnam. It recounted Kennedy's decision to support the coup that ousted President Diem in 1963 and resulted in Diem's death, causing General Maxwell Taylor to comment that one of our worst mistakes was our connivance in the Diem overthrow—"nothing but chaos came as a result." News reports said the document proved that Johnson had told the American people that he was not going to escalate the war, while privately planning an escalation from 17,000 to 185,000 American men. After the release of the papers James Reston wrote of the "deceptive and stealthy American involvement in the war under Presidents Kennedy and Johnson."

Nevertheless, publication of the Pentagon Papers was certain to hurt the whole Vietnam effort. Critics of the war would use them to attack my goals and my policies.

But to me, there was an even more fundamental reason

for taking action to prevent publication. An important principle was at stake in this case: it is the role of the government, not the New York *Times*, to judge the impact of a top secret document. Mel Laird felt that over 95 percent of the material could be declassified, but we were all still worried about whatever percent—even if it were only 1 percent—that should not be. If we did not move against the *Times* it would be a signal to every disgruntled bureaucrat in the government that he could leak anything he pleased while the government simply stood by.

The *Times*'s decision to publish the documents was clearly the product of the paper's antiwar policy rather than a consistent attachment to principle. In the early 1960s Otto Otepka, a State Department employee, had shown classified documents relating to lax security procedures in the department to senators who were investigating the problem. Otepka believed that his action was justified because it was the only way to correct what he considered a dangerous situation. The *Times* had no sympathy for Otepka's action and expressed its editorial indignation:

> Orderly procedures are essential if the vital division of power between legislative and executive branches is not to be undermined. The use of "underground" methods to obtain classified documents from lower-level officials is a dangerous departure from such orderly procedures.

The Washington *Post* had also been outraged:

> If any underling in the State Department were free at his own discretion to disclose confidential cables or if any agent of the Federal Bureau of Investigation could leak the contents of secret files whenever he felt like it, the Executive Branch of the Government would have no security at all.

When the *Times*'s publisher, Arthur Sulzberger, was asked about the government's concern that publication of the Pentagon Papers undermined the faith of foreign governments in our ability to deal in confidence, he was reported to have said, "Oh, that's a lot of baloney. I mean, really."

On Tuesday, June 15, the Justice Department moved to enjoin the *Times* from publication until the government could review the documents and verify that they caused no national security problems. In the meantime, the Washington *Post*, the Boston *Globe*, and the St. Louis *Post-Dispatch* had obtained copies and started publication on their own.

In court the *Times*'s counsel argued at one point that even if publication of the Pentagon Papers contributed to the delay of the return of our POWs, protection of the First Amendment made that a risk we should be willing to take. I was outraged. I did not consider that rights conveyed by the First Amendment for the publication of these documents superior to the right of an American soldier to stay alive in wartime.

At the outset I had hoped that former Presidents Truman and Johnson would join me in taking a strong public stand against such leaks of classified material. As far as I know, however, Truman made no comment. And after talking to Johnson, Bryce Harlow reported that Johnson felt that whatever he said now would be turned against him by the Washington *Post* and the New York *Times*. Those papers, he said, were merely trying to "re-execute" him. Harlow said Johnson had talked in bitter outbursts, accusing the "professors" who wrote the study of misconstruing contingency plans as actual presidential decisions. The authors of the study had all been involved in the actions they were "bitching" about now, Johnson had said, adding that he had never made a decision of any consequence on escalation or the use of troops without the full concurrence of McNamara and others in his administration.

On June 30, the Supreme Court ruled on our effort to prevent publication: the government lost, 6 to 3. One of the majority opinions agreed that the disclosures might have a serious impact on the national interest but said this was still no basis for sanctioning entire restraint on the press. Chief Justice Burger, in his dissent, criticized the undue haste of the Court's deliberation and the *Times*'s failure to consult the government: "To me it is hardly believable that a newspaper long regarded as a great institution in American lives would fail to perform one of the basic and simple duties of every citizen with respect to the discovery or possession of stolen property or secret government documents. . . . This duty rests on taxi drivers, justices, and the New York *Times*."

The Pentagon Papers leak came at a particularly sensitive time. We were just three and a half weeks away from Kissinger's secret trip to China, and the SALT talks were under way. Sir Robert Thompson had written in April saying that the major factor now influencing the course of the war was psychological: our military policy was working on the battlefield, but division in America was causing the North Vietnamese to stall in Paris. There had been violent demonstrations in Washington in May. On May 31, at the secret Paris talks, Kissinger offered our most far-reaching proposal yet. On June 13 the Pentagon Papers were published, and on June 22 the Senate voted its first resolution establishing a pull-out timetable for Vietnam. Before long, the North Vietnamese would slam the door on our new proposal and begin building up for a new military offense.

We had lost our court battle against the newspaper that published the documents, but I was determined that we would at least win our public case against the man I believed had stolen them, Daniel Ellsberg. A former Pentagon aide, Ellsberg had come under suspicion soon after the first installments from the study appeared. Whatever others may have thought, I considered what Ellsberg had done to be despicable and contemptible—he had revealed government foreign policy secrets during wartime. He was lionized in much of the media. CBS devoted a large segment of the network news to a respectful interview with him even while he was still a fugitive from the FBI.

On June 28, a Los Angeles grand jury indicted him on one count of theft of government property and one count of unauthorized possession of documents and writings related to national defense.

"I think I've done a good job as a citizen," Ellsberg told the throng of admirers outside the courthouse.

Kissinger, Haldeman, Ehrlichman, and I had met on the afternoon of June 17 to assess the situation. Kissinger had known Ellsberg at Harvard and said he was bright but emotionally unstable.

In various interviews Ellsberg had said he was convinced that I intended to escalate the war rather than pull troops out of Vietnam. He said that increased public opposition would be necessary to force unilateral withdrawal. I felt that there was serious reason to be concerned about what he

633

might do next. During his years at the Defense Department, he had had access to some of the most sensitive information in the entire government. And the Rand Corporation, where he had worked before he gave the Pentagon Papers to the *Times*, had 173,000 classified documents in its possession. I wondered how many of these Ellsberg might have and what else he might give to the newspapers.

Ellsberg was not our only worry. From the first there had been rumors and reports of a conspiracy. The earliest report, later discounted, centered on a friend of Ellsberg, a former Defense Department employee who was then a Fellow at the Brookings Institution. I remembered him from the early days of the administration when I had asked Haldeman to get me a copy of the Pentagon file on the events leading up to Johnson's announcement of the bombing halt at the end of the 1968 campaign. I wanted to know what had actually happened; I also wanted the information as potential leverage against those in Johnson's administration who were now trying to undercut my war policy. I was told that a copy of the bombing halt material and other secret documents had been taken from the Pentagon to Brookings by the same man. I wanted the documents back, but I was told that one copy of the bombing halt report had already "disappeared"; I was sure that if word got out that we wanted it, the copy at Brookings might disappear as well.

In the aftershock of the Pentagon Papers leak and all the uncertainty and renewed criticism of the war it produced, my interest in the bombing halt file was rekindled. When I was told that it was still at Brookings, I was furious and frustrated. In the midst of a war and with our secrets being spilled through printing presses all over the world, top-secret government reports were out of reach in the hands of a private think tank largely staffed with antiwar Democrats. It seemed absurd. I could not accept that we had lost so much control over the workings of the government we had been elected to run—I saw absolutely no reason for that report to be at Brookings, and I said I wanted it back right now—even if it meant having to get it surreptitiously. My determination only increased when I learned of a 1969 Brookings circular announcing a new study of Vietnam, due in 1971, to be based in part on "executive branch documents." The director of the study was Dr. Daniel Ellsberg.

We learned that an aide to Elliot Richardson at the State Department had given Ellsberg access to the current Vietnam documents in 1970. Even after the information in them was leaked, presumably by Ellsberg, Richardson had refused to remove the aide. It was also well known that a number of people on Kissinger's staff had friends and contacts at Brookings, and I wondered if any of them had provided Ellsberg and his friends with documents and materials.

In early July, John Mitchell reported that the Justice Department had continuing indications that Ellsberg had acted as part of a conspiracy; we received a report that the Soviet Embassy in Washington had received a set of the Pentagon Papers before they had been published in the New York *Times*; I was told that some of the documents provided to the newspapers were not even part of the McNamara study. Once again we were facing the question: what more did Ellsberg have, and what else did he plan to do?

In the meantime Ellsberg was successfully using the press, television talk shows, and antiwar rallies to promote the concept of unlawful dissent. Kissinger said that we were in a "revolutionary" situation.

Even as our concern about Ellsberg and his possible collaborators was growing, we learned that J. Edgar Hoover was dragging his feet and treating the case on merely a medium-priority basis; he had assigned no special task forces and no extra manpower to it. He evidently felt that the media would automatically make Ellsberg look like a martyr, and the FBI like the "heavy," if it pursued the case vigorously. Mitchell had been told that Hoover was sensitive about his personal friendship with Ellsberg's father-in-law. Finally, other agencies, principally the Defense Department, were conducting simultaneous investigations, and Hoover strongly resisted sharing his territory with anyone.

I did not care about any reasons or excuses. I wanted someone to light a fire under the FBI in its investigation of Ellsberg, and to keep the departments and agencies active in pursuit of leakers. If a conspiracy existed, I wanted to know, and I wanted the full resources of the government brought to bear in order to find out. If the FBI was not going to pursue the case, then we would have to do it ourselves. Ellsberg was having great success in the media with his efforts to justify unlawful dissent, and while I cared nothing for him personally, I felt that his views had to be discredited. I urged that we find out everything we could about his background, his motives, and his co-conspirators, if they existed.

I was also determined not to sit back while the Democratic architects of our Vietnam involvement tried to make me pay for the war politically. I wanted a good political operative who could sift through the Pentagon Papers as well as State and Defense Department files and get us all the facts on the Bay of Pigs, the Diem assassination, and Johnson's 1968 bombing halt. We were heading into an election year, in which the Vietnam war was almost certainly going to be the biggest issue. I wanted ammunition against the antiwar critics, many of whom were the same men who, under Kennedy and Johnson, had led us into the Vietnam morass in the first place. Finally, I wanted a revision of the classification system that would ensure that only legitimate foreign policy secrets were classified, but that those that were classified stayed secret.

On July 17, 1971, Ehrlichman assigned Egil "Bud" Krogh, a young lawyer on the Domestic Council staff, to head the leak project. David Young, a lawyer who was formerly a Kissinger aide, Howard Hunt, a former CIA agent, and G. Gordon Liddy, a former FBI man, worked with him. A year and a half later I learned for the first time that because their job was plugging leaks, Young had jokingly put up a sign establishing himself as a "Plumber."

On July 23, the morning before we were scheduled to present our formal position at the SALT talks in Helsinki, the New York *Times* carried a front-page leak of our fallback negotiating position. I tried to motivate Krogh in the strongest terms, and I told him, "We're not going to allow it. We just aren't going to allow it." The Plumbers pushed the departments to investigate with interviews and polygraph tests. An August 13 New York *Times* report was based on a CIA report we had received at the White House only a few days earlier. The information in the story was traceable to a highly secret CIA intelligence source. By fall the CIA reported that we were in the midst of the worst outbreak of leaks since 1953. I urged everyone to keep the pressure on.

On Labor Day weekend, 1971, Krogh's group organized a break-in at the office of Ellsberg's psychiatrist in an attempt to get information from his files on his motivation, his further intentions, and any possible co-conspirators.

I do not believe I was told about the break-in at the time, but it is clear that it was at least in part an outgrowth of my sense of urgency about discrediting what Ellsberg had done and finding out what he might do next. Given the temper of those tense and bitter times and the peril I perceived, I cannot say that had I been informed of it beforehand, I would have automatically considered it unprecedented, unwarranted, or unthinkable. Ehrlichman says that he did not know of it in advance, but that he told me about it after the fact in 1972. I do not recall this, and the tapes of the June-July 1972 period indicate that I was not conscious of it then, but I cannot rule it out.

Today the break-in at Ellsberg's psychiatrist's office seems wrong and excessive. But I do not accept that it was as wrong or excessive as what Daniel Ellsberg did, and I still believe that it is a tragedy of circumstances that Bud Krogh and John Ehrlichman went to jail and Daniel Ellsberg went free.

In hindsight I can see that, once I realized the Vietnam war could not be ended quickly or easily and that I was going to be up against an antiwar movement that was able to dominate the media with its attitudes and values, I was sometimes drawn into the very frame of mind I so despised in the leaders of that movement. They increasingly came to justify almost anything in the name of forcing an immediate end to a war they considered unjustified and immoral. I was similarly driven to preserve the government's ability to conduct foreign policy and to conduct it in the way that I felt would best bring peace. I believed that national security was involved. I still believe it today, and in the same circumstances, I would act now as I did then. History will make the final judgment on the actions, reactions, and excesses of both sides; it is a judgment I do not fear.

By late September the Plumbers unit began to disband. Before long, too, the natural cycle of concern over the Pentagon Papers ran its course and our thoughts turned to other matters.

It is an interesting sidelight of the Pentagon Papers episode that our efforts to document the role of the Kennedy administration in the Diem assassination and the Bay of Pigs did not prove easy. The CIA protects itself, even from Presidents. Helms refused to give Ehrlichman the agency's internal reports dealing with either subject. At one point he told Ehrlichman on the phone that even he did not have a copy of one of the key Bay of Pigs reports. He also expressed concern about all the people, and specifically Howard Hunt, who he said would like to run around in the agency's "soiled linen."

Helms finally brought me several of the items after I had requested them from him personally. I promised him I would not use them to hurt him, his predecessor, or the CIA. "I have one President at a time," he responded. "I only work for you." When Ehrlichman read the materials Helms had delivered, however, he found that several of the reports, including the one on the Bay of Pigs, were still incomplete.

The CIA was closed like a safe, and we could find no one who would give us the combination to open it.

1971: ECONOMIC CONTROLS

I have always believed that America's economy operates best with the least possible government interference. Yet in August 1971 I proposed a series of economic controls and reforms that left even long-time wage and price control advocates breathless.

The economy that Eisenhower had bequeathed to Kennedy in January 1961 was remarkably stable, with a rate of inflation of about 1.5 percent. By 1968, largely because of the effects of the Vietnam war, inflation had soared to 4.7 percent. But the war was not the only cause of inflation.

Johnson had tried to satisfy everyone; he had encouraged the American people to believe that even in time of war they could have butter as well as guns. The fact was that the expansion of the Great Society was financed by deficit spending.

The major theme of my economic policy in 1969 and 1970 was the rejection of government "jawboning" of business and labor as a way of restraining inflation. It had become clear during the Johnson administration that voluntary "guideposts" for wage and price increases were ineffective. I also strongly opposed mandatory government controls on wages and prices because I felt that controls would constitute interference in the free market and, once begun, would end up building a bureaucracy that would have dictatorial power to regulate business and labor.

By the end of 1969 there were hopeful signs that inflation was abating. But in the early spring of 1970 we ran into difficulty. Unemployment, fueled in part by the reduction in the armed services resulting from our troop withdrawals, rose to 5 percent; the inflation rate had still not declined and a sharp decline in the stock market further intensified apprehension about the economy.

Over my objections Congress sent me sweeping legislation that empowered the President to control prices, wages, and salaries. Since my strong opposition to controls was well known, I viewed the bill as a political ploy on the part of the Democratic Congress aimed at putting the ball publicly in my court. To a certain extent the ploy worked. Although I would not accept a complete move to a mandatory system of wage and price controls, I feared that if I refused to take some action I might exacerbate the general lack of confidence that was itself beginning to harm the economy and hamper its chances of recovery.

Therefore, in June 1970, I made a televised address on the economy that contained the basic steps I was proposing to try to slow the rate of inflation. I announced plans to appoint a National Commission on Productivity, with members to be chosen from business, labor, the general public, and the government. The job of the commission would be to achieve a balance between costs and productivity that would lead to more stable prices. I instructed the Council of Economic Advisers to issue periodic "inflation alerts" that would spotlight the significant areas of wage and price increases and to analyze their impact on price levels. This move was intended to test the idea that publicity about past or prospective price and wage increases would deter business and labor from inflationary behavior. I established an interagency Regulations and Purchasing Review Board to determine whether federal actions were driving up prices and costs and to bring about corrective actions if that were the case.

None of these steps had any significant effect on the economy in 1970. So I tried again. The budget I submitted in January of 1971 was set to be balanced at full employment and run a deficit to help take up the slack when unemployment was high. Along with this new "full employment" budget policy, there would have to be a rate of monetary expansion sufficient to move the economy up on the desired path.

When I briefed the Republican congressional leaders on this budget, which in effect endorsed the concept of deficit spending in periods of high unemployment, Congressman Les Arends of Illinois shook his head sadly and said, "Mr. President, I'll support you as I always do, but I'm going to have to burn up a lot of old speeches denouncing deficit spending."

I answered, "I'm in the same boat."

The economy remained sluggish in the early months of 1971. There were signs of improvement ahead, but patience had worn thin, and we ran out of time. Demands for action poured down on the White House from all sides. Media criticism of our policies became intense. Republicans as well as Democrats reflected the pressure they were receiving from their constituents and vociferously called for new policies to deal more positively with unemployment and inflation. Most of the critics and many of the economists hammered away on one theme: the need to have some program of mandatory government control of prices and wages.

On June 26, 1971, I met with my economic advisers at Camp David. We discussed the problems and our options for dealing with them at great length. After weighing all the factors, I decided to remain on the present course with one exception. For several months I had been concerned about conflicting views on the economy that filtered out of different parts of the administration and helped to create a sense of disarray and confusion in the country. My solution to the problem of too many voices was to designate a single voice: an economic spokesman who would be the authoritative source for my administration's economic policy. I selected John Connally for this role.

As Treasury Secretary, Connally was the senior Cabinet officer with economic responsibility. More important, he was an articulate speaker who could convey his determination to carry out presidential decisions vigorously.

On June 29 Connally briefed the White House press corps on the decisions we had reached at Camp David. He handed down what became known as the "four noes" when he announced that there would be no wage and price review board, no mandatory wage and price controls, no tax cut, and no increase in government spending.

In response to reporters' questioning, Connally forcefully insisted that the economy was expanding and that better days lay ahead. But even Connally's skills could not redeem the troubled economic, psychological, and political situation that had been building up over several years.

In the briefing I held for congressional leaders after my July 15 China announcement, I found that for every one who expressed support of that dramatic foreign initiative, at least twice as many used the opportunity to express concern about our domestic economic policies and to urge new actions to deal with the problems of unemployment and inflation. After this meeting Connally and I concluded that the time had come to act.

"If we don't propose a responsible new program, Congress will have an irresponsible one on your desk within a month," he said. I knew that he was right, and I authorized him to obtain privately the views of our senior economic advisers and then to prepare a report for me that included action options for me to consider.

Connally's report was ready on August 6. By nature he

always favored the "big play," so I had expected that he would recommend something bold. But even I was not prepared for the actions he proposed. He urged, in effect, total war on all economic fronts, including across-the-board wage and price controls. "I am not sure this program will work. But I *am* sure that anything less will not work," he said. He also advised me to let the issue "sit and simmer" for a while, even if it meant letting matters worsen a bit. If that happened then the actions I took would look all the better.

However, an unexpected development forced us to accelerate dramatically our economic timetable. In the second week of August the British ambassador appeared at the Treasury Department to ask that $3 billion be converted into gold. Whether we honored or denied this request, the consequences of our action would be fraught with danger: if we gave the British the gold they wanted, then other countries might rush to get theirs. If we refused, then that would be an admission of our concern that we could not meet every potential demand for conversion into gold. Connally deferred giving his answer, but we knew that we would very soon have to confront a major crisis concerning the international economic position of the United States.

Acting on Connally's recommendations, I called a high-level meeting at Camp David for August 13. Fifteen economic experts, White House staff members, and a speechwriter assembled there, some arriving by secret routes lest news of the meeting itself trigger a wave of international speculation.

These were the men who understood the intricate complexities of economics: John Connally, Arthur Burns, George Shultz, Paul McCracken, and Herbert Stein from my Council on Economic Advisers; Peter Peterson, head of the Council of International Economic Policy; and Paul Volcker, Treasury Undersecretary for Monetary Affairs. From my personal staff there were Haldeman, Ehrlichman, and Bill Safire.

I began by laying down the ground rules that I would insist upon being followed over the next few days until I officially announced my decision: "In the past, leaks have compromised our positions on various issues. Between now and Monday, no one here is to say anything."

I then turned the meeting over to Connally, who succinctly described the actions that the experts had been working on: closing the "gold window" and allowing the dollar to float; imposing a 10 percent import tax that would be mainly a bargaining chip to discourage foreign countries from depressing their currencies in order to promote their exports; reinstating the investment tax credit to stimulate the business community; providing new income tax relief; and repealing the excise tax on automobiles to encourage higher sales.

He left for last the action that would be perceived by the American people as the most dramatic and significant: a ninety-day freeze on wages and prices. No large or permanent bureaucracies would be created; these controls would be monitored for the duration by a Pay Board, a Price Board, and a Cost of Living Council.

Herbert Stein, who subsequently became Chairman of my Council of Economic Advisers, later wrote of those Camp David sessions:

> The tense psychological condition in the country, the remoteness and beauty of the Camp David setting, the orderly and disciplined conduct of the business there, and the surprising and sweeping character of the decisions taken make the August 13-15 meeting one of the most dramatic events in the history of economic policy.

While there was relatively strong, though skeptical, support among those present for the freeze and the other domestic actions, there was substantial disagreement on closing the gold window—in other words suspending the convertibility of the dollar into gold.

The strongest opposition came from Arthur Burns, Chairman of the Federal Reserve Board. He wanted us to wait. Even if all the arguments were right, he said, he still felt that there was no rush. He warned that I would take the blame if the dollar were devalued. "*Pravda* would write that this was a sign of the collapse of capitalism," he said. On the economic side he worried that the negative results would be unpredictable: the stock market could go down; the risk to world trade would be greater if the trade basis changed; and there might be retaliation by other countries.

I always gave great weight to Burns's opinions because of my respect for his superior intellect and because he always followed the practice he once described to me of "telling the President what he *needs* to hear, not just what he *wants* to hear." This was to be one of the few cases in which I did not follow his recommendations. I decided to close the gold window and let the dollar float. As events unfolded, this decision turned out to be the best thing that came out of the whole economic program I announced on August 15, 1971.

I decided to announce these decisions on Sunday night so that the new policy would be known before the stock markets opened on Monday morning.

As I worked with Bill Safire on my speech that weekend I wondered how the headlines would read: would it be *Nixon Acts Boldly?* Or would it be *Nixon Changes Mind?* Having talked until only recently about the evils of wage and price controls, I knew I had opened myself to the charge that I had either betrayed my own principles or concealed my real intentions. Philosophically, however, I was still against wage-price controls, even though I was convinced that the objective reality of the economic situation forced me to impose them.

The public reaction to my television speech was overwhelmingly favorable. On the networks, 90 percent of the Monday newscasts were devoted to it, and most of the focus was on the brilliant briefing that John Connally had given during the day. From Wall Street the news came in numbers: 33 million shares were traded on the New York Stock Exchange on Monday, and the Dow Jones average gained 32.93 points.

Over the next months the New Economic Policy began to take hold. The inflation rate in 1971, before the freeze, was 3.8 percent. It fell to 1.9 percent during the freeze, and then, after a bulge when the freeze ended, it ran around 3.0 percent for the rest of 1972. The unemployment rate, which had been 6.1 percent when the new policy was initiated, fell to 5.1 percent at the end of 1972.

A Harris poll taken six weeks after the announcement showed that, by 53 percent to 23 percent, Americans believed my economic policies were working.

Over the next two and a half years the economy went through three additional phases of wage and price controls before all controls were finally lifted in the spring of 1974.

Phase II, which began in November 1971, was our answer to getting out of the controls before they broke down or became permanent. In this phase the controls, although still mandatory and widespread, were much less comprehensive.

The switch into Phase III in January 1973, as we expected, caused some outcry as repressed prices began moving up. In June 1973, this time over the objection of many of my advisers, I reimposed a temporary, limited freeze to settle public anxiety, which by then was compounded by Watergate, and to dampen a rise in prices taking place simply because a freeze was anticipated. If this freeze only further complicated a bad situation, at least it produced a side benefit that was wryly summarized by George Shultz: "At least we have now convinced everyone else of the rightness of our original position that wage-price controls are not the answer," he said.

When mandatory wage and price controls came to a complete end in 1974, the aftermath was far from pleasant. Energy shortages and high food costs contributed to an increase in inflation and to recession, and the pressures that built up after the period of controls led into the destructive double-digit inflation that plagued the early months of the Ford administration. Three years after controls had completely ended, both unemployment and inflation hovered around 7 percent, and there was even nostalgia for the "good old days" in 1971 when we had only 4 percent inflation and 6 percent unemployment.

What did America reap from its brief fling with economic controls? The August 15, 1971, decision to impose them was politically necessary and immensely popular in the short run. But in the long run I believe that it was wrong. The piper must always be paid, and there was an unquestionably high price for tampering with the orthodox economic mechanisms.

In concentrating on the most urgent economic problem of my administration—the inflation-unemployment problem—I have tended to highlight the area in which we felt it necessary to depart dramatically from the free market and then painfully work our way back to it. But there were also a number of economic steps during my administration that better reflected my economic philosophy and that may be more important in the longer run.

For example, in 1969 we reduced income taxes and relieved more than six million low-income people from the burden of paying any income taxes at all. By 1973 we had freed agriculture of almost all production controls for the first time in thirty-five years. We abolished numerous controls on international capital movements that had been imposed in the 1960s, and we took the lead in establishing a worldwide system of free exchange rates. We pushed legislation through Congress authorizing negotiations for reduction of barriers to international trade, and the first of these negotiations was held in Tokyo in September 1973. We also began moves to reduce or eliminate regulations in the fields of transportation and finance that were burdensome on industry and expensive to consumers.

Some people think of the free market as a matter of concern only to businessmen. But when I came into office, one of the severest and most unfair restraints on the free market was the military draft, which is a way of compelling service from everyone rather than hiring service from those who supply it voluntarily. Thus the elimination of the draft and the introduction of a volunteer Army in January 1973 were also major steps to meaningful economic freedom.

Conservatives are always at a disadvantage when speaking about economics because their belief that some pain may be necessary now to save the patient later is conventionally interpreted by liberal politicians and commentators as "heartlessness" or "callous indifference to human suffering."

It is unfortunate that the *politics* of economics has come to dictate action more than the *economics* of economics. Not surprisingly, when prudence clashes with political reality, the latter sometimes triumphs. Like all oversimplifications, this one sounds too cynical; but I can personally attest to how even someone with strong economic ideas can be affected by the sting of criticism and the clamor of those who want a different policy.

Government enterprise is the most inefficient and costly way of producing jobs. Through the private enterprise system, with all its faults, the United States in its 200 years has waged the most successful war on poverty in the history of civilized man. Private enterprise is an instrument that produces change and encourages progress; government enterprise almost invariably discourages change and inhibits progress.

It is significant to note that our major Communist competitor, the Soviet Union, has found it necessary to turn to *our* way to increase production. At a time when the Communists are by necessity providing increased incentives for more efficient producers, the United States seems to be slowly but surely turning *their* way by discouraging incentives.

America today is at a watershed as far as our economic and political system is concerned. Federal, state, and local taxes now take 40 percent of our net national product. If this percentage continues to rise, we will soon reach a point at which people will be working more for the government than for themselves. If that day ever comes, then we will no longer have the private enterprise system that has made America the freest and most prosperous nation in the world. We can only hope that statesmen of both parties will see the danger of this situation and not allow it to come to pass.

SALT BREAKTHROUGH AND BERLIN SETTLEMENT

There were dire predictions that the announcement that I would be going to China, which I made on July 15, 1971, would seriously damage U.S.-Soviet relations. Exactly the opposite occurred. On October 12 a joint announcement issued in Washington and Moscow confirmed that I would visit the Soviet Union three months after returning from China.

A U.S.-Soviet summit was at last possible because of two achievements: progress in the Strategic Arms Limitation Talks before the China overture was revealed, and progress on a Berlin settlement after the China announcement had been made.

The SALT talks, which had begun at the end of 1969, had quickly bogged down because the two sides differed on the proper scope of an agreement. Stated in its simplest form, the Soviets wanted to conclude an agreement dealing only with the limitation of defensive ABM systems. We, however, wanted to conclude a comprehensive agreement covering not only defensive systems like the ABMs but also offensive weapons like Intercontinental Ballistic Missiles (ICBMs) and Multiple Independently-targetable Re-entry Vehicles (MIRVs).

On January 9, 1971, I sent a personal message to Brezhnev stressing the necessity of linking offensive and defensive weapons if an agreement were to be reached.

Two weeks later Kissinger met with Dobrynin, who had just returned from lengthy consultations with Brezhnev in Moscow. At this meeting Dobrynin suggested late summer for a summit meeting and indicated that a SALT agreement might be worked out along the compromise lines we had suggested: an ABM-only formula coupled with a freeze on offensive weapons while further talks took place.

On March 12, however, Dobrynin delivered a reply to our proposed SALT agreement that seemed to return to earlier hard-line insistence on ABM-only terms. After having made what appeared to be considerable progress in our relations, it looked as if we were in for another period of testing by the Soviets.

Perhaps this sudden about-face was one final test they felt they had to make, or perhaps Brezhnev was just covering his own flanks on the eve of a Party Congress. Whatever the reason, on March 26 Dobrynin received a new set of instructions from Moscow, and they embodied the breakthrough we had been waiting for: the Soviets would agree to continued talks and a freeze on offensive weapons after reaching an ABM agreement.

The SALT talks in Vienna, under the leadership of our chief negotiator, Gerard Smith, and the secret exchanges of messages through Kissinger and Dobrynin immediately became more intense and serious. The major problem, as I saw it, was going to be the American negotiating position. Congressional doves were treating the Soviet ABM-only proposal as a way to chalk up a belated victory over the administration on the ABM issue and urged that I accept immediately.

I felt that it would be disastrous to go into the final SALT negotiations in this position. I believed that the only effective way to achieve nuclear arms limitation was to confront the Soviets with an unacceptable alternative in the form of increased American armaments and the determination to use them.

On April 20 I met for an hour and a half in the Cabinet Room with a group of Senate Republicans. I said, "If SALT is to have a chance, we cannot give away in the Senate things we might want to negotiate with the Soviets. They will say, 'Why should we continue to negotiate SALT when the United States is going to take these actions unilaterally?' The Soviets have strong reasons to have an agreement, but we know for a fact that they will only deal from strength and that they only respect those who have strength; otherwise they have historically moved into the power vacuums."

On May 12 Dobrynin delivered to Kissinger the latest Soviet proposals regarding SALT. They had dropped the last remaining objectionable provision. Now we had our breakthrough. I appeared before the television cameras in the White House briefing room at noon on May 20.

"As you know," I began, "the Soviet-American talks on limiting nuclear arms have been deadlocked for over a year. As a result of negotiations involving the highest level of both governments, I am announcing today a significant development in breaking the deadlock." I read the statement, which was being released at the same moment in Moscow. Its wording was purposely vague: it said only that we had agreed to concentrate on an ABM agreement and that they had agreed on "certain measures" with respect to the limitation of offensive weapons.

The Berlin talks reached a successful conclusion in late August. After sixteen months of negotiation in which we were represented by our Ambassador to West Germany, Kenneth Rush, the United States, in cooperation with the United Kingdom and France, reached an agreement with the Soviets on Berlin that dissipated some of the tension accumulated over twenty-six years of the city's divided existence. The agreement contained provisions that would prevent harassment of travelers and visitors from West Berlin to East Berlin and East Germany, make available to West Berliners passports to the Communist-controlled section, and ensure West Berlin's representation abroad by the Bonn government. Before 1971 it was common to consider Berlin and the Middle East as the greatest stumbling blocks in U.S.-U.S.S.R. relations. By removing at least one of these obstacles we were able to clear the way for a summit meeting.

The announcement of the Soviet Summit for May 1972 came as a complete surprise. The Detroit *Free Press* titled its editorial *Another Rabbit from Hat of the Ever-Amazing Nixon*. The *Wall Street Journal* said that the scheduling of two summits "reflects the most optimistic view of world politics that any President has held for a good many years."

Not all the reactions were positive. George Meany, who had been able to restrain his enthusiasm for the China announcement, now suggested that I might also want to visit Allende in Chile and Castro in Cuba. "If he's going to visit the louses of the world," Meany asked, "why doesn't he visit them all?"

The important thing was that our patient preparation of linkage had paid off handsomely. We would have a Chinese trip and a Soviet Summit as well.

INDO-PAKISTAN WAR

On the morning of November 4 I met in the Oval Office with the Prime Minister of India, Indira Gandhi. Her visit to Washington came at a critical time. Eight months earlier there had been a rebellion in East Pakistan against the government of President Yahya Khan. Indian officials reported that nearly 10 million refugees fled from East Pakistan into India. We knew that Yahya Khan eventually would have to yield to East Pakistan's demands for independence, and we urged him to take a more moderate and conciliatory line. We could not have known the extent to which India would seize this opportunity not just to destroy Pakistan's control of East Pakistan but to weaken West Pakistan as well.

Mrs. Gandhi complimented me highly on the way I was winding down the war in Vietnam and on the boldness of the China initiative. We talked about the uneasy situation in Pakistan, and I stressed how important it was that India not take any actions that would exacerbate it.

She earnestly assured me that India was not motivated in any way by anti-Pakistan attitudes. "India has never wished the destruction of Pakistan or its permanent crippling," she said. "Above all, India seeks the restoration of stability. We want to eliminate chaos at all costs."

I later learned that, even as we spoke, Mrs. Gandhi knew that her generals and advisers were planning to intervene in East Pakistan and were considering contingency plans for attacking West Pakistan as well.

Even though India was officially neutral and continued to receive foreign aid from us, Mrs. Gandhi had gradually become aligned with the Soviets and received substantial economic and military aid from Moscow. President Ayub Khan and his successor, Yahya Khan, had responded by developing Pakistan's relations with the People's Republic of China. With Moscow tied to New Delhi and Peking tied to Islamabad, the potential for the subcontinent's becoming a dangerous area of confrontation between the Communist giants was great.

In our conversation that morning I was disturbed by the fact that although Mrs. Gandhi professed her devotion to peace, she would not make any concrete offers for deescalating the tension. Yahya Khan had agreed to move his troops away from the border if India would do the same, but she would not make a similar commitment.

I said, "Absolutely nothing could be served by the disintegration of Pakistan. For India to initiate hostilities would be almost impossible to understand." I said that in some respects the situation was similar to that in the Middle East: just as American and Soviet interests were involved there, so Chinese, Soviet, and American interests were at stake in South Asia and the Indian subcontinent. "It would be impossible to calculate precisely the steps which other great powers might take if India were to initiate hostilities," I said.

A month later, primed with Soviet weapons, the Indian Army attacked East Pakistan. Fighting also erupted along the border with West Pakistan, but it was impossible to tell whether the Indian objective there was to pin down Pakistani forces or whether the action was the prelude to a full-scale attack. Battle plans of such dimension are not formulated in less than a month, and I could not help thinking that Mrs. Gandhi had purposely deceived me in our meeting. I was also concerned that the Soviets had ignored several clear signals from us that we would react very unfavorably if they supported India in an invasion of Pakistan. I felt that one of the primary Soviet motives was to show the world that, despite the much heralded Sino-American rapprochement, the U.S.S.R. was still the premier Communist power. In fact, the Soviets moved troops to the Chinese border in an unsubtle attempt to tie up Chinese forces and prevent them from going to the aid of Pakistan.

I felt it was important to discourage both Indian aggression and Soviet adventurism, and I agreed with Kissinger's recommendation that we should demonstrate our displeasure with India and our support for Pakistan.

To coordinate our planning, Kissinger convened a meeting of the Washington Special Action Group (WSAG), composed of representatives from State, Defense, CIA, and the NSC. He found that the State Department felt that independence for East Pakistan was inevitable and desirable, and that India had limited aims in East Pakistan and no designs on West Pakistan. The risk of Soviet or Chinese intervention, according to this reasoning, was small. The State Department, therefore, argued that we should keep calm, sit back, and let the inevitable happen.

I completely disagreed with this bland assessment. I wanted to let the Soviets know that we would strongly oppose the dismemberment of Pakistan by a Soviet ally using Soviet arms. Kissinger, therefore, summoned Soviet Chargé Vorontsov to the White House and told him that this crisis had once again brought our relations to a watershed because we considered that promoting a war in the Indian subcontinent was inconsistent with improved relations between us.

Kissinger said that we wanted a cease-fire and the withdrawal of all Indian troops from Pakistan. Once the fighting had stopped, the parties could begin to negotiate a political settlement of the problem. We recognized that political autonomy for East Pakistan would be the probable outcome of a political solution, and we were willing to work in that direction. The main point was that the fighting should stop and the danger of a great power confrontation should be removed.

The next day I wrote a letter to Brezhnev that left no doubts about my feelings:

> The objective fact now is that Indian military forces are being used in an effort to impose political demands and to dismember the sovereign state of Pakistan. It is also a fact that your government has aligned itself with this Indian policy. . . .
> I am convinced that the spirit in which we agreed that the time had come for us to meet in Moscow next May requires from both of us the utmost restraint and the most urgent action to end the conflict and restore territorial integrity in the subcontinent.

At eleven that night, Vorontsov delivered a note replying to the points Kissinger had made the day before. It accused the United States of not having been active enough in maintaining peace, and it proposed an immediate cease-fire coupled with a demand that Pakistan immediately recognize the independence of East Pakistan. The Soviets clearly intended to play a hard line. What we had to do, therefore, was remain absolutely steadfast behind Pakistan. If we failed to help Pakistan, then Iran or any other country within the reach of Soviet influence might begin to question the dependability of American support. As Kissinger put it, "We don't really have any choice. We can't allow a friend of ours and China's to get screwed in a conflict with a friend of Russia's."

On December 9 Vorontsov arrived with a long letter from Brezhnev. In an attempt to put the shoe on the other foot, he said that the crux of the problem lay in finding ways to exert influence on Yahya Khan to give up East Pakistan. Kissinger felt that the cordial tone of the letter at least indicated some responsive movement on the Soviet side, but I expressed my doubts.

In the meantime, the crisis had taken a disturbing turn. Through intelligence sources we learned that at a meeting of the Indian Cabinet Mrs. Gandhi had led a discussion of plans to expand the war on the western front and to invade West Pakistan. Kissinger called in the Indian Ambassador, virtually told him that we knew his government's plans, and demanded that the Ambassador urge New Delhi to reconsider any precipitate action.

The Soviet Minister of Agriculture happened to be visiting Washington at this time. I knew he was a close friend of Brezhnev's, so I asked him to carry back a personal message to Brezhnev from me, conveying my seriousness in saying that it was incumbent upon the two of us as the leaders of the two nuclear superpowers not to allow our larger interests to become embroiled in the actions of our smaller friends.

Later that afternoon I authorized Admiral Moorer to dispatch a task force of eight ships, including the nuclear aircraft carrier *Enterprise*, from Vietnam to the Bay of Bengal.

The military situation in East Pakistan was hopeless. The numerically superior Indians had been joined by fierce Bengali rebels, and Yahya Khan's forces were in total retreat. The almost unbelievable cruelty of the fighting on both sides had turned the situation into a nightmare. Millions of people were left homeless before the fighting ended.

Finally, Yahya Khan recognized that he should follow the course of action we had been recommending: that he could no longer defend East Pakistan and that he should concentrate his forces in the defense of West Pakistan, in which event I indicated he would have my complete support. On December 9 Pakistan accepted the UN General Assembly's call for a cease-fire. India rejected it, however, and tension was still rising along the border in West Pakistan, as I wrote another letter to Brezhnev, calling on him to join me in ending the crisis before we ourselves were dragged into it. I began by stating that, in our view, his proposal for the political independence of East Pakistan had been met by Pakistan's own action. Then I wrote:

> This must now be followed by an immediate cease-fire in the West. If this does not take place, we would have to conclude that there is in progress an act of aggression directed at the whole of Pakistan, a friendly country toward which we have obligations.
>
> I therefore propose an immediate joint appeal for a complete cease-fire.
>
> Meanwhile, I urge you in the strongest terms to restrain India with which, by virtue of your treaty, you have great influence and for whose actions you must share responsibility.

On December 11 we waited all day for a reply from Brezhnev. This delay was intolerable, since the possibility of an Indian attack on West Pakistan increased with each passing hour. On December 12, shortly before I was to fly to the Azores for a Franco-American Summit with President Pompidou on the international monetary crisis, a brief reply arrived from Moscow, stating simply that the government of India had no intention of taking any military action against West Pakistan.

I immediately sent back a message that the Indian assurances lacked any concreteness. In view of the urgency of the situation and the need for concerted action, I proposed that we continue consultations through the secret Kissinger-Dobrynin channel. I added that I could not emphasize too strongly that time was of the essence to avoid consequences that neither of us wanted.

Despite the urgent tone of my message, the hot-line wires were cold until 5 A.M. the next day, when a three-sentence message arrived that the Soviets were conducting a "clarification" of the circumstances in India and would inform us of the results without delay.

In Washington on December 14 Vorontsov handed Haig another message from the Kremlin. Once again it offered only vague assurances that India had no intention of taking any military action against Pakistan. Since this reply offered no improvement over the earlier message I agreed with Kissinger that Haig should call Vorontsov and tell him so.

On the flight from the Azores back to Washington, Kissinger talked to the three pool reporters flying aboard *Air Force One*. One of them asked if there were any danger that the crisis might deteriorate to the point that it would affect my plans to go to the summit. "Not yet," Kissinger replied, "but we will have to wait and see what happens in the next few days." The reporters immediately realized that they had just been given a big story. "Should we infer from that statement that if the Russians don't begin to exercise a restraining influence very soon, the plans for the President's trip might be changed?" one asked.

Kissinger replied, "We are definitely looking to the Soviets to become a restraining influence in the next few days, and if they continue to deliberately encourage military actions, we might have to take a new look at the President's plans."

As soon as the plane landed, the reporters rushed to share their notes with their colleagues and file their stories. The early evening news programs flashed the report around the country and around the world.

Kissinger summoned Vorontsov to the White House and told him that I had been concerned that the Soviet leaders were not doing everything possible to arrive at a settlement. In view of their continued delays, I had begun to believe that they were dealing only in words, with the intention of letting events on the ground dictate the ultimate outcome.

"It is not President Nixon's style to threaten," Kissinger said. "He has long sought a genuine change in U.S.-Soviet relations. Despite his desire, however, your government has proceeded to equip India with great amounts of sophisticated armaments. If the Soviet government were to support or to pressure other foreign leaders to dismember or to divide an ally of the United States, how can they expect progress in our mutual relationships?"

The next day, Kissinger called Vorontsov back and showed him the text of a letter I had written to Kosygin urging that our countries take prompt and responsible steps to ensure that the military conflict not spread and that assurances be given against territorial acquisition by either side.

Vorontsov complained that the Indians were proving very resistant to Soviet pressure. Kissinger replied, "There is no longer any excuse. The President has made any number of personal appeals, all of which have been rejected, and it is now time to move."

Vorontsov said that the Soviets were prepared unconditionally to guarantee that there would be no Indian attack on West Pakistan or on Kashmir. But to do this publicly would mean that they were, in effect, speaking for a friendly country. In other words, the Soviets would urge the Indians to accept a cease-fire as long as they did not have to do so publicly. Without the prospect of Soviet support and aid, the Indians were almost certain to agree to a settlement.

The next day Yahya Khan's forces in East Pakistan surrendered unconditionally. On December 17 the explosive situation on the western front was also resolved when Pakistan accepted the Indian offer of a cease-fire there. By using diplomatic signals and behind-the-scenes pressures we had been able to save West Pakistan from the imminent threat of Indian aggression and domination. We had also once again avoided a major confrontation with the Soviet Union.

The Indo-Pakistan war involved stakes much higher than the future of Pakistan—and that was high enough. It involved the principle of whether big nations supported by the Soviet Union would be permitted to dismember their smaller neighbors. Once that principle was allowed, the world would have become more unstable and unsafe.

The Chinese played a very cautious role in this period. They had troops poised on the Indian border, but they would not take the risk of coming to the aid of Pakistan by attacking India, because they understandably feared that the Soviets might use this action as an excuse for attacking China. They consequently did nothing, but the presence of their forces probably had a deterrent effect on India.

Three days after the cease-fire was arranged, we sent the Chinese a brief description of its major points. We concluded, "It is the U.S. view that recent events in South

Asia involve sobering conclusions. The governments of the People's Republic of China and the United States should not again find themselves in a position where hostile global aims can be furthered through the use of proxy countries."

As a result of the Indo-Pakistan crisis, my respect and regard for Mrs. Gandhi diminished. A few months later, in March 1972, after having seen a film biography of Mahatma Gandhi—who was no relation to her—during a weekend at Key Biscayne, I dictated a brief reflection in the diary I had begun keeping in November 1971.

Diary
As I saw Gandhi's assassination and heard his words on violence, I realized how hypocritical the present Indian leaders are, with Indira Gandhi talking about India's victory wings being clipped when Shastri went to Tashkent, and her duplicitous attitude toward us when she actually had made up her mind to attack Pakistan at the time she saw me in Washington and assured me she would not. Those who resort to force, without making excuses, are bad enough—but those who resort to force while preaching to others about their use of force deserve no sympathy whatever.

––––––––––––

One of the most serious incidents of the Indo-Pakistan crisis occurred on our domestic front. On December 14, while we were still uncertain whether India would attack West Pakistan, syndicated columnist Jack Anderson published verbatim excerpts of the minutes of the WSAG meetings of December 2, 4, and 6. The minutes revealed Kissinger's statements to the group relaying my strong pressure to "tilt" toward Pakistan, which differed from the posture that had been adopted by some State Department sources as well as from the more neutral public position we embraced in order to exercise greater leverage on all parties. From a diplomatic point of view, the leak was embarrassing; from the point of view of national security, it was intolerable.

The leak came as a shock because WSAG meetings had been attended by only the highest-ranking members of the military intelligence organizations and the State Department. We learned that Rear Admiral Robert O. Welander believed that one of the leaked documents had to have come from his office, which handled liaison between the Joint Chiefs of Staff and the National Security Council. Bud Krogh and David Young were assigned to investigate.

Suspicion centered on a young Navy yeoman assigned to Welander's office. In the course of questioning, Young learned that for some time the yeoman had been making copies of secret NSC documents. He had regularly rifled burn bags for carbons or Xerox copies, and in some cases he actually took documents for copying out of Kissinger's and Haig's briefcases. On one occasion he copied a memo of Kissinger's conversation with Chou En-lai during the first secret mission to Peking. He passed these documents to his superiors in the Pentagon.

We were not able to establish beyond doubt that the yeoman was Anderson's source. However, circumstantial evidence was strong. They were personally acquainted and had met on several occasions. Whether or not he had disclosed classified information to Anderson, the fact remained that he had jeopardized the relationship of the JCS to the White House.

I was disturbed—although not perhaps really surprised—that the JCS was spying on the White House. But I was, frankly, very reluctant to pursue this aspect of the case because I knew that if it were explored, like so many other sensitive matters it would wind up being leaked to the media where it would be completely distorted, and we would end up doing damage to the military at a time when it was already under heavy attack.

The yeoman himself presented a similar problem. I felt the circumstantial evidence that he had provided information to Anderson was convincing, and I knew that such actions could not be tolerated.

Diary

What concerns me about this story is the Ellsberg complex that drove the yeoman to put out the information. His spying on the White House for the Joint Chiefs is something that I would not particularly be surprised at, although I don't think it's a healthy

659

practice. But his proceeding to put out top secret information to a newspaper columnist, because he disagreed with the policy on India, is the kind of practice that must, at all costs, be stopped.

I felt, however, that it would be too dangerous to prosecute the yeoman. He had traveled with Kissinger and others on a number of secret missions and had had access to other top-secret information, which, if disclosed, could have jeopardized our negotiations with China and with North Vietnam. In this respect he was a potential time bomb that might be triggered by prosecution. We had him transferred to a remote post in Oregon and kept him under surveillance, including wiretaps for a time, to make sure that he was not dispensing any more secret information. It worked: there were no further leaks from him.

SIX GREAT GOALS

Although Vietnam and other foreign problems dominated most of 1971, this was the year in which I challenged Congress to pass domestic legislation that would result in what I called a "New American Revolution." Undeterred by Congress's lack of interest in diffusing power and returning it to the people, I once again urged action on proposals—some of which I had first sent up in 1969—that would begin changing the whole size and shape of the federal government. In my State of the Union address on January 22, 1971, I used blunt language to describe the need for the programs I was proposing. "Let's face it," I said. "Most Americans today are simply fed up with government at all levels."

In a speech that I consider the most comprehensive and constructive statement on my domestic policy that I made as President, I listed six great goals for the American nation and the American people: welfare reform; full prosperity in peacetime; restoring and enhancing the natural environment; improving health care and making it available more fairly to more people; strengthening and renewing state and local government; and a complete reform of the federal government.

The response from Congress continued to be disappointing and frustrating. Welfare reform, government reorganization, the comprehensive health care programs, and dozens of other programs and pieces of legislation continued to be casualties of congressional inaction.

PAT

Most people would probably say that it takes stamina, strength, or determination to succeed in political life. Pat once said that what political life most requires is "heart"—and she is right. That is true of politics at its best and public life at its finest.

"Heart" is a combination of personal communication and human understanding that is based on a liking for people because you respect them rather than because you need their votes or their support. It is a quality that Pat possesses in abundance. It was her gift to the White House and to the country from the moment she became First Lady.

She stepped into the demanding new role without breaking stride. She set up staff offices in the East Wing and took a personal interest in every aspect of the operation of the White House. She was as concerned about having fresh flowers in the public rooms for the daily tours as she was in being completely briefed on every state visitor.

Each of us loved the White House and looked for ways to share its history and beauty with others, but it was Pat who made it happen.

She had loudspeakers set up near the fence on the South Grounds so that while they were waiting people standing in line for the tour could hear about the history of the rooms they were about to see. She arranged special tours for the blind that allowed them for the first time to touch the historic objects in the different rooms. Pat also recorded an introduction for the first "talking history" of the White House so that those who could not see it would nevertheless have a sense of sharing and belonging when they were there.

The girls reflected their mother's sense of caring and generosity. Tricia, who lived with us until her marriage, tutored young children from one of the city's elementary schools, and she thought of imaginative ways to bring young people into the White House—meeting with 1,000 Boy Scouts on the South Lawn, having a Halloween party for 350 children from less privileged areas of Washington. In the spring of 1970 she was the hostess for 2,000 children who blanketed the lawn for a concert by the D.C. Youth Orchestra. All this was in addition to her regular schedule of receptions, teas, and speaking engagements.

During our first summer in the White House, Julie volunteered as a guide at the Visitors Office, taking delighted tourists on special trips through the gardens and up to the historical rooms on the second floor. In the afternoons, she gave special tours for the handicapped. Even when she was studying for a master's degree and later while an editor for the *Saturday Evening Post*, she maintained a heavy schedule of speeches and visits throughout the country.

Pat arranged for private contributions so that the outside of the White House could be illuminated at night for the city's residents as well as for tourists. Inside, she transformed the House with her unerring sense of color and design, and her extraordinary energy. Working with White House Curator Clement Conger, and Edward V. Jones of Albany, Georgia, an authority on Federal period art, architecture, and furniture, she raised the money to bring more than 500 carefully selected pieces of early American furniture and art to the public rooms of the White House. With Carlisle Humelsine, the head of the Colonial Williamsburg Foundation, she was instrumental in the refurbishment of the West Wing of the White House.

The girls and I took great pride in the fact that after Pat was finished with her work, the many artists, historians, architects, and decorators who came to visit said that the White House had never looked more beautiful.

I can take credit for only one innovation in our White House redecorating program. One night as we were arriving home from some social function, I noticed that the flags were flying over many of the federal buildings but not over the White House. My military assistant, Don Hughes, informed me that the flag could be flown at night only if it were lighted. I asked him to have a floodlight installed on the roof and, from that time on, the flag flew over the White House day and night.

There is a deep common bond among all those who have shared in life at the White House. Pat and I particularly wanted to make the families of all former Presidents and Vice Presidents, regardless of their party or their politics, feel welcome.

Pat suggested that we compile a register of all living direct descendants of former Presidents, and over the years we invited many of them to White House functions. In this way we met Calvin Coolidge's son, some of Grover Cleveland's grandchildren, Roosevelts from Oyster Bay and Hyde Park, and dozens of Adamses.

We made sure that approval was given for the Johnson family to have additional Secret Service protection when they traveled abroad. I periodically called Johnson and Humphrey to ask their advice, and sometimes just to chat and let them know I understood the burdens they had borne.

Pat's idea of having a visitor to the White House was to visit with them. She has always disliked making formal speeches, and instead of dropping by a reception just long enough to say a few words for the benefit of the reporters and television cameras, she preferred spending her time mixing personally with the guests and talking to them. One afternoon it would be 450 dieticians, then 670 wives of financial leaders from foreign countries, or the 1,200 members of the White House Conference on Food, Nutrition, and Health, or the 350 American Farm Bureau Women.

It frustrated me that her backbreaking schedule received so little attention from the press. But all that mattered to her was that she had made people feel welcome.

Each morning Pat would go over some of the more than 1,000 letters she received every week and sign replies to them. She believed that if people took the time to write to her that they deserved a personal reply. In the afternoon, after her regular schedule of receptions and teas, she might take retarded children for a cruise on the *Sequoia,* or plan a special event such as the Thanksgiving dinner to which she invited hundreds of older citizens—not VIPs, but people who might never have a chance to see the White House otherwise. Then, in the evenings, she would often have some function at the White House or be scheduled to make an appearance somewhere in the city.

She left us all breathless. By our second year in the White House we had set a record of 50,000 guests.

There is a modern notion that every First Lady has to have a "project," one thing with which to be identified. Pat was dedicated to promoting the concept of volunteerism, the idea of people helping each other and not waiting for the government to do things they can do for themselves. But she bridled at the idea that volunteerism was her "project," or that her interests had to be compartmentalized. She once said, "People are my real project," and she proved it time and time again.

She traveled around the country talking with people in every kind of program—programs for young people, for old people, for the handicapped, programs to help children get a head start on reading, programs for city and community beautification. She made over 150 trips out into the country, some with me and many on her own. And not once did she lose sight of the fact that she was not meeting groups, but individuals, not constituencies, but people. I remember being told once about an afternoon when she had been on a tour of a medical facility and stopped to embrace a little girl blinded by rubella. For a few minutes, while the tour waited, she talked to the child and held her close. When someone came over and told her that the child was deaf as well as blind, Pat answered she had known that. "But she knows what love is," Pat said. "She can feel love."

Life in the White House is active and intense. For one thing, it is a city home and there is always the sense and sound of traffic outside. Sometimes there would be the sound of demonstrations. Inside, it often seemed as if there were never any real privacy as the household staff went about their work, and in the basement the kitchens were constantly bustling with preparations for the steady stream of breakfasts, luncheons, teas, receptions, and official dinners.

We tried at the beginning to cut back on some of the trappings. Pat and I agreed that we should reduce the number of stewards and aides who surround a President wherever he goes. I told Haldeman to have the two Navy medics who had served full time as the President's masseurs reassigned to some more productive duty. I immediately stopped what was to me the almost incredible practice of having the President's bed from the White House flown ahead whenever he traveled outside Washington so that he would never have to sleep in a strange bed. I said that I would need only Manolo and possibly one steward to take care of my clothes and meals when I went on weekend working trips to Camp David or Key Biscayne. We ordered the decommissioning of the two large Navy yachts that had been maintained exclusively for the President's use. We also tried to cut down on the numbers and security requirements of the Secret Service who were always with us.

But even so, life in the White House was confining, and this made the home we bought in summer 1969 for our retirement in San Clemente even more special for us. It is an old Spanish house situated on a beautiful high point directly above the beach. The constant sound of the waves gives it serenity, and the palm and eucalyptus trees surrounding it provide natural protection that made it possible for us to take at least semi-private walks. We named the house La Casa Pacifica—the Peaceful House. A small complex of offices was built on the Coast Guard station next door, and these became the Western White House.

Because of the distance we were able to visit San Clemente only a few times a year. More often we would go for a weekend to Key Biscayne or to Camp David. In some respects, Pat ran three households—in Washington, California, and Florida—and she made each of them a home for us even if we were there for only a few days.

Over the years of our life in politics, Pat's strength of character continued to grow, and her gentle sensitivity to people became even more acute. She was often criticized by feminist radicals of the women's liberation movement, but she held to her guiding principle: the right of a woman to choose her role in life. And by her actions she proved that it was possible to be both an independent woman and a supportive wife. She was not at all dismayed when she was sometimes accused of being inhibited. In personal encounters she is lively, informal, and witty, but she felt that it was important for a First Lady to be dignified. She recognized that the role is in many ways a representative one. She was traditional, but in a warm way that transcended time and place. And, most important, she was comfortable with herself, sure of herself in a world of rapidly changing values.

During the vice presidential years, Pat and I had traveled together to fifty-three countries. Eisenhower used to think of us as a team—and so did I. While I spent the days in meetings, she went to meet the local people in schools, hospitals, factories, orphanages. I remember the awe and respect on the faces of our hosts in Panama when she insisted on visiting and shaking hands with the tragic inhabitants of a leper colony there.

At night, she would come back to our rooms in time to change into a gown for glittering state dinners.

Pat became for thousands of people abroad the personification of American good will: it was there in her voice, her smile, her eyes. That spoke to the people in the countries we visited in a way that speeches, toasts, and communiqués never could.

Pat was the first First Lady to serve as the President's official diplomatic representative abroad. In this capacity she went to Peru to take supplies gathered by volunteer workers in America to the victims of a devastating earthquake. Braving danger and enduring fatigue, she climbed amid the rubble to embrace homeless children and bring a message of American love and concern. In gratitude for this trip, the President of Peru invested her with the Grand Cross of the Order of the Sun, the oldest decoration in the Americas. She was the first North American woman ever to receive this signal honor.

During our trips to China and the summits in the Soviet Union, Pat showed her mastery of the art of personal diplomacy. She shook hands with dancing bears at the circus, drew children to her in schools and hospitals, visited communes, factories, department stores, and danced a step with the Bolshoi Ballet school.

In 1974, she led the U.S. delegation to the inaugural ceremonies for the President of Venezuela and the President of Brazil. In 1972 she represented me in Africa at the inauguration of the President of Liberia and then traveled on for meetings with the heads of state in Ghana and the Ivory Coast. She returned home from Africa on January 9.

Diary

Pat was obviously elated by her trip. She was particularly impressed by the President of the Ivory Coast. She pointed out that he did not believe in using force against South Africa, and I realized that this is the reason that many in the State Department don't like him because he does not take the usual line which is totally anti-South Africa without regard to the consequences, even if it means a war which no one would win.

I have concluded, after having grave doubts about the independence movements in Africa, that perhaps it is best to allow these countries to start with their first faltering steps and learn to walk alone. They are going to mess a lot of things up but it allows them to have dignity and develop capability which comes only from having responsibility. They would never acquire it in a colonial status or in a dependent status.

The amazing thing is that Pat came back looking just as fresh as a daisy despite an enormously difficult, taxing schedule. She had press conferences in each country, had had conversations with the Presidents, and then carried it all off with unbelievable skill.

As Julie put it, what came through was love of the people of the countries she visited for her, and, on her part, love for them.

Sometimes our family was called square and as far as we were concerned, that was just fine. In the environment of Washington, "square" often means rooted in principles that ignore chic, transitory fashions.

On our first Sunday in the White House we held the first White House worship service in the East Room. It was our idea to have these short inspirational services, each conducted by a distinguished preacher of a different faith and with choirs from different parts of the country. Each time we would invite between two and three hundred people—from congressional leaders to White House policemen and telephone operators. The worship services meant Pat and I could avoid the exploitation of religion that too often took place when we attended regular church services outside and were accompanied by television crews and pursued by large numbers of tourists and curiosity-seekers who had no interest whatever in the service. This bothered me personally, and I thought that it must be an irritating nuisance and distraction to the others who had come to worship.

There was a flurry of criticism about the worship services. Traditionalists said that they were too watered down to be meaningful; nonbelievers said religion had no place in the White House; and editorialists complained that we were breaking down the separation between church and state. But Pat and I consider the worship services to have been among the high points of our years in the White House. They gave many thousands of people an opportunity to join us. More important, they set a national example of reverence.

Our whole family has always loved theatre, movies, and music. Our favorite relaxation after dinner at Camp David or in Florida or California was to watch a movie. Sometimes we would experiment with films we had never heard of; sometimes we would choose current hits; and sometimes old family favorites.

Pat and I looked forward to the evenings of entertainment at the White House as much as any of our guests. We felt that performers invited to entertain after state dinners should reflect the whole spectrum of American tastes—and, incidentally, our own eclectic preferences. Among the hundreds of memorable evenings, I particularly remember Golda Meir rushing impulsively to embrace Isaac Stern and Leonard Bernstein when they performed after a state dinner in her honor. Beverly Sills, Roberta Peters, Merle Haggard, and the Carpenters covered the range from classical to country and rock. Pearl Bailey was her warmly humorous and inimitable self; and Frank Sinatra, in his first appearance at the White House, had tears in his eyes when he thanked me afterward. Tony Bennett, Johnny Cash, Glen Campbell, Art Linkletter, and Bob Hope were among the others who came to perform.

In addition to the after-dinner entertainment, Pat initiated a series of special Evenings at the White House to which guests were invited to enjoy the artistry of a great performer, whether it was Nicol Williamson reading from *Hamlet*, Red Skelton cracking jokes, or Sammy Davis, Jr., singing and dancing. Sammy and his wife spent the night with us after his performance and—in fulfillment of a lifelong dream—he slept in the Lincoln Bedroom.

More than once, in performances that would have dismayed my Aunt Jane, I sat down at the piano for some rollicking sing-alongs of old favorites like "When Irish Eyes Are Smiling" and "God Bless America."

In addition to honoring the performing arts, Pat also took a special interest in handicrafts and the fine arts. She welcomed many craft groups to the White House and their work was often displayed in the East Wing corridor. Pat was also the first First Lady ever to arrange a one-man art exhibition at the White House, inviting Andrew Wyeth to show some of his paintings in the East Room.

Except for the POW dinner in 1973, which was a unique historical event, I think that the most memorable of all our White House social occasions was Duke Ellington's seventieth birthday on April 29, 1969, when I presented him with the country's highest civilian honor, the Medal of Freedom. We invited more than 200 guests, including Cab Calloway, Earl Hines, Billy Eckstine, Mahalia Jackson, Harold Arlen, and Richard Rodgers. In making the presentation, I said, "In the royalty of American music, no man swings more or stands higher than the Duke."

I braved the piano accompaniment to "Happy Birthday" and when the formal program was over, and some of the greatest jazz musicians had performed some of his greatest songs, I said, "I think we all ought to hear from one more pianist." I went over to Duke's chair and led him to the piano.

The room was hushed as he sat quietly for a moment. Then he said he would improvise a melody. "I shall pick a name—gentle, graceful—something like Patricia," he said.

And when he started to play it was lyrical, delicate, and beautiful—like Pat.

Index

Abadi (Djakarta), 165

ABC, 304, 305, 408, 412–13

Abernathy, Ralph, 539–540

ABM (Anti-ballistic missile system), 513–517, 648–49

Abrams, Creighton, 470, 557, 578

Acheson, Dean, 136, 138, 496, 504

Achilles, Ted, 230

Adams, Duque and Hazeltine, 285

Adams, Earl, 285

Adams, John, 173

Adams, Sherman, 105–106, 111, 118, 175, 203, 214, 215, 226, 238–45, 530

Adelson, Bill, 24–25

Adenauer, Konrad, 346–47

Adlai Stevenson of Illinois (Martin), 123

AFL-CIO, 46

Africa, 144
    RN's 1967 trip to, 345, 349–50

Agnew, Judy (Mrs. Spiro T.), 421

Agnew, Spiro T. "Ted," 342, 370–71, 384–90, 396, 400, 412, 421, 452, 473, 475, 497, 508–509, 528, 534, 554, 608–609, 614

Aiken, George, 117, 559

Alcorn, Meade, 241, 242–243, 244

Allende, Salvador, 606–607

Alliance for Progress, 349

Allyson, June, 95

Alsop, Stewart, 515

America-Japan Society, 158–59

American Exhibition, Moscow, 256–58

American Society of Newspaper Editors, 187, 248, 373

Americans for Democratic Action (ADA), 197

Anderson, Jack, 239, 658–59

Andrews, Bert, 70, 83, 85–86, 116, 130

Antiwar demonstrations and movements, 434, 441, 480, 492–99, 510–11, 554, 577, 580, 609–12, 616, 635, 637–38

Apollo program, 447, 487–88, 530–32
Arabs. *See specific countries:* Egypt; Iraq; Jordan; Lebanon; Syria
Arends, Les, 640
Argentina, 607
   RN's 1958 trip to, 228
Arlen, Harold, 669
Armstrong, Neil, 531
Army, U.S., and McCarthy hearings, 172–76, 180
ARVN [South Vietnamese Army], 556, 557, 562, 579, 580, 617–18
Associated Press (AP), 369, 499, 567, 583
Atlanta *Constitution,* 271
Attlee, Clement, 59
Australia, 186, 189, 338
   RN's 1953 trip to, 147
Austria
   RN's 1956 trip to, 224–25

Bailey, Pearl, 539
Baldwin, Lilly, 28
Ball, George, 403, 405
Bao Dai, 149–50
Barnum, Everett, 3–4
Bassett, Jim, 118, 269
Batista, Fulgencio, 248–50
Bay of Pigs, 287–88, 316, 636–38
Bayh, Birch, 520–21
Beam, Jacob, 592
Beeson, Alden, 10
Beeson, Harold, 10
Beeson, Jane (Mrs. Harold), 10
Beeson, Sheldon, 10
Bennett, D. V., 586
Bennett, Tony, 668
Bentley, Elizabeth, 63, 64
Berlin, 289–90, 427, 502, 551, 650
   RN's 1963 trip to, 307
   RN's 1969 trip to, 460
Bernstein, Leonard, 668
Bevan, Aneurin, 195
Bevin, Ernest, 59
Bewley, Kathryn (Mrs. Thomas W.), 34
Bewley, Thomas W., 34
"Big Five" coalition, 46

Birch Society. *See* John Birch Society
Black, Hugo, 523
Black Panthers, 564, 581–89
Blackmun, Harry A., 523
Blacks, 538–51
   student demands, 492
Bliss, Ray, 336
Block, Herbert, 200
Blount, Winton "Red," 420
Bo, Mai Van, 433, 489–90
Bobst, Elmer, 306
Boddy, Manchester, 90–91
Bohemian Grove, 98–99, 350–52
Bohlen, Charles E. "Chip," 171, 289, 502
Bolivia, 607
   RN's 1958 trip to, 229
Bonn
   RN's 1969 trip to, 460
Borman, Frank, 448, 531
Boston *Globe,* 499, 632
Braden, Tom, 299
Bradlee, Benjamin, 277
Brandon, Henry, 510
Brandt, Willy, 344
Brazil, 607
   RN's 1956 trip to, 228–29
Brezhnev, Leonid, 258, 427, 458, 648, 653, 655
Bricker, John, 109
Bridges, Styles, 110, 182, 320, 467
Briggs, Ellis, 154
Britain, 144, 149, 160, 166, 186–87, 188, 189, 220–21
   RN's 1947 trip to, 59, 60
   RN's 1958 trip to, 247–48
   RN's 1963 trip to, 309
   RN's 1969 trip to, 457–60, 487
Broder, David, 495–96
Brooke, Ed, 419
Brookings Institution, 634–35
Brosio, Manlio, 347
Brown, Pat, 291, 293–302, 458
Brown v. Board of Education, 543, 550
Brownell, Herbert, 103, 106, 196, 201–202, 217, 388, 518
Brussels
   RN's 1969 trip to, 458, 460
Buchanan, Frank, 51–52
Buchanan, Pat, 335, 338–41, 369;

383, 508, 607–608
Bundy, William, 171
Bunker, Ellsworth, 470, 557
Burger, Vera (Mrs. Warren), 125
Burger, Warren, 125, 519, 551,
560, 632–33
Burma
RN's 1953 trip to, 160, 167
Burns, Arthur, 423–24, 528, 642
Bush, George, 386
Byrnes, James, 77

Cabinet Committee on Education,
545
Caldwell, Trimble, and Mitchell,
345
Califano, Joseph, 403
Calley, William, Jr., 618–20
Calloway, Cab, 669
Cambodia, 318, 430, 451–56, 470–
75, 479, 512, 577, 578–79, 617
RN's 1953 trip to, 149, 150, 153
Campaigns. See Elections and
campaigns
Campbell, Glen, 668
Campus protests, 492–93, 495,
554, 564–67
Captive Nations resolution, 253,
254, 255
Carlson, Frank, 99
Carnegie Endowment for
International Peace, 64, 68,
69, 74, 79
Carswell, G. Harrold, 513, 522–23
Carter, Jimmy, 620
Case, Cliff, 284
Cash, Johnny, 668
Castro, Fidel, 248–50, 287–88,
426, 602
Cavers, David, 31
CBS, 408, 414, 499, 509, 633
Ceaușescu, Nicolae, 347–48,
488–89
Chafee, John, 388
Chamberlain, Neville, 572
Chambers, Esther (Mrs.
Whittaker), 68, 72, 80–81
Chambers, Whittaker, 63–84, 125,
136, 293, 295, 426
Chamoun, Camille, 240
Chandler, Kent, 122

Chapin, Dwight, 345, 383, 412–13
Chiang Kai-shek, Generalissimo,
154, 185, 271, 318, 348–49
Chiang Kai-shek, Madame, 154
Chicago Daily News, 105
Chicago Tribune, 123, 278
Chile, 606–07
China, Communist, 136, 488
expansion of, 146, 167, 184, 332,
352
and Indo-Pakistan war, 651–58
and Nationalist China, 154, 185,
318, 349
RN's 1972 trip to, 647–50
and Soviet Union, 144, 347, 460,
461, 502, 511
and United States, 422, 425,
430, 457, 461, 462, 502, 617
and Vietnam, 185, 319, 334,
336–37, 349, 352, 426, 427,
457, 579
See also Communists, Chinese;
Mao Tse-tung
Chotiner, Murray, 47, 106, 109,
113–31, 201, 304, 411, 412
Christian, George, 509–10
Church, Frank, 588
Churchill, Winston, 54, 64, 186,
191–95, 247–48, 327, 333,
572
CIA (Central Intelligence
Agency), 171, 229, 232, 248,
250, 272, 287, 346, 478, 553,
584–87, 606, 607, 629, 630,
636, 638
Civil rights, 331, 372, 391, 538–51
Civil Rights Act of 1964, 377, 538
Clark, Ramsey, 585
Clay, Lucius, 103
Cleaver, Eldridge, 581
Clifford, Clark, 403, 405, 416, 417
Coffin, J. Herschel, 18–19, 20
Cole, Al, 329, 336
Colmer, William, 435
Colombia
RN's 1958 trip to, 232
Colson, Chuck, 615
Committee of 100, 41, 49
Communism, 136, 263, 318, 347,
425, 426, 463
in Asia and Far East, 184,
186–87, 316, 318

Castro's attitude toward, 249
Churchill on, 194–95
in Cuba, 289
Dulles on, 253
in Europe, 53–54, 61–63, 85
in India and Pakistan, 162–63
in Indochina, 150–53
and McCarthy hearings, 168–84
RN on, 54–57, 167, 247
in South America, 229
in Soviet Union, 53–54
Truman and, 196–97
in United States, 46, 50, 54–57,
  67, 101, 108, 168–84
Communist Party
in Europe, 61, 63
in France, 346
in Italy, 346
RN on, 197
in Romania, 347–48
in South America, 229, 236
in Soviet Union, 251
in United States, 56, 57, 63–70,
  78, 79, 169
Communists, 101, 107, 165, 167,
  290
in Asia, 107
Chiang Kai-shek on, 318
in Communist China, 136, 154,
  185, 272, 348–49, 381, 427,
  511–12, 551
Churchill on, 194–95
in Cuba, 248–50, 316
in Europe, 54–56, 59–63, 107,
  136, 226, 260, 263, 291, 307,
  347, 425, 426, 555
and Hiss case, 63–81
in Indochina, 148–54, 160, 161,
  167, 184–91, 287, 291, 316,
  317, 332–33, 338, 340,
  347–49, 368, 381, 402, 404,
  430–32, 462–63, 469–506,
  552–62, 578–79, 580, 617, 618
in Indonesia, 148–49, 167
in Korea, 136, 148, 156, 158,
  185–86, 474–475, 476
and McCarthy hearings, 168–84
RN on, 160, 167
in South America, 606–607
in Soviet Union, 54, 263, 427,
  428, 511, 551, 647
in United States, 45–50, 54–56,
  93, 586
  See also China, Communist;
  Soviet Union
Conant, James Bryant, 171
Confessions of a Congressman
  (Voorhis), 49
Conger, Clement, 662
Congress, and Vietnam war
  appropriations, 190, 488, 504,
  507–508, 512, 616
Congress '66 committee, 336
Connally, John, 411
Constitution, U.S.
  Twenty-fifth Amendment, 228
Conversations with Kennedy
  (Bradlee), 277
Cooper-Church amendment, 579
COSVN (Central Office of South
  Vietnam), 556, 557
Council of Economic Advisers,
  640, 642–43
Council of International Economic
  Policy, 642–43
Cox, Dorothy, 91
Cox, Edward, 383
  wedding of, to Tricia Nixon,
  624–29
Crawford, Kenneth, 434
Cronin, Father John, 216
"Crosley, George," 72–79
CRP (Committee to Re-elect the
  President), 615
Cuba, 248–50, 272–73, 287–92,
  304, 316, 426, 533, 583,
  601–607, 616
Cutler, Robert, 189
Cyprus, 494
Czechoslovakia, 54, 226, 333, 449,
  488–89, 555

Daily People's World, 46
Daily Worker, 92
Daley, Richard, 275–76, 277,
  392–93, 410, 412
Davis, Sammy, Jr., 668–69
Day, Roy, 42, 43
Dayan, Moshe, 595
Dean, Arthur, 154
de Gaulle, Charles, 307, 346–47,
  457, 460–63, 476–77
de Gaulle, Madame, 461, 476

Dejean, Maurice, 152
Democratic National Committee
    (DNC), 114. 121–22, 134,
    198
Democratic National Conventions
    1956, 219
    1960, 266
    1968, 392
Democratic Party. See Elections
    and campaigns
Dent, Harry, 547
de Toledano, Ralph, 100
Detroit Free Press, 650
Dewey, Thomas, 68, 87, 96, 98,
    102–103, 111, 116–17, 119,
    125–26, 205, 245, 247, 294,
    359, 519
Diem, Ngo Dinh, 149, 316
Dien Bien Phu, fall of, 184–190
Dies, Martin, 53
Dirksen, Everett, 171, 173, 174,
    276, 400, 403–404, 541
Di Vittorio, Giuseppe, 59-60
Doar, John, 585
Dobrynin, Anatoly, 456, 457,
    483–84, 494, 501–502, 533,
    603–604, 648, 649, 655
Dong, Pham Van, 491, 492,
    496–97
Donovan, Leisure, Newton and
    Lombard, 26
Dorn, Evlyn, 34
Douglas, Helen Gahagan, 88–95
Douglas, Melvyn, 91
Douglas, Paul, 446
Downey, Sheridan, 87–88, 90, 92,
    95
Driscoll, Alfred, 109
Drown, Helene, 307
Drown, Jack, 307
Drown, Maureen, 307
Dulles, Allen, 69, 171, 248, 249,
    287
Dulles, John Foster, 64, 68, 69,
    77, 80, 86, 136–37, 158, 163,
    185–91, 193, 206, 214–15,
    220, 223–24, 228, 247, 250,
    252–53, 298, 421, 533, 555

Eban, Abba, 595
EC-121 incident, 472–76, 517
Eckstine, Billy, 669

Economist, The, 561
Ecuador,
    RN's 1958 trip to, 232
Eden, Anthony, 191–95
Edson, Peter, 112, 113–14
Education of a Public Man, The
    (Humphrey), 279
Edwards, Willard, 278
Efron, Edith, 408
Egypt, 220, 425, 591–600
    RN's 1963 trip to, 307–308
Ehrlichman, John, 498, 528, 536,
    568, 569, 577, 586, 634, 636,
    638, 643
Eisenhower, David, 353, 362–63,
    377, 381, 383, 409–13, 464,
    554, 558, 563
    wedding of, to Julie Nixon,
    444–49
Eisenhower, Dwight D., 144–45,
    174–76, 190–92, 223–24, 240,
    241, 243–44, 250, 253, 287,
    308, 341, 357, 358, 421, 428,
    446–47, 478, 515, 530, 533,
    621
    and Sherman Adams, 238–45
    death of, 464
    in elections and campaigns
        1952, 88–112, 114–35, 137,
        138, 424
        1954, 195–200
        1956, 204–23
        1958, 245–46
        1960, 264, 266–80
        1962, 293–95, 298
        1964, 321–24
        1966, 341, 379–80
        1968, 353, 381, 395
    heart attack, 201–204
    ileitis operation, 212–13
    and Lyndon B. Johnson, 354,
        357–58
    and Korea, 154–58
    and McCarthy, 170–83
    RN on, 418, 440, 441, 464–68
    and RN, 16–17, 164, 373, 415,
        448
    and RN's fund crisis, 114–35
    and RN's South America trip,
        228–38
    suffers stroke, 226–28
    and Vietnam, 185–91, 357

Eisenhower, Mamie (Mrs. Dwight D.), 107, 129, 193, 207, 274, 275, 446, 464
Eisenhower, Milton, 207
Eisler, Gerhart, 54–55
Elections and campaigns
    1946, 40–50
    1948, 87–88
    1950, 88–96
    1952, 96–139
    1954, 195–200
    1956, 204–223
    1958, 245–47
    1960, 264–81
    1962, 292–305
    1964, 319–25
    1966, 335–36, 337, 340–42
    1968, 342–45, 352–63, 367–415
    1970, 607–15
Elizabeth, Queen of England, 458
Ellington, Duke, 669
Elliott, William Y., 262
Ellsberg, Daniel, 633–37.
    See also Fielding, Lewis
Ellsworth, Robert, 345–46, 347
England. See Britain
Ervin, Sam, 148
Evans, Daniel, 386
Evans, Rowland, 495
Evans, Tom, 335
Executives Club of Chicago, RN's speech before, 287, 291–92

Fairlie, Henry, 437
Faisal, King of Iraq, 240
Family Assistance Plan (FAP), 513, 527–30
Fanfani, Amintore, 347
Farley, Frank "Hap," 384
Fawzi, Mahmoud, 592
FBI (Federal Bureau of Investigation), 70, 86, 481, 582–90, 633, 635, 636
Fielding, Lewis, 637. See also Ellsberg, Daniel
Finch, Bob, 269, 294, 295–96, 386–87, 406–407, 412, 420–21, 528, 586
Flanders, Ralph, 181
Flanigan, Peter, 329, 336, 344
Folger, Cliff, 295
Ford, Gerald, 125, 266, 304, 357,
509, 529, 542, 619
Foreign Affairs, 350, 352, 422
Formosa
    RN's 1953 trip to, 154
    See also Taiwan; Chiang Kai-shek
Fortas, Abe, 518, 519–20
France, 144, 149–54, 184–91, 220, 333, 346, 399, 457, 461, 462, 650
    RN's 1947 trip to, 60
    RN's 1963 trip to, 307
    RN's 1969 trip to, 457, 460–62
Franco, Francisco, 53–54, 307
Frank, John, 521
Freeman, John, 458
French Indochina. See Cambodia; Laos; Vietnam
Friendly Persuasion, The (West), 15
Friends Church. See Quakerism
Frondizi, Arturo, 228
Fulbright, William, 354, 420, 496, 559, 604–605

Gallup polls, 138, 181, 203, 205, 238, 268, 269–70, 273, 328, 358, 367, 390, 393, 409, 507, 508, 545, 551, 578.
    See also Harris polls; Polls
Gandhi, Indira, 162, 650–51, 654, 658
Gandhi, Mohandas, 16, 658
Garment, Len, 335, 383
Gayler, Noel, 586
Geneva peace conferences, 190, 213
Germany
    RN's 1947 trip to, 59
    RN's 1963 trip to, 307
    RN's 1967 trip to, 346
    RN's 1969 trip to, 460
Giap, Vo Nguyen, 332–33
Gibson, Dunn, and Crutcher, 124
Gist, Sam, 42
Goldfine, Bernard, 238–45
Goldwater, Barry, 238–39, 246–47, 267, 294, 309, 310, 315, 318, 319–25, 327–28, 330, 344, 354, 384, 419, 534, 547
Goodell, Charles, 388

Goodman, Julian, 509
Goodpaster, Andrew, 404
Graham, Billy, 355, 361–62, 391, 531–32, 548
Great Society, 330, 331, 395, 423, 436, 525, 527, 550, 585, 639
Greece, 85, 91, 92
    RN's 1947 trip to, 60
    RN's 1963 trip to, 309
Gregory, Dick, 510
Gridiron Dinner, March 12, 1966, 336
Griffin, Robert, 521
Gromyko, Andrei, 533
Guam
    RN's trip to, 1969, 487–88
Guildhall speech (London, 1958), 247, 255
Gurney, Ed, 547
Guylay, Lou, 203

Hagerty, James, 201, 207, 212–14, 238, 305
Haggard, Merle, 668
Haig, Alexander, 617, 656
Haldeman, H. R. "Bob," 298, 375, 383, 400–402, 409–13, 417, 531, 535, 536, 558, 577, 586, 634, 643
Hall, Len, 180, 196, 203–15, 295
Halleck, Charlie, 188
Hardin, Clifford, 420–21
Harlan, John, 523
Harlem riots, 538
Harlow, Bryce, 379, 403, 407, 412, 517, 632
Harriman, Averell, 502, 533
Harris, Herbert, 22
Harris polls, 409, 645. See also Gallup polls; Polls
Hatfield, Mark, 386
Hayakawa, S. I., 493
Haynsworth, Clement F., 495, 513, 520, 521
Hébert, Eddie, 67, 71, 435
Helms, Richard, 390, 416, 553, 586, 617, 638
Herter, Christian, 57, 146, 213–16, 248, 249, 272
Herter Committee, 57–63
Hesburgh, Rev. Theodore, 493
Hickel, Walter, 384, 566

Hiestand, Edgar, 298, 301
Hilliard, David, 510
Hillings, Pat, 128
Hillman, Sidney, 45
Hines, Earl, 669
Hiss, Alger, 57, 63–87, 88, 100, 108, 136, 168–71, 179, 304
Hiss, Priscilla (Mrs. Alger), 67, 69
Ho Chi Minh, 184, 432, 486, 487, 491, 492, 500
Ho Chi Minh trail, 317, 617
Hoffman, Paul, 124, 162
Hollywood Independent Citizens Committee of the Arts, Sciences, and Professions, 46
Hong Kong
    RN's 1953 trip to, 166
    RN's 1964 trip to, 316
Hoover, Herbert, 8, 84, 98–99, 117, 205, 294, 350
Hoover, J. Edgar, 26, 70, 183, 294, 312, 381, 443, 479, 582–88, 635
Hope, Bob, 668
Horack, H. Claude, 25
House Education and Labor Committee, 50–51
House Un-American Activities Committee, 53–86
Hughes, Don, 275, 662
Hughes Tool Company, 299, 300, 305
Hull, Cordell, 77
Humelsine, Carlisle, 662
Humphrey, Hubert H., 279, 336, 377, 392–414, 415–16, 419, 427, 434, 442, 443, 500, 608, 663
Humphrey, Muriel (Mrs. Hubert H.), 414
Hungary, 54, 220, 223, 224, 225, 488–89, 555
Hunt, E. Howard, 636, 638
Hussein, King of Jordan, 479, 591, 599, 600
Huston Plan, 583–84, 588, 589. See also Interagency Intelligence Report
Huston, Tom, 586, 587

ICBMs (Intercontinental Ballistic Missiles), 514, 648

Ikeda, Hayato, 319
Independent Voters of South
    Pasadena, 44, 46
India, 186
    RN's 1953 trip to, 161–63
    RN's 1969 trip to, 487
    Pakistan war, 650–58
    See also Pakistan
Indochina. See Burma; Cambodia;
    Laos; Malaysia; Thailand;
    Vietnam
Indonesia
    RN's 1953 trip to, 147–48, 165
    RN's 1969 trip to, 487
Interagency Intelligence Report,
    586
Internal Revenue Service (IRS),
    305
Iran
    and Soviet Union, 144
    RN's 1953 trip to, 163
Iraq, 240
Israel, 144. 220. 308. 425. 590–600
    RN's 1967 trip to, 350
Issues and Answers, 343
Italian Labor Confederation, 59
Italy
    RN's 1947 trip to, 59-60
    RN's 1963 trip to, 309
    RN's 1967 trip to, 347
    RN's 1969 trip to, 460, 463
Izvestia, 255

Jackson, Henry, 419, 516
Jackson, Mahalia, 669
Japan, 54, 155, 186, 348, 422, 425,
    480–81
    RN's 1953 trip to, 158–59, 167
    RN's 1964 trip to, 316, 319
    RN's 1967 trip to, 348
Jefferson, Thomas, 590
Jenner, Albert, 183
John Birch Society, 298, 301
Johnson, Lady Bird (Mrs. Lyndon
    B.), 336, 339–40, 391, 416,
    451
Johnson, Lyndon B., 228, 288,
    311, 417, 451–52, 455,
    466–67, 509–10, 530, 538,
    606, 663
    and bombing halt in Vietnam,
    398–406, 493

in elections
    1954, 176
    1960, 265, 268
    1964, 317–25
    1966, 337–43
    1968, 326, 353–58, 368–72,
    378–81, 390, 393, 397–407,
    411, 518, 520
    and Abe Fortas, 518, 519–20
    Great Society, 330, 436, 639
    leaks and wiretaps, 443, 455,
    478, 479–80, 631–33
    Manila Communiqué, 337–40,
    346
    and Soviet Union, 428, 532–34
    and tapes, 621–22
    and Vietnam war, 135–36, 317,
    331–35, 357–58, 416, 422,
    424, 429–30, 431, 433, 470,
    532–34, 567, 631, 632, 636
Johnston, Vic, 209
Jones, Charlie, 210
Jones, Edward V., 662
Jordan, 591, 599, 600
Jorgensen, Frank, 88
Judd, Walter, 104, 266
Justice Department, 81–85, 305,
    545, 547–48

Kai-shek, Chiang. See Chiang
    Kai-shek
Kanady, Johnson, 123
Katcher, Leo, 114
Kempton, Murray, 370
Kennedy, Caroline, 623
Kennedy, David, 420
Kennedy, John F., 51, 228, 238,
    294, 295, 300–301, 305, 308,
    346, 349, 422, 424, 437, 530,
    533, 606, 621, 623
    assassination of, 312–15
    and Bay of Pigs, 287–91, 601,
    638
    and Cuba missile crisis, 301
    debates with RN: 1947, 51;
    1960, 268–73
    in elections: 1960, 266–79; 1964,
    310
    and RN, 91–92, 112, 299, 309
    and Vietnam war, 287, 299, 316,
    431, 433, 630, 636
Kennedy, John F., Jr., 623

Kennedy, Robert, 279, 305, 319, 358, 370, 377–78, 381, 520–21, 621–22
Kennedy, Rose, 623
Kennedy, Ted, 378, 442, 517, 559
Kent State University, 565, 566, 567, 568, 577
Kersten, Charles, 52, 69
Key, Bill, 230
Khan, Ayub, 163, 316, 651
Khan, Yahya, 651–54, 657
Khmer, Rouge, 553
Khrushchev, Nikita, 220, 251–64, 271, 289–90, 301, 428, 602
Kim, Il-sung, 474
King, Bob, 224
King, Coretta (Mrs. Martin Luther, Jr.), 372
King, Martin Luther, Jr., 372, 539
Kishi, Nobusuke, 319, 348
Kissinger, Henry, 421–23, 492, 498, 516, 535, 536, 566, 568, 577, 634, 635, 660
   and Cuban crisis, September 1970, 601–605
   and EC-121 incident, 473–76
   and Indo-Pakistan War, 652–57
   and leaks, 479–80
   and Mideast: 1970—Jordanian War, 591–601
   at Paris peace talks, 432, 483–92, 551–54, 579–80
   at SALT talks, 648, 649
   and U.S.-Soviet relations, 429, 456, 494, 501, 503–504, 648, 649, 652–658
   and Vietnam war, 399–400, 404, 429, 470, 496–97, 504, 511, 554–58, 617
"Kitchen debate," 257–58
Kittikachorn, Thanom, 317
Klein, Herb, 298–303, 440
Kleindienst, Richard, 383, 384
Knight, Jack, 105
Knowland, Bill, 47, 97, 102, 104–105, 108, 109, 132, 173, 175, 178, 182, 239, 382
Korea, 144, 149, 185–86, 338, 447, 473–75, 488, 517, 533, 583
   RN's 1953 trip to, 154–58
Koslov, Frol, 254
Kosygin, Aleksei, 428, 458, 533, 593, 656–57
Kraft, Joseph, 394, 481
Krogh, Egil "Bud," 636–37, 659
Ku Klux Klan, 589
Kubitschek, Juscelino, 229

La Follette, Robert, 7
Labor unions, 45–46, 51, 393, 541–42, 558, 577–78
Laird, Mel, 357, 420, 470–75, 480, 484, 495, 504, 535, 553, 557, 566, 585, 617, 631
Lakeside Speech, of RN, 350–51
Lam Son, 618
Laos, 287, 290, 316, 317, 318, 334, 430, 551, 555, 616–18
   RN's 1953 trip to, 149–50, 153
Lasky, Victor, 100
"Last press conference," 303
Latin America, 144
   RN's 1967 trip to, 345–46, 349
Law and Contemporary Problems, 25
Leaks, 478–82
Leathers, Harlan, 26
Lebanon, 240
   RN's 1964 trip to, 316
Leonard, Jerris, 547
Lewis, Flora, 499
Life, 520
Lincoln, Abraham, 15–16, 121–22
Lindbergh, Anne Morrow (Mrs. Charles), 36
Lindbergh, Charles, 36
Lindsay, John, 386, 388, 577, 594
Linkletter, Art, 668
Lippmann, Walter, 251, 289–90
Lloyd, David, 32
Lodge, Henry Cabot, 98, 111, 266, 268, 274–75, 315–19, 328, 490, 496
Lon Nol, 553, 555, 579
Longworth, Alice Roosevelt, 26, 103–104, 210
Look, 534
Los Angeles Daily News, 90
Los Angeles Times, 88–89, 299, 356
Love, John, 386
Luce, Clare Boothe, 232
Lucke, Jane, 577
Lynch, John, 624

MacArthur, Douglas, 294
McCall, Harrison, 47
McCarran-Walter Act, 56, 225
McCarthy, Eugene, 358, 370–73, 377, 392, 398, 406
McCarthy, Jean (Mrs. Joseph), 180–81
McCarthy, Joseph, 57, 168–84, 195–98
McClellan, John, 435
McCracken, Paul, 642
McDowell, John, 67, 73
McGill, Ralph, 271
McGovern, George, 509, 529
McGrory, Mary, 304
McKinney, William J., 122
Macmillan, Harold, 247
McNamara, Robert, 533, 629, 632
Magsaysay, Ramón, 159
Mahon, George, 435
Making of the President 1960, The (White), 278
Malaysia
   RN's 1953 trip to, 148–49, 165, 192
   RN's 1964 trip to, 316
Manila Communiqué, 337–40, 346
Mansfield, Mike, 488, 505, 516–17, 559, 599
Mao Tse-tung, Madame. *See* Chiang Ching
Marcantonio, Vito, 56, 90, 93, 94
Marshall, George C., 57, 170, 192
Marshall Plan, 57, 62, 425
Marshburn, Olive, 4
Marshburn, Oscar, 4, 33
Martin, Jack, 173
Martin, Joe, 42, 53, 57, 110, 320
Martin, John Bartlow, 123
Mayo, Robert, 528
Meany, George, 393, 520, 542, 558, 650
Meet the Press, 80, 112, 334–35
Meir, Golda, 592–600, 668
Menzies, Robert, 147
Mikoyan, Anastas, 259, 260
Milhous, Almira Burdg, 15, 26, 33
Milhous, Elizabeth Price, 15
Milhous, Griffith, 10
Miller, William, 323
Millikin, Eugene, 467
Mills, Wilbur, 529

MIRVs (Multiple Independently-targetable Re-entry Vehicles), 648
Mitchell, Jim, 228, 266
Mitchell, John, 345, 382–88, 400–404, 411–413, 420, 421, 475, 479, 518–25, 536, 588, 612, 615, 635
Mitchell, Martha (Mrs. John), 413, 614
Mitchell, Stephen, 114, 121–22, 198
Mondale, Walter, 561
Montgomery, Sonny, 435
Moore, Richard, 524
Moorer, Thomas H., 617, 619–20, 654
Moratorium, 493, 495, 496–97, 498, 499, 501, 510
Morse, Wayne, 354
Morton, Rogers, 384, 387
Morton, Thruston, 266
Mosbacher, Bus, 594
Mossadegh, Mohammed, 163
Moynihan, Daniel Patrick, 423, 525–30, 540, 551
Mudge, Stern, Baldwin, and Todd, 306
Mundt, Karl, 55, 65, 67, 77, 117, 171, 174, 180–81
Mundt-Nixon bill, 55–56
Murphy, George, 353
Muskie, Edmund S., 392, 396, 415, 442, 452, 561, 612, 613, 616
My Lai, 619

NASA (National Aeronautics and Space Administration), 530–31
Nasser, Gamal Abdel, 148, 220, 308, 592
National Citizens Political Action Committee (NCPAC), 45–46
National Commission on Productivity, 640
National Security Agency, 586–87, 630
National Security Council (NSC), 184–90, 204, 248, 250, 422, 443, 478, 480, 481, 530, 555, 556, 558, 603

National Student Association, 565
National Welfare Rights
Organization, 529
NATO (North Atlantic Treaty
Organization), 136–37, 144,
346, 347, 422, 424–25,
457–58, 463,
NBC, 127, 341, 408, 411, 412,
414, 509
Nehru, Jawaharlal, 161
New Deal, 7–8, 21, 41, 43, 44, 58,
64, 330
New Economic Policy, 645
New Frontier, 436
New Mobe, 510
New Republic, The, 561
New Statesman, 458
New York *Herald Tribune,* 69,
115, 116, 117, 271
New York *Post,* 114, 134, 239, 370
New York *Times,* 79, 94, 166,
220, 271, 277, 305, 339, 393,
394, 478, 479, 480, 496, 561,
565, 582, 583, 603, 629–37
New Yorker, The, 246
New Zealand, 189, 338
RN's 1953 trip to, 147
Newman, Wallace "Chief," 23–24
News media, 278, 497, 509, 565,
595, 619
campaign uses of, 375–76
in 1968 election and campaign,
408
RN on, 273, 438–39
and Vietnam, 433–34
*See also specific publications and
networks.*
News Twisters, The (Efron), 408
Newsweek, 48–49, 114, 208–209,
219, 434, 495, 578, 609, 613
Newton, Huey, 581
Nixon, Arthur (brother), 9, 11–13,
313
Nixon, Clara Jane (Mrs. Francis
Donald), 34
Nixon, Edward (brother), 9, 34
Nixon, Francis Anthony "Frank"
(father), 3–20, 27, 34, 134,
216, 356
Nixon, Francis Donald "Don"
(brother), 4, 6, 9, 11, 13, 34,
134, 299, 305, 354

Nixon, Hannah Milhous (Mrs.
Francis Anthony), 4–19, 27,
31, 34, 118, 131–32, 134, 143,
216, 299, 305, 354–56
Nixon, Harold (brother), 6, 8, 9,
13–14, 313, 356
Nixon, Julie (Mrs. David
Eisenhower), 40, 146, 200,
275, 276, 280, 285–86, 292,
295–96, 306, 310, 326, 328,
353, 355, 356, 360, 363, 377,
383, 394–95, 409–15, 453–54,
464, 554, 558–61, 662, 667
South America trip, 1958,
232–42
Europe and Middle East trip,
1963, 306–309
wedding of, to David
Eisenhower, 444–47
Nixon, Pat (Mrs. Richard), 40,
193, 200, 203, 223–24, 240,
242, 285–86, 378, 524, 563
early life and marriage, 28–36, 39
in 1946 election, 40, 43, 48
in 1952 election, 103–38
during fund crisis, 117–34,
521–22
on Asia and Far East trip, 1953,
146, 147–65, 168
in 1954 election, 199
in 1956 election, 204–205, 210,
216, 218–22
on South America trip, 1958,
229–38
on Soviet Union trip, 1959,
250–63
in 1960 election, 274, 276, 280
family life, 292, 295–96, 306,
355, 356, 359, 448, 554
on Europe and Middle East trip,
1963, 306–309
and RN's political life, 310, 326,
328, 360, 363
in 1966 election, 335
in 1968 election, 369–70, 377,
382, 383, 388–89, 394–95,
408, 409, 411, 413, 414–15
at Julie Nixon's wedding,
444–47
life in White House, 451–55,
536–37
as First Lady, 661–69

Nixon, Richard
  childhood and early life, 3–16
  family, 5–6, 9–10, 15–16
  early influences, 7–20
  at Whittier College, 17–24
  at Duke Law School, 24–26
  at Wingert & Bewley, 27–28
  wedding of, to Pat Ryan, 30
  at Office of Price
    Administration, 31–32
  naval career, 32–36
  in 1946 election, 40–50
  on House Education and Labor
    Committee, 50–51
  on House Un-American
    Activities Committee, 53–87
  on Herter Committee, 57–63
  and Hiss case, 63–87
  in 1948 election, 87
  in 1950 election, 87–95
  in 1952 election, 96–139
  fund controversy, 112–35
  begins vice presidency, 143–45
  on Asia and Far East trip, 1953,
    145–68
  Joseph McCarthy, 168–84
  Indochina war, 184–91
  Churchill-Eden visit, 191–95
  in 1954 election, 195–201
  Eisenhower's heart attack,
    201–205
  Eisenhower's ileitis operation,
    212–213
  in 1956 election, 204–23
  Operation Mercy—Hungarian
    rebellion, 223–26
  Eisenhower's stroke, 226–28
  on South America trip, 1958,
    228–38
  Sherman Adams's resignation,
    238–45
  in 1958 election, 245–47
  Guildhall speech, (London,
    1958), 247–48
  on Soviet Union trip, 1959,
    250–64
  "kitchen debate," 257–58
  in 1960 election, 264–81
  in 1962 election, 292–305
  as private citizen—New York
    lawyer, 305–63
  at Nixon, Mudge, Rose,

  Baldwin & Todd, 306
  on Europe and Middle East trip,
    1964, 306–309
  in 1964 election, 319–25
  on Middle East and Far East
    trip, 1964, 316–19
  on Vietnam trip, 1965, 334–35
  in 1966 election, 335–42
  on Europe trip, 1967, 350
  on Asia, Latin America, Africa,
    and Middle East trips, 1967,
    348–50
  Lakeside speech (Bohemian
    Grove), 350–51
  Foreign Affairs article, 350, 352,
    422
  in 1968 election, 342–415
  presidential transition, 415–42
  Inauguration, January 20, 1969,
    451–53
  moving into White House, 453–
    56
  on Europe trip, 1969, 457–63
  de Gaulle meetings, 1969,
    460–62
  Cambodia bombing, March
    1969, 471–72
  May 14, 1969—Vietnam speech,
    474, 484
  EC-121 incident, 472–76
  Thieu meeting at Midway, June
    1969, 485
  on around-the-world trip, 1969,
    487–89
  Apollo XI moon landing, 487,
    530–31
  Nixon Doctrine, 488, 490
  Vietnam Moratorium, October
    15, 1969, 495–511
  November 3, 1969—Vietnam
    speech ("Silent Majority"),
    496–512
  New Mobe, November 15, 1969,
    510–11
  Supreme Court appointments,
    517–25
  welfare reform and domestic
    programs, 525–30
  civil rights, 538–51
  Cambodia operation, 551–63
  May 1971 protests, 567–77
  in 1970 election, 607–15

White House taping system, 620–22

Pentagon Papers, 629–38

Nixon, Tricia (Mrs. Edward Cox), 43, 146, 200, 275, 280, 286, 288, 292, 295, 296, 306, 310, 326, 328, 355, 360, 363, 377, 383, 394–95, 409–15, 446, 447, 453, 507, 661–62
  South America trip, 1958, 228–42
  Europe and Middle East trip, 1963, 306–309
  wedding of, to Edward Cox, 624–29

Nixon Doctrine, 488, 490

Nixon, Mudge, Rose, Guthrie, and Alexander, 306, 309

Nkrumah, Kwame, 148, 308

NLF (National Liberation Front), 490, 491

North Atlantic Council, 458

Novak, Robert, 495

Nuclear Weapons and Foreign Policy (Kissinger), 421–22

Oakland *Tribune,* 89

O'Brien, Larry, 412

Oceanside *Blade Tribune,* 299

Office of Price Administration (OPA), 31–32

Oishi, Gene, 396

Okinawa, 425, 480–81

Onassis, Jacqueline Kennedy, 313–15, 622–24

One World (Willkie), 345

OPA. *See* Office of Price Administration

Operation Breakfast, 469–72

Operation Mercy, 223–26

Operation Vulture, 184–85

Oregon Journal, 96

Oswald, Lee Harvey, 312

Oswald, Marina (Mrs. Lee Harvey), 312

Otepka, Otto, 631

Out of Debt, Out of Danger (Voorhis), 45

PAC (Political Action Committee), 45–47, 56

Pakistan, 161

India war, 650–59
  RN's 1953 trip to, 163
  RN's 1964 trip to, 316
  RN's 1969 trip to, 487
  See also India

Palestinian guerrillas, 599

Palmer, Kyle, 88–89

Paraguay
  RN's 1958 trip to, 229

Paris peace talks, 398–407, 416–17, 427, 432–33, 457, 471, 482–90, 503, 504, 506, 508, 551, 552–53, 554, 580, 616, 633

Passman, Otto, 435

Paul VI, Pope, 463

Payne, Fred, 239

Peale, Norman Vincent, 444, 448

Pearson, Drew, 134, 169–70, 239, 467–68

Peirce, Neal, 277

Pentagon Papers, 616, 629–38

People's President, The (Peirce), 277

People's Republic of China. *See* China, Communist

Percy, Chuck, 384, 385, 386

Perdue, William, 26

Peress, Irving, 173–74

Perón, Juan, 228

Perry, Herman L., 40–41

Persons, Jerry, 173, 175, 196, 202, 203, 207, 209, 466, 467–68

Peru
  RN's 1958 trip to, 230–31

Peters, Roberta, 668

Peterson, Peter, 642

Philadelphia Plan, 541–42

Philippines, 189, 338
  RN's 1953 trip to, 159, 164
  RN's 1964 trip to, 316
  RN's 1969 trip to, 487

Phoenix speech, 611–12

Phouma, Souvanna, 150

Plumbers, 636, 638

Poland, 220, 260, 347
  RN's 1959 trip to, 263

Political Action Committee (PAC), 45–47

Polls, 293, 298, 300, 310, 390, 395
  See also Gallup polls; Harris polls

Pompidou, Georges, 477, 593–94, 655
Pompidou, Madame, 594
Porter, William, 474
Potter, Charles, 171, 174
POWs, 431
Powell, Dick, 95
Powell, Lewis, 524–25
Prado, Manuel, 229
Pravda, 255, 262
Presidential disability plan, 227–28
Price, Raymond K., Jr., 345, 383
Price Waterhouse, 124, 127
Progressive AFL, 46
Pueblo, 447, 474
"Pumpkin papers," 83–84

Quakerism, 5, 9–10, 16, 19, 31, 32, 33, 35, 69
Quemoy and Matsu, 272

Rabin, Yitzhak, 350, 595, 597, 599, 601
Race riots, 538
Radford, Arthur, 184–90
Radio Free Europe, 224–25, 263
Railroad brotherhood, 46
Rajagopalachari, 162–63
Rand Corporation, 634
Rather, Dan, 499
Rayburn, Sam, 534
Reagan, Ronald, 325, 326, 344, 353–54, 374–78, 383–87
Real Majority, The (Scammon and Wattenberg), 607–608
Rebozo, Charles G. "Bebe," 305–306, 343, 361, 563, 577, 629
Red China. *See* China, Communist
"Red herring," 57, 65, 86
Regulations and Purchasing Review Board, 640
Rehnquist, William, 524
Religion, as issue in 1960 campaign, 265, 279
Renter, Marc, 31
Renter, Neva, 31
Republican Congressional Campaign Committee, 42, 341
Republican National Committee, 119, 121, 128, 129, 181, 196, 199, 241, 328, 336, 614

Republican National Conventions
1948, 87
1952, 102–10
1956, 213
1960, 266–68
1964, 319–20
1968, 382–91
Republican Party, 108, 145, 170, 195, 196, 221–22, 264–65, 320, 325–26, 330, 424, 442
See also Elections and campaigns
Reston, James, 79, 396, 631
Resurrection (Tolstoy), 18
Revolutionary Force 9, 582
Rhee, Syngman, 155–58
Rhodes, James, 383, 385, 563, 565
Ribicoff, Abraham, 530
Richardson, Elliot, 635
Riza Pahlevi, 163
Robb, Chuck, 629
Robinson, Claude, 266
Roche, John P., 567
Rockefeller, Nelson, 246–47, 266, 267, 293, 294–95, 306, 309–10, 319–25, 328, 344, 357, 367–75, 378–79, 382–86, 399, 412, 421, 422, 594
Rockefeller, Winthrop, 342
Rodgers, Richard, 415, 669
Rogers, Adele (Mrs. William P.), 202
Rogers, Ted, 127, 128, 270
Rogers, William P., 116, 117, 126, 128, 139, 172, 173, 201–202, 203, 224, 227–28, 419, 420, 470–75, 495, 504, 518, 535–36, 553, 557, 566, 591–93, 597, 600, 603, 617
"Rogers Plan," 592–93
Romania
RN's 1967 trip to, 347–48
RN's 1969 trip to, 487, 488–89
Romney, George, 311, 319, 323, 326, 344, 356–57, 367–68, 383, 386, 388, 420–21
Roosevelt, Eleanor, 52–53
Roosevelt, Franklin D., 7–8, 30, 39, 45, 53, 64, 122, 191, 621
Roosevelt, Theodore, 103–104, 135, 454
Rosenberg, Julius, 172

Rostow, Walt, 380, 416
Rousselot, John, 298, 301
Rovere, Richard, 246
Rubottom, Roy, Jr., 228–29, 236
Rush, Kenneth, 650
Rusk, Dean, 380, 390, 401, 416, 533, 630
Russell, Richard, 435, 472, 546
Russia. *See* Soviet Union

Safire, Bill, 643, 644
St. Louis *Globe-Democrat*, 335
St. Louis *Post-Dispatch*, 133, 271, 632
Sainteny, Jean, 433, 486, 489, 492
Sales Executives Club of New York
    RN's speech to, 333
SALT (Strategic Arms Limitation Talks), 428, 480, 616, 633, 636–37, 649
Saltonstall, Leverett, 175
San Francisco *Chronicle*, 89, 94
San Jose, California, rally, 610–11
San Marcos University, Lima, Peru, 229–30
Sanchez, Fina (Mrs. Manolo), 359, 363, 414–15
Sanchez, Manolo, 359, 363, 414–15, 569, 571, 665
Saragat, Giuseppe, 347
Sarasin, Pote, 317
Sato, Eisaku, 319, 348
Saturday Review, 510
Scammon, Richard, 549, 607–608
School desegregation and busing, 543–51
Scott, Hugh, 499–500, 542
Scranton, William, 311, 320, 323, 354
Seale, Bobby, 581
Sears, John P., 335–36
SEATO (Southeast Asia Treaty Organization), 630
Seaton, Fred, 115, 116–17, 266
Seeds of Treason (de Toledano and Lasky), 100
Senatorial and Congressional Campaign Committees, 121, 209
Shafer, Ray, 385
Shell, Joe, 294–95, 298

Sherwood, Jack, 231–35, 254, 275
Shriver, Sargent, 419
Shultz, George, 420–21, 513, 528, 541, 642, 645
Sidey, Hugh, 496
Sihanouk, Norodom, 153, 472, 553
"Silent Majority" speech, 496–512
Sills, Beverly, 668
Sinatra, Frank, 668
Sisco, Joseph, 591, 597
Six Crises (Nixon), 297
Skelton, Red, 668–69
Smith, Dana, 113, 114, 133
Smith, Gerard, 649
Smith, Howard K., 304
Smith, Margaret Chase, 516
Smith, Paul, 18, 20
Smith, Walter Bedell, 188, 244
Snyder, Howard, 274
Sobeloff, Simon, 520–21
"Social Issue," 607–10, 613
Souvanna Phouma, 150
Soviet Union
    and Berlin, 551
    and Cambodia, 578–79
    and China, 144, 347–48, 460, 502
    and Cuba, 387–88, 301, 533, 601–606
    and Czechoslovakia, 488–89
    disarmament talks, 478–79, 514–17, 593
    and Egypt, 308
    expansion, 167
    and Greece, 91
    and Hungary, 220, 223–24, 488–89
    and India, 163, 616, 650–57
    and Japan, 159
    and Korea, 533
    and Mideast crisis, 591–601
    post-World War II intentions, 45
    RN on, 351
    RN's 1959 trip to, 251–64
    RN's 1967 trip to, 346
    and Romania, 488–89
    and SALT, 648–50
    subversion in U.S., 86
    Summit I, 650
    and Turkey, 91
    and U-2 incident, 271

U.S. relations and détente, 251, 422, 425–31, 457–64, 483, 494, 501–504, 530, 592, 595, 616, 647

and Vietnam war, 188, 318, 332, 346–47, 371, 381, 427, 503, 511–12, 532–33

Spain

RN's 1963 trip to, 307, 309

Sparkman, John, 137–38

Sputnik, 136–37, 530

Srinivas, M. N., 564

Stalin, Joseph, 31, 54, 64, 259

Stans, Maurice, 298, 304, 329, 336, 344, 420–21, 542

Stanton, Frank, 509

Stassen, Harold, 77, 87, 98, 188, 205, 213–14

Stein, Herbert, 642–43

Stennis, John, 435, 472

Stephens, Tom, 178

Stern, Isaac, 668

Stevens, Robert, 172–76, 182

Stevenson, Adlai, 96, 114, 122–23, 128, 133, 136, 138, 177, 178, 179, 196, 198, 203, 205–22, 238–39, 288, 602

Stevenson, Adlai, III, 609

Stewart, Potter, 519

Strategic Hamlet Program, 318

Strauss, Lewis, 280

Stripling, Robert, 63, 66, 71–74, 82, 83

Students for a Democratic Society, 581

Submission of Recorded Presidential Conversations. See "Blue Book"

Subversive Activities Control Board, 56

Suez Canal. *See* Egypt

Sukarno, 148, 165, 308

Sulzberger, Arthur, 632

Sulzberger, C. L., 603

Summerfield, Arthur, 129, 132, 196

Supreme Court, 481–82, 495, 513, 517–25, 543–51, 632–33

Sweeney, Joe, 21

Syria, 240, 425, 590–601

Taft, Martha (Mrs. Robert A.), 101

Taft, Robert, 50, 87, 97–111, 117, 145, 196, 320

Taft-Hartley Act, 51, 100

Taiwan

RN's 1964 trip to, 316

RN's 1967 trip to, 348

See also Formosa; Chiang Kai-shek

Talbott, Harold, 103

Tapes, White House, 620–22

TASS, 605

Taylor, Maxwell, 630

Templer, Gerald, 149

Thailand, 189, 338

RN's 1964 trip to, 316, 317

RN's 1969 trip to, 487

Thieu, Nguyen Van, 149, 337–38, 406, 431–32, 480–85, 490, 558, 578–79

Tho, Le Duc, 485–86, 496, 551–52

Thomas, J. Parnell, 63, 77

Thompson, Llewellyn "Tommy," 224, 254, 262, 403, 533

Thompson, Robert, 500–501, 502, 511, 618, 633

Thomson, Dick, 22

Thornton, Dan, 104–105

Thurmond, Strom, 376–77, 383, 547

Thuy, Xuan, 487, 490, 551–52

Time, 49, 496

Tkach, Walter, 464, 576

Tolstoy, Leo, 18

Tower, John, 383, 386, 403–404, 547

Trieste

RN's 1947 trip to, 60–61

Triggs, Dean, 20

Trud, 255

Truman Doctrine, 92

Truman, Harry S., 44. 52–53, 57, 58, 65–88, 96–98, 104, 136, 137, 138, 145, 168, 184, 191–92, 218, 468, 632

Tunney, John, 609

Turkey, 85, 91, 92, 602

Unions. *See* Labor unions

United Nations (UN), 54, 64, 654

United Press, 81

U.S. Information Agency, 250

U.S. News & World Report, 519

Upton, Albert, 18, 20
Urban Affairs Council, 423, 512
Uruguay, 607
  RN's 1958 trip to, 229
USSR. *See* Soviet Union

Vance, Cyrus, 390
Venezuela
  RN's 1958 trip to, 232–38
Victory at Sea (Rodgers), 415
Vietcong, 317, 318, 334, 338, 339,
  402, 431, 619, 619
Vietminh, 149, 150–51, 154,
  184–85, 189–90, 317
Vietnam Situation Report, 456
Vietnam war, 317–18, 331–34,
  337–41, 426, 427, 429–34,
  462, 463, 469–72, 478–79,
  480, 481, 482–87, 488,
  489–94, 551–63, 577–81,
  617–20
  Chronology
  1953: RN's trip to Vietnam,
    149–54
  1954: April 16—RN's speech
    to American Society of
    Newspaper Editors,
    187–88
    May 7—surrender of Dien
    Bien Phu, 184–90
  1964: RN's trip to Vietnam,
    316–18
  1965: RN's trip to Vietnam,
    334–35
  1966: Manila Communiqué,
    337–40, 346
  1967: RN's trip to Vietnam,
    348–419
  1968: Vietnam war as a
    campaign issue, 357, 368,
    371, 393–94
    bombing halt, 380, 394,
    398–407
    Paris peace talks, 398–99,
    416–17, 427, 432–33,
  1969: administration efforts to
    negotiate settlement,
    469–72
    March—Cambodia
    bombing, 471–72
    May 14—RN's speech and
    new peace proposal,
      474–75, 484
    Vietnamization and
    withdrawal considered,
    485–86
    June—meeting of RN and
    Thieu at Midway,
    485–86
    RN's trip to Vietnam, 487
    July—Nixon Doctrine, 488,
    490
    August—Kissinger's first
    secret peace talks, 487
    October 15—Moratorium,
    495–511
    November 3—RN's speech
    ("Silent Majority"), 496–512
    November 15—New Mobe,
    510
  1970: March-April—
    Cambodia, 551–69,
    578–79
    April-May—Kent State,
    565–68
  1971: February—Lam Son,
    617–18
    March—Calley case,
    618–20
    June—Pentagon Papers,
    629–38
  See also Antiwar demonstrations
    and movements; China,
    Communist; Communists;
    Congress; Kissinger, Henry;
    Paris peace talks; Soviet
    Union; specific countries in
    Indochina
Vietnamization, 338, 484–85, 495,
  496, 501, 504, 506, 555–61,
  579, 580, 617, 618
Voice of America, 224–25
Volcker, Paul, 642–43
Volpe, John, 374, 386, 420–21
Voorhis, H. Jerry, 41–49, 304
Vorontsov, Yuli, 601, 652–53,
  656–57
Voting Rights Act of 1965, 538

Waggonner, Joe, 435
Wall Street Journal, 650
Wallace, George, 331, 358, 376,
  380, 386, 391–98, 410, 411,
  434, 538, 545, 620

Wallace, Henry, 50
Walters, Vernon, 231–34
Wardlaw, John, 281
Warren, Earl, 50, 87, 98, 102, 112, 205, 452, 517, 518, 520
Washington *Daily News*, 81
Washington *Post*, 80, 115, 116, 117, 198, 200, 271, 273, 396, 480, 495–96, 498, 510, 565, 632
Washington Special Action Group (WSAG), 652, 658–59
Washington *Star*, 201, 287, 481, 498
Washington Witch Hunt (Andrews), 69–70
Watkins, Arthur V., 181
Watkins Committee, 182
Wattenberg, Ben, 607–608
Watts, Phil, 146
Watts riots, 538
Weathermen, 581–82, 583, 586, 587, 588–89
Welander, Robert O., 659
Welch, Ola Florence, 17, 22, 23
Welch, Robert, 298
West, Jessamyn, 10, 15
Wheeler, Earle, 416, 471

White, Clifton, 382
White, Theodore H., 278
Whitman, Ann, 242
Wicker, Tom, 277, 393, 395
Wildermuth, Carrie, 11
Wilkinson, Bud, 407
Williamson, Nicol, 668–69
Willkie, Wendell, 30–31, 345
Wilson, Bob, 224
Wilson, Harold, 458
Wilson, Woodrow, 54
Winchester, Lucy, 628
Wingert, Bewley, and Nixon, 27
Wiretaps, 478–82
Woods, Rose Mary, 130, 146, 293, 305, 335, 338, 354, 363, 383, 417, 558
Woodward, Robert, 229
World Health Organization, 99
Wyeth, Andrew, 669

Young, David, 636, 659
Young, Whitney, 419

Zahedi, Fazollah, 163
Ziegler, Ron, 298, 440
Zwicker, Ralph, 173, 176, 182